Lecture Notes in Computer Science   11655

More information about this series at http://www.springer.com/series/7407

Ying Tan · Yuhui Shi · Ben Niu (Eds.)

Advances in Swarm Intelligence

10th International Conference, ICSI 2019
Chiang Mai, Thailand, July 26–30, 2019
Proceedings, Part I

 Springer

Editors
Ying Tan
Peking University
Beijing, China

Yuhui Shi
Southern University of Science
and Technology
Shenzhen, China

Ben Niu
Shenzhen University
Shenzhen, China

ISSN 0302-9743   ISSN 1611-3349 (electronic)
Lecture Notes in Computer Science
ISBN 978-3-030-26368-3   ISBN 978-3-030-26369-0 (eBook)
https://doi.org/10.1007/978-3-030-26369-0

LNCS Sublibrary: SL1 – Theoretical Computer Science and General Issues

This Springer imprint is published by the registered company Springer Nature Switzerland AG
The registered company address is: Gewerbestrasse 11, 6330 Cham, Switzerland

Preface

This book and its companion volumes, LNCS vols. 11655 and 11656, constitute the proceedings of the 10th International Conference on Swarm Intelligence (ICSI 2019) held during July 26–30, 2019, in Chiang Mai, Thailand.

The theme of ICSI 2019 was "Serving Life with Intelligence Science." ICSI 2019 provided an excellent opportunity and/or an academic forum for academics and practitioners to present and discuss the latest scientific results and methods, innovative ideas, and advantages in theories, technologies, and applications in swarm intelligence. The technical program covered most of the aspects of swarm intelligence and its related areas.

ICSI 2019 was the tenth international gathering in the world for researchers working on most of the aspects of swarm intelligence, following successful events in Shanghai (ICSI 2018), Fukuoka (ICSI 2017), Bali (ICSI 2016), Beijing (ICSI-CCI 2015), Hefei (ICSI 2014), Harbin (ICSI 2013), Shenzhen (ICSI 2012), Chongqing (ICSI 2011), and Beijing (ICSI 2010), which provided a high-level academic forum for participants to disseminate their new research findings and discuss emerging areas of research. It also created a stimulating environment for participants to interact and exchange information on future challenges and opportunities in the field of swarm intelligence research. ICSI 2019 was held in conjunction with the 4th International Conference on Data Mining and Big Data (DMBD 2019) held in Chiang Mai, Thailand, for sharing common mutual ideas, promoting transverse fusion, and stimulating innovation.

The ICSI 2019 was held in Chiang Mai, Thailand, which was founded in 1296 as the capital of the ancient Lanna Kingdom, located 700 km north of Bangkok in a verdant valley on the banks of the Ping River. Chiang Mai is a land of misty mountains and colorful hill tribes, a playground for seasoned travelers, a paradise for shoppers, and a delight for adventurers. Chiang Mai can expand visitors' horizons with Thai massage, cooking courses, variety of handicrafts, and antiques. Despite its relatively small size, Chiang Mai truly has it all. Today it is a place where past and the present seamlessly merge with modern buildings standing side by side with venerable temples.

ICSI 2019 took place at the Duangtawan Hotel in Chiang Mai, Thailand, which is located in the center of Night Bazaar, one of the famous shopping areas in downtown Chiang Mai. Surrounded by a night market where there is an ideal district for shopping, sightseeing, meeting, and commercial business, the hotel is only 15 minutes away from Chiang Mai International Airport, the main railway station, and Chiang Mai bus station. Guests can easily access the weekend walking streets, historical attractions, and traditional temples, while indulging in fascinating northern eateries, original handicrafts, souvenirs, and local entertainment. The hotel offers comfortable and convenient guestrooms overlooking Chiang Mai's vibrant city view, and a plentiful service of TAI-style restaurants and bars, as well as a complete service of MICE events towards a selection of our function rooms. Guests can enjoy the wide-panoramic view of an outdoor swimming pool, fully-equipped fitness center, and well-being Varee Spa.

ICSI 2019 received 179 submissions and invited submissions from about 429 authors in 30 countries and regions (Algeria, Australia, Austria, Bangladesh, Brazil, China, Colombia, Finland, Germany, Chinese Hong Kong, India, Iraq, Italy, Japan, Malaysia, Mexico, New Zealand, Norway, Portugal, Romania, Russia, Serbia, Singapore, South Africa, Spain, Sweden, Chinese Taiwan, Thailand, United Kingdom, United States of America) across 6 continents (Asia, Europe, North America, South America, Africa, and Oceania). Each submission was reviewed by at least two reviewers, and on average 2.6 reviewers. Based on rigorous reviews by the Program Committee members and reviewers, 82 high-quality papers were selected for publication in this proceedings volume with an acceptance rate of 45.81%. The papers are organized into 13 cohesive sections covering major topics of swarm intelligence research and its development and applications.

On behalf of the Organizing Committee of ICSI 2019, we would like to express our sincere thanks to Peking University, Southern University of Science and Technology, and Mae Fah Luang University for their sponsorship, and to Computational Intelligence Laboratory of Peking University, School of Information Technology of Mae Fah Luang University, and IEEE Beijing Chapter for its technical co-sponsorship, as well as to our supporters of International Neural Network Society, World Federation on Soft Computing, Beijing Xinghui Hi-Tech Co., and Springer Nature.

We would also like to thank the members of the Advisory Committee for their guidance, the members of the international Program Committee and additional reviewers for reviewing the papers, and the members of the Publications Committee for checking the accepted papers in a short period of time. We are particularly grateful to the proceedings publisher Springer for publishing the proceedings in the prestigious series of Lecture Notes in Computer Science. Moreover, we wish to express our heartfelt appreciation to the plenary speakers, session chairs, and student helpers. In addition, there are still many more colleagues, associates, friends, and supporters who helped us in immeasurable ways; we express our sincere gratitude to them all. Last but not the least, we would like to thank all the speakers, authors, and participants for their great contributions that made ICSI 2019 successful and all the hard work worthwhile.

June 2019

Ying Tan
Yuhui Shi
Ben Niu

Organization

General Co-chairs

Ying Tan	Peking University, China
Russell C. Eberhart	IUPUI, USA

Programme Committee Chair

Yuhui Shi	Southern University of Science and Technology, China

Advisory Committee Chairs

Xingui He	Peking University, China
Gary G. Yen	Oklahoma State University, USA
Benjamin W. Wah	Chinese University of Hong Kong, SAR China

Technical Committee Co-chairs

Haibo He	University of Rhode Island Kingston, USA
Kay Chen Tan	City University of Hong Kong, SAR China
Nikola Kasabov	Aukland University of Technology, New Zealand
Ponnuthurai Nagaratnam Suganthan	Nanyang Technological University, Singapore
Xiaodong Li	RMIT University, Australia
Hideyuki Takagi	Kyushu University, Japan
M. Middendorf	University of Leipzig, Germany
Mengjie Zhang	Victoria University of Wellington, New Zealand
Qirong Tang	Tongji University, China

Plenary Session Co-chairs

Andreas Engelbrecht	University of Pretoria, South Africa
Chaoming Luo	University of Mississippi, USA

Invited Session Co-chairs

Andres Iglesias	University of Cantabria, Spain
Haibin Duan	Beihang University, China
Junfeng Chen	Hohai University, China

Special Sessions Chairs

Ben Niu   Shenzhen University, China
Yan Pei   University of Aizu, Japan
Yinan Guo   China University of Mining and Technology, China

Tutorial Co-chairs

Milan Tuba   Singidunum University, Serbia
Junqi Zhang   Tongji University, China
Shi Cheng   Shanxi Normal University, China

Publications Co-chairs

Swagatam Das   Indian Statistical Institute, India
Radu-Emil Precup   Politehnica University of Timisoara, Romania

Publicity Co-chairs

Yew-Soon Ong   Nanyang Technological University, Singapore
Carlos Coello   CINVESTAV-IPN, Mexico
Yaochu Jin   University of Surrey, UK
Rossi Kamal   GERIOT, Bangladesh
Dongbin Zhao   Institute of Automation, CAS, China

Finance and Registration Chairs

Andreas Janecek   University of Vienna, Austria
Suicheng Gu   Google Corporation, USA

Local Arrangement Chair

Tossapon Boongoen   Mae Fah Luang University, Thailand

Conference Secretariat

Renlong Chen   Peking University, China
Xiangyu Liu   Peking University, China

Program Committee

Rafael Alcala   University of Granada, Spain
Esther Andrés   INTA, Spain
Sabri Arik   Istanbul University, Turkey
Carmelo J. A. Bastos Filho University of Pernambuco, Brazil
Sujin Bureerat   Khon Kaen University, Thailand

David Camacho	Universidad Autonoma de Madrid, Spain
Bin Cao	Tsinghua University, China
Mu-Song Chen	Da-Yeh University, Taiwan
Walter Chen	National Taipei University of Technology, Taiwan
Shi Cheng	Shaanxi Normal University, China
Prithviraj Dasgupta	U. S. Naval Research Laboratory, USA
Mingcong Deng	Tokyo University of Agriculture and Technology, Japan
Haibin Duan	Beijing University of Aeronautics and Astronautics, China
Andries Engelbrecht	University of Stellenbosch, South Africa
Zhun Fan	Technical University of Denmark, Denmark
Hongyuan Gao	Harbin Engineering University, China
Shangce Gao	University of Toyama, Japan
Shenshen Gu	Shanghai University, China
Ping Guo	Beijing Normal University, China
Ahmed Hafaifa	University of Djelfa, Algeria
Mo Hongwei	Harbin Engineering University, China
Weiwei Hu	Peking University, China
Xiaohui Hu	GE Digital, Inc., USA
Changan Jiang	Ritsumeikan University, Japan
Mingyan Jiang	Shandong University, China
Colin Johnson	University of Kent, UK
Dhou Khaldoon	University of Missouri-St. Louis, USA
Arun Khosla	National Institute of Technology, Jalandhar, India
Vivek Kumar	NUST-MISIS, Russia
Germano Lambert-Torres	PS Solutions, USA
Xiujuan Lei	Shaanxi Normal University, China
Bin Li	University of Science and Technology of China, China
Xiaodong Li	RMIT University, Australia
Yangmin Li	The Hong Kong Polytechnic University, SAR China
Jing Liang	Zhengzhou University, China
Fernando B. De Lima Neto	University of Pernambuco, Brazil
Ju Liu	Shandong University, China
Wenlian Lu	Fudan University, China
Wenjian Luo	University of Science and Technology of China, China
Jinwen Ma	Peking University, China
Chengying Mao	Jiangxi University of Finance and Economics, China
Bernd Meyer	Monash University, Australia
Carsten Mueller	Baden-Wuerttemberg Cooperative State University, Germany
Bijaya Ketan Panigrahi	IIT Delhi, India
Yan Pei	University of Aizu, Japan
Thomas Potok	ORNL, USA
Radu-Emil Precup	Politehnica University of Timisoara, Romania
Kai Qin	Swinburne University of Technology, Australia

Boyang Qu	Zhongyuan University of Technology, China
Guangchen Ruan	Indiana University Bloomington, USA
Kevin Seppi	Brigham Young University, USA
Ponnuthurai Suganthan	Nanyang Technological University, Singapore
Jianyong Sun	University of Nottingham, UK
Ying Tan	Peking University, China
Mario Ventresca	Purdue University, USA
Guoyin Wang	Chongqing University of Posts and Telecommunications, China
Yan Wang	The Ohio State University, USA
Ning Xiong	Mälardalen University, Sweden
Benlian Xu	Changshu Institute of Technology, China
Yingjie Yang	De Montfort University, UK
Peng-Yeng Yin	National Chi Nan University, Taiwan
Zhi-Hui Zhan	South China University of Technology, China
Chenggang Zhang	Tsinghua University, China
Jie Zhang	Newcastle University, UK
Junqi Zhang	Tongji University, China
Qieshi Zhang	Shenzhen Institutes of Advanced Technology, Chinese Academy of Sciences, China
Xingyi Zhang	Anhui University, China
Zili Zhang	Deakin University, Australia
Qiangfu Zhao	The University of Aizu, Japan
Xinchao Zhao	Beijing University of Posts and Telecommunications, China

Additional Reviewers

Chai, Zhengyi	Nguyen, Kieu Anh
Deng, Xiaodan	Sun, Xiaoxuan
Fan, Zhun	Thomas, Kent
Gao, Chao	Tian, Yanlling
Li, Li	Wang, Chunxia
Liu, Xiaoxi	Wang, Hongfeng
Liu, Yuxin	Wang, Jue
Lu, Yu	Xiao, Fuyuan
Luo, Juanjuan	Zhang, Peng
Mahmoud, Mohammed	Zhou, Kang

Contents – Part I

Fireworks Algorithms and Brain Storm Optimization

Swarm Intelligence Algorithms and Improvements

Genetic Algorithm and Differential Evolution

Swarm Robotics

Contents – Part II

Neural Networks

Machine Learning

Social Computing and Knowledge Graph

Service Quality and Energy Management

Novel Models and Algorithms for Optimization

Generative Adversarial Optimization

Ying Tan$^{(\boxtimes)}$ and Bo Shi

Key Laboratory of Machine Perception (Ministry of Education), School of Electronics Engineering and Computer Science, Peking University, Beijing 100871, China
{ytan,pkushibo}@pku.edu.cn

Abstract. Inspired by the adversarial learning in generative adversarial network, a novel optimization framework named Generative Adversarial Optimization (GAO) is proposed in this paper. This GAO framework sets up generative models to generate candidate solutions via an adversarial process, in which two models are trained alternatively and simultaneously, i.e., a generative model for generating candidate solutions and a discriminative model for estimating the probability that a generated solution is better than a current solution. The training procedure of the generative model is to maximize the probability of the discriminative model. Specifically, the generative model and the discriminative model are in this paper implemented by multi-layer perceptrons that can be trained by the back-propagation approach. As of an implementation of the proposed GAO, for the purpose of increasing the diversity of generated solutions, a guiding vector ever introduced in guided fireworks algorithm (GFWA) has been employed here to help constructing generated solutions for the generative model. Experiments on CEC2013 benchmark suite show that the proposed GAO framework achieves better than the state-of-art performance on multi-modal functions.

Keywords: Generative Adversarial Optimization (GAO) ·
Adversarial Learning · Generative adversarial network (GAN) ·
Guiding vector · Multi-modal functions

1 Introduction

Continuously-valued function optimization problem [20] has long been an important problem in mathematics and computer science. With the development of deep learning in recent years, continuously-valued function optimization problem has become more and more important [23,37]. For continuously-valued function optimization problems, gradient-based methods are commonly used, such as stochastic gradient descent (SGD), Newton's method, conjugate gradient (CG), BFGS and so on [33]. However, for more complex functions and multi-modal functions, gradient-based methods can only find local optimal solutions. For these problems, the algorithm needs to be able to better deal with the balance between exploration and exploitation [4].

© Springer Nature Switzerland AG 2019
Y. Tan et al. (Eds.): ICSI 2019, LNCS 11655, pp. 3–17, 2019.
https://doi.org/10.1007/978-3-030-26369-0_1

In order to solve the problem, more and more meta-heuristic algorithms have been proposed. Meta-heuristic algorithms are usually inspired by biological or human behaviors. By designing a sophisticated mechanism to guide algorithms to find solutions, so as to avoid local optimal solutions and find global optimal solutions. The most critical component for meta-heuristic algorithms is generating solutions and retaining solutions. For the part of generating solutions, the algorithm should generate better solutions as many as possible, but at the same time, it is also hoped that the generated solutions have a rich diversity and will not cluster in local optimal spaces. For the part of retaining solutions, the algorithm should retain better solutions, but it is also hoped that potential solutions which are not so good currently can be retained, because solutions which is better than the current optimal solution may be found in the local searches around them later.

In the early meta-heuristic algorithms, various methods to generate solutions were proposed. Particle swarm optimization (PSO) [19] mimics migration and clustering in the foraging of birds to generate solution. The genetic algorithm (GA) [8] targets all individuals in a group and uses randomization techniques to efficiently search a coded parameter space. The fireworks algorithm (FWA) [40] employs the fitness value of each firework to dynamically calculate the explosion radius and the number of sparks in an explosion as local search. In recent years, research on methods to generate solutions tends to be more refined. Guided firework algorithm (GFWA) [26] employs the fitness value information obtained by the explosion sparks to construct the guiding vector (GV) with promising direction and adaptive length, and an elite solution called guiding spark (GS) is generated by adding the guiding vector to the corresponding firework position.

In recent years, generative adversarial network (GAN) [13] has been proposed as a new generating model, with its outstanding performance proving its powerful ability in generative tasks. Different from the previous generative model, GAN guides a generator to automatically learn how to generate by setting a loss function. In GAN, a discriminator and a generator are alternatively trained, where the discriminator is used to discriminate between the generated sample and the real sample, the generator is used to generate samples as real as possible, so as to deceive the discriminator. GAN has been widely used in the fields of image generation [10,12,32], video synthesis [41,42], text generation [3,21,44], music generation [14], semi-supervised learning [5,9], medical image [7] and information security [16,35].

Inspired by the adversarial learning in GAN, a feasible optimization framework, so-called Generative Adversarial Optimization (GAO), is proposed in this paper. The framework sets up generative models to generate candidate solutions via an adversarial process, in which two models are trained alternatively and simultaneously, i.e., a generative model $\mathcal{G}$ to generate candidate solutions, and a discriminative model $\mathcal{D}$ to estimates the probability that a generated solution is better than a current solution. The training procedure for $\mathcal{G}$ is to maximize the probability of $\mathcal{D}$. In our case, $\mathcal{G}$ and $\mathcal{D}$ are defined by multi-layer perceptrons, which can be trained with back-propagation. To improve the quality of generated solutions, the guiding vectors introduced in GFWA are employed to help constructing generated solutions. Experiments on CEC2013 benchmark suite show that the proposed framework achieves impressive performance on multi-modal functions.

The main contributions of this paper are as follows:

1. Inspired by adversarial learning and GAN, a novel optimization framework so-called Generative Adversarial Optimization, GAO, for short, is proposed.
2. The guiding vectors introduced in GFWA [26] are employed to help constructing generated solutions, which improves the training stability and generative diversity of $\mathcal{G}$.
3. Experiments show that for GAO, multiple rounds of updates are necessary to obtain better generative capabilities.
4. Compared with current famous optimization algorithms, GAO achieves better than state-of-the-art performance on multi-modal functions.

The remainder of this paper is organized as follows. Section 2 presents related works of meta-heuristic algorithms and GAN. Section 3 describes the detail of GAO, a novel optimization framework proposed for continuously-valued function optimization. Experimental settings and results are presented and discussed in Sect. 4. Conclusions are given in Sect. 5.

2 Related Works

2.1 Meta-heuristic Algorithms

Inspired by biological and human behaviors, meta-heuristic algorithms are a kind of algorithms that can be used to better solve continuous optimization problems by simulating agents' behaviors in order to balance "exploration" and "exploitation" [4]. In recent years, researches on meta-heuristic algorithms for optimization problem have developed rapidly, more and more meta-heuristic algorithms have been proposed. According to the mechanism of the agents' behaviour, meta-heuristic algorithms can be divided into swarm intelligence algorithms [18] and evolutionary computation algorithms.

Swarm intelligence algorithms are usually inspired by the behavior of biological groups in natural world to seek the optimum in search space by employing programs to simulate the interaction among biological individuals. Swarm intelligence algorithms mainly focus on biological groups such as ant colony [11], bird flock [19], fish school [29], etc. In addition, some non-biological group systems also belong to the scope of the researches on swarm intelligence, such as multi-robot systems, fireworks [40] and other unnatural phenomena. there are many famous swarm intelligence algorithms such as particle swarm optimization (PSO) [19], ant colony optimization (ACO) [11], fireworks algorithm (FWA) [24–26, 39, 40, 45–47], etc. Specially, GFWA [26] proposed the guiding vector to help constructing solutions for the first time.

Evolutionary computation algorithms are primarily inspired by biological evolution, which solves the global optimal solution by simulating the evolution of organisms. Specific algorithms include genetic algorithm (GA) [8], evolution strategy (ES) [38], genetic programming, evolutionary programming, differential evolution (DE) [31], etc.

2.2 Generative Adversarial Networks

Generative adversarial network (GAN), which was first proposed by Goodfellow in 2014 [13], provides a new method of learning deep representations based on extensively unlabeled data. The basic idea of GAN is derived from the minimax two-player game in game theory, consisting of a generator $\mathcal{G}$ and a discriminator $\mathcal{D}$. GAN is trained by means of adversarial learning, with the goal of estimating the potential distribution of the data samples and generating new data samples. The discriminator $\mathcal{D}$ of the original GAN can be regarded as a function $\mathcal{D} : \mathcal{D}(x) \rightarrow (0, 1)$, which maps the sample to the discriminant probability that whether the sample is from the real data distribution or the generator distribution. The generator $\mathcal{G}$ is trained to reduce the discriminator's accuracy. If the generator distribution is sufficient to perfectly match the real data distribution, then the discriminator will be most confused and give a probability value of 0.5 to all inputs.

Since GAN was proposed, it has quickly become a hot research issue. A large number of researches based on GAN have sprung up, mainly focusing on optimizing GAN's structure [10,32,43] and loss function [1,28,30], proposing some tricks to assist the training of GAN [15,32,34], and using GAN to solve specific problems. GAN is widely used in many fields, and there are many impressive works on different tasks. For image Synthesis, there are LapGAN [10], DCGAN [32] and etc. For image-to-image translation, there are pix2pix [17], cycleGAN [48], etc. For super-resolution, there are SRGAN [22]. For text generation and NLP, there are seqGAN [44], maliGAN [3], Gumbel-softmax GAN [21], etc. For information security, there is MalGAN [16].

3 GAO: Generative Adversarial Optimization

GAO and its detailed implementation are presented in this section. First, the model architectures are described in Sect. 3.1, then the training procedure of GAO is discussed in details in Sect. 3.2.

3.1 Model Architectures

Different from the existing meta-heuristic algorithms which mainly adopt random sampling to generate elite solutions or guiding vectors [26], in GAO, we adopt a generative network $\mathcal{G}$ to generate effective guiding vectors for current solutions to move towards. Simultaneously, a discriminative network $\mathcal{D}$ is trained to evaluate whether the generated solution is better than a current one. The generative network $\mathcal{G}$ is trained by computing gradients from the feedback of $\mathcal{D}$, which means that $\mathcal{G}$ learns how to generate better guiding vectors under the guidance of $\mathcal{D}$.

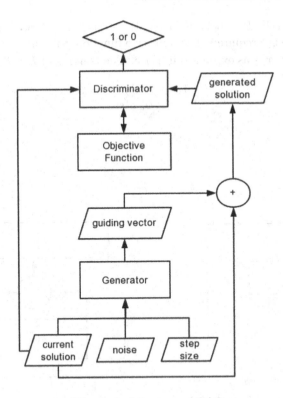

Fig. 1. Architecture of GAO

Given a objective function f, an optimization problem seeks to find the global minimum $x_* \in A$ which satisfies:

$$f(x_*) \leq f(x), \quad \forall x \in A \tag{1}$$

where A is the searching space.

As illustrated in Fig. 1, $\mathcal{G}$ gets the input, which includes a current solution x_c, a noise z and a step size l, and outputs a guiding vector g. This procedure can be expressed in Eq. 2:

$$g = \mathcal{G}(x_c, z, l) \tag{2}$$

Then the guiding vector g is added to the current solution x_c to get the generated solution x_g, as shown in Eq. 3:

$$x_g = x_c + g \tag{3}$$

$\mathcal{D}$ receives a current solution x_c and a generated solution x_g, then outputs a prediction p that whether the generated solution x_g is better than the current solution x_c as shown in Eq. 4. If the generated solution x_g is better than the current solution x_c, let $p = 1$, otherwise $p = 0$.

$$p = \mathcal{D}(x_c, x_g) = \begin{cases} 1, & x_g \text{ is better than } x_c \\ 0, & else \end{cases} \tag{4}$$

8   Y. Tan and B. Shi

In order to train $\mathcal{D}$, labels y^i for tuples of current solution and generated solution $\{x_c^i, x_g^i\}$ are required. The objective function f is employed to label the two-tuple set $\{x_c^i, x_g^i\}$ as expressed in Eq. 5. The training of $\mathcal{D}$ will be detailedly discussed in Sect. 3.2.

$$y^i = \begin{cases} 1, & if \ f(x_g^i) < f(x_c^i) \\ 0, & else \end{cases} \tag{5}$$

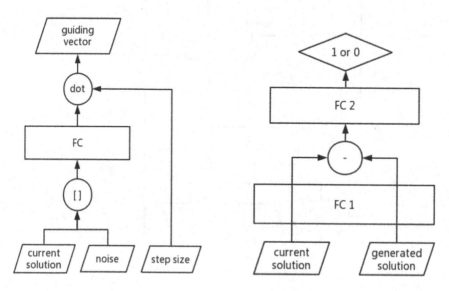

Fig. 2. Architecture of $\mathcal{G}$ **Fig. 3.** Architecture of $\mathcal{D}$

The architecture of $\mathcal{G}$ is illustrated in Fig. 2. First, $\mathcal{G}$ concatenate the current solution x_c and noise z included in the input, then feed the concatenated vector to a fully-connected layer (denoted as FC). Finally $\mathcal{G}$ dot the concatenated vector with step size l and get the guiding vector g as $\mathcal{G}$'s output. This procedure can be expressed in Eq. 6.

$$g = \mathcal{G}(x_c, z, l) = FC([x_c^T, z^T]^T) \cdot l \tag{6}$$

The architecture of $\mathcal{D}$ is illustrated in Fig. 3. First, $\mathcal{D}$ feed two solutions x_c, x_g to the same fully-connected layer denoted as FC_1, then subtract the output of x_c with the output of x_g. Finally, $\mathcal{D}$ feed the subtracted vector to a fully-connected layer denoted as FC_2 and get the prediction p as $\mathcal{D}$'s output. This procedure can be expressed in Eq. 7. The activation function for the final layer of FC_2 should be sigmoid function to regularize the prediction.

$$p = \mathcal{D}(x_c, x_g) = FC_2(FC_1(x_c) - FC_1(x_g)) \tag{7}$$

3.2   Training of GAO

The complete training procedure of GAO is shown in Algorithm 1. At the beginning, μ solutions are randomly sampled in searching space to make up the solution set $C = \{x_c^i, \ i = 1, 2, ..., \mu\}$, calculate each solution's fitness value $f(x_c^i)$ and initialize the step size l. Then we repeatedly do adversarial training of $\mathcal{D}$ and $\mathcal{G}$, select solutions to be retained and reduce step size l as the iteration progresses. When the termination criterion is met, the algorithm exit the loop. Since the time allowed to evaluate the solution using fitness function is limited as $MaxFES = 10000*D$, in which D is the evaluation dimension of fitness function [27], the termination criterion always refers to whether the limited evaluation time is used up. Details of training $\mathcal{D}$ and $\mathcal{G}$, selecting solutions and reducing step size are discussed below.

Algorithm 1. Training procedure of GAO

Require: μ: number of current solutions
Require: β: number of solutions generated at each iteration
Require: l_{init}: initial value of step size l
 1: randomly sample μ solutions in searching space A as set $C = \{x_c^i\}$
 2: calculate fitness value $f(x_c^i)$ for each solution x_c^i in C
 3: initialize the step size $l = l_{init}$
 4: **while** termination criterion is not met **do**
 5:     generate β solutions and train $\mathcal{D}$
 6:     train $\mathcal{G}$ with fitted $\mathcal{D}$
 7:     select μ solutions for next iteration from μ current solutions and β generated solutions
 8:     reduce step size l
 9: **end while**

Training of $\mathcal{D}$. $\mathcal{D}$ is trained to evaluate whether the generated solution x_g will be better than the current solution x_c. Train $\mathcal{D}$ requires employing $\mathcal{G}$ to generate solutions first. In this paper, the number of solutions to be generated totally at each iteration is denoted as β. Since $\mathcal{D}$ receives two solutions as input and output a prediction, training $\mathcal{D}$ requires triplets composed of two solutions x_c^i and x_g^i and a label y^i, in which y^i can be calculated with Eq. 5. For a triplet $\{x_c^i, x_g^i, y^i\}$, the loss function of $\mathcal{D}$ can be calculated with Eq. 8:

$$\max_{\mathcal{D}} \ loss_{\mathcal{D}} = y^i \log(D(x_c^i, x_g^i)) + (1 - y^i) \log(1 - D(x_c^i, x_g^i)) \qquad (8)$$

When training with batches, the loss of a batch is the average loss for each triplet in batch.

Training of $\mathcal{G}$. As mentioned above, $\mathcal{G}$ learns how to generate better guiding vectors under the guidance of $\mathcal{D}$, which means that $\mathcal{G}$ is trained by computing gradients from the feedback of $\mathcal{D}$. $\mathcal{G}$ is trained to generate elite guiding vectors for current solutions, so it's hoped that the generated solutions perform better than current solutions. For a current solution x_c^i, the loss function of $\mathcal{G}$ can be calculated with Eq. 9:

$$\max_{\mathcal{G}} \; loss_{\mathcal{G}} = \log(D(x_c^i, x_c^i + \mathcal{G}(x_c^i, z, l))) \tag{9}$$

In which, z is a random Gaussian noise, l is the step size. When training with batches, the loss of a batch is the average loss for each triplet in the batch.

Selecting Solutions. In general, solutions with better fitness values should be retained, so we calculate the probability to be selected for each solution x^i in Eq. 10 and select solutions using the calculated probability:

$$p_r(x^i) = \frac{\gamma_{f(x^i)}^{-\alpha}}{\sum_{i=1}^{n} \gamma_{f(x^i)}^{-\alpha}} \tag{10}$$

where $\gamma_{f(x^i)}$ means the rank of fitness value for x^i among all solutions, n is the total number of candidate solutions, α is a hyper-parameter to control the shape of the distribution. The larger α is, the probability of solutions with better fitness values is larger as well.

Reducing Step Size. In GAO, the guiding vector introduced in GFWA [26] is employed to control the searching radius at each iteration. In a general searching process, searching radius should be larger at the beginning and gradually reduced to a smaller value, which coincides with keeping the balance between exploration and exploitation. At the beginning, the algorithm needs to explore the searching space to avoid missing any local optimal region where the global optimum may exist. As the algorithm goes on, it has accumulated some information about the searching space and tends to exploit more in existing local optimal regions. Thus several different schemes to adjust step size are designed, for which the basic principle is to gradually decrease the step size as the algorithm goes on. The detailed introduction and experiments will be discussed in Sect. 4.

4   Experiments

In this section, principles on how to set parameters and construct $\mathcal{D}$ and $\mathcal{G}$ are given. In more detail, we first introduce the model architecture specifically and give principles for setting parameters. Secondly, the benchmark the experiment taken on is introduced. Finally, we compare GAO with other famous optimization algorithms.

In our experiment, the architecture of $\mathcal{D}$ and $\mathcal{G}$ are mainly fully-connected layers. In this section, we denote the number of hidden layers as L, the sizes of each hidden layer as H, the sizes of output layer as O ,the activation functions of each hidden layer as AH and the activation functions of output layer as AO.

each of them is introduced respectively as follows. For FC in $\mathcal{G}$, we set $L = 1$, $H = [64]$, $O = dimension\ of\ objective\ function$, $AH = [relu]$, $AO = tanh$. For $FC1$ in $\mathcal{D}$, we set $L = 2$, $H = [64, 64]$, $O = 10$, $AH = [relu, relu]$, $AO = relu$. For $FC2$ in $\mathcal{D}$, we set $L = 1$, $H = [10]$, $O = 1$, $AH = [relu]$, $AO = sigmoid$.

The number of solutions retained at each iteration is denoted as μ, which mainly keeps the balance between "exploration" and "exploitation" [4]. Since the time allowed to evaluate is limited to $MaxFES = 10000 * D$, where D is the dimension of the objective function, smaller μ allows more solutions to be generated from one solution, which focuses on "exploitation", while larger μ allows generating solutions from more locations in search space, which focuses on "exploration". In this paper, we follow the suggestion in [40] and set $\mu = 5$.

To train $\mathcal{D}$, we need to label the tuple of $\{x_c^i, x_g^i\}$ with y^i, which requires using objective function to evaluate the fitness value of x_g^i, since fitness value of x_c^i have been calculated at the former iteration. To make $\mathcal{D}$ learn how to generate solutions better, we not only generate x_g^i from $\mathcal{G}$, but also generate x_g^i from local search and global search at each iteration. When generating solution, x_g^i calculated from Eq. 3 have to be clipped to the boundary once it exceeds the search space. In this paper, we denote the number of solutions to be generated totally at each iteration as β. On account of the limit of $MaxFES$, the iteration number $MaxIter = \frac{MaxFES}{\beta}$. In this paper, we set $\beta = 30$.

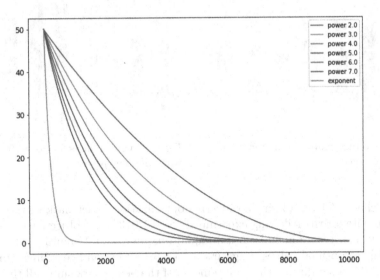

Fig. 4. How step size changes with different monotone functions

As discussed in Sect. 3.2, when selecting solutions, we calculate a probability to be selected for each solution x^i as expressed in Eq. 10 and select solutions in accordance with that probability. We denote the parameter controlling the shape of the distribution as α. The larger α is, the probability of solutions with better fitness values is larger as well. In this paper, we set $\alpha = 2$ as suggested in [24].

In our experiment, step size l have to be set as l_{init} at the beginning of the algorithm. In general, we set $l_{init} = \frac{1}{2} \cdot radius \; of \; search \; space$. Specifically for CEC2013 [27] in this paper, we set $l_{init} = 50$. To gradually reduce the step size as the algorithm goes on, we map the iteration count to $[\epsilon, l_{init}]$ with a monotone function F, here ϵ is a small positive number set to 10^{-20} in this paper. In practice, we compare exponential function and power function with different power. Figure 4 illustrates how step size changes with iteration count increases when using different functions. It shows that using exponential function make the step size drop rapidly. And when using power function, the step size drop faster as the power increases.

We compare different monotone functions on CEC2013 benchmark suite and the average ranks (ARs) are shown in Figs. 5 and 6, in which AR-uni, AR-multi and AR-all indicate average ranks for uni-modal, multi-modal and all functions, respectively. It shows that using power function performs better than exponential function and using 4.5 as power is comprehensively best. In this paper, we use power function and set power to 4.5.

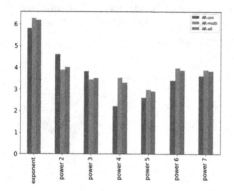

Fig. 5. Average ranks for different monotone functions

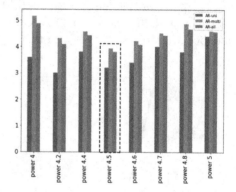

Fig. 6. Average ranks for power function with different power

We choose CEC2013 single objective optimization benchmark suite [27] as the test suite for the following experiments. CEC2013 single objective optimization benchmark suite includes 5 uni-modal functions and 23 multi-modal functions, whose optimal values range from -1400 to 1400 and searching range is $[-100, 100]$. According to the requirements of the benchmark suite, all the algorithms should run 51 times for each function to calculate average and variance. The maximal number of function evaluations in each run, which is denoted as $MaxFES$, is set as $10000*D$, where D is the dimension of the objective function. The benchmark suite supports 10, 30 and 50 as the dimension of the objective function.

Table 1. Mean error, standard variance and average ranks of the chosen algorithms on CEC2013 benchmark suite

CEC2013	ABC Mean	ABC Std	SPSO2011 Mean	SPSO2011 Std	IPOP-CMAES Mean	IPOP-CMAES Std	DE Mean	DE Std	LoT-FWA Mean	LoT-FWA Std	GAO Mean	GAO Std
1	**0.00E+00**	0.00E+00	**0.00E+00**	1.88E−13	**0.00E+00**	0.00E+00	1.89E−03	4.65E−04	**0.00E+00**	0.00E+00	**0.00E+00**	0.00E+00
2	6.20E+06	1.62E+06	3.38E+05	1.67E+05	**0.00E+00**	0.00E+00	5.52E+04	2.70E+04	1.19E+06	4.27E+05	1.02E+06	6.89E+05
3	5.74E+08	3.89E+08	2.88E+08	5.24E+08	**1.73E+00**	9.30E+00	2.16E+06	5.19E+06	2.23E+07	1.91E+07	7.98E+06	1.01E+07
4	8.75E+04	1.17E+04	3.86E+04	6.70E+03	**0.00E+00**	0.00E+00	1.32E−01	1.02E−01	2.13E+03	8.11E+02	3.17E+03	1.49E+03
5	**0.00E+00**	0.00E+00	5.42E−04	4.91E−05	**0.00E+00**	0.00E+00	2.48E−03	8.16E−04	3.55E−03	5.01E−04	2.95E−03	4.70E−04
AR. uni	4		3.4		1		3.2		3.8		3.4	
6	1.46E+01	4.39E+01	3.79E+01	2.83E+01	**0.00E+00**	0.00E+00	7.82E+00	1.65E+01	1.45E+01	6.84E+00	1.73E+01	1.53E+01
7	1.25E+02	1.15E+02	8.79E+01	2.11E+01	1.68E+01	1.96E+01	4.89E+01	2.37E+01	5.05E+01	9.69E+00	**1.08E+01**	8.15E+00
8	2.09E+01	4.97E−02	2.09E+01	5.89E−02	2.09E+01	5.90E−02	2.09E+01	5.65E−02	2.09E+01	6.14E−02	**2.09E+01**	6.96E−02
9	3.01E+01	2.02E+00	2.88E+01	4.43E+00	2.45E+01	1.61E+01	1.59E+01	2.69E+00	1.45E+01	2.07E+00	**1.09E+01**	2.10E+00
10	2.27E−01	6.75E−02	3.40E−01	1.48E−01	**0.00E+00**	0.00E+00	3.24E−01	1.97E−02	4.52E−02	2.47E−02	1.09E−02	1.05E−02
11	**0.00E+00**	0.00E+00	1.05E+02	2.74E+01	2.29E+00	1.45E+00	7.88E+01	2.51E+01	6.39E+01	1.04E+01	5.84E+01	1.84E+01
12	3.19E+02	5.23E+01	1.04E+02	3.54E+01	**1.85E+00**	1.16E+00	8.14E+01	3.00E+01	6.82E+01	1.45E+01	5.60E+01	1.26E+01
13	3.29E+02	3.91E+01	1.94E+02	3.86E+01	**2.41E+00**	2.27E+00	1.61E+02	3.50E+01	1.36E+02	2.30E+01	1.09E+02	2.61E+01
14	**3.58E−01**	3.91E−01	3.99E+03	6.19E+02	2.87E+02	2.72E+02	2.38E+03	1.42E+03	2.38E+03	3.13E+03	2.38E+03	4.39E+02
15	3.88E+03	3.41E+02	3.81E+03	6.94E+02	**3.38E+02**	2.42E+02	5.19E+03	5.16E+02	2.58E+03	3.83E+02	2.43E+03	4.78E+02
16	1.07E+00	1.96E−01	1.31E+00	3.59E−01	2.53E+00	2.73E−01	1.97E+00	2.59E−01	**5.74E−02**	2.13E−02	7.72E−02	4.24E−02
17	**3.04E+01**	5.15E−03	1.16E+02	2.02E+01	3.41E+01	1.36E+00	9.29E+01	1.57E+01	6.20E+01	9.45E+00	9.40E+01	1.80E+01
18	3.04E+02	3.52E+01	1.21E+02	2.46E+01	8.17E+01	6.13E+01	2.34E+02	2.56E+01	**6.12E+01**	9.56E+00	8.92E+01	2.64E+01
19	**2.62E−01**	5.99E−02	9.51E+00	4.42E+00	2.48E+00	4.02E−01	4.51E+00	1.30E+00	3.05E+00	6.43E−01	3.68E+00	8.05E−01
20	1.44E+01	4.60E−01	1.35E+01	1.11E+00	1.46E+01	3.49E−01	1.43E+01	1.19E−01	1.33E+01	1.02E+00	**1.10E+01**	6.91E−01
21	**1.65E+02**	3.97E+01	3.09E+02	6.80E+01	2.55E+02	5.03E+01	3.20E+02	8.55E+01	2.00E+02	2.80E−03	2.94E+02	6.29E+01
22	**2.41E+01**	2.81E+01	4.30E+03	7.67E+02	5.02E+02	3.09E+02	1.72E+03	7.06E+02	3.12E+03	3.79E+02	2.99E+03	5.34E+02
23	4.95E+03	5.13E+02	4.83E+03	8.23E+02	**5.76E+02**	3.50E+02	5.28E+03	6.14E+02	3.11E+03	5.16E+02	2.67E+03	6.25E+02
24	2.90E+02	4.42E+00	2.67E+02	1.25E+01	2.86E+02	3.02E+01	2.47E+02	1.54E+01	**2.37E+02**	1.20E+01	2.39E+02	6.32E+02
25	3.06E+02	6.49E+00	2.99E+02	1.05E+01	2.87E+02	2.85E+01	2.80E+02	1.57E+01	2.71E+02	1.97E+01	**2.60E+02**	1.74E+01
26	2.01E+02	1.93E−01	2.86E+02	8.24E+01	3.15E+02	8.14E+01	2.52E+02	6.83E+01	**2.00E+02**	1.76E−02	2.60E+02	4.32E−02
27	**4.16E+02**	1.07E+02	1.00E+03	1.12E+02	1.14E+03	2.90E+02	7.64E+02	1.00E+02	6.84E+02	9.77E+01	6.45E+02	5.58E+01
28	2.58E+02	7.78E+02	4.01E+02	4.76E+02	3.00E+02	0.00E+00	4.02E+02	3.90E+02	2.65E+02	7.58E+02	2.96E+02	2.77E+01
AR. multi	3.57		4.87		2.87		4.04		2.61		2.48	
AR. all	3.64		4.61		2.54		3.89		2.82		2.64	

We compared GAO with the famous optimization algorithms including the artificial bee colony algorithm (ABC), the standard particle swarm optimization 2011 (SPSO2011) [6], the restart CMA-ES with increasing population size (IPOP-CMA-ES) [2], the differential evolution algorithm (DE) [36] and the loser-out tournament based FWA (LoT-FWA) [24]. The parameters of these algorithms are set as suggested in [2,6,24,36]. All these algorithms are tested under same conditions with GAO. The mean errors, standard deviations and average ranks are shown in Table 1. Average ranks are calculated separately for uni-modal functions and multi-modal functions, denoted as AR.uni and AR.multi, respectively. Average rank for all functions are denoted as AR.all. The minimal mean errors for each function are shown in **bold**.

As illustrated in Table 1, on all functions, IPOP-CMA-ES performs best, followed by GAO and LoT-FWA, while SPSO2011 is the worst one. IPOP-CMA-ES, ABC, GAO and LoT-FWA achieve 11, 10, 6 and 5 of 28 minimal mean errors on all functions, respectively. Specifically on uni-modal functions, IPOP-CMA-ES performs best as well, followed by DE, SPSO2011 and GAO performing comparable, while ABC is the worst one. IPOP-CMA-ES achieves all minimal errors on uni-modal functions, while ABC, SPSO2011, LoT-FWA and GAO achieve 1 of 5 the minimal mean errors.

On multi-modal functions, GAO performs best, followed by LoT-FWA and IPOP-CMA-ES, while SPSO2011 is the worst one. ABC achieves 8 of 23 minimal mean errors on multi-modal functions, followed by IPOP-CMA-ES, GAO and LoT-FWA, achieving 6, 5, 4 of 23 minimal mean errors, respectively. SPSO2011 and DE performs worst, achieving none minimal mean errors on multi-modal functions. Although ABC achieves 8 minimal mean errors on multi-modal functions, it also achieves 10 maximal mean error, which shows that ABC is not stable enough. At the same time, GAO achieves none maximal mean errors on all functions, which shows that GAO is quite stable and can be adapted to various problems.

It turns out from the experimental results that the proposed GAO framework performs quite very well on multi-modal functions. This is mainly due to the adversarial learning procedure, which enables $\mathcal{G}$ to learn how to generate elite and diverse solutions under the supervision of $\mathcal{D}$, rather than to follow an artificially-designed meta-heuristic rule directly. In our implementation, the guiding vector introduced in GFWA [26] has been employed to improve the quality and diversity of generated solutions, which can also certainly be replaced by other feasible methods. In this paper, the exploration on hyper-parameters is greatly simplified, with a main focus on presenting the proposed optimization framework.

5   Conclusion

Inspired by the adversarial learning in generative adversarial network, this paper proposed a novel optimization framework, so-called GAO, for short, which is the first attempt to employ adversarial learning for continuously-valued function optimization. In order to improve the quality of generated solutions, a guiding vector appeared in GFWA is employed in this paper to help constructing generated solutions. Experiments on CEC2013 benchmark suite shew that the proposed GAO algorithm performs quite well, especially on multi-modal functions, it gave the best performance over some famous optimization approaches. Meanwhile, the performance of the GAO framework on uni-modal functions indicates that there is still room for improvement. It is worth noting that the proposed GAO framework should be further studied since it can be easily embedded into any iterative algorithms as an operator to generate solutions. We hope this paper can be regarded as a start point to attract more research on solving various optimization problems using adversarial learning strategy.

Acknowledgement. This work was supported by the Natural Science Foundation of China (NSFC) under grant no. 61673025 and 61375119 and also Supported by Beijing Natural Science Foundation (4162029), and partially supported by National Key Basic Research Development Plan (973 Plan) Project of China under grant no. 2015CB352302.

References

1. Arjovsky, M., Chintala, S., Bottou, L.: Wasserstein GAN. arXiv preprint arXiv:1701.07875 (2017)
2. Auger, A., Hansen, N.: A restart cma evolution strategy with increasing population size. In: 2005 IEEE Congress on Evolutionary Computation, vol. 2, pp. 1769–1776. IEEE (2005)
3. Che, T., et al.: Maximum-likelihood augmented discrete generative adversarial networks. arXiv preprint arXiv:1702.07983 (2017)
4. Chen, J., Xin, B., Peng, Z., Dou, L., Zhang, J.: Optimal contraction theorem for exploration-exploitation tradeoff in search and optimization. IEEE Trans. Syst. Man Cybern. Part A Syst. Hum. **39**(3), 680–691 (2009)
5. Chongxuan, L., Xu, T., Zhu, J., Zhang, B.: Triple generative adversarial nets. In: Advances in Neural Information Processing Systems, pp. 4088–4098 (2017)
6. Clerc, M.: Standard particle swarm optimisation from 2006 to 2011. Part. Swarm Cent. **253** (2011)
7. Dai, W., et al.: Scan: structure correcting adversarial network for chest X-rays organ segmentation. arXiv preprint arXiv:1703.08770 (2017)
8. Davis, L.: Handbook of Genetic Algorithms. Van Nostrand Reinhold, New York (1991)
9. Denton, E., Gross, S., Fergus, R.: Semi-supervised learning with context-conditional generative adversarial networks. arXiv preprint arXiv:1611.06430 (2016)
10. Denton, E.L., Chintala, S., Fergus, R., et al.: Deep generative image models using a Laplacian pyramid of adversarial networks. In: Advances in Neural Information Processing Systems, pp. 1486–1494 (2015)
11. Dorigo, M., Di Caro, G.: Ant colony optimization: a new meta-heuristic. In: Proceedings of the 1999 Congress on Evolutionary Computation-CEC 1999 (Cat. No. 99TH8406), vol. 2, pp. 1470–1477. IEEE (1999)
12. Ganin, Y., et al.: Domain-adversarial training of neural networks. J. Mach. Learn. Res. **17**(1), 2096–3030 (2016)
13. Goodfellow, I., et al.: Generative adversarial nets. In: Advances in Neural Information Processing Systems, pp. 2672–2680 (2014)

14. Guimaraes, G.L., Sanchez-Lengeling, B., Outeiral, C., Farias, P.L.C., Aspuru-Guzik, A.: Objective-reinforced generative adversarial networks (organ) for sequence generation models. arXiv preprint arXiv:1705.10843 (2017)
15. Gulrajani, I., Ahmed, F., Arjovsky, M., Dumoulin, V., Courville, A.C.: Improved training of Wasserstein GANs. In: Advances in Neural Information Processing Systems, pp. 5767–5777 (2017)
16. Hu, W.W., Tan, Y.: Generating adversarial malware examples for black-box attacks based on GAN (2017)
17. Isola, P., Zhu, J.Y., Zhou, T., Efros, A.A.: Image-to-image translation with conditional adversarial networks. In: Proceedings of the IEEE Conference on Computer Vision and Pattern Recognition, pp. 1125–1134 (2017)
18. Kennedy, J.: Swarm intelligence. In: Zomaya, A.Y. (ed.) Handbook of Nature-Inspired and Innovative Computing, pp. 187–219. Springer, Boston (2006). https://doi.org/10.1007/0-387-27705-6_6
19. Kennedy, J.: Particle swarm optimization. In: Sammut, C., Webb, G.I. (eds.) Encyclopedia of Machine Learning, pp. 760–766. Springer, Boston (2010). https://doi.org/10.1007/978-0-387-30164-8
20. Koziel, S., Yang, X.S.: Computational Optimization, Methods and Algorithms, vol. 356. Springer, Heidelberg (2011). https://doi.org/10.1007/978-3-642-20859-1
21. Kusner, M.J., Hernández-Lobato, J.M.: GANs for sequences of discrete elements with the Gumbel-softmax distribution. arXiv preprint arXiv:1611.04051 (2016)
22. Ledig, C., et al.: Photo-realistic single image super-resolution using a generative adversarial network. In: Proceedings of the IEEE conference on Computer Vision and Pattern Recognition, pp. 4681–4690 (2017)
23. Lehman, J., Chen, J., Clune, J., Stanley, K.O.: Safe mutations for deep and recurrent neural networks through output gradients. In: Proceedings of the Genetic and Evolutionary Computation Conference, pp. 117–124. ACM (2018)
24. Li, J., Tan, Y.: Loser-out tournament-based fireworks algorithm for multimodal function optimization. IEEE Trans. Evol. Comput. 22(5), 679–691 (2018)
25. Li, J., Zheng, S., Tan, Y.: Adaptive fireworks algorithm. In: 2014 IEEE Congress on Evolutionary Computation (CEC), pp. 3214–3221. IEEE (2014)
26. Li, J., Zheng, S., Tan, Y.: The effect of information utilization: Introducing a novel guiding spark in the fireworks algorithm. IEEE Trans. Evol. Comput. 21(1), 153–166 (2017)
27. Liang, J., Qu, B., Suganthan, P., Hernández-Díaz, A.G.: Problem definitions and evaluation criteria for the CEC 2013 special session on real-parameter optimization. Technical report 201212(34), Computational Intelligence Laboratory, Zhengzhou University, Zhengzhou, China and Nanyang Technological University, Singapore, pp. 281–295 (2013)
28. Mao, X., Li, Q., Xie, H., Lau, R.Y., Wang, Z., Paul Smolley, S.: Least squares generative adversarial networks. In: Proceedings of the IEEE International Conference on Computer Vision, pp. 2794–2802 (2017)
29. Neshat, M., Sepidnam, G., Sargolzaei, M., Toosi, A.N.: Artificial fish swarm algorithm: a survey of the state-of-the-art, hybridization, combinatorial and indicative applications. Artif. Intell. Rev. 42(4), 965–997 (2014)
30. Nowozin, S., Cseke, B., Tomioka, R.: f-GAN: training generative neural samplers using variational divergence minimization. In: Advances in Neural Information Processing Systems, pp. 271–279 (2016)
31. Qin, A.K., Huang, V.L., Suganthan, P.N.: Differential evolution algorithm with strategy adaptation for global numerical optimization. IEEE Trans. Evol. Comput. 13(2), 398–417 (2009)

32. Radford, A., Metz, L., Chintala, S.: Unsupervised representation learning with deep convolutional generative adversarial networks. arXiv preprint arXiv:1511.06434 (2015)
33. Ruder, S.: An overview of gradient descent optimization algorithms. arXiv preprint arXiv:1609.04747 (2016)
34. Salimans, T., Goodfellow, I., Zaremba, W., Cheung, V., Radford, A., Chen, X.: Improved techniques for training GANs. In: Advances in Neural Information Processing Systems, pp. 2234–2242 (2016)
35. Shi, H., Dong, J., Wang, W., Qian, Y., Zhang, X.: SSGAN: secure steganography based on generative adversarial networks. In: Zeng, B., Huang, Q., El Saddik, A., Li, H., Jiang, S., Fan, X. (eds.) PCM 2017. LNCS, vol. 10735, pp. 534–544. Springer, Cham (2018). https://doi.org/10.1007/978-3-319-77380-3_51
36. Storn, R., Price, K.: Differential evolution-a simple and efficient heuristic for global optimization over continuous spaces. J. Glob. Optim. **11**(4), 341–359 (1997)
37. Such, F.P., Madhavan, V., Conti, E., Lehman, J., Stanley, K.O., Clune, J.: Deep neuroevolution: genetic algorithms are a competitive alternative for training deep neural networks for reinforcement learning. arXiv preprint arXiv:1712.06567 (2017)
38. Tan, K.C., Chiam, S.C., Mamun, A., Goh, C.K.: Balancing exploration and exploitation with adaptive variation for evolutionary multi-objective optimization. Eur. J. Oper. Res. **197**(2), 701–713 (2009)
39. Tan, Y.: Fireworks Algorithm. Springer, Heidelberg (2015). https://doi.org/10.1007/978-3-662-46353-6
40. Tan, Y., Zhu, Y.: Fireworks algorithm for optimization. In: Tan, Y., Shi, Y., Tan, K.C. (eds.) ICSI 2010. LNCS, vol. 6145, pp. 355–364. Springer, Heidelberg (2010). https://doi.org/10.1007/978-3-642-13495-1_44
41. Tulyakov, S., Liu, M.Y., Yang, X., Kautz, J.: MoCoGAN: decomposing motion and content for video generation. In: Proceedings of the IEEE Conference on Computer Vision and Pattern Recognition, pp. 1526–1535 (2018)
42. Vondrick, C., Pirsiavash, H., Torralba, A.: Generating videos with scene dynamics. In: Advances In Neural Information Processing Systems, pp. 613–621 (2016)
43. Wu, J., Zhang, C., Xue, T., Freeman, B., Tenenbaum, J.: Learning a probabilistic latent space of object shapes via 3D generative-adversarial modeling. In: Advances in Neural Information Processing Systems, pp. 82–90 (2016)
44. Yu, L., Zhang, W., Wang, J., Yu, Y.: SeqGAN: sequence generative adversarial nets with policy gradient. In: Thirty-First AAAI Conference on Artificial Intelligence (2017)
45. Zheng, S., Janecek, A., Li, J., Tan, Y.: Dynamic search in fireworks algorithm. In: 2014 IEEE Congress on Evolutionary Computation (CEC), pp. 3222–3229. IEEE (2014)
46. Zheng, S., Janecek, A., Tan, Y.: Enhanced fireworks algorithm. In: 2013 IEEE Congress on Evolutionary Computation, pp. 2069–2077. IEEE (2013)
47. Zheng, S., Li, J., Janecek, A., Tan, Y.: A cooperative framework for fireworks algorithm. IEEE/ACM Trans. Comput. Biol. Bioinform. (TCBB) **14**(1), 27–41 (2017)
48. Zhu, J.Y., Park, T., Isola, P., Efros, A.A.: Unpaired image-to-image translation using cycle-consistent adversarial networks. In: 2017 IEEE International Conference on Computer Vision (ICCV) (2017)

Digital Model of Swarm Unit System with Interruptions

Eugene Larkin[1(✉)] and Aleksandr Privalov[2]

[1] Tula State University, Tula 300012, Russia
elarkin@mail.ru
[2] Tula State Lev Tolstoy Pedagogical University, Tula 300026, Russia
privalov.61@mail.ru

Abstract. Interruption regime of operation using in physical swarm units for input-output data, preventing of emergency mode of operation, acceleration of reaction on suddenly appearing dangerous external affects, etc., is considered. It is shown that for the proper planning of computation process in systems with interruption it is necessary to have a model, which permits to predict system state at any time. Approach to simulation, based on the representation of random time intervals, both interrupt quest generator, and interrupt handler, with discrete distributions is proposed. Method of time densities sampling is worked out. For discrete distributions formulae, describing competition are obtained. With use the Petri-Markov net notion complex model of system under investigation with discrete distributions, which takes into account the draw effect in competition, is built. Recursive procedure, which permits rather exactly simulate a functioning of the system as a whole, is worked out. Method of numerical analysis, arising from digital model is schematically described.

Keywords: Interruption · Interrupt quest generator · Interrupt handler · Petri-Markov net · Discrete distribution · Competition · Draw effect · Recursive procedure

1 Introduction

When managing the individual physical units of swarm (i.e. mobile robot, drone, etc. [1–3]), digital controllers, in which interruption regime of operation is realized for input data, rapid response to internal and external emergencies, are widely used [4]. Utilization of such regime requires additional hard and software, that, in turn, requires increasing of control system volume and energy consumption, so when design and especially optimization of swarm unit configuration, it is necessary to have the model, which permits describe system behavior in physical time. Usually interruption regime is realized as follows: on admission an interruption from external hardware, controller CPU discontinues main program interpretation and switches to interrupt handling, after completion of which it returns to execution of postponed program. So in computer system there is a competition [5–7] between CPU and external interrupt source, which was in detail considered in [8, 9]. Basic theories, used in to simulate system, namely the semi-Markov process theory [10] and the theory of Petri-Markov net [11], give exact,

Y. Tan et al. (Eds.): ICSI 2019, LNCS 11655, pp. 18–28, 2019.
https://doi.org/10.1007/978-3-030-26369-0_2

but rather complicated description of the process, which is suitable for analytical study of the system, but little avail to its practical numerical analysis.

2 Models of Interruption System Components

The primary operational model of components of computer system with interruptions is shown on the Fig. 1. Model includes Interrupt Quests Generator (IQG) and Interrupt Handler (IH).

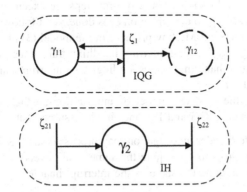

Fig. 1. Components of system with interruptions.

When IQG and IH not interact between them, then mathematical description of components operation may be represented as 2-parallel semi-Markov process as follows:

$$\Pi = \{\Pi_1, \ \Pi_2\}, \tag{1}$$

where Π is 2-parallel Petri-Markov net (PMN); Π_1 is PMN, described Interrupt quest generator; Π_2 is PMN, described interrupt handler.

In turn,

$$\Pi_1 = \{\Gamma_1, \ Z_1, \ I_1, \ O_1, \ \overline{\Phi}_1(t), \ \overline{\Lambda}_1\}; \tag{2}$$

$$\Pi_2 = \{\Gamma_2, \ Z_2, \ I_2, \ O_2, \ \overline{\Phi}_2(t), \ \overline{\Lambda}_2\}, \tag{3}$$

where $\Gamma_1 = \{\gamma_{11}, \gamma_{12}\}$, $\Gamma_2 = \{\gamma_2\}$ are sets of places; $Z_1 = \{\zeta_1\}$, $Z_2 = \{\zeta_{21}, \zeta_{22}\}$ are sets of transitions; $I_1 = \{I_1(\zeta_1)\}$, $I_2 = \{I_{21}(\zeta_{21}), \ I_{22}(\zeta_{22})\}$ are sets of transition input functions; $O_1 = \{O_1(\zeta_1)\}$, $O_2 = \{O_{21}(\zeta_{21}), \ O_{22}(\zeta_{22})\}$ are sets of transition output functions; $\overline{\Phi}_2(t) = [0, \ f(t)]$ are matrices of time densities of residence of corresponding semi-Markov processes in their places, before doing semi-steps into proper transitions; $\overline{\Lambda}_1 = [(\gamma_{11}, \zeta_1), \ (\gamma_{11}, \zeta_1)]$, $\overline{\Lambda}_2$ are matrices of logical conditions of doing semi-steps from proper transitions; $f(t)$ is the runtime of interrupt handler;

$$I_1(\zeta_1) = \{\gamma_{11}\}; \ O_1(\zeta_1) = \{\gamma_{11}, \gamma_{12}\};$$
$$I_{21}(\zeta_{21}) = \varnothing; \ I_{22}(\zeta_{22}) = \{\gamma_2\}; \ O_{21}(\zeta_{21}) = \{\gamma_2\}; \ O_{22}(\zeta_{22}) = \varnothing;$$
$$\overline{\Phi}_1(t) = \begin{bmatrix} g(t) \\ 0 \end{bmatrix}; \ \overline{\Lambda}_2 = \begin{bmatrix} b \\ 0 \end{bmatrix};$$

$g(t)$ is time interval density between two neighbor Interrupt quests; b is start of IH.

In the model (2) place γ_{11} simulates lag time between neighbor interrupt quests equal to $g(t)$. Place γ_{12} simulates interrupt handler, which absorbs interrupt quests; transition ζ_1 simulates «fork» type parallelism, when one process separated onto two ones; logical conditions $\overline{\Lambda}_1$ show, that two semi-steps are executed immediately after semi-step from the place γ_{11} to the transition ζ_1 is done. As it follows from (2) interrupt generation is an ergodic semi-Markov process. In the model (3) place γ_2 simulates lag time between starting and finishing interrupt handling; transitions ζ_{21} and ζ_{22} simulate starting and finishing of handling, correspondingly, so interrupt handling lasts during random time interval $f(t)$.

For working out the complex model of interruptions, which takes into account interaction of components IQG and IH, one should assume, that:

- the computer system under investigation may process data on K interruption levels;
- interrupt handling programs are quite the same at all levels;
- the main program is quite the same as the interrupt handler.

3 Sampling of Time Densities

In the most general case both $f(t)$ and $g(t)$ are continual functions, with the next common properties:

$$0 \leq t_{\min} \leq \ \text{arg}[\phi(t)] \leq t_{\max} < \infty \int_0^\infty \varphi(t)dt = 1, \qquad (4)$$

where $\phi(t) \in \{f(t), g(t)\}$; $t_{\min}$, $t_{\max}$ are lower and upper boundaries of function domain.

Time density $\phi(t)$ may be represented as a histogram. For this purpose domain $[t_{\min}, t_{\max}]$ should be divided onto K intervals, $0 \leq t < \tau_1, \ ..., \ \tau_{k-1} \leq t < \tau_k, \ ...,$ $\tau_{K-1} \leq t < \infty$, as it is shown on the Fig. 2. When sampling, two cases are possible: at first case lower and upper boundaries are clearly defined, so it is advisable to do all intervals of histogram digits quite the same, id est.

$$\Delta = \frac{t_{\max} - t_{\min}}{K}, \qquad (5)$$

where K is the number of histogram digits; at the second case the function $\phi(t)$ at lower boundary is as follows

$$\lim \frac{d^v \phi(t)}{dt^v} \bigg|_{t \to 0} = 0, v = 0, 1, 2, \ldots, \tag{6}$$

or at upper boundary is as follows

$$\lim \frac{d^v \phi(t)}{dt^v} \bigg|_{t \to \infty} = 0, v = 0, 1, 2, \ldots, \tag{7}$$

i.e. approaches to zero asymptotically, so intervals from τ_1 till τ_{K-1}, may be done the same and equal to

$$\Delta = \frac{\tau_1 - \tau_{K-1}}{K - 2}. \tag{8}$$

The first and last intervals may differ from others, and are appointed as follows

$$\Delta_1 = \tau_1 - 0; \Delta_K = \infty - \tau_{K-1}. \tag{9}$$

Such appointment of intervals for calculation of histogram digits nomination is necessary for reducing of a time complexity of computer system investigation. The width of all histogram digits, including first and last, expediently to appoint the same and equal to Δ (see Fig. 2), so histogram domain begins from the point $\tau_0 = \tau_1 - \Delta$ and ends at the point $\tau_K = \tau_{K-1} + \Delta$. Representative point of k-th histogram digits is situated at the middle of k-th digit, between points τ_{k-1} and τ_k:

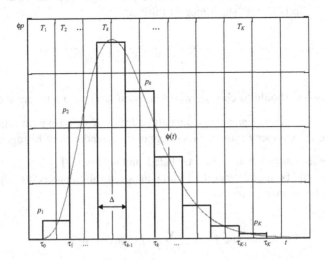

Fig. 2. Sampling of time density.

$$T_k = \tau_k - \frac{\Delta}{2}; \; \tau_k = \tau_0 + k \cdot \Delta \tag{10}$$

Histogram digit values may be defined as follows:

$$p_k = \Phi[\tau(k,r)] - \Phi[\tau(k,r)], \tag{11}$$

where $\Phi[\tau(k,r)] = \int_0^{\tau(k,r)} \phi(t)dt$ is the right border distribution function of the histogram

k-th digit; $\Phi[\tau(k,l)] = \int_0^{\tau(k,l)} \phi(t)dt$ is the left border distribution function of the histogram k-th digit;

$$\tau(k,l) = \begin{cases} \tau_1 + \Delta(k-2), & \text{when } 2 \le k \le K; \\ \tau_{\min}, & \text{when } k = 1, \text{ case 1;} \\ 0, & \text{when } k = 1, \text{ case 2;} \end{cases} \tag{12}$$

$$\tau(k,r) = \begin{cases} \tau_1 + \Delta(k-1), & \text{when } 1 \le k \le K - 1; \\ \tau_{\max}, & \text{when } k = K, \text{ case 1;} \\ \infty, & \text{when } k = K, \text{ case 2.} \end{cases} \tag{13}$$

In sampled model every digit of histogram is represented as weighted shifted degenerative distribution law, so function, described histogram, is as follows:

$$\widetilde{\phi}(t) = \sum_{k=1}^K p_k \cdot \delta(t - T_k), \tag{14}$$

where $\delta(\ldots)$ is the shifted Dirac function; p_k is the weight of Dirac function.

Due to (11), in (14) next stipulation is fulfilled:

$$\sum_{k=1}^K p_k = 1. \tag{15}$$

Parameters one should to choose, when function $\phi(t)$ sampling, are the next:

- in the case 1 - the only parameter, namely, number K of histogram digits;
- in the case 2 - number K, lower τ_0 and upper τ_K boundaries of histogram domain.

For proper assignment both parameter listed, and values p_k, $1 \le k \le K$, of histogram digits, latter should be slightly modified using an optimization procedure. Optimization criterion may be defined as follows:

$$\text{for the case 1} - \varepsilon = \sum_{k=1}^K \int_{\tau_{k-1}}^{\tau_k} |\phi(t) - p_k| dt; \tag{16}$$

$$\text{for the case } 2 - \varepsilon = \int\limits_{0}^{\tau_0} \phi(t)dt + \sum_{k=1}^{K} \int\limits_{\tau_{k-1}}^{\tau_k} |\phi(t) - p_k|dt + \int\limits_{\tau_K}^{\infty} \phi(t)dt, \qquad (17)$$

where τ_{k-1} and τ_k are lower and upper boundaries of histogram k-th digit.

When optimization procedure, at least next conditions must be met; restriction (15) for optimal values of histogram digits; equality of expectations of initial density $\phi(t)$ and distribution $\widetilde{\phi}(t)$, namely

$$\text{M} = \int\limits_{0}^{\infty} t \cdot \phi(t)dt = \int\limits_{0}^{\infty} t \cdot \widetilde{\phi}(t)dt = \widetilde{\text{M}}; \qquad (18)$$

equality of dispersions of initial density $\phi(t)$ and distribution $\widetilde{\phi}(t)$, namely

$$\int\limits_{0}^{\infty} (t - \text{M})^2 \cdot \phi(t)dt = \int\limits_{0}^{\infty} \left(t - \widetilde{\text{M}}\right)^2 \cdot \widetilde{\phi}(t)dt. \qquad (19)$$

Optimization may be carried out by any known method, for example numerically [12].

Due to $\phi(t) \in \{f(t), g(t)\}$, with substitutions $f(t) \to \widetilde{f}(t)$ and $g(t) \to \widetilde{g}(t)$ problem of interruption simulation is reduced to the task of simulation of parallel interactive semi-Markov processes with discrete distributions.

4   The United Model of the System with Interruptions

Models of interruption system components (1) may be united into complex PMN, shown on the Fig. 3:

$$\Pi_\Sigma = \{A, Z, \overline{W}(t), \overline{\Lambda}\}, \qquad (20)$$

where $A = \{a_0, {}^1A, \ldots, {}^kA_k, \ldots\}$ is the set of places; a_0 is the place, which simulates start of system operation; ${}^kA = \{{}^ka_1, {}^ka_2, {}^ka_3, {}^ka_4\}$ $k = 1, 2, \ldots$ are subsets of places, which simulate a competition [11] on the k-th level; ${}^ka_1$ are places which simulate IH operation (when $k = 1$ it is the main program), ${}^ka_3$ are places which simulate IQG operation; ${}^ka_3, {}^ka_4$ are pseudo-places, which simulate return onto previous levels of IH, ${}^1a_3$ is absorbing place, which simulates end of operation; $Z = \{z_0, \ldots, z_k, \ldots\}$ is the set of transitions, which define interruption level; $\overline{W}(t)$ is the matrix of time distributions; $\overline{\Lambda}$ is the matrix of logical conditions.

Anatomically PMN may be divided onto overlapping subnets, according to interruption levels. Every level simulates a competition between IQG and IH. Subnet structure of k-th level is as follows:

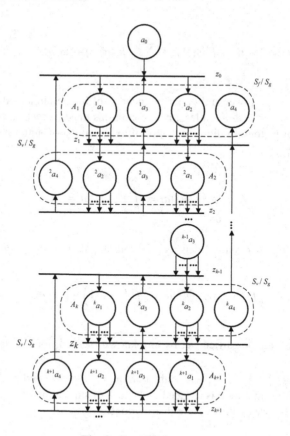

Fig. 3. Petri-Markov net.

$$\Pi_{\Sigma k} = \{A_k, \ Z_k, \overline{W}_k(t), \ \overline{\Lambda}_k\}, \ k = 1, 2, \ldots, \tag{21}$$

where $A_k = \{{}^k a_1, \ {}^k a_2, \ {}^k a_3, \ {}^k a_4, \ {}^{k+1} a_1, \ {}^{k+1} a_2\}$ is the subset of places; $Z_k = \{z_{k-2}, z_{k-1}, z_k\}$ is the subset of transitions; $\overline{W}_k(t)$ is the 6×3 matrix of time densities, which specifies time intervals of the subnet residence in states of subset A_k; $\overline{\Lambda}_k$ is the 3×6 matrix of logical conditions of doing semi-steps from transitions of subset Z_k.

Elements of matrix $\overline{W}_k(t)$ are as follows:

$$w_{13}(t) = {}^k \widetilde{\phi}_1(t); w_{23}(t) = {}^k \widetilde{\phi}_2(t); w_{32}(t) = \delta(t); w_{41}(t) = \delta(t), \tag{22}$$

where ${}^k \widetilde{\phi}_2, \ {}^k \widetilde{\phi}_2$ are auxiliary distributions; all other elements are equal to zero;

$$\widetilde{\phi}_1(t) = \sum_{k(1)=1(1)}^{K(1)} p_{1,k(1)} \cdot \delta(t - T_{1,k(1)}); \tag{23}$$

$$\widetilde{\phi}_2(t) = \sum_{k(2)=1(2)}^{K(2)} p_{2,k(2)} \cdot \delta\big(t - T_{2,k(2)}\big). \tag{24}$$

Stochastic summation in the right part of (23), (24) may be considered as $K(1)/K(2)$ possible realizations of time interval, which are randomly selected from sets $\big\{T_{1,1(1)}, \ldots, T_{1,k(1)}, \ldots, T_{1,K(1)}\big\}/\big\{T_{2,1(2)}, \ldots, T_{2,k(2)}, \ldots, T_{2,K(2)}\big\}$.

Elements of matrix $\overline{\Lambda}_k$ are as follows:

$$
\begin{gathered}
{}^k\lambda_{21}\big(z_{k-1}, {}^ka_1\big) = {}^k\lambda_{22}\big(z_{k-1}, {}^ka_1\big) = \big({}^ka_3, z_{k-1}\big); \\
{}^k\lambda_{33}\big(z_k, {}^ka_3\big) = \big({}^ka_1, z_k\big) \wedge \big({}^ka_2, z_k\big); \quad {}^k\lambda_{34}\big(z_k, {}^ka_4\big) = \big({}^ka_1, z_k\big); \\
{}^k\lambda_{35}\big(z_k, {}^{k+1}a_1\big) = {}^k\lambda_{36}\big(z_k, {}^{k+1}a_2\big) = \big({}^ka_2, z_k\big),
\end{gathered} \tag{25}
$$

where $(\cdots a_{\ldots}, z_{\ldots})$ is corresponding semi-step from place to transition; $(z_{\ldots}, \cdots a_{\ldots})$ is corresponding semi-step from transition to place; all other elements are equal to logical zero.

5   The Digital Competition

The PMN (21) permits to analyze operation of the system with interruption. The analysis is based on the theory of competition, and its development, theory of digital competition. Let processes (23) and (24) compete between them. Then distribution of competition outcome is as follows:

$$\varphi_w(t) = \frac{d}{dt}\Big\{1 - \big[1 - \widetilde{\Phi}_1(t)\big]\big[1 - \widetilde{\Phi}_2(t)\big]\Big\} = \theta_{w1}(t) + \theta_d(t) + \theta_{w2}(t), \tag{26}$$

where $\cdots\widetilde{\Phi}_{\ldots}(k,l) = \int_0^t \cdots\widetilde{\phi}_{\ldots}(\xi)d\xi$ is the distribution function; $\theta_{w1}(t)$ is the weighted distribution of winning the competition by first participant; $\theta_d(t)$ is weighted distribution of competition draw; $\theta_{w2}(t)$ is weighted distribution of winning the competition by second participant;

$$\theta_{w1}(t) = \sum_{k(1)=1(1)}^{K(1)-1} p_{1,k(1)}\delta\big[t - T_{1,k(1)}\big] \cdot \sum_{k(2)=K(2)}^{k(1)+1} p_{2,k(2)}; \tag{27}$$

$$\theta_d(t) = \sum_{[k(1)=k(2)]=1}^{\min[K(1),K(2)]} p_{1,k(1)}p_{2,k(2)}\delta\big[t - T_{1,k(1)}\big]; \tag{28}$$

$$\theta_{w2}(t) = \sum_{k(2)=1(2)}^{K(2)-1} p_{2,k(2)}\delta\big[t - T2_{2,k(2)}\big] \cdot \sum_{k(1)=K(1)}^{k(2)+1} p_{1,k(1)}. \tag{29}$$

Probabilities and pure distributions of different outcomes of competition are as follows:

$$\pi_{w1} = \sum_{k(1)=1(1)}^{K(1)-1} P_{1,k(1)} \cdot \sum_{k(2)=K(2)}^{k(1)+1} P_{2,k(2)}; \ \varphi_{w1}(t) = \frac{\theta_{w1}(t)}{\pi_{w1}}; \tag{30}$$

$$\pi_d = \sum_{[k(1)=k(2)]=1}^{\min[K(1),K(2)]} P_{1,k(1)} P_{2,k(2)} \delta\big[t - T_{1,k(1)}\big], \ \varphi_d(t) = \frac{\theta_d(t)}{\pi_d}; \tag{31}$$

$$\pi_{w2} = \sum_{k(2)=1(2)}^{K(2)-1} P_{2,k(2)} \cdot \sum_{k(1)=K(1)}^{k(2)+1} P_{1,k(1)}; \ \varphi_{w2}(t) = \frac{\theta_{w2}(t)}{\pi_{w2}}. \tag{32}$$

If in competition wins the one of participants, for example the first, he waits until the second participant complete the distance during the time [8]

$$\varphi_{1\to2}(t) = \frac{\eta(t) \int_0^\infty \tilde{\phi}_1(\tau) \cdot \tilde{\phi}_2(t+\xi)d\xi}{\int_0^\infty \tilde{\Phi}_1(t)d\tilde{\Phi}_2(t)}, \tag{33}$$

where $\eta(t)$ is the Heaviside function; ξ is an additional argument having the dimension of time.

When $\tilde{\phi}_1(\tau)$ and $\tilde{\phi}_2(\tau)$ have the same domain left $\tau_{1,0} = \tau_{2,0} = \tau_0$ and right $\tau_{1,K} = \tau_{2,K} = \tau_K$ border, and the same sampling interval Δ (see Fig. 1), then discrete variant of (30) is as follows:

$$\varphi_{1\to2}(t) = \frac{\sum_{k(1)=1}^{K(1)} \sum_{k(2)=k(1)}^{K(2)-k(1)+1} P_{1,k(2)} P_{2,k(1)+k(2)-1} \delta\{t - \Delta[k(1)-1]\}}{\sum_{k(1)=1}^{K(1)} \sum_{k(2)=k(1)}^{K(2)-k(1)+1} P_{1,k(2)} P_{2,k(1)+k(2)-1}}. \tag{34}$$

Similarly,

$$\varphi_{2\to1}(t) = \frac{\sum_{k(1)=1}^{K(1)} \sum_{k(2)=k(1)}^{K(2)-k(1)+1} P_{2,k(2)} P_{1,k(1)+k(2)-1} \delta\{t - \Delta[k(1)-1]\}}{\sum_{k(1)=1}^{K(1)} \sum_{k(2)=k(1)}^{K(2)-k(1)+1} P_{2,k(2)} P_{1,k(1)+k(2)-1}}. \tag{35}$$

Formulae obtained permit to describe recursive procedure of the system analysis. Recursive procedure begins from semi-step (a_0, z_0), which causes semi-steps $(z_0, {}^1a_1)$ and $(z_0, {}^1a_2)$, To execute such semi-steps substitutions

$$^1\varphi_1(t) := \widetilde{f}(t); {}^1\varphi_2(t) := \widetilde{g}(t), \tag{36}$$

should be done, which shows, that IH and IQG start simultaneously. When starting, time densities $^1\varphi_1(t)$ and $^1\varphi_2(t)$ begin compete between them. There are three possible outcomes of competition: $^1\varphi_1(t)$ wins, $^1\varphi_1(t)$ and $^1\varphi_2(t)$ draw; $^1\varphi_2(t)$ wins. For named outcomes probabilities of switches, weighted and pure time densities are described with formulae: (27), (30); (28), (31); (29), (32) correspondingly.

6 Conclusion

Digital model obtained permits to calculate main parameters, necessary when studying system with interruption, time interval, which system spend for wandering from one state to another and probability of such a walk. Simple algorithm of calculation permit use proposed method for optimization of system as a whole, for example for optimization of interrupt handler runtime. Further development of the method may be direct to optimization of sampling of standard distribution laws, alignment of samplings of IQG and IH, etc.

The research was carried out within the state assignment of the Ministry of Education and Science of Russian Federation (No. 2.3121.2017/PCH).

References

1. Tzafestas, S.G.: Introduction to Mobile Robot Control. Elsevier, Amsterdam (2014). 692 pp.
2. Kahar1, S., Sulaiman1, R., Prabuwono1, A.S., Akma, N. Ahmad, S.A., Abu Hassan, M.A.: A review of wireless technology usage for mobile robot controller. In: 2012 International Conference on System Engineering and Modeling (ICSEM 2012). International Proceedings of Computer Science and Information Technology (IPCSIT), vol. 34, pp. 7–12 (2012)
3. Cook, G.: Mobile Robots: Navigation, Control and Remote Sensing. Wiley-IEEE Press, Hoboken (2011). 319 pp.
4. Regehr, J., Duongsaa, U.: Preventing interrupt overload. In: Proceedings of the Conference on Languages, Compilers, and Tools for Embedded Systems, pp. 50–58 (2005)
5. Cleaveland, R., Smolka, S.: Strategic directions in concurrency research. ACM Comput. Surv. **28**(4), 607–625 (1996)
6. Valk, R.: Concurrency in communicating object petri nets. In: Agha, Gul A., De Cindio, F., Rozenberg, G. (eds.) Concurrent Object-Oriented Programming and Petri Nets. LNCS, vol. 2001, pp. 164–195. Springer, Heidelberg (2001). https://doi.org/10.1007/3-540-45397-0_5
7. Heymann, M.: Concurrency and discrete event control. IEEE Control Syst. Mag. **10**, 103–112 (1990)
8. Ivutin, A.N., Larkin, E.V.: Simulation of concurrent games. Bull. South Ural. State Univ. Ser. Math. Model. Program. Comput. Softw. Chelyabinsk **8**(2), 43–54 (2015)
9. Larkin, E.V., Ivutin, A.N., Kotov, V.V., Privalov, A.N.: Simulation of relay-races. Bull. South Ural. State Univ. Math. Model. Program. Comput. Softw. **9**(4), 117–128 (2016)
10. Korolyuk, V., Swishchuk, A.: Semi-Markov Random Evolutions. Springer, Dordrecht (1995). https://doi.org/10.1007/978-94-011-1010-5. 309 p.

11. Larkin, E.V., Lutskov, Y., Ivutin, A.N., Novikov, A.S.: Simulation of concurrent process with Petri-Markov nets. Life Sci. J. **11**(11), 506–511 (2014)
12. Squillante, M.S.: Stochastic Analysis and optimization of multiserver systems. In: Ardagna, D., Zhang, L. (eds.) Run-Time Models for Self-managing Systems and Applications. Autonomic Systems, pp. 1–24. Springer, Basel (2010). https://doi.org/10.1007/978-3-0346-0433-8_1
13. Larkin, E.V., Bogomolov, A.V., Privalov, A.N., Dobrovolsky, N.N.: Discrete model of paired relay-race. Bull. South Ural. State Univ. Ser. Math. Model. Program. Comput. Softw. **11**(3), 72–84 (2018)

Algorithm Integration Behavior
for Discovering Group Membership Rules

Jesús Silva[1]([✉]), Carlos Rondón Rodriguez[2], Cesar Ospino Abuabara[2],
Nadia León Castro[3], Leidy Pérez Coronell[3], Hugo Hernandez-P[3],
Osman Redondo Bilbao[3], and Danelys Cabrera[2]

[1] Universidad Peruana de Ciencias Aplicadas, Lima, Peru
jesussilvaUPC@gmail.com
[2] Universidad de la Costa, St. 58 #66, Barranquilla, Atlántico, Colombia
{crondon1, cospino1, dcabrera4}@cuc.edu.co
[3] Corporación Universitaria Latinoamericana, Barranquilla, Colombia
{nleon, lperez, hhernandez, oredondo}@ul.edu.co

Abstract. Information exploitation processes use different data mining algorithms for obtaining knowledge patterns from data obtained on the problem domain. One of the assumptions when working with these algorithms is that the complexity of the membership domain of the cases they use does not affect the quality of the obtained results. So, it is important to analyze the behavior of the information exploitation process through the discovery of group membership rules by using clustering and induction algorithms. This research characterizes the complexity of the domains in terms of the pieces of knowledge that describe them and information exploitation processes they seek to discover. The results of the experiments show that, in the case of the process for discovering group membership rules, the quality of the patterns differs depending on the algorithms used in the process and the complexity of the domains to which they are applied.

Keywords: Information exploitation engineering ·
Information exploitation process · Complexity of domains · Clustering ·
Induction algorithm performance

1 Introduction

Information exploitation is defined as the search for relevant patterns and regularities in large masses of information [1, 2]. Information exploitation based on intelligent systems [3] refers specifically to the application of intelligent system methods to discover and enumerate patterns in the information.

The authors in [4] have defined five information exploitation processes: discovery of behavioral rules, discovery of groups, discovery of significant attributes, discovery of group membership rules, and weighting of behavioral rules or group membership. The information exploitation processes use different data mining algorithms for obtaining knowledge patterns from the examples (instances) selected on the domain of problem. One of the implicit assumptions of these algorithms is that when the algorithms for the information exploitation process are fixed, the complexity of the domain

© Springer Nature Switzerland AG 2019
Y. Tan et al. (Eds.): ICSI 2019, LNCS 11655, pp. 29–38, 2019.
https://doi.org/10.1007/978-3-030-26369-0_3

on which information is applied does not impact on the quality of the patterns obtained. However, there is evidence [5] that the complexity of the domains, in terms of the pieces of knowledge that describe them and the information exploitation processes they seek to discover, emerges as a component to consider when analyzing the quality of the results to be obtained [6].

In this context, the research seeks to demonstrate through an experiment that, in the case of the information exploitation process in the discovery of group membership rules, the quality of the produced patterns differ depending on the complexity of the domains on which they are applied and the algorithms used in the process [7–9].

The following research questions emerge: Is the assumption that the performance of any pair of algorithms used to discover group membership rules independent of the complexity of the domain? In the case that this assumption is false: What is the pair that provides a better understanding about the situation according to the complexity of the domain?

2 Theoretical Review

2.1 Information Exploitation Process

Information Exploitation (DM for Data Mining) consists of the extraction of nontrivial knowledge that is implicit in the data available from different sources of information [Schiefer et al. 2004]. Such knowledge is previously unknown and can be useful for some processes [10]. For an expert, or the person responsible for a system, data are not usually the most relevant issue but the knowledge that is enclosed in their relations, fluctuations, and dependencies.

This discipline encompasses a set of techniques aimed at the extraction of actionable knowledge, implicit in the Data Warehouse (DW) or another storage system of the organization. The bases of these techniques can be found in the statistical analysis and intelligent systems. Information Exploitation addresses the solution of problems related to prediction, classification, and segmentation [11, 12].

A process of information, or an information exploitation process [13] can be defined as a set of logically related tasks running to achieve, from a set of information with a degree of value for the organization, another set of information with a degree of value greater than the initial one [13]. Each information exploitation process defines a set of input, a set of transformations, and a set of output information. An information exploitation process can be part of a larger process or can include other information exploitation processes that must be included in it, allowing a view from several levels of granularity [14].

For this paper, it is important to describe the process of discovering group membership rules using clustering and induction algorithms for the knowledge extraction.

The process of discovering group membership rules applies when the business problem requires identifying the characteristics, described in terms of attributes, and their possible values from a set of a priori classes that are unknown but are in the mass of the available information about the domain of problem. The process can be described as follows: the first step is to identify the existing sources of information in the organization that offer relevant data about the addressed problem. After identifying the variables, they are included in the same source of information called integrated data [15–17].

Clustering algorithms are applied once the data are integrated, obtaining a partition of the set of records in different groups that are called identified groups, subsequently generating files associated with each identified group, which are referred to as ordered groups. The attribute *group of each ordered group* is used as the class attribute of that group, later becoming a file with identified class attribute (GR). Finally, an induction algorithm is implemented to obtain a set of rules that define the behavior of each group [18, 19].

2.2 Domain Classification by Complexity

To address the issue of complexity of domains, in [8], it is characterized in terms of pieces of knowledge (rules) that explain the membership of an instance (example) to a specific domain. So, the complexity of domain is characterized by the number of classes that describe it, the number of rules that define the membership to each class, the number of attributes that each rule can have, and the number of values (different) of each attribute.

Based on classification attributes set out and the classification protocol of proposed domains, the authors in [7, 20, 21] classify the domains according to their complexity in the following types:

Simple Complexity Domains: Those domains in which the increase in number of examples by rule improves the coverage of rules independent of other used dimensions.

Medium Complexity Domains: Those domains explained by examples with few attributes and few classes, or few attributes and many classes, or few classes and few rules per class.

Oscillating Domains: Those domains that are explained with examples where the number of attributes by example can vary, or number of examples supported by a rule, or common values of attributes in a set of examples covered by the same rule.

Complex Domains: Those domains that are explained with examples with few attributes and many possible values per attribute, or with many attributes and few possible values per attribute, or with many attributes and many possible values per attribute.

Hypercomplex Domains: Those domains that are explained with examples where there can be a variation in the number of possible values that can be taken by the attributes, the number of attributes that cover examples, the number of rules that cover examples, or the number of classes.

3 Method

A tool based on the test bench or experimental design is proposed in [9]. This tool was developed in JAVA 2.2.1 and PostgreSQL 11.2 as database manager.

The tool allows to set the complexity of the domain on which the experimentation will be conducted. For this purpose, the parameters of the relevant domain must be defined manually (or the system allows the automatic allocation), so generating the free variables (without restrictions in their values) at random. The basic parameters to be defined for the determination of the domain complexity are shown in Table 1.

Table 1. The basic parameters to be defined for determining the domain complexity.

Item	Description
Number of Classes (CC)	The number of different classes that will be created by the tool; each class will have a set of rules and therefore a set of examples; the number of classes will dictate the number of groups where all the examples generated in an experiment will be grouped
Number of Attributes (CA)	The number of attributes that the examples to be generated will have; at the same time, each attribute will have a certain number of possible values
Number of Possible Values per Attribute (CVA)	The number of different values that an attribute can take both at the time of generating a rule that will impose a condition on a certain attribute (in this case, the number of possible values will be limited, as shown later) or when generating the examples
Percentage of Possible Values per Attribute in Rules (PCVA)	The percentage of the number of possible values per attribute that will be considered to create the rules
Percentage of Examples used for Training the Algorithms (PENT)	The percentage of generated examples that will be used for training the clustering and induction algorithms before completely running them; the training examples are randomly selected from the full set of examples
Number of Rules to be generated for each class (CRC)	The number of rules that is generated for each class; the generated rules describe each class since the examples of domain are generated from them
Number of Examples to be generated for each rule (CER)	The number of examples to be generated for each rule; it should be considered that the number of examples will depend on the number of classes that have been defined, the number of rules to generate per class as defined, and this parameter; therefore, the number of examples generated will quickly rise depending on the values assigned to the parameters
Number of attributes to use in each rule (CAR).	This parameter can be understood as the number of conditions that each rule generated by the tool will have; the value of this parameter must be less than or equal to the number of defined attributes
Seed for generation of Random Numbers (SEM)	The seed that will be used by the tool to generate random numbers that feed the whole process of experimentation

The definition of domains in laboratory conditions involves the generation of a set of "original" rules. Based on these rules, examples will be generated to support it. Each rule presents the following format "if att1 = val1 and att2 = val2... and attn = valn then Cn". The number of rules to be generated and the number of conditions of the rules, as well as the number of classes, attributes, and values are defined based on the values set by the experiment parameters. The experiment is composed of 3 steps:

[i] The first step defines the complexity of the domain to be analyzed and determines its parameters. As a result of this case, the rules of domain and the number of cases that support these rules are generated.

[ii] The second step consists in the implementation of each of the possible pairs of data mining algorithms, thus obtaining the set of discovered rules.

[iii] The third and final step consists in the comparison between the set of classification rules generated in the first step and the rules discovered in the second step. The percentage of rules discovered in the right way defines the success of the experiment [9, 22, 23].

4   Results

For the experimental development, 7500 experiences were conducted (300 scenarios for each of the 5 types of domains) to perform the analysis of 30 possible combinations of algorithm pairs. The variables of each scenario were defined at random according to the possible variations between the domains listed in [9]. Categories were defined to establish the variation of values for each relevant variable (Table 2), the relationship between these categories (per parameter), and the complexity of the domain (Table 3).

Table 2. Categorization of variable variation

Variables	Low	Medium	High
CC	2–4	5–7	8–10
CRC	1–5	6–10	11–15
CER	1–7	8–14	15–21
CAR	1–2	3–4	5–6
CVA	1–4	5–7	8–10
PCVA	1–40	41–70	71–100
CA	1–4	5–7	8–10

Table 3. Relation between complexity and independent variables according to the variation range

Complexity/variables	CC	CRC	CAR	CVA	CER	PCVA	CA
Simple					High		
Medium	Low	Low	Low				Low-medium
Oscillating			Medium-high	High	High		
Complex			Medium	Low-medium	High	Medium	Medium
Hypercomplex	Low	Low		High	High	High	Low

Table 3 derives the possible compositions of each scenario according to its complexity. Simple Complexity Scenarios: for simple scenarios of complexity, the variable CER varies from 15 to 21 while holding fixed the value of the rest of variables [24, 25].

Medium Complexity scenarios: in these scenarios, variables vary. Number of classes in the range from 2 to 4; Number of rules per Class in the range from 1 to 5, Number of Rule attributes in the range from 1 to 2; and number of attributes in the range from 1 to 5.

Oscillating Complexity Scenarios: in these scenarios, variables vary. Number of Rule Attributes in the range from 3 to 6; Number of Attribute values in the range from 8 to 10; and number of examples by rule in the range from 15 to 21.

Complex Complexity Scenarios: for these scenarios, variables vary. Number of Rule Attributes in the range from 3 to 4, Number of Attribute Values in the range from 4 to 7, number of examples per rule in the range from 15 to 21, Percentage of Possible Attribute Values in the range from 45 to 70, and the Number of Attributes in the range from 5 to 7.

Hypercomplex Complexity Scenarios: in these scenarios, the variables vary. Number of Classes in the range from 2 to 4, Number of Rules per Class in the range from 1 to 5, Number of Attribute Values in the range from 8 to 10, Number of Examples per Rule in the range from 15 to 21, Percentage of Possible Values Attribute in the range from 75 to 100, and Number of Attributes in the range from 2 to 4.

The development of the experiment generated a matrix of complexity which details the average results of success of each pair of algorithms from the generated 100 cases. Tables 4, 5, 6, 7 and 8 present the results.

Table 4 shows the average results obtained for Simple complexity domains with each combination of algorithms. Note that the best combination for this type of complexity are the SOM and ID3 algorithms with a 73.8% of rules properly covered on average, followed by the combination Farthest First and ID3 with 67.55%.

The higher results from the point of view of induction can be seen in the Column of the ID3 algorithm and, from the point of view of clustering, in the row that belongs to the SOM algorithm with their respective combinations. The lower results are found in the combinations of clustering algorithms with induction algorithms AQ15 and CN2.

Table 4. Simple complexity results

	PART	J48	ID3	A priori	CN2	AQ15
KMeans	51.5	57.45	60.38	52.37	16.25	9
EM	39.75	40.77	39.14	63.75	11.12	9
Farthest First	46.35	49.1	67.13	62.12	10.37	6.75
SOM	51.86	62	**73.8**	49.75	25.12	10.87
KNN	36.11	40	53.23	52.5	12.37	8.5

Table 5 shows the average results obtained for the domains of medium complexity. The best combination of algorithms for this type of complexity was Farthest First and ID3 with 53.31% of rules properly covered on average, followed by the combination SOM and ID3 with 51.87%. In general, it can be observed that, for this type of complexity, results are fewer in relation to those obtained for domains of other complexities.

Table 5. Medium complexity results

	PART	J48	ID3	A priori	CN2	AQ15
KMeans	40.27	45.73	51.01	43.03	18.39	12.85
EM	32.84	34.97	41.72	49.43	15.18	9.71
Farthest First	36.05	38.11	**53.31**	46.08	15.70	8.84
SOM	40.62	46.16	51.87	40.12	18.09	11.26
KNN	38.66	41.45	45.58	34.10	18.87	13.01

Table 6 shows the average results obtained for Oscillating complexity domains. The best combination of algorithms for this type of complexity was KNN and a priori with 95.13% of rules correctly covered on average, followed by the combination EM and a priori with 90.14%. From the point of view of the induction algorithms, the combinations of the A priori algorithm present the highest results, while, from the point of view of the clustering algorithms, the KMeans algorithm with its respective combinations has the highest averages. Note that combinations of AQ15 algorithm were the lowest and combinations of the CN2 algorithm increased again.

Table 6. Oscillating complexity results

	PART	J48	ID3	A priori	CN2	AQ15
KMeans	49.5	59.75	70.25	83.75	25.5	13.25
EM	40.62	48.5	48.75	90.14	21.83	11.13
Farthest First	48.75	53.5	71.5	83.75	22.37	9.25
SOM	29.12	30.87	61.62	84	21.12	2.5
KNN	9.62	9.37	19.5	**95.13**	14	1.5

Table 7 shows the average results obtained for complex complexity domains. The best combination of algorithms for this type of complexity was EM and a priori with 91.15% of rules correctly covered on average, followed by the combination KNN and A priori with 88.3%. Again, in this type of complexity, the highest results are in the combinations of the A priori algorithm with the clustering algorithms. Note that, for this complexity, the combinations of ID3 also present high values and, from the point of view of clustering algorithms, the best combinations are those where the Farthest First algorithm is present.

Table 7. Complex complexity results

	PART	J48	ID3	A priori	CN2	AQ15
KMeans	50	53.37	68.87	81.75	19	12.37
EM	22.13	24.12	27.87	**91.15**	16.4	6
Farthest First	54.75	54.63	77.75	82.5	16.75	10.75
SOM	46.62	51	72.25	80.62	17.37	8.25
KNN	27.12	27.25	54.62	88.3	16.87	4.625

Table 8 shows the average results obtained for Hypercomplex complexity domains with each combination of algorithms. The best combination of algorithms for this type of complexity was EM and A priori with 77.14% of rules correctly covered on average, followed by the combination Farthest First and A priori with 71.90%. In this type of complexity, the highest results are for the combinations with the CN2 algorithm, reaching and sometimes exceeding the combinations of the PART algorithm.

Table 8. Hypercomplex complexity results

	PART	J48	ID3	A priori	CN2	AQ15
KMeans	36.74	41.60	49.21	66.86	37.14	18.24
EM	25.54	28.64	29.65	**77.14**	30.19	10.97
Farthest First	31.31	35.46	40.65	71.90	31.81	12.81
SOM	34.67	40.96	52.17	61.34	37.051	19.65
KNN	22.65	25.12	34.24	70.31	32.051	12.9

5 Conclusions

From the previous results, it is possible to assert that the performance achieved by the pairs of algorithms varies according to the complexity of the domain. The best pairs are ordered by complexity in an increasing way: <SOM, ID3>, <Farthest First; ID3>, <KNN, A PRIORI>, <EM, A PRIORI> and <EM, A PRIORI>. It can also be noted in the results that the A PRIORI algorithm presents significant improvements for the last 3 complexities regardless of the clustering algorithm with which it is matched, high-lighting that they show the highest level of performance.

Although the pair presents the best levels of performance in the last 2 complexities of domain, all of them present acceptable levels of success. The PART and J48 algorithms present the highest level of general success in the simplest domain. CN2 and AQ15 algorithms present the lowest levels of success, for all complexities and combinations of algorithms in a global way. The CN2 algorithm presents improvements in its results as the complexity increases, although all of them are significantly below the performance.

References

1. Khella, R., Abu-Naser, S.S.: Rule based system for chest pain in infants and children. Int. J. Eng. Inf. Syst. 1(4), 138–148 (2017)
2. Abu Naser, S.S., Baraka, M.H., Baraka, A.R.: A proposed expert system for guiding freshman students in selecting a major in Al-Azhar University, Gaza. J. Theor. Appl. Inf. Technol. 4(9) (2008)
3. Azaab, S., Abu Naser, S., Sulisel, O.: A proposed expert system for selecting exploratory factor analysis procedures. J. Coll. Educ. 4(2), 9–26 (2000)
4. Abu-Nasser, B.S.: Medical expert systems survey. Int. J. Eng. Inf. Syst. 1(7), 218–224 (2017)
5. AlZamily, J.Y., Abu-Naser, S.S.: A cognitive system for diagnosing musa acuminata disorders. Int. J. Acad. Inf. Syst. Res. (IJAISR) 2(8), 1–8 (2018)
6. Abu Naser, S.S.: Predicting learners performance using artificial neural networks in linear programming intelligent tutoring system. Int. J. Artif. Intell. Appl. 3(2), 65 (2012)
7. Elzamly, A., Hussin, B., Abu Naser, S.S., Shibutani, T., Doheir, M.: Predicting critical cloud computing security issues using Artificial Neural Network (ANNs) algorithms in banking organizations. Int. J. Inf. Technol. Electr. Eng. 6(2), 40–45 (2017)
8. El Agha, M., Jarghon, A., Abu Naser, S.S.: Polymyalgia rheumatic expert system. Int. J. Eng. Inf. Syst. (IJEAIS) 1(4), 125–137 (2017)
9. Abu Naser, S.S., Zaqout, I.S.: Knowledge-based systems that determine the appropriate students major: In the faculty of engineering and information technology. World Wide J. Multidiscip. Res. Dev. 2(10), 26–34 (2016)
10. Abu Naser, S., Akkila, A.N.: A proposed expert system for skin diseases diagnosis. J. Appl. Sci. Res. 4(12), 1682–1693 (2008)
11. Kamatkar, S.J., Kamble, A., Viloria, A., Hernández-Fernandez, L., Cali, E.G.: Database performance tuning and query optimization. In: Tan, Y., Shi, Y., Tang, Q. (eds.) DMBD 2018. LNCS, vol. 10943, pp. 3–11. Springer, Cham (2018). https://doi.org/10.1007/978-3-319-93803-5_1
12. Viloria, A., Robayo, P.V.: Virtual network level of application composed IP networks connected with systems-(NETS Peer-to-Peer). Indian J. Sci. Technol. 9(46) (2016)
13. Torres-Samuel, M., Vásquez, C.L., Viloria, A., Varela, N., Hernández-Fernandez, L., Portillo-Medina, R.: Analysis of patterns in the university world rankings Webometrics, Shanghai, QS and SIR-SCimago: case Latin America. In: Tan, Y., Shi, Y., Tang, Q. (eds.) DMBD 2018. LNCS, vol. 10943, pp. 188–199. Springer, Cham (2018). https://doi.org/10.1007/978-3-319-93803-5_18
14. Huggins, J., Campbell, T., Broderick, T.: Coresets for scalable bayesian logistic regression. In: Lee, D.D., Sugiyama, M., Luxburg, U.V., Guyon, I., Garnett, R. (eds.) Advances in Neural Information Processing Systems 29, pp. 4080–4088. Curran Associates, Inc. (2016)

15. Munteanu, A., Schwiegelshohn, C., Sohler, C., Woodruff, D.: On coresets for logistic regression. In: Bengio, S., Wallach, H., Larochelle, H., Grauman, K., Cesa-Bianchi, N., Garnett, R. (eds.) Advances in Neural Information Processing Systems 31, pp. 6562–6571. Curran Associates, Inc. (2018)

16. Ostrovsky, R., Rabani, Y., Schulman, L.J., Swamy, C.: The effectiveness of Lloyd-type methods for the k-means problem. In: 47th Annual IEEE Symposium on Foundations of Computer Science, FOCS 2006, pp. 165–176. IEEE (2006)

17. Trelles, O., Prins, P., Snir, M., Jansen, R.C.: Big data, but are we ready? Nat. Rev. Genet. **12** (3), 224 (2011)

18. Torres-Samuel, M., et al.: Efficiency analysis of the visibility of Latin American universities and their impact on the ranking web. In: Tan, Y., Shi, Y., Tang, Q. (eds.) DMBD 2018. LNCS, vol. 10943, pp. 235–243. Springer, Cham (2018). https://doi.org/10.1007/978-3-319-93803-5_22

19. Alaei, A.R., Becken, S., Stantic, B.: Sentiment analysis in tourism: capitalizing on big data. J. Travel. Res. **58**(2), 175–191 (2019). https://doi.org/10.1177/0047287517747753

20. Abu Naser, S.S., Shaath, M.Z.: Expert system urination problems diagnosis. World Wide J. Multidiscip. Res. Dev. **2**(5), 9–19 (2016)

21. Boyd, D., Crawford, K.: Six Provocations for big data. In: A Decade in Internet Time: Symposium on the Dynamics of the Internet and Society (2011). SSRN: http://ssrn.com/abstract=1926431 or http://dx.doi.org/10.2139/ssrn.1926431

22. Moreno, A., Moro, E.: Big data versus small data: the case of 'gripe' (flu) in Spanish. Procedia Soc. Behav. Sci. **198**, 339–343 (2015)

23. Liu, B.: Sentiment Analysis and Opinion Mining. Morgan and Claypool, Chicago (2012)

24. Garcia, D., Garas, A., Schweitzer, F.: Positive words carry less information than negative words. EPJ Data Sci. **1**, 3 (2012). http://www.epjdatascience.com/content/1/1/3

25. Lazer, D., Kennedy, R., King, G., Vespignani, A.: Big data. The parable of Google Flu: traps in big data analysis. Science **343**(6176), 1203–1205 (2014)

Success-History Based Position Adaptation in Co-operation of Biology Related Algorithms

Shakhnaz Akhmedova$^{(\boxtimes)}$, Vladimir Stanovov, and Eugene Semenkin

Reshetnev Siberian State University of Science and Technology,
"Krasnoyarskiy Rabochiy" Av. 31, 660037 Krasnoyarsk, Russia
shahnaz@inbox.ru,
{vladimirstanovov,eugenesemenkin}@yandex.ru

Abstract. Previously, a meta-heuristic approach called Co-Operation of Biology Related Algorithms or COBRA based on a fuzzy logic controller for solving real-parameter optimization problems was introduced and described. COBRA's basic idea consists in a cooperative work of well-known bio-inspired algorithms with similar schemes, while the fuzzy logic controller determines which bio-inspired algorithms should be included in the co-operative work at a given moment for solving optimization problems using the COBRA approach. COBRA's performance has been evaluated on a set of test functions and its workability demonstrated. However, COBRA's search efficiency depends significantly on its ability to keep the balance between exploration and exploitation when solving complex multimodal problems. In this study, a new technique for generating potential solutions in biology-inspired algorithms is proposed. This technique uses a historical memory of successful positions found by individuals to guide them in different directions and thus to improve the exploration and exploitation abilities. The proposed method was applied to the components of the COBRA approach. The modified meta-heuristic as well as its original variant and components (with and without the proposed modification), were evaluated on a set of various well-known test functions. The obtained experimental results are presented and compared. It was established that the fuzzy-controlled COBRA with success-history based position adaptation allows better solutions with the same computational effort to be found. Thus, the usefulness of the proposed position adaptation technique was demonstrated.

Keywords: Optimization · Biology-inspired algorithms · Cooperation · External archive · Probabilistic distribution

1 Introduction

Co-Operation of Biology Related Algorithms or COBRA is a meta-heuristic approach developed for solving unconstrained real-parameter optimization problems [1]. Its basic idea consists in the cooperative simultaneous work of different biology-inspired algorithms with similar schemes. In the original version of the COBRA approach, six well-known bio-inspired heuristics were used as component-algorithms, namely the Particle Swarm Optimization Algorithm (PSO) [2], the Wolf Pack Search Algorithm

© Springer Nature Switzerland AG 2019
Y. Tan et al. (Eds.): ICSI 2019, LNCS 11655, pp. 39–49, 2019.
https://doi.org/10.1007/978-3-030-26369-0_4

(WPS) [3], the Firefly Algorithm (FFA) [4], the Cuckoo Search Algorithm (CSA) [5], the Bat Algorithm (BA) [6] and, finally, the Fish School Search Algorithm (FSS) [7].

However, there are various other algorithms which could be used as components for COBRA. Moreover, previously conducted experiments demonstrated that even the bio-inspired algorithms which had already been chosen could be combined in different ways. Later, the fuzzy-controlled COBRA was proposed, where the component-algorithms and their population sizes were automatically determined by the fuzzy controller [8]. This modification was called COBRA-f and its workability was demonstrated in [9].

The COBRA-f approach was originally developed for continuous variable space, but despite its effectiveness compared to the above-listed biology-related algorithms (its components and the original COBRA), the COBRA-f meta-heuristic still needs to address the exploration (visiting entirely new regions of the search space) and exploitation (visiting regions of the search space within the neighbourhood of previously visited points) of the search space [10].

A variety of ideas has been proposed to seek the balance between exploration and exploitation of the population-based algorithms, which includes parameter adaptation methods, population size control, island models and many others (for example, [11] or [12]). One of the valuable ideas proposed for the DE algorithm in [13] is to use an archive of potentially good solutions, which is limited in size and updated as the search proceeds. This idea is similar to the external non-dominated set of solutions used in multi-objective optimizers such as SPEA or SPEA2 [14].

The advantage of the archive is that it contains promising solutions that appear to have valuable information about the search space and its promising regions, thereby indicating the history of algorithms' successful searches [13]. The idea of using such information could be applied to any population-based method. In this paper, the idea of applying the success-history based archive of potentially good solutions is applied to the biology-inspired component-algorithms of the COBRA-f approach.

Therefore, in this paper firstly the COBRA-f meta-heuristic approach is described, and then a description of the modified fuzzy-controlled COBRA is presented. In the next section, the experimental results obtained by the fuzzy-controlled COBRA-f and its new modification as well as results obtained by components with and without the external archive are discussed and demonstrated. Finally, some conclusions are given in the last section.

2   Fuzzy-Controlled COBRA

The meta-heuristic approach called Co-Operation of Biology Related Algorithms or COBRA [1] was developed based on six optimization methods, namely Particle Swarm Optimization (PSO) [2], the Wolf Pack Search (WPS) [3], the Firefly Algorithm (FFA) [4], the Cuckoo Search Algorithm (CSA) [5], the Bat Algorithm (BA) [6] and the Fish School Search (FSS) [7] (hereinafter referred to as "component-algorithms"). The proposed approach consists in the generation of one population for each biology-inspired algorithm, giving six populations, which are then executed in parallel, cooperating simultaneously with each other.

The fuzzy-controlled COBRA is a self-tuning meta-heuristic, so there is no need to choose the population size for each component-algorithm [8]. The number of individuals in the population of each algorithm can increase or decrease depending on the fitness values. To be more specific, the success rates of component-algorithms were used as the fuzzy controller's inputs and the population size changes as outputs [8].

The fuzzy controller had seven input variables, including six success rates, one for each component and an overall success rate, and six output variables, i.e. the number of solutions to be added to or removed from each component. The success rate for the first six input variables is the best fitness value of a given population. The last input variable is determined as the ratio of the number of iterations during which the best found fitness value was improved to a given number of iterations, which is a pre-defined constant. Thus, the process of population growth is automated by the fuzzy controller [8].

The Mamdani-type fuzzy inference is used to obtain the output values. The rule base contained 21 fuzzy rules and had the following structure: each three rules described the case when one of the components gave better results than the others (as there are six components, 18 rules were established); the last three rules used the overall success of all components (variable 7) to add or remove solutions from all components, i.e. to regulate the computational resources [8].

The input variables were always in the range [0, 1], and fixed fuzzy terms of triangular shape were used for this case. In addition to the three classical fuzzy sets A_1, A_2 and A_3, the "Don't Care" (DC) condition and the A_4 term with the meaning "larger than 0" (opposite to A_1) were also used to decrease the number of rules and make them simpler [8]. For the outputs, three fuzzy terms of triangular shape were used. The output fuzzy terms were symmetrical, and the positions and shapes were determined by two values, encoding the left and right position of the central term, as well as the middle position of the side terms in one value, and the left and right positions of the side term in another value. These values were optimized using the PSO algorithm and the parameters $[-12, -2, 0, 19]$ were obtained according to [8]. The defuzzification procedure is performed by calculating the centre of mass of the shape received by fuzzy inference.

In addition, all populations communicated with each other with the aim of preventing their preliminary convergence to the local modes. The communication was determined in the following way: populations exchanged individuals in such a way that a part of the worst individuals of each population was replaced by the best individuals of other populations. Thus, the group performance of all algorithms could be improved.

The performance of the fuzzy-controlled COBRA was evaluated on a set of benchmark problems with 10 and 30 variables taken from [15] and the experiments showed that COBRA-f works successfully and is reliable on different benchmarks [8, 9]. Besides, the meta-heuristic COBRA-f was compared with its component-algorithms and with the original COBRA, and simulations and the comparison showed that COBRA-f is superior to these biology-inspired algorithms when the dimension grows or when complicated problems are solved [8].

3 Proposed Modification

In this study, the success-history based position adaptation of potential solutions for improving the search diversity of the biology-inspired component-algorithms of the COBRA approach and consequently COBRA's efficiency is introduced. The key concept of the proposed technique can be described as follows.

First of all, the initial population for a given biology-inspired component-algorithm is generated. To be more specific, the set of potential solutions called individuals and represented as real-valued vectors with length D, where D is the number of dimensions for a given optimization problem, is randomly generated. Additionally, the external archive for best found positions is created. The maximum size of this archive is chosen by the end-user and stays the same during the work of the component-algorithm, but at the beginning the external archive is empty.

For each individual in each population, the local best found position (the best found position by a given individual) in the search space is also saved. Thus, the local best for each individual is initially its current coordinates. If later the improved position is discovered, then it will be used as the local best and the previous one will be stored in the external archive.

The process of the external archive update for component-algorithms can be described with the following pseudo-code for a minimization problem:

```
A is the external archive with maximum size |A|
The current number of individuals stored in A is k
The individuals stored in the archive are Aᵢ, i = 1,…,k
N is the population size
The individuals in the population are Pⱼ, j = 1,…,N
The local best for each Pⱼ is localⱼ, j = 1,…,N
The objective function is f
For each individual Pⱼ (j = 1,…,N)
   If f(Pⱼ) < f(localⱼ)
      If (k + 1) ≤ |A|
         Aₖ₊₁ = localⱼ
         k = k + 1
      End If
      If (k + 1) > |A|
         Randomly choose the integer r from 1 to |A|
         If f(localⱼ) < f(Aᵣ)
            Aᵣ = localⱼ
         End If
      End If
      localⱼ = Pⱼ
   End If
End For
```

As was mentioned earlier, firstly six populations for component-algorithms are generated. For each component-algorithm, an external archive is created, and then all component-algorithms are executed in parallel. Later, when individuals change their position in the search space according to the formulas given for the considered component-algorithm, they can use the individuals stored in the archive with some probability p_a.

Despite the fact that there is one renewable external archive for each component-algorithm, only three of them use archives during their execution. This is because previously conducted research demonstrated that only the Firefly Algorithm, the Cuckoo Search Algorithm and the Bat Algorithm show statistically better results by using an archive for an individual's position adaptation [16]. Firstly, let's consider the Bat Algorithm [6]. Each i-th individual from the population in the Bat Algorithm is represented by its coordinates x_i and velocity v_i. The following formulas are used for updating velocities and locations/solutions in the BA approach:

$$v_i(t+1) = v_i(t) + (x_i(t) - x^*) \cdot f_i. \tag{1}$$

$$x_i(t+1) = v_i(t+1) + x_i(t). \tag{2}$$

where t and $(t+1)$ are the numbers which indicate the current and the next iterations, x^* is the current best found solution by the whole population, and f_i is the frequency of the emitted pulses for the i-th individual [6]. Thus, with the probability p_a instead of x^* the randomly chosen individual A_i from the external archive (if it is not empty) will be used. This is done with the expectation that individuals will move in multiple directions and, therefore, will be able to find better solutions.

For the other two algorithms, FFA and CSA, the archive is used in the same way: with probability p_a the current point of attraction x^* is changed to the stored solution A_i. To be more specific, in the CSA approach, individuals are sorted according to the objective function. Then part of the worst ones is removed from the population and new individuals are generated instead of them using the external archive with a given probability p_a. On the other hand, in the FFA approach, a firefly or individual moves towards another firefly or individual if the latter has a better objective function value [4]. Thus, while using the proposed technique for the FFA approach, the firefly can be moved also towards individuals from the external archive.

After the simultaneous execution of all component-algorithms, the fuzzy controller makes a decision about the population sizes of components. To be more specific, each population's size can decrease to a minimal value chosen by the end-user or increase (the maximum population size is also established beforehand). While increasing the population size, new individuals can be generated using the following scheme:

```
padd_i is the probability for using normal distribution
N(a, σ) with mean value a and standard deviation σ
|Ac_i| is the current archive size of the i-th population
alg_best_i is the currently best found position by the i-
th population
Generate random number rand from the interval [0, 1]
If rand ≤ padd_i and |Ac_i| > 0
    Generate random integer r from [1,|Ac_i|]
    a = 0.5·(Ac_ir + alg_best_i)
    σ = |Ac_ir - alg_best_i|
    Generate new individual ind_new = N(a, σ)
End If
Else
    Generate new individual ind_new around the alg_best_i
End Else
```

As was mentioned earlier, populations also communicate with each other. However, in this version of the fuzzy-controlled COBRA, part of the worst individuals of each population is replaced by new individuals generated by a scheme similar to the one described above, but instead of alg_best_i the currently best found position by all populations is used.

Thus, the position adaptation strategy of success-history based potential solutions depends on the probability p_a (there are three values for this probability, specifically one value for each component-algorithm that uses its archive during the execution), the maximum archive size $|A|$ and probabilities $padd_i$ (one for each component-algorithm).

4 Experimental Results

To check the efficiency of the proposed algorithm, the modified COBRA-f algorithm, called COBRA-fas, was tested on a set of 23 classical test problems. These functions have been widely used in literature, for instance [17], and their descriptions are given in [18]. The set of mentioned benchmark functions includes classical benchmark functions such as Ackley's, Rastrigin's, Griewank's, Sphere, Swefel's and Rosenbrock's functions. They span a diverse set of features and are separated into three groups: unimodal, high-dimensional and low-dimensional multimodal benchmark functions.

The performance of the suggested algorithm COBRA-fas was compared with other state-of-the-art algorithms like PSO [2], WPS [3], FFA [4], CSA [5], BA [6] and FSS [7]. These algorithms have several parameters that should be initialized before running. The optimal control parameters usually depend on problems and they are unknown without prior knowledge. Therefore, the initial values of the necessary parameters for all algorithms were taken from the original papers dedicated to them.

For all mentioned biology-inspired algorithms except COBRA-fas, the initial population size was equal to 100 on all 23 benchmark functions for comparison, while the maximum number of iterations was equal to 1000. Thus, to check the efficiency of the proposed algorithm COBRA-fas, the maximum number of function evaluations was set to 100000.

In order to show the advantage of the modification COBRA-fas more clearly, it was also compared with the fuzzy-controlled COBRA-f. For COBRA-f the maximum number of function evaluations was also set to 100000. Parameters for the COBRA-fas approach were found by PSO in the same way as for the COBRA-f algorithm [8], with the following parameters being obtained: $[-3, -2, 0, 10]$. The maximum archive size $|A_i|$ for each component-algorithm of the COBRA-fas meta-heuristic was equal to 50. The minimum population size for each component was set to 0, but if the total sum of population sizes was equal to 0, then all population sizes increased up to 10. Additionally, the maximum total sum of population sizes was set to 300.

Previously conducted experiments showed that the probability of using the external archive should have the following values for FFA, CSA and BA: 0.75, 0.6 and 0.15 respectively [16]. For the rest of the component-algorithms, the probability of using the external archive was set to 0 (the archive was not used specifically during the execution of a given component-algorithm but was updated). The probability $padd_i$ for the i-th component-algorithm was set to 0.25, where $i = 1, ..., 6$.

COBRA-fas was also compared with modified versions of FFA, CSA and BA: each modification used the external archive for position adaptation of individuals [16]. For these modifications (FFA-a, CSA-a and BA-a), the same maximum archive size as for COBRA-fas was chosen. For them, the initial population size was equal to 100 on each benchmark function and the maximum number of iterations was equal to 1000.

Each of the 23 problems was solved by all the mentioned algorithms and the experimental results such as average and standard deviation (SD) values are reported. Statistical parameter results are presented in Table 1. The outcomes are averaged over 30 program runs and the best results are shown in bold type in Table 1.

From Table 2 it can be observed that the proposed approach COBRA-fas outperformed state-of-the-art approaches and their modifications as well as COBRA-f on five unimodal functions (f_1, f_2, f_3, f_6 and f_7) in terms of the mean and standard deviation of the results. Regarding function f_4, COBRA-fas was outperformed only by the fuzzy-controlled COBRA-f in terms of the mean and standard deviation of the results. However, the median value obtained by COBRA-fas for f_4 was the best among all the others. Finally, regarding function f_5, COBRA-fas was outperformed only by the modification CSA-a.

For multimodal functions f_8–f_{13} with many local minima, the final results are more important because these functions can reflect the algorithm's ability to escape from local optima. For functions f_9, f_{10} and f_{11}, COBRA-fas was successful in finding the global minimum. For function f_8, CSA's modification with the external archive CSA-a gave the best results, but the median value found by COBRA-fas was equal to the global minimum. Regarding f_{10}, several algorithms gave the same results, with COBRA-fas and COBRA-f being among them. For function f_{12}, the proposed modification CSA-a produced better results compared to the others. Regarding function f_{13}, CSA-a outperformed the others in terms of the mean and standard deviation of the

Table 1. Minimization results of 23 benchmark functions

f		PSO	WPS	FSS	CSA	FFA	BA	CSA-a	FFA-a	BA-a	COBRA-f	COBRA-fas
1	ave	1.59E-06	5.79E-06	0.000757	5.18E-06	0.00313	0.000388	2.35E-05	0.001314	7.78E-05	3.00E-10	**9.75E-33**
	sd	2.43E-06	4.19E-06	7.54E-05	6.99E-06	3.73E-05	0.000332	7.21E-05	0.000367	6.51E-05	9.00E-10	**5.16E-32**
2	ave	0.186667	0.227403	0.028172	0.001134	0.403881	0.035159	0.003197	0.281052	0.031517	5.06E-05	**3.37E-32**
	sd	0.076303	0.012788	0.012715	0.000682	1.03462	0.022733	0.000603	0.461951	0.024053	0.000111	**1.81E-31**
3	ave	0.002586	0.238068	0.028531	0.079277	0.095334	0.016487	0.003036	0.023881	0.004284	3.15E-08	**2.00E-24**
	sd	0.004729	0.051457	0.004659	0.095424	0.145768	0.020547	0.001282	0.043687	0.003749	1.70E-07	**1.07E-23**
4	ave	0.787991	0.225498	0.033573	0.040128	0.232527	0.002159	0.003279	0.088004	0.002697	**1.77E-18**	2.94E-14
	sd	0.072534	0.037601	0.010726	0.020981	0.097467	0.001356	0.000519	0.127233	0.001475	**1.73E-18**	1.32E-13
5	ave	24.3935	26.768	30.9688	0.044777	32.9873	0.562678	**0.001852**	29.8896	0.54081	0.632481	0.709068
	sd	1.17226	0.260772	0.397344	0.011904	6.95187	0.38868	**0.000402**	2.73287	0.334356	1.59647	0.651327
6	ave	4.37E-07	0	0	0.00084	0.069408	0	0.000856	0.035759	0	0	0
	sd	3.80E-07	0	0	0.000306	0.001029	0	0.000246	0.011896	0	0	0
7	ave	0.022798	0.011072	0.034065	0.001386	0.119858	0.000363	0.000299	0.023482	0.000283	0.000971	**0.000164**
	sd	0.009644	0.006379	0.006115	0.000726	0.024429	0.000916	7.16E-05	0.009803	0.000455	0.002437	**0.000184**
8	ave	-3365.88	-3715.84	-1953.42	-3833.45	-2004.41	-4113.93	**-4189.83**	-2233.67	-4095.29	-4080.25	-4129.2
	sd	348.708	0.365664	349.539	102.134	34.4298	241.696	0	218.254	340.29	297.391	325.696
9	ave	25.1497	0.443485	25.9596	0.001061	31.1039	0.014076	1.42E-05	5.25703	0.012228	0	0
	sd	14.569	0.150292	9.92443	0.000993	7.9054	0.014305	2.47E-06	3.8853	0.013029	0	0
10	ave	2.33524	0.286503	0.022724	0.007219	2.19393	-4.44E-16	0.001914	1.87908	-4.44E-16	-4.44E-16	-4.44E-16
	sd	5.22105	0.107099	0.006266	0.033985	0.56606	0	0.00014	0.675231	0	0	0
11	ave	0.022367	0.667855	0.02914	0.007411	1.3761	6.23E-06	0.003739	0.330717	7.38E-06	6.68E-12	0
	sd	0.012069	0.06976	0.007509	0.009916	0.1058	4.95E-06	0.003676	0.249647	6.54E-06	3.60E-11	0
12	ave	0.832804	0.002054	0.030286	0.007105	1.23821	0.285361	**1.62E-05**	1.11234	0.165609	0.000471	0.00015
	sd	2.41123	0.000881	0.010161	0.025964	0.474751	0.303834	**8.53E-06**	0.538147	0.136602	0.001761	0.000607

(continued)

Table 1. (continued)

f		PSO	WPS	FSS	CSA	FFA	BA	CSA-a	FFA-a	BA-a	COBRA-f	COBRA-fas
13	ave	0.069719	0.038975	0.030959	2.46E-05	0.836476	0.292157	**1.47E-05**	0.477642	0.399484.	0.002164	0.001114
	sd	0.134767	0.017712	0.013819	8.74E-05	0.120599	0.204197	**7.57E-06**	0.239367	0.206086	0.00597	0.004535
14	ave	**0.998**	0.998	1.5642	0.998	1.9947	0.998	0.998	1.0157	0.998	**0.998**	**0.998**
	sd	0	7.08E-12	0.892633	1.57E-16	0.979812	1.75E-16	9.90E-16	0.06081	4.74E-16	0	0
15	ave	0.000641	0.005924	0.000524	0.000366	0.001927	0.003983	0.000324	0.000864	0.003981	0.000566	**0.000310**
	sd	0.000216	0.008707	2.17E-19	8.05E-05	0.000119	0.002392	6.55E-05	0.000977	0.002794	0.000269	**1.13E-05**
16	ave	**-1.0316**	-1.0316	-1.0316	-1.03159	-1.0281	-1.0316	-1.0316	-1.0316	-1.0316	**-1.0316**	**-1.0316**
	sd	0	1.97E-07	6.66E-16	2.69E-05	0.00149	5.51E-16	5.20E-08	3.98E-06	2.88E-07	0	0
17	ave	**0.39789**	0.39789	**0.39789**	0.398604	0.39809	0.39789	0.39789	0.39789	0.39789	**0.39789**	**0.39789**
	sd	0	1.34E-08	0	0.001596	2.64E-08	2.01E-15	5.42E-15	2.12E-05	3.19E-16	0	0
18	ave	**3.00E+00**	3.00001	3.0145	3.08097	3.02798	3.00E+00	3.01732	3.00011	3.00E+00	**3.00E+00**	**3.00E+00**
	sd	2.22E-15	1.41E-06	8.88E-16	0.032441	0.081617	2.86E-14	0.003692	0.000416	1.42E-14	0	0
19	ave	-3.8628	-3.8628	-3.8617	-3.86268	-3.8312	-3.2190	-3.8472	-3.8627	-3.8628	**-3.8628**	**-3.8628**
	sd	3.11E-15	2.76E-07	0.000558	8.61E-05	0.022515	0.638175	0.016026	0.000430	1.46E-06	0	0
20	ave	-3.2429	**-3.3223**	-3.3137	-3.20118	-3.2179	-3.3192	-3.2523	-3.2908	**-3.3223**	-3.3221	**-3.3223**
	sd	0.056194	**5.58E-05**	0.002282	0.001506	0.371432	0.016419	0.078632	0.117259	8.15e-05	0.001024	0.000126
21	ave	-4.42594	**-10.1532**	-10.147	-10.1531	-9.67012	-10.153	**-10.1532**	-10.1231	-9.74075	-10.153	-10.153
	sd	3.1596	1.64E-05	8.88E-15	4.68E-05	1.21432	0.000913	2.23E-05	0.138499	1.55633	0	0.001217
22	ave	-5.27308	**-10.4029**	-10.3966	-10.4027	-9.89302	-9.46839	**-10.4029**	-10.3104	-9.85423	-10.4028	**-10.4029**
	sd	0.952733	**6.63E-06**	0.002702	0.000178	0.100572	2.11049	2.21E-05	0.406034	1.59768	0.000272	5.62E-05
23	ave	-4.03078	-10.5364	-10.531	-10.5362	-9.37719	-10.2025	-10.5364	-10.4969	-10.5309	-10.5227	**-10.5364**
	sd	2.9128	1.07E-05	0.002013	0.000154	1.6799	1.20832	5.06E-05	0.16659	0.029262	0.073438	0

Table 2. Results of the Mann-Whitney statistical test with $p = 0.01$

	PSO	WPS	FSS	CSA	FFA	BA	CSA-a	FFA-a	BA-a	COBRA-f
+	15	12	17	17	23	12	11	13	11	8
−	0	0	0	1	0	0	2	0	0	1
=	5	8	3	2	0	11	7	7	12	11

results. However, the median value obtained by COBRA-fas for this function was the best. Therefore, it can be concluded that the proposed algorithm also has a high exploration ability.

For f_{14}–f_{23} with only a few local minima, the dimension of the function is also small. For functions f_{14}, f_{15}, f_{16}, f_{17}, f_{18}, f_{19} and f_{23}, COBRA-fas was successful in finding the global minimum. Regarding f_{14} and f_{16}, PSO, COBRA-f and COBRA-fas produced the same results. For function f_{17}, PSO, FSS, COBRA-f and COBRA-fas also gave the same values. Regarding f_{18} and f_{19}, COBRA-f and COBRA-fas produced the same mean, standard deviation and median values. From Table 1, it can be observed that the COBRA-fas approach performs better than the other algorithms on the multimodal low-dimensional benchmarks.

In Table 2, the results of comparison between COBRA-fas and the other mentioned algorithms according to the Mann-Whitney statistical test with significance level $p = 0.01$ are presented. The following notations are used in Table 2: "+" means that COBRA-fas was better compared to a given algorithm, similarly, "–" means that proposed algorithm was statistically worse, and "=" means that there was no significant difference between their results.

Thus, the comparison demonstrates that proposed modification COBRA-fas significantly outperforms other algorithms. Therefore, it can be used for solving the optimization problems instead of the other algorithms used in this study.

5 Conclusions

In this paper, a new modification of the meta-heuristic COBRA, namely the COBRA-fas meta-heuristic, is proposed for solving real-valued unconstrained optimization problems. This algorithm is compared with others using a set of 23 test functions. The experimental results show that the performance of the proposed algorithm is superior to that of the other biology-inspired algorithms: it is better at exploiting the search space and also has advantages in exploration.

In future research, real-world problems will be solved using the COBRA-fas approach to determine whether the modification provides good results in real cases with the parameters obtained in this study. This algorithm could also be considered for usage in multi-objective and constrained optimization problems.

Acknowledgments. Research is performed with the support of the Ministry of Education and Science of the Russian Federation within State Assignment project № 2.1680.2017/ПЧ.

References

1. Akhmedova, S., Semenkin, E.: Co-operation of biology related algorithms. In: IEEE Congress on Evolutionary Computation, pp. 2207–2214 (2013)
2. Kennedy, J., Eberhart, R.: Particle swarm optimization. In: IEEE International Conference on Neural Networks, IV, pp. 1942–1948 (1995)
3. Yang, Ch., Tu, X., Chen, J.: Algorithm of marriage in Honey Bees Optimization based on the Wolf Pack Search. In: International Conference on Intelligent Pervasive Computing, pp. 462–467 (2007)
4. Yang, X.S.: Firefly algorithms for multimodal optimization. In: 5th Symposium on Stochastic Algorithms, Foundations and Applications, pp. 169–178 (2009)
5. Yang, X.S., Deb, S.: Cuckoo search via Levy flights. In: World Congress on Nature & Biologically Inspired Computing, pp. 210–214. IEEE Publications (2009)
6. Yang, X.S.: A new metaheuristic bat-inspired algorithm. In: González, J.R., Pelta, D.A., Cruz, C., Terrazas, G., Krasnogor, N. (eds.) NICSO 2010. SCI, vol. 284, pp. 65–74. Springer, Heidelberg (2010). https://doi.org/10.1007/978-3-642-12538-6_6
7. Bastos, F.C., Lima, N.F.: Fish school search: an overview. In: Chiong, R. (ed.) Nature-Inspired Algorithms for Optimisation. SCI, vol. 193, pp. 261–277. Springer, Heidelberg (2009). https://doi.org/10.1007/978-3-642-00267-0_9
8. Akhmedova, S., Semenkin, E., Stanovov, V., Vishnevskaya, S.: Fuzzy logic controller design for tuning the cooperation of biology-inspired algorithms. In: Tan, Y., Takagi, H., Shi, Y., Niu, B. (eds.) ICSI 2017. LNCS, vol. 10386, pp. 269–276. Springer, Cham (2017). https://doi.org/10.1007/978-3-319-61833-3_28
9. Akhmedova, S., Semenkin, E., Stanovov, V.: Semi-supervised SVM with fuzzy controlled cooperation of biology related algorithms. In: 14th International Conference on Informatics in Control, Automation and Robotics, vol. 1, pp. 64–71 (2017)
10. Črepinšek, M., Liu, S., Mernik, M.: Exploration and exploitation in evolutionary algorithms: a survey. ACM Comput. Surv. **45**(3) (2013). Article no. 35
11. Zaharie, D.: Critical values for control parameters of differential evolution algorithm. In: The 8th International Mendel Conference on Soft Computing, pp. 62–67 (2002)
12. Kumar, A., Misra, R., Singh, D.: Improving the local search capability of effective butterfly optimizer using covariance matrix adapted retreat phase. In: IEEE Congress on Evolutionary Computation, pp. 1835–1842 (2017)
13. Zhang, J., Sanderson, A.: JADE: adaptive differential evolution with optional external archive. IEEE Trans. Evol. Comput. **13**(5), 945–958 (2009)
14. Zitzler, E., Thiele, L.: Multiobjective evolutionary algorithms: a comparative case study and the strength Pareto approach. IEEE Trans. Evol. Comput. **3**, 257–271 (1999)
15. Liang, J.J., Qu, B. Y., Suganthan P.N., Hernandez-Diaz, A.G.: Problem definitions and evaluation criteria for the CEC 2013 special session on real-parameter optimization. Technical report, Computational Intelligence Laboratory, Zhengzhou University, Zhengzhou China, and Nanyang Technological University, Singapore (2012)
16. Akhmedova, S., Stanovov, V., Erokhin, D., Semenkin, E.: Position adaptation of candidate solutions based on their success history in nature-inspired algorithms. Int. J. Inf. Technol. Secur. **11**(1), 21–32 (2019)
17. Mirjalili, S.: SCA: a Sine Cosine Algorithm for solving optimization problems. Knowl. Based Syst. **96**, 120–133 (2016)
18. Nenavath, H., Jatoth, R.K., Das, S.: A synergy of the sine-cosine algorithm and particle swarm optimizer for improved global optimization and object tracking. Swarm Evol. Comput. **43**, 1–30 (2017)

An Inter-Peer Communication Mechanism Based Water Cycle Algorithm

Ben Niu[1,2(✉)], Huan Liu[1,2], and Xi Song[2]

[1] College of Management, Shenzhen University, Shenzhen 518060, China
drniuben@gmail.com
[2] Greater Bay Area International Institute for Innovation, Shenzhen University,
Shenzhen 518060, China

Abstract. As a nature inspired metaheuristic algorithm, Water Cycle Algorithm (WCA) has been applied to some real-world problems for its excellent optimization performance. However, in standard WCA, each individual only learns information from a higher level individual but lacks communication among inter peers, which leads to the loss of some important information. In order to address this problem, an inter-peer communication mechanism based Water Cycle Algorithm (IPCWCA) is presented in this paper. In IPCWCA, besides getting information from higher level individual, each stream and river communicate with one of their peers to increase the diversity of whole population and enhance the efficiency of optimization. To explore the efficiency of IPCWCA, other four heuristic algorithms are involved to test on eight benchmark functions. Experimental results show that IPCWCA performs better on solving different types of problems compared with other four algorithms.

Keywords: Standard water cycle algorithm ·
Inter-peer communication mechanism · IPCWCA

1 Introduction

Water Cycle Algorithm (WCA) was inspired by the nature phenomenon of water cycle and presented by Eskandar et al. [1], describing the processes including water cycle and the flow among streams, rivers and sea in detail. In WCA, initial individuals are generated at first and then chosen as sea, rivers and streams according to the fitness values. Then, flow step makes streams flow to sea and rivers and makes rivers flow to sea. Last, as important portions of water cycle, evaporation and raining start, which avoid WCA being trapped into local optima.

Recently, WCA has attracted the attention of scholars widely. For the purpose of enhancing the original WCA's performance, many variances and real-world applications of it are presented. To modify the original WCA, Seyed et al. [2] proposed an improved WCA by introducing a local optimization operator. Wang et al. [3] presented a binary encoding water cycle algorithm to solve the Bayesian network structures learning problem. Ahmed et al. [4] proposed a novel WCA (MWCA) to address Directional Over Current Relays' optimal coordination problems. Besides, improved

© Springer Nature Switzerland AG 2019
Y. Tan et al. (Eds.): ICSI 2019, LNCS 11655, pp. 50–59, 2019.
https://doi.org/10.1007/978-3-030-26369-0_5

WCAs have been applied to many areas, such as electrical power systems [5], traveling salesman problem [6], traffic light scheduling problem [7] and so on.

In this paper, an inter-peer communication mechanism based Water Cycle Algorithm (IPCWCA) is proposed to promote the information communication among individuals and then improve the performance of WCA. This inter-peer communication mechanism requires each stream and river to select a peer randomly before flowing to a higher level individual and learn from some dimensions of its peer. After learning from a peer, the position of each stream and river will be updated.

The rest of the paper is organized as follows: Sect. 2 introduces the principle of original WCA briefly. The proposed IPCWCA is presented in Sect. 3. In Sect. 4, some algorithms and the proposed WCA were tested on a series of benchmark functions. Finally, Sect. 5 draws conclusions and gives future work.

2 Water Cycle Algorithms

Water Cycle Algorithm (WCA) is a new metaeuristic optimization approach to solve the constrained engineering optimization problems, which simulates the processes of water cycle and the flow among streams, rivers and sea.

WCA can be summarized as:

(i) **Initialization.** WCA creates initial population firstly and then calculates the fitness value of all individuals. Among these individuals, sea is the best one owing the best fitness value. Later, some rivers whose fitness values are closest to the sea's are selected. After choosing the sea and rivers, the remaining individuals are regarded as streams and then will flow to the rivers and sea.

(ii) **Flow.** The intensity of flow to rivers and sea, using

$$NS_n = \text{round}\left\{ \left| \frac{C_n}{\sum_{n=1}^{N_{sr}} C_n} \right| \times N_{Streams} \right\}, n = 1, 2, \ldots, N_{sr} \qquad (1)$$

The new position of a stream after flowing to the rivers and sea, using

$$X_{Stream}(t+1) = X_{Stream}(t) + rand \times C \times (X_{Sea}(t) - X_{Stream}(t)) \qquad (2)$$

$$X_{Stream}(t+1) = X_{Stream}(t) + rand \times C \times (X_{River}(t) - X_{Stream}(t)) \qquad (3)$$

and then exchange the position of specific river/sea with a stream if the stream has better fitness value.

The new position of a river after flowing to the sea, using

$$X_{River}(t+1) = X_{River}(t) + rand \times C \times (X_{Sea}(t) - X_{River}(t)) \qquad (4)$$

and then exchange the position of sea with a river if the river has better fitness value.

(iii) **Evaporation and Raining.** This process is defined to prevent WCA from getting into local optima and improve the performance of WCA. In WCA, evaporation leads individuals to evaporate and then rain as streams. The new streams are generated, using:

$$X_{Stream}^{New}(t+1) = LB + rand \times (UB - LB) \tag{5}$$

3 Inter-Peer Communication Mechanism Based Water Cycle Algorithm

As mentioned above, the individuals in standard WCA consist of three roles, including sea, river and stream. Then, the streams flow to specific river and sea will be decided according to the fitness value of the river and sea. To be more specific, take an example, there are 10 streams flow to a river. 10 streams' position will be updated after flowing and the river will be replaced by a stream if the stream's fitness value is better than the river's. Therefore, several rivers represent some local best individuals in their own group and sea is the global best individual.

In original WCA, as an information exchange way, flow step helps streams learn from rivers or sea and urges rivers learn from sea. It means that each stream and river can get some useful information from high level individual, which is beneficial for them to improve their performance. Unfortunately, there is no information communication among inter streams and inter rivers. The lack of inter-peer communication may cause some important information loss and then influence the exploration performance of the algorithm.

To avoid the loss of significant information, especially from excellent peer individuals, an inter-peer communication mechanism is presented in this paper to improve the performance of WCA. Just like us human beings, besides learning from superiors, we tend to study some advantages of our peers to improve our own abilities. Similarly, in addition to follow high level individuals' example, streams and rivers in the new communication mechanism will learn from one of their peers before flow step. The structure of original WCA is shown in Fig. 1 while IPCWCA is in Fig. 2. The yellow circle, green circle and blue circle represents sea, river and stream respectively. Arrow among inter streams or inter rivers means potential information communication. Table 1 shows the pseudo code of IPCWCA.

In IPCWCA, the peer is selected randomly among all streams or rivers. Thus, this peer may be the best individual or the worst individual, which is useful to improve diversity of the population. In other words, each stream and river in IPCWCA can get information from any other peer to update itself before flow step. At each iteration, the peer of a stream (X_i) or a river (X_j) will be selected by the random index I:

$$I_{stream} = fix(rand * (S - NSr)) + 1 \qquad I_{stream} \neq X_i \tag{6}$$

$$I_{river} = fix(rand * (Nsr - 1)) + 1 \qquad I_{river} \neq X_j \tag{7}$$

Where S is the number of individuals, Nsr is the total number of rivers and sea. Therefore, the index I_{stream} ranges from 1 to $S - Nsr$ and the index I_{river} ranges from 1 to $Nsr - 1$. After choosing a learning peer, a Gauss method is used to give a new position:

$$Position_{stream}(1,d) = Position_{stream}(1,d). * gauss$$
$$gauss = N(0, |Position_{I_{stream}}(1,d)|) \tag{8}$$

$$Position_{river}(1,d) = Position_{river}(1,d). * gauss$$
$$gauss = N(0, |Position_{I_{river}}(1,d)|) \tag{9}$$

For streams, "gauss" represents a normal distribution with a mean of 0 and a variance of the I_{stream}'s dth dimension's absolute value and the same is true for rivers. Instead of learning from all dimensions, each stream and river only acquire information from some dimensions of their peer. The number of dimensions and specific dimensions are also determined randomly. After getting information from a peer, a new position will be created and each stream or river will adopt this new position.

Table 1. The pseudo code of IPCWCA

Initialize paramesters and population
For i=1: it_max :
    For j=1: $(S$-$Nsr)$:
        Each stream learns from one of its peer by (8) and update its position;
        Each specific stream flows to sea by (2) and calculate the stream's fitness value;
        IF *Fitness_stream < Fitness_sea*
            Sea and stream exchange position and fitness value.
        End
    End
    For j=1: $(S$-$Nsr)$:
        Each stream learns from one of its peer by (8) and update its position;
        Each specific stream flows to connected river by (3) and calculate the stream's fitness value;
        IF *Fitness_stream < Fitness_river*
            River and stream exchange position and fitness value.
            IF *Fitness_river < Fitness_sea*
                Sea and river exchange position and fitness value.
            End
        End
    End
    For j=1: $(Nsr$-1$)$:
        Each river learns from one of its peer by (9) and update its position;
        Each river flows to sea by (4) and calculate the river's fitness value;
        IF *Fitness_river < Fitness_sea*
            Sea and river exchange position and fitness value.
        End
    End
    IF Evaporation condition is satisfied
        Create new streams by (5);
    End
End
Output the sea's position and fitness value

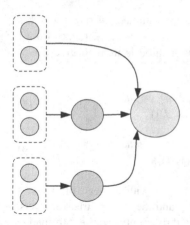

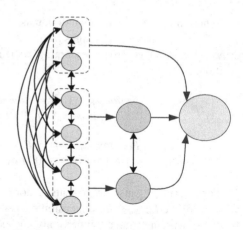

Fig. 1. The structure of WCA

Fig. 2. The structure of IPCWCA (Color figure online)

4 Experiments and Analysis

4.1 Benchmark Functions Parameter Settings

To test the efficiency of IPCWCA, eight benchmark functions are chosen [8, 9], including five unimodal benchmark functions (Powers, Sphere, Sumsquares, Zakharov, Schwefel 2.22) and three multimodal benchmark functions (Schwefel, Ackley, Weierstrass). The minimum values of all functions are the same and are equal to zero. Meanwhile, other four algorithms including original Water Cycle Algorithm, Hydrologic Cycle Optimization [10], Particle Swarm Optimization [11] and Bacterial Foraging Optimization [12] are chosen to compare with our proposed algorithm. The number of individuals for all algorithms are 50, the number of dimension is set as 10 and 30 (10D and 30D) respectively, the running time is 30, the maximum number of iterations is 2000, and other related parameters about these algorithms are shown as follows. WCA and IPCWCA: $Nsr = 4$, $dmax = 1e{-}16$. HCO: $maxFT = 3$, $P_{eva} = 0.1$. PSO: $\omega_{max} = 0.9$, $\omega_{min} = 0.7$, $C1 = C2 = 2$, $Vmin = 0.1 \times Lb$, $Vmax = 0.1 \times Ub$. BFO: $Ned = 4$, $Nre = 5$, $Nc = 100$, $Csz = 0.1$, $Ns = 10$, $Sr = Npop/2$, $Ped = 0.25$.

4.2 Experimental Results

After running 30 times, the results are shown. Tables 2 and 3 describe numerical results including the mean value, standard deviation, the minimum value and the maximum value while Figs. 3 and 4 show convergence characteristics.

For the first five unimodal benchmark functions, in both 30D and 10D experiments, IPCWCA obtains all minimum value of the mean value, standard deviation, the minimum value and the maximum value, especially on Powers, Sphere and Sumsquares functions for which IPCWCA can find the best value of zero on both four values.

As for the last three multimodal benchmark functions, IPCWCA performs differently. For Schwefel function, IPCWCA doesn't get the best value. Maybe it is because

IPCWCA is not good at optimizing this function and trapped into the local optima. For Ackley and Weierstrass functions, compared with four other algorithms, IPCWCA performs best no matter in the mean value or other values.

In general, among these five algorithms, HCO and IPCWCA have better performance. Although HCO performs well and gets the global best value on some benchmark functions, IPCWCA has a faster convergent speed on most benchmark functions and acquires the best value in almost all test functions.

Table 2. Numerical results of eight benchmark functions for 30D

	IPCWCA	WCA	HCO	PSO	BFO
Powers	**0**	2.5984e−28	**0**	6.6328e−17	5.6413e−04
	0	1.4111e−27	**0**	1.7281e−16	2.1207e−04
	0	2.0490e−37	**0**	3.2228e−21	1.6824e−04
	0	7.7310e−27	**0**	7.1097e−16	1.1000e−03
Sumsquares	**0**	1.0222e−19	2.5115e−140	8.4000e−03	7.1376e+00
	0	2.9501e−19	1.1513e−139	6.4000e−03	9.9880e−01
	0	2.6248e−24	1.0371e−155	1.7000e−03	4.3918e+00
	0	1.4961e−18	6.2125e−139	3.1400e−02	8.7403e+00
Sphere	**0**	5.9790e−19	6.3254e−141	2.3900e−02	5.6157e+03
	0	3.0209e−18	2.4906e−140	1.4900e−02	4.0051e+02
	0	1.1465e−23	3.6395e−159	6.1000e−03	4.6122e+03
	0	1.6580e−17	1.2456e−139	6.3000e−02	6.5628e+03
Zakharov	**3.3218e−128**	2.8411e−08	2.0089e−19	1.1689e+02	3.6456e+01
	1.8194e−127	5.7918e−08	6.0838e−19	7.1114e+01	6.4301e+00
	4.7496e−197	4.0432e−10	4.0184e−25	5.8400e−02	2.7430e+01
	9.9654e−127	2.7434e−07	2.7725e−18	3.3097e+02	5.0585e+01
Schwefel 2.22	**1.6623e−244**	5.9704e−07	5.8646e−123	2.0500e−01	5.4255e+01
	0	3.2515e−06	2.0627e−122	9.5700e−02	2.9359e+01
	6.7130e−291	2.9959e−12	3.6115e−131	5.1300e−02	7.0728e+00
	4.9859e−243	1.7813e−05	8.5786e−122	5.1510e−01	1.1220e+02
Schwefel	3.1176e+03	3.4081e+03	**1.2705e+03**	5.3998e+03	5.1234e+03
	4.3308e+02	7.7276e+02	2.3430e+02	8.3766e+02	**8.6769e+01**
	2.1981e+03	1.9026e+03	**8.2907e+02**	4.0673e+03	4.9124e+03
	4.2465e+03	5.8674e+03	**1.6985e+03**	7.2659e+03	5.3133e+03
Ackley	**8.8818e−16**	1.6820e−01	5.3883e−15	2.0767e+00	1.9473e+01
	0	3.8190e−01	1.5979e−15	5.0040e−01	6.3700e−02
	8.8818e−16	1.2874e−10	4.4409e−15	9.4010e−01	1.9263e+01
	8.8818e−16	1.1552e+00	7.9936e−15	3.0295e+00	1.9561e+01
Weierstrass	**0**	1.0629e+01	**0**	9.1903e+00	3.6403e+01
	0	2.5344e+00	**0**	2.1960e+00	1.2772e+00
	0	6.3341e+00	**0**	4.6499e+00	3.3760e+01
	0	1.9318e+01	**0**	4.3156e+00	3.8494e+01

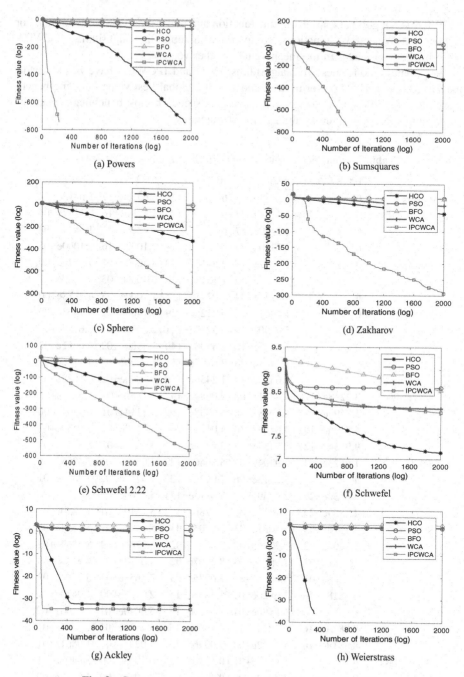

Fig. 3. Convergence characteristics of five algorithms for 30D

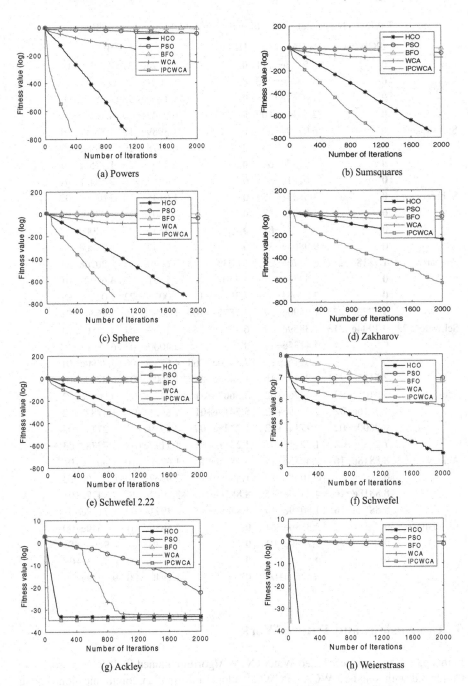

Fig. 4. Convergence characteristics of five algorithms for 10D

Table 3. Numerical results of eight benchmark functions for 10D

	IPCWCA	WCA	HCO	PSO	BFO
Powers	0	8.5176e−111	0	2.0824e−21	2.2787e−04
	0	4.5646e−110	0	1.1081e−20	9.2549e−05
	0	1.0261e−138	0	1.1400e−28	4.7856e−05
	0	2.5016e−109	0	6.0742e−20	4.7239e−04
Sumsquares	0	6.0739e−37	0	1.8989e−19	1.8540e−01
	0	2.9561e−36	0	6.0078e−19	3.4900e−02
	0	8.9237e−60	0	1.2797e−25	1.2250e−01
	0	1.6181e−35	0	3.1744e−18	2.4640e−01
Sphere	0	3.6823e−38	0	1.0135e−18	3.6800e−02
	0	1.8227e−37	0	4.9803e−18	1.0300e−02
	0	9.4577e−62	0	1.3531e−23	1.7400e−02
	0	9.9804e−37	0	2.7339e−17	5.7200e−02
Zakharov	**1.7518e−274**	6.6776e−29	1.6039e−105	3.6040e−17	2.2020e−01
	0	2.5288e−28	8.7301e−105	1.8391e−16	4.6600e−01
	0	2.2706e−35	8.3979e−127	3.0075e−22	1.0370e−01
	4.9773e−273	1.3590e−27	4.7826e−104	1.0094e−15	3.8650e−01
Schwefel2.22	**9.1904e−313**	1.3859e−17	6.3036e−249	9.1869e−04	5.7030e−01
	0	4.4135e−17	0	2.4000e−03	6.8800e−02
	0	4.0116e−25	7.3470e−268	4.6735e−06	4.2890e−01
	2.5121e−311	2.2613e−16	1.7488e−247	1.2600e−02	6.8750e−01
Schwefel	3.0105e+02	8.5276e+02	**3.5667e+01**	1.0324e+03	9.5609e+02
	1.9616e+02	2.9169e+02	**5.5419e+01**	1.8925e+02	1.4782e+02
	6.9600e−02	2.1714e+02	**1.2728e−04**	7.8959e+02	9.2777e+02
	7.2689e+02	1.3241e+03	**1.2251e+02**	1.7177e+03	1.7378e+03
Ackley	**8.8818e−16**	7.4015e−15	3.4935e−15	1.6229e−10	1.6073e+01
	0	2.1035e−15	1.5979e−15	2.9967e−10	6.5520e−01
	8.8818e−16	4.4409e−15	**8.8818e−16**	3.2907e−12	1.4438e+01
	8.8818e−16	1.5099e−14	4.4409e−15	1.4971e−09	1.7142e+01
Weierstrass	0	7.3880e−01	0	2.6650e−01	8.3649e+00
	0	9.7830e−01	0	3.4530e−01	4.9460e−01
	0	0	0	3.9500e−02	6.9718e+00
	0	3.6251e+00	0	1.1940e+00	9.0979e+00

5 Conclusions and Future Work

In this paper, an inter-peer based Water Cycle Algorithm named IPCWCA is proposed. Compared with standard WCA, IPCWCA adopts information communication among peers, which is beneficial to avoid useful information loss and increase the diversity of whole population.

During this inter-peer communication mechanism, each stream and river select one peer to communicate and update its position. In order to test the performance of IPCWCA, several heuristic algorithms are used to compare with it on eight benchmark functions. As a result, IPCWCA shows good efficiency and outperforms other algorithms on different functions both in 10D and 30D experiments. In the future, we will continue to improve the ability of IPCWCA and try to apply it to some real-world problems, like Portfolio Problems, Nurse Scheduling Problems and so on.

Acknowledgements. This work is partially supported by the Natural Science Foundation of Guangdong Province (2016A030310074), Project supported by Innovation and Entrepreneurship Research Center of Guangdong University Student (2018A073825).

References

1. Eskandar, H., Sadollah, A., Bahreininejad, A., Hamdi, M.: Water cycle algorithm–a novel metaheuristic optimization method for solving constrained engineering optimization problems. Comput. Struct. **110–111**(10), 151–166 (2012)
2. Pahnehkolaei, S.M.A., Alfi, A., Sadollah, A., Kim, J.H.: Gradient-based water cycle algorithm with evaporation rate applied to chaos suppression. Appl. Soft Comput. **53**, 420–440 (2017)
3. Wang, J., Liu, S.: Novel binary encoding water cycle algorithm for solving Bayesian network structures learning problem. Knowl. Based Syst. **150**, 95–110 (2018)
4. Ahmed, K., Salah, K., Abdel, Y., Francisco, J.: Modified water cycle algorithm for optimal direction overcurrent relays coordination. Appl. Soft Comput. **74**, 10–25 (2019)
5. Heidari, A.A., Abbaspour, R.A., Jordehi, A.R.: Gaussian bare-bones water cycle algorithm for optimal reactive power dispatch in electrical power systems. Appl. Soft Comput. **57**, 657–671 (2017)
6. Eneko, O., Javier, D.S., Ali, S., Miren, N.B., David, C.: A discrete water cycle algorithm for solving the symmetric and asymmetric traveling salesman problem. Appl. Soft Comput. **71**, 277–290 (2018)
7. Gao, K.Z., Zhang, Y.C., Sadollah, A., Lentzakis, A., Su, R.: Jaya, harmony search and water cycle algorithms for solving large-scale real-life urban traffic light scheduling problem. Swarm Evol. Comput. **37**, 58–72 (2017)
8. Tan, L.J., Yi, W.J., Yang, C., Feng, Y.Y.: Adaptive structure-redesigned-based bacterial foraging optimization. In: Huang, D.-S., Jo, K.-H. (eds.) ICIC 2016. LNCS, vol. 9772, pp. 897–907. Springer, Cham (2016). https://doi.org/10.1007/978-3-319-42294-7_80
9. Niu, B., Liu, H., Yan, X.: Hydrologic cycle optimization Part II: experiments and real-world application. In: Tan, Y., Shi, Y., Tang, Q. (eds.) ICSI 2018. LNCS, vol. 10941, pp. 350–358. Springer, Cham (2018). https://doi.org/10.1007/978-3-319-93815-8_34
10. Yan, X., Niu, B.: Hydrologic cycle optimization Part I: background and theory. In: Tan, Y., Shi, Y., Tang, Q. (eds.) ICSI 2018. LNCS, vol. 10941, pp. 341–349. Springer, Cham (2018). https://doi.org/10.1007/978-3-319-93815-8_33
11. Kennedy, J.: Encyclopedia of Machine Learning. Springer, Boston (2010)
12. Passino, K.M.: Biomimicry of bacterial foraging for distributed optimization and control. IEEE Control Syst. Mag. **22**(3), 52–67 (2002)

Cooperation-Based Gene Regulatory Network for Target Entrapment

Meng Wu[1], Yun Zhou[1], Xiaomin Zhu[1,2(✉)], Li Ma[1], Yutong Yuan[1,3], Taosheng Fang[1], Ji Wang[1], Weidong Bao[1], and Zhun Fan[3]

[1] College of Systems Engineering, National University of Defense Technology, Changsha 410073, China
{wumeng15,zhouyun007,xmzhu,mali10,wangji,wdbao}@nudt.edu.cn,
fts1787353110@163.com
[2] State Key Laboratory of High Performance Computing, Changsha, China
[3] Department of Electronic Engineering, Shantou University, Shantou 515063, China
{17ytyuan,zfan}@stu.edu.cn

Abstract. Multi-agent systems are applied to a variety of scenarios, in which target entrapment has become a primary research area in recent decades. In order to solve the problem of intelligent swarm behavior control, the hierarchical gene regulation network (H-GRN) is proposed. However, the networks in H-GRN rely solely on target information for behavioral control, and interaction with surrounding partners only involves avoiding physical collisions. To benefit from the cooperation with partners, we design a cooperation-based gene regulatory network (C-GRN) for target entrapment. Following the hierarchical gene regulatory network, we use the agent's own sensor to get the companion information, and add information to the network by controlling changes in the corresponding protein concentration. In addition, a self-organizing obstacle avoidance control method is also proposed. A series of empirical evaluations index comparison show that C-GRN can cooperate with partners. The experimental results indicate that the total time to complete task and average thickness of the target's encirclement is obviously optimized in a simulation experiment.

Keywords: Cooperation-based gene regulatory network ·
Target entrapment · Swarm agents · Pattern formation ·
Self-organization

1 Introduction

The development in self-organising multi-agent systems has become attractive in recent years. Because of their properties such as robustness in dynamic environment, the systems have found a wide range of successful applications, including cluster search and rescue operation [1,2], large objects handling [3,4], cooperative positioning and mapping [5,6], cluster area shape coverage [7,8]. Among these, self-organized target entrapment with a swarm of simple agents is a promising

© Springer Nature Switzerland AG 2019
Y. Tan et al. (Eds.): ICSI 2019, LNCS 11655, pp. 60–69, 2019.
https://doi.org/10.1007/978-3-030-26369-0_6

research topic with numerous applications, where entrapping a dangerous target is an important mission of a agent swarm, or sub-task of further collective operations.

For target entrapment, due to its stability and robustness, considerable attention has been paid to its various applications, which leads to the development of regional coverage methods. Pattern formation algorithms for swarm agents can be largely divided into five categories: (a) leader-follower and virtual structure, in which the leaders are firstly specified or identified, and the followers keep relative position to the leader [9,10]; (b) behavioural approach: rules are applied to relatively important agents to control group behavior [11–13]; (c) morphogen diffusion: morphogen-like signals are used to provide agents with information of others relative locations [14–16]. (d) reaction-diffusion model: several morphogens in cells begin to react with morphogens in other adjacent cells to produce interesting patterns [17,18]; (e) gene regulatory network: multi-cellular systems are used to control multi-agent systems [19,20].

Despite the large body of research on multi-agent pattern formation, self-organizing multi-agent systems still have many unresolved problems. First, there is a large amount of communication between agents to obtain environmental information. In existing research, behavioral control often requires a global coordinate system to achieve collaboration between agents or completely ignore cooperation with surrounding agents and only consider collision avoidance [24]. Apart from that, when entrapping a target, the agent easily loses the information of the target in a complex environment because the target may be good at escaping the encirclement. A hierarchical gene regulatory network [25] was proposed to adapt to dynamic targets. However, they have not fully utilized cooperation with partners but only use them as restrictions on action.

As for gene regulatory network, Guo et al. [21] proposed a decentralized control algorithm for multi-agent shape construction by establishing a metaphor between multi-cellular systems and multi-agent systems. They use a multi-objective evolutionary algorithm to evolve to GRN model, which was also improved to eliminate the dependence on the availability of the global coordinate system [22]. In addition, a hierarchical gene regulatory network (H-GRN) [24] was proposed, where the first layer is responsible for adaptive pattern generation, while the second is a control mechanism that drives the agents on to the generated pattern. By using this network, the agents can cover the pattern formed around the target to achieve the goal of entrapping the target. However, it costs too much time to forming an encirclement around the target.

To solve these problems, in this paper, we introduce a cooperation-based gene regulatory network for target entrapment, named C-GRN, to enhance the cooperation with partners. We assume that the agent can use the sensor to receive information about surrounding partners. Then recording them in the agent's own coordinate system. When pattern is formed, the partner's position will be used as input to lead changes in protein concentration. Thus, a pattern showing the unstable position is generated to guide the agent's actions.

In our proposed model, partners are considered when pattern is generating. By adding to the pattern based on the target proposed before, the performance of targets entrapment is optimized, with less completion time and higher entrapment quality.

2   The Proposed Framework

The framework C-GRN is presented in this section. We first give the overview of C-GRN. Then we detail two key modules: (1) cooperation with partner in the upper layer model, (2) the differentially obstacle avoidance mechanism.

2.1   Overall Structure

The overview of C-GRN is given in Fig. 1. Undoubtedly, using agent swarm to catch a target is becoming a trend. To better complete a entrapment task, more cooperations between partners should be considered. Thereby, we jointly consider the partner information and target information when entrapment pattern is generating, so agents can be reinforced to weak areas faster.

In the overall structure of C-GRN, the information of targets and agents is used as input to cause changes in protein concentration. Protein concentration is expressed in a blue circle with words. The protein concentration S guides the formation of guidance model. And in the layer 2, protein concentration P_i and G_i change according to pattern with the aim of guiding the motion of agents.

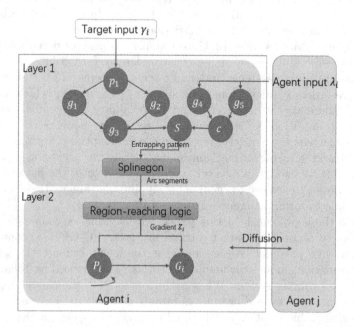

Fig. 1. Overview of a two-layer C-GRN structure for target entrapment under the help of partner and obstacle

Obstacle cannot be perceived entirely in a proximate scenario. It is obvious that much information is needed if an agent tends to avoid obstacles using a pattern generated in the upper layer. Further, original methods have less adaptation when the obstacles appear or move suddenly. So a self-organizing obstacle avoidance mechanism is proposed, which expects to keep away from obstacles by using its own sensor.

2.2   Cooperation with Partners

In order to apply the model to the target entrapment scenario and improve its performance, we propose a model that considers peer collaboration. This model enables an agent to generate pattern depends on the information from not only the targets but also the partners. Thus, the agent can spot the weak parts of the encirclement and reinforce it.

An improved frame is proposed in the upper layer of the model (see Fig. 1). By applying gene regulation network, agents can simply interact with others through the protein concentration in the environment. They get the protein concentration p in the environment which is produced by all the detected targets [24], and this integrated protein will activate the internal protein concentrations. Similarly, an agent also gets the protein concentration c_i produced by the perceived agent. The protein concentration c_i includes $g_{4,j}$ and $g_{5,j}$ produced when detected nearby agent j for agent i.

As for a swarm of agents with sensors, they are able to gain the knowledge about the protein concentration by using position sensors. In this way, protein concentration can diffuse through agents [23] using the following equation:.

$$\frac{dg_{4,j}}{dt} = -g_{4,j} + e^{-\lambda_j}. \tag{1}$$

$$\frac{dg_{5,j}}{dt} = -g_{5,j} + [(1 - sig(\lambda_j, \varepsilon_1, \alpha_1)) + sig(\lambda_j, \varepsilon_2, \alpha_2)]. \tag{2}$$

$$\frac{dc_i}{dt} = -c_i + k_1 \sum_{j=1}^{n_{tj}} g_{4,j} + k_2 \sum_{j=1}^{n_{tj}} g_{5,j}. \tag{3}$$

$$sig(x, z, k) = \frac{1}{1 + e^{-k(x-z)}}. \tag{4}$$

where c_i is the protein concentration got from neighbouring in agent i, λ_j is the input from agent j, and n_{tj} is the number of agents that are communicationally connected to agent i. $g_{4,j}$ and $g_{5,j}$ represent the protein concentration produced by homologous gene which is activated by environment input λ_j from agent j. Parameter k_1 and k_2 represent the impact of protein concentration $g_{4,j}$ and $g_{5,j}$ for agent i, respectively. For a two-dimensional scene, its computational complexity is $O(n^2)$.

A common phenomenon in biology is that every agent has a source of protein concentration $g_{5,j}$, and it diffuses through the exponential curve, refer to Fig. 2(a). However, because it is sensitive to noise and disturbance at the part of low slope, an effective solution is provided by Werfel [23]. They put a small diffusion source at the opposite side, then the two protein concentrations interact with each other, which results in a linear concentration gradient of the first protein concentration diffusion, shown as Fig. 2(b). Similarly, we assume a negative protein $g_{5,j}$ is also produced when getting the partner j's input, and its concentration is defined as Eq. (2). By combining the two proteins, the diffusion will avoid from low slope and be more robust to the environment.

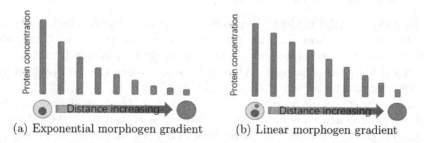

(a) Exponential morphogen gradient   (b) Linear morphogen gradient

Fig. 2. Comparing the concentration pattern of diffusion mechanism.

To be more robust to noise and disturbance, protein concentration c is diffused following Eq. (5). The final pattern depends on the input of target and partner, according to the following formula.

$$S = \sum_{i=1}^{N} a_i D_i. \tag{5}$$

where S is an integrated protein concentration that represents the synthesis of all protein effects, also the final parameter that will be delivered to the lower layer and used to form the pattern by agent itself. N is the number of protein species which directly impacts protein concentration S. a_i is the influence of protein concentration D_i of i-th kind of protein. In this part, S consists of the cooperation protein c and target protein g_3.

$$S = g_3 + c. \tag{6}$$

The target protein g_3 is activated by the integrated protein p and protein concentration g_2 and g_3. Where p_j represents the protein concentration produced by the j-th target input γ_j and p is the sum of concentrations of all detected n_t targets.

$$\frac{dp_j}{dt} = -p_j + \nabla^2 p_j + \gamma_i, p = \sum_{j=1}^{n_t} p_j. \tag{7}$$

$$\frac{dg_1}{dt} = -g_1 + sig(p, \theta_1, k). \tag{8}$$

$$\frac{dg_2}{dt} = -g_2 + [1 - sig(p, \theta_2, k)]. \tag{9}$$

$$\frac{dg_3}{dt} = -g_3 + sig(g_1 + g_2, \theta_3, k). \tag{10}$$

New pattern generated under the upper layer, as shown in the white part of the Fig. 3. It shows two examples of a target entrapping pattern from protein concentration g_3 and c when the entrapping task is unfinished (Fig. 3(a)) and completed (Fig. 3(b)). Agents are represented by white points, the target is represented by a white asterisk, and the gradient of the pattern is represented by different colors. Agents tend to be employed in lighter areas in the pattern, where the encirclement of the target is unstable and easy to break.

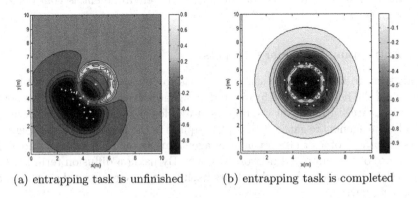

(a) entrapping task is unfinished   (b) entrapping task is completed

Fig. 3. Examples of a target entrapping pattern from protein concentration S generated by the upper layer of the C-GRN. (Color figure online)

2.3 Self-organizing Obstacle Avoidance Mechanism

To enhance adaptivity capacity of agents to avoid obstacles in a dynamic environment, in our study, self-organizing obstacle avoidance is added in lower layer. It can be applied when the obstacles move fast or appear suddenly, i.e., the pattern generated from upper layer has no time to change. So in our proposed mechanism, the loss cased by wrong pattern can be avoided.

This mechanism is based on the agent's own sensor. The agent determines the speed and direction of the movement at next step through the C-GRN network. Then, the agent detects the situation in this direction. If it is safe, which means no obstacles or attackers, the agent can move forward according to the original plan. If there are things that might harm the agent, then the agent detects the left and right direction, whose angle with this direction is the random degree. The mechanism compares the detection results on both sides until there is something on one side, but not on the other side. Then proceeds from the original direction and continue to increase the angle detection, until the angle is found at which the obstacle is not detected. The agent will record this angle and the next step is to proceed at this angle.

Therefore, agents can quickly avoid obstacles, only through their own sensors and self-organizing obstacle avoidance mechanisms.

3 Experimental Analysis

Numerical simulations have been performed using scenarios containing either stationary or moving targets to evaluate the feasibility and benefit of the proposed algorithm. Parameters for the upper layer of the C-GRN are set up as $k_1 = 0.6$, $k_2 = -0.4$, and for the lower layer as $a = 6.5$, $m = 4.2$, $c = 9.9$, $r = 4.3$, and $b = 3.5$. These values in the lower layer adopt the settings in [25]. In addition, the speed of the agent is $1\,\mathrm{m/s}$ considering the agents' physical capability. Changing the speed according to the environment is considered in the future work.

3.1 Entrapping Stationary Targets

In this section, the designed task of agents is to entrap two stationary targets. The size of the field is set to [15, 15], and an agent is represented by a blue point. The targets are stationary at the upper left and lower right corners, respectively. Initially, the agents are gathered in a [2, 2] square in the lower left corner. Figure 4 shows snapshots of a situation where 40 agents are trapping 2 targets, under the governance of the improved network C-GRN. By using a diffusion term Eq. (5), the C-GRN dynamics inherently adapts itself to the environmental changes, i.e., the moving partners.

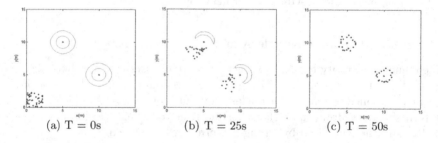

(a) T = 0s   (b) T = 25s   (c) T = 50s

Fig. 4. 40 agent (blue point) entrapping 2 targets (denoted by ×). The pattern is simply represented by a red NURBS curve. (Color figure online)

Figure 4 shows that the agents trap targets with faster spreading speed. In the end, both goals are completely entrapped. To quantitatively evaluate the pattern formation performance, we performed a set of simulations to examine the time cost to complete the encirclement. The time cost is defined to be the time when every unit of the target is occupied, it also means the target has no direction to escape.

The experiment was done many times with different numbers of agents and the experimental results are listed in Table 1, which are average over 25 independent runs. From the table, we can conclude that the agents can move faster under the cooperation between agents.

Table 1. Average entrapping time cost(s)

	No. of agents		
	40	50	60
Network			
H-GRN	57 (s)	55 (s)	52 (s)
C-GRN	48 (s)	45 (s)	42 (s)

4 Conclusions and Future Work

In this paper, a cooperation-based gene regulatory network is presented for target entrapment. The main new feature of the proposed model is that the target pattern generated by the agent not only depends on the information of the target, but also considers the influence of the surrounding agents. Therefore, agents can enhance the cooperation with other agents by using their sensors exclusively. This ability of cooperation is not available in the H-GRN model, nor in any existing models for distributed agent swarm control, to the best of our knowledge. The proposed model in our study enables a cooperative self-organization of multi-agent systems and enhanced performance of target entrapment. Empirical results show that the performance of the system in terms of the time needed for completing a entrapment task obviously decreases due to the using of the whole framework.

However, it should be pointed out that this network requires precise positioning of surrounding agents, so that high demands on the sensor is requested. We are considering to propose other computational methods for sensors with poor performance to adapt to the proposed network in the future work.

A few quite conservative assumptions are still made in this model, including the reliance on global coordinate system. In this model, the agent needs to know the position of its target and other agents in the global coordinate system. A more realistic implementation is to establish the agent's own polar coordinate system and locate various objects in it. Apart from that, the agent needs to calculate all the partners within the detection range, which requires the computing power and storage capacity of the agent.

The use of encirclement consisting of unmanned equipment to entrap targets is a common application of current unmanned systems. The C-GRN proposed in this work can be conceivably extended to complete dangerous missions such as reclamation thieves or terrorists. The salient features of such missions are complex environments, many obstacles, dangerous targets and easy escape. For example, at a terrorist base, terrorists are dangerous and good at using environmental obstacles to escape. In this scenario, using this network can make better use of surrounding agent to arrest. In short, this network is suitable for all multi-agent swarm systems to enhance collaboration between agents.

Acknowledgements. This work was supported in part by the National Natural Science Foundation of China under Grants 61872378, and 91648204, in part by the National Defense Technology Innovation Special Zone Projects

References

1. Baxter, J., Burke, E., Garibaldi, J., et al.: Multirobot search and rescue: a potential field based approach. In: Proceedings of the IEEE/RSJ International Conference on Intelligent Robots and Systems, pp. 9–16 (2007)
2. Bakhshipour, M., Jabbari Ghadi, M., Namdari, F.: Swarm robotics search & rescue: a novel artificial intelligence-inspired optimization approach. Appl. Soft Comput. **57**, 708–726 (2017). 2017:S1568494617301072
3. Martinoli, A., Easton, K., Agassounon, W.: Modeling swarm robotic systems: a case study in collaborative distributed manipulation. Int. J. Robot. Res. **23**(4), 415–436 (2004)
4. Chen, J., Gauci, M., Li, W., et al.: Occlusion-based cooperative transport with a swarm of miniature mobile robots. IEEE Trans. Robot. **31**(2), 307–321 (2017)
5. Madhavan, R., Fregene, K., Parker, L.E.: Distributed heterogeneous outdoor multi-robot localization. In: Proceedings of the 2002 IEEE International Conference on Robotics and Automation, pp. 374–381 (2002)
6. Arnold, R.D., Yamaguchi, H., Tanaka, T.: Search and rescue with autonomous flying robots through behavior-based cooperative intelligence. J. Int. Humanit. Action **3**(1), 18 (2018)
7. Dierks, T., Jagannathan, S.: Neural network output feedback control of robot formations. IEEE Trans. Syst. Man Cybern. Part B Cybern. **40**(2), 383–399 (2010)
8. Arezoumand, R., Mashohor, S., Marhaban, M.H.: Efficient terrain coverage for deploying wireless sensor nodes on multi-robot system. Intell. Serv. Robot. **9**(2), 163–175 (2016)
9. Loria, A., Dasdemir, J., Jarquinalvarez, N.: LeaderCFollower formation and tracking control of mobile robots along straight paths. IEEE Trans. Control Syst. Technol. **24**(2), 727–732 (2016)
10. Dingjiang, Z., Zijian, W., Mac, S.: Agile coordination and assistive collision avoidance for quadrotor swarms using virtual structures. IEEE Trans. Robot. **34**, 1–8 (2018)
11. Doctor, S., Venayagamoorthy, G.K., Gudise, V.G.: Optimal PSO for collective robotic search applications. In: IEEE Congress on Evolutionary Computation, vol. 2, pp. 1390–1395. IEEE (2004)
12. Scharf, D.P., Hadaegh, F.Y., Ploen, S.R.: A survey of spacecraft formation flying guidance and control. Part II: control. In: American Control Conference, vol. 4. pp. 2976–2985. IEEE (2004)
13. Beard, R.W., Lawton, J., Hadaegh, F.Y., et al.: A coordination architecture for spacecraft formation control. IEEE Trans. Control Syst. Technol. **9**(6), 777–790 (2001)
14. Yeom, K.: Bio-inspired automatic shape formation for swarms of self-reconfigurable modular robots. In: IEEE Fifth International Conference on Bio-Inspired Computing: Theories and Applications (BIC-TA), pp. 469–476 (2010)

15. Kondacs, A.: Biologically-inspired self-assembly of two-dimensional shapes using global-to-local compilation. In: International Joint Conference on Artificial Intelligence, pp. 633–638 (2003)
16. Nagpal, R., Kondacs, A., Chang, C.: Programming methodology for biologically-inspired self-assembling systems. In: AAAI Spring Symposium on Computational Synthesis, pp. 173–180 (2003)
17. Schroeder, A.M., Kumar, M.: Design of decentralized chemotactic control law for area coverage using swarm of mobile robots. IEEE Trans. **261**, pp. 189–192 (2016)
18. Lee, I.-H., Cho, U.-I.: Pattern formations with turing and HOPF oscillating pattern in a discrete reaction-diffusion system. Bull. Korean Chem. Soc. **21**, 1213–1216 (2000)
19. Jin, Y., Meng, Y.: Morphogenetic robotics: an emerging new field in developmental robotics. IEEE Trans. Syst. Man Cybern. Part C Appl. Rev. **41**(2), 145–160 (2011)
20. Taylor, T., Ottery, P., Hallam, J.: Pattern formation for multi-robot applications: robust, self-repairing systems inspired by genetic regulatory networks and cellular self-organisation. Informatics Research Report (2006)
21. Guo, H., Meng, Y., Jin, Y.: A cellular mechanism for multi-robot construction via evolutionary multi-objective optimization of a gene regulatory network. BioSystems **98**(3), 193–203 (2009)
22. Guo, H., Jin, Y., Meng, Y.: A morphogenetic framework for self-organized multi-robot pattern formation and boundary coverage. ACM Trans. Auton. Adapt. Syst. **7**(1), 1–23 (2012)
23. Werfel, J.: Biologically realistic primitives for engineered morphogenesis. In: Dorigo, M., et al. (eds.) ANTS 2010. LNCS, vol. 6234, pp. 131–142. Springer, Heidelberg (2010). https://doi.org/10.1007/978-3-642-15461-4_12
24. Jin, Y., Guo, H., Meng, Y.: A hierarchical gene regulatory network for adaptive multirobot pattern formation. IEEE Trans. Syst. Man Cybern. Part B Cybern. **42**(3), 805 (2012). A Publication of the IEEE Systems Man & Cybernetics Society
25. Oh, H., Jin, Y.: Adaptive swarm robot region coverage using gene regulatory networks. In: Mistry, M., Leonardis, A., Witkowski, M., Melhuish, C. (eds.) TAROS 2014. LNCS (LNAI), vol. 8717, pp. 197–208. Springer, Cham (2014). https://doi.org/10.1007/978-3-319-10401-0_18

Population-Based Metaheuristics for Planning Interval Training Sessions in Mountain Biking

Iztok Fister Jr.[1]([✉]), Dušan Fister[1], Andres Iglesias[2,3], Akemi Galvez[2,3], Samo Rauter[4], and Iztok Fister[1]

[1] Faculty of Electrical Engineering and Computer Science, University of Maribor, Koroška cesta 46, Maribor, Slovenia
iztok.fister1@um.si
[2] Toho University, 2-2-1 Miyama, Funabashi 274-8510, Japan
[3] University of Cantabria, Avenida de los Castros, s/n, 39005 Santander, Spain
[4] University of Ljubljana, Ljubljana, Slovenia

Abstract. Stochastic population-based nature-inspired metaheuristics have recently revealed that they are a very robust tool for planning sport training sessions in various sports, e.g. running, cycling, triathlon. Most of the existing solutions in literature are focused on planning training sessions for a particular training cycle. Until recently, no special attention was paid to planning interval training sessions, where the high-intensity intervals are followed by low-intensity periods of recovery. This kind of training sessions increases the aerobic capacity of an athlete. In this paper, we propose planning interval training sessions using stochastic population-based nature-inspired metaheuristics. The proposed bat algorithm was tested on an archive of interval training sessions realized by a younger mountain biker, where two different scenarios were taken into account.

Keywords: Planning sport training sessions · Metaheuristics · Optimization

1 Introduction

Sport trainers are crucial components in the process of an athlete's sports training, that is a required precondition for achieving success in the sport competitions. The primary task of the modern sport trainer is offering assistance for athletes, helping them by planning sport training sessions, analyzing the past training sessions, and also racing. Typically, it is very difficult to become an excellent sport trainer. Therefore, the majority of them are past athletes with many training, as well as racing, experiences. Besides these experiences, each good trainer must have a deep knowledge about nutrition, human anatomy, sociology, psychology, and so on.

Nowadays, we live in a society where modern Information Technology (IT) can be found in almost every domain of life. Therefore, it is no wonder that the

Y. Tan et al. (Eds.): ICSI 2019, LNCS 11655, pp. 70–79, 2019.
https://doi.org/10.1007/978-3-030-26369-0_7

modern computer technology has also been applied into the domain of Sport. A recent book [4] has introduced the concept of the Artificial Sport Trainer (AST), based on stochastic population-based nature-inspired metaheuristics [3,6]. Automatic planning of the sport training sessions that is a part of the AST is still considered as a very hard task. For an efficient automatic planning of sports training sessions, algorithms have to deal with archives of existing sports training sessions, which were obtained by measuring the performance data obtained during the real ones by wearable mobile devices (e.g., sports watches, mobile phones). Additionally, these algorithms are able to deal with several constraints that could arise during the process of sport training. In some cases, athletes are injured and the existing training plan needs to be adapted accordingly.

Until recently, no special attention was devoted to automatic planning of interval training sessions, where the high-intensity intervals are interspersed with recovery periods, due to increasing the aerobic capacity of the athlete in sports training. In this paper, the automatic planning of interval training sessions in mountain biking presents the main challenge. Thus, this planning is represented as an optimization problem, which combines the high-intensity intervals and corresponding low-intensity recovery periods from existing interval training sessions collected within an archive, such that the sum of all *TRIMP* values of the proposed intervals does not exceed the prescribed maximum value. Let us notice that the *TRIMP* value represents an intensity measure of the specific interval training session expressed as a product of average Heart Rate (HR) by its duration (t).

Although the proposed algorithm could be implemented using any stochastic population-based nature-inspired algorithm [5], the Bat Algorithm (BA) [12] was selected due to its simplicity. The algorithm for planning the interval training sessions was applied to an archive of 40 existing interval training sessions produced by a young mountain cyclist. However, the results were commented by real cyclist trainers, who confirmed that these training plans could be applied in practice. To the authors' knowledge, this is the first study that operates with population-based metaheuristics for the interval training sessions planning.

In summary, this paper presents the following main novel contributions:

- to elucidate the problem of planning the interval training sessions,
- to present planning the interval training sessions as an optimization problem,
- to propose a new method for particular problem based on the BA.
- to apply the proposed algorithm on a real archive of collected interval training sessions.

The structure of this paper is as follows: Sect. 2 deals with the fundamentals of interval training in mountain biking. In Sect. 3, the optimization problem of planning the interval training sessions is discussed in detail. Experiments and results are subjects of Sect. 4, while Sect. 5 summarizes the performed work and outlines directions for the future work.

2   Fundamentals of Interval Training in Mountain Bike

Interval training has a very long tradition. In general, for successful endurance athletes must balance the overall frequency and volume of training with the high-intensity interval training sessions [11]. The interval training session intersperses the high-intensity intervals (i.e., exercises of intensity equal to or higher than the maximal lactate steady-state threshold) with recovery periods (i.e., low-intensity exercises or recovery). Interval training was first described by Reindell and Roskamm [2], and was popularized by the Olympic Champion Emil Zatopek in the 1950s. Indeed, aerobic interval training is defined as an interval training which elicits aerobic metabolism at a higher ratio than anaerobic metabolism.

The Olympic format of cross-country mountain bike racing (XCO) is a fairly different sport in comparison to road cycling, because it changes also the basic principles of mountain bike training by including high-intensity workouts beside the endurance ones. A cycling race requires cyclists to possess the ability to generate a relatively high power output of short duration during steep climbing and in accelerations [10]. It can be characterized as a high-intensity, intermittent activity that requires riders to compete over varying terrains, including rocky paths, a technical single-track, and open forestry roads. Frequently, this also includes obstacles such as jumps and vertical drops, with high-intensity, high-power ascending sections that are separated by relatively lower-intensity descents [1,7,8].

In sports theory, it is well known that mountain bikers need to adapt, and to simulate competitive conditions during their training sessions. Especially, there are a lot of short periods of acceleration. Typically, mountain bikers have to overcome up to 120 of such accelerations within 90 min of racing. Consequently, special attention needs to be paid to the development of speed (with emphasis on high intensity training), as well as specific strength (special strength training) and coordination, which becomes particularly important during the downhills [9].

A typical endurance training session consists of repeated 1 to 8 min runs at 90 % to 100 % speed of maximal oxygen uptake, with recovery intervals of 2 to 3 min). This is the most effective program for improving maximal oxygen uptake and performance for endurance athletes [2]. On the other hand, studies of anaerobic intervals divide the interval training into two categories. The first category (the older studies) examined this kind of training at a fixed work-rate. Thus, the time limit, or the number of repetitions, was suitable to sustain a different pause duration. The intensities used in these studies were not at the highest intensity level, but were at about 130 % to 160 % of the maximal oxygen uptake speed. Moreover, they used high-intensity intervals of 10 to 15 s in duration that were interrupted by short recovery intervals of 15 to 40 s in duration. The second category (the more recent studies) demanded that the high-intensity intervals of 30 s be interspersed with different recovery intervals of 4 to 5 min in duration. These studies examined the changes in maximal dynamic power during successive exercise periods, and characterized the associated metabolic changes in muscle [2].

3   Problem Definition and Proposed Solution Method

An interval training consists of a sequence of exercises, where each high-intensity exercise is followed by a low-intensity exercise that is dedicated to resting. For instance, if the typical interval training session in cycling lasts 60 min and there are 10 intervals, the duration of each interval is 6 min, where the high-intensity interval lasts 5 min and the low-intensity one 1 min. Formally, each interval of an interval training session can be expressed as $IT_i = \langle I_i, R_i \rangle$, where the high-intensity period is defined as couple $I_i = \langle HR_i^{(I)}, t_i^{(I)} \rangle$, and the low-intensity period as $R_i = \langle HR_i^{(R)}, t_i^{(R)} \rangle$. In both couples, the first element $HR_i^{(.)}$ determines the average heart rate, while the second element $t_i^{(.)}$ the duration of i-th interval. In summary, the whole interval training session is defined as:

$$IT = \left[\left\langle HR_1^{(I)}, t_1^{(I)}, HR_1^{(R)}, t_1^{(R)} \right\rangle, \ldots, \left\langle HR_n^{(I)}, t_n^{(I)}, HR_n^{(R)}, t_n^{(R)} \right\rangle \right], \quad (1)$$

where n describes the number of intervals in the interval training session IT.

All the interval training sessions realized in one training cycle are accumulated into an archive of interval training sessions, in other words:

$$A = \begin{cases} IT_1 = \left[\left\langle HR_{1,1}^{(I)}, t_{1,1}^{(I)}, HR_{1,1}^{(R)}, t_{1,1}^{(R)} \right\rangle, \ldots, \left\langle HR_{1,n}^{(I)}, t_{1,n}^{(I)}, HR_{1,n}^{(R)}, t_{1,n}^{(R)} \right\rangle \right], \\ \quad\quad\quad\quad\quad\quad \ldots \\ IT_m = \left[\left\langle HR_{m,1}^{(I)}, t_{m,1}^{(I)}, HR_{m,1}^{(R)}, t_{m,1}^{(R)} \right\rangle, \ldots, \left\langle HR_{m,n}^{(I)}, t_{m,n}^{(I)}, HR_{m,n}^{(R)}, t_{m,n}^{(R)} \right\rangle \right], \end{cases} \quad (2)$$

where m determines the number of interval training sessions in archive A.

3.1   Problem Definition

Planning the interval training sessions in mountain biking is presented as an optimization problem in the following way: Let us assume, an archive of interval training sessions in mountain biking to be A, and the desired values $TRIMP_0$ are given, where the measure $TRIMP$ determines the intensity of the interval training session according to the following equation:

$$TRIMP = HR \cdot t. \quad (3)$$

Then, the total intensity of the interval training session is expressed as follows:

$$TRIMP(IT) = \sum_{j=1}^{n} \left(HR_{k_j}^{(I)} \cdot t_{k_j}^{(I)} + HR_{k_j}^{(R)} \cdot t_{k_j}^{(R)} \right), \quad (4)$$

subject to

$$\sum_{j=1}^{n} \left(t_{k_j}^{(I)} + t_{k_j}^{(R)} \right) \leq TD, \text{ and} \quad (5)$$

$$t_0^{(I)} \leq t_{k_j}^{(I)} < 0, \text{ for } j = 1, \ldots, n, \quad (6)$$

where k_j determines the j-th interval of the selected k-th interval training session from the archive A, TD is the duration of the interval training (typically ≤ 60 min), and $t_0^{(I)}$ the maximum duration of the high-intensity interval that cannot be zero.

Objective function is expressed as:

$$f(IT) = |TRIMP(IT) - TRIMP_0|. \tag{7}$$

The task of the optimization algorithm is to find the minimum value of the objective function, in other words:

$$f^*(IT) = \min f(IT). \tag{8}$$

In the remainder of the section, the design of the stochastic population-based nature-inspired algorithm for planning the interval training is illustrated in detail.

3.2   Algorithm for Planning the Interval Training

As said before, the algorithm for planning interval training can be any stochastic population-based nature-inspired algorithm. However, the BA [12] was used in our study, due to its simplicity. The following modifications must be applied to the original algorithm.

Representation of Individuals. The individuals representing the interval training session IT are represented as vectors:

$$\mathbf{x}_i = [x_{i,1}, \ldots, x_{i,n}], \quad \text{for } i = 1, \ldots, Np, \tag{9}$$

where each of $x_{i,j} \in [0,1]$ for $j = 1, \ldots, n$ determines the index of the interval training session, from which the $IT_{k,j}$ elements of the interval training k belonging to the specific interval j are taken, n is a dimension of the problem, and Np denotes the number of individuals within the population.

Evaluation of Objective Function. The objective function is expressed by Eq. (7). In order to evaluate this function, each element of the vector $x_{i,j}$ needs to be mapped into the corresponding elements of the interval training $IT_{k,j}$ according to the following equation:

$$k_j = \lfloor x_{i,j} \cdot m \rfloor + 1, \tag{10}$$

where $k_j \in [1, m]$ determines the j-th interval of the k-th interval training session within the archive A.

Repairing the Infeasible Solutions. Often, the solution generated by the stochastic population-based nature-inspired algorithms, can be infeasible, when the constraints according the inequalities in Eqs. (5) and (6) are violated. Let us assume that we generate 10 intervals that must be finished in one hour. When the generated interval training exceeds the limitation of one hour, the constraint presented in Eq. (5) is violated. In this case, the infeasible solution is repaired, such that one of the intensity intervals in the violating solution is selected randomly. This interval is then modified with the interval of lower duration in the randomly selected interval training from the archive.

The second constraint violation occurs when the duration of the high-intensity interval exceeds the maximum duration $t_0^{(I)}$. Also, in that case, the randomly selected high-intensity interval violating constraint is changed with the high-intensity interval from the randomly selected interval training from the archive that does not violate the constraint.

However, the additional constraints could be incorporated into Eq. (4) that determine the characteristics of the interval training in more detail. Obviously, the constraints remain as a direction for the future.

Comment. The principle of the proposed algorithm is simple: Actually, it selects the most suitable values of the HR and t for the specific interval from the interval training sessions accumulated into the archive. Thereby, this does not generate new values that were not realized in practice. Consequently, if we want to generate the interval training with maximum values, this could be achieved only to a certain extent, i.e., when all the maximum values were not achieved in the same interval training. This means that the algorithm never prescribes values which the athlete does not achieve in real training, but it is expected that the results of particular intervals will overcome the prescribed "hard" interval training sessions. Thus, the athlete increases the level of his/her achievements due to archiving each activity into the archive.

4   Experiments and Results

The aim of the experimental work was to evaluate the proposed stochastic population-based nature-inspired algorithm for planning interval training sessions. In line with this, two scenarios were defined:

- scenario A: deals with interval training of low-intensity *TRIMP*,
- scenario B: deals with interval training of high-intensity *TRIMP*.

Characteristics of both scenarios are described in detail in the remainder of the section. The results of scenarios were obtained by applying the BA for planning the interval training using the parameter setting as illustrated in Table 1.

The proposed BA was applied on an archive of interval training sessions consisting of $m = 40$ interval training sessions, realized by the professional young mountain biker. Part of the archive is presented in Table 2. Let us notice that

Table 1. Parameter setting of the BA

Nr.	Parameter name	Value
1	Population size	$Np = 50$
2	Individual size	$n = 10$
3	Pulse rate	$r_i = 0.5$
4	Loudness	$A_i = 0.5$

Table 2. Part of the archive

ID	$HR_{\mathrm{ID}}^{(I)}$	$t_{\mathrm{ID}}^{(I)}$	$HR_{\mathrm{ID}}^{(R)}$	$t_{\mathrm{ID}}^{(I)}$
1	185	5	147	3
2	186	5	148	2
3	186	4	149	2
4	187	5	148	3
5	188	4	150	2

the archive comprises interval training sessions of a wide spectrum, i.e., from the low-intensity and short-duration toward the high-intensity and long-duration. The same is also true for the resting period, where they are spread from shorter-duration to longer-duration. The intensities of this period are similar, and, therefore, can be ignored.

Although 25 runs of the proposed BA were performed for each scenario, we are interested only in the best solution according to the Eq. (8).

4.1   Scenario A

The characteristics of the interval training sessions in this scenario are used to generate an interval training plan of lower-intensity $TRIMP$. This means that the rational algorithm for planning the interval training session needs to select both the observed training periods (i.e., intensity and recovery) of either low-intensity or short-duration. Thus, the desired total intensity of the generated interval training was set to $TRIMP_0 = 9,000$. However, the interval training plan must be generated with $n = 10$ intensity and recovery periods.

Table 3. Generated interval training plan of lower-intensity $TRIMP$

ID	$HR_{\mathrm{ID}}^{(I)}$	$t_{\mathrm{ID}}^{(I)}$	$HR_{\mathrm{ID}}^{(R)}$	$t_{\mathrm{ID}}^{(I)}$	$TRIMP_{\mathrm{ID}}^{(I)}$	$TRIMP_{\mathrm{ID}}^{(R)}$	$TRIMP_{\mathrm{ID}}$
1	183	5	140	2	915	280	1195
2	187	3	161	1	561	161	722
3	188	3	161	1	564	161	725
4	184	3	160	1	552	160	712
5	187	3	161	1	561	161	722
6	186	5	148	2	930	296	1226
7	183	5	140	2	915	280	1195
8	188	3	161	1	564	161	725
9	188	4	150	2	752	300	1052
10	188	3	161	1	564	161	725
$\sum$	186.2	37	154.3	14	6,878	2,121	8,999

The results of Scenario A are presented in Table 3, from which it can be seen that the total intensity of the best generated interval training amounts to $TRIMP = 8,999$. This means that the algorithm found the solution of intensity $TRIMP$, differing from the desired one by less than 1 % (more precisely 99.99 % matching). On the other hand, this training session is also of short-duration, due to endurance of $37 + 14 = 51$ min, where the average heart rate of the intensity period is 186.2 bpm, and the recovery period 154.3 bpm.

The comment of the real sports trainer is as follows: Results in the table shows a high level of correlation with aerobic interval training, which is performed by mountain bikers very often, especially in preparation periods for competitions. The first type of training plan consists of repeated 3–5 min high intensity intervals with a relatively short-time of recovery (1–2 min). This training method ensures a successful adaptation to the level of high acidose by the athletes, which represents a similar effort as usually presented in the mountain bike races.

4.2   Scenario B

In this scenario, two demands were tested: (1) drastic increase of the demanded interval training intensity to $TRIMP_0 = 15,000$, and (2) at least one intensity period to be longer or equal to $t_{k_j}^{(I)} \geq 9$ min. Now, the BA must prefer the intensity and recovery periods of longer-duration on the one hand, and of higher-intensity on the other. Also here, the interval training must consist of 10 intensity, as well as recovery periods.

The results of Scenario B are depicted in Table 4, from which it can be seen that the total intensity of the best interval training needs to be realized at the intensity $TRIMP = 14,960$, that means 99.73 % matching with the demanded intensity. The slightly worse results than in Scenario A is a consequence of more constrained problem substituted with additional objectives. In this case, the total duration of

Table 4. Generated interval training plan of higher-intensity $TRIMP$

ID	$HR_{ID}^{(I)}$	$t_{ID}^{(I)}$	$HR_{ID}^{(R)}$	$t_{ID}^{(I)}$	$TRIMP_{ID}^{(I)}$	$TRIMP_{ID}^{(R)}$	$TRIMP_{ID}$
1	179	5	120	6	895	720	1,615
2	188	5	151	2	940	302	1,242
3	178	6	148	3	1,068	444	1,512
4	174	8	138	4	1,392	552	1,944
5	186	4	143	2	744	286	1,030
6	172	9	131	5	1,548	655	2,203
7	185	4	145	2	740	290	1,030
8	177	7	135	4	1,239	540	1,779
9	186	5	148	2	930	296	1,226
10	187	5	148	3	935	444	1,379
$\sum$	181.2	58	140.7	33	10,431	4,529	14,960

the interval training increases to $58 + 33 = 91$ min, while the average heart rate of the intensity period settles at 181.2 bpm, and the recovery period 140.7 bpm.

The comment of the real sports trainer is now as follows. The second type of training consists of repeated 4–9 min intensity intervals, with recovery periods that last approximately 50 % less time than the intensity phase. Although this type of interval training slightly differs from the above mentioned Scenario A, it is the most effective for improving the maximal oxygen uptake and racing performance of the mountain bikers.

5   Conclusion

There is no doubt that stochastic population-based nature-inspired metaheuristics are a robust tool for planning the training sessions in various sports. In past, these metaheuristics have appeared for planning sports training sessions, where this training plan was generated for longer training periods.

In this paper, we investigated the possibility of planning the interval training sessions that consist of different intervals, and each interval is composed of an intensity interval and recovery period. Additionally, each intensity interval and recovery period are determined by the average heart rate and duration. The planning is represented as an optimization problem, where all intervals (i.e., intensity interval and recovery period) are composed from an archive of the interval training sessions, such that the total intensity of the training according to value $TRIMP$ does not exceed the desired intensity $TRIMP_0$. Let us mention that, in this preliminary phase, we do not generate the training plan for the whole training cycle, but for one interval training session only.

Although the algorithm for planning the interval training sessions could be implemented in any stochastic population-based nature-inspired algorithm, the BA was applied in this study. Experiments using the algorithm were divided into two scenarios, e.g. Scenario A and Scenario B, where both were conducted on an archive consisting of 40 interval training sessions realized by a younger mountain biker. The results confirmed our assumption that population-based metaheuristics can be applied for such type of planning.

The future of this area is still full of opportunities. Firstly, we should focus on the feedback of athletes who train on the training plan proposed by our method. Secondly, we should take into account more information about the already realized training sessions. From the initial observations, we see that there are many differences among athletes in the realm of endurance or speed. For that reason, some athletes prefer more interval sessions of more duration over intensity, while others vice-versa.

Acknowledgments. I. Fister Jr. acknowledges the financial support from the Slovenian Research Agency (Research Core Founding No. P2-0057). I. Fister acknowledges the financial support from the Slovenian Research Agency (Research Core Founding No. P2-0041). A. Iglesias and A. Galvez would like to thank the financial support from the projects TIN2017-89275-R (AEI/FEDER, UE) and PDE-GIR (H2020, MSCA program, ref. 778035).

References

1. Abbiss, C.R., et al.: The distribution of pace adopted by cyclists during a cross-country mountain bike world championships. J. Sports Sci. **31**(7), 787–794 (2013)
2. Billat, L.V.: Interval training for performance: a scientific and empirical practice. Sports Med. **31**(1), 13–31 (2001)
3. Engelbrecht, A.P.: Computational Intelligence: An Introduction. Wiley, Chichester (2007)
4. Fister, I., Fister Jr., I., Fister, D.: Computational Intelligence in Sports. ALO, vol. 22. Springer, Cham (2019). https://doi.org/10.1007/978-3-030-03490-0
5. Fister Jr., I., Yang, X.S., Fister, I., Brest, J., Fister, D.: A brief review of nature-inspired algorithms for optimization. Elektrotehniški vestnik **80**(3), 116–122 (2013)
6. Hassanien, A.E., Emary, E.: Swarm Intelligence: Principles, Advances, and Applications. CRC Press, Boca Raton (2018)
7. Impellizzeri, F.M., Marcora, S.M.: The physiology of mountain biking. Sports Med. **37**(1), 59–71 (2007)
8. Macdermid, P.W., Stannard, S.: Mechanical work and physiological responses to simulated cross country mountain bike racing. J. Sports Sci. **30**(14), 1491–1501 (2012)
9. Prins, L., Terblanche, E., Myburgh, K.H.: Field and laboratory correlates of performance in competitive cross-country mountain bikers. J. Sports Sci. **25**(8), 927–935 (2007)
10. Rauter, S.: New approach for planning the mountain bike training with virtual coach. Trends Sport Sci. **25**(2), 69–74 (2018)
11. Seiler, S., Sylta, Ø.: How does interval-training prescription affect physiological and perceptual responses? Int. J. Sports Physiol. Perform. **12**(Suppl 2), S2–80 (2017)
12. Yang, X.S.: A new metaheuristic bat-inspired algorithm. In: González, J.R., Pelta, D.A., Cruz, C., Terrazas, G., Krasnogor, N. (eds.) NICSO 2010. Studies in Computational Intelligence, vol. 284, pp. 65–74. Springer, Heidelberg (2010). https://doi.org/10.1007/978-3-642-12538-6_6

Comparison of Infrastructure and AdHoc Modes in Survivable Networks Enabled by Evolutionary Swarms

George Leu[✉] and Jiangjun Tang

School of Engineering and IT, UNSW Canberra, Canberra, Australia
{g.leu,j.tang}@adfa.edu.au

Abstract. This paper investigates how the communication architecture of a ground swarm of agents contributes to the survivability level when trying to solve the problem of survivable ground networks via UAV support. The paper considers the two most important conceptual communication architectures, infrastructure and adhoc, and compares the levels of survivability obtained by each of them when we use a mobility model for the UAVs which is based on evolutionary swarm intelligence. Results show that systems which operate in infrastructure mode tend to exhibit higher levels of survivability, which is somewhat counter-intuitive but can be explained through the way the mobility model implements the behavior of the supporting UAVs.

Keywords: Evolutionary swarm intelligence · Survivable networks · Communication architectures

1 Introduction

Swarm intelligence has been increasingly used in recent years in the field of survivable networks, where the wireless communication between mobile unmanned agents operating on the ground (UGV) is facilitated by a swarm of unmanned aerial vehicles (UAVs) that act as mobile aerial communication relays. The concept of survivability refers to the extent to which the UGVs remain connected when various obstructions occur in the ground wireless communication, thanks to the convenient positioning of the UAVs.

Research in survivable networks is mainly focused on the mobility models adopted by the UAVs as part of the aerial swarms used for ensuring network survivability. These refer to the decision-making mechanisms that provide the optimal air trajectories and/or positions, to ensure communication within the UGV swarm. While mobility models aim to improve the network survivability levels, they also contribute to other aspects such as the scalability of the overall systems, or the level of operational integration between the UAV and UGV swarms [12,18]. The investigations in survivable networks domain propose swarm intelligence methods for ground systems of interest that use certain given communication (conceptual) architectures [2,12] or technologies [7,8]. These investigations demonstrate the ability of the proposed methods to ensure network

© Springer Nature Switzerland AG 2019
Y. Tan et al. (Eds.): ICSI 2019, LNCS 11655, pp. 80–89, 2019.
https://doi.org/10.1007/978-3-030-26369-0_8

survivability when applied to the respective given systems, but do not investigate the possibility of being applied to systems using different communication architectures/technologies. However, we argue that working solely on improving the swarm behaviors that lead to network survivability may not be sufficient, since the communication architecture (and/or technology) used by the ground system of interest may have as well a significant impact. Thus, another question to be answered is, if a certain swarm intelligence method is given for guiding the UAV swarms, then what would be the communication architecture that the ground system should employ to maximize the performance of the method. Analyzing this aspect is crucial especially when the system considered from a network survivability perspective does not exist yet, and a decision on its future design needs to be made.

This paper considers the two most important conceptual communication architectures adopted by the existing networked systems, i.e. infrastructure and adhoc, and compares the levels of survivability obtained when a swarm intelligence method is applied to each of them. To perform the comparison between the two communication architectures, we use one of the most recent swarm intelligence UAV mobility models used in survivable networks, which was proposed in [12]. This mobility model uses a bio-inspired approach that combines swarm intelligence and evolutionary computation, where the UAVs and ground agents are modelled as a boids-like dual air-ground swarm, and the UAVs' movements are optimized by a real-time genetic algorithm.

The rest of the paper is organized as follows. Section 2 briefly discusses the main achievements reported in the literature in relation to the swarm intelligence methods used in survivable networks. Then, Sect. 3 describes the methodology used to compare the two communication architectures, and Sect. 4 presents and discusses the experiment results. In the end, Sect. 5 summarises the findings and concludes the paper.

2   Background

The survivable network problem is not exclusively related to contexts where mobile aerial support is used by the swarming ground agents. Historically, mobile ground relays have been initially used to connect mobile ground agents. However, with the ever increasing needs of communication, and the broader contexts where ground swarming was adopted, aerial relays became necessary. Satellites and high-altitude fixed-wing aircraft have been proposed in the early days, but they have substantial limitations, especially related to their ability to follow the ground agents in difficult locations like forests, urban areas, indoors or underground. As a result, the subsequent studies on survivability could only be performed on very low numbers of agents, where the concept of swarming can be hardly considered. In [3,7] very low scale systems are investigated, with one relay agent and two ground agents. In [6] few relay agents support the communication between a single mobile ground agent and a fixed base station. Attempts to investigate larger systems have been reported in [2,8,9], however, they are still limited to few relay agents and few ground agents.

The leap towards using true swarm intelligence in survivable networks contexts came with the advances in drone technology. The availability of miniaturized, versatile and low-cost rotary-wing UAVs (i.e. multicopter drones) made possible the investigation of a wider range of swarm intelligence mobility models for the UAVs, which have been applied to systems with higher number of agents. With respect to survivable networks domain, the increased number of agents also posed the question about the type of information available to UAVs from both the air and ground side. The information can be global, where map-based or global positioning systems inputs have been proposed [4,11], or local as in boid-like swarms [14], where inputs come only from the neighboring agents [2,6]. While studies that use global information exists, the bulk of the literature in survivable networks concentrates on models that use local information. Thus, the literature discussed below refers exclusively to models that rely on local information.

Chaos-enhanced mobility models, which build on early approaches like random trajectories [11], generated a considerable amount of research in the literature [15]. Parametric approaches with fixed pre-tuned parameters have been also proposed over time, especially in early studies on survivable network research [2,8,10] Another category of mobility models is based on nature-inspired swarming behaviours, such as ant colony pheromone-based mobility [11], bat algorithms [16], or boids-based finite state machines [2]. Models based on artificial evolution principles have been also reported in the literature, where evolutionary computation techniques are used to evolve parameters of the controllers used in the aerial agents [6]; though, this direction has been less investigated. This is in essence because of the challenges imposed by the use of evolutionary computation techniques in real-time contexts, i.e. due to their relatively slow convergence [17], especially when they need to optimize large numbers of parameters.

Recently, hybrid methods have been proposed, which use boids-based flocking behaviour (i.e. Reynolds' boids [14]) to implement UAVs' movement and evolutionary computation to optimise their movement towards increased ground network survivability. Such hybrid method is proposed in [12], where the authors take a step froward and model both UAVs and ground agents as boids guided by the classic boids forces [14]—cohesion, alignment and separation—to obtain a dual air-ground swarm. The air and ground swarms are in fact a single swarm, with the UAVs and ground agents having the parameters tuned differently. The evolutionary computation technique takes the form of a genetic algorithm that optimizes the parameters of the UAV boids towards improving the ground network survivability. Given that the number of parameters of the boids is low, the genetic algorithm runs well in real-time; thus, the use of boids rules with the genetic algorithm avoids the slow convergence issues.

In terms of the communication architecture/technology used by the systems under investigation, some of the existing studies work with the adhoc mode [8,9] while others work with the infrastructure mode [2,12]. To the best of our knowledge, no study exists to date to compare the two communication architectures in the context of survivable networks when swarm intelligence mobility models are used. Thus, we perform this comparison using a modified version of the hybrid mobility model proposed in [12]. This modification is in the way the genetic algorithm works. In [12] the authors intend to demonstrate the viability of their approach for any type of movement pattern of the UGVs. In this paper, we are interested in the comparison of the two communication architectures and adopt only the core algorithm from [12], but we use it for a different set of scenarios, with different operational environment and agent settings, as explained below.

3 Methodology

In this paper we consider a test-bed environment that has been largely used for survivable networks investigations [2,5,12]. This is a flat $2D$ rectangular surface S with length L and width W, which has no obstacles. The UGVs can move freely on the surface, but must avoid collision with each other. Above this surface fly the UAVs at a constant low altitude that does not affect communication with the ground; this means the communication is only affected by the horizontal movement. There are n_a UAVs and n_g UGVs in the environment. Both UAVs and UGVs are modelled based on Reynolds' boids model [14] and use the two key boids concepts: the neighborhood-based interaction and the three forces— cohesion, alignment and separation. All forces are defined and calculated exactly as in Reynolds' paper, while the neighborhood is calculated slightly differently, as explained below.

The ground network survivability is typically evaluated based on the "connectivity" concept. This uses the graph theoretical concept of connected network component [1], which denotes a sub-graph where any two nodes are connected to each other. We define connectivity as the number of connected components that exist at a moment in time within the swarm of UGVs. Ideally, when the ground swarm is fully connected, the connectivity has the value 1, i.e. there is only one sub-graph which is equal to the entire ground network. In practice, more than one connected components are accepted in survivable networks, due to the nature of the problem. However, among them one or several giant connected components should exist [13]. In this paper, we measure the survivability by calculating the size of the giant components throughout the simulation.

3.1 The Agents

The UGVs are modelled as a boids-based swarm, and follow the three classic boids rules, which are applied as a result of the influence received from their ground neighbors, where the neighborhood is defined by agents' vision distance v_d and vision angle v_α.

The forces are calculated like in Reynolds original study [14], and then, the velocity V and position P of a UGV at time step t are updated using Eqs. 1 and 2, respectively.

$$V(t) = V(t-1) + W_C \cdot C(t) + W_A \cdot A(t) + W_S \cdot S(t) \qquad (1)$$

$$P(t) = P(t-1) + V(t) \tag{2}$$

where W_C, W_A, and W_S are weights corresponding to cohesion, alignment, and separation forces. These weights are constant, because the movement pattern of the UGVs is fixed (i.e. they perform a specific task). We recall that in survivable networks contexts the UGVs operate in the field to accomplish a certain task, and are not aware or concerned about the UAVs' activity.

When the ground swarm is in infrastructure mode, no direct communication exists between UGVs; they can only communicate indirectly via the UAVs. When the ground swarm is in adhoc mode, an omnidirectional ground communication range R_g is considered. The communication range is only used to determine the adhoc links, not to define the neighborhood.

The UAVs are also modelled as a boids-based swarm, but with slightly different interactions. The interaction in the air, between UAVs, follows the three classic boids forces showing the influence from the neighboring UAVs. In addition, an interaction with the ground is considered, and modelled via two additional forces that represent the influence from the neighboring ground agents. We recall that the purpose in survivable networks is for the UAVs to move according to the UGVs' movement, so that they facilitate communication. Thus, an UAV is influenced by the movement of the UGVs situated in its neighborhood through the cohesion and alignment forces. The separation force is not considered, because there is no risk of collision between UAVs and UGVs.

Unlike the UGVs (i.e. classic vision-based boids), UAVs' neighborhood is defined using an omnidirectional air communication range R_a, and is different for the infrastructure and adhoc modes. Thus, the UAV swarm is not a classic vision-based swarm, but an adhoc networked swarm where links are established within the R_a range. When the ground swarm is in infrastructure mode, the neighbors of an UAV are the UAVs and UGVs situated within the air communication range R_a. When the ground swarm is in adhoc mode, the neighbors of an UAV are the UAVs situated within R_a, the UGVs situated within R_a (we call them primary air-ground neighbors—PAGN), plus the UGVs that are outside R_a but are adhoc connected to the PAGNs (i.e. they are within R_g from the PAGNs).

With the five forces calculated as in Reynodls' study according to the corresponding neighborhood, the velocity $V_{A_i}(t)$ and position $P_{A_i}(t)$ of each UAV A_i are updated as in Eqs. 3 and 4, respectively.

$$\begin{aligned} V_{A_i}(t) =\ & V_{A_i}(t-1) \\ & + W_{C_A} C_{A_i}(t) + W_{A_A} A_{A_i}(t) + W_{S_A} S_{A_i}(t) \\ & + W_{C_{AG}} C_{AG_i}(t) + W_{A_{AG}} A_{AG_i}(t) \end{aligned} \tag{3}$$

$$P_{A_i}(t) = P_{A_i}(t-1) + V_{A_i}(t) \tag{4}$$

where C_A, A_A and S_A are the three air-air forces, C_{AG} and A_{AG} are the two air-ground forces, and Ws denote the weights of the forces. Unlike the UGVs, the force weights of the UAVs are not constant, since their movement must adapt continuously to the movement of the UGVs. Thus, an optimization of the force weights at each time step is needed, so that the best connectivity for the UGVs is achieved. The optimization algorithm is described in detail in Sect. 3.2.

3.2 The Optimization Method

A decentralized real-time GA is used to optimize the force weights in the update rules of the UAVs, so that the resultant movements lead to high network survivability. Each UAV runs the GA separately to obtain its own set of optimal force weights at each time step. Thus, each UAV optimizes independently its own five force weights plus the speed, with the purpose of providing better connectivity to the ground agents. In theory, each UAV should run the GA at each time step of the simulation; however, in practice a certain time is needed for the evolution to reach meaningful results. For this reason the UAVs run their GAs every t' time steps. The GAs run in time windows of duration t', where the duration is the stopping condition. This affects the quality of the optimal solution at each GA run, but ensures the overall simulation runs in real-time. The time windows allow a historical period of duration t', as well as a future prediction period of duration t' to be used for optimization as part of the fitness function (which is explained below).

The structure of the chromosomes is the same for all UAVs in the simulation. They are vectors with 6 components $[s, W_{GA}, W_{GC}, W_{AA}, W_{AC}, W_{AS}]$, where Ws are force weights and s is the speed. The value ranges for the genes in the chromosomes are: speed between 0 (hovering) and 5, separation weight between 0.5 and 2, all other weights (i.e. $W_{GA}, W_{GC}, W_{AA}, W_{AC}$) between 0 and 0.5.

The fitness function is based on the number of UGVs covered by an UAV and its neighbors (i.e. one hop aerial network links), with the consideration of both historic and predicted periods.

$$ F = \sum_{k=t-t'}^{t} N_G(k) + N_G(t + t') \tag{5} $$

where N_G is the total number of ground agents covered by an UAV and its neighbouring UAVs.

The GA aims to maximize the fitness, which means, to increase the UAV's individual coverage as well as the number of neighbouring connections for establishing better connectivity. Further, selection, crossover, and mutation operators are applied for producing offspring. Selection uses the binary tournament with elitism, and reproduction employs single point crossover at a rate of 0.8, and mutation at a rate that is the reciprocal of the chromosome length ($\frac{1}{m_a \times 6}$).

4   Experiments and Results

4.1   Experimental Setup

The numbers of agents are $n_g = 100$ UGVs and $n_a = 4$ UAVs. They operate in an environment of size 1000×1000 units for a duration of 22000 time steps. UGVs are initialized with random positions, and the weights of their forces are: $W_C = 0.01$, $W_A = 0.125$ and $W_S = 1$. Their neighborhood is defined by $v_d = 30$ units, and $v_\alpha = 360°$. The communication range for the adhoc scenario is $R_g = v_d$, for convenience. UAVs are initialized to form a 300×300 units square situated in the center of the environment. The UAV communication range is $R_a = 300$. Each UAV initializes 50 chromosomes randomly (the size of the population in the GA) and runs the GA repeatedly in t' time windows to optimize the weights of its forces.

There are a total of 30 random number generator seeds used for initialing the environment and agents, which means, 30 runs for each scenario, to ensure statistical validity of the results. Two scenarios are used, as explained earlier in the paper: infrastructure mode and adhoc mode.

4.2   Discussion of Results

As explained earlier in the paper, we measure the ground network survivability by calculating the size of the giant components throughout the simulation, for the system operating in infrastructure and adhoc modes. Figure 1 shows the top 3 largest components for the two scenarios. Of these three, the most relevant is the largest component. The other two, while still accounting for the overall quality of the communications within the UGV swarm, have sizes that do not qualify them as giant components [13]. However, when analyzing these two components we can see that they are smaller in infrastructure mode. Arguably, we can expect that since less nodes are in the second and third largest components, then more nodes will be part of the largest component. This confirms if we analyse the curve illustrating the largest component. From a survivability perspective the levels for the largest component match those reported in previous studies [2,12]. However, from a comparison perspective it is still difficult to decide which communication architecture is better, even though visually the infrastructure mode seems better.

To clarify this, we would like to investigate how much time out of the total simulation time the largest component has a certain size. Figure 2 illustrates the results of this investigation, where higher values on the right side of the plot indicate better survivability. We can see clearly that throughout the simulation the largest component contains between 95 and 100 nodes for more than 40% of the time in infrastructure mode compared to approx. 25% in adhoc mode. It can be also seen that in infrastructure mode the largest component has over 80 nodes for a relatively high percentage of time compared to the adhoc mode. In addition, the adhoc mode also has periods of time when the largest component contains as few as 30 to 40 nodes, which does not happen in infrastructure mode.

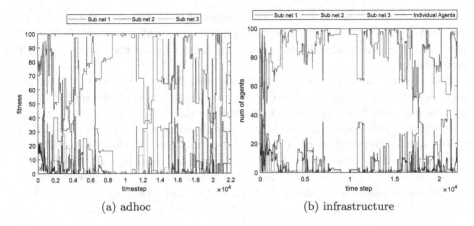

(a) adhoc   (b) infrastructure

Fig. 1. The number of agents in TOP 3 largest sub-networks.

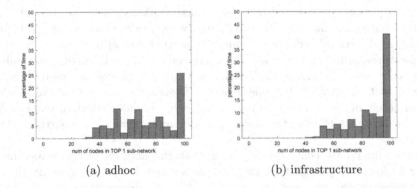

(a) adhoc   (b) infrastructure

Fig. 2. The number of agents over time (percentage) in the largest sub-network.

With the above simulation results, if becomes apparent that if the UGV swarm uses infrastructure as a communication architecture, the resultant survivability is higher compared to the adhoc case. This may be counter-intuitive at a first sight, since having the possibility to connect any UGV to any other UGV directly, without UAV support, seems to be more beneficial for the overall connectivity. However, in reality, we recall that the survivable network problem is focused on situations when communication is disrupted for various reasons. As such, the high dynamics of the ground swarm and the potential disruptions still lead to the network being broken in numerous subnetworks despite the adhoc architectural approach; which further means that aerial support is still needed. Then, the UAVs need to react to the movement of the various adhoc subnetworks via the boids forces, as explained in the methodology. We recall that if an UAV has a neighbor in a subnetwork, in adhoc mode this UAV is attracted by all UGVs in the subnetwork, whereas in infrastructure mode it is attracted only by that particular neighbor. This means that if clusters of UGVs are in the field and are far away from each other, they may pull away and disconnect the UAVs from each other leading to a much larger loss of the system's overall connectivity.

The above results and their rationale are nevertheless pertinent to the mobility model use in this paper. Indeed, the conclusions may be different if other models are used. However, the hybrid models that employ evolutionary swarm intelligence are the most recent and, arguably, the most comprehensive in relation to the survivable networks problem; hence, we may assume that the infrastructure mode could be the better performer in general, regardless of the mobility model. Whilst this is an assumption at the moment, more investigation would be needed the evaluate its validity in other contexts, which is an important direction of future work resulting from this paper.

5   Conclusion

In this paper, we investigated how the communication architecture of a ground swarm agents contributes to the survivability level in the context of survivable networks. We considered the two most important conceptual communication architectures, infrastructure and adhoc, and compared the levels of survivability obtained when a hybrid swarm intelligence mobility model was used. Results showed that the system that operates in infrastructure mode tends to exhibit higher levels of survivability, which is somewhat counter-intuitive but can be explained through the way the mobility model implements the supporting UAVs behavior.

In summary, we conclude by saying that the findings of this paper have some limitations through that they might be bounded to the mobility model used; however, this is a preliminary study which considered the influence of the communication architecture on the survivable networks problem for the first time, and opens the way for significant future work in this direction.

References

1. Albert, R., Barabási, A.L.: Statistical mechanics of complex networks. Rev. Mod. Phys. **74**, 47–97 (2002). https://doi.org/10.1103/RevModPhys.74.47
2. Basu, P., Redi, J., Shurbanov, V.: Coordinated flocking of UAVs for improved connectivity of mobile ground nodes. In: 2004 IEEE MILCOM 2004. Military Communications Conference, vol. 3, pp. 1628–1634, October 2004. https://doi.org/10.1109/MILCOM.2004.1495182
3. Elliot, M., Stevens, T.: Dynamic range extension using harlequin and hail. In: MILCOM 2016–2016 IEEE Military Communications Conference, pp. 835–841, November 2016. https://doi.org/10.1109/MILCOM.2016.7795433
4. Elston, J., Frew, E.W.: Hierarchical distributed control for search and tracking by heterogeneous aerial robot networks. In: 2008 IEEE International Conference on Robotics and Automation, pp. 170–175, May 2008. https://doi.org/10.1109/ROBOT.2008.4543204

5. Gaudiano, P., Bonabeau, E., Shargel, B.: Evolving behaviors for a swarm of unmanned air vehicles. In: Proceedings 2005 IEEE Swarm Intelligence Symposium, 2005. SIS 2005, pp. 317–324, June 2005. https://doi.org/10.1109/SIS.2005.1501638

6. Hauert, S., Zufferey, J.C., Floreano, D.: Evolved swarming without positioning information: an application in aerial communication relay. Auton. Robots **26**(1), 21–32 (2009). https://doi.org/10.1007/s10514-008-9104-9

7. Hui, K., Phillips, D., Kekirigoda, A.: Beyond line-of-sight range extension with opal using autonomous unmanned aerial vehicles. In: MILCOM 2017–2017 IEEE Military Communications Conference (MILCOM), pp. 279–284, October 2017. https://doi.org/10.1109/MILCOM.2017.8170774

8. Hui, K., Pourbeik, P., George, P., Phillips, D., Magrath, S., Kwiatkowski, M.: Opal - a survivability-oriented approach to management of tactical military networks. In: 2011 - MILCOM 2011 Military Communications Conference, pp. 1127–1132, November 2011. https://doi.org/10.1109/MILCOM.2011.6127450

9. Hunjet, R., Stevens, T., Elliot, M., Fraser, B., George, P.: Survivable communications and autonomous delivery service a generic swarming framework enabling communications in contested environments. In: MILCOM 2017–2017 IEEE Military Communications Conference (MILCOM), pp. 788–793, October 2017. https://doi.org/10.1109/MILCOM.2017.8170775

10. Kar, K., Banerjee, S.: Node placement for connected coverage in sensor networks. In: WiOpt 2003: Modeling and Optimization in Mobile, Ad Hoc and Wireless Networks, March 2003. https://hal.inria.fr/inria-00466114. poster

11. Kuiper, E., Nadjm-Tehrani, S.: Mobility models for UAV group reconnaissance applications. In: 2006 International Conference on Wireless and Mobile Communications (ICWMC 2006), p. 33, July 2006. https://doi.org/10.1109/ICWMC.2006.63

12. Leu, G., Tang, J.: Survivable networks via uav swarms guided by decentralized real-time evolutionary computation. CoRR abs/1902.07860 (2019). https://arxiv.org/abs/1902.07860

13. Newman, M.E.J.: Assortative mixing in networks. Phys. Rev. Lett. **89**, 208701 (2002). https://doi.org/10.1103/PhysRevLett.89.208701

14. Reynolds, C.W.: Flocks, herds and schools: a distributed behavioral model. SIGGRAPH Comput. Graph. **21**(4), 25–34 (1987). https://doi.org/10.1145/37402.37406

15. Rosalie, M., Danoy, G., Chaumette, S., Bouvry, P.: From random process to chaotic behavior in swarms of UAVs. In: Proceedings of the 6th ACM Symposium on Development and Analysis of Intelligent Vehicular Networks and Applications, pp. 9–15. DIVANet 2016. ACM, New York (2016). https://doi.org/10.1145/2989275.2989281. http://doi.acm.org/10.1145/2989275.2989281

16. Suarez, P., Iglesias, A., Galvez, A.: Make robots be bats: specializing robotic swarms to the bat algorithm. Swarm Evol. Comput. (2018). https://doi.org/10.1016/j.swevo.2018.01.005

17. Tang, Y., Gao, H., Kurths, J., Fang, J.: Evolutionary pinning control and its application in UAV coordination. IEEE Trans. Industr. Inf. **8**(4), 828–838 (2012). https://doi.org/10.1109/TII.2012.2187911

18. Zeng, Y., Zhang, R., Lim, T.J.: Wireless communications with unmanned aerial vehicles: opportunities and challenges. IEEE Commun. Mag. **54**(5), 36–42 (2016). https://doi.org/10.1109/MCOM.2016.7470933

Particle Swarm Optimization

An Analysis of Control Parameter Importance in the Particle Swarm Optimization Algorithm

Kyle Robert Harrison[1(✉)], Beatrice M. Ombuki-Berman[2],
and Andries P. Engelbrecht[3]

[1] Department of Electrical, Computer, and Software Engineering,
University of Ontario Institute of Technology, Oshawa, Canada
kharrison@outlook.com
[2] Department of Computer Science, Brock University, St. Catharines, Canada
bombuki@brocku.ca
[3] Department of Industrial Engineering and Division of Computer Science,
Stellenbosch University, Stellenbosch, South Africa
engel@sun.ac.za

Abstract. Particle swarm optimization (PSO) is a stochastic search algorithm based on the social dynamics of a flock of birds. The performance of the PSO algorithm is known to be sensitive to the values assigned to its control parameters, and appropriate tuning of these control parameters can greatly improve performance. This paper employs function analysis of variance (fANOVA) to quantify the importance of each of the three conventional PSO control parameters, namely the inertia weight (ω), the cognitive acceleration coefficient (c_1), and the social acceleration coefficient (c_2), according to their respective variances associated with the fitness. Results indicate that the inertia value, ω, has the greatest sensitivity to its assigned value and thus is the most important parameter to tune when optimizing PSO performance for low dimensional problems.

Keywords: Particle swarm optimization · Self-adaptive ·
Control parameter tuning · fANOVA · Response surface

1 Introduction

It is widely accepted that an effective search technique should strike a balance between exploration, which focuses on examining unexplored regions of the search space, and exploitation, which focuses on improving (promising) known solutions. In the particle swarm optimization (PSO) algorithm [20], the exploration and exploitation can be controlled by appropriately setting the values of the three primary control parameters [1,2,5,6,29]. In turn, the performance of PSO can be greatly improved when the parameters are tuned with respect to the current problem [3,7,19,23].

© Springer Nature Switzerland AG 2019
Y. Tan et al. (Eds.): ICSI 2019, LNCS 11655, pp. 93–105, 2019.
https://doi.org/10.1007/978-3-030-26369-0_9

While there is a clear benefit associated with effective control parameter tuning in the PSO algorithm, the tuning process is typically time-consuming and cumbersome given that a large number of candidate control parameter configurations must be analyzed. Fortunately, there have been a number of studies that have suggested general-purpose control parameter values based on empirical evidence [5,7,10,14,18,23,29,32].

To alleviate the issue of manual parameter tuning, numerous self-adaptive PSO (SAPSO) algorithms that adapt their control parameter values over time have been proposed [25,26,28,30,31]. Despite their reported successes, a large majority of these SAPSO algorithms have been shown to exhibit poor performance [12,13,33]. It is hypothesized that the poor performance of SAPSO algorithms is due to their simultaneous need to optimize two continuous problems, namely the primary optimization problem and the control parameter tuning problem. Furthermore, poor performance in the control parameter tuning problem will most certainly lead to poor performance in the primary optimization problem. Therefore, any reduction in the difficulty of the control parameter tuning problem will likely lead to major improvements in the performance of SAPSO algorithms. One potential avenue for reducing the difficulty of the control parameter tuning problem is to identify which of the control parameters are most influential in the tuning process. If any of the control parameters are found to be more influential towards the overall performance, more resources can be allocated to optimizing their values. Similarly, control parameters that have little influence on the overall performance can be allocated less resources when optimizing their values.

To this end, the primary objective of this study is to determine the relative importance of each of the three PSO control parameters. Functional analysis of variance (fANOVA) [27], which examines the variance of a response relative to each of its inputs, is employed to analyze the importance of each of the PSO control parameters across a suite of 20 benchmark problems in both 10 and 30 dimensions. A total of 8400 PSO control parameter configurations are examined on both 10D and 30D problems to provide a comprehensive analysis of the effects of each control parameter. Note that the purpose of this study is not to identify well-performing control parameter configurations. Rather, this study presents a meta-analysis of the control parameters to identify their relative importance for the purposes of tuning.

The remainder of this paper is structured as follows. Section 2 provides the necessary background on PSO, the control parameter tuning problem, and the fANOVA procedure. Section 3 describes the experimental procedure used in this work, while Sect. 4 presents the experimental results. Finally, Sect. 5 provides concluding remarks and avenues for future work.

2 Background

This section provides the necessary background for the remainder of this paper. Section 2.1 introduces the PSO algorithm. The control parameter tuning problem is formally described in Sect. 2.2 while Sect. 2.3 describes common automated parameter tuning methods. Section 2.4 provides a description of the fANOVA procedure.

2.1 Particle Swarm Optimization

The PSO algorithm [20] consists of a collection of particles, which each represents a candidate solution to an optimization problem. Each particle retains three pieces of information, namely its current position, its velocity, and its (personal) best position found within the search space. Particle positions are updated each iteration by calculation and subsequent addition of a velocity vector to the particle's current position.

A particle's velocity is influenced by the attraction towards two promising locations in the search space, namely the best position found by the particle itself and the best position found by any particle within the particle's neighbourhood [21], in addition to a momentum term. The neighbourhood of a particle is defined as the other particles within the swarm from which it may take influence, most commonly the entire swarm, or the two immediate neighbours when the particles are arranged in a ring structure [21].

According to the inertia weight model [26], the velocity is calculated for particle i as

$$
\begin{aligned}
v_{ij}(t+1) = {} & \omega v_{ij}(t) + c_1 r_{1ij}(t)(y_{ij}(t) - x_{ij}(t)) \\
& + c_2 r_{2ij}(t)(\hat{y}_{ij}(t) - x_{ij}(t)),
\end{aligned}
\tag{1}
$$

where $v_{ij}(t)$ and $x_{ij}(t)$ are the velocity and position in dimension j at time t, respectively. The inertia weight is given by ω, while c_1 and c_2 represent the cognitive and social acceleration coefficients, respectively. The stochastic component of the algorithm is provided by the random values $r_{1ij}(t), r_{2ij}(t) \sim U(0,1)$, which are independently sampled each iteration for all components of each particle's velocity. Finally, $y_{ij}(t)$ and $\hat{y}_{ij}(t)$ denote the personal and neighbourhood best positions in dimension j, respectively. Particle positions are then updated according to

$$
x_{ij}(t+1) = x_{ij}(t) + v_{ij}(t+1).
\tag{2}
$$

2.2 Formalized Control Parameter Tuning

Given an algorithm A that has n_p control parameters with domains $\Theta_1, ..., \Theta_{n_p}$, respectively, the configuration space of A is defined as $\Theta = \Theta_1 \times ... \times \Theta_{n_p}$. The notation N_p is used to refer to the set $\{p_1, ..., p_{n_p}\}$ of all control parameters of algorithm A. A (complete) instantiation of the control parameters is then given by a vector $\theta_i = (\theta_{p_1}, ..., \theta_{p_{n_p}})$. The general goal of control parameter tuning is to find a configuration $\theta_i \in \Theta$ that minimizes the performance metric $m(\theta_i, \pi_j)$ over a set of k problems $\pi_1, \pi_2, ..., \pi_k$. The performance metric $m(\theta_i, \pi_j)$ can be any metric that quantifies the performance of A with respect to a parameter configuration $\theta_i \in \Theta$ on a problem π_j. The control parameter tuning problem can then be summarized as finding the parameter configuration θ^* that minimizes the overall performance of A, given by

$$\theta^* = \arg\min f(\theta_i) := \sum_{j=1}^{k}(m(\theta_i, \pi_j)), \tag{3}$$

assuming that the performance metric m is to be minimized.

2.3   Automated Control Parameter Tuning Methods

Configuring a heuristic optimizer is a complicated, labour-intensive process. Recently, there has been considerable research efforts devoted to creating automated parameter tuning methods. These tools are generally model-free and can be applied to arbitrary optimization algorithms and objective functions. Generally, automated parameter configuration techniques are based on the assumption that the response surfaces are smooth and that the performance of nearby parameter configurations are correlated – an assumption that has not been verified, in general [24]. Therefore, improving the underlying assumptions used in automated control parameter tuning methods can be of large benefit. Three of the most prominent parameter configuration methods used in practice are ParamILS [17], Iterated F-Race [4], and Bayesian Optimization [22], each of which are briefly described below.

ParamILS is an iterated local search procedure that begins with an initial parameter configuration and randomly samples candidate configurations, retaining the best found, which is then refined via a local search procedure and a perturbation (i.e., mutation) to escape local optima [17]. Furthermore, the search is reinitialized at random, according to a fixed probability. This process continues until no further improvements can be made. The search process is conducted over a fixed set of training instances, with further extensions that can adaptively vary the number of target runs needed for each candidate parameter configuration.

Iterated F-Race is based on racing techniques from machine learning, whereby a large set of candidate configurations are examined under a fixed computational budget and those that show promise are allocated more of the computation time [4]. At each iteration, each of the candidate configurations are evaluated in parallel and poor performing configurations are removed from consideration as soon as statistical evidence is gathered against their performance, thereby allowing the promising configurations a larger computational budget. In Iterated F-Race, the surviving candidate configurations are used to bias the selection of new candidate configurations to consider. This process is repeated until some termination criterion is satisfied.

Bayesian optimization, which is very prominent in machine learning contexts, is a global optimization technique that models an objective function (e.g., the performance of a control parameter configuration) using a Bayesian statistical model, and subsequently uses an acquisition function to decide the regions of the search space to sample next [22]. A statistical model, which is typically a Gaussian process, provides a probability distribution to describe the potential performance associated with any particular parameter configuration and as new configurations are examined, the distribution is updated accordingly. An expected improvement process is typically used as the acquisition function, whereby new configurations to examine are selected with respect to a trade-off between those expected to perform well and those with high uncertainty.

2.4   fANOVA

Optimization techniques, such as PSO, often behave strikingly different when the configurations of their control parameters are varied [3,7,19,23]. To quantify the overall effect of each control parameter, the fANOVA technique [27] is a classical statistical approach that is used to decompose the variance of a response value into additive components associated with each subset of its inputs [16]. In the context of this paper, fANOVA is used to quantify the performance associated with a partial instantiation of the algorithm's control parameters, in regards to all instantiations of the remaining control parameters.

Using the definitions provided in Sect. 2.2, let $\theta_\phi = (\theta_{\phi_1}, ..., \theta_{\phi_m})$ be a partial instantiation of $m \leq n_p$ control parameters of A, such that $\{\theta_{\phi_1}, ..., \theta_{\phi_m}\} = \Phi \subseteq N_p$. The extension set of θ_ϕ, denoted by $X(\theta_\phi)$, is then defined as the set of control parameter configurations that form a complete instantiation when combined with θ_ϕ, denoted by θ_T where $T = N_p \setminus \Phi$.

The marginal performance of θ_ϕ, denoted by $\hat{m}(\theta_\phi)$, is then defined as the expected (i.e., predicted) performance of θ_ϕ with respect to all instantiations of the remaining control parameters, as given by

$$\hat{m}(\theta_\phi) = \frac{1}{||\Theta_T||} \int \hat{y}(\theta_T) d\theta_T, \tag{4}$$

where $\hat{y} : \Theta \mapsto \mathbb{R}$, and $||\Theta_T|| = \prod_{i=1}^{k} ||\Theta_{T_i}||$. Assuming that Θ_{T_i} is defined as a closed interval $[u, l]$, which is true for the PSO control parameters examined in this paper, then $||\Theta_{T_i}|| = u - l$. In simpler terms, the marginal performance given by Eq. (4) quantifies the performance of a (particular) partial instantiation of control parameters, θ_ϕ, over the set of all instantiations of the remaining control parameters T.

Given that exact calculation of the marginal performance would require enumerating and sampling an infinite number of possible parameter configurations[1], a random forest model is used to approximate the marginal performance in linear time [16]. The key principle underlying the prediction technique is that each regression tree defines a partitioning of the configuration space Θ, such that the marginal prediction of the entire forest is the average prediction over each tree [16].

The fANOVA procedure uses the predicted marginal performance to partition the observed variation of a response value (i.e., the performance of an

---

[1] Assuming the control parameter values are continuous.

algorithm) into additive components associated with subsets of its inputs (i.e., control parameter values). In the context of this paper, fANOVA is used to partition the model $\hat{y}$ into additive components that depend only on partial instantiations θ_ϕ. The importance of each partial instantiation θ_ϕ (i.e., subset of control parameters), can then be quantified by the fraction of variance of $\hat{y}$ associated with θ_ϕ [16]. A larger fraction of variance associated with a particular control parameter indicates a higher sensitivity to the values of that control parameter. Therefore, control parameters with higher values for the variance are more influential, and thus should have a higher priority when tuning control parameter values.

3   Experimental Setup

To examine the effect of each of the PSO control parameters, values for each control parameter were sampled in increments of 0.1 in the following ranges: $\omega \in [-1.0, 1.0]$, $c_1 \in [0.1, 2.0]$, and $c_2 \in [0.1, 2.0]$, producing a total of 8400 parameter configurations. These ranges were chosen to approximately coincide with the boundaries of the theoretically stable region [9]. Selecting parameter values outside of the theoretically stable region is not recommended as these parameter values generally lead to worse performance than random search [8]. Each parameter configuration was examined on a suite of 20 minimization problems, summarized in Table 1, in both 10 and 30 dimensions. Each experiment made use of synchronous updates and ran for 5000 iterations with a swarm size of 30. Experiments were repeated 30 times using the gbest topology. To prevent invalid attractors, personal best positions were only updated if the new position was feasible and had a better fitness than the previous personal best position. Particles were initialized uniformly within the feasible region and had an initial velocity of **0** [11]. The response values, for use in the fANOVA procedure, were taken as the average fitness values after 5000 iterations.

According to the definitions provided in Sect. 2.2, algorithm A is the PSO algorithm, the training instances π_i are problems provided in Table 1, and the performance metric $m(\theta, \pi_i)$ is the average fitness of PSO after 5000 iterations on problem π_i using configuration θ_j. Therefore, these experiments examine the influence of each control parameter on the overall fitness of the PSO algorithm.

4   Results

This section presents the results of the aforementioned experimental procedure. Section 4.1 presents the proportion of variance in fitness associated with each control parameter, while Sect. 4.2 presents the response surfaces visually.

4.1   Variance in Fitness

Table 2 presents the proportion of variance in fitness associated with each of the three control parameters in both 10 and 30 dimensions where bold entries

Table 1. Benchmark problems

Problem	Domain	Problem	Domain
Absolute Value	$[-100, 100]^d$	Quartic	$[-1.28, 1.28]^d$
Ackley	$[-32.768, 32.768]^d$	Rastrigin	$[-5.12, 5.12]^d$
Alpine	$[-10, 10]^d$	Rosenbrock	$[-30, 30]^d$
Egg Holder	$[-512, 512]^d$	Saloman	$[-100, 100]^d$
Elliptic	$[-100, 100]^d$	Schaffer 6	$[-100, 100]^d$
Griewank	$[-600, 600]^d$	Schwefel 1.2	$[-100, 100]^d$
Hyperellipsoid	$[-5.12, 5.12]^d$	Shubert	$[-10, 10]^d$
Michalewicz	$[0, \pi]^d$	Spherical	$[-5.12, 5.12]^d$
Norwegian	$[-1.1, 1.1]^d$	Step	$[-100, 100]^d$
Quadric	$[-100, 100]^d$	Vincent	$[0.25, 10]^d$

denote the control parameter that has the highest variance for a particular problem. Note that the variances do not sum to 1 because the fANOVA procedure calculates the variance associated with each subset of parameters, while Table 2 only presents the results for each control parameter independently. From Table 2, it is evident that the ω parameter had the greatest variance for all 20 problems in both dimensionalities, with the exception of the Elliptical problem in 30D. On average, the inertia component accounted for 55.1% of the variance in 10D problems and 42.1% on 30D problems. Thus, the influence of the inertia component was more pronounced in 10D problems. The cognitive acceleration coefficient was the least important parameter to tune, accounting for only 0.9% and 0.4% of the variance in 10D and 30D problems, respectively. The social acceleration coefficient accounted for 7.5% and 12.4% of the variance in 10D and 30D problems, respectively.

It is noteworthy that the variance associated with the ω control parameter was significantly below the average, at only 19.0% and 17.2% for 10D and 30D, when considering the Elliptic problem, while the c_2 control parameter was significantly above the average, at 17.6% and 27.8% for this problem. The exact reason that the results for the Elliptic problem are anomalous is not yet known.

For the objective functions considered in this paper, these results provide strong evidence that the inertia weight is the most influential control parameter, with respect to overall fitness, in the PSO algorithm for low dimensional problems. Additionally, this suggests that the cognitive acceleration coefficient is the least influential control parameter while the social control parameter is only moderately influential. This may explain the tendency for SAPSO algorithms to focus solely on the inertia weight [15].

Table 2. Proportion of variance in fitness for PSO control parameters

Problem	10D			30D		
	ω	c_1	c_2	ω	c_1	c_2
Absolute Value	**0.645021**	0.001677	0.038427	**0.446099**	0.001371	0.094186
Ackley	**0.610086**	0.000370	0.023532	**0.414973**	0.002505	0.066243
Alpine	**0.662894**	0.002883	0.043359	**0.532597**	0.002557	0.071407
Egg Holder	**0.508794**	0.010904	0.023919	**0.512384**	0.000663	0.046083
Elliptic	**0.189763**	0.005530	0.176589	0.172190	0.008921	**0.278671**
Griewank	**0.616815**	0.001870	0.095774	**0.410851**	0.003300	0.177518
Hyperellipsoid	**0.600843**	0.002612	0.098467	**0.406675**	0.004425	0.183428
Michalewicz	**0.607955**	0.010827	0.015676	**0.550291**	0.001364	0.015341
Norwegian	**0.567687**	0.003638	0.085906	**0.606357**	0.008016	0.046624
Quadric	**0.571072**	0.004573	0.109951	**0.417776**	0.010275	0.195691
Quartic	**0.481665**	0.001954	0.150146	**0.322408**	0.005273	0.256089
Rastrigin	**0.632356**	0.000798	0.057356	**0.555449**	0.001185	0.067148
Rosenbrock	**0.469396**	0.002248	0.153637	**0.333712**	0.004969	0.251373
Saloman	**0.610867**	0.000264	0.059487	**0.391126**	0.000982	0.139879
Schaffer 6	**0.494144**	0.027852	0.028585	**0.455864**	0.005774	0.003785
Schwefel 1.2	**0.570365**	0.004249	0.107213	**0.419636**	0.010159	0.196484
Shubert	**0.310248**	0.109850	0.019874	**0.080289**	0.014961	0.004335
Spherical	**0.603515**	0.002277	0.098588	**0.411410**	0.003379	0.177229
Step	**0.610909**	0.001599	0.101479	**0.406908**	0.002340	0.188080
Vincent	**0.653907**	0.001226	0.018588	**0.572382**	0.000508	0.017953
Mean	0.550915	0.009860	0.075328	0.420969	0.004646	0.123877
Std. Dev	0.118774	0.024342	0.049636	0.128060	0.003957	0.090519

4.2   Response Surface Analysis

Figures 1, 2 and 3 present, for each of the ω, c_1, and c_2 control parameters, the average fitness values associated with the different values of that particular control parameter. These plots are henceforth referred to as the response surfaces. In these figures, the solid line through the middle indicates the average fitness while the larger region indicates one standard deviation above and below the average. These figures give an overview of the control parameter values that lead to the best performance, while also providing a visual indication of their influence.

Figure 1 presents the average fitness, with respect to ω, for selected problems in 10D and 30D. It is evident from these figures that the ω control parameter had the largest variability, thereby supporting the fANOVA results. Visually, an inertia value of approximately 0.8 lead to the best overall fitness. Values above 0.8 tended to rapidly deteriorate in fitness, while values below 0.8 demonstrated

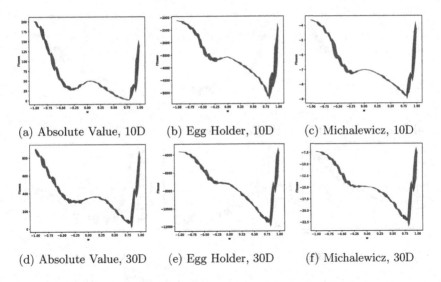

Fig. 1. Average fitness, with respect to ω, on various problems.

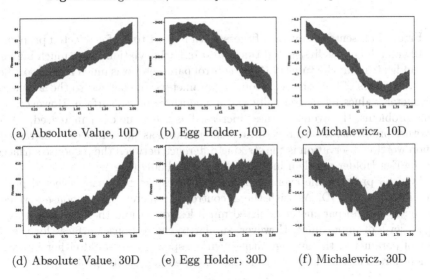

Fig. 2. Average fitness, with respect to c_1, on various problems.

relatively smooth deterioration in fitness as the inertia value decreased. Note that the overall shape of the plots were largely the same regardless of the problem and, furthermore, that the same general shape was observed for both 10D and 30D problems. Additionally, the small standard deviations indicate a low deviation, which suggests that the values of c_1 and c_2 had significantly less impact on the performance than the value of ω.

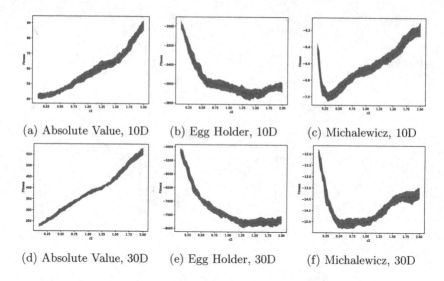

(a) Absolute Value, 10D   (b) Egg Holder, 10D   (c) Michalewicz, 10D

(d) Absolute Value, 30D   (e) Egg Holder, 30D   (f) Michalewicz, 30D

Fig. 3. Average fitness, with respect to c_2, on various problems.

Figure 2 presents the average fitness, with respect to c_1, for selected problems in 10D and 30D. It is first noted that the standard deviations were much higher. This indicates that the value of the c_1 control parameter was much less important than the values of the other two control parameters. In contrast to the ω control parameter, values for c_1 generally had a smooth response surface. However, for some problems, the average fitness increased as the value of c_1 increased, while for other problems, the average fitness deteriorated as the values of c_1 increased. A noteworthy observation is the striking difference between the response surfaces for the Egg Holder problem in 10D (Fig. 2b) and 30D (Fig. 2e).

Figure 3 presents the average fitness, with respect to c_2, for selected problems in 10D and 30D. As with the ω control parameter, the response surfaces for the c_2 control parameter depicted much less deviation, thereby indicating a higher level of importance. However, similar to the response surfaces for the c_1 control parameter, the average fitness with respect to c_2 would either improve or deteriorate as the value of c_1 increased, depending on the problem.

5   Conclusions

This paper investigated the relative importance of the three main control parameters, namely ω, c_1, and c_2, for the particle swarm optimization (PSO) algorithm. A total of 8400 parameter configurations were examined on a benchmark suite of 20 minimization problems in both 10 and 30 dimensions. The functional analysis of variance (fANOVA) procedure was executed to indicate the variance in fitness associated with each of the control parameters. Response surfaces were plotted to visually inspect the effect of various values of each control parameter.

For the objective functions considered in this paper, the results suggest that the inertia control parameter, ω, accounts for 55.1% and 42.1% of the variance in fitness, on average, for 10D and 30D problems, respectively. The cognitive acceleration coefficient, c_1, was the least important control parameter and accounts for less that 1% of the variance in fitness, on average. Therefore, when tuning a PSO algorithm, the value of the inertia weight control parameter is by far the most important to tune. Visual inspection of the response surfaces also indicated that the response surface of the inertia weight is largely uninfluenced by the problem itself or the dimensionality, while the same can not be said for the other two control parameters. These results have major implications for the design of future self-adaptive PSO algorithms (SAPSO) as they provide concrete evidence that tuning the inertia weight will reap the largest benefit, while tuning the cognitive acceleration is of little benefit.

An immediate avenue of future work is to determine the variance associated with each subset of control parameters, thus determining their influence in combination with one another. Furthermore, investigating problems with larger dimensionalities, different PSO topologies, and other PSO variants is also warranted.

References

1. Beielstein, T.: Tuning PSO parameters through sensitivity analysis. Technical report, Universitat Dortmund (2002)
2. van den Bergh, F., Engelbrecht, A.P.: A study of particle swarm optimization particle trajectories. Inf. Sci. **176**(8), 937–971 (2006)
3. Bergh, F.V.D.: An analysis of particle swarm optimizers. Ph.D. thesis, University of Pretoria (2001)
4. Birattari, M., Yuan, Z., Balaprakash, P., Stützle, T.: F-Race and iterated F-Race: an overview. In: Bartz-Beielstein, T., Chiarandini, M., Paquete, L., Preuss, M. (eds.) Experimental Methods for the Analysis of Optimization Algorithms, pp. 311–336. Springer, Heidelberg (2010). https://doi.org/10.1007/978-3-642-02538-9_13
5. Bonyadi, M., Michalewicz, Z.: Impacts of coefficients on movement patterns in the particle swarm optimization algorithm. IEEE Trans. Evol. Comput. **21**(3), 1–1 (2016)
6. Bratton, D., Kennedy, J.: Defining a standard for particle swarm optimization. In: 2007 IEEE Swarm Intelligence Symposium, pp. 120–127. IEEE (2007)
7. Carlisle, A., Dozier, G.: An off-the-shelf PSO. In: Proceedings of the Workshop on Particle Swarm Optimization, vol. 1, pp. 1–6. Purdue School of Engineering and Technology (2001)
8. Cleghorn, C.W., Engelbrecht, A.: Particle swarm optimizer: the impact of unstable particles on performance. In: 2016 IEEE Symposium Series on Computational Intelligence, pp. 1–7. IEEE (2016)
9. Cleghorn, C.W., Engelbrecht, A.P.: Particle swarm stability: a theoretical extension using the non-stagnate distribution assumption. Swarm Intell. **12**, 1–22 (2017)
10. Eberhart, R., Shi, Y.: Comparing inertia weights and constriction factors in particle swarm optimization. In: Proceedings of the 2000 Congress on Evolutionary Computation, vol. 1, pp. 84–88. IEEE (2000)

11. Engelbrecht, A.: Particle swarm optimization: velocity initialization. In: 2012 IEEE Congress on Evolutionary Computation, pp. 1–8. IEEE (2012)
12. Harrison, K.R., Engelbrecht, A.P., Ombuki-Berman, B.M.: Inertia weight control strategies for particle swarm optimization. Swarm Intell. **10**(4), 267–305 (2016)
13. Harrison, K.R., Engelbrecht, A.P., Ombuki-Berman, B.M.: The sad state of self-adaptive particle swarm optimizers. In: Proceedings of the 2016 IEEE Congress on Evolutionary Computation, pp. 431–439. IEEE (2016)
14. Harrison, K.R., Engelbrecht, A.P., Ombuki-Berman, B.M.: Optimal parameter regions and the time-dependence of control parameter values for the particle swarm optimization algorithm. Swarm Evol. Comput. **41**, 20–35 (2018)
15. Harrison, K.R., Engelbrecht, A.P., Ombuki-Berman, B.M.: Self-adaptive particle swarm optimization: a review and analysis of convergence. Swarm Intell. **12**(3), 187–226 (2018)
16. Hutter, F., Hoos, H., Leyton-brown, K.: An efficient approach for assessing hyperparameter importance. In: Proceedings of the 31st International Conference on Machine Learning, vol. 32, pp. 754–762. ACM (2014)
17. Hutter, F., Hoos, H.H., Leyton-Brown, K., Stützle, T.: ParamILS: an automatic algorithm configuration framework. J. Artif. Intell. Res. **36**, 267–306 (2009)
18. Jiang, M., Luo, Y., Yang, S.: Particle swarm optimization - stochastic trajectory analysis and parameter selection. In: Swarm Intelligence, Focus on Ant and Particle Swarm Optimization, pp. 179–198. No. December, I-TechEducation and Publishing (2007)
19. Jiang, M., Luo, Y., Yang, S.: Stochastic convergence analysis and parameter selection of the standard particle swarm optimization algorithm. Inf. Process. Lett. **102**(1), 8–16 (2007)
20. Kennedy, J., Eberhart, R.: Particle swarm optimization. In: Proceedings of the International Conference on Neural Networks, vol. 4, pp. 1942–1948. IEEE (1995)
21. Kennedy, J., Mendes, R.: Population structure and particle swarm performance. In: Proceedings of the 2002 Congress on Evolutionary Computation, vol. 2, pp. 1671–1676. IEEE (2002)
22. Kushner, H.J.: A new method of locating the maximum point of an arbitrary multipeak curve in the presence of noise. J. Fluids Eng. **86**(1), 97–106 (1964)
23. Liu, Q.: Order-2 stability analysis of particle swarm optimization. Evol. Comput. **23**(2), 187–216 (2015)
24. Pushak, Y., Hoos, H.: Algorithm configuration landscapes. In: Auger, A., Fonseca, C.M., Lourenço, N., Machado, P., Paquete, L., Whitley, D. (eds.) PPSN 2018. LNCS, vol. 11102, pp. 271–283. Springer, Cham (2018). https://doi.org/10.1007/978-3-319-99259-4_22
25. Ratnaweera, A., Halgamuge, S., Watson, H.: Self-organizing hierarchical particle swarm optimizer with time-varying acceleration coefficients. IEEE Trans. Evol. Comput. **8**(3), 240–255 (2004)
26. Shi, Y., Eberhart, R.: A modified particle swarm optimizer. In: Proceedings of the 1998 IEEE International Conference on Evolutionary Computation, pp. 69–73. IEEE (1998)
27. Sobol, I.: Sensitivity estimates for nonlinear mathematical models. Math. Modell. Comput. Exper. **1**(4), 407–414 (1993)
28. Tanweer, M., Suresh, S., Sundararajan, N.: Self regulating particle swarm optimization algorithm. Inf. Sci. **294**, 182–202 (2015)
29. Trelea, I.C.: The particle swarm optimization algorithm: convergence analysis and parameter selection. Inf. Process. Lett. **85**(6), 317–325 (2003)

30. Xu, G.: An adaptive parameter tuning of particle swarm optimization algorithm. Appl. Math. Comput. **219**(9), 4560–4569 (2013)
31. Zhan, Z.H., Zhang, J., Li, Y., Chung, H.S.H.: Adaptive particle swarm optimization. IEEE Trans. Syst. Man Cybern. Part B (Cybern.) **39**(6), 1362–1381 (2009)
32. Zhang, W., Ma, D., Wei, J.J., Liang, H.F.: A parameter selection strategy for particle swarm optimization based on particle positions. Expert Syst. Appl. **41**(7), 3576–3584 (2014)
33. van Zyl, E.T., Engelbrecht, A.P.: Comparison of self-adaptive particle swarm optimizers. In: Proceedings of the 2014 IEEE Symposium on Swarm Intelligence, pp. 1–9. IEEE (2014)

Parameters Optimization of Relay Self-oscillations Sampled Data Controller Based on Particle Swarm Optimization

Eugene V. Larkin, Sergey V. Feofilov, and Andrew Kozyr[(⊠)]

Tula State University, 300012 Tula, Russia
Kozyr_A_V@mail.ru

Abstract. The applied task of synthesis of digital self-oscillating control system is considered. Problem of correction devices parameters search is considered as the task of finite-dimensional optimization task. For its solution parallel swarm optimization algorithm is worked out. Algorithm is applied to parametric optimization of actuator digital control self-oscillating system. The proposed approach had superior features, including easy implementation, stable convergence characteristic, and good computational efficiency. When control system digital realization synthesis the exact algorithm of determination of periodical movement in relay system is worked out. Method of self-oscillations stability analysis in such a system is proposed. Optimization task is solved with taking into account the criterion of stability of self-oscillations in the system under consideration. Effectiveness of proposed methods and PSO algorithms was shown on the example of synthesis of digitally controlled relay system for an electro-pneumatic servo-mechanism. On the model example it is shown that the use of the PSO algorithm as compared with the genetic algorithm (GA) have better convergence.

Keywords: Digital control system · Particle Swarm Optimization · Self-oscillation · Stability · Actuator · Relay controller

1 Introduction

Methods of swarm intelligence are widely used in the field of computing and artificial intelligence now. Swarm conception, based on social behavioral model had been introduced for investigation of distributed intellectual systems [1]. Swarm includes set of homogeneous simple agents, which execute simple operations and interact between them and/or environment without any external control. Swarm social behavior is formed as the consequence of self-organizing and local interaction [2]. Swarm intelligence permit rather effective solve the tasks of global optimization [1–4]. At first particle swarm optimization (PSO) algorithm had been proposed at 1995 [3]. Its simplest realization may be performed as follows: in n–dimensional space with those or that method set of points, named the swarm, is created. Points shifted in space, and at every location point, optimization criterion is calculated. Optimal solution is best solution by points position and by points itself. The PSO technique can generate a quality solution within shorter calculation time and stable convergence characteristic

© Springer Nature Switzerland AG 2019
Y. Tan et al. (Eds.): ICSI 2019, LNCS 11655, pp. 106–117, 2019.
https://doi.org/10.1007/978-3-030-26369-0_10

than other stochastic methods [5, 6]. Many practical optimization tasks are subject to constraints, which means that not an arbitrary solution to the problem is searched for, but a solution that complies with certain restrictions. The use of the PCO algorithm for optimization of problems with constraints is considered in [7, 8]. The most common approach for solving constraints optimization (CO) problems is the use of a penalty function [9]. In this paper, the performance of the Particle Swarm Optimization method (PSO), in solving CO problems is investigated. This approach may be applied to synthesis of relay self-oscillating system with digital control and various restrictions. Relay systems are widely used in servo control systems. Studies on the use of such systems are to numerous publications [10–12]. The main works deal with the analysis of periodic processes and the assessment of their stability and linearization for systems operating in continuous time. Currently, self-oscillating relay control systems are being designed in digital form [13, 14]. The traditional design of such systems is based on a finite-dimensional optimization of the controller parameters. The criterion for the synthesis of a relay feedback system is the minimization of phase lag [14]. When use the PSO algorithm for synthesis multiple calculation of criterion is executed. It is important, that computational procedure is performed as soon as possible. The paper proposes an approach to the calculation of the quality indicator for a linearized model of a relay system with a sampled. Control system digital realization causes significant influence on self-oscillating system operation parameters [14, 16], this is why it is necessary to take into account sampling influence.

The rest of this paper is organized as follows. The formal definition of the problem under study is given in Sect. 2. In the 3rd and 4th section, the problems of identifying periodic motions and assessing their stability are considered. In Sect. 5, the parameters of the relay controller are optimized using the PSO and GA method. Section 6 concludes with a brief summary of this paper.

2 Mathematical Description of System Under Investigation

Flowchart of relay control system (RCS) with linear controllable object is shown on the Fig. 1.

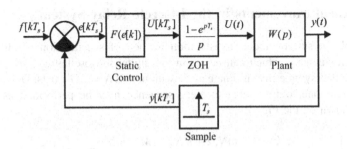

Fig. 1. Block diagram of the sampled-data relay control system.

On the flowchart, the function $F(e[kT_s])$ determines static characteristic of two-position relay (TPR) with hysteresis (Fig. 2). To the input of this element is applied sequence $e[kT_s] = f[kT_s] - y[kT_s]k = 0, 1, 2, \ldots$, where $f[kT_s]$ is discrete input signal; $y[kT_s]$ is the feedback signal, obtained from feedback continual signal $y(t)$ by means of sampling with regular sampling period T_s. At every time interval $kT_s \leq t < (k+1)T_s, k = 0, 1, 2, \ldots$ to controllable object signal $U(t) = U[kT_s]$ is applied. Mathematical model of closed system in the space of states is as follows

$$\begin{cases} \mathbf{x}[(k+1)T_s] = \mathbf{\Phi}\mathbf{x}[kT_s] + \mathbf{\Psi}U[kT_s], \\ y[kT_s] = \mathbf{C}^T[kT_s]. \end{cases} \tag{1}$$

where $\mathbf{x}$ is the phase variable vector. System matrices are determined with well-known dependencies:

$$\mathbf{\Phi} = e^{AT_s}, \mathbf{\Psi} = \int_0^{T_s} e^{At}dt\mathbf{B}. \tag{2}$$

where A, B are matrices of continual object under control of corresponding size.

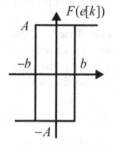

Fig. 2. Static characteristic hysteresis relay.

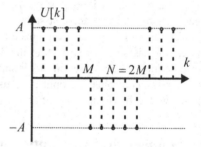

Fig. 3. Output signal of a relay element.

3   Periodical Movements in the Discrete Relay System

Let us apply to system under investigation method of specification of all possible periodical movements, which can be set in the digital self-oscillating system. Let us also assume that symmetrical ultimate cycle with period $N = 2M$ exists. Due to system is the discrete one, output relay element sequence may be performed as discrete function, shown on the Fig. 3:

$$\begin{cases} U[k] = A, k = 1 + mN, 2 + mN, \ldots M + mN, \\ U[k] = -A, k = M + 1 + mN, \ldots, N + mN. \end{cases}, m = 0, 1, 2, \ldots. \tag{3}$$

Periodical signal (3) may be transformed onto Fourier series [13]

$$U[k] = \frac{1}{N}\sum_{n=1}^{N} C_n e^{jn\omega_0 k} \tag{4}$$

where $\omega_0 = \frac{2\pi}{N}$; C_n is the complex coefficient:

$$C_n = \sum_{k=1}^{N} U[k]e^{-jn\omega_0 k} = \sum_{k=1}^{M} e^{\frac{-jmnk}{M}} - \sum_{k=M+1}^{N} e^{\frac{-jmnk}{M}}.$$

When n is even, then C_n is equal to zero, otherwise

$$C_n = (1 - (-1)^n)\frac{je^{-jn\pi/N}}{\sin(n\pi/N)}. \tag{5}$$

Output signal of the continual part of the system, when input signal is as (4) is as follows

$$y[k] = \frac{1}{N}\sum_{n=1}^{N} W(e^{jn\omega_0})C_n e^{jn\omega_0 k} = \frac{j}{N}\sum_{n=1}^{N} (1 - (-1)^n)\frac{e^{-jn\pi/N}}{\sin(n\pi/N)}e^{2jnk/N}. \tag{6}$$

Similarly to continual case [10], let us introduce notion phase locus of discrete relay system. Components of phase locus are named R-characteristics, they are functions of semi-period of oscillation and determine nominations of phase variables at the moment of switching of relay element from negative to positive value. In such a way, phase locus is the vector function $x^*(M)$, which depends on parameter M and describes all symmetrical periodical movements. Due to the fact, that in periodical movement there is a symmetry $y[0] = -y[MT_s]$ then with taking into account (6)

$$y[M] = -\frac{1}{M}\sum_{n=1}^{M} \frac{(1 - (-1)^n)}{\sin\left(\frac{n\pi}{N}\right)}\operatorname{Im}\left(W(jn\omega_0)e^{\frac{jm(M-0.5)}{M}}\right). \tag{7}$$

Relay switch condition in the discrete system quite differ from continual case. In continual system self-oscillation are determined from condition of trajectory $y(t)$ attachment to switching surface $y(t) = -b$ at time moment t. When discrete case discrete function $y[k]$ causes switching only at moments, aliquot integer values of sampling interval $MT_s \geq t$. Conditions switch relay element into a sample data relay systems

$$\begin{cases} y[M] \geq -b, \\ y[M-1] \geq -b. \end{cases} \tag{8}$$

To search for all limit cycles in a given relay feedback system, you can use expression (7) and check the inequality (8). The search for all possible symmetric periodic motions in systems can be performed graphically. Based on the delay in switching the relay $\in [0, T_s]$, the R-characteristics [14] (7) will take the form

$$y[M, \tau] = -\frac{1}{M}\sum_{n=1}^{M} \frac{(1-(-1)^n)}{\sin\left(\frac{n\pi}{N}\right)} \mathrm{Im}\left(W(jn\omega_0)e^{-jn\omega_0\tau}e^{-\frac{j\pi n(M-0.5)}{M}}\right). \tag{9}$$

Possible symmetric periodic movements with a period N are determined by the graphical solution of the equation $y[M, \tau] = -b$. Time discretization leads to the occurrence of various periodic motions in relay control systems.

4   Stability of Self-oscillation in the Digital Relay System and Linearization

In the case of RCS relay switches only at time moments, which are aliquot integer values T_s, but disturbances at initial conditions $\tilde{y}[k] = y[k] + \Delta$ may not adduct to changing of relay switching moment. Such a situation is shown on the Fig. 4, where $[t_1, t_2]$ are moments of switching of undisturbed trajectory $y[k]$ and disturbed trajectory $\tilde{y}[k]$ correspondingly. Relay output signal $U[k]$ switches at the moment MT_s, similarly to the case of undisturbed trajectory.

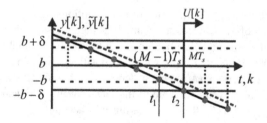

Fig. 4. Periodic trajectory of a disturbed and undisturbed system

Initial periodical solution $y[k] = C^T x[k]$ intersects switching surface $-b$ at time moments t_1. Let us introduce small disturbance Δ to periodical trajectory $y(t)$ and suppose that disturbed periodical trajectory $\tilde{y}(t) = C^T(x(t) + \Delta)$ will intersect switching surface at the time moment t_1. If both solutions intersect switching surface during the same interval of the set

$$t_1 \wedge t_2 \in ([M-1], M)T_s \tag{10}$$

then relay switches at the same time moment MT_s, both in the case of undisturbed and in the case of small disturbance Δ. If (10) will be fulfilled for further switches, then trajectory will be asymptotically convergent to ultimate cycle. If in discrete system there is stable ultimate cycle, then for it there is some domain of disturbances Δ, at which control signal $U[k]$ do not change. For periodical trajectory stability analysis in RCS it is necessary to evaluate set of values Δ, at which condition (10) will be fulfilled.

Domain of permissible disturbances, at which shifting of switching moments does not occur may be obtained as follows. Let us suppose that in the relay system there is symmetrical ultimate cycle with the period NT_s, and matrix A is the Hurwitz matrix In this case all solutions with initial conditions $\tilde{x}_N^* = x_N^* + \Delta$, where $\Delta \in D_I$ will be asymptotically converged to the stable limit cycle. In such a way the problem of definition of admissible set of disturbances is quite equivalent to the task of definition of set of attainability of discrete system. Method of searching of such a set is expounded in [15, 17].

As was shown, time sampling leads to a delay in switching the relay with the continuous case. Using the expression 9 can determine the equivalent time delay τ. It is possible to assess the stability of the sample relay system using the equivalent system with a delay [18].

Proposition 1. Periodic motions in a closed relay system will be asymptotically orbitally stable if all the eigenvalues of the product of matrices $W_1 W_2$ are in a circle of unit radius.

$$W_1 = \left(I - \frac{A^{n-}\left(Ax_m^* + BA\right)C}{CA^{n-}\left(Ax_m^* + BA\right)} \right) e^{A(\tau + T_0)} \tag{11}$$

$$W_1 = \left(I - \frac{A^{n+}\left(Ax_m^* + BA\right)C}{CA^{n+}\left(Ax_m^* + BA\right)} \right) e^{A(\tau + T_0)} \tag{12}$$

τ – equivalent delay, x_m^* – the initial value belongs to the maximum limit cycle, identity matrix by dimension $(n \times n)$, n_- and n_+ positive integers that are determined and solutions of the next system

$$\begin{cases} CA^{i+1}x_m^* + CA^i BA = 0, i = 0, \ldots, n_+, \\ CA^{n_+ +1}x_m^* + CA^{n_+} BA < 0, \\ CA^{j+1}x_m^* + CA^j BA = 0, i = 0, \ldots, n_-, \\ CA^{n_- +1}x_m^* + CA^{n_-} BA < 0. \end{cases} \tag{13}$$

The condition presented allows us to estimate the stability of periodic motions in a relay system with a delay.

4.1   Linearization of Relay Sampled-Data Feedback Systems

Tracking mode accuracy of the relay control system is estimated from the frequency response of a closed feedback systems. At the stage of optimization of the controller parameters is important to quickly calculate the criterion. Linearization allows a simple way to study the tracking mode for the input signals in the relay system. The paper considers the linearization of the relay equivalent transmission coefficient (see Fig. 5) [10].

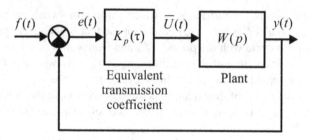

Fig. 5. Linearization relay feedback systems

In the case of a sample-data relay feedback system, the relay transfer ratio will be variable $K_p(\tau) \in [K_1, K_2, \ldots, K_m]$, K_m–corresponds to the maximum limit cycle. The equivalent transmission coefficient is calculated on the basis of a relay system with delay τ.

$$K_p(\tau) = \left(\frac{2\pi}{N}\sum_{k=1}^{M}(-1)^k \mathrm{Re}\left(W\left(\frac{j\pi k}{M}\right)e^{-\frac{j\pi k}{M}\tau}\right)\right). \tag{14}$$

The accuracy of the tracking mode is estimated by the amplitude-frequency and phase frequency response

$$A(\omega, \tau) = \left|\frac{K_p(\tau)W(p)}{1 + K_p(\tau)W(p)}\right|, \tag{15}$$

$$\varphi(\omega, \tau) = \arg\left[\frac{K_p(\tau)W(p)}{1 + K_p(\tau)W(p)}\right]. \tag{16}$$

A designed relay controller must maintain the desired frequency of self-oscillations and minimize phase lag and meet the requirements of the amplitude-frequency characteristic. Tuning the controller parameters is performed by the finite-optimization. in the paper describes the method of optimizing the swarm of particles with constraints is considered.

5 Optimization of RCS with Use PSO Method

Let us consider global PSO algorithm. On the first stage at the parametric space randomly swarm of initial points is created. Every point moves in some direction with a speed, which is defined as follows:

$$V_i[k+1] = wV_i[k] + C_1 r_1(p_i[k] - S_i[k]) + C_1 r_1(g[k] - S_i[k]). \tag{17}$$

Next position of point in the space may be defined as follows:

$$S_i[k+1] = S_i[k] + V_i[k+1], i = 1, 2, \ldots, n. \tag{18}$$

where $S_i[k]$ is the current position of i-th searching point, $V_i[k]$ is the speed of i-th point; n is number of points in the swarm, p_i is the best value of optimization criterion for i-th point, g is the best value from all points, $\omega_{min} \le \omega \le \omega_{max}$ is the weight coefficient, $\omega_{min}, \omega_{max}$ are minimal and maximal values of weight coefficient; $r_1, r_2 \in (0, 1]$. C_i is i-th point inertia coefficient [6, 7];

$$C_i = \omega_{max} - \frac{(\omega_{max} - \omega_{min})k}{k_{max}} \tag{19}$$

As criterion of algorithm stopping one use error of convergence of swam points $\sum_{k=1}^{n} var(p_k) < \varepsilon$, where ε is permissible accuracy of convergence. The constraints on the parameters in the optimization algorithm are implemented as penalty functions. The use of penalty functions is one of the most common approaches to deal with constraints in evolutionary computation. If a minimization problem is assumed, the objective function f is modified to f_{new}

$$f_{new}(x) = \begin{cases} f(x), \text{if } x \in X, \\ +\infty, \text{otherwise.} \end{cases}$$

X - set of possible values. Simple parallel realization of algorithm is possible (Fig. 6).

6 Example

As an example let us consider simplified model of actuator, flowchart of which is shown on the Fig. 7. In the model rigid mechanical limiters are not taken into consideration, so assumption, that system operates in linear domain are made.

On flowchart: $f[kT_s]$ is the input signal; $W_{filter}(z) = \frac{a_1 z}{z - a_2}$ is discrete correction device, $W_{freq}(z) = \frac{K_f z + T_f}{z^2 - 1.762z + 0.8187}$ device of discrete self-oscillation frequency correction; $U[k]$ is the signal from output of relay; $b = 0.001$ is the relay hysteresis; δ is the output shaft rotation angle; $T_s = 0.001$ (s) is the sampling period. Plant parameters: $K_1 = 7$, $T_1 = 0.001$, $K_m = 1.0$, $T_M = 0.004$, $\xi_M = 0.8$, $T_g = 0.025$, $M = 0.68$. The filter $W_{filter}(z)$ provides frequency correction. The filter $W_{freq}(z)$ provides stabilization of self-oscillation frequency. As the criterion of actuator operation effectiveness maximal phase lag in working interval of frequencies of input signals

$$f_{new}(a_1, a_2, T_1, K_1) = \max_{\omega_{min} \le \omega \le \omega_{max}} \varphi(\omega, \tau) \tag{20}$$

Calculation of optimization criterion conveniently to do with use linear model (See Fig. 5). Parallel PSO optimization algorithm implemented in MatLab. Using the electro-pneumatic actuator as an example, the controller is optimized using the PSO

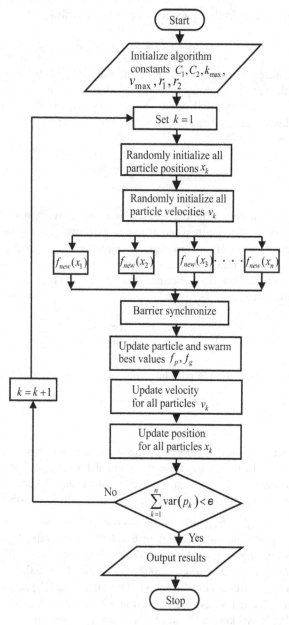

Fig. 6. Algorithm PSO

method and the standard GA method. The constraints on the parameters of the controller are the conditions for the stability of self-oscillations and the physical release of the controller (Table 1).

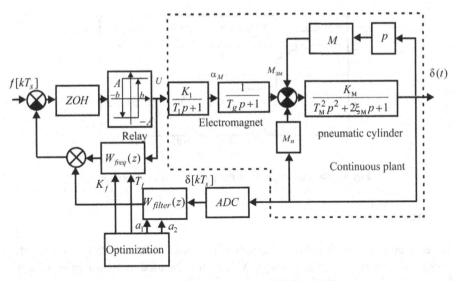

Fig. 7. Electro-pneumatic servomechanism.

Table 1. Results of the relay controller parameter tuning.

GA	PSO
$W_{filter}(z) = \frac{1.106z - 1.104}{z - 0.9979}$	$W_{filter}(z) = \frac{1.714z - 1.711}{z - 0.9971}$
$W_{freq}(z) = \frac{0.02249z + 0.002088}{z^2 - 1.732z + 0.8007}$	$W_{freq}(z) = \frac{0.002067z + 0.001934}{z^2 - 1.762z + 0.8187}$

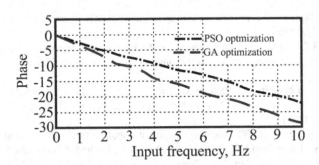

Fig. 8. Phase frequency characteristic of electro-pneumatic-servomechanism synthesized optimized by methods PSO and GA.

From the above simulation result, it illustrates that PSO has the better performance and faster convergence speed compared with the basic GA in relay controller parameters tuning problem. The particle swarm algorithm converges in 250 iterations (Figs. 8 and 9).

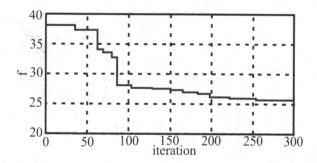

Fig. 9. The convergence of the particle swarm algorithm.

7 Conclusion

The result obtained confirms high efficiency of proposed method of PSO for solving the problem of relay control system design. Method may be used for optimization of wide class of digital relay control systems with self-oscillations.

Further investigation development in this area may be aimed on working out the method of selection of the direction of swarm unit movement during optimal solution search, which accelerate runtime of PSO algorithm.

Acknowledgement. The research was carried out within the state assignment of the Ministry of Education and Science of Russian Federation (No 2.3121.2017/PCH).

References

1. Marini, F., Walczak, B.: Particle swarm optimization (PSO). A tutorial. Chem. Intell. Lab. Syst. **149**, 153–165 (2015)
2. Eberhart, R.C., Shi, Y.: Particle swarm optimization: developments, applications, and resources. In: Proceedings of the 2001 Congress on Evolutionary Computation, pp. 81–86 (2001)
3. Kennedy, J., Eberhart, R.: Particle swarm optimization. In: Proceedings of the IEEE International Conference on Neural Networks, vol. IV, pp. 1942–1948. IEEE Press, Piscataway (1995)
4. Cui, Z., Zeng, J., Sun, G.: adaptive velocity threshold particle swarm optimization. In: Wang, G.-Y., Peters, James F., Skowron, A., Yao, Y. (eds.) RSKT 2006. LNCS (LNAI), vol. 4062, pp. 327–332. Springer, Heidelberg (2006). https://doi.org/10.1007/11795131_47
5. Wang, Y.-B., Peng, X., Wei, B.-Z.: A new particle swarm optimization based auto-tuning of PID controller. In: 2008 International Conference on Machine Learning Cybernetics, vol. 4, pp. 12–15, July 2008
6. Eberhart, R.C., Shi, Y.: Comparison between genetic algorithms and particle swarm optimization. In: Proceedings of IEEE International Conference on Evolutionary Computation, Anchorage, AK, pp. 611–616 (1998)
7. Helwig, S.: Particle swarms for constrained optimization. Ph.D. Thesis, University of Erlangen-Nurnberg (2010)

8. Paquet, U., Engelbrecht, A.P.: A new particle swarm optimiser for linearly constrained optimization. In: Proceedings of the Congress on Evolutionary Computation, CEC 2003, Piscataway, vol. 1, pp. 227–233. IEEE Service Center, Canberra (2003)

9. Floudas, Christodoulos A., Pardalos, Panos M.: A Collection of Test Problems for Constrained Global Optimization Algorithms. LNCS, vol. 455. Springer, Heidelberg (1990). https://doi.org/10.1007/3-540-53032-0

10. Morzhov, A.V., Faldin, N.V..: J. Comput. Syst. Sci. Int. **46**, 337 (2007). https://doi.org/10. 1134/S106423070703001X

11. Hetel, L., Fridman, E., Floquet, T.: Variable structure control with generalized relays: a simple convex optimization approach. IEEE Trans. Autom. Control **60**(2), 497–502 (2015)

12. Garulli, A., Giannitrapani, A., Leomanni, M.: Minimum switching limit cycle oscillations for systems of coupled double integrators. In: 2014 IEEE 53rd Annual Conference on Decision and Control (CDC), pp. 4655–4660 (2014)

13. Bazanella, A.S., Parraga, A.: Limit cycles in sampled-data relay feedback systems. Int. J. Control Autom. Electr. Syst. **27**(3), 237–249 (2016). https://doi.org/10.1007/s40313-016-0239-1

14. Feofilov, S.V., Kozyr, A.V.: Analysis of periodic motions in digital self-oscillating control systems. Mekhatronika, Avtomatizatsiya, Upravlenie **19**(8), 587–594 (2018). https://doi.org/ 10.17587/mau.19.587-594

15. Koch, S., Horn, M.: Frequency domain analysis of sampled variable structure systems. In: IEEE 56th Annual Conference on Decision and control, pp. 6664–6670, December 2017

16. Galias, Z., Yu, X.: Euler's discretization of single input sliding-mode control systems. IEEE Trans. Autom. Control **52**(9), 1726–1730 (2007)

17. Gilbert, E.G., Tan, K.T.: Linear systems with state and control constraints: the theory and application of maximal output admissible sets. IEEE Trans. Autom. Control **36**(9), 1008–1020 (1991). 310 pages (2005)

18. Lin, C., Wang, Q.-G., Lee, T.H., Lam, J.: Local stability of limit cycles for time-delay relay-feedback systems. IEEE Trans. Circuits Syst. Part I **49**(12), 1870–1875 (2002)

Niching Particle Swarm Optimizer with Entropy-Based Exploration Strategy for Global Optimization

Dongyang Li[1], Weian Guo[2(✉)], and Lei Wang[1]

[1] Department of Electronics and Information Engineering,
Tongji University, Shanghai 201804, China
lidongyang0412@163.com, wangle_tj@126.com
[2] Sino-German College of Applied Sciences,
Tongji University, Shanghai 201804, China
guoweian@tongji.edu.cn

Abstract. As a kind of evolutionary algorithms, particle swarm optimization is famous for its simplicity and efficiency in optimization. However, for complex problems, PSO is prone to be trapped into the local optima. To address this issue, a particle swarm optimizer with niching strategy and entropy-based exploration strategy (PSO-NE) is proposed in this paper. To be specific, on one hand, a distance based niching strategy and the competitive learning strategy are adopted to design the exploitation in PSO-NE; on the other hand, the exploration in PSO-NE is achieved by an entropy based exploring strategy. With such kind of designs, the exploitation and exploration in PSO-NE can be dependently adjusted, which is beneficial for balancing these two factors. To validate the effectiveness of the proposed algorithm, extensive experiments have been conducted based on 28 benchmarks from CEC' 2013. The proposed algorithm shows its competitive performance with comparing to six other typical variants of PSO.

Keywords: Particle swarm optimizer · Global optimization · Niching strategy · Competitive learning · Entropy

1 Introduction

As a kind of evolutionary algorithms (EAs), particle swarm optimization (PSO) has attracted a huge amount of attentions since its advent [1, 2]. The basic PSO keeps a number of particles each of which includes two attributes, the velocity and position which are iteratively updated according to the following equations

$$v_i^d(t+1) = w \cdot v_i^d(t) + c_1 \cdot r_1 \cdot \left(pbest_i^d(t) - p_i^d(t)\right) + c_2 \cdot r_2 \cdot \left(gbest^d(t) - p_i^d(t)\right) \quad (1)$$

$$p_i^d(t+1) = p_i^d(t) + v_i^d(t+1) \quad (2)$$

where t is the generation number; p_i^d and v_i^d are the dth dimensions of the position and velocity of ith particle respectively; $pbest_i^d$ represents the dth dimension of the best position searched by ith particle in current generation while $gbest^d$ are the best position

Y. Tan et al. (Eds.): ICSI 2019, LNCS 11655, pp. 118–127, 2019.
https://doi.org/10.1007/978-3-030-26369-0_11

of the whole swarm in current generation; w is the inertia weight, c_1 and c_2 are the acceleration coefficients; r_1 and r_2 are two randomly generated number within $[0, 1]$. Due to its simplicity and efficiency, PSO has been widely used in many studies areas, such as antenna designs [3], feature selection [4], robot path planning [5], and power system [6].

But many researchers have found that PSO lacks efficiency in solving complex optimizations. Thus, a lot of studies can be found in past two decades. First, many researchers focus on the adjustment of the parameters in PSO including the deterministic control methods [7–9] and the adaptive control strategies [10, 11]. Second, some efforts are made to diversify the exemplars for particles, such as the fully informed particle swarm optimization [12], the comprehensive learning particle swarm optimizer [13], and the competitive swarm optimizer (CSO) [17]. Besides, hybridization with other techniques is also much accounted by many studies such as particle swarm optimizer with crossover [18] and cooperatively coevolutionary strategy [19].

However, PSO and its variants still always fail to find the global optima in many cases. That's mainly because the existing PSO variants usually can't get a good balance between exploitation and exploration. For example, CSO enhances the exploration by learning the mean position of the whole swarm. However, such mean position is shared by all the particles to be updated [17], which results in a highly coupled relationship between exploration and exploitation in such kind of learning strategy.

To address this issue, this paper aims to reduce the coupling between exploitation and exploration in PSO and the main contributions in this paper are in following.

(1) A niching strategy is adopted to classify the particles into several sub-groups based on the distances among particles; then, a competitive learning strategy is employed to exploit each sub-group.
(2) An entropy based exploring strategy is proposed to enhance the exploration of PSO.

The rest of this paper is organized as follows. A brief overview of the related works on PSO will be presented in Sect. 2. In Sect. 3, the details of the proposed algorithm are introduced. The experiments and the results analyses are conducted in Sect. 4 and we end this paper with the conclusion in Sect. 5.

2 Related Works

For improving the performance of PSO, the existing works can be mainly categorized into following three classes.

2.1 Modified Updating Strategies

In such kind of variants, the main idea is to propose new learning strategy to improve the search ability of PSO. Mendes and Kennedy designed a fully informed learning strategy where particles learn to the contracted exemplars based on their neighbors [12]. Liang proposed comprehensive learning which allows each particle's *pbest* to be a leader [13]. Chen and Zhang proposed ALCPSO in which the *gbest* can be challenged and replaced by another generated particle in some cases leading to a more diverse global leader [20]. Cheng and Sun proposed FBE which includes two sub-swarms and a fitness value based competition. They identify the weak particles and the strong particles at each generation, then each weak particle is leaded by the best and another randomly selected particles from another sub-swarm while the strong particles are subjected to a mutation operation [14]. Later in 2015, Cheng and Jin proposed the competitive swarm optimizer which shows promising performance both in low dimensional and large scale optimization [17]. In the same year, Cheng and Jin proposed SL-PSO allowing particles to learn from each particles that better than themselves [15]. Last year, Yang and Chen proposed DLLSO in recently [16]. DLLSO grades particles base on the fitness values, and every particle chooses two different exemplars from superior levels. By this way, particles in DLLSO can get more diverse exemplars than CSO.

2.2 Parameter Control Strategies

The parameters are essential for controlling the convergence and diversity of PSO. Shi proposed a linear control methods and a fuzzy control strategy for the adjustment of the inertia weight [21, 22]. Ratnaweera and Halgamuge proposed HPSO-TVAC, where the acceleration coefficients are varying during the run of the algorithm [8]. APSO proposed by Zhan adjusts the acceleration coefficients according to an evolutionary state estimation strategy [10].

2.3 Hybridization with Other Techniques

The hybridization with other techniques is to utilize other techniques to enhance the search ability of the basic PSO. Such as the $CCPSO\text{-}S_K$ and $CCPSO\text{-}H_K$ integrated the co-operative co-evolutionary framework into PSO [23, 24]. Following this idea, Li and Yao put forward CCPSO2 in which the Gaussian and Cauchy distribution are used to update individuals to make a balance between exploitation and exploration [25]. Qin and Cheng proposed a PSO variant by dividing the whole swarm into learned and learning sub-swarms at each generation. And the learning sub-swarm will learn from the learned sub-swarm with a random probability [26]. The genetic learning particle swarm optimization put forward by Gong and Li uses crossover and mutation operators to enhance the exploration ability of PSO [27]. Similar to this idea, Chen and Li designed two different crossover operations to breed promising exemplars in their recent work [18].

More about the development of PSO can be found in [28]. Although these works have promoted PSO in various kinds of optimizations, PSO and its variants are still less effective for complex optimization. As discussed in Sect. 1, this is mainly because most of the existing methods still cannot achieve a good balance between exploitation and exploration, especially in solving problems with high complexity.

Thus, to further decouple the exploitation and exploration and get more reasonable balance between these two factors for PSO. This paper proposed a novel variant of PSO with introducing a niching method, the competitive learning strategies and an entropy-based exploration tactics. The details will be presented in the following section.

3 Proposed Algorithm

As discussed above, one can found that PSO still need to be further improved in balancing its exploitation and exploration. Thus, we proposed a novel variant of PSO as following.

3.1 Exploitation Operator

Exploitation is important for PSO because it can help the algorithm to refine the located promising areas. However, for the basic PSO, the current global best position of the swarm at each generation may be not in the most promising area in the search space under some cases during the optimization, especially for the multi-modal optimization. This can be illustrated by Fig. 1.

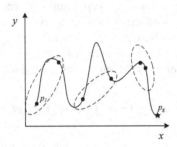

Fig. 1. A potential function with one decision variable.

As shown in Fig. 1, the true global best solution is p_g while the current global best position is p_1. And in the basic PSO, all the particle will be attracted by p_1 which will lead to missing of the true global best solution. To address this issue, it is better to group the swarm to different sub-groups as shown in Fig. 1. By this way, more promising solutions can be exploited which can potentially address the aforementioned issue. To achieve this, a niching method and the competitive learning strategy are adopted which will be introduced following.

Algorithm 1. Niching strategy: Clustering for Speciation [29]

Input : Population P, cluster size M

Step 1: Sort P according to fitness;

Step 2: While P is not empty

           Select the best individual P_{best} in P as a new seed;

           Build a species containing P_{best} and M-1 individuals nearest to it;

           Eliminate these M individuals from P;

      End While

Output: A set of species

Then, in each group, for a thorough exploitation, the competitive learning strategy proposed in [17] is used to identify the particles to be updated and the corresponding exemplars. Consequently, the velocity of a particle to be updated in subgroup in the exploitation phase will be updated by using (3)

$$v_{m,l,i}^d(t+1) = r_1 \cdot \left(p_{m,w,i}^d(t) - p_{m,l,i}^d(t) \right) \tag{3}$$

where $v_{m,l,i}^d(t)$ and $p_{m,l,i}^d(t)$ denote the dth dimension of the ith particle to be updated in mth subgroup and the corresponding information of the exemplars; r_1 holds the same meaning with that in (1).

3.2   Exploration Operator

For exploration, a commonly used way is to keep the particles uniformly dispersed in the search space. To achieve this, this paper suggests an entropy based exploring strategy because entropy is an effective measure to evaluate the scatter degree of a set of random variables. Specifically, we adopt a modified entropy measurement based on the design proposed in [30], where the particles will be first sorted according to their fitness values and then the entropy for ith particle is defined as following

$$entropy_i = -normal\{(pro_{i,1}\log_2(pro_{i,1}) + pro_{i,2}\log_2(pro_{i,2}))\} \cdot normal\left\{\frac{L_i}{L}\right\} \tag{4}$$

$$pro_{i,1} = \frac{fitness_i - fitness_{i-1}}{L_i} \tag{5}$$

$$pro_{i,2} = \frac{fitness_{i+1} - fitness_i}{L_i} \tag{6}$$

$$L_i = fitness_{i+1} - fitness_{i-1} \tag{7}$$

$$L = \max(fitness) - \min(fitness) \tag{8}$$

where $normal\{\vec{z}\}$ is a normalize operator by dividing each element in $\vec{z}$ by the maximum value of $\vec{z}$. From (4)–(8) one can find that the proposed method takes both the uniform degree and the search space of particles in fitness landscape, which results in a more reasonable measurement for the uniform degree of particles. However, it is obvious that this method cannot compute the entropy for the best and worst particles, in this paper, such kind of particles' entropy are set to 0. Due to the space limitation, the detailed analysis for the benefits of the entropy-based crowding measurement will be not presented here, one can find it in [30].

Besides, to further enhance the flexibility of the search behavior of particles, a social learning based strategy is embedded in the exploration operator. The velocity updating of ith particle in exploration phase can be expressed in (9)

$$v_i^d(t+1) = c_2 \cdot r_2 \cdot \left(p_j^d(t) - p_i^d(t)\right) \tag{9}$$

where p_j^d is the dth dimension of the jth particle that randomly selected in the set in which all the particles' entropy is larger than ith particle; c_2 and r_2 hold the same meaning with that in (1).

In summary, the proposed velocity updating strategy for ith particle in mth subgroup that to be updated can be shown in (10) and (11)

$$v_{m,l,i}^d(t+1) = w \cdot v_{m,l,i}^d(t) + r_1 \cdot \left(p_{m,w,i}^d(t) - p_{m,l,i}^d(t)\right) + c_2 \cdot r_2 \cdot \left(p_j^d(t) - p_{m,l,i}^d(t)\right) \tag{10}$$

$$p_{m,l,i}^d(t+1) = p_{m,l,i}^d(t) + v_{m,l,i}^d(t+1) \tag{11}$$

To this end, the pseudo code of the proposed PSO-NE is shown in Algorithm 2.

Algorithm 2. Proposed algorithm: PSO-NE

Input : Population P, cluster size M, parameter c_2

Step 1: Swam initialization;

Step 2: Compute the *fitness* for P;

Step 2: While terminal criterion is false

      Sort P according to *fitness*

      Execute the niching strategy according to Algorithm 1;

      Computing the *entropy* for particles using (4)-(8);

      Update swarm using (10)-(11);

      Compute the *fitness* for P;

    End While

Output: Best particle

---

4 Experiments and Discussions

4.1 Experiments Settings

To validate the performance of PSO-NE, 28 benchmark functions from CEC's 2013 are employed to conduct the experiments. More details about the benchmarks can be find in [31]. Six other popular variants of PSO are adopted to compare with PSO-NE including ALCPSO [20], CLPSO [13], CSO [17], HPSO-TVAC [8], and FIPS [12], DLLSO [16].

In the experiments, the dimensionality D of the functions is set to 50. Each algorithm has a population size N of 40. The maximum fitness evaluations *MaxFEs* is set to $10000 \cdot D$, the search range is $[-100\ 100]$. For parameter settings, the cluster size M in PSO-NE is set to 10 while the parameter c_2 is set to 1 to 0.4 during the run. For the other five algorithms, we adopt the default parameter settings as following. In ALCPSO, w varies from 0.9 to 0.4 while $c_1 = c_2 = 1.49$; In CLPSO, w also varies

Table 1. The experimental results with fitness evaluations of 5e5.

Function	Property	ALCPSO	CLPSO	CSO	HPSO-TVAC	LIPS	DLLSO	PSO-NE
1	mean	3.19E-12	3.18E-13	2.27E-13	6.63E-12	6.79E-11	1.06E+01	2.27E-13
	pvalue	8.68E-05	7.81E-03	1.00E+00*	8.82E-05	8.84E-05	8.86E-05	-
2	mean	3.02E+07	3.53E+07	2.67E+06	7.71E+06	4.95E+07	5.01E+07	1.96E+06
	pvalue	8.86E-05	8.86E-05	2.50E-03	8.86E-05	1.20E-04	8.86E-05	-
3	mean	1.95E+09	3.65E+09	2.47E+09	2.33E+09	4.83E+09	2.83E+10	4.60E+05
	pvalue	8.86E-05	8.86E-05	8.86E-05	8.86E-05	8.86E-05	8.86E-05	-
4	mean	4.97E+03	3.42E+04	5.06E+04	2.40E+04	1.18E+05	1.29E+05	1.87E+03
	pvalue	1.03E-04	8.86E-05	8.86E-05	8.86E-05	8.86E-05	8.86E-05	-
5	mean	1.88E-12	3.87E-13	7.91E-11	1.33E-06	1.43E-08	1.48E+02	3.12E-13
	pvalue	8.81E-05	2.07E-03	1.28E-03	8.86E-05	8.86E-05	8.86E-05	-
6	mean	5.96E+01	4.62E+01	5.60E+01	9.28E+01	5.93E+01	1.59E+02	4.57E+01
	pvalue	3.04E-02	2.32E-01*	1.26E-01*	2.93E-04	3.19E-03	8.86E-05	-
7	mean	1.19E+02	1.19E+02	6.23E+01	1.75E+02	1.17E+02	1.06E+02	8.11E-01
	pvalue	8.86E-05	8.86E-05	8.86E-05	8.86E-05	8.86E-05	8.86E-05	-
8	mean	2.11E+01	2.11E+01	2.11E+01	2.11E+01	2.11E+01	2.11E+01	2.11E+01
	pvalue	8.23E-01*	1.91E-01*	7.37E-01*	6.27E-01*	3.32E-01*	7.37E-01*	-
9	mean	5.35E+01	5.39E+01	2.89E+01	5.83E+01	4.80E+01	3.94E+01	9.88E+00
	pvalue	8.86E-05	8.86E-05	8.86E-05	8.86E-05	8.86E-05	8.86E-05	-
10	mean	9.32E-01	1.47E+01	1.18E+00	2.41E+00	1.16E+00	3.30E+02	7.15E-02
	pvalue	8.86E-05	8.86E-05	8.86E-05	8.86E-05	1.69E-02	8.86E-05	-
11	mean	2.69E+01	7.39E-14	7.62E+01	8.11E+01	2.10E+02	1.37E+02	2.62E+01
	pvalue	9.70E-01*	8.84E-05	8.86E-05	8.86E-05	8.86E-05	8.86E-05	-
12	mean	3.17E+02	3.22E+02	7.68E+01	5.46E+02	2.40E+02	1.62E+02	1.71E+02
	pvalue	1.63E-04	1.03E-04	2.19E-04	8.86E-05	1.71E-03	3.70E-01*	-
13	mean	4.58E+02	4.13E+02	1.96E+02	6.78E+02	4.52E+02	3.77E+02	1.93E+02
	pvalue	8.86E-05	8.86E-05	6.81E-01*	8.86E-05	8.86E-05	8.86E-05	-
14	mean	1.04E+03	8.97E-01	2.13E+03	1.45E+03	4.64E+03	4.84E+03	1.05E+03
	pvalue	5.50E-01*	8.86E-05	8.86E-05	3.19E-03	8.86E-05	8.86E-05	-
15	mean	9.28E+03	8.25E+03	5.08E+03	8.40E+03	6.95E+03	6.91E+03	7.70E+03
	pvalue	7.19E-03	3.51E-01*	6.81E-04	1.91E-01*	2.18E-01*	1.17E-01*	-
16	mean	3.05E+00	1.89E+00	7.24E-01	2.75E+00	7.48E-01	5.66E-01	3.40E+00
	pvalue	3.59E-03	8.86E-05	8.86E-05	4.55E-03	8.86E-05	8.86E-05	-
17	mean	1.24E+02	5.08E+01	8.86E-05	2.57E+02	3.49E+02	2.11E+02	9.34E+01
	pvalue	2.54E-04	8.86E-05	8.97E-03	8.86E-05	8.86E-05	8.86E-05	-
18	mean	3.83E+02	4.07E+02	1.03E+02	8.21E+02	3.73E+02	2.79E+02	3.70E+02
	pvalue	5.50E-01*	8.86E-05	8.86E-05	8.86E-05	8.81E-01*	1.03E-04	-
19	mean	1.46E+01	5.47E-01	1.47E+01	1.94E+01	9.34E+01	6.00E+01	6.59E+00
	pvalue	8.86E-05	8.86E-05	1.89E-04	8.86E-05	8.86E-05	8.86E-05	-
20	mean	2.45E+01	2.36E+01	2.06E+01	2.24E+01	2.21E+01	2.34E+01	2.03E+01
	pvalue	8.86E-05	8.86E-05	6.81E-01*	1.20E-04	2.19E-04	8.86E-05	-
21	mean	7.74E+02	2.33E+02	6.18E+02	8.66E+02	3.78E+02	1.27E+03	9.36E+02
	pvalue	1.91E-01*	8.86E-05	6.90E-03	8.23E-01*	2.19E-04	3.66E-02	-
22	mean	2.68E+03	2.45E+01	2.65E+03	1.84E+03	6.68E+03	6.10E+03	1.18E+03
	pvalue	8.86E-05	8.86E-05	8.86E-05	1.89E-04	8.86E-05	8.86E-05	-
23	mean	9.78E+03	1.00E+04	5.74E+03	1.04E+04	9.07E+03	8.80E+03	8.56E+03
	pvalue	6.20E-02*	4.00E-02	1.71E-03	3.04E-02	5.02E-01*	7.37E-01*	-
24	mean	3.53E+02	3.51E+02	2.92E+02	3.81E+02	3.54E+02	3.22E+02	2.15E+02
	pvalue	8.86E-05	8.86E-05	8.86E-05	8.86E-05	8.86E-05	8.86E-05	-
25	mean	3.89E+02	3.90E+02	3.29E+02	3.77E+02	4.15E+02	3.60E+02	2.90E+02
	pvalue	8.86E-05	8.86E-05	1.40E-04	8.86E-05	8.86E-05	8.86E-05	-
26	mean	4.38E+02	2.04E+02	3.53E+02	4.22E+02	2.76E+02	4.00E+02	3.01E+02
	pvalue	8.86E-05	3.90E-04	2.51E-02	5.17E-04	2.47E-01*	6.81E-04	-
27	mean	1.74E+01	1.60E+03	1.18E+03	2.09E+03	1.74E+03	1.44E+03	5.19E+02
	pvalue	8.86E-05	1.89E-04	8.86E-05	8.86E-05	8.86E-05	8.86E-05	-
28	mean	2.14E+03	4.00E+02	7.25E+02	3.95E+03	8.76E+02	1.59E+03	4.00E+02
	pvalue	8.84E-05	8.86E-05	2.98E-05	8.86E-05	8.68E-05	8.86E-05	-
w/l/t		21/1/6	18/7/3	17/6/5	24/1/3	22/1/5	22/2/4	-

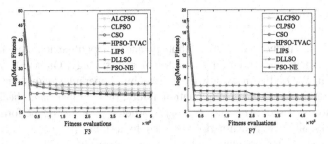

Fig. 2. The convergence figure on F3 and F7.

from 0.9 to 0.4, $c = 1.49445$ and $m = 7$; In CSO, *phi* is set to 0; In HPSO-TVAC, w varies from 0.9 to 0.4, c_1 varies from 0.5 to 2.5 while c_2 varies from 2.5 to 0.5; In FIPS, $\chi = 0.729$ and $\sum c_i = 0.41$; In DLLSO the level number set is $\{4, 6, 8, 10, 20\}$ and $\varphi = 0.4$. We run 20 simulations of each algorithm on each benchmark to get representative performance.

4.2 Results and Discussions

In this part, we record the difference between the obtained best fitness value and the real global optima in each run. Then the mean optimization results and the p-value obtained by Wilcoxon test are shown in Table 1, while Fig. 2 shows the convergence curve of these algorithms, due to the limitation of the space, we just draw the convergence figure on F_3 and F_7 which are unimodal and multimodal function respectively. In Table 1, the best results of mean performance are high lightened by gray; the p-value marked by bond and "*" indicate PSO-NE significantly better than and statistically equivalent to the compared algorithm on the corresponding function and. w/l/t at the bottom of the tables represent that how many times PSO-NE wins/loses/ties in the competitions with comparing to the corresponding algorithms.

From Table 1 we can see that the proposed PSO-NE wins for 16 functions with the mean fitness comparison. To be specific, for all the unimodal functions, PSO-NE obtains the best results, especially for F_2, F_3, PSO-NE performs much better than all the other algorithms; for the multi-modal functions, PSO-NE wins the first place on 6 functions; besides, the proposed PSO-NE performs competitive on the composition Functions as shown in Table 1.

For the p-value results, PSO-NE wins 21, 18, 17, 24, 22, 22 times over the corresponding algorithms, which stochastically demonstrates the competitive performance of PSO-NE. Additionally, the convergence figures also demonstrate the promising exploitation ability of PSO-NE.

In summary, the results shown in Table 1 turn out that the proposed strategy is effective for improving PSO in low dimension optimization.

5 Conclusions

In this paper, we propose a niching strategy and competitive learning based local exploitation strategy and an entropy based exploring strategy. On one hand, because the particles in PSO-NE can exploit local areas by cooperating with their neighbors, PSO-NE has a more reasonable exploitation ability; on the other hand, because of the designed entropy based exploring strategy, particles in PSO-NE perform better in exploration. Finally, 28 benchmarks are used to test the proposed algorithm with comparing to six other popular PSO variants. The results finally demonstrate the proposed algorithm is effective to deal with optimization problems.

Acknowledgments. This work was sponsored by the National Natural Science Foundation of China under Grant no. 71771176 and 61503287.

References

1. Eberhart, R., Kennedy, J.: A new optimizer using particle swarm theory. In: 6th Proceedings of the Sixth International Symposium on Micro Machine and Human Science, pp. 39–43, IEEE, Nagoya (1995)
2. Eberhart, R., Kennedy, J.: Particle swarm optimization. In: Proceedings of the IEEE International Conference on Neural Networks, vol. 4, pp. 1942–1948. IEEE, Australia (1995)
3. Jin, N., Rahmat-Samii, Y.: Advances in particle swarm optimization for antenna designs: real-number, binary, single-objective and multiobjective implementations. IEEE Trans. Antennas Propag. **55**(3), 556–567 (2007)
4. Ghamisi, P., Benediktsson, J.A.: Feature selection based on hybridization of genetic algorithm and particle swarm optimization. IEEE Geosci. Remote Sens. Lett. **12**(2), 309–313 (2015)
5. Das, P.K., Behera, H.S., Panigrahi, B.K.: A hybridization of an improved particle swarm optimization and gravitational search algorithm for multi-robot path planning. Swarm Evol. Comput. **28**, 14–28 (2016)
6. Koad, R.B.A., Zobaa, A.F., El-Shahat, A.: A novel MPPT algorithm based on particle swarm optimization for photovoltaic systems. IEEE Trans. Sustain. Energy **8**(2), 468–476 (2017)
7. Zheng, Y., Ma, L., Zhang, L., et al.: Empirical study of particle swarm optimizer with an increasing inertia weight. In: The 2003 Congress on Evolutionary Computation, vol. 1, pp. 221–226. IEEE, Canberra, ACT, Australia (2003)
8. Ratnaweera, A., Halgamuge, S.K., Watson, H.C.: Self-organizing hierarchical particle swarm optimizer with time-varying acceleration coefficients. IEEE Trans. Evol. Comput. **8**(3), 240–255 (2004)
9. Chatterjee, A., Siarry, P.: Nonlinear inertia weight variation for dynamic adaptation in particle swarm optimization. Comput. Oper. Res. **33**(3), 859–871 (2006)
10. Zhan, Z.H., Zhang, J., Li, Y., et al.: Adaptive particle swarm optimization. IEEE Trans. Syst. Man Cybern. Part B (Cybern.) **39**(6), 1362–1381 (2009)
11. Taherkhani, M., Safabakhsh, R.: A novel stability-based adaptive inertia weight for particle swarm optimization. Appl. Soft Comput. **38**, 281–295 (2016)

12. Mendes, R., Kennedy, J., Neves, J.: The fully informed particle swarm: simpler, maybe better. IEEE Trans. Evol. Comput. **8**(3), 204–210 (2004)
13. Liang, J.J., Qin, A.K., Suganthan, P.N., et al.: Comprehensive learning particle swarm optimizer for global optimization of multimodal functions. IEEE Trans. Evol. Comput. **10** (3), 281–295 (2006)
14. Cheng, R., Sun, C., Jin, Y.: A multi-swarm evolutionary framework based on a feedback mechanism. In: 2013 IEEE Congress on Evolutionary Computation, pp. 718–724. IEEE, Cancun (2001)
15. Cheng, R., Jin, Y.: A social learning particle swarm optimization algorithm for scalable optimization. Inf. Sci. **291**, 43–60 (2015)
16. Yang, Q., Chen, W.N., Da Deng, J., et al.: A level-based learning swarm optimizer for large-scale optimization. IEEE Trans. Evol. Comput. **22**(4), 578–594 (2018)
17. Cheng, R., Jin, Y.: A competitive swarm optimizer for large scale optimization. IEEE Trans. Cybern. **45**(2), 191–204 (2015)
18. Chen, Y., Li, L., Xiao, J., et al.: Particle swarm optimizer with crossover operation. Eng. Appl. Artif. Intell. **70**, 159–169 (2018)
19. Tang, R.L., Wu, Z., Fang, Y.J.: Adaptive multi-context cooperatively coevolving particle swarm optimization for large-scale problems. Soft. Comput. **21**(16), 4735–4754 (2017)
20. Chen, W.N., Zhang, J., Lin, Y., et al.: Particle swarm optimization with an aging leader and challengers. IEEE Trans. Evol. Comput. **17**(2), 241–258 (2013)
21. Shi, Y., Eberhart, R.C.: Empirical study of particle swarm optimization. In: Proceedings of the 1999 Congress on Evolutionary Computation, vol. 3, pp. 1945–1950. IEEE, Washington (1999)
22. Shi, Y., Eberhart, R.C.: Fuzzy adaptive particle swarm optimization. In: Proceedings of the 2001 Congress on Evolutionary Computation, vol. 1, pp. 101–106. IEEE, South Korea (2001)
23. van den Bergh, F., Engelbrecht, A.: A cooperative approach to particle swarm optimization. IEEE Trans. Evol. Comput. **8**(3), 225–239 (2004)
24. den Bergh, F.V.: An analysis of particle swarm optimizers. Ph.D. dissertation, Dept. Comput. Sci., Univ. Pretoria, Pretoria, South Africa (2002)
25. Li, X., Yao, X.: Cooperatively coevolving particle swarms for large scale optimization. IEEE Trans. Evol. Comput. **16**(2), 210–224 (2012)
26. Qin, Q., Cheng, S., Zhang, Q., et al.: Particle swarm optimization with interswarm interactive learning strategy. IEEE Trans. Cybern. **46**(10), 2238–2251 (2016)
27. Gong, Y.J., Li, J.J., Zhou, Y., et al.: Genetic Learning Particle Swarm Optimization. IEEE Trans. Cybern. **46**(10), 2277–2290 (2017)
28. Bonyadi, M.R., Michalewicz, Z.: Particle swarm optimization for single objective continuous space problems: a review. Evol. Comput. **25**(1), 1–54 (2017)
29. Sheng, W., Swift, S., Zhang, L., Liu, X.: A weighted sum validity function for clustering with a hybrid niching genetic algorithm. IEEE Trans. Syst. Man Cybern. Part B (Cybern.) **35** (6), 1156–1167 (2005)
30. Wang, Y.N., Wu, L.H., Yuan, X.F.: Multi-objective self-adaptive differential evolution with elitist archive and crowding entropy-based diversity measure. Soft. Comput. **14**(3), 193–209 (2010)
31. Liang, J.J., Qu, B.Y., Suganthan, P.N., et al.: Problem definitions and evaluation criteria for the CEC 2013 special session on real-parameter optimization. Computational Intelligence Laboratory, Zhengzhou University, Zhengzhou, China and Nanyang Technological University, Singapore, Technical Report, 201212(34): 281–295 (2013)

A Study on Designing an Aperiodic Antenna Array Using Boolean PSO

Waroth Kuhirun[(✉)]

Electrical Engineering Department, Faculty of Engineering,
Kasetsart University, Bangkok 10900, Thailand
fengwrk@yahoo.com
http://www.ee.ku.ac.th

Abstract. Wireless communication systems play a major role in communication systems, especially in modern communication systems. An antenna is one of the most important part of wireless communication systems. An Antenna is a device for transmitting or receiving signals. Antennas can be broadly divided into two types, antenna elements and antenna arrays. Antenna elements function in transmitting or receiving signals. Antenna arrays are actually an array of antenna elements. Analytical approach for designing an antenna element is possible for an antenna array with a simple configuration. An example is a 2-element array. However, for designing complicated antenna arrays, it is a very difficult task, especially aperiodic arrays. A design problem can be regarded as an optimization problem. There are various optimization techniques; one of which is particle swarm optimization. Particle swarm optimization is one of optimization based on the behavior of social animals, i.e., fishes, birds and bees. For particle swarm optimization, each bee travel from place to place to find the highest density of honeybees. The bees and the highest density of honeybees are analogous to potential solutions and the position with optimal fitness function. Particle swarm optimization allows designing aperiodic antenna arrays more convenient and flexible. This paper presents a study on designing an aperiodic antenna array using boolean particle swarm optimization, a version of particle swarm optimization.

Keywords: Antennas · Arrays · Fitness function ·
Boolean particle swarm optimization · Aperiodic

1 Introduction

Wireless communication systems play a major role in communication systems, especially in modern communication systems. An antenna is one of the most important part in wireless systems. An antenna is a device for transmitting or receiving signals. Antennas can be broadly divided into two types, antenna elements and antenna arrays.

Supported by Kasetsart University Research and Development Institute.

Y. Tan et al. (Eds.): ICSI 2019, LNCS 11655, pp. 128–138, 2019.
https://doi.org/10.1007/978-3-030-26369-0_12

1.1   Antenna Arrays

Antenna arrays are actually an array of antenna elements. In this article, antenna arrays are briefly discussed. Further literature may be found in [1–5]. In general, antenna elements of an antenna array are identical and oriented in the same direction. The total electric field intensity $\boldsymbol{E}$ and magnetic field intensity $\boldsymbol{H}$ in the far-field generated by all antenna elements of an N-element antenna array can be expressed as

$$\boldsymbol{E}_{total} = \sum_{n=1}^{N} \boldsymbol{E}_n \quad \text{and} \quad \boldsymbol{H}_{total} = \sum_{n=1}^{N} \boldsymbol{H}_n \qquad (1)$$

Since all antenna elements are identical and oriented in the same direction, the total electric field intensity $\boldsymbol{E}_{total}$ and the total magnetic field intensity $\boldsymbol{H}_{total}$ can be factor out and are of the form.

$$\boldsymbol{E}_{total} = \boldsymbol{E}_0 AF(\theta, \varphi) \quad \text{and} \quad \boldsymbol{H}_{total} = \boldsymbol{H}_0 AF(\theta, \varphi) \qquad (2)$$

where $\boldsymbol{E}_0$ and $\boldsymbol{H}_0$ are electric field intensity and magnetic field intensity generated by an antenna element. In addition, the factor $AF(\theta, \varphi)$ is called "array factor".

The array factor $AF(\varphi, \theta)$ can be expressed as

$$AF(\theta, \varphi) = \sum_{n=1}^{N} I_n e^{jk\boldsymbol{r}_n.\hat{n}+\beta_n} \qquad (3)$$

or

$$AF(\theta, \varphi) = \sum_{n=1}^{N} I_n e^{jkr_n \sin\theta \cos(\varphi-\varphi_n)+\beta_n} \qquad (4)$$

where θ is elevation angle whereas φ is azimuthal angle in the spherical coordinates as shown in Fig. 1. In addition, k is the wavenumber and I_n, β_n is the relative current excitation and relative phase, respectively, of the nth element. Finally, $\hat{n}$ is the unit vector in the direction of observation (θ, φ) and $\boldsymbol{r}_n$ is the position vector of the nth antenna element. In spherical coordinates, the nth antenna element is located at the spherical coordinates $(r_n, \theta_n, \varphi_n)$.

The array factor pattern can illustrate how well the antenna array can direct to a specified direction. There is another parameter which is closely related to the array factor mentioned earlier. The directivity D is defined by [1,3]

$$D = \frac{|AF(\theta, \varphi)|^2_{max}}{\frac{1}{4\pi} \int_0^\pi \int_0^{2\pi} |AF(\theta, \varphi)|^2 \sin\theta \, d\varphi d\theta} \qquad (5)$$

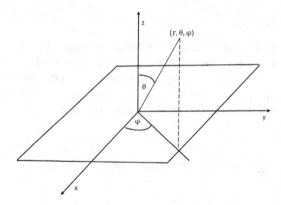

Fig. 1. Spherical coordinates.

Kuhirun [3] demonstrated that

$$D = \frac{\left(\sum\limits_{n=1}^{N} I_n\right)^2}{\sum\limits_{n=1}^{N} I_n^2 + 2\sum\limits_{m=2}^{N}\sum\limits_{n=1}^{m-1} I_n I_m \dfrac{sin\left(k|\boldsymbol{r}_n - \boldsymbol{r}_m|\right)}{\left(k|\boldsymbol{r}_n - \boldsymbol{r}_m|\right)}} \qquad (6)$$

The proof can be found in [3].

For a simple antenna array (i.e, two-element array), analytical approach may be utilized. However, it is difficult for more complicated antenna array. Optimization techniques [6–11] can be used in practice. One of the most popular optimization techniques used in antenna engineering is particle swarm optimization [6,9,11].

1.2   Particle Swarm Optimization

Particle swarm optimization is one of stochastic optimization techniques based on behavior of social animals. Examples are fishes, birds, and bees. For particle swarm optimization, each bee (potential solution) travels from place to place in the search space to find the place with highest density of honeybees (optimal solution). Direction and velocity of each bee are determined stochastically by inertia factor- the inertia of each bee, cognitive factor-the past experience of each bee and social factor-the past experience of the whole population of bees. More detail can be found in [6,9,11].

2   Setup of Computer Simulation

First of all, encode each bee (potential solution) using binary number described in Sect. 2.1 and set the fitness function described in Sect. 2.2. Next, perform computer simulation using matlab code shown in Sect. 2.3.

2.1 Encoding

Shown in Fig. 2, the nth antenna element in the ith N-element array is located at the coordinates (x_i, y_i). x_i and y_i where $A \leq x_i \leq B$ and $C \leq y_i \leq D$ are represented by an n-binary number $x_{b,i}$ and $y_{b,i}$, respectively.

$$x_{b,n} = \left[x_{b,n}^{n_x} \ldots x_{b,n}^1 \right] \quad \text{and} \quad y_{b,n} = \left[y_{b,n}^{n_y} \ldots y_{b,n}^1 \right] \tag{7}$$

$$x_n = d \sum_{j=1}^{n_x} x_{b,i}^j 2^{j-1} + A \quad \text{and} \quad y_n = w \sum_{j=1}^{n_y} y_{b,i}^j 2^{j-1} + C \tag{8}$$

$$d = \frac{B-A}{2^{n_x} - 1} \quad \text{and} \quad w = \frac{D-C}{2^{n_y} - 1} \tag{9}$$

where n_x and n_y are the numbers of bits of $x_{b,n}$ $y_{b,n}$, respectively. Also, x_i and y_i represent x_n and y_n, respectively. In addition, $X_{b,i} = [x_{b,1} \ldots x_{b,N}], Y_{b,i} = [y_{b,1} \ldots y_{b,N}], n_X = n_x N$ and $n_Y = n_y N$

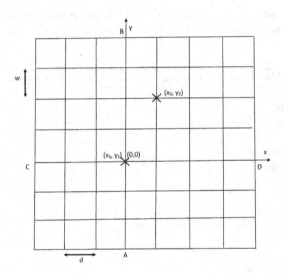

Fig. 2. Figure to show coding. This figure show an example of a 2-element array where $n_x = 3, n_y = 3, x_{b,1} = [011], x_{b,2} = [100], y_{b,1} = [011]$ and $y_{b,2} = [101]$. That is, $Xb, i = [x_{b,1}x_{b,2}] = [011100], Yb, i = [y_{b,1}y_{b,2}] = [011101], n_X = 2 \times 3 = 6$ and $n_Y = 2 \times 3 = 6$

2.2 Fitness Function

We aim to maximize the directivity D whereas to keep the spacings between adjacent elements large enough so that the mutual effect between elements is negligible. The fitness function f is described by

$$f = c_1 f_1 + c_2 f_2 \tag{10}$$

where f_1 corresponds to the directivity D and f_2 corresponds to the minimum distance between adjacent elements.

The fitness function f is set as follows:

$$f = -c_1 \frac{\left(\sum\limits_{n=1}^{N} I_n\right)^2}{\sum\limits_{n=1}^{N} I_n^2 + 2 \sum\limits_{m=2}^{N} \sum\limits_{n=1}^{m-1} I_n I_m \frac{sin\left(k|\boldsymbol{r}_n - \boldsymbol{r}_m|\right)}{\left(k|\boldsymbol{r}_n - \boldsymbol{r}_m|\right)}} + c_2 max(min_{threshold} - |\boldsymbol{r}_n - \boldsymbol{r}_m|, 0)$$

(11)

where $c_1 = 1$ and $c_2 = 5000$

It is of importance to note that we intend select the constants c_1 and c_2 in that $c_2 >> c_1 > 0$. The reason behind this is that f_2 dominates f_1 when f_2 is not zero.

2.3   Algorithm for Computer Simulation

The computer simulation is performed using boolean particle swarm optimization [12]. The algorithm for computer simulation is shown below.

Algorithm 1. Algorithm for Boolean Particle Swarm Optimization

time $t \leftarrow 0$
for $i = 1 : N_a$ **do**
   Evaluate Fitness Function of array i
end for
for $i = 1 : Na$ **do**
   Initialize p_i^t and v_i^t
   $p_{i,best}^t \leftarrow p_i^t$
end for
Locate G_{best}^t
while Terminating Criteria are not met **do**
   $t \leftarrow t + 1$
   for $i = 1 : N_a$ **do**
      for $n = 1 : N_b$ **do**
         randomise ω, α_1 and α_2
         $v_{i,n}^t = \omega v_{i,n}^{t-1} + \alpha_1(p_{i,n,best}^{t-1} \oplus p_{i,n}^{t-1}) + \alpha_2(G_{n,best}^{t-1} \oplus p_{i,n}^{t-1})$
         $p_{i,n}^t = p_{i,n}^t \oplus v_{i,n}^t$
      end for
      Update $p_{i,best}^t$
   end for
   Update G_{best}^t
end while

Table 1. Table for comparison between the optimized 9-element antenna array and the standard 9-element square antenna array with minimum distance of λ

Type of arrays	Minimum threshold	Minimum distance	Value of fitness function	Directivity
Optimized antenna array	λ	0.502λ	2477	11.2455
	0.8λ	0.668λ	647	11.7102
	0.5λ	0.490λ	39.3532	10.9987
Standard square array	-	λ	-	8.7264

Table 2. Table for comparison between the optimized 25-element antenna array and the standard 25-element square antenna array with minimum distance between elements of 0.5λ

Type of arrays	Minimum threshold	Minimum distance	Value of fitness function	Directivity
Optimized antenna array	0.5λ	0.15λ	1744.1	11.9401
Standard square array	-	0.5λ	-	15.2779

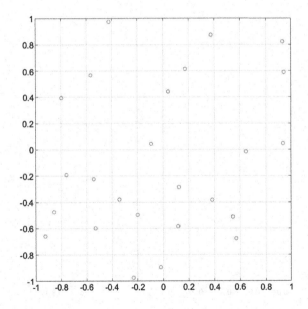

Fig. 3. Optimized 9-element antenna array with minimum threshold of λ. Each antenna element is represented by "o" and the coordinates is shown in wavelength λ

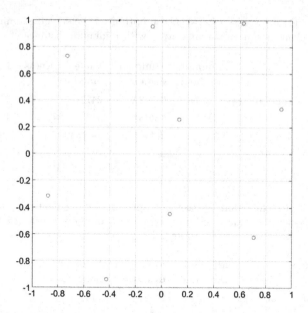

Fig. 4. Optimized 9-element antenna array with minimum threshold of 0.8λ. Each antenna element is represented by "o" and the coordinates is shown in wavelength λ

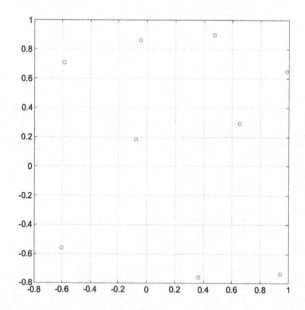

Fig. 5. Optimized 9-element antenna array with minimum threshold of 0.5λ. Each antenna element is represented by "o" and the coordinates is shown in wavelength λ

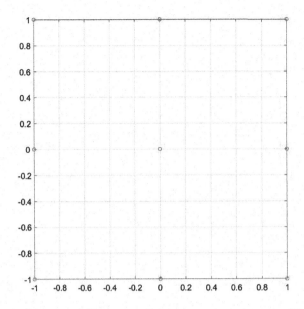

Fig. 6. Standard 9-element square antenna array with minimum distance of λ. Each antenna element is represented by "o" and the coordinates is shown in wavelength λ

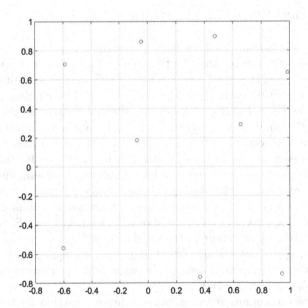

Fig. 7. Optimized 25-element antenna array with minimum threshold of 0.5λ. Each antenna element is represented by "o" and the coordinates is shown in wavelength λ

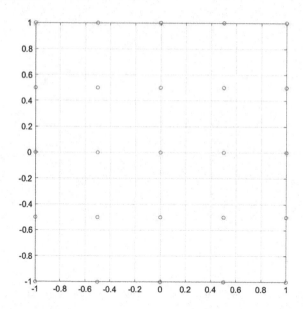

Fig. 8. Standard 25-element square antenna array with minimum distance of 0.5λ. Each antenna element is represented by "o" and the coordinates is shown in wavelength λ

3 Simulation Setup and Results

Both arrays optimized by boolean particle swarm optimization and standard square antenna array are confined by the area of $2\lambda \times 2\lambda$, that is, $X_{min} = A = -\lambda, X_{max} = B = \lambda, Y_{min} = C = -\lambda, Y_{max} = D = \lambda$. The numbers of bits n_x and n_y representing each x_i and y_i are both 30. The number N_a of array population is 30. For designing an aperiodic antenna array using particle swarm optimization, the number of iterations for particle swarm optimization is set to be 500. Minimum threshold $min_{threshold}$ is varied for each optimization case.

Table 1 shows minimum distance, value of fitness function for the optimized antenna array associated with each value of minimum thresholds. For comparison, the directivity of the standard square antenna array for a fixed minimum distance of λ is shown. Optimized antenna arrays for minimum threshold ($min_{threshold}$) of $\lambda, 0.8\lambda$ and 0.5λ are shown in Figs. 3, 4 and 5, respectively, whereas standard square antenna array is shown in Fig. 6. The number of elements for both optimized antenna array and standard square antenna array is 9. It follows that the minimum distance between adjacent elements of standard square array shown in Fig. 6 is λ.

Table 2 shows minimum distance, value of fitness function for the optimized antenna array. For comparison, the directivity of the standard 25-element square antenna array for a fixed minimum distance of 0.5λ is shown. Optimized antenna arrays for minimum threshold $min_{threshold}$) of 0.5λ is shown in Fig. 7 whereas standard 25-element square antenna array is shown in Fig. 8. The number of elements for both optimized antenna array and standard square antenna array is

25. It follows that the minimum distance between adjacent elements of standard square array shown in Fig. 8 is 0.5λ.

4 Conclusion

Designing an antenna array using particle swarm optimization allows more flexible, especially for antenna arrays with more complicated structure, i.e., aperiodic antenna arrays. However, it is known that to obtain the global optimized solution using particle swarm optimization is not guaranteed. There are several possible reasons; one of which is that the optimized solution obtained using particle swarm optimization gets trapped locally or, possibly, there exists no good solution. The optimization result may not as good as it is supposed to be. One possible way is to relax the constraint, that is, to reduce the minimum threshold. This is a trade-off since too low minimum distance between elements may result in too much interference between elements. Another possible way is to enlarge the confined area of optimized antenna arrays to make more possible antenna array configurations.

References

1. Balanis, C.A.: Antenna Theory: Analysis and Design, 3rd edn. Wiley, Hoboken (2005)
2. Bencivenni, C.: Aperiodic Array Synthesis for Telecommunications. Chalmers University of Technology, Gothenburg (2017)
3. Kuhirun, W.: A new design methodology for modular broadband arrays based on fractal tilings. The Pennsylvania State University (2003)
4. Anselmi, N., Rocca, P., Salucci, M., Massa, A.: Irregular phased array tiling by means of analytic schemata-driven optimization. IEEE Trans. Antennas Propag. 65(9), 4495–4510 (2017)
5. Werner, D.H., Kuhirun, W., Werner, P.L.: Fractile arrays: a new class of tiled arrays with fractal boundaries. IEEE Trans. Antennas Propag. 52(8), 2008–2018 (2004)
6. Silabut, W., Kuhirun W.: Design of a miniaturized dual-band antenna using particle swarm optimization. In: 2009 Asia Pacific Microwave Conference, Singapore, pp. 1887–1889. IEEE (2009)
7. Gregory, M.D., Werner, D.H.: Next generation electromagnetic optimization with the covariance matrix adaptation evolutionary strategy. In: 2011 IEEE International Symposium on Antennas and Propagation (APSURSI), Spokane, Washington, USA, pp. 2423–2426. IEEE (2011)
8. Gregory, M.D., Martin, S.V., Werner, D.H.: Improved electromagnetics optimization: the covariance matrix adaptation evolutionary strategy. IEEE Antennas Propag. Mag. 57(3), 48–59 (2015)
9. Robinson, J., Rahmat-Samii, Y.: Particle swarm optimization in electromagnetics. IEEE Trans. Antennas Propag. 52(2), 397–407 (2004)
10. Gregory, M.D., Bayraktar, Z., Werner, D.H.: Fast optimization of electromagnetic design problems using the covariance matrix adaptation evolutionary strategy. IEEE Trans. Antennas Propag. 59(4), 1275–1285 (2011)

11. Kuhirun, W., Silabut, W., Boonek, P.: Particle swarm optimisation for antenna element design. In: Tan, Y. (ed.) Swarm Intelligence Volume 3: Applications, 1st edn, pp. 369–402. Institute of Engineering and Technology, Stevenage (2018)
12. Marandi, A., Afshinmanesh, F.: Boolean particle swarm optimization and its application to the design of a dual-band dual-polarized planar antenna. In: 2006 IEEE Congress on Evolutionary Computation, Sheraton Vancouver Wall Centre Hotel, Vancouver, BC, Canada, pp. 3212–3217 (2006)

Building Energy Performance Optimization: A New Multi-objective Particle Swarm Method

Yong Zhang[1], Li-juan Yuan[1(✉)], and Shi Cheng[2]

[1] School of Information and Control Engineering,
China University of Mining and Technology, Xuzhou, China
yongzh401@126.com, ljyuan310@163.com
[2] School of Computer Science, Shaanxi Normal University, Xi'an, China
cheng@snnu.edu.cn

Abstract. Good energy performance of buildings can decrease energy consumption. The optimization of building energy performance is a typical multi-objective problem. The purpose of this paper is to propose a powerful and easy-to-use multi-objective optimization approach for building energy performance. In this work, an improved multi-objective particle swarm optimization algorithm with less control parameters is proposed and coupled with EnergyPlus building energy simulation software to improve the energy performance of buildings. Applied the proposed approach into a typical office building located at Beijing in China, and compared with three representational algorithms, experimental results show that the proposed approach is a very powerful and useful tool.

Keywords: Building performance optimization · Particle swarm optimization · Multi-objective · EnergyPlus

1 Introduction

Energy is one of the most important resources in society. With the development of industrial, energy consumption continues to increase. Among the total energy consumption, the buildings and construction are energy-intensive, accounting for about 40% of the total energy consumption. Now, the energy consumption mechanism of the whole building has become an international issue [1].

In the early stage of studying building energy, most studies focus on the prediction models or strategies on energy consumptions due to the lack of effective simulation tools [2–5]. In recent years, due to the increase of running speed of energy consumption simulation software and the improvement of calculation accuracy, scholars have begun to focus on studying model-based building energy optimization. Part of typical evolutionary optimization technologies, such as genetic algorithm [6–8], distributed evolutionary optimization [9], ant colony optimization [10], have been successfully applied to building energy performance optimization problems. However, they all treat the building energy optimization problem as a single-objective optimization problem.

The optimization of building energy performance is a typical multi-objective problem, which includes at least two objectives, i.e., maximizing the user comfort and minimizing the energy consumption [11–13]. In view of this, a few of multi-objective approaches based on evolutionary algorithms have been studied [12–17]. Particle swarm optimization (PSO) is a relatively new evolutionary optimization technique [18]. Compared with the traditional evolutionary optimization techniques, PSO has the advantages of simple concept and fast convergence speed, and has been widely used in various practical problems [19–21]. However, few studies apply it to the energy consumption optimization of the building. Recently Delgarm [1] studied the application of multi-objective PSO in building performance design problem. However, since needing decision makers repeatedly to modify control parameters for obtaining good optimization solutions, this method is too sensitive to the setting of control parameters, such as inertia weights and learning factors.

In this paper, a multi-objective particle swarm optimization algorithm with few control parameters is proposed and coupled with EnergyPlus building energy simulation software to improve the capability of PSO on solving building energy performance optimization problems. The main contributions of this paper are as follows: (1) considering both the user comfort and minimizing the energy consumption, a more generalized multi-objective optimization model of building energy performance is introduced; (2) a new PSO-based multi-objective optimization algorithm with few control parameters is proposed and applied to the above model; (3) a PSO-based simulation platform for building energy preference design is established.

2   Related Work

2.1   Multi-objective Optimization

A typical multi-objective optimization problem can be defined as: finding decision vectors $X^* = [x_1^*, x_2^*, \cdots, x_n^*]$ to satisfy the following condition [22–24]:

(1) $x_i^L \leq x_i \leq x_i^U$, $i = 1, 2, \cdots, n$, where $X = (x_1, x_2, \cdots, x_n)$;
(2) J equations or inequality constraints,

$$h_j(X) = (\leq) \, 0, \quad j = 1, 2, \cdots, J \tag{1}$$

(3) Simultaneously minimizing the objective vector function

$$F(X) = (f_1(X), f_2(X), \ldots, f_M(X)) \tag{2}$$

In the definition, $F(X)$ is objective function, and X is decision variable. The boundary values of all the decision variables constitute the decision space $\mathbf{S} \in \Re^n$ of the problem, and the output values of the M objective functions constitute the target space $\mathbf{Z}$ of the problem.

To compare the quality between solutions, the concept of Pareto dominance is proposed [25–27].

Definition 1 (Pareto dominance). A vector $Y = (y_1, y_2, \cdots, y_M)$ is said to dominate $Y' = (y_1', y_2', \cdots y_M')$ (denoted by $Y \prec Y'$), if Y is partially less than Y', $y_i \leq y_i'$, $\forall i \in \{1, 2, \cdots, M\}$, and there exists $j \in \{1, 2, \cdots, M\}$, such that $y_j < y_j'$.

Definition 2 (Pareto optimal). For a multi-objective optimization problem $F(X)$, a solution vector X^* is Pareto optimal if it has any solution $X \in \mathbf{F}$ satisfying the following conditions:

$$\forall i \in \{1,2,\ldots.M\}, f_i(X^*) \leq f_i(X) \ \& \ \exists j \in \{1,2,\ldots.M\}, f_j(X^*) < f_j(X). \quad (3)$$

2.2 Particle Swarm Optimization

PSO is initialized with a set of random particles, and then iteratively searches for the optimal solution of the problem. In each iteration, each particle updates its position mainly by learning two empirical knowledge. One is the optimal position found by the particle itself, i.e. the personal best position or the personal leader, and the other is the optimal position found by its neighboring particle so far, i.e. the global best position or global leader.

Taking the global version of PSO as example, and assuming that the i-th particle in the swarm is $X_i = (x_{i,1}, x_{i,2}, \cdots, x_{i,n})$, the global best position is $Gb = (gb_1, gb_2, \cdots, gb_n)$ and its personal best position is $Pb_i = (pb_{i,1}, pb_{i,2}, \cdots, pb_{i,n})$, the new position and velocity of this particle is as follows:

$$v_{i,j}(t+1) = wv_{i,j}(t) + c_1 r_1 (pb_{i,j}(t) - x_{i,j}(t)) + c_2 r_2 (gb_j(t) - x_{i,j}(t)) \quad (4)$$

$$x_{i,j}(t+1) = x_{i,j}(t) + v_{i,j}(t+1) \quad (5)$$

where t is the iteration times; w is the inertia weight, c_1 and c_2 are two learning factor, r_1 and r_2 are two random numbers in [0, 1].

3 The Proposed PSO-Based Multi-objective Approach

This section presents a powerful multi-objective PSO optimization approach with less control parameters for optimizing the building energy performance. Firstly, a new multi-objective optimization model is given by introducing new key parameters, such as lighting power density and personnel density. Next, an improved bare-bones multi-objective PSO algorithm with few control parameters are proposed to balance the convergence and diversity of the swarm. Finally, the improved algorithm is applied to building energy performance model, and a running platform of the algorithm is built by integrating the software Matlab and EnergyPlus.

3.1 Multi-objective Optimization Model of Building Energy Performance

The building energy consumption (BEC) and the user discomfort (UDC) are two main indicators or objectives in building energy saving design. Based on EnergyPlus, this paper establishes the multi-objective optimization model of building energy performance. Specifically, this model considers 12 optimization parameters or decision variables, i.e. building orientation x_{or}, window length x_{wl}, window height x_{wh}, glazing heat transfer coefficient x_{ghtc} (Glazing u-factor), solar heat gain coefficient of the glazing x_{shgc} (Glazing solar heat gain coefficient), thickness of the outer insulation layer of wall x_{tolw}, solar radiation absorption rate of the external wall x_{srar} (Wall solar absorptance), personnel density x_{pd} (people per zone floor area), lighting power density x_{lpd} (watts per zone floor area of the light), equipment power density x_{epd} (watts per zone floor area of the equipment), heating and cooling setpoint temperature of air conditioning system, x_{hst} and x_{cst}.

After giving a building and setting the values of these parameters, the EnergyPlus software will be able to calculate the annual energy consumption of this building and the uncomfortable hours of users. Based on this, the multi-objective optimization model of building energy performance can be described as follows:

$$\min F = (BEC(X), UDC(X))$$
$$s.t. X = (x_{or}, x_{wl}, x_{wh}, x_{ghtc}, x_{shgc}, x_{tolw}, x_{srar}, x_{pd}, x_{lpd}, x_{epd}, x_{hst}, x_{cst})$$

(6)

3.2   The Improved Bare-Bones Multi-objective PSO Algorithm

Due to the need to adjust the inertia weight and the learning factors to control the global exploration and the local exploitation of the algorithm, most of multi-objective PSO methods have the shortcoming of being sensitive to the control parameters. Focused on this, in our previous work we proposed a multi-objective particle swarm optimization algorithm with few control parameters, called the bare-bones multi-objective PSO (BB-MOPSO) [28]. However, we find by analyzing the particle update strategy of BB-MOPSO that: when the global best position and the personal best position are very close or even equal, the particles in BB-MOPSO will stop evolving ahead of time. To this end, this section presents an improved update strategy based on adaptive perturbation:

$$x_{i,j}(t+1) = \begin{cases} N\left(\frac{r_3 \times Pb_{i,j}(t) + (1-r_3) \times Gb_{i,j}(t)}{2}, \ \left|Pb_{i,j}(t) - Gb_{i,j}(t)\right| + \delta_j\right), & \text{if } U(0,1) < 0.5 \\ Gb_{i,j}(t), & \text{otherwise} \end{cases}$$

(7)

$$\delta_j = \begin{cases} (x_j^{up} - x_j^{low}) \times e^{(-5t/T)}, & pro\_d \geq rand \\ 0, & \text{otherwise} \end{cases}$$

(8)

$$pro\_d = 0.5 \times \left(1 - \frac{1}{M} \sum_{m=1}^{M} \left|\frac{f_m(Pb_i(t)) - f_m(Gb_i(t))}{f_m^{\max} - f_m^{\min}}\right|\right)$$

(9)

Where T is the maximum iteration times of the algorithm, x_j^{up} and x_j^{low} are the upper and lower bounds of the j-th decision variable value; $f_m^{\max}$ and $f_m^{\min}$ are the maximum and minimum values of the m-th objective function obtained by the archive; $f_m(Gb_i(t))$ and $f_m(Pb_i(t))$ are the m-th objective value of Gb_i and Pb_i respectively; pro_d is a perturbation probability determined by the degree of similarity between Gb_i and Pb_i;

δ_j is the disturbance factor determined by the similarity of Gb_i and Pb_i, and the iteration time of the swarm.

Based on the above work, steps of the improved multi-objective PSO algorithm (BBMOPSO-A) are described as follows:

Step 1: Set related parameters, including the particle swarm size N, the maximum iteration time T;

Step 2: Initialization. Generate the initial positions of N particles randomly in the variable space, set the personal best position of each particle to its own; Set the archive set Ar to an empty set;

Step 3: Calculate the objective values for all particles. In this paper, the position of each particle is a set of feasible system parameters. Write the values of these parameters into EnergyPlus, and then run the software to obtain the values of two objective functions, BEC and UDC;

Step 4: Update the external archive based on the crowded distance technology in [29];

Step 5: Update the global best position and the personal best position of each particle by the method in [28];

Step 6: Update the position of each particle by the formula (7);

Step 7: Determine whether the maximum iteration time T is reached. If yes, stop the algorithm and output the Pareto optimal solutions saved in the archive; otherwise, continue to step 3.

4   Experiments and Analyses

4.1   Application Cases

This experiment takes the design of a typical office room as examples. This office room locates in Beijing of China. Beijing has not only densely population, but also has very densely office buildings [12]. Using the SketchUp software to create the architectural shape of a common office, Fig. 1 shows the base style of the office. The length, width and height of this model are 8.8 m, 3.6 m and 3.9 m. The initial length and height of the window are 1.7 m and 1.6 m. Considering the 12 decision variables listed in the Eq. (7), Table 1 gives the ranges of these decision variables.

4.2   Comparison Algorithm and Performance Index

This section applies the proposed BBMOPSO-A algorithm to the above office room in Beijing, and compares it with three typical evolution computation-based building energy-saving methods. Three typical multi-objective methods are the NSGA-II-based multi-objective optimization algorithm (NSGA-II) proposed in [11], the artificial bee colony optimization-based multi-objective optimization algorithm (MOABC) proposed in [16], and the PSO-based multi-objective optimization algorithm (MOPSO) proposed in [1]. For a fair comparison, we set the same population size $N = 50$ and the same maximum number of iterations $T = 20$ for all the algorithms. Table 2 shows the detailed parameter settings for all the algorithms.

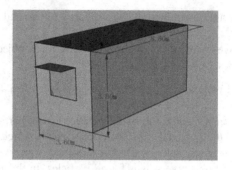

Fig. 1. Outline of the Laboratory Office

Table 1. Decision variables and their range of values

Decision variables	Unit	Range	Reference value
Building orientation	°	[0, 360)	0
Window length	m	(0, 3.6)	1.7
Window height	m	(0, 3.9)	1.6
Glazing u-factor	$w/(m^2 \cdot k)$	(2, 6)	4.3
Glazing solar heat gain coefficient	–	(0, 0.7)	0.65
Thickness	m	(0, 0.1)	0.1
Wall solar absorptance	–	(0.1, 1)	0.6
Personnel density	–	(0.1, 1)	0.2
Lighting power density	w/m^2	[6, 12]	9
Equipment power density	\ w/m^2	[10, 18]	14
Heating setpoint temperature	°C	[18, 23]	20
Cooling setpoint temperature	°C	[24, 28]	26

This paper uses EnergyPlus to simulate the building energy consumption behavior, uses Matlab to implement the proposed multi-objective PSO algorithm, and uses a Visual C ++ based interface program to embed new solutions from Matlab into EnergyPlus. This paper uses the hyper-volume measure (HV) [30] to evaluate the performance of an algorithm. This measure can simultaneously evaluate the distribution and convergence of a set of optimal solutions.

Table 2. Parameter settings for all the algorithms

Algorithms	Parameter setting
NSGA-II	Cross ratio 0.7, Variation ratio 0.4, Mutation rate 0.02, Tolerance 0.001
MOABC	The maximum number of searches per food is 5
MOPSO	Acceleration coefficients $c1$ and $c2$ are taken as 2; Inertia weight is 0.5; The archive size $Na = 50$
BBMOPSO-A	The archive size $Na = 50$

4.3 Comparison with NSGA-II, MOABC and MOPSO

Running the four algorithms 20 times respectively, Table 3 shows their HV values for the office room. Table 4 shows the *SC* values obtained by different algorithms. In the Table, *SC* (*A1*, *A2*) indicates the proportion of the results of the algorithm *A2* dominated by the algorithm *A1*. We can see that:

(1) Comparing the performance of NSGA-II with the other three algorithms, the average value of NSGA-II is significantly inferior to that of BBMOPSO-A, MOABC and MOPSO in terms of the HV measure. The convergence of the solutions obtained by BBMOPSO-A is significantly better than that of NSGA-II, where SC (BBMOPSO-A, NSGA-II) = 1 and SC (NSGA-II, BBMOPSO-A) = 0.

(2) Comparing the performance of BBMOPSO-A and MOABC, MOABC achieves the smallest variance in terms of the HV measure, but its average is significantly inferior to the average HV value of BBMOPS0-A. Moreover, comparing their SC values, BBMOPSO-A dominates 30.61% solution of the MOABC algorithm, SC (BBMOPSO-A, MOABC) = 0.3061, but the ratio of optimal solutions of MOABC dominated by BBMOPSO-A is only 13.33%, SC (MOABC, BBMOPSO-A) = 13.33. Therefore, the performance of BBMOPSO-A is better than the MOABC algorithm.

(3) Comparing the performance of BBMOPSO-A and MOPSO, BBMOPSO-A show better performance than MOPSO in terms of the HV measure. The average HV value of BBMOPSO-A is significantly better than that of MOPSO. Moreover, comparing their SC measure values, BBMOPSO-A dominates 36.96% solution of MOPSO, SC (BBMOPSO-A, MOPSO) = 0.3696, but the ratio of optimal solutions of MOPSO dominated by BBMOPSO-A is only 8.67%, SC (MOPSO, BBMOPSO-A) = 0.0867. This indicates that the convergence of the solutions obtained by BBMOPS0-A is better than that of MOPSO.

Table 3. HV values obtained by different algorithms for the Beijing case

Algorithm	HV(Best)	HV(Worst)	HV(Average)	HV(Std)
NSGA-II	29654	15115	21566	6194
MOABC	28929	27350	27788	**998**
MOPSO	29930	23083	27166	3609
BBMOPSO-A	**31153**	**28086**	**29200**	1697

Table 4. SC values obtained by different algorithms for the Beijing case

Algorithm	SC(BBMOPSO-A, *)		SC(*, BBMOPSO-A)	
	Average	Std	Average	Std
NSGA-II	1	0	0	0
MOABC	**0.3061**	0.0204	0.1333	0.0216
MOPSO	**0.3696**	0.0697	0.0867	0.0502

5   Conclusions

To solve the problem of building energy performance design, a multi-objective particle swarm optimization algorithm with few control parameters, called BBMOPSO-A, is proposed. Integrating the proposed algorithm with the simulation software EnergyPlus, we established a powerfully and easy-to-use simulation platform for building energy performance design. Taking a typical office room located in Beijing as examples, experimental results show that the proposed BBMOPSO-A algorithm can obtain Pareto optimal solutions with good convergence and distribution, is a highly competitive optimization method for solving building energy performance design.

Acknowledgments. This work was jointly supported by the National Natural Science Foundation of China (No. 61876185, 61573361, 61876184).

References

1. Delgarm, N., Sajadi, B., Kowsary, F., et al.: Multi-objective optimization of the building energy performance: a simulation-based approach by means of particle swarm optimization (PSO). Appl. Energy **170**, 293–303 (2016)
2. Liu, Y., Yan, H., Lam, J.C.: Thermal comfort and building energy consumption implications-a review. Appl. Energy **115**(4), 164–173 (2014)
3. White, J.A., Reichmuth R.: Simplified method for predicting building energy consumption using average monthly temperatures. In: Proceedings of the 31st Intersociety Energy Conversion Engineering Conference, Washington, pp. 1834–1839. IEEE, (2002)
4. Yao, R., Steemers, K.: A method of formulating energy load profile for domestic buildings in the UK. Energy Build. **37**(6), 663–671 (2005)
5. Yik, F.W.H., Burnett, J., Prescott, I.: Predicting air-conditioning energy consumption of a group of buildings using different heat rejection methods. Energy Build. **33**(2), 151–166 (2001)
6. Junghans, L., Darde, N.: Hybrid single objective genetic algorithm coupled with the simulated annealing optimization method for building optimization. Energy Build. **86**, 651–662 (2015)
7. Yang, C., Li, H., Rezgui, Y., et al.: High throughput computing based distributed genetic algorithm for building energy consumption optimization. Energy Build. **76**, 92–101 (2014)
8. Sun, X.Y., Gong, D.W., Jin, Y.C., Chen, S.S.: A new surrogate-assisted interactive genetic algorithm with weighted semisupervised learning. IEEE Trans. Cybern. **43**(2), 685–698 (2013)
9. Scott, B., Vasken, D.: Distributed evolutionary algorithm for co-optimization of building and district systems for early community energy masterplanning. Appl. Soft Comput. **63**, 14–22 (2018)
10. Bamdad, K., Cholette Michael, E., Guan, L., et al.: Ant colony algorithm for building energy optimisation problems and comparison with benchmark algorithms. Energy Build. **154**, 404–414 (2017)
11. Delgarm, N., Sajadi, B., Delgarm, S., et al.: A novel approach for the simulation-based optimization of the buildings energy consumption using NSGA-II: case study in Iran. Energy Build. **127**, 552–560 (2016)

12. Zhang, A.X., Bokel, R., Andy, V.D.D., et al.: Optimization of thermal and daylight performance of school buildings based on a multi-objective genetic algorithm in the cold climate of China. Energy Build. **139**, 371–384 (2017)
13. Bre, F., Fachinotti, V.D.: A computational multi-objective optimization method to improve energy efficiency and thermal comfort in dwellings. Energy Build. **154**, 283–294 (2017)
14. Ascione, F., Bianco, N., Masi, R.F.D., et al.: Energy retrofit of educational buildings: transient energy simulations, model calibration and multi-objective optimization towards nearly zero-energy performance. Energy Build. **144**, 303–319 (2017)
15. Ascione, F., Bianco, N., Stasio, C.D., et al.: CASA, cost-optimal analysis by multi-objective optimisation and artificial neural networks: a new framework for the robust assessment of cost-optimal energy retrofit, feasible for any building. Energy Build. **146**, 200–219 (2017)
16. Delgarm, N., Sajadi, B., Delgarm, S., et al.: Multi-objective optimization of building energy performance and indoor thermal comfort: a new method using artificial bee colony (ABC). Energy Build. **131**(11), 42–53 (2016)
17. Hamdy, M., Nguyen, A.T., Hensen, J.L.M.: A performance comparison of multi-objective optimization algorithms for solving nearly-zero-energy-building design problems. Energy Build. **121**, 57–71 (2016)
18. Kennedy, J., Eberhart, R.: Particle swarm optimization. In: IEEE International Conference on Neural Networks, pp. 1942–1948. IEEE, Perth (1995)
19. Zhang, Y., Gong, D.W., Cheng, J.: Multi-objective particle swarm optimization approach for cost-based feature selection in classification. IEEE/ACM Trans. Comput. Biol. Bioinf. **14**(1), 64–75 (2017)
20. Zhang, Y., Gong, D.W., Zhang, J.H.: Robot path planning in uncertain environment using multi-objective particle swarm optimization. Neurocomputing **103**(2), 172–185 (2013)
21. Hu, W.W., Tan, Y.: Prototype generation using multiobjective particle swarm optimization for nearest neighbor classification. IEEE Trans. Cybern. **46**(12), 2719–2731 (2016)
22. Guo, Y.N., Cheng, J., Luo, S., Gong, D.W., Xue, Y.: Robust dynamic multi-objective vehicle routing optimization method. IEEE/ACM Trans. Comput. Biol. Bioinf. **15**(6), 1891–1903 (2018)
23. Cai, X.Y., Li, Y.X., Fan, Z., Zhang, Q.F.: An external archive guided multiobjective evolutionary algorithm based on decomposition for combinatorial optimization. IEEE Trans. Evol. Comput. **19**(4), 508–523 (2015)
24. Zhang, Y., Gong, D.W., Sun, J.Y., Qu, B.Y.: A decomposition-based archiving approach for multi-objective evolutionary optimization. Inf. Sci. **430**, 397–413 (2018)
25. Taghdisian, H., Pishvaie, M.R., Farhadi, F.: Multi-objective optimization approach for green design of methanol plant based on CO2-efficiency indicator. J. Clean. Prod. **103**, 640–650 (2015)
26. Guo, Y.N., Zhang, P., Cheng, J., Wang, C., Gong, D.W.: Interval multi-objective quantum inspired cultural algorithms. Neural Comput. Appl. **30**(3), 709–722 (2018)
27. Gong, D.W., Sun, J., Ji, X.F.: Evolutionary algorithms with preference polyhedron for interval multi-objective optimization problems. Inf. Sci. **233**(1), 141–161 (2013)
28. Zhang, Y., Gong, D.W., Ding, Z.H.: A bare-bones multi-objective particle swarm optimization algorithm for environmental/economic dispatch. Inf. Sci. **192**, 212–227 (2012)
29. Deb, K., Pratap, A., Agarwal, S., Meyarivan, T.: A fast and elitist multiobjective genetic algorithm: NSGA-II. IEEE Trans. Evol. Comput. **6**(2), 182–197 (2002)
30. Sengupta, S., Das, S., Nasir, M., et al.: An evolutionary multiobjective sleep-scheduling scheme for differentiated coverage in wireless sensor networks. IEEE Trans. Syst. Man Cybern. Part C (Appl. Rev.) **42**(6), 1093–1102 (2012)

A Novel PSOEDE Algorithm for Vehicle Scheduling Problem in Public Transportation

Hong Wang, Lulu Zuo[(⊠)], and Xuesen Yang

College of Management, Shenzhen University, Shenzhen 518060, China
ghllu.zuo@gmail.com

Abstract. One of the problems in public transportation is the vehicle scheduling problem (VSP), which can reduce the bus company cost and meet the demand of passengers' minimum waiting time. This paper proposes an ensemble differential algorithm based on particle swarm optimization (abbreviated as PSOEDE) to solve the VSP. In PSOEDE algorithm, the mutation process is designed by dividing the original process into two parts: the first part combines the PSO operator with the improved mutation strategy to enhance the global search ability, while the second part is to randomly select two mutation strategies (i.e. random learning and optimal learning) to improve the diversity of population. In addition, the random selection methods of the parameters and crossover strategies are proposed and applied in the total PSOEDE algorithm. The effectiveness and superiority of the proposed PSOEDE algorithm in dealing with the VSP are verified using the simulation experiments and six comparison algorithms.

Keywords: Particle swarm optimization · Differential evolution algorithm · Vehicle scheduling problem

1 Introduction

Vehicle scheduling problem (VSP), known as a complex NP-Hard problem, has become the most noteworthy issue in operating of public transportation system [1]. In the past, classical optimization methods are applied in dealing with VSP, including variable neighborhood search (VNS) [2], adaptive memetic algorithm (AMA) [3], first in and first out algorithm (FIFO) [4] and so on. However, satisfactory solutions are still hard to find in terms of performance and efficiency. Therefore, many improved evolutionary computation approaches are proposed to solve VSP, e.g. genetic algorithm (GA) [5–7], ant colony optimization (ACO) [8], particle swarm optimization (PSO) [9], and differential evolution (DE) [10]. Though the superior performances of independent optimization algorithms have been verified, the shortcoming of premature convergence still exists.

Earlier studies mostly focused on the independent evolutionary computation algorithms to handle VSP. This paper incorporates PSO operator in the ensemble DE algorithm (PSOEDE) to enhance the global best performance in solving VSP. To enhance the population diversity, random selection methods of mutation strategies (i.e. random learning and optimal learning) are applied in the proposed PSOEDE algorithm. Random learning can guide the individual to explore more widely while the optimal learning can lead the individual to explore deeper.

© Springer Nature Switzerland AG 2019
Y. Tan et al. (Eds.): ICSI 2019, LNCS 11655, pp. 148–155, 2019.
https://doi.org/10.1007/978-3-030-26369-0_14

The remaining paper is organized as follows. Section 2 describes an introduction of VSP model. The proposed algorithm is given in Sect. 3. In Sect. 4, the experimental results of a case of VSP are provided. Section 5 is the conclusion.

2 Vehicle Scheduling Problem

In VSP model [10–12], one single-goal problem is formed by merging two objectives (i.e. the operation cost of bus company and the satisfaction of passenger's waiting time) using the weight coefficients (i.e. α and $1-\alpha$) in Eq. (1). In addition, the constraints, i.e. departmental requirement, the conditions of passenger safety and bus company interest guarantee are displayed in Eqs. (2)–(4) respectively.

$$fit = \alpha \times \frac{\sum_{m=1}^{M} (T_m/\Delta t_m)}{T_s/\Delta t_{min}} + (1-\alpha)$$
$$\times \frac{(\sum_{m=1}^{M} \sum_{n=1}^{N} (T_m/\Delta t_m) \times \rho_{mn} \times \Delta t_m \times \Delta t_m/2)/ \sum_{m=1}^{M} \sum_{n=1}^{N} \lambda_{mn}}{\Delta t_{max}} \quad (1)$$

s.t.

$$h_{m\,min} \leq \Delta t_m \leq h_{m\,max} \quad (2)$$

$$\sum_{m=1}^{M} \sum_{n=1}^{N} \lambda_{mn}/(Q \times \sum_{m=1}^{M} (T_m/\Delta t_m) \geq P \quad (3)$$

$$C_p \sum_{m=1}^{M} \sum_{n=1}^{N} \lambda_{mn} > C_q \times L \times \sum_{m=1}^{M} (T_m/\Delta t_m) \quad (4)$$

where $m = (1...m...M)$ is the mth period and $n = (1...n...N)$ is the nth platform. Δt_m means the time interval during the mth period. T_s is the day's total operation time and T_m is the time during the mth period. λ_{mn} and ρ_{mn} represent the number of the arrival passengers and the passengers' arrival rate on the nth platform during the mth period, respectively. The range of time interval during the mth period is from $h_{m\,min}$ to $h_{m\,max}$. Q is the capacity of every vehicle. C_p is the unit ride fee of every passenger and C_q is the operational cost of every vehicle in a unit of mileage. P is the full load rate of every vehicle. α is bus company cost's weight coefficient.

3 The Proposed PSOEDE Algorithm

Based on the advantages of PSO [13] (i.e. fast speed of convergence and fewer parameters) and superior exploration capability of DE [14], a novel hybrid algorithm (named as PSOEDE) is proposed in this paper, including PSO operator in mutation step and ensemble strategy of random parameters.

3.1   PSO Operator in Mutation Step

In the mutation process, the multi-population cooperative strategy [15, 23] is applied to enhance the population diversity. At the beginning of each iteration, two subpopulations (P_1 and P_2) are generated from two independent methods (particles updating method from PSO (Eqs. (5)–(7) [16]) and improved mutation method from DE (Eq. (8)). The number of every subpopulation is NP. The mutation method is improved by following the strategy of individual optimal learning (i.e. the best position of the ith particle $pbest_i$), which is beneficial for expanding the disturbance of the group.

The better individuals of these two subpopulations are preserved by comparing with the previous population. However, the number of population is constant. Finally, a

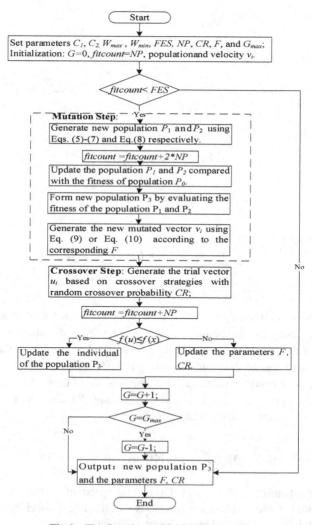

Fig.1. The flowchart of PSOEDE algorithm

new population P_3 is generated according to evaluating the fitness values of the two subpopulations.

$$v_i^{G+1} = \omega v_i^G + c_1 rand(0,1)(pbest_i^G - x_i^G) + c_2 rand(0,1)(gbest^G - x_i^G) \qquad (5)$$

$$x_i^{G+1} = x_i^G + v_i^{G+1} \qquad (6)$$

$$\omega = \omega_{max} - (\omega_{max} - \omega_{min}) * G/G_{max} \qquad (7)$$

$$x_i^G = F^G(pbest_i^G - x_i^G) + F^G(x_a^G - x_b^G), \; i = 1...NP \qquad (8)$$

where $G = 1...G...G_{max}$ is G^{th} iteration. x_i^G and v_i^G are the ith particle and its corresponding velocity at G^{th} iteration. $gbest$ is the best position of population at each iteration. c_1 and c_2 are acceleration factors. ω is the inertia weight. The range of it is ω_{min} to ω_{max}. F is the scaling factor. a and b are indexes selected from $[1, NP]$ and are not i.

3.2 Ensemble Strategy of Random Parameters

The effectiveness of DE algorithm depends on the mutation and crossover strategies. The suitable strategies can make DE algorithm apply in various problems [17]. In mutation process of PSOEDE algorithm, the mutation strategies are randomly selected from two methods (random learning, i.e. Eq. (9) [18] and optimal learning, i.e. Eq. (10) [19]) except the PSO operator and improved mutative strategy. Random learning can improve exploration in breadth while optimal learning can enhance the exploration in depth. In PSOEDE, the selection method of mutation strategy is consistent with the random method of parameter (i.e. scaling factor F). The scaling factor is given two values, which are assigned to every individual of the population [23]. In order to improve the population diversity, Binomial crossover and exponential crossover [20] are used to renew the trial vector u_i in proposed PSOEDE algorithm. The selection method of these two crossover strategies corresponds the random method of parameters (i.e. crossover probability CR). Three values of CR is embedded in PSOEDE.

$$v_i^G = x_i^G + K \cdot (x_{r1}^G - x_i^G) + F^G \cdot (x_{r2}^G - x_{r3}^G) \qquad (9)$$

$$v_i^G = x_i^G + K \cdot (gbest^G - x_i^G) + F^G \cdot (x_{r4}^G - x_{r5}^G) \qquad (10)$$

where K is a value between 0 to 1. $r1, r2, r3, r4$ and $r5$ are randomly selected from $[1, NP]$. They are different from each other and are not i.

After mutation and crossover step, the greedy selection method is employed to update the population by evaluating the fitness value. The termination criteria in proposed algorithm is the maximum function evaluations' number FES. The flowchart of PSOEDE is shown in Fig. 1.

4 Simulation Test and Discussion

4.1 Parameters Setting and Encoding

Every individual in proposed algorithm is seen as a potential solution for VSP and fitness function is combined by object function and constraints using penalty function. The basic variables of VSP model are described in [11]. Some well-exploit algorithms (i.e. PSO [16], DE and comprehensive learning PSO (CLPSO) [21]) and recently proposed algorithms (i.e. DE with ensemble of parameters and mutation strategies (EPSDE) [17] and ensemble PSO (EPSO) [22]) are compared to verify the performance of PSOEDE. The maximum function evaluations' number FES is 300000 is and swarm size is 40. Scaling factors F are 0.5 and 0.9, while 0.1, 0.5 and 0.9 are selected as value of crossover probabilities CR. Other parameters are set from [23].

4.2 Experiment Results and Discussion

Table 1 displays the experiment results and the bold type is used to underline the optimal solution obtained by comparing six optimization algorithms. Figure 2 shows the convergence curves of different weight coefficients α.

Table 1. The fitness values of six algorithms with different weight coefficient α

α	PSO	EPSO	CLPSO	DE	EPSDE	PSOEDE
0.1	3.8845E−02 ±4.9069E−03	3.4284E−02 ±2.1276E−03	3.6142E−02 ±1.9494E−03	6.0009E−02 ±3.0663E−03	**3.1108E−02** ±1.1196E−17	**3.1108E−02** ±8.2471E-8
0.2	7.6578E−02 ±8.9614E−03	6.6907E−02 ±3.9351E−03	7.2487E−02 ±6.2626E−03	1.2252E−01 ±3.9463E−03	6.2999E−02 ±1.6221E−03	**6.1505E−02** ±2.4380E−17
0.3	1.0866E−01 ±1.1677E−02	1.0111E−01 ±5.5718E−03	1.0781E−01 ±6.7674E−03	1.7951E−01 ±8.9369E−03	9.3433E−02 ±1.6644E−03	**9.1903E−02** ±1.7094E−17
0.4	1.4447E−01 ±1.3254E−02	1.3278E−01 ±6.8579E−03	1.4054E−01 ±7.2986E−03	2.3759E−01 ±9.8380E−03	1.2369E−01 ±1.5097E−03	**1.2261E−01** ±1.6613E−03
0.5	1.8541E−01 ±2.1622E−02	1.6809E−01 ±8.2172E−03	1.7696E−01 ±9.4040E−03	2.9039E−01 ±1.3940E−02	1.5444E−01 ±1.1580E−03	**1.5283E−01** ±6.5007E-4
0.6	2.1036E−01 ±1.5634E−02	1.9759E−01 ±1.0881E−02	2.0625E−01 ±9.8602E−03	3.5215E−01 ±2.1629E−02	1.8455E−01 ±8.9394E−04	**1.8323E−01** ±5.0425E−04
0.7	2.5580E−01 ±1.9072E−02	2.3030E−01 ±1.3606E−02	2.4131E−01 ±1.5349E−02	4.2371E−01 ±1.7950E−02	2.1469E−01 ±6.0645E−04	**2.1379E−01** ±6.0643E−04
0.8	2.9067E−01 ±2.3327E−02	2.6203E−01 ±1.2944E−02	2.8407E−01 ±1.3766E−02	4.5565E−01 ±2.8916E−02	2.4472E−01 ±3.7668E−04	**2.4452E−01** ±2.3649E−03
0.9	3.3142E−01 ±4.3105E−02	2.9355E−01 ±1.6126E−02	3.1900E−01 ±2.2112E−02	5.3183E−01 ±2.5341E−02	2.7469E−01 ±2.0215E−04	**2.7455E−01** ±2.4847E−04
1	3.6052E−-01 ±3.1712E−02	3.2204E−01 ±1.2050E−02	3.3402E−01 ±1.5374E−02	5.7309E−01 ±3.2697E−02	**3.0469E−01** ±2.7273E−17	3.0469E−01 ±3.6891E−11

As shown in Table 1, the proposed PSOEDE algorithm succeeds to perform well in comparison with other five algorithms. In addition, the results of PSO, DE, CLPSO and EPSO are not better than PSOEDE and EPSDE. The optimal solution of the PSOEDE algorithm is same as the EPSDE algorithm on the weight coefficients of bus company cost $\alpha = 0.1$ and $\alpha = 1$. In Fig. 2, the superior performance of the proposed PSOEDE algorithm can be clearly seen on the weight coefficients $\alpha = 0.3$ and $\alpha = 0.5$. Compared with the EPSDE algorithm, the PSOEDE algorithm avoids the local convergence and is conductive in more in-depth exploration.

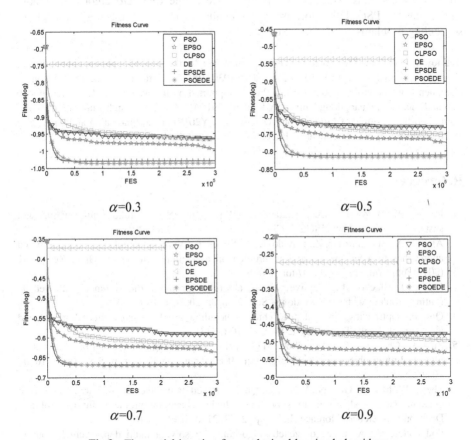

Fig.2. The partial iteration figure obtained by sixed algorithms

The main reason that proposed PSOEDE algorithm performs better than other five algorithms on solving VSP are as follows: (1) In PSOEDE algorithm, the PSO operator and improved mutation strategy is applied to enhance the disturbance diversity; (2) The ensemble mutation strategies (i.e. random learning and optimal learning) are proposed to improve exploration capability of PSOEDE algorithm.

5 Conclusion

In this paper, a novel ensemble differential algorithm with PSO operator (PSOEDE) is proposed to solve the problem of vehicle scheduling. In PSOEDE algorithm, the mutation process is divided into two parts to avoid the premature convenience. The experiment results illustrate that PSOEDE algorithm shows the superiority in obtaining the better time interval scheduling to reduce the cost and improve the passengers' satisfactory. In terms of search accuracy, the PSOEDE algorithm is slightly better than other five algorithms. The superior performance of the EPSODE algorithm demonstrates that the PSOEDE algorithm is potentially applicable to the VSP and sets of scheduling problems similar to VSP.

Acknowledgements. This work is partially supported by the Natural Science Foundation of Guangdong Province (2018A030310575, 2016A030310074), Natural Science Foundation of Shenzhen University (85303/00000155), Project supported by Innovation and Entrepreneurship Research Center of Guangdong University Student (2018A073825), Research Cultivation Project from Shenzhen Institute of Information Technology (ZY201717) and Innovating and Upgrading Institute Project from Department of Education of Guangdong Province (2017GWTSCX038).

References

1. Miller, P., Barros, A.G.D., Kattan, L., Wirasinghe, S.C.: Public transportation and sustainability: a review. KSCE J. Civ. Eng. **20**(3), 1076–1083 (2016)
2. Anokić, A., Stanimirović, Z., Davidović, T., Stakić, Đ.: Variable neighborhood search based approaches to a vehicle scheduling problem in agriculture. Int. Trans. Oper. Res. 1–31 (2017). https://doi.org/10.1111/itor.12480
3. Nalepa, J., Blocho, M.: Adaptive memetic algorithm for minimizing distance in the vehicle routing problem with time windows. Soft Comput. **20**(6), 1–19 (2016)
4. Qiu, F.: Optimizing single-depot vehicle scheduling problem: fixed-interval model and algorithm. J. Intell. Transp. Syst. **19**(3), 1–10 (2013)
5. Zuo, X., Chen, C., Tan, W., Zhou, M.C.: Vehicle scheduling of an urban bus line via an improved multi-objective genetic algorithm. IEEE Trans. Intell. Transp. Syst. **16**(2), 1030–1041 (2015)
6. Zheng, D., Mao, J., Guo, N., Wang, C., Qu, W.: Based on two element neighborhood search quantum genetic algorithm to solve the vehicle scheduling problem. In: Control and Decision Conference, Florence, Italy, pp. 2147–2150. IEEE (2016)
7. Podgorelec, V.: A survey of genetic algorithms for solving multi depot vehicle routing problem. Appl. Soft Comput. **27 (C)**, 519–532 (2015)
8. Yao, B., Yu, B., Hu, P., Gao, J., Zhang, M.: An improved particle swarm optimization for carton heterogeneous vehicle routing problem with a collection depot. Ann. Oper. Res. **242** (2), 303–320 (2016)
9. Sharma, R., Kumari, A.: A review on traffic route optimizing by using different swarm intelligence algorithm. Int. J. Comput. Sci. Mob. Comput. **4**(5), 271–277 (2015)
10. Wang, H., Zuo, L., Liu, J., Yang, C., Li, Y., Baek, J.: A comparison of heuristic algorithms for bus dispatch. In: Tan, Y., Takagi, H., Shi, Y., Niu, B. (eds.) ICSI 2017. LNCS, vol. 10386, pp. 511–518. Springer, Cham (2017). https://doi.org/10.1007/978-3-319-61833-3_54

11. Fang, Z.X.: Study on bus scheduling based on trend guidance for bacterial foraging optimization. Doctoral dissertation, Northeastern University (2013). (in Chinese)
12. Ding, Y., Jiang, F., Wu, Y.Y.: Application of genetic algorithm in public transportation scheduling. Comput. Sci. **43**(S2), 601–603 (2016)
13. Kennedy, J., Eberhart, R.C.: Particle swarm optimization. In: IEEE International Conference on Neural Networks, Piscataway, pp. 1942–1948 (1995)
14. Storn, R., Price, K.: Differential evolution – a simple and efficient heuristic for global optimization over continuous spaces. J. Global Optim. **11**(4), 341–359 (1997)
15. Niu, B., Zhu, Y., He, X.: Multi-population cooperative particle swarm optimization. In: Capcarrère, M.S., Freitas, A.A., Bentley, P.J., Johnson, C.G., Timmis, J. (eds.) ECAL 2005. LNCS (LNAI), vol. 3630, pp. 874–883. Springer, Heidelberg (2005). https://doi.org/10.1007/11553090_88
16. Shi, Y., Eberhart, R.: A modified particle swarm optimizer. In: IEEE International Conference on Evolutionary Computation Proceedings. IEEE World Congress on Computational Intelligence, pp. 69–73. IEEE (1998)
17. Mallipeddi, R., Suganthan, P.N.: Differential evolution algorithm with ensemble of parameters and mutation and crossover strategies. In: Panigrahi, B.K., Das, S., Suganthan, P.N., Dash, S.S. (eds.) SEMCCO 2010. LNCS, vol. 6466, pp. 71–78. Springer, Heidelberg (2010). https://doi.org/10.1007/978-3-642-17563-3_9
18. Iorio, A.W., Li, X.: Solving rotated multi-objective optimization problems using differential evolution. In: Webb, G.I., Yu, X. (eds.) AI 2004. LNCS (LNAI), vol. 3339, pp. 861–872. Springer, Heidelberg (2004). https://doi.org/10.1007/978-3-540-30549-1_74
19. Price, K.V., Storn, R.M., Lampinen, J.A.: Differential Evolution: A Practical Approach to Global Optimization. NCS. Springer, Heidelberg (2005). https://doi.org/10.1007/3-540-31306-0
20. Wong, J.Y.Q., Sharma, S., Rangaiah, G.P.: Design of shell-and-tube heat exchangers for multiple objectives using elitist non-dominated sorting genetic algorithm with termination criteria. Appl. Therm. Eng. **93**, 888–899 (2016)
21. Liang, J.J., Qin, A.K., Suganthan, P.N., Baskar, S.: Comprehensive learning particle swarm optimizer for global optimization of multimodal functions. IEEE Trans. Evol. Comput. **10**(3), 281–295 (2006)
22. Lynn, N., Suganthan, P.N.: Ensemble particle swarm optimizer. Appl. Soft Comput. **55**, 533–548 (2017)
23. Wang, H., Zuo, L.L., Liu, J., Yi, W.J., Niu, B.: Ensemble particle swarm optimization and differential evolution with alternative mutation method. Nat. Comput. 1–14 (2018). https://doi.org/10.1007/s11047-018-9712-z

Hierarchical Competition Framework for Particle Swarm Optimization

Qidong Chen[1], Jun Sun[1(✉)], Vasile Palade[2], Chao Li[1], Zhongjie Mao[1], and Hao Wu[1]

[1] School of IoT, Jiangnan University, No. 1800, Lihu Avenue, Binhu District, Wuxi, Jiangsu, China
sunjun_wx@hotmail.com
[2] School of Computing, Electronics and Mathematics, Coventry University, Priory Street, Coventry CV1 5FB, UK

Abstract. Particles in PSO algorithms evolve only in one group, or in many groups but without interaction between different groups. Inspired by the concept of social class evolution process, a hierarchical competition framework is proposed in this paper. Through the competition mechanism, particles can flow dynamically between different levels, and this can reduce the probability of top-level particles leading to a wrong direction and in this way enhance the global search ability. In this paper, the proposed framework is tested in combination with the canonical PSO and one of the most famous variant particle warm optimizers, named quantum-behaved particle swarm optimizer. All the experiments are run on the CEC'2013 benchmark function database, and the results show that the global search ability and the convergence speed are both improved compared to the basic optimizers.

Keywords: Global optimization ·
Hierarchical competition framework · Particle swarm optimize

1 Introduction

PSO begins with a population of candidate solutions, also called particles group, and then it improves each candidate solution iteratively until the termination condition is reached. Since particles aggregate to their local best position and the global best position, sometimes the algorithm falls into the local optima and in some situations premature convergence and stagnation occur [2,12,15]. At the same time, the performance of PSO also depends on the algorithm parameters [18]. Generally, particle swarm optimization models can be divided into two types, according to whether the particles exchange the information with whole population, and we can have global optimization models and local optimization models [10]. Kennedy [9] proved that the global model has a faster convergence speed, but it is more easily to trap it into local optima. In order to overcome the above shortcomings, researchers have proposed various improvements. These can

Y. Tan et al. (Eds.): ICSI 2019, LNCS 11655, pp. 156–166, 2019.
https://doi.org/10.1007/978-3-030-26369-0_15

be divided into four categories: particle swarm initialization [8,17], neighbourhood topology [9–11], parameter selection [4,5], and blending strategies [16].

For neighbourhood topology improvement measurements, common neighbourhood topologies like Ring topology [13], von Neumann topology [7], and Moore topology [6] are widely used these days. However, these topologies only consider the influence from neighbourhood and the global candidate solution, they do not consider that particles should also learn from particles from other groups. In addition, it is not sensible that the importance of all the particles are equally. Moreover, these topology only have one layer, which increases the probability of being trapped into local optima.

In a human management social system, people often can be divided into three classes, namely, lower class, middle class and top class. People from the top class have to make plans to guide the middle class people, and people from middle class need to guide the lower class. Besides, lower class person can enter to upper class through competition, upper class person may lose its power and enter the lower class. Such a dynamic system can ensure that society can develop in the right direction.

Considering the above shortcomings, and inspired by the concept of human social class evolution process, we propose a novel three layer topology called hierarchical competition framework for particle swarm optimization. The differences are as follows: First, the numbers of particles in different layers are different, and particles are distributed hierarchically in the proposed framework; that is, an upper layer has fewer particles than a lower layer. Second, competition not only exists in the same group, but also occurs between adjacent layers.

We have applied the proposed hierarchical competition framework with canonical PSO and quantum-behaved particle swarm optimizers, and named them hierarchical competition particle framework based swarm optimization algorithm (HCPSO), and hierarchical competition framework based quantum-behaved particle swarm optimization algorithm (HCQPSO), respectively. Then, we have compared HCPSO and HCQPSO with their corresponding basic algorithm, PSO and QPSO, respectively.

The rest of paper is organized as follows: In Sect. 2, the standard particle swarm optimization and quantum-behaved particles swarm optimization algorithm are described. In Sect. 3, we demonstrate the proposed method named hierarchical competition framework in detail. In Sect. 4, the dataset we used in the experiment is shortly described, and the experiment results are analyzed in this section as well. Finally, conclusions and future work are discussed in Sect. 5.

2 Canonical Particle Swarm Optimizer and Quantum-Behaved Particle Swarm Optimizer

2.1 Canonical Particle Swarm Optmizer

It is common that each particle in the search-space has its own position and velocity, and all particles change their position and velocity around the search-space according to some simple mathematical formulae. The most classical formulae are:

$$v_i(t+1) = w(t) \cdot v_{ij}(t) + c_1 \cdot r_1 \cdot (pbest_i(t) - x_i(t))$$
$$+ c_2 \cdot r_2 \cdot (gbest(t) - x_i(t)) \,. \tag{1}$$

$$x_i(t+1) = x_i(t) + v_i(t+1) \,. \tag{2}$$

where $v_i(t)$ is the velocity value at time t, $x_i(t)$ is the position at time t. $pbest_i(t)$ and $gbest(t)$ are the personal best candidate solution position and the global best candidate solution at time t, respectively. c_1 and c_2 are cognitive acceleration parameters and social acceleration parameter, respectively, always set to 2. r_1 and r_2 are random numbers in the range of $[0, 1]$. At time $t + 1$, the position of particles are changed as in Eq. (2). Each particle is influenced by its local best-known position and is guided to the global best-known position. Parameter $w(t)$ is set to control the balance of the global and social candidate solution, and is usually decreases linearly by:

$$w(t) = w_{init} - t \cdot (w_{init} - w_{end})/T \,. \tag{3}$$

where w_{init} and w_{end} are the initial weight and the end weight of w, respectively, and are usually set to 0.9 and 0.4. T is the maximum number of iterations.

2.2 Quantum-Behaved Particle Swarm Optimize

Recently, researchers proposed various local models [9, 11] to overcome the shortcomings of the global model, and quantum-behaved swarm optimizer (QPSO) is one of the most efficient global particle swarm optimizers motivated by the theory of quantum mechanics [19].

Clerc [3] analyzed the convergence of PSO and proved that each particle is attracted by the attractor position, the update formula of traditional PSO can then also be written as:

$$A_i(t) = \varphi_{i,j}(t) \cdot pbest_i(t) + \varphi_{i,j}(t) \cdot gbest(t) \,. \tag{4}$$

where $\varphi_{(i,j)}(t)$ is a randomly generated number in the range from 0 to 1.

The novelty of QPSO was to build up an attractor in each particle position. It should be noted that the velocity and the position of particles cannot be determined at the same time in the quantum space, so the state of particle can only be described by a wave function $\Psi(X, t)$ [1] defined as,

$$\psi(X, t)dxdydz = Qdxdydz \,. \tag{5}$$
$$Q = (x, y, z) \,. \tag{6}$$

where Q is the position in the 3-dimensional quantum space.

In QPSO, the Monte Carlo method is used to generate the position randomly. The position of the ith particle at time $(t + 1)$ iteration can be obtained by:

$$x_i(t+1) = A_i(t) \pm 0.5 \cdot L_i(t) \cdot ln(\frac{1}{u_i(t)}) \,. \tag{7}$$

where $u_i(t)$ is a random number uniformly distributed in $[0, 1]$. $L_i(t)$ is defined as:

$$L_i(t) = 2 \cdot \alpha_t \cdot |mbest_i(t) - x_i(t)| . \tag{8}$$

$$\alpha_t = \alpha_0 + (\alpha_1 - \alpha_0) \cdot \frac{i_t}{I} . \tag{9}$$

where $mbest_i(t)$ means the mean position of personal best candidate solution of particle i at time t, D is the dimension of the problem, N is the number of the particles. α_t is the parameter to control the convergence speed, which is always set by a linear decreasing function. i_t is the iteration number at time t and I is the maximum fitness evaluation number. According to Eqs. 8, 9, each particle in the QPSO algorithm can be updated by:

$$x_i(t+1) = A_i(t) \pm \alpha_t \cdot |mbest_i(t) - x_i(t)| \cdot ln(\frac{1}{u_i(t)}) . \tag{10}$$

The Pseudocode of the QPSO is given in Algorithm 1 below.

3   Hierarchical Competition Framework Based PSO Algorithm

The hierarchical competition framework described here is inspired by a social phenomenon named social class division. In the human society, people can be divided into three classes, namely, lower class, middle class and top class. Therefore, we established a three layer hierarchical competition framework as Fig. 1 shows.

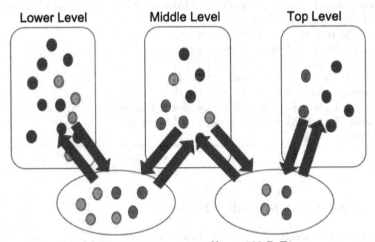

(a) The convergence profile on 100-D F1.

Fig. 1. Experimental results of convergence profiles on 100-D functions. (Color figure online)

Similar to this phenomenon, particles in the same level have to compete with each other in each iteration, several winner particles in this level have a chance to evolve to the upper-level (red points in Fig. 1) and the losers from the upper level may be moved to the lower-level (green points in Fig. 1). In detail, winner particles from the lower-level and loser particles from the upper-level will be put into a pool to have another competition, and the winner particles in this pool will finally evolve to the upper-level, and the loser particles be moved to the lower-level.

In addition, like a leader in the human society, the upper-level particles have to guide the lower-level particles to a right direction. Meanwhile, persons from lower classes have an opportunity to enter the upper class through competition. Therefore, in the proposed framework, the particles from a lower-level that finally entered an upper-level can influence the search direction of the upper-level.

Through this competition mechanism, particles can flow dynamically between different levels, which can reduce the probability of top-level particles leading to a wrong direction and can enhance global search ability.

It should be noted that the particles' numbers in different layers are different. According to the phenomenon of human social class evolution, the quantities of particles are increased from Top-level to Lower-level. The ratio of the three levels are set to 0.6, 0.3 and 0.1 from the total population. The number of exchange particles between adjacent level particles are usually set to half of quantities of upper layer in the experiments. Furthermore, we use mean personal best-known solution of upper level to guide the lower level particles.

Algorithm 1. Pseudocode of the proposed framework

1: Generate an initial population randomly and calculate fitness value;.
2: Separate the whole particles group into three subgroups according to fitness value.
3: Initial $pbest_{ij}$, $gbest$, $mbest_{upper}(t)$;
4: **while** The termination condition is not met **do**
5:    Update $pbest_i$ and $gbest$, $mbest_{upper}t$;
6:    Level 1: Update particles using MQPSO;
7:    Level 2: Update particles using MQPSO;
8:    Exchange particles between Level 1 and Level 2;
9:    Level 3: Update particles using canonical QPSO or PSO;
10:   Exchange particles between Level 2 and Level 3;
11: **end while**

3.1 Combined with Canonical PSO

We first combine hierarchical competition framework with canonical PSO, and called it HCPSO. We have mentioned that we use the mean personal best-known solution of upper level to guide the lower level particles. Therefore, the velocity update formula of particles in the lower level can be rewritten as,

$$v_i(t+1) = w(t) \cdot v_{ij}(t) + c_1 \cdot r_1 \cdot (pbest_i(t) - x_i(t))$$
$$+ c_2 \cdot r_2 \cdot (mbest_{upper}(t) - x_i(t)). \qquad (11)$$

where $mbest_{upper}(t)$ means the mean personal best-known solution of adjacent upper level. The others parameters are not changed. We call it modified PSO (MPSO) in this paper.

For the top layer, particles are influenced by the personal best solution and global best solution as usual. In order to describe the algorithm more clearly, we use level 1, level 2 and level 3 to present lower, middle and top level.

3.2   Combined with QPSO

Then, we combine hierarchical competition framework with QPSO, and we called it HCQPSO. Similar to the change in PSO, the update formula in Level 1 and Level 2 can be rewritten as,

$$A_i(t) = \varphi_{i,j}(t) \cdot pbest_i(t) + \varphi_{i,j}(t) \cdot mbest_{upper}(t). \qquad (12)$$

The modified QPSO is called MQPSO in this paper. The Pseudocode of the proposed framework is given in Algorithm 2.

4   Experiments

In order to test our hypothesis that the hierarchical competition framework based algorithm would be at least as good as the standard PSO and QPSO, we ran 51 runs of experiments on the CEC'2013 standard benchmark functions with 30-D decision variables. The maximum fitness evaluations (FEs) is 30000. The following sections describe the benchmark database, parameters we set in the experiments and the results.

4.1   Database Summary and Parameters Set

The results are shown in Tables 2 and 3. The letter w, l, and e represent win, lose and comparable result in the table. Table 2 shows the results of HCPSO and PSO, and we see that HCPSO has better mean value results on 15 benchmark functions, and one comparable result. HCPSO also obtained better best value result and the standard deviation value is smaller than PSO on most functions.

The CEC'2013 [14] benchmark suitet has 20 functions, with 5 unimodal functions and 15 basic multimodal functions, as Table 1 shows. In our experiments, we use this 20 functions with 30-D decision variables to test the performance of the proposed method. In order to maintain fairness in comparison, all the parameters are set the same as set in the original paper of PSO and QPSO.

In hierarchical competition framework, we only have to set particles ratios (for the 3 levels) and the exchange probability. The ratio of lower level, middle level, and top level are set to 0.6, 0.3 and 0.1, respectively. The number of exchange particles between adjacent level particles, we usually set it to half of the quantities of upper layer in the experiments.

Table 1. CEC'2013 dataset conclusion

	No	Functions	fi* = fi(x*)
Unimodal functions	1	Sphere Function	−1400
	2	Rotatet High Conditioned Elliptic Function	−1300
	3	Rotated Bent Cigar Function	−1200
	4	Rotated Discus Function	−1100
	5	Different Powers Function	−1000
Basic multimodal functions	6	Rotated Rosenbrock's Function	−900
	7	Rotated Schaffers F7 Function	−800
	8	Rotated Ackley's Function	−700
	9	Rotated Weierstrass Function	−600
	10	Rotated Griewank's Function	−500
	11	Rastrigin's Function	−400
	12	Rotated Rastrigin's Function	−300
	13	Non-Continuous Rotated Rastrigin's Function	−200
	14	Schwefel's Function	−100
	15	Rotated Schwefel's Function	100
	16	Rotated Katsuura Function	200
	17	Lunacek $Bi_R astrigin Function$	300
	18	Rotated Lunacek $Bi_R astrigin$ Function	400
	19	Expanded Griewank's plus Rosenbrock's Function	500
	20	Expanded Scaffer's F6 Function	600

4.2   Results and Analysis

Table 3 shows the results of HCQPSO and QPSO, where HCQPSO performs better than the basic algorithm and it has better mean value result on 13 benchmark functions, and one comparable result. HCQPSO also find better best value result and the Standard deviation value is smaller than QPSO on most functions. These results prove that the hierarchical competition framework based algorithms can improve the global search ability and has stable convergence.

In order to further prove the stable convergence rate and good global search ability of the algorithm, we have plotted the convergence profile on function 2 and function 5, respectively. In the top two figures, we can see that the convergence rate of HCPSO is decreased in a stable manner compared to PSO, and finds a better global value in the end. Meanwhile, we known that QPSO has a strong global search ability but the convergence rate is low, but HCQPSO has improved this shortcoming. Two figures below in Figs. 2 and 3 has shown its strong global search capability with a faster convergence rate.

The main reason is, through this competition mechanism, particles can flow dynamically between different levels, which can make the diversity explode and reduce the probability of top-level particles leading to a wrong direction and can enhance global search ability. Furthermore, we use mean solution of upper level as the attractor point to guide the lower level particles that limited the search space of lower layer to speed up the convergence rate.

Table 2. Experimental results of hierarchiacal competition framework based PSO algorithm

Function number	PSO	HCPSO	PSO	HCPSO	PSO	HCPSO
	Mean value		Best value		Std value	
1	3.30E−13	**9.09E−14**	2.27E−13	0.00E+00	1.14E−13	1.13E−13
2	5.59E+06	**1.06E+06**	1.90E+05	3.50E+05	4.86E+06	7.04E+05
3	3.42E+07	**5.08E+06**	7.14E+05	8.13E+04	5.52E+07	8.24E+06
4	4.15E+02	**4.77E+01**	9.23E+01	2.25E+01	2.71E+02	1.70E+01
5	2.81E−13	**1.02E−13**	1.14E−13	0.00E+00	7.99E−14	4.74E−14
6	8.89E+01	**8.22E+01**	4.58E−03	1.62E−01	4.22E+01	3.08E+01
7	4.00E+01	**5.00E+00**	1.24E+01	1.21E+00	1.33E+01	2.42E+00
8	2.08E+01	**2.08E+01(≈)**	2.07E+01	2.07E+01	5.54E−02	5.21E−02
9	2.45E+01	**1.41E+01**	1.88E+01	8.62E+00	3.45E+00	3.03E+00
10	1.73E−01	**1.42E−01**	2.71E−02	4.19E−02	1.08E−01	7.26E−02
11	1.02E+01	**9.07E+00**	3.98E+00	2.98E+00	3.13E+00	2.60E+00
12	7.05E+01	**5.44E+01**	3.28E+01	7.96E+00	2.12E+01	5.24E+01
13	1.30E+02	**5.69E+01**	7.18E+01	3.98E+00	2.84E+01	3.92E+01
14	4.41E+02	1.51E+03	2.41E+01	2.80E+02	1.90E+02	1.56E+03
15	6.32E+03	**6.12E+03**	3.85E+03	5.25E+03	5.90E+02	3.40E+02
16	1.76E+00	1.82E+00	9.78E−01	1.21E+00	3.49E−01	2.45E−01
17	4.65E+01	5.47E+01	3.80E+01	3.31E+01	4.68E+00	2.73E+01
18	1.71E+02	**1.61E+02**	7.40E+01	1.31E+02	4.65E+01	8.83E+00
19	2.55E+00	3.36E+00	1.34E+00	2.04E+00	6.45E−01	1.09E+00
20	1.08E+01	**1.02E+01**	9.06E+00	9.16E+00	9.48E−01	4.60E−01
w/l/e		15/4/1				

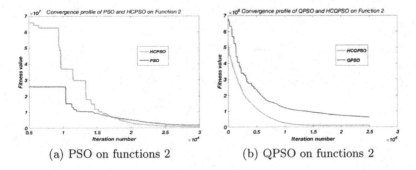

(a) PSO on functions 2   (b) QPSO on functions 2

Fig. 2. Convergence profile on functions 2.

164   Q. Chen et al.

Table 3. Experimental results of hierachiacal competetion framework based qpso algorithm

Function number	QPSO	HCQPSO	QPSO	HCQPSO	QPSO	HCQPSO
	Mean value		Best value		Std	
1	0.00E+00	**0.00E+00**	0.00E+00	0.00E+00	0.00E+00	0.00E+00
2	5.83E+05	**1.17E+05**	6.46E+04	5.07E+04	3.52E+05	3.55E+04
3	1.66E+06	**8.67E+05**	1.01E+02	1.73E+01	4.52E+06	1.44E+06
4	1.69E−03	6.27E−01	7.12E−06	1.09E−01	2.40E−03	4.85E−01
5	6.69E−14	**0.00E+00**	0.00E+00	0.00E+00	5.65E−14	0.00E+00
6	2.68E+01	**1.30E+01**	6.90E−02	2.31E−01	2.55E+01	1.25E+01
7	4.74E+00	**1.59E+00**	4.17E−01	1.76E−01	4.07E+00	1.46E+00
8	2.09E+01	**2.09E+01(≈)**	2.07E+01	2.06E+01	4.63E−02	5.67E−02
9	1.20E+01	**1.11E+01**	5.44E+00	7.14E+00	4.20E+00	1.84E+00
10	8.12E−02	1.42E−01	2.46E−02	3.20E−02	3.72E−02	7.73E−02
11	6.23E+00	**2.21E+00**	1.00E+00	0.00E+00	3.00E+00	1.40E+00
12	3.91E+01	**1.09E+01**	1.53E+01	5.97E+00	2.32E+01	4.75E+00
13	6.86E+01	**2.69E+01**	2.27E+01	1.09E+01	2.65E+01	1.30E+01
14	2.46E+03	3.63E+03	3.99E+02	8.54E+02	2.00E+03	2.15E+03
15	6.36E+03	**4.66E+03**	5.19E+03	1.51E+03	3.30E+02	1.71E+03
16	1.99E+00	2.08E+00	1.25E+00	1.53E+00	2.52E−01	1.80E−01
17	6.41E+01	6.61E+01	3.48E+01	3.27E+01	2.70E+01	4.04E+01
18	1.75E+02	**1.56E+02**	1.47E+02	1.32E+02	1.03E+01	8.63E+00
19	2.46E+00	2.93E+00	1.29E+00	2.20E+00	5.90E−01	4.87E−01
20	1.05E+01	**9.63E+00**	8.80E+00	8.24E+00	6.25E−01	4.89E−01
w/l/e		**13/6/1**				

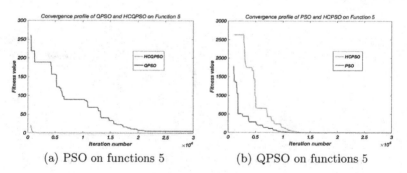

(a) PSO on functions 5   (b) QPSO on functions 5

Fig. 3. Convergence profile on functions 5.

5   Conclusion

In this paper, motivated by the human social class mobility, we proposed a general method named hierarchical competition framework for particle swarm optimization, which can improve the global search ability and enhance the convergence performance. In the future, we will pay more attention to combining this framework with other algorithms and then test its performance on high dimensional and large scale optimization problems.

References

1. Bjorken, J.D., Drell, S.D.: Relativistic Quantum Mechanics. McGraw-Hill, New York (1965)
2. Clerc, M.: Stagnation analysis in particle swarm optimisation or what happens when nothing happens (2006)
3. Clerc, M., Kennedy, J.: The particle swarm-explosion, stability, and convergence in a multidimensional complex space. IEEE Trans. Evol. Comput. **6**(1), 58–73 (2002)
4. Del Valle, Y., Venayagamoorthy, G.K., Mohagheghi, S., Hernandez, J.C., Harley, R.G.: Particle swarm optimization: basic concepts, variants and applications in power systems. IEEE Trans. Evol. Comput. **12**(2), 171–195 (2008)
5. Fan, H.: Study on Vmax of particle swarm optimization. In: 2001 Proceedings of the Workshop on Particle Swarm Optimization (2001)
6. Fernandes, C.M., Rosa, A.C., Laredo, J.L., Cotta, C., Merelo, J.J.: A study on time-varying partially connected topologies for the particle swarm. In: 2013 IEEE Congress on Evolutionary Computation, pp. 2450–2456. IEEE (2013)
7. Figueiredo, E.M., Ludermir, T.B.: Effect of the PSO topologies on the performance of the PSO-ELM. In: 2012 Brazilian Symposium on Neural Networks, pp. 178–183. IEEE (2012)
8. Glerc, M.: Initialisations for particle swarm optimization (2008). http://clerc. maurice.free.fr/pso
9. Kennedy, J.: Small worlds and mega-minds: effects of neighborhood topology on particle swarm performance. In: Proceedings of the 1999 Congress on Evolutionary Computation-CEC99 (Cat. No. 99TH8406), vol. 3, pp. 1931–1938. IEEE (1999)
10. Kennedy, J.: Swarm intelligence. In: Zomaya, A.Y. (ed.) Handbook of Nature-Inspired and Innovative Computing, pp. 187–219. Springer, Boston (2006). https:// doi.org/10.1007/0-387-27705-6_6
11. Kennedy, J., Mendes, R.: Population structure and particle swarm performance. In: Proceedings of the 2002 Congress on Evolutionary Computation. CEC'02 (Cat. No. 02TH8600), vol. 2, pp. 1671–1676. IEEE (2002)
12. Langdon, W.B., Poli, R.: Evolving problems to learn about particle swarm and other optimisers. In: 2005 IEEE Congress on Evolutionary Computation, vol. 1, pp. 81–88. IEEE (2005)
13. Li, X.: Niching without niching parameters: particle swarm optimization using a ring topology. IEEE Trans. Evol. Comput. **14**(1), 150–169 (2010)
14. Liang, J., Qu, B., Suganthan, P., Hernández-Díaz, A.G.: Problem definitions and evaluation criteria for the cec 2013 special session on real-parameter optimization. Computational Intelligence Laboratory, Zhengzhou University, Zhengzhou, China and Nanyang Technological University, Singapore, Technical Report, vol. 201212, no. 34, pp. 281–295 (2013)

15. Ling, S.H., Iu, H.H.C., Leung, F.H.F., Chan, K.Y.: Improved hybrid particle swarm optimized wavelet neural network for modeling the development of fluid dispensing for electronic packaging. IEEE Trans. Industr. Electron. **55**(9), 3447–3460 (2008)
16. Panda, A., Mallipeddi, R., Das, S.: Particle swarm optimization with a modified learning strategy and blending crossover. In: 2017 IEEE Symposium Series on Computational Intelligence (SSCI), pp. 1–8. IEEE (2017)
17. Richards, M., Ventura, D.: Choosing a starting configuration for particle swarm optimization. In: IEEE International Joint Conference on Neural Networks, vol. 3, pp. 2309–2312 (2004)
18. dos Santos Coelho, L., Herrera, B.M.: Fuzzy identification based on a chaotic particle swarm optimization approach applied to a nonlinear Yo-yo motion system. IEEE Trans. Industr. Electron. **54**(6), 3234–3245 (2007)
19. Sun, J., Xu, W., Feng, B.: A global search strategy of quantum-behaved particle swarm optimization. In: 2004 IEEE Conference on Cybernetics and Intelligent Systems, vol. 1, pp. 111–116. IEEE (2004)

Study on Method of Cutting Trajectory Planning Based on Improved Particle Swarm Optimization for Roadheader

Suyu Wang$^{(\boxtimes)}$, Dengcheng Ma, Ze Ren, Yuanyuan Qu,
and Miao Wu

China University of Mining and Technology (Beijing), Beijing 100083, China
blueapple772233@163.com

Abstract. Robotic tunneling is urgently needed to be developed for the safety and efficiency of coal mining. This paper have studied one of the key technologies, which was cutting trajectory planning method of roadheader. It could reduce the cost of tunneling, improve the cutting efficiency of coal and rock, and reduced casualties. The improved particle swarm optimization (PSO) is adopt to plan the cutting trajectory and the features of the improvements are reflected in multi-targets and multi-group of particle swarm. The fitness value is redefined to reflect multiple targets of cutting, which are avoiding the dirt band, shortest and section forming. It could most represent the real cutting process. And the multi-group search region segmentation are adopt to maintain the diversity of the group, prevent the algorithm from falling into a local optimum and improve the efficiency of the algorithm. Finally, for real cutting, the collision avoidance is corrected by expansion operation. Results of simulation experiments showed that the proposed method could plan out the optimal cutting trajectories for roadheader which was suitable for actual automatic control.

Keywords: Cutting trajectory planning · PSO · Multi-target · Multi-group · Roadheader

1 Introduction

In recent years, the automation and intelligence of coal mine have progressed rapidly [1]. The technology and workmanship of unmanned coal mining working face have gradually matured and more than 30 have been put into used. However, the development of fully-mechanized tunneling has lagged far behind. A roadheader is the core equipment used for the tunneling. The under holing, coal cutting, loading, temporary support, drilling and paving nets, and permanent anchoring are the six main production processes linked for the fully-mechanized excavation work surface [2]. In view of the difficulties in obtaining coal and rock properties, equipment postures, and operating condition parameters in the process, there are various challenges, such as accurate and reliable measurement and control, and safe and efficient formation of sections under the circumstances of floor inclined and complex and load unknown and suddenly changed. The realization of unmanned excavation in coal mine underground is currently the

© Springer Nature Switzerland AG 2019
Y. Tan et al. (Eds.): ICSI 2019, LNCS 11655, pp. 167–176, 2019.
https://doi.org/10.1007/978-3-030-26369-0_16

forefront technology pursued by the international coal industry, and it is also a technological leap for the safe and efficient mining in China [3].

In many engineering field, path planning is an important part of automatic control. Liu designed a novel inchworm robot which was used in inspection and maintenance of gas and liquid supply pipelines. And its optimized motion planning was presented using the genetic algorithm (GA) [4]. To solve the shortest path design problem (SPDP) on bidirectional path topology for automated guided vehicles, Hamzheei developed an integer linear programming model and proposed an ant colony system (ACS) algorithm [5]. Lebedev introduced a new type of neural network which named the dynamic wave expansion neural network (DWENN) for path generation of both mobile robots and robotic manipulators in a dynamic environment [6]. While Qu studied global path planning for multiple mobile robots [7]. Chu [8] and Huang [9] both studied path planning methods for tool of computer aided manufacturing machine.

For roadheader, it also needs to plan the path for walking and cutting to realize robotic tunneling. This paper studies the cutting trajectory planning of the roadheader, which mainly aimed at the cutting process, totally different from the walking path planning. The cutting of the roadheader is carried out by cutting arm and trajectory is formed by movement of cutting head. It needs to be planned according to a certain set of performance indicators (such as time, specific point, accuracy, etc.) to get the optimal one which could cut out the most regular section without collision.

Because the particle swarm optimization (PSO) is fast, easy to be implemented, and only a few parameters need to be adjusted [10–12], this paper studies an improved PSO for cutting trajectory planning of roadheader. According to the section shape and cutting procedure, the basic PSO is improved to plan the optimal target trajectory that meets the planning goals. The trajectory planning method proposed in this paper could provide a solution for the planning and automatic control of full-coverage trajectories for large-scale equipment in confined space.

2   The Principle of Basic PSO

The basic idea of the PSO algorithm is that birds are abstracted as "particles" without mass and volume. The solution group is equivalent to a bird group. All particles have a fitness value that is determined by the function being optimized. Each particle has a speed that determines the direction and distance they fly. Then the particles follow the current optimal particle and search in the solution space.

The PSO algorithm initializes a group of particles randomly and then finds the optimal solution iteratively. In each iteration, the particle updates its own extremum by tracking these two "extreme values". One is the individual extremum (*Pbest*) that each particle have achieved by itself in the history search process. The other is the global extremum (*gbest*) that all particles achieved in the entire particle swarm. At the same time, each particle constantly changes its speed in the solution space to determine its own direction and flight distance, and fly toward the area pointed by *Pbest* and *gbest* as soon as possible.

Suppose that in the N dimensional target search space, there are m particles that make up a community. The position formula of the i th particle in the t th iteration is:

$$\vec{x}_i(t) = \left(x_{i,1}(t), x_{i,2}(t), \cdots, x_{i,N}(t)\right) \quad i = 1, 2, \cdots, m. \tag{1}$$

Its velocity formula is:

$$\vec{v}_i(t) = \left(v_{i,1}(t), v_{i,2}(t), \cdots, v_{i,N}(t)\right) \quad i = 1, 2, \cdots, m. \tag{2}$$

The fitness value is:

$$fitness_i(t) = f(\vec{x}_i(t)). \tag{3}$$

In the $t+1$ th iteration, the update equation for the position and velocity of the particle's d th dimension component $(1 \leq d \leq N)$ are as follows:

$$v_{id} = w \times v_{id} + c_1 r_1 \times \left(x_{id}^{Pbest} - x_{id}\right) + c_2 r_2 \times \left(x_{id}^{gbest} - x_{id}\right). \tag{4}$$

$$x_{id} = x_{id} + v_{id}. \tag{5}$$

In the equation, v_{id} is the d th dimension component of the i th particle's flight velocity vector; x_{id} is the d th dimension component of the i th particle's position vector; x_{id}^{Pbest} is the best position experienced by the d th dimension component of the i th particle; x_{id}^{gbest} represents the best position that the current particle group experiences in solution space; r_1 and r_2 are random numbers between $[0, 1]$; c_1 and c_2 are the acceleration coefficients; ω is inertia weight.

3   Cutting Trajectory Planning Based on Improved PSO

During the continuous excavation operation, the disturbance of the coal seam unsteady factors (such as the dirt band, changes of coal and rock properties at the roof and bottom boundaries of the cut section) will affect the cutting path of the unmanned tunneling equipment. While the cutting trajectory is closely related with roadheader operational stability, efficiency and power consumption. In the cutting process, when the hardness of coal rock changes abruptly, because the rotation speed of the cutting motor cannot be changed, if the cutting arm's swing speed cannot be adjusted quickly, it will easily cause damages of picks, gears, and joints of driving cylinders, and cutting motor will also be shutdown with greatly overloaded current or even damaged. In the case of a relatively large volume dirt band, the body of the roadheader will generate violent vibration, and will cause a large error of its position and posture, resulting in a large offset of the tunneling section. Therefore, the dynamic correction and real-time planning of the cutting trajectory and the adaptive control of the cutting process are the key to achieve accurate and efficient automatic cutting.

The central task of the PSO-based cutting trajectory planning is to find a path from the starting point to the ending point in an already established grid map. This trajectory should be reasonably avoided the dirt band and shortened to guarantee the section profiled. For this purpose, the basic PSO needs to be improved as follows.

(1) Multi-target of cutting trajectory planning

The overall goal of the cutting trajectory planning is to form the section, that is, to ensure that the section is completely covered and to ensure the formation quality of the two boundaries. The local goal is to reasonably avoid the dirt band when the dirt band is large and make it the shortest.

To this end, each particle represents a solution to the planned trajectory which is set to be a number of one-dimensional arrays. Each point in the array represents the number of the grid in space which is one-to-one correspondence with its position. The array represents the entire trajectory of the particle and its connection can cover the entire section. Let a large number of particles find together, and the optimal trajectory could be found after a few iterations.

The fitness function of the improved PSO considers three performance indexes which are the length of the experienced trajectory, the trajectory validity, and the trajectory integrity, shown in formula (6). The smaller the fitness value, the shorter the trajectory, and the best the particle.

$$f = \omega_1 fit_1 + \omega_2 fit_2 + \omega_3 fit_3 \quad 0 < \omega_1, \omega_2, \omega_3 < 1. \tag{6}$$

In the formula, $\omega_1, \omega_2, \omega_3$ are adjustment parameters; $fit_1 = \sum_{i=1}^{n} \sqrt{(x_{i+1} - x_i)^2 + (y_{i+1} - y_i)^2}$ represents the length of the experienced trajectory; $fit_2 = \begin{cases} 1 & \text{Valid} \\ 0 & \text{Invalid} \end{cases}$ represents the trajectory validity; $fit_2 = \begin{cases} 1 & \text{Full cover} \\ \infty & \text{Others} \end{cases}$ represents the trajectory integrity.

(2) Particle initialization and multi-group search region segmentation

In order to maintain the diversity of the group and prevent the algorithm from falling into a local optimum, each particle is randomly initialized, and according to the coal mining cutting process, the starting point of all particles are set as a uniform starting point. For example, when encountering a relatively medium-hard coal, the process in general is drilling the coal wall from the left bottom corner, sweeping the bottom, and then cutting from the bottom up. Therefore, the starting point of all particles are need to be set at the left bottom corner of the grid.

At the same time, when iterating, a multi-group parallel evolution is adopted, and different groups are arranged in different feasible regions of the search space. As shown in Fig. 1, the entire cross section is divided into 3 parts by dividing the area near the dirt band and each part is searched by one group separately. If the current section does not have a dirt band, one group is still used for searching. The number of each group particles are the same. The advantage is that the search efficiency can be improved. For the part with the dirt band, the search trajectory is the shortest and avoiding the dirt band, and the validity of the trajectory should be considered. In other parts, the search is relatively simple, so as to ensure the requirements of the section forming.

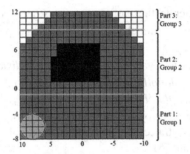

Fig. 1. Schematic diagram of multi-group search region segmentation

(3) Effectiveness of particles

The neighborhood of a grid normally included the up, down, left, right, left up, left down, right up, and right down ones. However, the boundary points of the section are rather special. Their neighborhoods are different according to their locations, excluding the neighborhood points outside the boundary.

For complex sections with dirt bands, because the cutting head cut step by step, while the search of particles is random and may not be a continuous path, it needs to determine whether the particles are valid by examining two adjacent points of the found trajectory in order according to the grids neighborhood. If the neighboring points on the connection between two adjacent points not passed through the dirt band region, the trajectory between the two points is valid. If from the start point to the end point are all valid, the trajectory of the particle is considered valid, and the particle invalid should be searched again.

Specific steps of roadheader cutting trajectory planning based on improved PSO are as follows:

Step 1: Use grid method to model the environment and create a two-dimensional array $chart_{[a][b]}$ which representing environmental information. The total number of grids is $m = a \cdot b$.

Step 2: Parameters initialization
Set the group size as N, inertial weight ω, acceleration coefficients C_1 and C_2, maximum number of iterations $N_{\max}$ and maximum velocity $V_{\max}$. At the same time, define the particle trajectory array as $Group_{[N][m]}$, particle velocity array $Velocity_{[N][m]}$, local optimal trajectory array $IndividualBest_{[N][m]}$, global optimal trajectory array $GlobalBest_{[m]}$, local optimal fitness value $IndividualBestFitness_{[N]}$, global optimal fitness $GlobalBestFitness$.

Step 3: Randomly generate the particle trajectory array $Group_{[N][m]}$ and velocity array $Velocity_{[N][m]}$. Set the initial starting point of all particles according to the cutting procedure: $Group_{[N][1]} = s$.

Step 4: Check each particle validity. Calculate the $IndividualBestFitness_{[N]}$ using formula (6) and get the $GlobalBestFitness$. According to the fitness values, if better than before, update $IndividualBest_{[N][m]}$ and $GlobalBest_{[m]}$, otherwise not.

Step 5: Increase the number of iterations, each trajectory respectively exchanged with the local optimal trajectory, the global optimal trajectory and velocity according to Eqs. (4) and (5).

Step 6: If reaches the maximum number of iterations or meet the system accuracy requirements, stop the algorithm, otherwise go to Step 4.

4   Simulation and Results

To verify the effectiveness of the proposed algorithm, a large number of simulation experiments has been performed using MATLAB. The initial parameters of the simulation are set as: 4 m * 4 m rectangular roadway section, position of the dirt band in the environment is given, group size $N = 500$, inertial weight $\omega = 0.96 - n/N_{max}$, acceleration coefficients $C_1 = 0.4$ and $C_2 = 0.4$, maximum number of iterations $N_{max} = 200$, speed maximum $V_{max} = 40$. Randomly set the position of the dirt band, the simulation results are as shown in Fig. 2. It can be seen that all particles could find the optimal trajectory within 105 times iteration.

Since the cutting head is large, the optimal trajectory obtained by the particle will cause collision and damage to the pick during actual cutting. For this reason, in collision avoidance correction, the dirt band is firstly subjected to an expansion operation, and one grid is outwardly expanded (gray grids in Fig. 2). In the process of particle optimization, the gray grids should also forbidden to be selected. At the same time, when the roadheader is automatically cutting, the cutting head is controlled to stop 1 grid away from the boundary of the dirt band after expansion.

Take the EBZ200 type roadheader as an example. The diameter of the cutting head is 800 mm. Assume the projections of the cutting head on the roadway sections are approximately circular. The experiments and results of the optimization in actual cutting are shown in Fig. 3. From the simulation results, it can be seen that when the roadheader is controlled cutting automatically, adopting the trajectory planning and correction method, the section can be effectively cut avoiding dirt band collision and the full cover forming can be ensured.

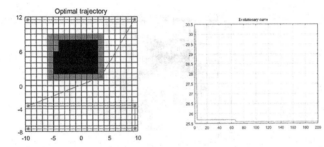

a)   Optimal trajectory and evolutionary curve of section with dirt band on the left

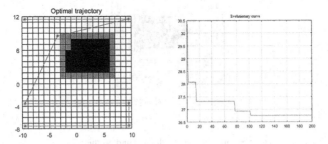

b) Optimal trajectory and evolutionary curve of section with dirt band on the right

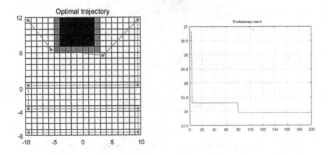

c) Optimal trajectory and evolutionary curve of section with dirt band on the roof

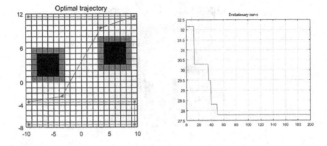

d) Optimal trajectory and evolutionary curve of section with two dirt bands

Fig. 2. Simulation results of cutting trajectory planning using improved PSO

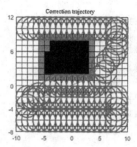

a) Correction trajectory with dirt band on the left

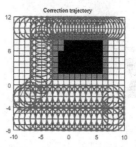

b) Correction trajectory with dirt band on the right

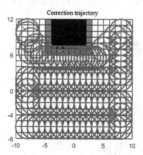

c) Correction trajectory with dirt band on the roof

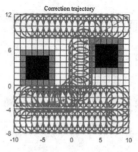

d) Correction trajectory with two dirt bands

Fig. 3. Simulation results of autonomous cutting trajectory correction method

5 Conclusion

Since path planning is an important part to fulfill robotic tunneling, this paper proposed a cutting trajectory planning method based on improved PSO in order to realize the automatic and intelligent cutting of the roadheader.

The features of the improvements are reflected in multi-targets and multi-group of particle swarm. The fitness value is redefined to reflect multiple targets of cutting, which are avoiding the dirt band, shortest and section forming. It could most represent the real cutting process. And the multi-group search region segmentation are adopt to maintain the diversity of the group, prevent the algorithm from falling into a local optimum and improve the efficiency of the algorithm. Finally, for real cutting, the collision avoidance is corrected by expansion operation. The simulation experiments are carried out and the results show the correctness of the method.

At present, cutting trajectory planning has just made initial progress. The simulation of rectangular sections have been carried out, while sections with other shapes still needs to be continued. At the same time, this paper only designs the algorithm for the global static environment, that is, the position and shape of dirt bands are given and fixed. The dynamic optimization problem still needs further research. The successful solution of cutting trajectory planning can provide the optimal trajectory for the automatic control of cutting, and automatically control the cutting arm's swing speed to adapt to the hardness of cutting. It could reduce the cost of tunneling, improve the cutting efficiency of coal and rock, and reduced casualties. So, it has an important research significance.

Acknowledgements. This work is supported by the National Natural Science Foundation of China Grant no. 51874308 and no. 61803374.

References

1. Chen, H., Qi, H., Long, R., et al.: Research on 10-year tendency of China coal mine accidents and the characteristics of human factors. Saf. Sci. **50**(4), 745–750 (2012)
2. Park, Y.T., Choi, S.W., Park, J.H., et al.: Excavation mechanism of roadheader and statistical analysis of its key design parameters based on database. Tunn. Undergr. Space **23**(5), 428–441 (2013)
3. Saleh, J.H., Cummings, A.M.: Safety in the mining industry and the unfinished legacy of mining accidents: safety levers and defense-in-depth for addressing mining hazards. Saf. Sci. **49**(6), 764–777 (2011)
4. Liu, Q., Chen, Y., Ren, T., et al.: Optimized inchworm motion planning for a novel in-pipe robot. Proc. Inst. Mech. Eng., Part C J. Mech. Eng. Sci. **228**(7), 1248–1258 (2014)
5. Hamzheei, M., Farahani, R.Z., Rashidi-Bajgan, H.: An ant colony-based algorithm for finding the shortest bidirectional path for automated guided vehicles in a block layout. The Int. J. Adv. Manuf. Technol. **64**, 1–11 (2013)
6. Lebedev, D.V., Steil, J.J., Ritter, H.J.: The dynamic wave expansion neural network model for robot motion planning in time-varying environments. Neural Netw. **18**(3), 267–285 (2005)

7. Qu, H., Xing, K., Alexander, T.: An improved genetic algorithm with co-evolutionary strategy for global path planning of multiple mobile robots. Neurocomputing **120**, 509–517 (2013)
8. Chu, C.H.: Particle swarm optimisation (PSO)-based tool path planning for 5-axis flank milling accelerated by graphics processing unit (GPU). Int. J. Comput. Integr. Manuf. **24**(7), 676–687 (2011)
9. Huang, X., Xi, F., Li, J., et al.: Optimal layout and path planning for flame cutting of sheet metals. Int. J. Comput. Integr. Manuf. **22**(1), 30–41 (2009)
10. Masehian, E., Sedighizadeh, D.: Multi-objective PSO-and NPSO-based algorithms for robot path planning. Adv. Electr. Comput. Eng. **10**(4), 69–76 (2010)
11. Couceiro, M.S., Machado, J.A.T., Rocha, R.P., et al.: A fuzzified systematic adjustment of the robotic Darwinian PSO. Robot. Auton. Syst. **60**(12), 1625–1639 (2012)
12. Zhang, Y., Gong, D.W., Zhang, J.H.: Robot path planning in uncertain environment using multi-objective particle swarm optimization. Neurocomputing **103**, 172–185 (2013)

Variants and Parameters Investigations of Particle Swarm Optimisation for Solving Course Timetabling Problems

Thatchai Thepphakorn[1] and Pupong Pongcharoen[2(✉)]

[1] Faculty of Industrial Technology, Pibulsongkram Rajabhat University,
Phitsanulok 65000, Thailand
[2] Centre of Operations Research and Industrial Applications (CORIA),
Department of Industrial Engineering, Faculty of Engineering,
Naresuan University, Phitsanulok 65000, Thailand
pupongp@nu.ac.th

Abstract. University course timetabling problem (UCTP) is well known to be Non-deterministic Polynomial (NP)-hard problem, in which the amount of computational time required to find the optimal solutions increases exponentially with problem size. Solving the UCTP manually with/without course timetabling tool is extremely difficult and time consuming. A particle swarm optimisation based timetabling (PSOT) tool has been developed in order to solve the real-world datasets of the UCTP. The conventional particle swarm optimisation (PSO), the standard particle swarm optimisation (SPSO), and the Maurice Clerc particle swarm optimisation (MCPSO) were embedded in the PSOT program for optimising the desirable objective function. The analysis of variance on the computational results indicated that both main effect and interactions were statistically significant with a 95% confidence interval. The MCPSO outperformed the other variants of PSO for most datasets whilst the computational times required by all variants were moderately difference.

Keywords: Course timetabling · Particle swarm · Metaheuristic · Parameter setting

1 Introduction

University course timetabling problem (UCTP) is one of the most challenging scheduling problems and also classified into combinatorial optimisation problems due to its complexity and constraints [1]. This problem arises every semester and is solved either manually by academic staff or using automatic course timetabling tool [2, 3]. Solving large course timetabling problems without efficient timetabling program is extremely difficult and may require a group of experts to work for several days [4].

Swarm intelligence (SI) has received great attention in the communities of optimisation, computer science, computational intelligence, bio-inspired algorithms, and SI-based algorithms [5]. SI-based algorithms such as ant colony optimisation (ACO), artificial bee colony (ABC) algorithm, firefly algorithm (FA), cuckoo search (CS), and particle swarm optimisation (PSO) have become very popular to solve large-scale

© Springer Nature Switzerland AG 2019
Y. Tan et al. (Eds.): ICSI 2019, LNCS 11655, pp. 177–187, 2019.
https://doi.org/10.1007/978-3-030-26369-0_17

combinatorial optimisation problems [5]. These algorithms have been widely adopted to solve NP hard problems within acceptable computational time, but they do not guarantee optimum solutions [6]. Among the intelligent algorithms, PSO has been successfully applied to solve problems in several domains such as clustering problem, image processing, function optimisation, etc. This is because of PSO algorithm has a few parameters to adjust and requires little memory for computation, easy to understand and implement [7].

We have conducted a comprehensive literature survey on articles indexed in Scopus databases covering the period from the past to February 2019 using "course timetabl*" and "particle swarm*" as keywords, several variants of PSO were found to be applied to solve the UCTP. For examples, the conventional PSO (called PSO) has been applied to generate the optimal course timetables for 16 lecturers, 10 classrooms, and 10 classes [8]. The standard PSO using inertia weight factor (called SPSO) has been also developed to solve the UCTP both real world datasets [9] and benchmarking datasets [10]. Another variant of PSO introduced by Maurice Clerc (called MCPSO) has been wildly applied to deal with the UCTP [11–14]. However, there is no report related with the performance comparison among three variants of PSO to solve the UCTP. Moreover, parameter values of PSOs found on all articles have been set by using ad hoc fashion approach [10–14] or one factor at a time experimental strategy [8, 9]. The factorial experiment is one of the best statistical approaches for identifying optimal parameter setting especially when considering several factors [15].

The objectives of this paper were to: (i) develop a particle swarm optimisation based timetabling (PSOT) tool for solving real-world UCTP in Thailand; (ii) investigate the appropriate parameter settings of PSOs using statistical experimental design and analysis; and (iii) compare the performances of the conventional particle swarm optimisation (CPSO), the standard particle swarm optimisation (SPSO), and the Maurice Clerc particle swarm optimisation (MCPSO) in terms of the solution quality and computational time. The next section of this paper briefly explains the PSO algorithm. Section 3 describes the UCTP followed by the procedures of the PSOT tool in Sect. 4. Section 5 presents the experimental results and analysis followed by conclusions.

2 Particle Swarm Optimisation (PSO)

Particle Swarm Optimisation (PSO) was inspired by swarm behaviour in nature, such as bird flocking, fish schooling, and proposed by Kennedy and Eberhart in 1995 [16]. PSO has become one of the most widely used swarm-intelligence-based algorithms to solve every area in optimisation, computational intelligence, and design applications due to its simplicity and flexibility [17].

According to the conventional PSO procedures, the objective function $F(x)$ at an initial process is specified. Each particle x_i ($i = 1, 2,..., P$) is generated randomly and evaluated its fitness. The iteration best solution (P_{best}) and the global best solution (G_{best}) are identified by following Eq. (1) [18].

$$P_{best}(i,t) = \arg \min_{k=1,2,\ldots,t}[F(X_i^k)], i \in (1,2,3,\ldots,P),$$

$$G_{best}(t) = \arg \min_{\substack{i=1,2,\ldots,P \\ k=1,2,\ldots,t}}[F(X_i^k)], \tag{1}$$

Where i is index of particles, P is population (particle) size, t is current iteration, and $F(x)$ is objective function. For each generation of conventional PSO, generating new solutions x_i^{t+1} for each particle i is updated by using velocity and position vectors according to Eqs. (2) and (3), respectively [19].

$$V_i^{t+1} = V_i^t + c_1 r_1(P_{best}(i,t) - X_i^k) + c_2 r_2(G_{best}(i,t) - X_i^k). \tag{2}$$

$$X_i^{t+1} = X_i^t + V_i^{t+1}. \tag{3}$$

Where V_i denotes the velocity, c_1 and c_2 are positive constant parameters called acceleration coefficients, and r_1 and r_2 are uniformly distributed random variables within range from 0 to 1 [18]. For standard PSO (called SPSO), generating new solutions x_i^{t+1} is produced by using velocity and position vectors according to Eqs. (4) and (3) [18, 19]. Another variant of PSO introduced by Maurice Clerc is called MCPSO, in which applies Eqs. (5)–(6), and (3) for velocity and position updates [19].

$$V_i^{t+1} = \omega V_i^t + c_1 r_1(P_{best}(i,t) - X_i^k) + c_2 r_2(G_{best}(i,t) - X_i^k). \tag{4}$$

$$V_i^{t+1} = K(V_i^t + c_1 r_1(P_{best}(i,t) - X_i^k) + c_2 r_2(G_{best}(i,t) - X_i^k)). \tag{5}$$

$$K = \frac{2}{\left|2 - \phi - \sqrt{\phi^2 - 4\phi}\right|}, \quad \phi = c_1 + c_2, \quad \phi > 4. \tag{6}$$

Where ω is the inertia weight used to balance the global exploration and local exploitation [18], K is constriction factor to control the velocity of particles [19], and φ is a positive parameter depending on the acceleration coefficients. After preforming the movement strategies of PSO, the fitness value of new solution x_i or $F(x_i)$ is evaluated. The new x_i will be replaced to the P_{best} if the $F(x_i)$ is better than the $F(P_{best})$. Moreover, if the $F(x_i)$ is also better than the $F(G_{best})$, The new x_i will be replaced to the G_{best}. These processes are repeated until getting to the maximum iteration (G) or stop criterion.

Parameters required for any metaheuristic algorithm play a significant role for the algorithm's performance [20]. Parameters have to be tuned due to the optimal values for the parameters depend on the problem domain, the instance, and the computational time to solve [21]. A comprehensive literature survey on Scopus database covering the period from the past to February 2019 focused on the application of PSO on UCTP has been conducted and summarised in Table 1. There are many parameters to be assigned before computational executions including: (i) the number of population (particle) sizes (P); (ii) the acceleration coefficients (c_1 and c_2); and (iii) the inertia weight (ω). Due to an ad hoc fashion, most of research articles have not reported on the investigation of the best parameter setting of PSO via the appropriate statistical design and analysis.

Table 1. Comprehensive literature review of PSO's parameter settings to solve the UCTP

Authors	PSO variants	PSO's parameter settings to solve the UCTP			
		No. of Particles	c1	c2	ω
Oswald and Anand Deva Durai [11]	MCPSO	10	2.5	1.5	1/(2 * log(2))
Ahandani and Vakil Baghmisheh [10]	SPSO	60	0.8	0.8	0.3
Chen and Shih [8]	SPSO, PSO	30	2	2	0.8
Kanoh and Chen [9]	SPSO	200	5	2	0.05
Irene, Safaai, Mohd and Zaiton [12]	MCPSO	10	2.8	1.3	1/(2 * log(2))
Irene, Deris and Mohd Hashim [13]	MCPSO	10	2.8	1.3	1/(2 * log(2))
Sheau Fen Ho, Safaai and Siti Zaiton [14]	MCPSO	10	2.8	1.3	1/(2 * log(2))
Range		10–200	0.8–5	0.8–2	0.05–1.66

3 University Course Timetabling Problem (UCTP)

Timetabling courses and examinations in educational institutions is a crucial activity, which assigns appropriate timeslots for students, lecturers, and classrooms [22]. In this research, the real-world university course timetabling data obtained from previous research was considered [23]. Generally, the constraints found in course timetabling can be classified into two types: hard constraints (HC) and soft constraints (SC) [6]. Hard constraints are the most important and must be satisfied to have a feasible timetable whereas soft constraints are more relaxed as some violations are acceptable. However, the number of SC violations should be minimised [22]. Both HC and SC constraints considered in this research can be described as following [23].

The considered HC were: (i) all lectures within a course must be scheduled and assigned to distinct periods (HC_1); (ii) students and lecturers can only attend one lecture at a time (HC_2); (iii) only one lecture can take place in a room at a given time (HC_3); (iv) lecturers and students must be available for a lecture to be scheduled (HC_4); (v) all courses must be assigned into the classrooms according to their given requirements including building location, room facilities, and room types (HC_5); and (vi) all lectures within a course required consecutive periods must be obeyed (HC_6).

In additions, The considered SC were: (i) all courses should be scheduled in the appropriate classroom in order to avoid unnecessary operating or renting costs (hour)

(SC_1); (ii) the courses taught by the given lecturer(s) should be assigned into their available or preferred day and periods in order to save the hiring costs (hour) (SC_2); and (iii) the classrooms should be scheduled in consecutive working periods of a day in order to reduce the number of times to clean or setup after using the rooms (times) (SC_3).

HC_1–HC_6 determine whether potential solutions are feasible. HC_1–HC_3 are the fundamental timetabling constraints (called "event-clash") that can be found in almost all university timetabling problems [6] whilst HC_4–HC_6 are individual requirements and timetabling policy found in many universities in Thailand. This research, SC_1–SC_3 are considered as the objective function, which aim to minimise the total university operating costs considered from the candidate timetables following (7);

$$Minimise \quad F(X_i^k) = W_1SC_1 + W_2SC_2 + W_3SC_3. \tag{7}$$

$$Subject\ to : HC_h = 0, \quad \forall h, \tag{8}$$

Equation (7) is the objective functions that evaluate the total university operating costs of the SC_1–SC_3, called $F(X_i^k)$. The weightings (W_1–W_3) for each SC are not restricted and depend upon the user preferences for each institution. In this work, W_1–W_3 were specified at 50 (currency units per hour), 300 (currency units per hour), and 2.5 (currency units per times), respectively. Equation (8) checks a timetable to be a feasible timetable, in which all HCs must be satisfied. Where h is an index relating to the hth hard constraint ($h = 1, 2, 3,..., H$), where H is the number of hard constraints.

4 Particle Swarm Optimisation Based Timetabling (PSOT) Tool

The PSOT program has been coded in modular style using a general purpose programming language called TCL/TK with C extension [24]. It was developed in order to solve the real world UCTP by using three variants of particle swarm optimisation (PSO) including: (i) conventional PSO (PSO); (ii) standard PSO (SPSO), and (iii) Maurice Clerc PSO (MCPSO). The main procedures within the PSOT program are included in five steps and shown in Fig. 1.

Step 1: after uploading course timetable data and assigning PSO's parameters, the total number of events (n) is determined from the number of teaching periods required for all modules (courses). Then, an event list containing a set of n events was initialised. The event sequence in the list was sorted by using the Largest unpermitted period degree (LUPD) first heuristic [25]. This rule reduces the probability of getting infeasible timetables that generally occur in the process of solution initialisation. Next process is to create an empty timetable or solution. The length of that is calculated taking into account the number of timeslots per day, working day per week, and given classrooms. Then, all events according to the sorted list were inserted into an empty timetable in order to produce an initial population x_i ($i = 1, 2, 3, ..., P$) that represents a set of possible timetables. Next step is to create a new list having the same length of

```
Begin                                                    /*Step 1*/
    Input data and Set PSO's parameters
    Sort a list of courses using heuristic orderings
    Create initial population, x_i (i = 1,2,…,P)
    Generate random keys for each x_i
    While t < Max_Iteration(I) do                        /*Step 2*/
        For (i=1, i<= Max_Pop(P), i++) do
            Pick random numbers: r1, r2 ~ U(0,1)
            If PSO do Update particle's velocity x_i' using Eq.(2)
            If SPSO do Update particle's velocity x_i' using Eq.(4)
            If MCPSO do Update particle's velocity x_i' using Eq.(5)
            Update particle's position x_i' using Eq.(3)
        If (x_i' = an infeasible timetable) do
            Repair x_i' to be a feasible timetable   /*Step 3*/
        Evaluate objective functions F(x_i')         /*Step 4*/
        If F(x_i') > F(P_best),do Replace P_best by the new solution x_i
        If F(x_i') > F(G_best),do Replace G_best by the new solution x_i
    Output results and visualisation of G_best           /*Step 5*/
End
```

Fig. 1. Pseudo code of the PSOT tool

solution, in which each timeslot of a new list is assigned random numbers uniformly distributed between 0 and 1. This process is called a random key technique [26].

Step 2: this is the evolution process of the PSO algorithm. Each particle x_i is selected to update particle's velocity based on the variants of PSO. Particle's velocity of the CPSO, SPSO, and MCPSO are produced by using Eqs. (2), (3), and (4), respectively. Next process, particle's position of x_i' for all variants of PSO are updated by using Eq. (6). Step 3: after evolution process, a new solution (x_i') may be either feasible or infeasible timetable. The repair process was therefore design and embedded in the PSOT program in order to rectify infeasible solutions. Step 4: the solution quality of the x_i' can be measured by using Eq. (7). If $F(x_i')$ is better than $F(P_{best})$, a particle P_{best} is replaced by the x_i' whereas a particle P_{gest} is replaced by the x_i' if its solution quality is better. This processes will be repeated until all particles in the population are improved. Step 5: These processes (Step 2 to Step 4) will be repeated until reach the maximum iterations before showing the best so far results.

5 Experimental Results and Analysis

The objective of the PSOT program is to construct course timetables with the lowest total operating costs (Z). The aims of the computational experiments were to: (i) identify which main factors and their interactions were statistically significant for three variants of PSO; and (ii) explore and compare the performance of the PSO with difference movement strategies including the conventional PSO, the standard PSO (called SPSO), and the Maurice Clerc PSO (called MCPSO). Personal computer with Core 2 Quad 3.00 GHz CPU and 4 GB RAM was used to determine the computational time required to execute experimental runs. Five real-world university course time-tabling datasets obtained from the previous research [23] were used in the computational experiment.

5.1   PSO Parameters Investigation

The experiment was aimed to investigate which factors and first level interactions were statistically significant; and to identify the best settings for these factors. The main factors of the PSO, SPSO, and MCPSO included (i) the combination of population (particle) sizes and the number of generation (*PG*), which determines the total number of solutions generated (or amount of search) and the execution time, this computational experiments the value was fixed at 24,000 to limit the time taken for computational search; (ii) the acceleration coefficients (c_1 and c_2); and (iii) the inertia weight (ω) for the SPSO and the MCPSO, excepted the conventional PSO. The experimental design for all PSO's variants, shown in Table 2 was used together with data from dataset number 1. The range of available values for each parameter of PSO were considered from comprehensive literature reviews (shown in Table 1).

Table 2. Experimental factors and levels for the PSO variants

Factors	Levels	SPSO Factor values			PSO Factor values			MCPSO Factor values		
		−1	*0*	*+1*	*−1*	*0*	*+1*	*−1*	*0*	*+1*
PG	3	10 * 2400	60 * 400	200 *120	10 * 2400	60 * 400	200 * 120	10 * 2400	60 * 400	200 * 120
c1	3	0.8	2.8	5	0.8	2.8	5	2.8	4	5
c2	3	0.8	1.3	2	0.8	1.3	2	1.3	1.5	2
ω	3	0.05	0.8	1.66	–	–	–	–	–	–

A full factorial experiment based on the design in Table 2 was considered for this experiment. Thus, the total number of runs required for the PSO and MCPSO would be $3^3 = 27$ runs per replication whereas the total runs for the SPSO would be $3^4 = 81$ runs per replication. The first instant problem was selected and replicated ten times using different random seeds for all PSO's variants. The computational results obtained from the SPSO ($3^4 * 10 = 810$ runs), the PSO ($3^3 * 10 = 270$ runs), and MCPSO ($3^3 * 10 = 270$ runs) were analysed by using a general linear model form of analysis of variance (ANOVA). Table 3 shows the ANOVA table, which shows the source of variation (*Source*), degrees of freedom (*DF*), F-value, and P-value.

Table 3 shows the PSO parameters in terms of the main effect and first level interactions. *PG*, *PG* * *c2*, and *PG* * ω were statistically significant with a 95% confidence interval. The random seed number (*Seeds*) did not statistically affect the PSO performance. Moreover, the most influential factor in this experiment was *PG* because it had the highest F-value. After ANOVA analysis, the appropriate parameter settings for each variant of PSO were determined by using the lowest mean obtained from main effect and interaction plots. For example shown in Fig. 2, the best parameter settings for SPSO are: *PG* = 200 * 120, *c1* = 0.8–5.0, *c2* = 0.8, and ω = 0.8. Moreover, the best settings for PSO parameters are: *PG* = 200 * 120, *c1* = 0.8, and *c2* = 0.8. However, the best settings for MCPSO are: *PG* = 10 * 2,400, *c1* = 2.8, and *c2* = 1.5.

Table 3. ANOVA analysis of PSOs parameters

Source	DF	SPSO		PSO		MCPSO	
		F-value	P-value	F-value	P-value	F-value	P-value
PG	2	92.15	0.000	19.36	0.000	1.490	0.228
c1	2	0.00	1.000	1.17	0.311	0.600	0.548
c2	2	2.50	0.083	0.80	0.449	0.580	0.563
ω	2	0.90	0.407	–	–	–	–
Seeds	9	1.65	0.097	1.02	0.426	1.150	0.326
PG * c1	4	0.00	1.000	0.27	0.899	0.730	0.574
PG * c2	4	8.04	**0.000**	0.24	0.917	1.410	0.230
c1 * c2	4	0.00	1.000	0.53	0.714	0.490	0.740
PG * ω	4	5.23	**0.000**	–	–	–	–
c1 * ω	4	0.00	1.000	–	–	–	–
c2 * ω	4	1.47	0.210	–	–	–	–
Error	768						
Total	809						

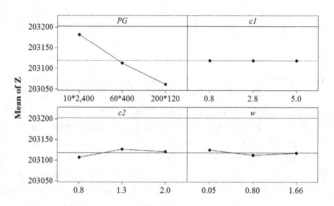

Fig. 2. Example of SPSO's main effect plots of *PG*, *c1*, *c2*, and ω factors

5.2 Performance of PSO's Variants

The objective of this experiment was to explore and compare the performance of the PSO with difference movement strategies including PSO, SPSO, and MCPSO in term of the quality of the solutions. The appropriate parameter settings for three variants of PSO were adopted from previous experiment. Five course timetabling datasets were used to test and compare the performance of these algorithms to find the course timetable with the lowest penalty Z. The computational run for each instance was repeated ten times by using different random seeds. The computational results were analysed in terms of *Avg* (currency unit), *SD*, and *Time* (minute unit) as shown in Table 4.

Table 4. Performance comparisons between three variants of PSO

Dataset No.	SPSO			PSO			MCPSO		
	Avg	SD	T	Avg	SD	T	Avg	SD	T
1	203,098.75	41.28	7.37	**202,944.90**	410.98	6.60	203,030.80	134.34	6.44
2	382,899.98	364.81	24.23	382,918.73	218.27	21.61	**382,744.20**	391.59	22.82
3	306,721.83	213.26	41.03	306,854.75	163.04	35.26	**305,400.33**	596.58	36.55
4	310,214.98	382.26	31.10	310,000.63	464.64	30.05	**308,821.35**	597.81	26.75
5	**492,891.90**	409.66	50.04	492,910.05	197.49	41.72	493,002.15	500.36	47.81

From Table 4, it can be seen that the average values of the best so far solutions (timetables) generated by MCPSO were better than those values generated by both PSO and SPSO for most problems. The PSO outperformed the other methods for problem number 1 whereas the SPSO outperformed both PSO and MCPSO for problem number 5. Moreover, the SD values and the averages of the computational times obtained from both methods were moderately different for all problems.

6 Conclusions

A particle swarm optimisation based timetabling (PSOT) tool has been developed in order to solve the real-world university course timetabling problems. The conventional PSO, the SPSO, and the MCPSO were embedded in the PSOT program for constructing the desirable timetables with minimal objective function. Full factorial experimental designs and ANOVA were adopted to investigate the statistically influential factors for each variant of PSO before identifying its best parameter settings. It was found that the PSOs' parameters in terms of the main effect and interactions including PG, $PG * c2$, and $PG * \omega$ were statistically significant with a 95% confidence interval. The most influential factor in this experiment was PG because it had the highest F-value. Moreover, the MCPSO outperformed the other variants of PSO for most datasets whereas the SPSO and PSO outperformed the other variants only one dataset. However, the computational times required by the proposed PSO variants were moderately difference.

Acknowledgements. This work was part of research project supported by the Thailand Research Fund (TRF) and Office of the Higher Education Commission (OHEC) under grant number MRG6080066.

References

1. Jat, S.N., Yang, S.: A guided search non-dominated sorting genetic algorithm for the multi-objective university course timetabling problem. In: Merz, P., Hao, J.-K. (eds.) EvoCOP 2011. LNCS, vol. 6622, pp. 1–13. Springer, Heidelberg (2011). https://doi.org/10.1007/978-3-642-20364-0_1
2. Thepphakorn, T., Pongcharoen, P., Hicks, C.: Modifying regeneration mutation and hybridising clonal selection for evolutionary algorithms based timetabling tool. Math. Probl. Eng. **2015**, 16 (2015). Article Number 841748
3. Lutuksin, T., Pongcharoen, P.: Best-worst ant colony system parameter investigation by using experimental design and analysis for course timetabling problem. In: 2nd International Conference on Computer and Network Technology, ICCNT 2010, pp. 467–471 (2010)
4. MirHassani, S.A.: A computational approach to enhancing course timetabling with integer programming. Appl. Math. Comput. **175**, 814–822 (2006)
5. Yang, X.-S.: Swarm intelligence based algorithms: a critical analysis. Evol. Intel. **7**, 17–28 (2014)
6. Lewis, R.: A survey of metaheuristic-based techniques for university timetabling problems. OR Spectrum **30**, 167–190 (2008)
7. Rana, S., Jasola, S., Kumar, R.: A review on particle swarm optimization algorithms and their applications to data clustering. Artif. Intell. Rev. **35**, 211–222 (2011)
8. Chen, R.M., Shih, H.F.: Solving university course timetabling problems using constriction particle swarm optimization with local search. Algorithms **6**, 227–244 (2013)
9. Kanoh, H., Chen, S.: Particle Swarm Optimization with Transition Probability for Timetabling Problems. In: Tomassini, M., Antonioni, A., Daolio, F., Buesser, P. (eds.) ICANNGA 2013. LNCS, vol. 7824, pp. 256–265. Springer, Heidelberg (2013). https://doi.org/10.1007/978-3-642-37213-1_27
10. Ahandani, M.A., Vakil Baghmisheh, M.T.: Hybridizing genetic algorithms and particle swarm optimization transplanted into a hyper-heuristic system for solving university course timetabling problem. WSEAS Trans. Comput. **12**, 128–143 (2013)
11. Oswald, C., Anand Deva Durai, C.: Novel hybrid PSO algorithms with search optimization strategies for a university course timetabling problem. In: Proceedings of the 5th International Conference on Advanced Computing, ICoAC 2013, pp. 77–85 (2014)
12. Irene, H.S.F., Safaai, D., Mohd, H., Zaiton, S.: University course timetable planning using hybrid particle swarm optimization. In: Proceedings of the 1st ACM/SIGEVO Summit on Genetic and Evolutionary Computation, GEC 2009, pp. 239–245 (2009)
13. Irene, S.F.H., Deris, S., Mohd Hashim, S.Z.: A combination of PSO and local search in university course timetabling problem. In: Proceedings - 2009 International Conference on Computer Engineering and Technology, ICCET 2009, pp. 492–495 (2009)
14. Sheau Fen Ho, I., Safaai, D., Siti Zaiton, M.H.: A study on PSO-based university course timetabling problem, pp. 648–651 (2009)
15. Montgomery, D.C.: Design and Analysis of Experiments. Wiley, Hoboken (2012)
16. Kennedy, J., Eberhart, R.: Particle swarm optimization. In: IEEE International Conference on Neural Networks, pp. 1942–1948 (1995)
17. Yang, X.-S.: Nature-Inspired Optimization Algorithms. Elsevier, Amsterdam (2014)
18. Zhang, Y., Wang, S., Ji, G.: A comprehensive survey on particle swarm optimization algorithm and its applications. Math. Prob. Eng. **2015**, 38 (2015)
19. Thangaraj, R., Pant, M., Abraham, A., Bouvry, P.: Particle swarm optimization: hybridization perspectives and experimental illustrations. Appl. Math. Comput. **217**, 5208–5226 (2011)

20. Chiroma, H., Herawan, T., Fister, I., Fister, I., Abdulkareem, S., Shuib, L., Hamza, M.F., Saadi, Y., Abubakar, A.: Bio-inspired computation: recent development on the modifications of the cuckoo search algorithm. Appl. Soft Comput. **61**, 149–173 (2017)
21. Talbi, E.-G.: Metaheuristics: From Design to Implementation. Wiley, Hoboken (2009)
22. Thepphakorn, T., Pongcharoen, P., Hicks, C.: An ant colony based timetabling tool. Int. J. Prod. Econ. **149**, 131–144 (2014)
23. Thepphakorn, T., Pongcharoen, P., Vitayasak, S.: A New Multiple Objective Cuckoo Search for University Course Timetabling Problem. In: Sombattheera, C., Stolzenburg, F., Lin, F., Nayak, A. (eds.) MIWAI 2016. LNCS (LNAI), vol. 10053, pp. 196–207. Springer, Cham (2016). https://doi.org/10.1007/978-3-319-49397-8_17
24. Ousterhout, J.K., Jones, K.: Tcl and the Tk Toolkit, 2nd edn. Addison-Wesley, Boston (2009)
25. Thepphakorn, T., Pongcharoen, P.: Heuristic ordering for ant colony based timetabling tool. J. Appl. Oper. Res. **5**, 113–123 (2013)
26. Khadwilard, A., Chansombat, S., Thepphakorn, T., Thapatsuwan, P., Chainate, W., Pongcharoen, P.: Application of firefly algorithm and its parameter setting for job shop scheduling. J. Ind. Technol. **8**, 49–58 (2012)

Ant Colony Optimization

Multiple Start Modifications of Ant Colony Algorithm for Multiversion Software Design

Mikhail V. Saramud[1,2(✉)], Igor V. Kovalev[1,2], Vasiliy V. Losev[1], and Anna A. Voroshilova[1]

[1] Reshetnev Siberian State University of Science and Technology, Krasnoyarsky Rabochy Av. 31, Krasnoyarsk 660037, Russian Federation
msaramud@gmail.com
[2] Siberian Federal University, 79 Svobodny Avenue, Krasnoyarsk 660041, Russian Federation

Abstract. The paper discusses the use of an optimization algorithm based on the behaviour of the ant colony to solve the problem of forming the composition of a multiversion fault-tolerant software package. A model for constructing a graph for the implementation of the ant algorithm for the selected task is proposed. The modifications of the basic algorithm for both the ascending and the descending design styles of software systems are given. When optimizing for downstream design, cost, reliability, and evaluation of the successful implementation of each version with the specified characteristics are taken into account. When optimizing for up-stream design, reliability and resource intensity indicators are taken into account, as there is a selection from already implemented software modules. A method is proposed for increasing the efficiency of the ant algorithm, which consists in launching a group of "test" ants, choosing the best solution from this group and further calculating on the basis of it. A software system that implements both modifications of the basic ant algorithm for both design styles, as well as the possibility of applying the proposed multiple start technique to both modifications, is considered. The results of calculations obtained using the proposed software tool are considered. The results confirm the applicability of ant algorithms to the problem of forming a multiversion software package, and show the effectiveness of the proposed method.

Keywords: Ant algorithm · Multiversion programming · Reliability · Optimization · Software design · Architecture

1 Introduction

Recently, the development of genetic algorithms, which are optimization algorithms based on natural decision-making mechanisms, has been very actively developing [1]. One of such algorithms is the ant colony algorithm (an optimization algorithm for imitating an ant colony, Ant Colony Optimization - ACO) [2]. This algorithm is a product of cooperation of scientists studying the behaviour of social insects and specialists in the field of computer technology. The basis of this algorithm is the behaviour of ants, or rather their ability to find the shortest paths to the food source.

© Springer Nature Switzerland AG 2019
Y. Tan et al. (Eds.): ICSI 2019, LNCS 11655, pp. 191–201, 2019.
https://doi.org/10.1007/978-3-030-26369-0_18

The main idea of ant algorithms is to use the principles of self-organization of real ants to coordinate artificial "agents" who cooperate in performing computational tasks. The essence of ant algorithms (AA) is artificial stigmergy - a mechanism of spontaneous indirect interaction between individuals, which consists in leaving environmental labels to individuals that stimulate the further activity of other individuals to coordinate sets of artificial "agents". One of the most successful applications of AA is the optimization algorithm of the ant colony imitation. It imitates the principles of collecting food used by ants in anthills.

The ant colony is a multi-agent system, and, despite the simplicity of its individual representatives, this system is capable of solving complex problems. Each representative of the colony is trying to find the shortest way to the source of food, while it cannot get access to information obtained by other representatives of the colony, so they must have a mechanism that would allow combining their knowledge. This mechanism is the ability of ants to mark the path with the help of pheromone. If in the process of searching the ant finds a source of food, then on the way back it will mark its route with a pheromone [3]. Other ants will rely on this signal when searching for food. The higher the pheromone value marks the path, the more likely the ant will choose this route in its search. This self-organization mechanism formed the basis of the ant colony algorithm.

Agents mark the traversed path with pheromone, increasing the chances of this path when choosing alternatives. In order for the algorithm not to roll into the region of local extremum, there is a mechanism such as pheromone evaporation. This mechanism is responsible for ensuring that the paths, mistakenly chosen as a solution, gradually lose their attractiveness due to the evaporation of pheromone on them.

2   The Problem of Designing Multiversion Software Systems

In recent years, industries have actively developed, requiring reliable, fault-tolerant real-time control systems. These include high-tech production using composite and hazardous materials, autonomous unmanned objects - from multi-rotor systems to cars with autopilot function and motorized seats for people with disabilities. Software is an integral part of modern control systems, however, only simple software can be guaranteed to be created without errors. Modern software of control systems is used for solving more and more complex tasks, the volume of the processed information increases in an avalanche manner. Increasing software complexity causes probability of errors [4].

The issue of designing fault-tolerant software systems of control systems is becoming increasingly important. The most relevant approach today is multiversion programming. Multiversion programming [5] offers parallel execution of N independently developed functionally equivalent versions with the choice of a correct exit by the decision block, as a rule, on the basis of voting.

In the process of applying the methodology of multiversion programming in the task of designing software, it becomes necessary to form the optimal composition of the multiversion software components. Depending on the design style used, the layout task also changes. In the case of top-down design, we know the required functionality, but there are no ready-made implementations of software components yet. In this case, the problem of selecting the optimal software modules and their specific versions for implementation arises.

In the case of an ascending design style, we already have implementations of software components, often with already known characteristics. The problem arises of the optimal layout of the existing components, and, if necessary, the development of the missing ones.

To solve both of these tasks, it is advisable to apply actively developing today evolutionary algorithms, namely, the optimization algorithm of the ant colony imitation.

3   Architecture of the Designed Software

To increase the fault tolerance of software systems, software redundancy in the most critical modules for reliability is introduced into them. There are usually several such modules, in our case we will consider a software package with 10 modules (m1–m10). The probability of activation of modules can be different and depends on the archi-tecture of the software package and the frequency of calling a specific functional implemented by the modules. Let us consider the architecture of the software, which will be described in this paper in Fig. 1.

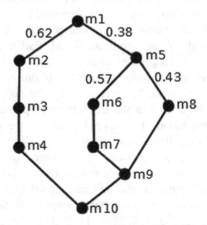

Fig. 1. Architecture of the considered software

Why do we need to know the architecture of the designed software? It affects the calculation of the most important parameter - reliability, or rather, estimates of the probability of failure-free operation for a given period of time [6]. This is a probabilistic characteristic taking values from 0 to 1, where 0 is an absolutely unreliable system, and 1 is an absolutely reliable one. The architecture is not used to calculate the total cost of implementing the software and the probability of its successful implementation. Let us consider the architecture under consideration (Fig. 1). It is clearly seen from the scheme that the modules m1 m10 are always used, the modules m2–m4 are activated with a probability of 0.16, and the module m8 with a probability of 0.16 (0.38 * 0.43). The overall reliability will be calculated using the formula

$$P_{rel} = P_{m1} * (0.62 * (P_{m2} * P_{m3} * P_{m4}) + 0.38 * P_{m5} * (0.57 * (P_{m6} * P_{m7}) + 0.43 * P_{m8}) * P_{m9}) * P_{m10}.$$

As it becomes clear from the formula, the change in the reliability of different modules will not equally affect the reliability of the entire software package. For example, the reliability of the modules m1 and m10 is more important than the reliability of the module m8.

The formation of the multiversion software package is an important optimization problem that can be solved in various ways, from simple enumeration to recently gaining popularity of evolutionary algorithms.

4 Modification of the Ant Algorithm for Descending Design

In solving the problem of descending design, we know the requirements for the versions that need to be developed. The following parameters will be used for optimization: the cost of the version implementation, the reliability of the version, the probability of a successful version implementation (the probability that the version will be implemented with a given reliability for the expected cost).

Our case will differ from the traveling salesman problem, which is most often cited as an example of the work of ant algorithms [7, 8]. Earlier we described the construction of a graph for the ant algorithm when solving the problem of optimizing the composition of a multiversion software package [9]. In our case, it will be a directed graph in which the ant will make M decisions - by the number of modules in the system, in this example 10. Each time the arcs will be all possible implementations of this module. For implementation of multiversion voting, the number of versions N 3 is necessary, we have only 10 versions of versions, so we will consider all possible combinations of these versions in the module with N from 3 to 10. Each version can be included in the module only one time, therefore we cannot build a module of more than 10 non-repeating versions. We will take into account all theoretically possible combinations with given restrictions on the number of versions. With N from 3 to 10: {1; 2; 3} … {1; 4; 8; 9; 10} … {2; 3; 5; 7; 8; 9} … {1; 2; 3; 4; 5; 6; 7; 8; 9; 10}, the total of such combinations will be 968 for each module, that is, the ant will choose from 968 arcs at each step. The total system implementation options will be 968 m, where m is the number of modules in the system.

The weight of each arc will be calculated by the formula $W_{ij} = \frac{(R*V)^\beta}{C} C$, and the probability of transition along this arc is $P_{ij} = \frac{\tau_{ij}^\alpha * W_{ij}}{\sum (\tau_{ij}^\alpha * W_{ij})}$, where τ_{ij} is the pheromone value on this arc, α and β are coefficients affecting the operation of the algorithm, the larger α is, the stronger the ant's decision depends on the pheromone level, the larger β, the more ant's decision depends on the weight of the arc [10]. The effect of α and β

coefficients on the operation of the algorithm was studied in [9]. It is important to note that in our case the arc has no length, as in the classical algorithm, and the weight is rather an inverse characteristic - the more weight, the "more attractive" the arc.

In the classical model, after the ant successfully passes the route, it leaves a trace on all the ribs, inversely proportional to the length of the path. In our implementation, the pheromone value will increase by the specified values in two cases - if an ant chooses a composition that satisfies the constraints (for example, when optimizing at cost, there are restrictions on the minimum reliability and evaluation of the successful implementation of the system) and when the composition replaces the optimal solution. This change was made for reasons of the same number of edges passed by all ants (by the number of modules, each arc is a specific combination of versions in the module) and the absence of a length indicator, which is replaced by a weight indicator. In addition, traces of pheromone evaporate, that is, the intensity of the pheromone on all edges decreases at each iteration of the algorithm. Thus, at the end of each iteration, it is necessary to update the intensity values.

5 Modification of the Ant Algorithm for Upstream Design

Using the modification proposed above, we solve the task of arranging the optimal composition of the multiversion software package only for top-down design, when we know the requirements and architecture of the software being developed, but the functional modules themselves have not yet been developed.

However, there is often a need to develop on the principle of bottom-up design, when we already have developed components, of which it is necessary to make the optimal structure of the developed software system. Such an approach can significantly reduce both the time and material costs of software development by re-using the previously developed software code.

In this case, the value of the previously developed module ceases to matter, since its reuse will be conditionally free. Such a parameter as the probability of successful implementation of the component, since it has already been developed, the cost of its development, functional and reliability characteristics also loses its meaning. Thus, we need to change again the formula for calculating the weights of the arcs. The calculation of the probability of transitions and the general logic are preserved - arcs with more weight remain more "attractive".

Since we choose from the modules that have already been tested, we already know not only their assessment of reliability, but also the functional characteristics, including the resources consumed. Thus, for an upstream design, the weight of each arc will be calculated by the formula $W_{ij} = \frac{(R)^\beta}{T}$, where T is the assessment of resource intensity, determined by the consumption of a critical resource for this project and the importance factor of resource intensity. It is necessary to clarify this point. If we leave the evaluation of resource intensity in the denominator without a coefficient, and β equals to 1, then the component with twice the reliability, but with twice the resource intensity will be equally attractive from the point of view of the system. This should be avoided, because in a real situation, as a rule, the requirements for resources are not as critical as for reliability, and in the case of the availability of resources, a more reliable component should always be chosen. Therefore, it is necessary to enter the coefficient when calculating the resource intensity estimate and set the coefficient β to be greater than 1.

6 Software Implementation

Let us consider the software implementation of the proposed ant algorithm modifications. The program interface is shown in Fig. 2, the screenshot shows the optimization result for reliability for the top-down design.

The program allows loading the characteristic values of versions from a file or generate values randomly. Randomly generated values can also be written to a file and used later. The form sets the minimum and maximum values of versions and all other parameters required for the calculation: coefficients α and β, evaporation coefficient, the number of ants in one "run", restrictions on cost, reliability, probability of successful implementation, resource intensity, the amount of pheromone added for the path that satisfies the conditions and for the path that has improved the optimal solution. Also on the right is the number of "test ants" for the multiple-run mode. Optimization modes, maximization of reliability, probability of successful implementation of the system, their work, or minimization of system cost for top-down design are selected from the drop-down lists, reliability maximization and resource consumption minimization for upstream design.

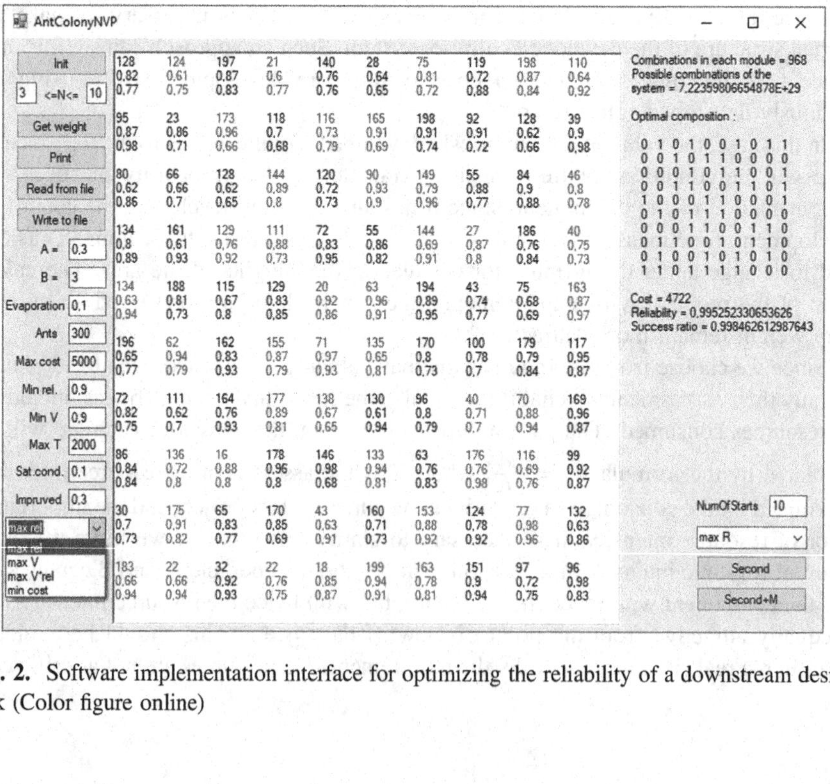

Fig. 2. Software implementation interface for optimizing the reliability of a downstream design task (Color figure online)

The characteristics of all available versions are displayed in the main area, while optimizing the selected versions are highlighted in red. The characteristics used for optimization in this mode are displayed, in Fig. 2 the optimization for the descending design is presented, in Fig. 3 - for the upward design.

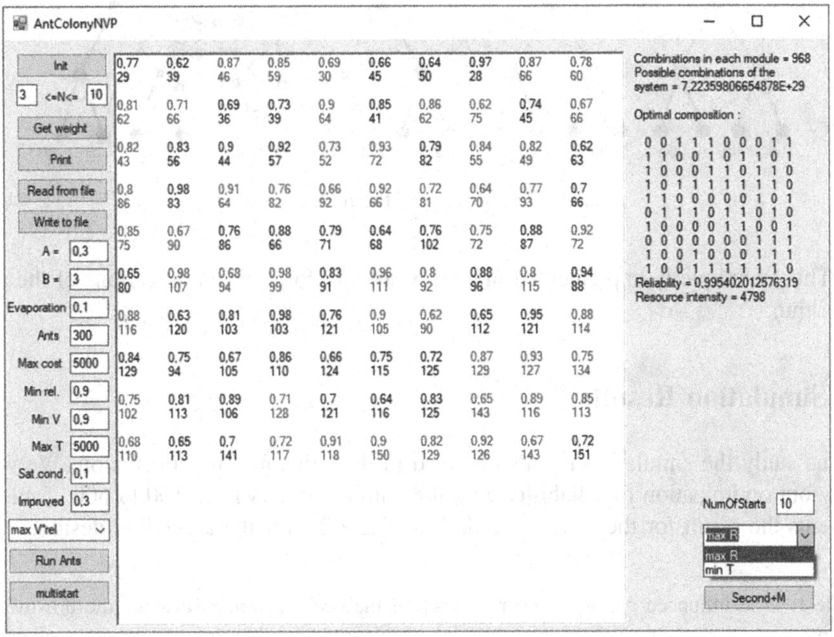

Fig. 3. Software implementation interface for optimization of the upstream design task (Color figure online)

7   Method of Multiple Algorithm Start

As the simulation shows in the proposed software environment, the result of the ant algorithm strongly depends on the passage of the first group of ants, which is almost random, since the pheromone values at the beginning are the same, and the weights of the arcs have relatively close values. When the first ants choose paths that are far from optimal, however, improving the solution, these arcs will receive an increase in the pheromone value, and from the truly optimal, but not used arcs, the pheromone will evaporate, which will reduce the chance of finding a really optimal solution. To further improve the operation of the algorithm, we can offer the following option: run the first few groups of ants, compare the result obtained by them at the first iteration, choose the best one and continue further modeling only with the best group. This does not significantly complicate the calculations, however, it will allow to exclude cases when, at the beginning of the simulation, the far-from-optimal arc solutions received a high pheromone value and even a large number of further iterations do not improve the solution.

The proposed method of increasing the efficiency of the ant algorithm consists in launching a group of "test" ants, choosing the best solution from this group and further calculating based on it. The scheme of work of a technique is presented in Fig. 4.

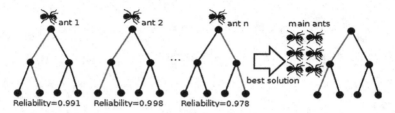

Fig. 4. The scheme of the multiple start

This technique is implemented in a software tool for both modifications of the ant algorithm.

8   Simulation Results

Let us study the simulation results obtained in the software implementation. We will carry out optimization of reliability with the number of ants from 100 to 600. Table 1 presents the result for the downward design, Table 2 - for the ascending design.

Table 1. The influence of the number of ants on the optimization results for the downward design

Ants	100	200	300	600	300-10
Cost	3272	3327	3481	3495	3360
Reliability	0.9421	0.9395	0.9557	0.9628	0.9628
Succ. ratio	0.9997	0.9999	0.9999	0.9999	0.9998

As it is clearly seen from the results presented in Table 1, an increase in the number of ants leads to finding a more optimal solution. However, due to the randomness inherent in the principle of the algorithm, its work depends on the passage of the first group of ants. From the results it can be seen that 100 ants have found a more optimal solution than 200. This is due to the fact that the first group of 200 ants went farther from the optimal solution than at 100, and even twice the number of ants did not allow us to find a more optimal solution.

As it is seen from the results presented in Table 2, for the upstream design, the same patterns are preserved - an increase in the number of ants leads to finding a more optimal solution.

Table 2. The effect of the number of ants on optimization results for upstream design

Ants	50	100	200	300	600
Reliability	0.9912	0.9934	0.9941	0.9952	0.9954
Resource intensity	4408	4362	4698	4585	4798

Table 3 presents the results of the optimization in reliability for the descending design with 600 ants. In the first column, the method of multiple starts was not used, in the rest 10, 30, 50 and 100 test ants were used. The total number of ants has always been 600, that is, with 50 test ants for the best of their solutions, 550 ants passed for further optimization. Thus, the total number of ants in all cases is 600, which allows us to objectively compare the results, and the use of the multiple start technique does not lead to an increase in the resource intensity of the algorithm.

Table 3. The effect of the number of test ants with multiple start (600 ants)

Ants	0	10	30	50	100
Cost	2955	3494	3401	3411	3480
Reliability	0.9845	9824	0.9862	0.9872	0.9874
Succ. ratio	0.9998	0.9996	0.9993	0.9991	0.9996

The results in Table 3 show that 10 ants are not enough to eliminate the probability, but already at 30 ants there is a more optimal solution that improves with an increase in the number of ants used for multiple start. Despite the smaller number of ants participating in the main optimization, the algorithm with the use of multiple start all finds a more optimal solution.

Table 4. The effect of the number of test ants with multiple start (300 ants)

Ants	0	10	30	50	100
Cost	3403	3356	3266	3247	3409
Reliability	0.9809	9776	0.9804	0.9826	0.9786
Succ. ratio	0.9995	0.9999	0.9992	0.9992	0.9981

The results in Table 4 show that for 300 ants, the effectiveness of the multiple start technique is not so high, since the number of ants for the main optimization is significantly reduced. In the case of 100 test ants, a less optimal solution was obtained. However, it should be noted that multiple experiments show that in case of using multiple starts with 30 or more test ants, the algorithm shows more stable results, "outliers" disappear - a much less optimal solution caused by a bad route of the first group of ants.

The results in Table 5 show that for the upstream design, the multiple start technique is effective. It is noteworthy that in the case of 10 and 30 test ants the same solution was found.

Table 5. The effect of the number of test ants in multiple start for upstream design

Ants	0	10	30	50
Reliability	0.9919	0.9931	0.9931	0.9942
Resource intensity	3710	3700	3700	3978

Many further experiments have shown a general trend - the use of the multiple-start technique makes the solution of the ant algorithm much more stable. If in the classical implementation there are often "outliers" - solutions that are far from optimal, then when applying the multiple start technique with a sufficient number of test ants, the system always gives a suboptimal solution.

9   Conclusion

The simulation results in the proposed software environment show the applicability of ant algorithms to the problem of designing the optimal composition of a multiversion software for both top-down and bottom-up design. The proposed modifications of the ant algorithm have a good performance, since they allow an acceptable solution to be obtained in 100–600 iterations, which is significantly faster than comparing 968 m (in our case, m = 10) combinations for the classical search for an optimal solution using the search method. The results show the effectiveness of the proposed method of multiple starts. This technique allows getting rid of the main drawback of ant algorithms - a strong dependence on the trajectory of the first group of ants, which is almost random, since the pheromone values at the beginning are the same, and the weights of the arcs have relatively close values. The use of the technique of multiple starts makes the ant algorithms more "stable", eliminating the emergence of solutions that are far from optimal, while almost without increasing the complexity of the algorithm calculation.

Acknowledgments. This work was supported by Ministry of Education and Science of Russian Federation within limits of state contract № 2.2867.2017/4.6

References

1. Dorigo, M., Birattari, M.: Swarm intelligence. Scholarpedia 2(9), 1462 (2007)
2. Dorigo, M., Di Caro, G., Gambardella, L.M.: Ant algorithm for discrete optimization. Artif. Life 5(2), 137–172 (1999)
3. Zhai, Y., Xu, L., Yang, Y.: Ant colony algorithm research based on pheromone update strategy. In: 2015 7th International Conference on Intelligent Human-Machine Systems and Cybernetics, vol. 1, pp. 38–41 (2015)

4. Yin, M.-L., Peterson, J., Arellano, R.R.: Software complexity factor in software reliability assessment. In: Annual Symposium Reliability and Maintainability, pp. 190–194 (2004)
5. Fisher, M.S.: Software Verification and Validation: An Engineering and Scientific Approach. Springer, New York (2007). https://doi.org/10.1007/978-0-387-47939-2. 172 p.
6. Kovalev, I., Losev, V., Saramud, M., Petrosyan, M.: Model implementation of the simulation environment of voting algorithms, as a dynamic system for increasing the reliability of the control complex of autonomous unmanned objects. In: MATEC Web of Conferences, 31 October 2017, vol. 132, no. 04011 (2017)
7. Dorigo, M., Gambardella, L.M.: Ant colonies for the travelling salesman problem. BioSystems 43(2), 73–81 (1997)
8. Yang, X., Wang, J.-S.: Application of improved ant colony optimization algorithm on traveling salesman problem. In: 2016 Chinese Control and Decision Conference (CCDC), pp. 2156–2160 (2016)
9. Saramud, M.V., Kovalev, I.V., Losev, V.V., Karaseva, M.V., Kovalev, D.I.: On the application of a modified ant algorithm to optimize the structure of a multiversion software package. In: Tan, Y., Shi, Y., Tang, Q. (eds.) ICSI 2018. LNCS, vol. 10941, pp. 91–100. Springer, Cham (2018). https://doi.org/10.1007/978-3-319-93815-8_10
10. Dorigo, M., Blum, C.: Ant colony optimization theory: a survey. Theoret. Comput. Sci. 344, 243–278 (2005)

Ant Colony Algorithm for Cell Tracking Based on Gaussian Cloud Model

Mingli Lu$^{(\boxtimes)}$, Benlian Xu, Xin Dong, Peiyi Zhu, and Jian Shi

Changshu Institute of Technology, Changshu 215500, China
luml@cslg.edu.cn

Abstract. The investigate of the cell image data are able to obtain the correlation between many diseases and abnormal cell behavior by tracking their trajectories. In this paper, a novel Ant Colony Algorithm for cell tracking based on Gaussian cloud model is proposed. In order to speed up the search and improve the accuracy, pheromone prediction strategy based on Gaussian cloud model is utilized. Experiment results show the effectiveness of our approach and it is competitive with some of the existing methods presented in recent literature.

Keywords: Ant Colony Optimization · Cell tracking · Gaussian cloud model

1 Introduction

In recent years, research on cell tracking has become a hot topic and it has been widely applied in cancer metastasis, developmental biology, immunology response, etc. Manual analysis is a simple and straightforward method to track moving cells. However, with the increasing of cell datasets, manual work is becoming heavy workload and inefficiency. Automated track processing can extract a richness of information far beyond what a manual work can observe. So, automated cell tracking method has attracted extensive research attentions.

The tracking of cells in microscopic image sequence is very challenging, such as poor signal-to-noise ratios images, cell deformations, cell's diversity of behaviors. To overcome these difficulties aforementioned, plenty of work has been carried out, which can be generally divided into three categories, such as detection-based association methods [1], model-based evolution methods [2] and stochastic filtering methods [3, 4]. The detection-based association methods involve two steps. At first, cells in each frame will be segmented, and then associate the segmented objects in association steps. Finally, lineages of cells are established in adjacent frames. These algorithms will not work well when segmentation is less accurate. Model-based evolution methods detect and track the cells simultaneously. The key idea of stochastic filtering methods is to establish a model for each cell to predict the next status. In general, this type of methods works well when the objects can be modeled in a Bayesian framework.

ACO [5] is a swarm intelligence-based method inspired by the behaviors of ants' foraging food. Under the guidance of pheromones, ants are more likely to choose shorter paths between the nest and food, which further leads to different amounts of pheromones in different paths. This algorithm has the characteristics of parallel

Y. Tan et al. (Eds.): ICSI 2019, LNCS 11655, pp. 202–209, 2019.
https://doi.org/10.1007/978-3-030-26369-0_19

computing and heuristic search. Now based on the great development, ACO have been used by a number of investigators as tools for studying image processing problems [6], traveling salesman problems (TSP) [7] and vehicle routing problems [8, 9].

In the ant colony algorithm for cell tracking, searching for interest cells is looked upon as an ant colony foraging process. However, similar with other nature-inspired algorithms, ACO also has its own shortcomings. The major weakness is that it searches speed slowly at the initial step and takes more time to cluster around their favored regions. In order to fill up with the research gap, pheromone prediction strategy based on Gaussian cloud model is utilized to reduce the processing time of ACO.

The remainder of this paper is structured as follows. In Sect. 2, the cell tracking method is described in details. Section 3 presents the experimental results of cell tracking. Finally, the fourth section includes the concluding remarks.

2 The Algorithm

In this paper, we present a novel Ant Colony Algorithm for cell tracking based on Gaussian cloud model to reduce the computation time and improve the accuracy

2.1 Gaussian Cloud Model

Cloud model is proposed based on the traditional fuzzy mathematics and probability statistics theory, which can converse model between qualitative concept and quantitative values [10]. Because two-dimensional cloud model can represent a large number of uncertainties phenomenon. So it has been widely used. In two dimensional cloud model theory, a qualitative concept is characterized by three numerical characteristics namely, expectation (Ex_1, Ex_2), standard entropy (En_1, En_2) and hyper standard entropy (He_1, He_2). (Ex_1, Ex_2) represents expectation of cloud droplets distribution in the domain, (En_1, En_2) represents uncertainty of qualitative concept, and (He_1, He_2) is Uncertainty Measures of the entropy. Given the parameters $(Ex_1, Ex_2, En_1, En_2, He_1, He_2)$, the Gaussian cloud model can be generated. The digital characteristics of the cloud are shown in Fig. 1.

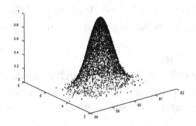

Fig. 1. The schematic diagram of two-dimension cloud model

2.2 Algorithm Description

2.2.1 Initialization of the Algorithm

The initialization step is performed at the beginning. A number of ants are randomly assigned on image potential region and assigning the initial pheromone values is performed.

In our algorithm, a local pheromone field corresponds to a potential cell. In general way, in terms of the resulting pheromone field, the more pheromone the pixel, the greater the probability of the existence of cells. To help the ACO work faster in finding cells, the spatiotemporal information is utilized to generate predicted pheromone field. Since the cloud model has the characteristics of randomness and uncertain concepts, and that the bell shape of clouds, is most useful in representing the shape of pheromone field.

The two-dimensional cloud model integrates the information of pheromone quantity and pixel spatial position perfectly, which not only shows the uncertainty of pheromone quantity, but also the uncertainty of pixel spatial position. So, we use the Gaussian cloud distribution to predictive the pheromone field evolution model of the cell.

Position values of pheromone field mapping to Cells are estimated at every time step. Then, predicting the current pheromone field position of each cell by using the previous frame estimated values. Suppose the position of pheromone field τ_{k-1}^i corresponding to ant colony i is (Ex_{k-1}^i, Ey_{k-1}^i). The pheromone on every pixel corresponds to a cloud droplet. Then, Gaussian cloud model with numerical characteristics $((Ex^i, Ey^i, En_1^i, En_2^i, He_1^i, He_2^i)$ is generated for the predicted pheromone field $\tau_{k|k-1}^i$ of headings should be numbered. Lower level headings remain unnumbered; they are formatted as run-in headings.

$$\tau_{k|k-1,j}^i \sim \text{cloud drop}(x_j, y_j, \mu_j) \ (j = 1, 2, \ldots, D), \tag{1}$$

$$\mu_j^i = e^{-\frac{(x_j - Ex_k^i)^2}{2(En_1^i)^2} - \frac{(y_j - Ey_k^i)^2}{2(En_2^i)^2}}, \tag{2}$$

where (Ex_k^i, Ey_k^i) is expectation of distribution of cloud drops i in the domain, corresponding to the center of pheromone field. We set $(Ex_k^i, Ey_k^i) = F(Ex_{k-1}^i, Ey_{k-1}^i)^T$, F is the state transition matrix. (x_j, y_j) represents the 2-D position of cloud drops (pixel), μ_j^i is the membership degree of j-th cloud drops in cloud model i, which represents the amount of pheromone. D is the number of cloud drops. (En_1^i, En_2^i) and (He_1^i, He_2^i) is standard entropy and Uncertainty Measures of the entropy, respectively.

2.2.2 Movement of the Ants

Ants operate is the current cell image. During search process, an ant chooses which cell to move to according to heuristics and the pheromone intensity of the four surrounding pixels. Assume ant at the current position of pixel i, it selects the next pixel using the following probabilistic formula:

$$p_{i \to j}^{a}(t) = \begin{cases} \dfrac{[\tau_{j}(t)]^{\alpha}[\eta_{j}]^{\beta}}{\sum\limits_{j \,\in H(i)} [\tau_{j}(t)]^{\alpha}[\eta_{j}]^{\beta}}, & \textit{if } j \in H(i) \\ 0, & \textit{otherwise} \end{cases} \tag{3}$$

In the equation, $p_{i \to j}^{a}$ is the probability with which ant a chooses to move from the pixel i to the pixel j at the t-th iteration. $H(i)$ is the set of all available neighbors of pixel, τ_{j} is equal to the amount of pheromone on pixel j at the t-th iteration, and η_{j} is heuristic value representing the degree of similarity between the current pixel and the target pixel. Heuristic information η_{j} is estimated based on gradient information of image. α and β are the parameters to adjust the effects of the pheromone value and heuristic value, respectively. α determines the relatively importance of the track, reflecting the effect of accumulated information of the ant in the course of movement. β weighs the comparative importance of heuristic information.

2.2.3 Pheromone Updating
Pheromone record accumulates historical experience and helps the search more directed. Under the guidance of pheromone, ants search in the neighborhood of pixels. In this work, we considered two kinds of pheromone, diffusive pheromone and accumulative pheromone. Diffusive pheromone is the propagated information from the different channels of the neighbor pixels. Accumulative pheromone is the accumulative information in each iteration. After all ants have moved once, the pheromone level of each pixel is updated according to the following formula:

$$\tau_{j}(t) \leftarrow (1 - \rho)\tau_{j}(t - 1) + \sum_{a} \Delta u_{j}^{a}(t - 1) + g_{j}(t - 1), \tag{4}$$

where $\rho(0 < \rho < 1)$ is the coefficient representing pheromone evaporation. $\sum\limits_{a} \Delta u_{j}^{a}(t - 1)$ represents accumulative pheromone, $\Delta u_{j}^{a}(t - 1)$ is the amount of pheromone laid by ant a on pixel j. Term $g_{j}(t - 1)$ models all diffusion input to pixel.

Once the searching behavior of each ant is finished, the resulting pheromone field is build. Then, the multimodality of pheromone field is utilized to extract cell state [11].

2.2.4 Algorithm Structure
In this section, to visualize our proposed algorithm in a full view, we represent the flowchart of the proposed algorithm. The algorithm contains three parts: Initialization, Movement of the ants and Pheromone Update, shown in Fig. 2.

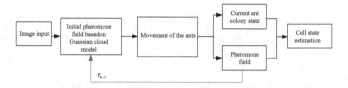

Fig. 2. The main framework of our proposed method

3 Experiments

In this section, we will discuss the implementation process in detail to verify the validity of our proposed method. All experiments were performed in MATLAB (R2016a) on a 1.7 GHz processor computer with 4G random access memory.

We defined three metrics to measure the performance of the tracking framework. The label switching rate (LSR) is the number of label switching events normalized over total number of ground truth tracks. The lost tracks ratio (LTR) is the number of tracks lost over total number of ground truth tracks. The false tracks ratio (LSR) is the number of false objects that are tracked over total number of ground truth tracks [12]. It is noted that cells partially entering and leaving the image are not considered when we compute the above measures.

To intuitively show how our method able to track the cells, the trajectories of on the cells in 2D space is shown in Fig. 3. Figure 4 presents the position estimates of each cell in each frame in x and y-directions. From the result we can obtain the exact locations of cells in each frame and the knowledge of the life cycle of each cell. we can see that the proposed method worked well when the cell mitosis, changing shape, cluster together and cell's diversity of behaviors happen in poor image sequences.

Figure 5 shows the velocity results of each cell in each frame in x and y-directions. It can be seen that cell 1 undergoes fast motion, and cell 5 also moves rapidly both in x and y directions, while the velocities of other cells are very small such as cell 9. Although the motion of each cell changes drastically, our algorithm can still accurately track all cells.

To illustrate the effectiveness of the proposed approach, we compare our algorithm with other techniques, such as the multi-Bernoulli filter [3] and the particle filter(PF) [13]. We record all LSR, LTR and FTR in each frame over 100 Monte-Carlo simulations, and their averaged values are listed in Table 1. From the result we can see that the averaged LSR, LTR and FTR are only 6.44%, 7.89% and 1.37%, respectively, using our algorithm. The comparison results show that our algorithm performs better than other methods when cells are mitosis, changing shape, cluster together and cell's diversity of behaviors happen.

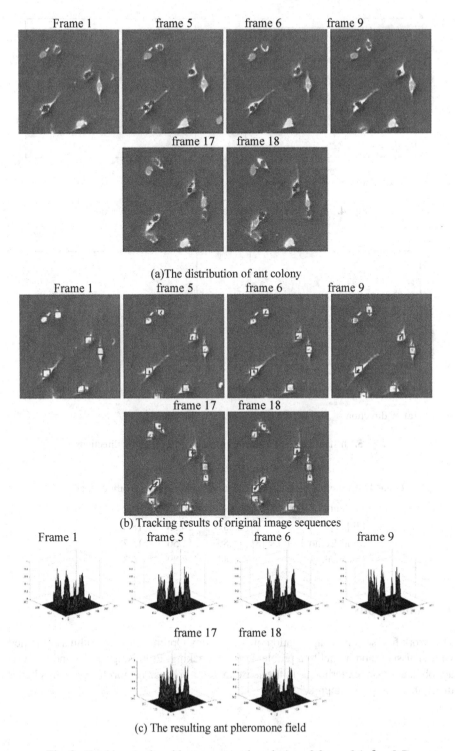

Fig. 3. Tracking results with our proposed mode ($\rho = 0.3, \alpha = 0.1, \beta = 0.5$)

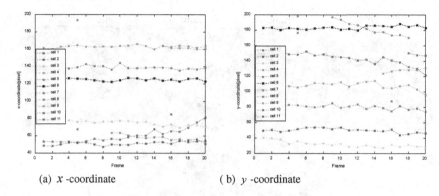

(a) x-coordinate   (b) y-coordinate

Fig. 4. Position estimate of each cell in x and y directions

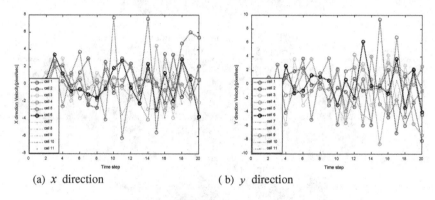

(a) x direction   (b) y direction

Fig. 5. Instant velocity estimate of each cell in x and y directions

Table 1. Comparison results for tracking performance of various methods

Method	LSR (%)	LTR (%)	FTR (%)
PF [11]	22.3	20.33	18.56
Multi-Bernoulli filter [3]	11.89	14.56	15.78
Our method	6.44	7.89	1.37

4   Conclusions

This work focuses on the application of Ant Colony Optimization algorithms combined with Gaussian clod model to a problem of cell tracking. Promising results and analysis are obtained from experiment, in the sense that our proposed algorithm performs better than other compared approaches.

Acknowledgments. This work is supported by national natural science foundation of China (No. 61876024 and No. 61673075), and partly by the project of talent peak of six industries (2017-DZXX-001), Jiangsu Laboratory of Lake Environment Remote Sensing Technologies Open Project Fund (JSLERS-2017-006) and The Science and Technology Development Plan Project of Chang Shu (CR0201711).

References

1. Liu, M., Xiang, P., Liu, G.: Robust plant cell tracking using local spatiotemporal context. Neurocomputing **208**, 309–314 (2016)
2. He, C., Wang, Y., Chen, Q.: Active contours driven by weighted region-scalable fitting energy based on local entropy. Sig. Process. **92**(2), 587–600 (2012)
3. Hoseinnezhad, R., Vo, B.-N., Vo, B.-T., Suter, D.: Visual tracking of numerous targets via multi-Bernoulli filtering of image data. Pattern Recogn. **45**, 3625–3635 (2012)
4. Rezatofighi, S.H., et al.: Multi-target tracking with time-varying clutter rate and detection profile: application to time-lapse cell microscopy sequences. IEEE Trans. Med. Imaging **34**(6), 1336–1348 (2015)
5. Dorigo, M., Maniezzo, V., Colorni, A.: Ant system: optimization by a colony of cooperating agents. IEEE Trans. Syst. Man Cybern. **26**(1), 29–41 (1996)
6. Miria, A., Sharifianb, S., Rashidib, S., Ghodsca, M.: Medical image denoising based on 2D discrete cosine transform via ant colony optimization. Optik **156**, 938–948 (2018)
7. Zhou, Y.: Runtime analysis of an ant colony optimization algorithm for TSP instances. IEEE Trans. Evol. Comput. **13**(5), 1083–1092 (2009)
8. Huanga, S.H., Huangb, Y.H., Blazquezc, C.A., Paredes-Belmarda, G.: Application of the ant colony optimization in the resolution of the bridge inspection routing problem. Appl. Soft Comput. **65**, 443–461 (2018)
9. Wang, X., Choi, T.-M., Liu, H., Yue, X.: Novel ant colony optimization methods for simplifying solution construction in vehicle routing problems. IEEE Trans. Intell. Transp. Syst. **17**(11), 3132–3141 (2016)
10. Wang, G., Xu, C., Li, D.: Generic normal cloud model. Inf. Sci. **280**, 1–15 (2014)
11. Xu, B., Lu, M., Zhu, P., et al.: Multi-task ant system for multi-object parameter estimate and its application in cell tracking. Appl. Soft Comput. **35**, 449–469 (2015)
12. Lu, M., Xu, B., et al.: Automated tracking approach with ant colonies for different cell population density distribution. Soft Comput. **21**, 3977–3992 (2017)
13. Smal, I., Carranza-Herrezuelo, N., Klein, S., Wielopolski, P., Moelker, A., Springeling, T., et al.: Reversible jump MCMC methods for fully automatic motion analysis in tagged MRI. Med. Image Anal. **16**, 301–324 (2012)

Physarum-Based Ant Colony Optimization for Graph Coloring Problem

Lingyan Lv[1], Chao Gao[1], Jianjun Chen[1], Liang Luo[1], and Zili Zhang[1,2(✉)]

[1] School of Computer and Information Science, Southwest University,
Chongqing 400715, China
{cgao,zhangzl}@swu.edu.cn
[2] School of Information Technology, Deakin University,
Locked Bag 20000, Geelong, VIC 3220, Australia

Abstract. Graph coloring problem (GCP) is a classical combinatorial optimization problem and has many applications in the industry. Many algorithms have been proposed for solving GCP. However, insufficient efficiency and unreliable stability still limit their performance. Aiming to overcome these shortcomings, a physarum-based ant colony optimization for solving GCP is proposed in this paper. The proposed algorithm takes advantage of the positive feedback mechanism of the physarum mathematical model to optimize the pheromone matrix updating in the ant colony optimization. Some experiments are implemented to estimate the efficiency and stability of the proposed algorithm compared with typical ant colony optimization and some state-of-art algorithms. According to these results, in terms of the efficiency, stability and computational cost, we can daringly infer that the improved ant colony optimization with the physarum model performs better than the aforementioned for graph coloring. In particular, it is recommended that the model is of rationality and the proposed algorithm is of validity, which will foster a science of color number and computational cost in GCP.

Keywords: Physarum-based ant colony optimization ·
Graph coloring problem · Physarum mathematical model ·
Ant colony algorithm

1 Introduction

The graph coloring problem (GCP) is one of the most studied combinatorial optimization problems in the graph theory [1]. The main purpose of this kind of problems is to find a coloring of vertices with the minimum number of colors such that any two adjacent vertices have different colors [2]. It has a wide spread of real-world applications in the timetabling, resource assignment, network design, crew assignment and register allocation [3].

Since it has been proved that the graph coloring problem belongs to a typical NP-hard problem in which the computational cost to obtain the optimal solution

© Springer Nature Switzerland AG 2019
Y. Tan et al. (Eds.): ICSI 2019, LNCS 11655, pp. 210–219, 2019.
https://doi.org/10.1007/978-3-030-26369-0_20

increases exponentially as the problem size increases as possible, and the research for the problem mainly focuses on the intelligent algorithm [4]. But there is no exact polynomial algorithm for NP-hard problems, many scholars have proposed various methods for solving approximate solutions from the perspective of modern bionic algorithms, such as DNA algorithm [5], ant colony algorithm [6,7], and particle swarm optimization [8]. Among them, the ant colony algorithm is widely used and has achieved ideal results in solving the graph coloring problem due to its pheromone update mechanism. However, some shortcomings, such as the insufficient efficiency and unreliable stability still limit the performance of ant colony-based algorithms [9,10].

Physarum, which is a simple multinucleated and unicellular slime mold, shows an intelligence in the network designing due to its internal positive feedback mechanism [11]. Furthermore, inspired by the intelligence of physarum, a physarum mathematical model (hereinafter referred to as PMM strategy) is proposed by Tero [12]. Inspired by the positive feedback mechanism of PMM, a physarum pheromone matrix update strategy (hereinafter referred to as PM strategy) is proposed in this paper to optimize the pheromone matrix of ant colony algorithm. Based on PM, the physarum-based ant colony optimization for GCP is proposed to overcome the insufficient efficiency, unreliable stability and redundant computational cost to some extend. And a series of represented experiments are implemented to estimate the performance of PM-ACO.

The remaining parts of this paper are organized as follows: Sect. 2 describes the graph coloring problem and introduces the basic ant colony algorithm about how to solve GCP. Section 3 proposes the PM and a physarum-based ant colony algorithm (PM-ACO) for GCP. Section 4 reveals that the basic ACO [13], some advanced algorithms in [14] with the benchmark datasets on website[1] are used to estimate the efficiency and stability of PM-ACO. Finally, Sect. 5 concludes this paper.

2   Related Works

According to the aforementioned works, focusing on many real-world applications, currently, the graph coloring problem is divided into three categories: vertex coloring, edge coloring and graph full coloring [1]. With certain transformation, the edge coloring and graph full coloring can be equivalent to the vertex coloring [2]. Therefore, this paper mainly focuses on the vertex coloring.

The graph coloring problem (GCP) can be defined as follows: let $G = (V, E)$ be a graph, where V is a set of vertices and E is a set of edges. The graph coloring problem is to divide V into K color groups. Each group forms an independent set, that is, there are no adjacent vertices. Our goal is to find the K. $K = min\{k_1, k_2 \ldots k_n\}$, where $k_1, k_2 \ldots k_n$ are obtained in each iteration.

Many algorithms have been proposed to solve GCP, however, ant colony optimization is someone to do for it, which has strong robustness and is of ability

---

[1] https://mat.tepper.cmu.edu/COLOR/instances.html.

to search a better resolution. On the contrast, it depends on parameters and computational cost greatly. Thus, insufficient efficiency and unreliable stability limit its performance. As a result, it is essential for ACO to improve and modify its core to overcome the dilemma.

In the face of these intractable problems, one of the most significant explanations for the performance directed at algorithm cannot be nothing but the color number K which negatively correlated. Thus the optimized version is intended to get the minimum K value. At the same time, the computational cost is the other important evaluation indicator.

In mathematics, ant colony optimization for graph coloring problem is defined as follows: in a graph G, a set of vertices V is denoted as $v_1, v_2, \ldots, v_n$. $C = \{c_1, c_2, \ldots, c_n\}$ is a set of colors and the maximum vertex degree is Max_degree. When solving GCP based on ant colony optimization, m ants are used to color the vertices in graph.

$A(n \times n)$ represents the adjacency matrix of graph $G(V, E)$, then:

$$A(n \times n) = \begin{cases} 1, & \text{a vertex } v_i \text{ is connected with } v_j \\ 0, & \text{otherwise} \end{cases} \tag{1}$$

$\tau(i \times j)$ denotes the pheromone matrix, $\tau(i, j)$ is the current pheromone between vertex v_i and v_j. And each edge follows the pheromone volatilization rule:

$$\tau_{ij}(i, j) = (1 - \rho)\tau_{ij}(i, j) + \Delta\tau(i, j) \tag{2}$$

where ρ indicates the pheromone volatility, $\Delta\tau(i, j)$ represents the pheromone left by an ant on a path (i, j), which is defined by Eq. (3).

$$\Delta\tau(i, j) = F/M \tag{3}$$

F is the pheromone intensity and M indicates the number of nodes colored. η_{ij} is the heuristic information defined in Eq. (4).

$$\eta_{ij} = 1/M \tag{4}$$

p_{ij} represents the transition probability of an ant while choosing the next vertex, then colors this node randomly based on Eq. (5).

$$p_{ij} = \frac{\tau_{ij}^{\alpha}\eta_{ij}^{\beta}}{\Sigma\tau_{ij}^{\alpha}\eta_{ij}^{\beta}} \tag{5}$$

And, inspired by the intelligence of the physarum, it is a combination about physarum and ACO, which is proposed to solve GCP.

3   Physarum-Based Ant Colony Optimization

In this subsection, Sect. 3.1 first introduces the physarum positive feedback mechanism and corresponding mathematical model. Section 3.2 proposes the basic core of physarum-based ant colony optimization and describes the details of PM-ACO.

3.1 The Physarum Mathematical Model

As mentioned above, the physarum positive feedback mechanism is inspired by the physarum, a simple multinucleated and unicellular slime mold. In the labyrinth test, the physarum protoplast pipeline would cover the entire maze first. Then the dead end pipeline would disappear, and the longer pipeline would disappear. Finally, the protoplasmic pipeline would converge to the shortest path [15]. Further research by Tero et al. [16] has found that during the convergence of protoplasmic pipelines, the radius of the protoplast pipeline and the flow in the pipeline have shown a positive feedback relationship, that is, the higher the flowing flux in a tube is, the thicker the tube becomes, vice versa.

On this basis, Tero et al. [12] have used the Poiseuille's equation to characterize the relationship between the pipe radius and flow. Based on the Kirchhoff's law, a positive feedback system is established to simulate the positive feedback mechanism (the physarum mathematical model PMM) [17].

The basic PMM model is used to find the shortest path between two points [18]. It is assumed that the edge in network is a pipe with water flow, N_{in} is the water inlet, and N_{out} is the water outlet. The conductivity D of the pipe connecting the vertex i and j, is used to reflect the radius of the pipe. The relationship between flux Q and continuity D is characterized by the Poiseuille equation as shown in Eq. (6), where P_i presents the pressure of vertex i and L_{ij} denotes the length of a pipe (i, j).

$$Q_{ij} = \frac{D_{ij}}{L_{ij}} |P_i - P_j| \qquad (6)$$

According to the Kirchhoff's law as shown in Eq. (7), the pressures and fluxes can be obtained at each time step.

$$P_i = \sum_i Q_{ij} = \begin{cases} I_0, & \text{if } v_i \text{ is an inlet} \\ -I_0, & \text{if } v_i \text{ is an outlet} \\ 0, & \text{otherwise} \end{cases} \qquad (7)$$

$$D_{ij}^{t+1} = f\left(|Q_{ij}^t|\right) - rD_{ij}^t \qquad (8)$$

The positive feedback relationship is characterized by Eq. (8). In time step t, the flux Q feeds back to the conductivity D^{t+1} based on Eq. (8). And then the conductivity D^{t+1} feeds back to Q^{t+1} again. In the wake of such feedback process, the network finally converges to a stable state.

More specifically, $f\left(|Q_{ij}^t|\right)$ has two forms, as shown in Eqs. (9) and (10) [19]. Equation (9) has a good effect on solving the shortest path. And Eq. (10) is better for network design implemented in our scheme.

$$f(Q) = Q^u \qquad (9)$$

$$f(Q) = \frac{(1+a)Q^u}{1+aQ^u} \qquad (10)$$

3.2   The Physarum-Based Ant Colony Optimization

In PM-ACO, assuming that flows in the physarum network is pheromone. The physarum pheromone is considered in the renewal process of pheromone matrix in ACO. This update strategy for physarum pheromone matrix is denoted as PM strategy.

In PM-ACO, the positive feedback mechanism is defined as Eq. (11). Where a pipe flux Q_{ij} is replaced by the average flux $\overline{Q_{ij}}$ as shown in Eq. (12). M denotes the number of edges. In time step t, both ends of each edge in graph are regarded as the inlet and outlet respectively. The pressure of each vertex and flux of each edge can be obtained by Eqs. (6) and (7). And the initial flux is defined as I_0, which means $\frac{2 \times F}{n \times (n-1)}$. The average flux $\overline{Q_{ij}}$ is measured by Eq. (12). Then the flux $\overline{Q_{ij}^t}$ feeds back to the conductivity D_{ij}^{t+1} based on Eq. (11).

$$\frac{d}{dt} D_{ij} = \frac{|Q_{ij}|}{1 + |Q_{ij}|} - D_{ij} \tag{11}$$

$$\overline{Q_{ij}} = \frac{1}{M} \sum_{m=1}^{M} |Q_{ij}^{(m)}| \tag{12}$$

After that, the pheromone obtained by PM strategy is used to update the pheromone matrix in ACO as shown in Eq. (13). Where ϵ is the influence factor of the physarum pheromone on total pheromone. And the *tempsteps* represents the number of steps affected by PM strategy during the algorithm operation. According to the mathematical analysis of PM model in [20], the evolution rate of PM model is relatively fast, and the evolution ends between 100 and 300 iterations. Therefore, it is appropriate to take *tempstep* $\in [100, 300]$.

$$\Delta \tau_{ij}(t) = \rho \left[\frac{F}{M} + \epsilon \frac{\overline{Q_{ij}(t)} \times M}{F} \right] \tag{13}$$

$$\epsilon = 1 - \frac{1}{1 + \lambda^{\frac{temsteps}{2} - (t+1)}} \tag{14}$$

Based on PM strategy, the physarum-based ant colony optimization is designed for the graph coloring in this paper, described as Algorithm 1.

4   Experiments

For the purpose of the validity of assessing the efficiency and stability of PM-ACO based on the benchmark datasets (See footnote 1), especially color number and computational cost, three representative experiments have been schemed for aforementioned insufficient deficiencies. In Sect. 4.2, the typical ACO [13], Exh [21] and AGA [21] are compared with PM-ACO in order to validate the efficiency of PM-ACO based on four cross-sectional datasets (*queen16_16*, *queen8_12*,

---

Algorithm 1: The Physarum-based Ant Colony Optimization

Input: *The Graph(node : n, edge)*
Output: *Number of colors : K, Algorithm runtime*
Initialization: flux Q, continuity D, ants m, proportion factor α, β, λ,
pheromone volatility ρ, pheromone matrix τ_{ij}, *visited_color_set*,
unvisited_color_set
for *iteration* $= 1 : N$ **do**
   for *point* $= 2 : n$ **do**
      for *ant* $= 1 : m$ **do**
         Selection probability p_{ij} is calculated for point based on Eq. (5);
         One point is selected based on the roulette mechanism;
         Update corresponding parameters: I_0, Q, D, P, $\Delta\tau(i,j)$;
         Colour the current point:
         if *collision* **then**
            | colour the point with random color in *visited_color_set*
         else
            | colour the point with random color in *unvisited_color_set*
         end
      end
      update the local pheromone $\tau(i,j)$
   end
   update the global pheromone $\tau(i,j)$
end

---

*queen*10_10 and *queen*12_12). In Sect. 4.3, with the purpose of verifying the stability, typical ACO, PM-ACO and some advanced algorithms MCOACL, ABAC, BEECOL in [14] have been tested on twenty benchmark datasets to move downward a deep step. Section 4.4 further discusses the computational cost of PM-ACO.

4.1 Datasets

The experimental data used in this paper, is derived from the graph coloring international standard database, and details are described in website (See footnote 1).

4.2 Efficiency

With comparison about efficiency, typical algorithms ACO [13], Exh [21] and AGA [21] are compared with PM-ACO on four representative datasets. The experimental results are shown in Table 1. According to our results, PM-ACO is superior to other algorithms. As for the dataset *queen*8_12, PM-ACO has found the best K. And pointing to the dense graph (i.e., *queen*12_12 and *queen*16_16), which is quite difficult to color nodes, PM-ACO has also done great performance. Distinctly, it shows that PM-ACO presents excellent performance.

Table 1. Comparison among PM-ACO, ACO, Exh and AGA

Graph	Best K	PM-ACO	ACO	Exh	AGA
queen16_16	18	**18**	20	25	25
queen8_12	12	**12**	14	16	16
queen10_10	11	**12**	13	18	18
queen12_12	13	**14**	15	22	22

4.3   Stability

To further verify the efficiency and the stability of PM-ACO, sort of experiments have been implemented around these two elements. The advanced algorithms MCOACL, ABAC, BEECOL in [14] and PM-ACO have been tested upon twenty benchmark datasets as shown in Table 2. According to the experimental results, PM-ACO reveals a better performance even if compared with the advanced algorithms. For the datasets *David, Huck, myciel3, myciel4, myciel5, myciel6, myciel3* and *queen5_5*, PM-ACO and contrastive algorithms have found the best K. For the rest datasets, the color number obtained by PM-ACO is much closer to the best K compared to the contrastive algorithms. It can be seen that PM-ACO can stably find a better color number for various kinds of datasets. Consequently, PM-ACO holds the excellent efficiency and stability to some extend for solving GCP.

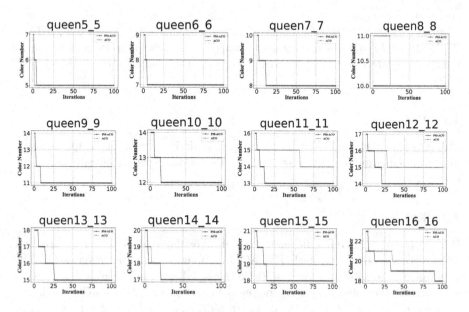

Fig. 1. Result analysis of color number and convergence

Table 2. Contrastive performances

Graph	Best K	PM-ACO	MCOA COL	AB AC	BEE COL	ACO	Graph	Best K	PM-ACO	MCOA COL	AB AC	BEE COL	ACO
David	11	11	11	11	11	11	queen8_12	12	12	13	12	12	14
Huck	11	11	11	11	11	11	queen8_8	9	10	10	9	10	10
Jean	10	11	11	11	11	11	queen9_9	10	11	11	10	11	12
myciel3	4	4	4	4	4	4	queen10_10	/	12	12	11	12	13
myciel4	5	5	5	5	5	5	queen11_11	11	13	14	13	13	14
myciel5	6	6	6	6	6	6	queen12_12	/	14	15	14	14	15
myciel6	7	7	7	7	7	7	queen13_13	13	15	16	15	15	16
queen5_5	5	5	5	5	5	5	queen14_14	/	17	17	16	16	18
queen6_6	7	7	8	7	8	8	queen15_15	/	18	18	17	18	19
queen7_7	7	8	7	7	8	9	queen16_16	/	18	19	18	19	20

4.4 Computational Cost

This section implements a series of deeper emulational experiments involved computational cost to test the speed of PM-ACO. Basic ACO [13] and PM-ACO are used to test 20 times upon the *queen* series datasets. Then computational cost of each generation can be obtained to evaluate the speed of these algorithms. Taking the experimental results into account, visibly, it is outstanding that PM-ACO has acquired preferable color number than basic ACO as shown in Fig. 1. As well as the computational cost, PM-ACO has superior performance compared to basic ACO based on Table 3. For the small-scale datasets, such as *queen5_5* and *queen6_6*, the computational cost of ACO is close to PM-ACO. However, processing from the dataset *queen10_10*, with the size of the dataset increases, the gap between the computational cost of ACO and PM-ACO exposes wider, and PM-ACO reveals much more sufficient capacity than ACO. Especially for the large-scale datasets *queen15_15* and *queen16_16*, PM-ACO requires less computational cost than ACO.

Table 3. Computational cost of ACO and PM-ACO

Graph	Best K	PM-ACO K	Time (s)	ACO K	Time (s)	Graph	Best K	PM-ACO K	Time (s)	ACO K	Time (s)
queen5_5	5	5	0.02	5	0.03	queen11_11	11	13	0.50	14	2.42
queen6_6	7	7	0.04	8	0.08	queen12_12	/	14	0.77	15	3.86
queen7_7	7	8	0.07	9	0.20	queen13_13	13	15	1.09	16	6.38
queen8_8	9	10	0.12	10	0.40	queen14_14	/	17	1.56	18	9.61
queen9_9	10	11	0.21	12	0.75	queen15_15	/	18	2.23	19	14.45
queen10_10	/	12	0.32	13	1.46	queen16_16	/	18	3.09	20	20.62

218   L. Lv et al.

5 Conclusion

GCP is a classical NP-hard problem, and many algorithms have been proposed for solving it. However, insufficient efficiency and unreliable stability still limit their performance. Aiming to overcome these shortcomings, a Physarum-based Ant Colony Optimization for solving GCP is proposed in this paper. Based on PM, PM-ACO takes advantage of the positive feedback mechanism of the physarum mathematical model to optimize the pheromone matrix updating in ant colony optimization. Three representative experiments with sort of famous benchmark datasets have been implemented to prove the assumption that the improved ACO with PM strategy holds better performance in terms of the efficiency, stability and computational cost. Deriving from experimental consequences, we can infer a brand new potency in GCP that PM-ACO can seek the best K or suboptimal color number in a great bucks of types of graph with the valuable computational cost around this area.

Acknowledgments. This work is supported by the National Natural Science Foundation of China (Nos. 61732019, 61762020), CQ CSTC(Nos. cstc2015gjhz40-002, cstc2018jcyjAX0274) and CERNET Innovation Project (No. NGII20170110). Prof. Chao Gao and Prof. Zili Zhang are the corresponding authors of this paper.

References

1. Tayarani-N, M.-H., Prugel-Bennett, A.: On the landscape of combinatorial optimization problems. IEEE Trans. Evol. Comput. **18**(3), 420–434 (2014)
2. Checco, A., Leith, D.J.: Fast, responsive decentralized graph coloring. IEEE/ACM Trans. Netw. **15**(6), 3628–3640 (2017)
3. Topcuoglu, H.R., Demiroz, B., Kandemir, M.: Solving the register allocation problem for embedded systems using a hybrid evolutionary algorithm. IEEE Trans. Evol. Comput. **11**(5), 620–634 (2007)
4. Bessedik, M., Laib, R., Boulmerka, A., Drias, H.: Ant colony system for graph coloring problem. In: International Conference on Computational Intelligence for Modelling Control and Automation, pp. 786–791 (2005)
5. Liu, Y.C., Xu, J., Pan, L.Q., Wang, S.Y.: DNA solution of a graph coloring problem. J. Chem. Inf. Comput. Sci. **42**(3), 524–528 (2002)
6. Lintzmayer, C.N., Mulati, M.H., Silva, A.F.: Toward better performance of colorant ACO algorithm. In: 30th International Conference of the Chilean Computer Science Society, pp. 256–264 (2011)
7. Mosa, M.A., Hamouda, A., Marei, M.: Graph coloring and ACO based summarization for social networks. Expert Syst. Appl. **74**, 115–126 (2017)
8. Qin, J., Yin, Y.X., Ban, X.J.: Hybrid discrete particle swarm algorithm for graph coloring problem. J. Chem. Phys. **6**(6), 1175–1182 (2011)
9. Liu, Y.X., et al.: Solving NP-hard problems with Physarum-based ant colony system. IEEE/ACM Trans. Comput. Biol. Bioinf. **14**(1), 108–120 (2017)
10. Zhang, Z.L., Gao, C., Liu, Y.X., Qian, T.: A universal optimization strategy for ant colony optimization algorithms based on the physarum-inspired mathematical model. Bioinspir. Biomim. **9**(3), 036006 (2014)

11. Gao, C., et al.: Does being multi-headed make you better at solving problems? A survey of Physarum-based models and computations. Phys. Life Rev. (2018). https://doi.org/10.1016/j.plrev.2018.05.002

12. Tero, A., Kobayashi, R., Nakagaki, T.: A mathematical model for adaptive transport network in path finding by true slime mold. J. Theor. Biol. **244**(4), 553–564 (2007)

13. Dorigo, M., Maniezzo, V., Colorni, A.: Ant system: optimization by a colony of cooperating agents. IEEE Trans. Syst. Man Cybern. B Cybern. **26**(1), 29–41 (1996)

14. Mahmoudi, S., Lotfi, S.: Modified cuckoo optimization algorithm (MCOA) to solve graph coloring problem. Appl. Soft Comput. **33**, 48–64 (2015)

15. Nakagaki, T., Yamada, H., Agota, T.: Intelligence: Maze-solving by an amoeboid organism. Nature **407**(6803), 470–470 (2000)

16. Tero, A., Kobayashi, R., Nakagaki, T.: A coupled-oscillator model with a conservation law for the rhythmic amoeboid movements of plasmodial slime molds. Physica D. **205**(1), 125–135 (2005)

17. Gao, C., Liang, M.X., Li, X.H., Zhang, Z.L., Wang, Z., Zhou, Z.L.: Network community detection based on the Physarum-inspired computational framework. IEEE/ACM Trans. Comput. Biol. Bioinf. **15**(6), 1916–1928 (2018)

18. Gao, C., Chen, S., Li, X.H., Huang, J.J., Zhang, Z.L.: A Physarum-inspired optimization algorithm for load-shedding problem. Appl. Soft Comput. **61**, 239–255 (2017)

19. Jones, J.: Characteristics of pattern formation and evolution in approximations of physarum transport networks. Artif. Life **16**(2), 127–153 (2010)

20. Miyaji, T., Ohnishi, I.: Mathematical analysis to an adaptive network of the Plasmodium system. Hokkaido Math. J. **36**(2), 445–465 (2007)

21. Li, K.: An improved genetic algorithm for solving graph coloring problem. Comput. Mod. **2**, 6–11 (2017)

Ant Colony Algorithm Based Scheduling with Lot-Sizing for Printed Circuit Board Assembly Shop

Zilong Zhuang, Zizhao Huang, Daili Song, and Wei Qin[✉]

School of Mechanical Engineering,
Shanghai Jiao Tong University, Shanghai, China
wqin@sjtu.edu.cn

Abstract. This paper investigates a multi-stage hybrid flow shop scheduling problem in a real-world printed circuit board (PCB) assembly shop. Some distinct characteristics such as calendar constraints, sequence-dependent setup times, unrelated parallel machines and stage skipping are taken into account. Besides, lot-sizing is introduced to split an order of PCBs into a number of smaller sub-lots to improve the utilization of the assembly lines. This article develops an effective hierarchical approach to reduce the complexity of such a complicated PCB scheduling problem by decomposing it into two highly coupled sub-problems of job sequencing and batch scheduling with lot-sizing. A two-stage ant colony algorithm with lot-sizing is proposed to evolve best results for makespan criterion. Extensive computational experiments have been conducted to compare the performance with two other algorithms. The results demonstrate that the proposed two-stage ant colony algorithm with lot-sizing is competitive in terms of computational result, computational time and stability.

Keywords: Hybrid flow shop · PCB assembly shop scheduling ·
Ant colony algorithm · Lot sizing

1 Introduction

Printed circuit boards (PCBs) are used as components for facsimiles, personal computers, printers, and other electrical/electronic devices. However, most of the PCB manufacturers are facing the challenge to improve the production efficiency in order to cope with the fierce competition.

According to the theory of operations scheduling, the PCB assembly process in the factory can be regarded as a hybrid flow shop (HFS) scheduling problem. Different from ordinary HFS scheduling problem, some characteristics emerged in PCB assembly shop significantly substantiates the complexity of the HFS scheduling problem. Two distinctive features are summarized as follows:

1. **Lot sizing:** Considering that the machine setup times are required between processing of different PCBs, the orders are always split into a small number of sub-lots. PCBs are produced in batches to enhance the utilization of the machines and the assembly lines. Each batch consists of identical PCBs with the same due date.

© Springer Nature Switzerland AG 2019
Y. Tan et al. (Eds.): ICSI 2019, LNCS 11655, pp. 220–231, 2019.
https://doi.org/10.1007/978-3-030-26369-0_21

All batches have the same sequence of stations to visit, since the PCBs have the same route. Each lot of a PCB type is processed till completion.

2. **Calendar constraints:** The calendar is a tool to set the work shifts of all the machines. This work shift is also called a *capacity* which is a segment of continuous available times of a machine. In the investigated PCB assembly shop, this means the machines such as screen printers, refold machines, inspection equipment, and also different types of placement machines are available only at working times in the calendar.

Besides, the setup times for the jobs depend on the sequence of PCBs to be processed. Also, the machines in each stage are unrelated, i.e., the processing times for different machines to complete the same sub-lot are different. The stage skipping is also allowed because not all jobs are required to go through all the stages.

These factors are generally considered separately as reported in the literature. The PCB scheduling problem considered in this paper can be described against the literature along the following directions: (1) PCB assembly shop scheduling; (2) scheduling with lot-sizing; and (3) scheduling with limited machine availability.

Many researchers have developed different algorithms, either mathematical or heuristic, to optimize different factors in PCB assembly. Ji et al. [1] formulated the problem of allocating components to a PCB assembly line as a minimax-type integer programming (IP) model. Alkaya and Duman [2] adopted metaheuristic approach to optimize the chip shooter component placement machines by decomposing the problem into placement sequencing and feeder configuration. Tóth et al. [3] presented a two-step optimisation method for the machine reconfiguration and workload balancing in the case of multiple PCB batches of different sizes and PCB types.

The technique of lot-sizing has been widely used for scheduling in recent years. Truscott [4] mentioned several potential benefits of lot streaming. Huang and Yu [5] developed an improved ant colony optimization to resolve multi-objective job shop scheduling problem with equal-size lot splitting. Wang et al. [6] studied integrated batching and lot streaming problem with variable sub-lots, incompatible job families, and sequence-dependent setup times, and developed heuristics for an efficient solution. From the literature, we can see that most works only indicate the condition of the job grouping or assumption that the job batches already exist. Very limited references are available that addresses the creation of job batches.

The traditional scheduling problem assumes that the machines are continuously available for processing throughout the planning horizon. However, in a real-life industry, this availability may not be true due to machine breakdowns (stochastic) or preventive maintenance or calendar capacity (deterministic). Allaoui and Artiba [7] studied two-stage hybrid flow shop with availability constraints. Yaurima et al. [8] proposed modified genetic algorithm for the hybrid flow shop with unrelated machines, sequence-dependent setup times, availability constraints, and limited buffers. Gholami et al. [9] incorporated simulation into genetic algorithm approach for a hybrid flow shop scheduling problems with sequence-dependent setup times and machines with random breakdowns. Seidgar et al. [10] investigated a two-stage assembly flow shop problem which considers machines breakdown, and presented a genetic algorithm and new self-adapted differential evolutionary algorithm. Han et al. [11] proposed an evolutionary multi-objective robust scheduling algorithm for blocking lot-streaming flow shop scheduling problems with machine breakdowns.

Based on the above brief literature review, we find that few researchers discussed the combination of these factors in one model, and there is a gap between theoretical development and practical application for such a complicated PCB assembly scheduling problem. Although a broad body of literature on PCB assembly shop scheduling has been published, only few works have implemented on industrial practice. Since the literatures lay particular stress on the model and algorithm, some real-life restrictions are either simplified or ignored. This research is an attempt to bridge this gap by proposing a comprehensive solution to this complicated scheduling problem which can coordinate all the necessary characteristics.

The remainder of this paper is organized as follows. Section 2 addresses the description of the investigated scheduling problem. Section 3 describes the basic ant colony algorithm and summarized the process of formulation and the main characteristics of the proposed algorithm. Section 4 reports the outcomes of the experimental study. Finally, some concluding remarks are presented in Sect. 5.

2   Problem Statement

The detailed layout of the assembly shop in our collaborating company is depicted in Fig. 1. All the PCBs go through 5 stages of manufacturing (assembly) process: surface mounting, reflow soldering, automatic/manual insertion, wave soldering and inspection by burn-in. The PCBs composed by small electronic elements might skip the insertion stage.

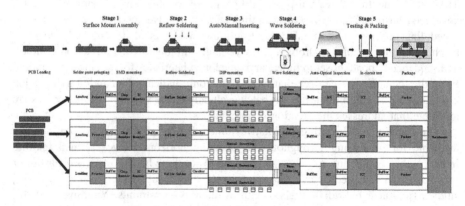

Fig. 1. Layout of the PCB assembly shop.

Suppose there are n jobs and m stages in the PCB assembly shop where each job is available at time zero and contains a lot of items of the same kind. Each stage can be processed by several machines, which are capacitated. The capacity, which is limited, will be consumed in producing an item. The target is to minimize the makespan. Assumptions and constraints for the scheduling problem are as follows:

1. All jobs are independent and available for processing at the initial time of scheduling.
2. Each job contains identical items with the same ready time and due date and can be separated into several sub-lots.
3. One machine can process only one job at a time and one job can be processed by only one machine at any time.
4. All the items in a sub-lot should be processed on the same machine.
5. A new sub-lot can start only after the completion of the previous sub-lot produced on the same machine, i.e., preemption is not allowed.
6. The machines in every stage are unrelated, i.e., the processing times for different machines to complete the same sub-lot are different.
7. Not all jobs are required to go through all stages, e.g., some jobs might skip some production stages.

3 Ant Colony Algorithm with Lot-Sizing

Due to the high complexity of the hybrid flow shop scheduling problem with lot sizing and calendar constraints, the exact method cannot obtain a feasible solution in an acceptable computational time. Although many heuristic algorithms based on dispatching rules have been employed with higher efficiency, the quality of the solution often deteriorates as the problem size increases because of the existence of many local optima. An intelligent algorithm has obvious advantages in solving complex production scheduling problems due to its optimization goal of seeking satisfactory solutions, easy integration of problem knowledge and expert experience, and procedure robustness. As a promising swarm intelligence algorithm, the ant colony algorithm (ACA) has been widely used to solve large-scale combinatorial optimization problems since its first introduction by Dorigo [12], due to its positive feedback, concurrency, robustness, global search, and independent of strict mathematical properties, etc. As an algorithm aiming to search for an optimal path in a graph, ACA has been widely used to solve the combinatorial problem, especially scheduling problem.

3.1 Two-Stage Structure and Algorithm Flow Chart

Considering the complexity of the investigated problem, we decompose it into two highly coupled sub-problems, which are job sequencing and lot scheduling of a job. This method is similar to that proposed in Arnaout et al. [13]. As described above, ACA has been proved to be a prominent tool for scheduling problem. We adopt the ACA to solve the sub-problems and propose a two-stage ant colony algorithm with lot-sizing (TSACAWLS). The flow chart of proposed algorithm is shown in Fig. 2.

Figure 3 illustrates the structure of the proposed two-stage ant colony algorithm. As shown in the figure, the investigated problem is divided into two highly coupled stages: at stage 1, we determine the sequence of jobs. And at stage 2, we assign all the sub-lots to the machines after separating the production stages of each job into multiple sub-lots. We manage each of these stages with an ant system scheme.

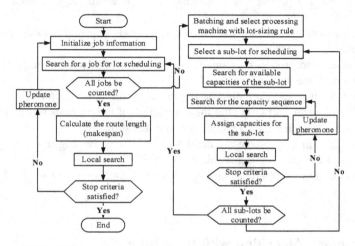

Fig. 2. Flow chart of two-stage ant colony algorithm with lot-sizing

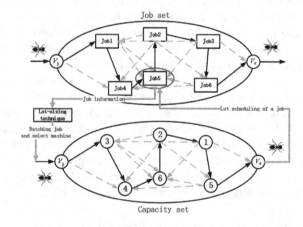

Fig. 3. Structure of two-stage ant colony algorithm with lot-sizing

3.2   Job Sequencing

Stage 1 mainly deals with job sequencing problem to minimize the makespan of all jobs. We express the output of first stage with a vector (S1) that contains n entries and each entry representing a job. The sub-lots of jobs to machines are arranged according to the sequence in the vector. We introduce $\tau_{i,j}^I$ and $\eta_{i,j}^I$ to express the pheromone trail and the visibility of ant respectively. The possibility to select job j after i and the value of $\eta_{i,j}^I$ are calculated as follows:

$$P_{i,j}^I = \frac{\left(\tau_{i,j}^I\right)^\alpha \cdot \left(\eta_{i,j}^I\right)^\beta}{\sum_{l\in\Phi}\left(\tau_{i,l}^I\right)^\alpha \cdot \left(\eta_{i,l}^I\right)^\beta}. \tag{1}$$

$$\eta_{i,j}^I = 1/Set_{i,j}. \tag{2}$$

Where $Set_{i,j}$ is the setup time between job i and j.

After all the ants complete their paths, we update the pheromone amounts in each link locally by reducing the amount due to evaporation and globally by increasing the amounts of pheromone in the routes constructed by the ant that produces the best objective function (OF^{best}). This is estimated according to the following formulas:

$$\tau_{i,j}^I \leftarrow (1-\rho)\tau_{i,j}^I + \rho\Delta\tau_{i,j}^{I,best}. \tag{3}$$

$$\Delta\tau_{i,j}^{I,best} = \begin{cases} 1/OF^{best} & \text{if } arc(i,j) \text{ is used by best ant} \\ 0 & \text{otherwise} \end{cases}. \tag{4}$$

Where OF^{best}, representing the makespan of the best job sequence, is the objective function with respect to the best vector S_1^{best}. Objective function of a job sequence is calculated through stage 2.

3.3 Batch Scheduling and Lot-Sizing

In order to calculate the objective function of a job sequence given by stage 1, we schedule the sub-lots in stage 2 after separating the production stages of the job into several sub-lots. Stage 2 can be separated into two highly coupled sub-problems: sub-lots scheduling problem and lot-sizing problem. We schedule each stage of a job with an AS scheme and express the output with a vector (S_2) that contains m entries and each entry representing a capacity. After that, a sub-lot will be arranged to the capacity according to the sequence in the vector. As we had described previously, several machines are capable of process a production stage $O_{i,j}$, it's vital to choose a suitable machine to process the job at the production stage. We assume the set of machines for stage $O_{i,j}$ to be $E_{i,j}$ and entitle each machine in $E_{i,j}$ with an objective value OV. Machine with the largest OV are selected for the production stage.

$$OV = N / \sum_{c=1}^{N} \sum_{l\in L_{i,j-1}} \alpha_l T_c \quad \forall i \in n, j \in m. \tag{5}$$

$$\alpha_l = Q_i / \sum_{k=1}^{l} Q_{i,j-1,k} \quad \forall i \in n, j \in m. \tag{6}$$

$$T_c = \begin{cases} S_{i,j}(c) - Max(C_{i,j-1,k}) & \text{if } S_{i,j}(c) \geq Max(C_{i,j-1,k}) \\ 0 & \text{otherwise} \end{cases} \quad \forall i \in n, j \in m, k \in L_{i,j-1} \tag{7}$$

Where α_l is the weight of quantity to the objective, T_c is the weight of capacity c to the objective, N is the available number of capacity whose start time is later than the earliest end time of the previous stage and end time earlier than the due date, and $S_{i,j}(c)$ is the start time of capacity c.

The pheromone trail $\left(\tau_{i,j}^{II}\right)$ is defined in this stage to indicate latest completion time of the production stage. In addition to the pheromone, we introduce $\eta_{i,j}^{II}$ to express the visibility of ant. The possibility to select capacity j after i and the value of $\eta_{i,j}^{II}$ is calculated as follows:

$$P_{i,j}^{II} = \frac{\left(\tau_{i,j}^{II}\right)^{\alpha} \cdot \left(\eta_{i,j}^{II}\right)^{\beta}}{\sum_{l\in\Phi}\left(\tau_{i,l}^{II}\right)^{\alpha} \cdot \left(\eta_{i,l}^{II}\right)^{\beta}}. \tag{8}$$

$$\eta_{i,j}^{II} = 1/End_j. \tag{9}$$

Where End_j is the end time of capacity j.

After all ants finish their paths, we will update the pheromone locally and globally with the similar manner of AS scheme in stage1.

$$\tau_{i,j}^{II} \leftarrow (1 - \rho)\tau_{i,j}^{II} + \rho\Delta\tau_{i,j}^{II,best}. \tag{10}$$

$$\Delta\tau_{i,j}^{II,best} = \begin{cases} 1/OV^{best} & \text{if } arc(i,j) \text{ is used by best ant,} \\ 0 & \text{otherwise.} \end{cases} \tag{11}$$

Where OV^{best} is the objective value of the best vector in stage2, representing the minimum completion time of the stage. It can be calculated by the vector S_2 combined with the lot-sizing technique below.

In order to separate the stage into multiple sub-lots and calculate the completion time of the production stage, we proposed a lot-sizing method. The detailed flow chart of stage 2 with lot-sizing is shown in Fig. 4.

3.4 Local Search Strategy

It is known that ACA usually provides very competitive solutions when integrated with a local search algorithm. Therefore, we include a local search algorithm in our implementation of ACA. After the ant k finishes its route search process, we generate neighbouring solutions for the ant in S_1 and S_2. If the local search generates a better solution at that particular iteration, we use the local search solution at that iteration to update the pheromone. The neighbouring solution for S_1 is generated by rotating a random entry in the vector to the first position while that for S_2 by swapping two randomly generated entries in the vector.

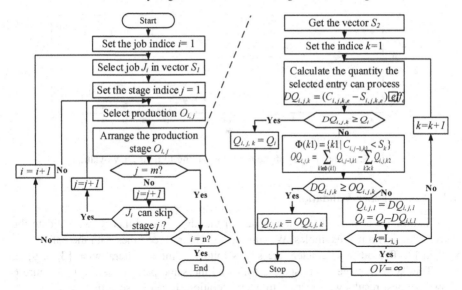

Fig. 4. Flow chart of batch scheduling and lot-sizing

4 Computational Results

To investigate the effectiveness of the proposed two-stage ant colony algorithm with lot-sizing, algorithms are coded in Microsoft Visual Studio 2008 and experiments are executed on Window 7 with a Core2 E8400 CPU and 2 GB RAM.

4.1 Parameters Setting

The factors considered in this experiment along with four different levels, respectively are as follows: α: (1, 2, 3, 4), β: (2, 3, 4, 5) and ρ: (0.1, 0.2, 0.3, 0.4); where ρ is the pheromone evaporation. To reduce the number of runs but reach sound conclusions, uniform experiment are utilized, which has been shown to be an effective design. Table 1 shows the final combination parameters of the factors. We denote the 16 groups of parameters in this table to be Com1, Com2,..., Com16 respectively. The value $DEV = \frac{x-min}{max-min}$ is defined to weigh the results, where x is the current value, *min* is the known optimal value and *max* is the known worst value. The results with lower DEV are better. The results are shown in Fig. 5. It can be clearly seen the Com 11 makes the best performance. In order to get the most optimal result, the parameters in Com 11 are adopted.

Table 1. Design of uniform experiment

Com	1	2	3	4	5	6	7	8	9	10	11	12	13	14	15	16
α	1	2	3	4	1	2	3	4	1	2	3	4	1	2	3	4
β	2	4	3	5	5	3	4	2	3	5	2	4	4	2	5	3
ρ	.3	.1	.2	.4	.2	.4	.3	.1	.1	.3	.4	.2	.4	.2	.1	.3

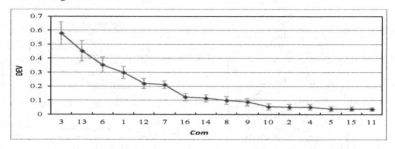

Fig. 5. Sorted results of the Coms according to their DEVs value

4.2 Convergence Validation

As it is difficult to prove the convergence of the algorithm in theory, we validate the convergence with real examples. We run the algorithm three times with the parameters in Com11. The other parameters are set as follows: Ant = 5, Iteration = {3, 6, 9,..., 99}. The ACA in stage 1 and stage 2 followed the same parameters setting. Figure 6 shows the best results with respect to every iteration. It can be seen that the algorithm converges to an optimal value when the iteration approaches 66.

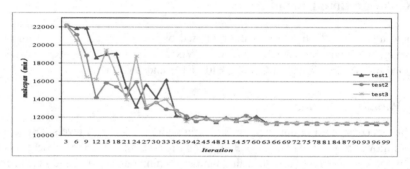

Fig. 6. Verify the convergence of the algorithm

4.3 Comparisons with Other Heuristics

As mentioned above, few works have dealt with hybrid flow shop scheduling problem with lot sizing and calendar constraints. For lack of benchmark instances and comparison algorithms, we attempt to prove the priority of ACA and lot-sizing respectively. We compare the TSACAWLS to two-stage Simulated Annealing with lot-sizing (TSSAWLS) in order to validate the superiority of the ACA algorithm and make a comparison with two-stage ant colony algorithm (TSACA) to verify the effectiveness of the lot-sizing technique.

Two metrics are used to compare the three meta-heuristic algorithms; namely: stability and speed to get a near-optimal solution. The stability of one algorithm can be calculated by: δ = avg $-$ min. The second metric is obtained by the average of computation time (CPU time) to get a near-optimal solution.

Figure 7 shows the stability of the meta-heuristic algorithms. It can be seen that TSACAWLS and TSACA outperforms TSSAWLS for all problem sizes and TSACA performs better than TSACAWLS when the number of jobs excess 11. Figure 8 depicts the average computational time of all algorithms. All algorithms require less time than 45000 ms which is acceptable in reality. TSACA and TSACAWLS require less time to get a near-optimal solution than TSSAWLS, and TSACA consumes less time than TSACAWLS. Though TSACA performs better than TSACAWLS in stability and computational time, their differences are not significant.

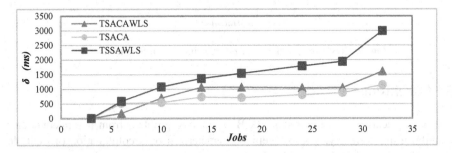

Fig. 7. Stability of all algorithms

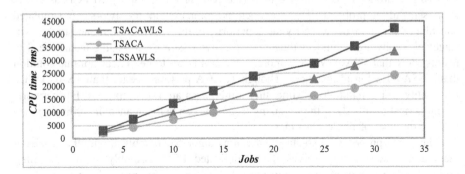

Fig. 8. Computational time for all algorithms

To further verify that the lot-sizing can enhance the utilization and balance the load of bottle machines, we calculate the utilization (η) of every machine and record the results in Fig. 9. It is clear that the algorithm considering lot-sizing (TSSAWLS and TSACAWLS) performs better in improving the utilization and balancing the load of bottle machines.

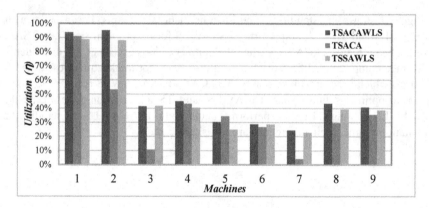

Fig. 9. Result of the lines utilization using four different methods

5   Conclusions

This study deals with a multi-stage PCB scheduling problem from a semiconductor manufacturing company. The problem is characterized by a combination of multiple features such as lot sizing, calendar constraints, sequence-dependent setup times, unrelated parallel machines and stage skipping. A two-stage ant colony algorithm with lot-sizing is proposed to minimize the makespan for this complicated PCB assembly shop scheduling problem. The approach is compared to the two-stage simulated annealing with lot-sizing to verify the superiority of its ACA algorithm, and to the two-stage ant colony algorithm to validate the effectiveness of the lot-sizing technique. The results show that TSACAWLS is more stable and faster to get a near-optimal solution than TSSAWLS for all instances. Though TSACA performs better than TSACAWLS in stability and computational time, their differences are not significant. Furthermore, the numerical results show the lot-sizing technique can help enhance the utilization and balance the load of bottle machines.

This paper proposes a two-stage ant colony algorithm combined with the lot-sizing method and successfully solves the complicated PCB assembly shop scheduling problem by decomposing them into two sub-problems. This research on this subject makes an important contribution to the overall knowledge in the field of PCB assembly shop scheduling, and the development of the multi-stage ACA approach also expands the application scope of ant colony optimization in the complex production scheduling field. Although the research has dealt with several academically challenging issues, further work is still needed. The first extension is that the multiple objectives especially related with the due date, such as total tardiness, needs to be considered. Furthermore, due to the influence of dynamic interrupts in actual production process, real-time scheduling or rescheduling based on the up-to-date shop floor information is one of our research directions in future.

References

1. Ji, P., Sze, M.T., Lee, W.B.: A genetic algorithm of determining cycle time for printed circuit board assembly lines. Eur. J. Oper. Res. **128**, 175–184 (2001)
2. Alkaya, A.F., Duman, E.: Combining and solving sequence dependent traveling salesman and quadratic assignment problems in PCB assembly. Discrete Appl. Math. **192**, 2–16 (2015)
3. Tóth, A., Knuutila, T., Nevalainen, O.S.: Machine configuration and workload balancing of modular placement machines in multi-product PCB assembly. Int. J. Comput. Integr. Manuf. **31**(9), 815–830 (2018)
4. Truscott, W.G.: Production scheduling with capacity-constrained transportation activities. J. Oper. Manag. **6**(3–4), 333–348 (1986)
5. Huang, R.H., Yu, T.H.: An effective ant colony optimization algorithm for multi-objective job-shop scheduling with equal-size lot-splitting. Appl. Soft Comput. **57**, 642–656 (2017)
6. Wang, S., Kurz, M., Mason, S.J., et al.: Two-stage hybrid flow shop batching and lot streaming with variable sublots and sequence-dependent setups. Int. J. Prod. Res., 1–15 (2019)
7. Allaoui, H., Artiba, A.: Scheduling two-stage hybrid flow shop with availability constraints. Comput. Oper. Res. **33**(5), 1399–1429 (2006)
8. Yaurima, V., Burtseva, L., Tchernykh, A.: Hybrid flowshop with unrelated machines, sequence-dependent setup time, availability constraints and limited buffers. Comput. Ind. Eng. **56**(4), 1452–1463 (2009)
9. Gholami, M., Zandieh, M., Alem-Tabriz, A.: Scheduling hybrid flow shop with sequence-dependent setup times and machines with random breakdowns. Int. J. Adv. Manuf. Technol. **42**(1–2), 189–201 (2009)
10. Seidgar, H., Rad, S.T., Shafaei, R.: Scheduling of assembly flow shop problem and machines with random breakdowns. Int. J. Oper. Res. **29**(2), 273–293 (2017)
11. Han, Y., Gong, D., Jin, Y., et al.: Evolutionary multiobjective blocking lot-streaming flow shop scheduling with machine breakdowns. IEEE Trans. Cybern. **99**, 1–14 (2017)
12. Dorigo, M.: Optimization, learning and natural algorithms. Ph.D. Thesis, Politecnico di Milano (1992)
13. Arnaout, J.P., Rabadi, G., Musa, R.: A two-stage ant colony optimization algorithm to minimize the makespan on unrelated parallel machines with sequence-dependent setup times. J. Intell. Manuf. **21**(6), 693–701 (2010)

Variable Speed Robot Navigation by an ACO Approach

Tingjun Lei[1], Chaomin Luo[1(✉)], Gene Eu Jan[2], and Kevin Fung[3]

[1] Department of Electrical and Computer Engineering,
Mississippi State University, Mississippi State, MS 39762, USA
Chaomin.Luo@ece.msstate.edu
[2] Graduate Institute of Animation and Film Art,
Tainan National University of the Arts, Tainan, Taiwan
[3] Department of Industrial Engineering and Engineering Management,
National Tsing Hua University, Hsinchu, Taiwan

Abstract. A variable-speed-based navigation and map building method of an autonomous mobile robot is developed in this paper in cooperation with an ant colony optimization algorithm (ACO). In real-world applications, an autonomous mobile robot is expected to operate at variable speed. It should slow down in vicinity of obstacles, whereas moving at high speed in open areas. A LIDAR-based local navigator algorithm integrated with a variable speed module is implemented for local navigation and obstacle avoidance. A variable speed navigation paradigm is developed in integration with the ACO algorithm to dynamically adapt its speed to the environment scenarios. In addition to the variable speed ACO based navigation, grid-based map representations are imposed for real-time autonomous robot navigation. Simulation and comparison studies demonstrate effectiveness of the proposed real-time variable-speed-based ACO approach of an autonomous mobile robot.

Keywords: Variable speed navigation · Ant colony optimization (ACO) ·
Map building · LIDAR-based local navigator

1 Introduction

Ant colony optimization algorithm (ACO) is a probabilistic technique for solving computational problems to finding suitable routes through graphs, which has successfully applications to robot navigation [1]. Real-time collision-free navigation and map building of an autonomous mobile robot is one of the most crucial issues in robotics. Populated with a variety of obstacles in an environment, mission of navigation and map building is involved in searching a suitable collision-free trajectory of an autonomous robot to move from a starting point to a final target while the robot constructs a map.

There have been many models proposed for autonomous robot navigation and mapping such as learning-based method [2], fuzzy logic [3], neural networks [4–6], tree-based model [7], brain storm optimization method [8, 9], bacterial foraging

© Springer Nature Switzerland AG 2019
Y. Tan et al. (Eds.): ICSI 2019, LNCS 11655, pp. 232–242, 2019.
https://doi.org/10.1007/978-3-030-26369-0_22

optimization algorithm [10], graph-based method [11], particle swarm optimization method [10, 12], ant colony optimization [13, 14], genetic algorithms [15], etc.

Pfeiffer *et al.* developed a model that combines expert demonstrations, imitation learning (IL) and deep reinforcement learning (RL) for robot navigation, in which a deep reinforcement learning of the learned navigation policy is used in real-world environments [2]. Kayacan *et al.* proposed a type-2 fuzzy logic model for autonomous navigation of an agricultural robot that involves the control of dynamic subsystems [3]. Chen *et al.* [4] proposed a neural network based adaptive dynamic control to solve the trajectory tracking issues, in which a leader–follower relation-invariable persistent formation control is imposed, and the global leader navigates the mission trajectory. Yang and Luo [5] developed a real-time autonomous robot coverage navigation model with obstacle avoidance in a non-stationary environment through a bio-inspired neural network method. It is computationally efficient [5]. Luo *et al.* extended the bio-inspired neural network into multi-robot navigation [6]. Sanz *et al.* [7] proposed an expert-guided kinodynamic (EGK) Rapidly-Exploring Random Trees (RRT) path planner.

Recently, plenty of evolutionary computation approaches have been explored to resolve the robot motion planning and navigation issues. As an example, Tuba *et al.* [8] applied brain storm optimization (BSO) method to the robot motion planning, from which the improved BSO model is enforced to enhance the accuracy and validity of the motion planning. BSO algorithm decrements computational time through local search procedure, where each new candidate solution trends to the local best position [9]. Roy *et al.* [10] used bacterial foraging optimization (BFO) algorithm to develop a robot path planner model with obstacle avoidance. A graph-based method that is a sort of enhanced Voronoi Diagram was utilized for robot motion planning in association with Vector Field Histogram (VFH) algorithm based on the LIDAR sensor information to locally guide the vehicle [11]. Particle swarm optimization method is applicable for the robot motion planning issue [12]. Ant colony optimization (ACO) algorithms have been studied to mimic the behavior of ants to provide heuristic solutions for optimization problems [13, 14]. Ma *et al.* [13] presented a nature-inspired ant colony optimization algorithm to search the optimal trajectory, in which the ACO model is imposed to aggregate the collision risk, length, and energy consumption, into the objective function as well as incorporate the steering window constraint [14].

Some researchers integrated two or three algorithms to performance of algorithms for robot motion planning. For instance, Fu *et al.* [12] developed a hybrid method, denoted as DEQPSO, which combines the differential evolution (DE) with quantum-behaved particle swarm optimization (QPSO) for the unmanned aerial vehicle (UAV) navigation, to further enhance the performance of both algorithms. Chen *et al.* [15] developed a hybrid algorithm that incorporates genetic algorithms and ant colony optimization. Luo and Yang proposed a biologically inspired neural network model for motion planning that integrates a neural network model and a heuristic algorithm under unknown environments [18, 21].

However, approaches aforementioned have not taken the robot speed into account in the motion planning and mapping. In real-world applications, an autonomous mobile robot is presumed to operate at variable speed. It should slow down in vicinity of obstacles, whereas moving at high speed in free areas. In this paper, a variable speed navigation and map building method of an autonomous mobile robot is developed in cooperation with an ACO algorithm (ACO). A LIDAR-based local navigator algorithm is implemented for local navigation and obstacle avoidance. Grid-based map representations are imposed for real-time autonomous robot navigation [16].

2   ACO Algorithms for Robot Path Planning

Ants in terms of the ACO are intelligent agents in the robot navigation and mapping, which walk from one waypoint to another navigated by pheromone trails through an a *priori* available heuristic information. In this paper, ant colony optimization is applied for the robot navigation and mapping. The agent (ant) is initially placed in a waypoint. Ant pheromone strength, $\tau_{ij}(t)$, a numerical information, defined with each arc (i,j) is updated in the ACO algorithm, in which t is the iteration counter. At each iteration phase, a probabilistic action select rule is imposed to an agent, or, a mobile robot, k. The probability of a robot k, currently at waypoint i, which traverses to waypoint j at the t th iteration of the algorithm, is achieved as follows in Eq. (1).

$$p_{ij}^k(t) = \frac{[\tau_{ij}(t)]^\alpha \times [\vartheta_{ij}]^\beta}{\sum_{l \in \aleph_i^k} [\tau_{il}(t)]^\alpha \times [\vartheta_{il}]^\beta} \quad \text{if } j \in \aleph_i^k \tag{1}$$

where $\aleph_i^k$ is the feasible adjacent waypoint of the robot k, the set of cities which the robot k has not visited yet. Parameters α and β determine the relative influence of the pheromone trail and the heuristic information. The $\vartheta_{ij} = 1/d_{ij}$ is an a *priori* available heuristic value, and d_{ij} is the distance between two waypoints. Parameter α represents importance factor of the pheromone, which matches a classical stochastic greedy algorithm. Parameter β is an importance factor of the heuristics function. If the larger parameter β becomes, the more likely it is that the robot moves to the closest waypoint driven by the heuristic function. If a parameter ρ is defined as the pheromone trail evaporation, $0 < \rho < 1$ to prevent the pheromone trails from accumulating unlimitedly; it allows the ACO algorithm to neglect unreasonably bad decisions previously made.

At each iteration step, $\Delta\tau_{ij}^k(t)$, the amount of pheromone robot k places on the arcs it has visited is dynamically updated by decreasing the pheromone strength on all arcs by

```
Procedure ACO algorithm for Robot Navigation
        Set parameters, initialize pheromone trail
    while (termination condition not met) do
        ConstructSolutions
        ApplyLocalSearch
        UpdateTrails
    end
    end ACO algorithm for Robot Navigation
```

Fig. 1. ACO algorithm for robot path planning

a constant factor before enabling each robot to supplement pheromone on the arcs. The pheromone strength τ_{ij} is dynamically updated as Eq. (2).

$$\begin{cases} \tau_{ij}(t+1) = (1-\rho) \cdot \tau_{ij}(t) + \Delta\tau_{ij} \\ \Delta\tau_{ij} = \sum_{k=1}^{n} \Delta\tau_{ij}^{k} \end{cases}, \quad 0 < \rho < 1 \qquad (2)$$

The amount of pheromone $\Delta\tau_{ij}^{k}(t)$, is defined as three modes [13, 14]:

(1) Ant cycle system mode:

$$\Delta\tau_{ij}^{k}(t) = \begin{cases} \frac{Q}{L^{k}(t)} & \text{if arc } (i,j) \text{ is used by robot } k \\ 0 & \text{otherwise} \end{cases}$$

(2) Ant quantity system mode:

$$\Delta\tau_{ij}^{k}(t) = \begin{cases} \frac{Q}{d_{ij}(t)} & \text{if arc } (i,j) \text{ is used by robot } k \\ 0 & \text{otherwise} \end{cases}$$

(3) Ant density system mode:

$$\Delta\tau_{ij}^{k}(t) = \begin{cases} Q & \text{if arc } (i,j) \text{ is used by robot } k \\ 0 & \text{otherwise} \end{cases}$$

$L^{k}(t)$ is the length of the kth robot's tour. $d_{ij}(t)$ is the distance between waypoints i and j. Here Q is constant representing the total amount of the pheromone. The ACO algorithm for motion planning is summarized as Fig. 1 [13, 14].

3   Variable Speed Navigation and Map Building

Concurrent map building and navigation are the essence of successful robot navigation under unknown environments. Map building is a fundamental task in order to achieve high levels of autonomy and robustness in robot navigation that makes it possible for autonomous robots to make decision in positioning with obstacle avoidance. Therefore, in terms of robotics navigation, 2D grid-based map filled with equally-sized cells, marked as either occupied or free, is built as a mobile robot walks in an unknown environment [19].

In our navigation system, it is decomposed of two layers, one is an ACO global path planner, and the other is a histogram-based local navigator. Efficiency and flexibility motivate ACO to be adapted to motion planning and map building of an autonomous robot. The local navigation aims to create velocity commands for the autonomous mobile robot to move towards a target. The inclusion of a sequence of markers in the motion planning, which decomposes the global route generated by the ACO global planner into a sequence of segments, makes the model especially efficient for the workspace densely populated by obstacles. A histogram-based Vector Field Histogram (VFH) approach for robot navigation was developed by Ulrich and

Borenstein [17]. VFH is utilized in this paper as our LIDAR-based local navigator. The polar histogram of obstacles in workspace with VFH is shown in Fig. 2.

Variable speed robot navigation aims to move the robot at a variable speed. In our navigation system, the histogram-based local navigator senses the obstacles through the on-board 270° LIDAR with a radius of 2.5 shown in Fig. 3. In most circumstances, a maneuverable autonomous mobile robot may be considered as a point robot in comparison with the size of the robot and its maneuvering possibilities to the size of the free workspace. The robot moves in the open areas, at a fast speed in our model whereas it moves slowly in the vicinity of obstacles. Once an obstacle area is sensed by the 270° LIDAR such as a segment of red boundary of the obstacle, the robot will decrease its speed in the vicinity of obstacles (see Fig. 3). The variable speed module has been integrated into the VFH local navigation algorithm. While the robot approaches vicinity of obstacles, the robot movement is represented by serried circles in Fig. 3. The robot moving in the open areas are illustrated by sparse circles in Fig. 3.

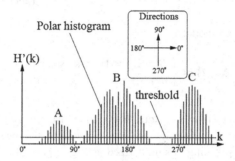

Fig. 2. Polar histogram of obstacles in workspace with VFH method (redrawn from [17])

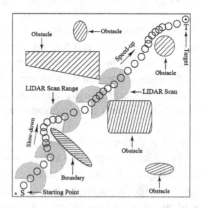

Fig. 3. Illustration of variable speed robot navigation (Color figure online)

4   Simulation and Comparison Studies

Simulation and comparison studies are carried out to validate the effectiveness and efficiency of proposed real-time variable-speed-based ACO autonomous robot navigation and mapping, in this section.

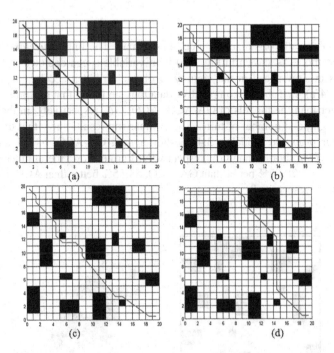

Fig. 4. Illustration of robot navigation with various models. (a) the proposed model; (b) GA-ACO model; (c) ACO model; (d) GA model.

4.1   Comparison of the Proposed Variable Speed Model with GA-ACO Algorithm

The proposed variable-speed-based ACO algorithm associated with VFH local navigation is used to compare with GA, ACO and GA-ACO models, respectively. Recall that Chen *et al.* [15] proposed a hybrid model combining GA and ACO approaches to resolve robot motion planning issue. However, their model has not carried out the local navigation that is necessary for the autonomous robot navigation systems. A comparison study is described in this section to evaluate the efficiency of the proposed model. The proposed model compares with others in terms of the minimum trajectory length, and number of turns [15].

The trajectories of robot motion planning are illustrated about the proposed model, GA-ACO, ACO and GA, respectively, in Fig. 4. The workspace has a size of 20 × 20,

Table 1. Comparison of path length and turns (Fig. 11 in [15])

Models	Minimum length	Number of turns
Proposed model	28.042	5
GA-ACO	29.038	7
ACO	29.524	11
GA	32.147	6

which is topologically organized as a cell-based map. The final *trajectory* planned by our proposed model is shown in Fig. 4(a) with variable speed depicted in Fig. 3. The robot moves at slow speed in the vicinity of obstacles, but it accelerates in the open areas in Fig. 4(a). In Table 1, comparative data may be found that our proposed model is much better than the models of GA-ACO, ACO, GA, respectively, in the minimum trajectory length, and number of turns. The comparison results show that the trajectory length by our proposed model is 3.43% shorter than GA-ACO, 5.02% shorter than ACO, and 12.77% shorter than GA, respectively. Furthermore, the number of turns of proposed model is 28.57% better than GA-ACO, 54.55% better than ACO, and 16.67% better than GA, respectively.

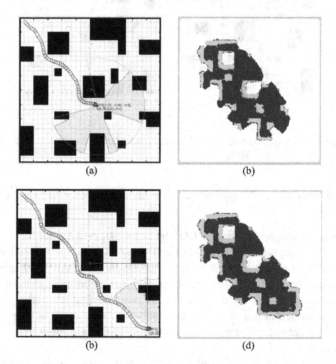

(a)

(b)

(b)

(d)

Fig. 5. Illustration of robot navigation and mapping in various stages by the improved ACO model (a) trajectory generated in the middle stage; (b) map built in the middle stage; (c) trajectory generated at the end; (d) map built at the end. (Color figure online)

The robot is able to traverse from the initial point to plan a reasonable collision-free route to reach the final designation. The robot moves at the variable speed while it constructs the map with 270° LIDAR. The trajectory generated by the robot is shown in Fig. 5(a) whereas the map built is illustrated in Fig. 5(b) at the middle of the travel of the robot. In this simulation, the robot is guided in an unknown environment populated with obstacles depicted in Fig. 5(c), which shows that the robot traverses from starting point to the final designation with successful obstacle avoidance. The built map while the robot moves in the unknown environment with 270° LIDAR scan is illustrated in Fig. 5(d). The yellow portions are detected obstacles in Fig. 5(b) and (d).

4.2 Comparison of the Variable Speed ACO with Others

The proposed model is then applied to a test scenario with populated obstacles in comparison of the test scenario identical as Fig. 6 of [20] shown in Fig. 6(a) in this context. The workspace has a size of 20×20, which is topologically organized as a cell-based map. The parameters of our improved ACO algorithm are selected as follows: $\alpha = 1$; $\rho = 0.3$ and $\beta = 5$. Initially, the starting point is located at S (13, 19) whereas the robot moves toward the goal at T (7, 1). The trajectory planned when using our proposed ACO model is illustrated in Fig. 6(b). The generated trajectory length, numbers of turns, and steps to complete by the robot are listed in Table 2 in comparison with Zhang's model [20].

Table 2. Comparison of path length, turns and steps (Fig. 6 in [20])

Models	Minimum length	Turns	Steps
Proposed model	22.07	3	20
Zheng's model [20]	27.49	8	25

The shorter and safer trajectory is generated by our ACO model illustrated in Fig. 6(b). The trajectory length produced by our ACO model is 19.7% shorter than the one by Zhang's model summarized in Table 2. It is observed that our model outperforms over theirs in terms of the trajectory length, and number of steps and turns. The number of turns of our model is 62.5% better than theirs. The resulting trajectory length, number of turns and steps are illustrated in Fig. 6(c). Consequently, our proposed method, in total, with the improved ACO algorithm has better performance. While the robot approaches vicinity of obstacles, the robot moves slowly. The robot moves in the open areas at high speed.

With VFH-based local navigator, the built map from the initial position S (13, 19) and the final trajectory planned, and final map built exactly when the robot reaches the final target are illustrated in Fig. 6(d). The white fields indicate detected obstacles, but the black portion of image represents explored zones by the 270° LIDAR scans.

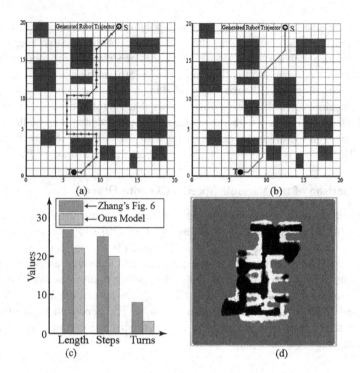

Fig.6. Comparison studies with Zhang's model. (a) planned trajectory by Zhang's model (redrawn from [20]); (b) planned trajectory by our model for the scenario of (c); comparison of path length steps and turns; (d) Illustration of mapping and navigation by the proposed scheme.

5 Conclusion

An efficient variable-speed-based ACO algorithm has been developed for real-time robot navigation and map building in this paper. A LIDAR-based local navigator algorithm has been implemented for local navigation and obstacle avoidance. A variable-speed navigation paradigm has been presented in integration with the ACO algorithm to dynamically adapt its speed to the environment scenarios. In addition to the variable speed ACO based navigation, grid-based map representations are imposed for real-time autonomous robot navigation. Simulation and comparison studies have demonstrated effectiveness of the proposed real-time variable speed ACO approach of an autonomous mobile robot.

References

1. Wang, L., Luo, C.: A hybrid genetic Tabu search algorithm for mobile robot to solve AS/RS path planning. Int. J. Robot. Autom. **33**(2), 161–168 (2018). https://doi.org/10.2316/journal. 206.2018.2.206-5102. ISSN: 0826-8185
2. Pfeiffer, M., et al.: Reinforced imitation: sample efficient deep reinforcement learning for mapless navigation by leveraging prior demonstrations. IEEE Robot. Autom. Lett. **3**(4), 4423–4430 (2018). https://doi.org/10.1109/lra.2018.2869644

3. Kayacan, E., Kayacan, E., Ramon, H., Kaynak, O., Saeys, W.: Towards agrbots: trajectory control of an autonomous tractor using type-2 fuzzy logic controllers. IEEE/ASME Trans. Mech. **20**(1), 287–298 (2015)
4. Chen, C.L.P., Yu, D., Liu, L.: Automatic leader-follower persistent formation control for autonomous surface vehicles. IEEE Access **7**, 12146–12155 (2019)
5. Yang, S.X., Luo, C.: A neural network approach to complete coverage path planning. IEEE Trans. Syst. Man Cybern. Part B **34**(1), 718–725 (2004)
6. Luo, C., Yang, S.X., Li, X., Meng, M.Q.H.: Neural dynamics driven complete area coverage navigation through cooperation of multiple mobile robots. IEEE Trans. Ind. Electron. **64**(1), 750–760 (2017)
7. Sanz, J.M., Hernani, M., Zaragoza, G., Brunete, A.: Expert-guided kinodynamic RRT path planner for non-holonomic robots. In: 2018 IEEE/RSJ International Conference on Intelligent Robots and Systems (IEEE-IROS), Madrid, pp. 6540–6545 (2018)
8. Tuba, E., Strumberger, I., Zivkovic, D., Bacanin, N., Tuba, M.: Mobile robot path planning by improved brain storm optimization algorithm. In: 2018 IEEE Congress on Evolutionary Computation (IEEE-CEC), Rio de Janeiro, pp. 1–8 (2018)
9. Cheng, S., Shi, Y., Qin, Q., Ting, T.O., Bai, R.: Maintaining population diversity in brain storm optimization algorithm. In: 2014 IEEE Congress on Evolutionary Computation (IEEE-CEC 2014), Beijing, China, pp 3230–3237 (2014)
10. Roy, D., Maitra, M., Bhattacharya, S.: Study of formation control and obstacle avoidance of swarm robots using evolutionary algorithms. In: 2016 IEEE International Conference on Systems, Man, and Cybernetics (IEEE-SMC), Budapest, pp. 3154–3159 (2016)
11. Luo, C., Krishnan, M., Paulik, M., Cui, B., Zhang, X.: A novel LIDAR-driven two-level approach for real-time unmanned ground vehicle navigation and map building. In: SPIE Conference on Intelligent Robots and Computer Vision: Algorithms and Techniques, February 2014, vol. 9025, pp. 902503-1–902503-11 (2014)
12. Fu, Y., Ding, M., Zhou, C., Hu, H.: Route planning for unmanned aerial vehicle (UAV) on the sea using hybrid differential evolution and quantum-behaved particle swarm optimization. IEEE Trans. Syst. Man Cybern. Syst. **43**(6), 1451–1465 (2013). https://doi.org/10.1109/tsmc.2013.2248146
13. Ma, Y., Gong, Y., Xiao, C., Gao, Y., Zhang, J.: Path planning for autonomous underwater vehicles: an ant colony algorithm incorporating alarm pheromone. IEEE Trans. Veh. Technol. **68**(1), 141–154 (2019)
14. Wang, L., Luo, C., Li, M., Cai, J.: Trajectory planning of an autonomous mobile robot by evolving an ant colony system. Int. J. Robot. Autom. **32**(4), 406–413 (2017). https://doi.org/10.2316/journal.206.2017.4.206-4917
15. Chen, J., Xie, S., Li, H., Luo, J., Feng, K.: Robot path planning based on adaptive integrating of genetic and ant colony algorithm. Int. J. Innov. Comput. Inf. Control **11**(3), 833–850 (2015)
16. Luo, C., Jan, G.E., Zhang, J., Shen, F.: Boundary aware navigation and mapping for a mobile automaton. In: IEEE International Conference on Information and Automation, Ningbo, China, 31 July 2016–4 August 2016, pp. 561–566 (2016)
17. Ulrich, I., Borenstein, J.: VFH+: reliable obstacle avoidance for fast mobile robots. In: IEEE International Conference on Robotics and Automation, Leuven, Belgium, 16–21 May 1998, pp. 1572–1577 (1998)
18. Luo, C., Yang, S.X.: A bioinspired neural network for real-time concurrent map building and complete coverage robot navigation in unknown environments. IEEE Trans. Neural Netw. **19**(7), 1279–1298 (2008)

19. Liu, L., Luo, C., Shen, F.: Multi-agent formation control with target tracking and navigation. In: IEEE International Conference on Information and Automation (IEEE ICIA2017), Macau SAR, China, 18–20 July 2017, pp. 98–103 (2017)
20. Zhang, Y., Cao, Y., Han, Z.: Path planning of vehicle based on improved ant colony algorithm. In: 2012 International Conference on Modelling, Identification and Control, 24–26 June 2012, pp. 797–801 (2012)
21. Luo, C., Yang, S.X., Krishnan, M., Paulik, M.: An effective vector-driven biologically motivated neural network algorithm to real-time autonomous robot navigation. In: IEEE International Conference on Robotics and Automation, pp. 4094–4099 (2014)

Solving Scheduling Problems in PCB Assembly and Its Optimization Using ACO

Vijay Pandey[1], Akshaye Malhotra[1], Rajeev Kant[1],
and Sudip Kumar Sahana[2]([✉]) [ID]

[1] Department of Mechanical Engineering, Birsa Institute of Technology, Sindri,
Dhanbad, Jharkhand, India
vpandeybit@rediffmail.com, malhotra.akshaye@gmail.com,
kant.rajeev@gmail.com
[2] Department of Computer Science and Engineering,
Birla Institute of Technology, Mesra, Ranchi, Jharkhand, India
sudipsahana@bitmesra.ac.in

Abstract. The focus of this paper is to schedule printed circuit board (PCB) assembly process while minimizing the mean flow time as well as work-in-process inventories. Here, problem for scheduling different types of PCBs on a single sequential pick-and-place automatic machine is considered in which the total number of different components required to process each type of PCBs exceeds the capacity of the feeder rack. The above objective is achieved through minimizing the number of feeder rack changes or component switches and sequential placement of components. A component switch refers to removal of one type of component from the feeder rack and a different type of component is placed on it, and may occur when changing to next type of PCB. In order to reduce component switches, group technology is applied following the counts of new components needed to add for successive group formation. Mathematical models are developed for PCB grouping and PCB group sequencing problem and integrated as multi-functional model to determine the optimal sequence of component placements. Ant colony optimization (ACO) technique is used to solve the proposed model and the results are compared with the different component grouping methods available in the literature.

Keywords: Scheduling · Printed circuit board · Pick-and-place · Grouping · Group sequencing · Ant colony optimization

1 Introduction

Scheduling can be defined as "prescribing when and where each operation necessary to manufacture the product is to be performed". The main aim of scheduling is to plan the sequence of work so that production can be systematically arranged towards the end of completion of all the products by due date. It is one of the vital components of production planning system that closely works with the material requirement planning and shop floor to optimize the resource utilization throughout the production.

A scheduling strategy involves both job and resource related parameters [1], which sets multi criterion objectives for a scheduling problem; job related – meeting the due

© Springer Nature Switzerland AG 2019
Y. Tan et al. (Eds.): ICSI 2019, LNCS 11655, pp. 243–253, 2019.
https://doi.org/10.1007/978-3-030-26369-0_23

dates and minimizing the completion time, resource related – maximizing resource utilization and minimizing work in process. Although these objectives are conflicting in nature, the solutions of multi objective problems provide deeper insights to the decision maker than those of single-objective problems. In the present work, multi-objective scheduling problem in PCB assembly process is considered to minimize the mean flow time as well as work-in-process inventories.

The paper is structured as follows: Sect. 2 describes the PCB assembly process and the working of an automated pick and place machine is illustrated. Section 3 explores the literature pertaining to the development of the related work done on scheduling and grouping of PCBs. Section 4 introduces ACO and is devoted to the development of the proposed approach. In Sect. 5, the proposed methodology is validated using a test problem from the available literature and the results are compared with existing methodologies in Sect. 6. Finally, the Sect. 7 concludes the present work.

1.1 PCB Assembly

PCB assembly is a discrete manufacturing process in which a number of electronic components are mounted on laminated boards. Assembly of printed circuit boards mainly consists of: (i) Printing of circuit on a clad board (laminated copper board), (ii) Placing electronic component on board, and (iii) Soldering of component (tin-lead allow). In PCB assembly line, the entire operations are performed to manufacture a PCB. Placing the components on a board involves several movements. In the present study, a sequential automatic placement machine, such as the pick-and-place (PAP) machine that performs the pick-up and placement operations one-by-one. The configuration of the PAP machine used in this work consists of three components: a table to which the PCB is attached, a feeder rack that holds components, and a head that picks components from the feeder and places them on the PCB. A complete board cycle is assumed in which the head starts from a given home position, moves between feeders (on the machine) and placement locations (on the PCB) until all the components have been mounted. The head returns to the home position once all the components required for a board have been placed on the board.

The machine has a robotic arm, which has one or more heads. Heads pick up components from the reels on the feeder racks and place them on the PCB, by means of using an appropriate tool. Each component type can be picked up with a subset of tools, that is, one head with a specific tool can only pick up components from a limited set of component types. Tools are changed in the automatic tool changer (ATC) when the next component cannot be picked up with the current tool.

2 Literature Review

A memetic algorithm was developed combining Genetic Algorithm (GA) and local search procedure to solve the combinatorial problem. Ho and Ji [2] considered distance travelled by the placement head for picking and placing the components and developed a hybrid GA for determining the optimal sequence of component placements and assignment of component types to feeder racks simultaneously for a sequential PAP placement mechanism. In their another work, Ho and Ji [3] formulated several mathematical models for determining the optimal sequence of component placements and assignment of component types to feeders simultaneously and employed genetic algorithm to solve the models while minimizing the total distance traveled by the placement head. Another hybrid GA was developed by Ho et al. [4] combining two improved heuristics, the nearest neighbour heuristic and iterated swap procedure, to minimize the total assembly time. In a recent study, Noroozi and Mokhtari [5] presented a GA based intelligent optimization techniques incorporated with Monte Carlo simulation to minimize the make span under uncertain processing times considering the feeders capacity. Though, Hardas et al. [6] presented a custom application of GA to demonstrate the effectiveness of GA for solving the component placement sequencing problem, several other meta-heuristic based approaches have been demonstrated by researchers. Chen and Lin [7] showed that the performance of particle swarm optimization (PSO) is not worse than the performance of GA in terms of the distance traveled by the placement head. Zeng and Guo [8] proposed a two-stage approach for optimizing PCB assembly on the sequential pick-and-place machine wherein the first stage, the distance score with weights selection (DSWS) method was used to select a suited set of slots to load feeders then a novel swarm intelligence approach, called the elimination with decay-based swarm intelligence approach (EDSIA) was employed for assignment of feeders to the selected slots and the placement sequence of the components. Another swarm based intelligent technique Cuckoo search37 was proposed for PCB drill path optimization by Wei Chen in 2014.

A survey carried by Crama et al. [9] revealed that many researchers [10] introduced group technology (GT) to the sequencing problem to minimize the setup times for different PCBs and so to minimize make span

In the present work, the PCB grouping is done first based on the similar component requirements followed by PCB group sequencing to reduce the total number of feeder reconfiguration. Although various intelligent computational techniques such as different heuristics and meta-heuristics (GA, PSO, Cuckoo Search) were adopted by researchers in quest to better results, the authors in the present work have investigated another efficient computational technique ACO for PCB scheduling problem.

3 Ant Colony Optimization

Ant colony optimization is a population based meta-heuristic that is inspired by the collective behavior of ants for finding the shortest path between the ant colony and the food [11].

Informally, an ACO algorithm can be imagined as the interplay of three procedures: (i) Construct ants solutions, (ii) Update pheromones, and (iii) Daemon actions.

Construct ants solutions manages a colony of ants that concurrently and asynchronously visit adjacent states of the considered problem by moving through neighbour nodes of the problem. *Update pheromones* is the process by which the pheromone trails are modified. The trails value can either increase, as ants deposit pheromone on the components or connections they use, or decrease, due to pheromone evaporation.

Daemon actions is the final procedure used to implement centralized actions which cannot be performed by single ants. The success of ACO in different large-scale application areas [12–14] motivated us for selecting ACO as solution strategy.

3.1 Assumption

The following assumptions were implied prior to the mathematical model formulation:

(i)   Number of slots in the feeder rack is known.
(ii)   Each reel carries only one component type.
(iii)   Only one slot in the feeder rack is occupied by the reel carrying a component type.
(iv)   The total number of different component types required for processing a group of PCBs is less than the feeder rack capacity for atleast one group to initialize grouping.

The Mathematical Model for PCB Grouping

This problem provides a set of groups 'G' of PCB types in such a way that the number of resulting groups $|G|$ is minimized without exceeding the number of component types 'S' that a machine can accommodate.

Notation

Types of PCBs to be processed = N
Types of components required for processing 'N' PCBs = $M \geq N$
Number of components in $PCB_i = M_i \leq M$

Decision Variable

$a_{ki} =$ 1, if component type k is used in PCB type i
    0, otherwise
$p_{ij} =$ 1, if PCB type i is assigned to group j
    0, otherwise
$q_j =$ 1, if group j is formed
    0, otherwise

$$r_{kj} = \left[\frac{1}{M} \sum_{i=1}^{N} p_{ij} a_{ki} \right] \tag{1}$$

$$\min_{p_{ij}, q_j, r_{kj}} |G| = \sum_{q=1}^{N} q_j \tag{2}$$

Subject to,

$$\sum_{k=1}^{M} r_{kj} q_j = S \tag{3}$$

$$\sum_{J=1}^{N} p_{ij} q_j = 1 \tag{4}$$

$$p_{ij}, q_j, r_{kj} \in \{0, 1\} \tag{5}$$

Equation (1) indicates if the component type k is used by at least one PCB in group j. Equation (2) states the PCB grouping subjected to constraints represented by Eqs. (3), (4) and (5). Equation (3) states the criteria for new group formation i.e. number of component types in each group should exceed the number of available slots present in the feeder rack. Equation (4) assures that one PCB type must be assigned to only one group while Eq. (5) represents the integrity constraints.

The Mathematical model for PCB group sequencing

This problem consists of sequencing the groups in 'G' such that the total number of feeder changes 'C' is minimized.

Decision Variable

$x_{jl} =$ 1, if PCB group l is manufactured after PCB group j
          0, otherwise

$C_{il} =$ 1, if PCB group 'j' and 'l' does not use the same component type 'k'
          0, otherwise

$$\min_{x_{jl} \in \{0,1\}} C_{il} = \sum_{j \in G} \sum_{l \in G} \sum_{k=1}^{M} \left(r_{kj} - r_{kl} \right)^2 x_{jl} \tag{6}$$

Subject to,

$$\sum_{l \in G} x_{jl} = 1, \ \forall j \in G \tag{7}$$

$$\sum_{j \in G} x_{jl} = 1, \ \forall j \in G \tag{8}$$

Equation (6) provides the changes in the feeder rack when finishing the manufacturing of PCB group 'j' and starting with PCB group 'l'. Equations (7) and (8) present the constraints imposed for PCB group sequencing. Equation (7) implies that one PCB group must be manufactured right after the group 'j' and Eq. (8) states that one PCB group must be manufactured right after group 'l'.

Strategy for Grouping PCBs

Grouping of PCBs is done involving the principle of collecting the PCBs that require similar components for assembly under a single group. Assumption (iv) is used to initialize grouping PCBs in different groups. A new group is to be formed when the feeder rack capacity is exceeded. The PCB that adds the minimum number of components will be chosen for next group. At each grouping stage, the group would be evaluated on the counts of new components needed to add for successive group formation.

The PCB groups are then subsequently sequenced using ACO by optimizing Eqs. (2) and (6) under corresponding constraints.

4 An ACO Algorithm for PCB Grouping

STEP 1: Determine the staring SEED PCB. SEED is the PCB requiring the maximum number of components (maximum global similarity) for assembly.

STEP 2: Start with an empty group 'G' and assign SEED PCB as the first member of the group and load the components in the feeder rack that are required for its assembly.

STEP 3: For finding the next element of the group, find that unallocated PCB having the maximum number of similar components as compared to SEED. Load all the extra components needed to assemble this PCB and proceed until the feeder rack capacity is exceeded.

STEP 4: When the feeder rack capacity is exceeded, make another empty group and repeat steps 2–4.

STEP 5: Repeat the above steps until either each PCB forms a part of a group or forms a group of its own.

4.1 ACO Algorithm for PCB Group Sequencing

STEP 1: Set the different parameters and initialize the pheromone trails.

STEP 2: Calculate the number of similar elements in each group.

STEP 3: Start iteration 1. Each ant is positioned at the starting node according to the distribution strategy (each node has at least one ant).

STEP 4: For k = 1 to m (k = number of ants, m = number of nodes), move each ant to different route and repeat until all nodes are visited once.

STEP 5: Compute candidate list according to the heuristic information.

STEP 6: Select the node to be visited next (from candidate list).

STEP 7: A local pheromone updating rule is applied until ant k has completed tour.

STEP 8: When all the ants have completed their tour, pheromone is updated by the global updating rule also, considering the evaporation of pheromone.

STEP 9: Update the heuristic parameters until end condition is met or an optimal solution is obtained

5 Validation

An industrial scheduling problem is considered to test the efficiency of the developed algorithm. The data regarding this study are available at Catay et al. [14]. These prior studies (and datasets) are cited at relevant place within the text as references [14]. Table 1 shows the different parameters of the test problem and Table 2 shows the component incidence matrix.

Table 1. Data taken from industrial scenarios [14]

Parameter	Average data drawn from industry source
Number of PCB types	12
The total number of different component types required for each PCB type	30
Capacity of master spool to hold different component types	20
Average number of each component type required by each PCB type	13.5

Before any PCB is processed all the components are removed from the master spool or considering it empty. All the components are generally removed from the rack to fully load the rack with maximum of its capacity. This helps further during the entire assembly process. Since the capacity of the rack to hold different component is 20, so at the start of the assembly process all 20 different components will loaded on the feeder rack when first PCB is about to be assembled. So, loading the feeder rack at start means 20 components switch over at the start of the assembly process. Once feeder rack is loaded than next component switch over depends upon the schedule of the PCB's. Minimum the switching of the component minimum will be the total assembly time.

Table 2. Component incidence matrix

Component No.	PCB No.											
	1	2	3	4	5	6	7	8	9	10	11	12
1	1	0	1	0	1	1	1	0	1	0	0	0
2	0	0	0	0	0	1	0	0	0	1	0	0
3	1	1	1	1	0	0	1	1	0	0	0	0
4	0	0	1	1	1	0	1	0	1	1	0	0
5	1	0	0	1	1	0	1	0	1	0	1	1
6	1	0	0	0	0	0	0	0	0	1	1	1
7	0	0	1	0	0	1	0	1	0	1	1	0
8	1	1	1	1	1	1	0	0	0	1	0	1

(continued)

Table 2. (*continued*)

PCB No.												
9	1	1	0	0	1	0	1	1	0	0	0	0
10	1	0	0	0	0	0	0	1	1	0	0	1
11	1	0	0	0	0	0	0	1	0	1	1	0
12	0	1	0	0	1	0	1	1	0	1	0	1
13	0	1	0	0	0	1	1	0	0	0	1	1
14	0	0	1	1	0	0	0	0	1	0	0	0
15	1	0	0	1	1	0	0	0	0	1	1	1
16	1	0	0	0	1	0	1	1	0	1	0	0
17	0	0	1	1	1	0	1	0	0	0	0	1
18	0	0	0	0	0	0	1	0	0	0	0	0
19	0	0	0	0	0	1	0	0	0	0	0	0
20	0	0	0	1	0	1	1	0	1	0	0	1
21	0	1	0	1	0	0	0	0	0	1	0	0
22	1	1	0	0	0	1	1	0	0	0	1	1
23	0	1	0	0	0	0	0	1	0	1	1	0
24	0	0	0	0	0	0	1	1	1	0	1	1
25	1	0	1	0	1	0	1	1	1	0	1	1
26	0	1	0	1	0	1	1	0	1	0	0	1
27	0	0	1	0	0	1	0	0	0	0	0	0
28	0	1	1	1	0	0	1	0	1	1	0	0
29	1	1	1	1	0	1	0	1	1	0	0	0
30	0	1	1	1	0	0	1	1	0	1	0	0
$\sum$	13	12	12	13	10	11	17	12	11	13	10	13

According to the first step of the grouping algorithm, SEED PCB is determined. The PCB with the maximum number of components is selected as SEED (PCB 7). Place this PCB as the first element of the empty group G1. Second element of the group is selected having the maximum number of similar components with the SEED PCB i.e. PCB 5. If another element is placed in the group G1 then the feeder rack capacity will be exceeded therefore a new empty group G2 is formed. This process continues until all the unallocated PCBs are assigned to different groups or forms a group of its own. Following the steps of the algorithm, total six groups are formed as shown in Table 3, having two PCBs each considering the feeder rack capacity is not exceeded.

Table 3. PCB groups and their member PCBs

Group No.	PCB No.	Component types required S ≤ 20
G1	7,5	19
G2	12, 11	16
G3	1, 8	18
G4	4, 9	17
G5	10, 2	19
G6	3, 6	18

6 Results and Comparisons

The proposed method assembles a lot of 12 PCBs in 6 PCB groups with 49 feeder rack changes which is less as compared with the results of the previous methods developed as shown in Table 4.

Table 4. Comparison with different component grouping methods

Method proposed by	No. of feeder rack changes	No. of groups formed
Hashiba and Chang [10]	62	6
Maimon and Stub [15]	66	7
Bhaskar and Narendran [16]	60	7
Narayanaswami and Iyengar [17]	56	6

When the developed algorithm is applied to the grouping schemes from the previous work, their results further improved as shown in Table 5. In addition to this, the proposed ACO algorithm provides the optimal sequence for processing these PCB groups while maintaining the feeder rack capacity.

Table 5. Number of feeder rack changes without and with proposed ACO

Method proposed by	No. of feeder rack changes without using ACO algorithm	No. of feeder rack changes after using ACO algorithm
Hashiba and Chang [10]	62	46
Maimon and Stub [15]	66	52
Bhaskar and Narendran [16]	60	51
Narayanaswami and Iyengar [17]	56	46

7   Conclusion

In this paper, problem for scheduling N type of PCBs on single sequential pick-and-place automatic machine was discussed in which the total number of different components required to process each type of PCBs exceeds the capacity of the feeder rack. An ACO based approach was developed in combination with application of group technology for efficient scheduling of PCBs to minimize the number of component switches. The problem comprises of two stages; grouping of PCBs followed by PCB group sequencing. The PCB grouping strategy involved the criteria of similar component requirement. The proposed approach yield better result when compared with other existing methodologies. Also, the ACO algorithm computed the solution in relatively very small time. Hence, model developed could be employed for solving highly complex industry-size PCB scheduling problems more efficiently.

The ACO described here can be extended to use for multiple machines augmented with different performance criteria. While the ACO approach presented in this article showed a better performance, it still remains an open question whether a more efficient methodology can be developed with other grouping strategy.

References

1. Framinan, M., Leisten, R., Garcia, R.R.: Manufacturing Scheduling Systems: An Integrated View on Models, Methods and Tools. Springer, Heidelberg (2014). https://doi.org/10.1007/978-1-4471-6272-8
2. Ho, W., Ji, P.: A genetic algorithm to optimise the component placement process in PCB assembly. Int. J. Adv. Manuf. Technol. **26**, 1397–1401 (2005)
3. Ho, W., Ji, P.: An integrated scheduling problem of PCB components on sequential pick-and-place machines: mathematical models and heuristic solutions. Expert Syst. Appl. **36**, 7002–7010 (2009)
4. Ho, W., Ji, P., Wu, Y.: A heuristic approach for component scheduling on a high-speed PCB assembly machine. Prod. Plan. Control **18**(8), 655–665 (2007)
5. Noroozi, A., Mokhtari, H.: Scheduling of printed circuit board (PCB) assembly systems with heterogeneous processors using simulation-based intelligent optimization methods. Neural Comput. Appl. **26**, 857–873 (2015)
6. Hardas, C.S., Doolen, T.L., Jensen, D.H.: Development of a genetic algorithm for component placement sequence optimization in printed circuit board assembly. Comput. Ind. Eng. **55**, 165–182 (2008)
7. Chen, Y.-M., Lin, C.-T.: A particle swarm optimization approach to optimize component placement in printed circuit board assembly. Int. J. Adv. Manuf. Technol. **35**, 610–620 (2007)
8. Zeng, K., Guo, Y.: A two-stage approach optimising PCB assembly on the sequential pick-and-place machine by a score-based slot selection method and a swarm intelligence approach. Int. J. Mater. Struct. Integrity **8**(1–3), 185–207 (2014)
9. Crama, Y., Klundert, J.V.D., Spieksma, F.C.R.: Production planning problems in printed circuit board assembly. Discrete Appl. Math. **123**, 339–361 (2002)
10. Hashiba, S., Chang, T.C.: PCB assembly setup reduction using group technology. Comput. Ind. Eng. **21**(1–4), 453–457 (1991)
11. Dorigo, M., Stutzle, T.: Ant Colony Optimization. MIT Press, Cambridge (2004)

12. Srivastava, S., Sahana, S.K.: Nested hybrid evolutionary model for traffic signal optimization. Appl. Intell. **46**(1), 113–123 (2016)
13. Sahana, S.K., AL-Fayoumi, M., Mahanti, P.K.: Application of modified ant colony optimization (MACO) for multicast routing problem. Int. J. Intell. Syst. Appl. **8**(4), 43–48 (2016)
14. Catay, B., Asoo, J.V., SelcukErenguc, S.: Printed circuit board scheduling in an open shop manufacturing environment. Int. J. Adv. Manuf. Technol. **29**, 980–989 (2006)
15. Maimon, O.Z., Shtub, A.: Grouping methods for printed circuit board assembly. Int. J. Prod. Res. **29**(7), 1379–1390 (1991)
16. Bhaskar, G., Narendran, T.T.: Grouping PCBs for set-up reduction: A maximum spanning tree approach. Int. J. Prod. Res. **34**(3), 621–632 (1996)
17. Narayanaswami, R., Iyengar, V.: Setup reduction in printed circuit board assembly by efficient sequencing. Int. J. Adv. Manuf. Technol. **26**, 276–284 (2005)

Fireworks Algorithms and Brain Storm Optimization

Accelerating Fireworks Algorithm with Weight-Based Guiding Sparks

Yuhao Li[1], Jun Yu[1,2], Hideyuki Takagi[3(✉)], and Ying Tan[4]

[1] Graduate School of Design, Kyushu University, Fukuoka 815-8540, Japan
li.yuhao.698@s.kyushu-u.ac.jp, yujun@kyudai.jp
[2] Japan Society for the Promotion of Science, Tokyo, Japan
[3] Faculty of Design, Kyushu University, Fukuoka 815-8540, Japan
h.takagi.457@m.kyushu-u.ac.jp
[4] School of Electronics Engineering and Computer Science, Peking University,
Beijing 100871, China
ytan@pku.edu.cn
http://www.design.kyushu-u.ac.jp/~takagi/

Abstract. We introduce two strategies into the guided fireworks algorithm (GFWA) to further improve its performance by generating one or more weight-based guiding spark individual(s) for each firework individual. The first strategy assigns different weights to spark individuals under each firework individual according to their fitness and then calculates one or more guiding vector(s) to guide the firework individual to evolve into potential directions. The second strategy decides the number of weight-based guiding spark individuals dynamically based on the evolution of a firework individual, i.e. if a firework individual does not evolve and survive in the next generation, then the second strategy reduces the number of spark individuals generated around the firework individual and generates the same reduced number of weight-based guiding spark individuals additionally. We design a controlled experiment to evaluate the performance of our proposal using CEC 2013 benchmark functions with five different dimensions. The experiment results confirm that the proposed strategies can provide effective guidance information to improve the GFWA performance significantly, and its acceleration effect for higher dimensional tasks is more obvious.

Keywords: Fireworks algorithm · Meta-heuristic algorithm ·
Weight-based guiding sparks · Acceleration

1 Introduction

The fireworks algorithm (FWA) [1] is a new family member of evolutionary computation community and simulates explosion process of real fireworks repeatedly

---

This work was supported in part by Grant-in-Aid for Scientific Research (17H06197, 18K11470, 19J11792).

Y. Tan et al. (Eds.): ICSI 2019, LNCS 11655, pp. 257–266, 2019.
https://doi.org/10.1007/978-3-030-26369-0_24

to find the global optimum. Many powerful variants of FWA have been sprung up like mushrooms by incorporating various effective search mechanisms, such as enhanced FWA (EFWA) [2], dynamic FWA (dynFWA) [3], adaptive FWA (AFWA) [4], guided FWA (GFWA) [5] and others [6–9]. They have also solved many complex real-world applications successfully, including multilevel image thresholding [10], RFID network planning [11] and privacy preserving [12], etc., thanks to their excellent characteristics. Although they have achieved gratifying results, there is still plenty of room to further improve FWA performance.

The primary objective of this paper is to propose a new type of weight-based guiding spark individuals to accelerate the convergence of FWA. The first strategy gives different weights to spark individuals to generate proposed weight-based guiding spark individuals, and the second strategy focuses on deciding the number of the guiding spark individuals dynamically, while GFWA always uses only one. The secondary objective is to analyze the effect of our proposal as well as their applicability and point out some open topics for discussion.

Following this introductory section, we roughly summarize optimization principles of FWA and a short introduction of GFWA in the Sect. 2. The proposed two strategies are comprehensively described in the Sect. 3. We evaluate the performance of our proposal using 28 benchmark functions of 5 different dimensions in the Sect. 4. Finally, we analyze some topics coming from the evaluation results in the Sect. 5 and conclude our works in the Sect. 6.

2   Optimization Mechanisms of Fireworks Algorithm

There are many generated sparks around a real firework launched into the sky, which can be considered as a local search pattern around a specific point. Inspired by this explosion process, FWA assigns different explosion amplitude and number of generated spark individuals to each firework individual to balance exploitation

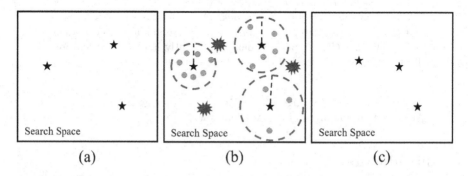

Fig. 1. Search process of FWA. (a) The initial firework individuals are generated randomly, (b) explosion spark individuals (blue solid points) and mutation spark individuals (green irregular points) are generated and (c) firework individuals in the next generation are selected from all individuals in the (b). The (b) and (c) are iterated until a termination condition is satisfied. (Color figure online)

and exploration. These explosion processes are repeated until a termination condition is satisfied. The Fig. 1 demonstrates the general framework of the FWA consisting of three major operations: explosion, mutation and selection.

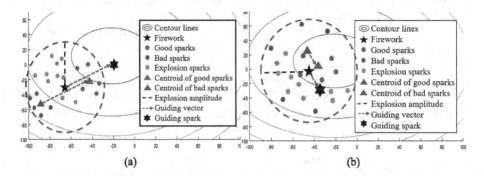

(a)   (b)

Fig. 2. (a) A guiding spark is calculated by adding a guiding vector information from a firework. The guiding vector is a vector from the centroid of poor spark individuals to that of better spark individuals. (b) An example case of a guiding vector pointing to a wrong direction.

GFWA is one of the most powerful variants of FWA, and its core idea is to divide spark individuals into two groups according to their fitness, determine a guiding vector from the centroid of the poor group to that of the better group, and evolve a firework individual to the guiding direction (Fig. 2(a)). However, an incorrect guiding vector may hinder the convergence of a firework individual as shown in Fig. 2(b). Since we do not focus on GFWA itself, the detailed implementations can refer to the [5]. We propose two strategies to avoid poor guidance by generating multiple high precision guiding vectors.

3   Two Proposed Strategies for GFWA

We propose two strategies to further improve the GFWA performance by introducing the concept of weights and generating multiple potential guiding vectors. The first strategy, *weight-based guiding strategy*, assigns different weights to generated spark individuals according to their fitness, which is expected to find a more effective guiding direction. The second strategy, *quantitative increase strategy*, may increase the number of weight-based guiding spark individuals to avoid falling into a local area based on previous searches.

3.1 Weight-Based Guiding Strategy

Top σ spark individuals among those generated by a firework individual $\boldsymbol{x}^i$ based on fitness rank are copied into a pool, and $\hat{N}$ spark individuals are randomly selected from the pool to calculate a guiding vector, i.e. we can obtain $\hat{N}$ vectors from the firework individual to these selected spark individuals.

The next problem is how to handle weights. There are many methods to assign weights to these vectors. In this paper, we simply use the fitness difference between a firework individual and a selected spark individual to determine weights, which means the more potential directions are, the more weight they are given. Thus, the i-th guiding spark individual $\boldsymbol{g}^i$ is calculated by weighting these vectors using Eq. (1). The i-th guiding vector is defined as a vector from the i-th firework individual $\boldsymbol{x}^i$ to the guiding spark individual $\boldsymbol{g}^i$.

$$
\boldsymbol{g}^i = \sum_{j=1}^{\hat{N}} \frac{\left| f(\boldsymbol{s}_j^i) - max\, f(\boldsymbol{s}_j^i) \right|}{\sum_{j=1}^{\hat{N}} \left| f(\boldsymbol{s}_j^i) - max\, f(\boldsymbol{s}_j^i) \right|} \times (\boldsymbol{s}_j^i - \boldsymbol{x}^i) + \boldsymbol{x}^i \tag{1}
$$

where $\boldsymbol{s}_j^i$ is the j-th spark individual generated by the i-th firework individual $\boldsymbol{x}^i$ $(1 \le j \le \hat{N})$, and $f()$ is a fitness function.

Note that

- if the i-th firework individual does not survive in the next generation, the pool is cleared. Otherwise, the pool is kept and generated better spark individuals are recorded into the pool until the upper limit is met. Once the pool becomes full, newcomers update poorer ones in the pool in turn.
- $\hat{N}$ is less than the pool size.
- if the j-th spark individual $\boldsymbol{s}_j^i$ is worse than the i-th firework individual $\boldsymbol{x}^i$, the weight of the vector from the firework individual to the spark individual, $\boldsymbol{s}_j^i - \boldsymbol{x}^i$, is set to 0.

3.2 Quantitative Increase Strategy

The second strategy is used only when a firework individual has not evolved and survived to the next generation. Multiple guiding sparks then are generated by using the first strategy to help the firework individual to evolve. Suppose the total number of spark individuals generated by the firework individual is M in the coming explosion operation. When the case mentioned in the above happens, we reduce the number of spark individuals generated by the explosion operation to $\alpha \times M$ and pack the number by generating $(1 - \alpha) \times M$ guiding spark individuals. We set α as 0.9 in our experimental evaluations.

The next key problem is how to generate multiple guiding vectors. Since a pool can provide a variety of spark individuals, we randomly select half of spark individuals from the pool to calculate a guiding vector and repeat this operation $(1 - \alpha) \times M$ times to provide multiple different guiding sparks.

Algorithm 1 outlines the flow of FWA combined with our proposed strategies.

Algorithm 1. The general framework of our proposed strategies combined to general FWA.

1: Randomly initialize n firework individuals in a search space.
2: Evaluating the fitness of firework individuals.
3: **while** a termination condition is not satisfied **do**
4:     Calculating an explosion amplitude for each firework individual.
5:     Calculating the number of spark individuals generated by firework individuals.
6:     Reassigning the proportion of spark individuals if the second strategy is executed.
7:     Generating spark individuals by an explosion operation.
8:     Generating guiding sparks for each firework using the first strategy.
9:     Evaluating the fitness of all generating spark individuals.
10:    Choose the best individual as a firework individual in the next generation.
11:    Randomly choose other $n-1$ firework individuals among the rest of individuals.
12: **end while**

4   Experimental Evaluations

To evaluate the performance of our proposed strategies, we combine the original guiding strategy in the [5] and our proposal with three different FEW variants, EFWA [2], dynFWA [3] and AFWA [4], respectively. Each benchmark function from the CEC2013 benchmark test suit [13] is run 51 times independently in 5 dimension settings of $D = 10, 30, 50, 70$ and 100.

These functions are designed for real parameter single-objective optimization, and their landscape characteristics include shifted, rotated, global on bounds, unimodal and multi-modal. The parameter settings used in our experimental evaluations showed as following; the number of firework individuals is set to 1, and the total number of spark individuals is set to 200. σ used for selecting top spark individuals is set to 0.2. The explosion amplitude used in EFWA is set to 80. All other parameter settings of EFWA, dynFWA and AFWA are exactly the same with original references [2,3] and [4], respectively. The dimension selection mechanism is not used in these evaluations to increase population diversity.

We use the number of fitness calls rather than generations to evaluate convergence fairly. The maximal number of evaluations, i.e. termination condition, of each run is $10,000 \times D$. We apply the Wilcoxon signed-rank test and the Holm's multiple comparison test on the fitness values at the termination condition to check significant difference between the original guiding Strategy in the [5] and our proposed strategies. Tables 1, 2 and 3 show results of statistical tests.

5   Discussions

5.1   Discussion on the Proposed Strategies

We begin our discussion from an explanation of the superiority of our proposal. The first strategy, *weight-based guiding strategy*, uses only spark individuals

Table 1. Wilcoxon signed-rank test and Holm's multiple comparison test results for average fitness of 3 methods for 51 trial runs. $\gg$, $>$, and $\approx$ mean that there are significant differences with significant levels 1%, 5%, and no significance, respectively. \ means that there is no significant difference among them. 0, 1, and 2 mean (EFWA + the original guiding strategy in the [5]), (EFWA + the proposed strategy 1), and (EFWA + the proposed strategies 1 and 2), respectively.

Func.	10-D	30-D	50-D	70-D	100-D
$f1$	$2 \gg 1 \gg 0$	$1 \gg 2 \gg 0$	$1 \gg 2 \gg 0$	$1 \gg 2 \gg 0$	$1 \gg 2 \gg 0$
$f2$	$2 \gg 1 \gg 0$	$2 \gg 1 \gg 0$	$2 \gg 1 \gg 0$	$2 \approx 1 \gg 0$	$1 \gg 2 \gg 0$
$f3$	$1 \approx 0 \gg 2$	$2 \gg 1 \gg 0$	$1 \gg 2 \gg 0$	$2 \gg 0 \gg 1$	$2 \gg 1 \approx 0$
$f4$	$2 \gg 1 \approx 0$	$2 \gg 1 \gg 0$	$2 \gg 1 \gg 0$	$2 \gg 1 \gg 0$	$2 \gg 1 \gg 0$
$f5$	$2 \gg 1 \approx 0$	$2 \gg 1 \gg 0$	$1 \gg 2 \gg 0$	$1 \gg 2 \gg 0$	$1 \gg 2 \gg 0$
$f6$	\	$1 \gg 2 \gg 0$	$1 \gg 2 \gg 0$	$1 \gg 2 \approx 0$	$1 \approx 0 \gg 2$
$f7$	$0 \approx 1 \gg 2$	$2 \gg 1 \approx 0$	$2 \gg 1 \gg 0$	$2 \gg 1 \gg 0$	$2 \gg 1 \approx 0$
$f8$	\	\	\	\	\
$f9$	$0 \approx 2 > 1$	$0 \gg 1 \approx 2$	$2 \approx 0 \gg 1$	$0 \approx 2 \gg 1$	$0 \gg 1 \approx 2$
$f10$	$2 \gg 1 \gg 0$	$1 \gg 2 \gg 0$	$1 \gg 2 \gg 0$	$1 \gg 2 \gg 0$	$1 \gg 2 \gg 0$
$f11$	$2 \gg 1 \gg 0$	$2 \gg 1 \gg 0$	$2 \gg 1 \gg 0$	$2 \gg 1 \gg 0$	$2 \gg 1 \gg 0$
$f12$	$2 \gg 1 \gg 0$	$2 \gg 1 \gg 0$	$2 \gg 1 \gg 0$	$2 \gg 1 \gg 0$	$2 \gg 1 \gg 0$
$f13$	$2 \gg 1 \gg 0$	$2 \gg 1 \gg 0$	$2 \gg 1 \gg 0$	$2 \gg 1 \gg 0$	$2 \gg 1 \gg 0$
$f14$	\	\	$2 \gg 0 \approx 1$	$2 \gg 0 \approx 1$	$2 \gg 0 \approx 1$
$f15$	$2 \gg 0 \approx 1$	$2 \gg 0 \approx 1$	$2 \gg 0 \approx 1$	$2 \gg 0 \approx 1$	$2 \gg 1 \approx 0$
$f16$	\	\	\	\	\
$f17$	$2 \gg 1 \gg 0$	$2 \gg 1 \gg 0$	$2 \gg 1 \gg 0$	$2 \gg 1 \gg 0$	$1 \gg 2 \gg 0$
$f18$	$2 \gg 1 \gg 0$	$2 \gg 1 \gg 0$	$2 \gg 1 \gg 0$	$2 \gg 1 \gg 0$	$1 > 2 \gg 0$
$f19$	$2 \gg 1 \gg 0$	$1 \gg 2 \gg 0$	$1 \gg 2 \gg 0$	$1 \gg 2 \gg 0$	$1 \gg 0 \gg 2$
$f20$	$0 \approx 1 \gg 2$	$2 \gg 0 \approx 1$	$2 \gg 0 \approx 1$	$2 \gg 1 \gg 0$	\
$f21$	$2 \approx 1 \gg 0$	\	$0 \gg 1 \approx 2$	$1 \gg 0 \gg 2$	$1 \gg 2 \gg 0$
$f22$	$2 > 1 \approx 0$	$2 \gg 0 \approx 1$	$2 \gg 0 \approx 1$	$2 \gg 0 \approx 1$	$2 \gg 0 \approx 1$
$f23$	$2 \gg 0 \approx 1$	$2 \gg 0 \approx 1$	$2 \gg 0 > 1$	$2 \gg 0 \approx 1$	$2 \gg 1 \approx 0$
$f24$	$1 \approx 2 > 0$	$2 \gg 1 \gg 0$	$2 \gg 1 \gg 0$	$2 \gg 1 \gg 0$	$2 \gg 1 \gg 0$
$f25$	$2 > 1 \gg 0$	\	$0 \gg 1 \gg 2$	$2 \gg 1 \approx 0$	$0 \gg 1 \gg 2$
$f26$	$2 \gg 1 \gg 0$	$2 \gg 1 \gg 0$	$0 \approx 1 \gg 2$	$1 \approx 2 \gg 0$	$2 \gg 1 \gg 0$
$f27$	$2 \gg 1 \gg 0$	$2 \gg 1 \gg 0$	$2 \gg 1 \gg 0$	$2 \gg 1 \gg 0$	$2 \gg 1 \gg 0$
$f28$	$0 \approx 2 \gg 1$	$2 \gg 1 \gg 0$	$1 \gg 2 \gg 0$	$1 \gg 2 \gg 0$	$2 \gg 1 \gg 0$

which fitness are better than that of a firework individual to construct multiple vectors from the firework individual to selected spark individuals. Different weights based on their fitness differences are given to these potential vectors

Table 2. Wilcoxon signed-rank test and Holm's multiple comparison test results for average fitness of 3 methods for 51 trial runs. The symbols used in this Table have same mean with the Table 1. 0, 1, and 2 mean (dynFWA + the original guiding strategy in the [5]), (dynFWA + the proposed strategy 1), and (dynFWA + the proposed strategies 1 and 2), respectively.

Func.	10-D	30-D	50-D	70-D	100-D
$f1$	\	\	\	\	\
$f2$	$2 \gg 1 > 0$	$2 \gg 1 \approx 0$	$2 \gg 1 > 0$	$2 \gg 1 \gg 0$	$2 \approx 1 \gg 0$
$f3$	$1 \approx 2 \gg 0$	$2 > 1 > 0$	$2 \gg 1 \gg 0$	$2 \approx 1 \gg 0$	$2 > 1 \gg 0$
$f4$	$2 \gg 1 \gg 0$	$2 \gg 0 \gg 1$	$0 \gg 2 \gg 1$	$0 \approx 2 \gg 1$	$0 \gg 2 \gg 1$
$f5$	$2 \gg 0 \gg 1$	$2 \gg 0 \gg 1$	$2 \gg 0 \gg 1$	$0 \gg 2 \gg 1$	$0 \gg 2 \approx 1$
$f6$	\	\	$1 \gg 2 \gg 0$	\	\
$f7$	$2 \approx 1 \gg 0$	$2 \gg 1 \approx 0$	$2 \gg 1 \gg 0$	$2 \gg 1 \gg 0$	$2 \gg 1 \gg 0$
$f8$	$1 \gg 2 \approx 0$	$1 \gg 2 \approx 0$	$1 \approx 2 > 0$	\	$1 \gg 2 \approx 0$
$f9$	$2 \gg 1 > 0$	$2 \approx 1 \gg 0$	$2 \approx 1 \gg 0$	$2 > 1 \gg 0$	$2 \gg 1 \gg 0$
$f10$	$2 \approx 1 > 0$	$2 \approx 1 \gg 0$	\	\	$1 > 0 \approx 2$
$f11$	$2 \gg 1 \gg 0$	$2 \gg 1 \gg 0$	$2 \gg 1 \gg 0$	$2 \gg 1 \gg 0$	$2 \approx 1 \gg 0$
$f12$	$2 \gg 1 > 0$	$2 \gg 1 \gg 0$	$2 \gg 1 \gg 0$	$2 \gg 1 \gg 0$	$2 > 1 \gg 0$
$f13$	$2 \gg 1 \approx 0$	$2 \gg 1 \gg 0$	$2 > 1 \gg 0$	$2 \gg 1 \gg 0$	$2 \gg 1 \gg 0$
$f14$	\	\	$1 \approx 2 \gg 0$	\	\
$f15$	\	\	\	$2 \approx 1 > 0$	$2 \approx 1 \gg 0$
$f16$	\	\	$1 \approx 2 > 0$	\	\
$f17$	$2 \gg 0 \approx 1$	$2 \gg 0 > 1$	$2 \approx 0 > 1$	\	\
$f18$	$2 \gg 1 \approx 0$	$2 \gg 0 \approx 1$	$2 \approx 0 \gg 1$	\	\
$f19$	$2 \gg 1 \approx 0$	$2 \gg 1 > 0$	$2 \gg 1 \gg 0$	$2 \gg 1 \gg 0$	$2 \gg 1 \gg 0$
$f20$	\	\	$2 \approx 1 \gg 0$	$2 \gg 1 \gg 0$	\
$f21$	\	\	$0 \gg 2 \approx 1$	$0 \gg 1 \approx 2$	$1 > 2 \approx 0$
$f22$	$2 \approx 1 > 0$	\	$1 \approx 2 \gg 0$	\	\
$f23$	$2 > 1 \approx 0$	\	$1 > 2 > 0$	$1 \approx 2 \gg 0$	$2 \approx 1 \gg 0$
$f24$	$2 > 0 \approx 1$	$2 \gg 1 \gg 0$	$2 \approx 1 \gg 0$	$2 \approx 1 \gg 0$	$2 \gg 1 \gg 0$
$f25$	\	$2 \approx 1 \gg 0$	$2 \approx 1 \gg 0$	$1 \approx 2 \gg 0$	$2 > 1 \gg 0$
$f26$	$2 \gg 1 \approx 0$	$2 \gg 1 \gg 0$	$2 \gg 1 \gg 0$	$2 \gg 1 \gg 0$	$2 \gg 1 \gg 0$
$f27$	$2 \approx 1 > 0$	$2 \gg 1 \gg 0$	$2 \gg 1 \gg 0$	$2 \gg 1 \gg 0$	$2 > 1 \gg 0$
$f28$	$0 \gg 1 \gg 2$	$2 > 1 \approx 0$	\	\	$2 \approx 1 > 0$

to calculate a guiding vector. The possibility of getting a better guiding spark individual by using the guiding vector from the firework individual becomes high.

A guiding spark individual has an anti-noise property to avoid over-preference for a certain direction because of aggregating multiple potential directions.

Table 3. Wilcoxon signed-rank test and Holm's multiple comparison test results for average fitness of 3 methods for 51 trial runs. The symbols used in this Table have same mean with the Table 1. 0, 1, and 2 mean (AFWA + the original guiding strategy in the [5]), (AFWA + the proposed strategy 1), and (AFWA + the proposed strategies 1 and 2), respectively.

Func.	10-D	30-D	50-D	70-D	100-D
$f1$	\	$1 \approx 2 \gg 0$	$1 \approx 2 \gg 0$	$1 \gg 2 \gg 0$	$1 \gg 2 \gg 0$
$f2$	$2 \approx 1 \gg 0$	$2 \approx 1 \gg 0$	$1 \approx 2 \gg 0$	$2 \approx 1 \gg 0$	$1 \approx 2 \gg 0$
$f3$	\	$2 \approx 1 \gg 0$	$2 \approx 1 \gg 0$	$2 \approx 1 \gg 0$	$2 \gg 1 \gg 0$
$f4$	$2 \gg 1 \approx 0$	$1 \gg 2 \approx 0$	$1 \approx 2 \gg 0$	$1 \approx 2 \gg 0$	$2 \gg 1 \gg 0$
$f5$	$1 > 0 \approx 2$	$1 \gg 2 \gg 0$	$1 \approx 2 \gg 0$	$1 > 2 \gg 0$	$1 \approx 2 \gg 0$
$f6$	\	$2 > 1 \gg 0$	$1 \gg 2 \gg 0$	$1 \approx 2 \gg 0$	$2 \gg 1 \gg 0$
$f7$	\	$1 \approx 2 \gg 0$	$2 \approx 1 \gg 0$	$2 \approx 1 \gg 0$	$2 \gg 1 \gg 0$
$f8$	$2 \gg 1 \approx 0$	$1 \approx 2 > 0$	\	$2 \gg 0 \gg 1$	\
$f9$	\	$2 \approx 1 > 0$	$2 \approx 1 > 0$	$2 \gg 1 \approx 0$	$2 \gg 0 \gg 1$
$f10$	\	$1 \approx 2 \gg 0$	$1 \gg 2 \gg 0$	$1 > 2 \gg 0$	$1 > 2 \gg 0$
$f11$	$2 > 1 \approx 0$	$1 \approx 2 \gg 0$	$1 \approx 2 \gg 0$	$1 > 2 \gg 0$	$1 \gg 2 \gg 0$
$f12$	$2 \gg 0 \approx 1$	$1 \approx 2 \gg 0$	$2 \approx 1 \gg 0$	$1 > 2 \gg 0$	$1 \gg 2 \gg 0$
$f13$	$2 \gg 0 \approx 1$	$2 \approx 1 \gg 0$	$1 \approx 2 \gg 0$	$1 \approx 2 \gg 0$	$1 \gg 2 \gg 0$
$f14$	\	$2 \approx 0 \gg 1$	$0 \gg 2 \gg 1$	$2 \approx 0 \gg 1$	$2 \gg 0 \gg 1$
$f15$	$2 \gg 0 \approx 1$	$2 \approx 0 \gg 1$	$2 \approx 0 \gg 1$	$2 \approx 0 \gg 1$	$2 \gg 0 > 1$
$f16$	\	$0 \gg 2 \gg 1$	$0 \gg 2 \gg 1$	$2 \gg 0 \gg 1$	$2 \approx 0 \gg 1$
$f17$	$2 \gg 1 \approx 0$	\	$0 \gg 1 \approx 2$	\	$1 \gg 2 \gg 0$
$f18$	$2 \gg 0 \approx 1$	\	\	$1 \gg 2 > 0$	$1 \gg 2 \gg 0$
$f19$	$2 > 1 \approx 0$	$2 \gg 1 \gg 0$	$2 \approx 1 \gg 0$	$1 \approx 2 \gg 0$	$1 > 2 \gg 0$
$f20$	\	$2 \approx 0 \gg 1$	$2 \gg 0 \gg 1$	\	\
$f21$	\	$1 \gg 2 \gg 0$	$2 \approx 1 \gg 0$	$1 \gg 2 \gg 0$	$1 \approx 2 \gg 0$
$f22$	\	$2 \approx 0 \gg 1$	$0 \approx 2 \gg 1$	$2 \approx 0 \gg 1$	$2 \gg 0 > 1$
$f23$	\	$2 \gg 0 \gg 1$	$2 \gg 0 \gg 1$	$2 > 0 \gg 1$	$2 \gg 1 \approx 0$
$f24$	\	$1 \approx 2 \gg 0$	$1 \gg 2 \gg 0$	$1 \gg 2 \gg 0$	$2 > 1 \gg 0$
$f25$	\	$2 \gg 1 > 0$	$2 \gg 1 \approx 0$	$2 \gg 1 \approx 0$	$2 \gg 1 \approx 0$
$f26$	\	$0 \approx 1 \gg 2$	$1 \approx 0 \gg 2$	$2 \approx 1 \gg 0$	$1 \approx 2 \gg 0$
$f27$	\	$1 > 2 \gg 0$	$2 \approx 1 \gg 0$	$1 \gg 2 \gg 0$	$1 \gg 2 \gg 0$
$f28$	\	$1 \gg 2 \gg 0$	$2 \gg 1 \gg 0$	$1 \approx 2 \gg 0$	$1 \gg 2 \gg 0$

Although the first strategy increases computing costs, i.e. weight processing operation, it is acceptable to add only one additional fitness operation. We can say that it is a *low cost, high return* strategy from the cost-performance view.

The second strategy, *quantitative increase strategy*, is to reduce the number of spark individuals generated by an explosion operation and generate the same number of guiding spark individuals to speed up unevolved firework individuals. Since the guiding operation is more likely to favor potential directions rather than a random search, multiple guiding vectors may be beneficial for a firework individual to jump out of the current local area.

To solve the key problem of how to generate diversified guidance vectors, a spark pool is adopted to efficiently use information by storing many excellent spark individuals generated in the past. This strategy does not need additional fitness calculations, but it simply redistributes the proportion of two different types of spark individuals. We can say that it is a *low risk, easy-to-use* strategy.

5.2   Discussion on Experimental Result

The next discussion is on the effectiveness and applicability of our proposal. To evaluate its performance, we compare it with the original guiding strategy in the [5], and apply them to three different baseline algorithms, EFWA, AFWA and dynFWA, respectively. We apply the Wilcoxon signed-rank test and Holm's multiple comparison test to the average fitness of 51 trial runs at the termination condition and check significant differences between two guiding methods. From the results of these statistical tests, we found that our proposed strategies had better performance in both unimodal and multimodal tasks on all 5 different dimensions. It may be because our proposal can provide more precise multiple guiding directions to accelerate convergence of FWA. The results show that our proposal can be applied to various variants of FWA successfully and implies that they have a wide range of applicability.

Finally, we discuss several potential approaches to further improve the performance of our proposed strategies. As the next improvement, we may use fitness gradient information instead of fitness difference to handle weights. How to further improve the accuracy of guiding spark individuals and how to use them to accelerate FWA are also our future works.

6   Conclusion

We proposed two effective strategies to improve a guiding information of the original GFWA and further increase its optimization ability. The first strategy uses existing and historical information to construct guiding vectors more reasonably, and the second strategy increases the number of guiding spark individuals to provide multiple potential guiding spark individuals. The experiments confirmed that our proposal can improve the performance of the GFWA significantly.

In our future work, we will continue to explore and exploit the hidden information to accelerate convergence and propose new methods to handle the weights reasonably. Besides, we will use them to solve practical problems.

References

1. Tan, Y., Zhu, Y.: Fireworks algorithm for optimization. In: Tan, Y., Shi, Y., Tan, K.C. (eds.) ICSI 2010. LNCS, vol. 6145, pp. 355–364. Springer, Heidelberg (2010). https://doi.org/10.1007/978-3-642-13495-1_44
2. Zheng, S., Janecek, A., Tan, Y.: Enhanced fireworks algorithm. In: 2013 IEEE Congress on Evolutionary Computation, Cancun, Mexico, pp. 2069–2077 (2013)
3. Zheng, S., Janecek, A., Li, J., Tan, Y.: Dynamic search in fireworks algorithm. In: 2014 IEEE Congress on Evolutionary Computation, Beijing, China, pp. 3222–3229 (2014)
4. Li, J., Zheng, S., Tan, Y.: Adaptive fireworks algorithm. In: 2014 IEEE Congress on Evolutionary Computation, Beijing, China, pp. 3214–3221 (2014)
5. Li, J., Zheng, S., Tan, Y.: The effect of information utilization: introducing a novel guiding spark in the fireworks algorithm. IEEE Trans. Evol. Comput. 21(1), 153–166 (2017)
6. Yu, J., Takagi, H.: Acceleration for fireworks algorithm based on amplitude reduction strategy and local optima-based selection strategy. In: Tan, Y., Takagi, H., Shi, Y. (eds.) ICSI 2017. LNCS, vol. 10385, pp. 477–484. Springer, Cham (2017). https://doi.org/10.1007/978-3-319-61824-1_52
7. Yu, J., Takagi, H., Tan, Y.: Accelerating the fireworks algorithm with an estimated convergence point. In: Tan, Y., Shi, Y., Tang, Q. (eds.) ICSI 2018. LNCS, vol. 10941, pp. 263–272. Springer, Cham (2018). https://doi.org/10.1007/978-3-319-93815-8_26
8. Yu, J., Tan, Y., Takagi, H.: Scouting strategy for biasing fireworks algorithm search to promising directions. In: The Genetic and Evolutionary Computation Conference Companion, Kyoto, Japan, pp. 99–100 (2018)
9. Yu, J., Takagi, H., Tan, Y.: Multi-layer explosion-based fireworks algorithm. Int. J. Swarm Intell. Evol. Comput. 7(3) (2018). https://doi.org/10.4172/2090-4908. 1000173
10. Tuba, M., Bacanin, N., Alihodzic, A.: Multilevel image thresholding by fireworks algorithm. In: The 25th International Conference Radioelektronika, Pardubice, Czech Republic, pp. 326–330 (2015)
11. Tuba, M., Bacanin, N., Beko, M.: Fireworks algorithm for RFID network planning problem. In: The 25th International Conference Radioelektronika, Pardubice, Czech Republic, pp. 440–444 (2015)
12. Rahmani, A., Amine, A., Hamou, R.M., Rahmani, M.E., Bouarara, H.A.: Privacy preserving through fireworks algorithm based model for image perturbation in big data. Int. J. Swarm Intell. Res. 6(3), 41–58 (2016)
13. Liang, J., Qu, B., Suganthan, P.N., Alfredo, G.H.: Problem definitions and evaluation criteria for the CEC 2013 special session on real-parameter optimization (2013). http://al-roomi.org/multimedia/CEC_Database/CEC2013/RealParameter Optimization/CEC2013_RealParameterOptimization_TechnicalReport.pdf

Last-Position Elimination-Based Fireworks Algorithm for Function Optimization

JunQi Zhang[1,2(✉)] and WeiZhi Li[1,2]

[1] Department of Computer Science and Technology,
Tongji University, Shanghai, China
{zhangjunqi,1631737}@tongji.edu.cn
[2] Key Laboratory of Embedded System and Service Computing,
Ministry of Education, Shanghai, China

Abstract. As rising swarm intelligence, fireworks algorithm (FWA) is designed to search the global optimum by the cooperation between the firework with the best fitness named as core firework (CF) and the other non-CFs. Loser-out tournament based fireworks algorithm (LoTFWA) is the most pioneering variant characterized by using competition as a new manner of interaction. However, its independent selection operator may prevent non-CFs from aggregating to CF in the late evolutionary phase if they fall into different local optima. This work proposes a last-position elimination-based fireworks algorithm which allocates more fireworks in the initial process of the optimization to search and locate the scattered local optima. Then for every fixed number of generations, the firework with the worst performance is eliminated and its budget of sparks is reallocated to other fireworks. In the final stage of optimization, only CF survives with all the budget of sparks and thus the aggregation of non-CFs to CF is ensured. Extensive experimental results performed on both CEC2013 and CEC2015 benchmarks covering 43 functions show that the proposed algorithm significantly outperforms most of the state-of-the-art FWA variants.

Keywords: Fireworks algorithm · Swarm intelligence ·
Independent selection · Elimination mechanism

1 Introduction

Fireworks algorithm (FWA) proposed by Tan [6], as a rising SI optimization algorithm, is inspired by the explosion process of fireworks in the sky. Zheng et al. [8] propose an enhanced fireworks algorithm (EFWA) with five modifications to FWA. Based on the work of EFWA, Zheng et al. [7] propose the dynamic search fireworks algorithm (dynFWA). In it, the firework with best fitness in each generation is called core firework (CF) and others are called non-core fireworks (non-CFs). Li et al. [1] present an adaptive fireworks algorithm

© Springer Nature Switzerland AG 2019
Y. Tan et al. (Eds.): ICSI 2019, LNCS 11655, pp. 267–275, 2019.
https://doi.org/10.1007/978-3-030-26369-0_25

(AFWA) by using adaptive amplitude. Li et al. [2] propose a guided fireworks algorithm (GFWA) by introducing a novel guiding spark to improve FWA performance. Zheng et al. [9] propose a cooperative framework for fireworks algorithm (CoFFWA) which can greatly enhance the exploitation ability of non-CFs by using an independent selection operator and increase the exploration capacity by a crowdness-avoiding cooperative strategy among the fireworks. Li and Tan [3] propose a loser-out tournament based fireworks algorithm (LoTFWA) which also utilizes an independent selection operator to select fireworks for the next generation. However, its independent selection operator may prevent non-CFs from aggregating to CF in the late evolutionary stage. This work proposes a novel Last-position Elimination-based fireworks algorithm (LEFWA). At first, it allocates more fireworks at the initial phase to search and locate scattered local optima. Then for every G (>1) generations, the firework with the worst fitness is eliminated and its budget of sparks is reallocated to other fireworks. At the final stage of optimization, only CF survives with all the budget of sparks and thus the aggregation of non-CFs to CF is guaranteed. This elimination mechanism reinforces exploitation by eliminating unpromising areas along with an evolution process and reveals where the true global optimum locates.

The rest of this paper is organized as follows. Section 2 introduces the related work. Section 3 describes and analyzes the proposed algorithm in detail. Section 4 presents the experimental settings and results. Conclusions are given in Sect. 5.

2 Related Work

In LoTFWA, the number of sparks for each firework depends on the ranking of its fitness value rather than the fitness value itself, it is calculated as follows:

$$S_i = M \cdot \frac{r_i^{-\alpha}}{\sum_{i=1}^{n}(r_i^{-\alpha})} \tag{1}$$

where r_i is the fitness ranking of firework i, α is a parameter to control the shape of the distribution. The larger α is, the more explosion sparks good fireworks generate. M and n represent the total number of sparks and fireworks, respectively.

Secondly, LoTFWA adopts a dynamic amplitude update strategy for each firework which is first introduced in the dynFWA [7]. The amplitude of each firework is calculated as follows:

$$A_i(t) = \begin{cases} A_i(t-1) \cdot \rho^+ & \text{if } f(X_i(t)) - f(X_i(t-1)) < 0 \\ A_i(t-1) \cdot \rho^- & \text{otherwise} \end{cases} \tag{2}$$

where $X_i(t)$ and $A_i(t)$ are the position and the amplitude of i-th firework at generation t, respectively. $\rho^+ \in (1, +\infty)$ and $\rho^- \in (0,1)$ are the coefficients of amplification and reduction, respectively.

Finally, the explosion sparks are generated uniformly within a hypercube. The radius of the hypercube is the explosion amplitude and the center of the hypercube is the position of the firework. **Algorithm 1** shows how the explosion sparks are generated for each firework.

Algorithm 1. Generating explosion sparks for X_i

1: **for** $j = 1$ to S_i **do**
2:   **for** $d = 1, 2, ..., D$ **do**
3:     $s_{i,j}^d = X_i^d + A_i \cdot rand(-1, 1)$
4:     **if** $s_{i,j}^d < B_L$ or $s_{i,j}^d > B_U$ **then**
5:       $s_{i,j}^d = B_L + rand(0, 1) \cdot (B_U - B_L)$
6:     **end if**
7:   **end for**
8: **end for**
9: **return** all the $s_{i,j}$

LoTFWA utilizes a recently proposed guiding spark [2] as the mutation operator which is simple and efficient. **Algorithm 2** shows how the guiding sparks are generated for each firework. σ is a parameter to control the proportion of adopted explosion sparks. Note that only one guiding spark is generated for each firework.

Algorithm 2. Generating the guiding spark for X_i

1: Sort the sparks by their fitness values $f(s_{i,j})$ in the ascending order
2: $\Delta_i = X_i + \frac{1}{\sigma S_i}(\sum_{j=1}^{\sigma S_i} s_{i,j} - \sum_{j=S_i-\sigma S_i+1}^{S_i} s_{i,j})$
3: $gs_i = X_i + \Delta_i$
4: **return** gs_i

LoTFWA adopts an independent selection operator to enhance the exploitation ability of non-CFs. In LoTFWA, each firework and its sparks are regarded as a group. The best candidate $\mathbf{x}_i^*$ in group i in the current generation is selected as a new firework for the next generation.

The search manner of the conventional fireworks algorithm is based on the cooperation of several fireworks. While in LoTFWA, the competition becomes a new manner of interaction, in which the fireworks are compared with each other not only according to their current status but also according to their progress rate. The progress rate of the i-th firework in generation g is calculated as follows:

$$\delta_i^g = f(X_i^{g-1}) - f(X_i^g) \geq 0 \tag{3}$$

The prediction of its fitness in the final generation g_{max} is calculated as follows:

$$f(\widetilde{X_i^{g_{max}}}) = f(X_i^g) - \delta_i^g(g_{max} - g) \tag{4}$$

The i-th firework is considered as a loser and will be reinitialized if the prediction is worse than the current best one, i.e., $f(\widetilde{X_i^{g_{max}}}) > min_j f(X_j^g)$. **Algorithm 3** shows how the loser-out tournament mechanism works in every generation.

Algorithm 3. Loser-out tournament

1: **for** $i = 1$ to n **do**
2:    **if** $f(X_i^g) < f(X_i^{g-1})$ **then**
3:        $\delta_i^g = f(X_i^{g-1}) - f(X_i^g)$
4:    **end if**
5:    **if** $f(X_i^g) - \delta_i^g(g_{max} - g) > min_j f(X_j^g)$ **then**
6:        reinitialize the i-th firework
7:    **end if**
8: **end for**

Integrating the above mechanisms, the main process of LoTFWA is described in **Algorithm 4**.

Algorithm 4. LoTFWA

1: Initialize n fireworks and evaluate their fitness
2: **while** (stopping criterion not met) **do**
3:    **for** $i = 1$ to n **do**
4:        Calculate the number of sparks using (1)
5:        Calculate explosion amplitude using (2)
6:        Generate explosion sparks using **Algorithm 1**
7:        Generate the guiding spark using **Algorithm 2**
8:        Evaluate all the sparks
9:        Select the new firework independently
10:   **end for**
11:   Perform the loser-out tournament using **Algorithm 3**
12: **end while**

---

3   Proposed Algorithm

In order to solve the problem of LoTFWA that non-CFs cannot aggregate to CF in the final stage, this work proposes LEFWA which adopts a last-position elimination mechanism based on LoTFWA. The description and analysis of the proposed algorithm are given in this section.

3.1   LEFWA

At the initial phase, LEFWA initializes n fireworks randomly in a search space and evaluates their fitness. At each generation, same as LoTFWA, the number of sparks and explosion amplitude of each firework are calculated. After each firework generates its explosion sparks and the guiding spark, the independent selection operator and loser-out tournament strategy are adopted. Then, the last-position elimination mechanism is introduced in the proposed LEFWA. For every G (>1) generations, the firework with the worst fitness is eliminated and G is calculated as follows:

$$G = \frac{(F_{max} - n)/M}{n} \tag{5}$$

where F_{max} is the maximum number of fitness evaluations, M is the total number of sparks and n is the initial number of fireworks. $(F_{max} - n)/M$ calculates a rough total number of generations. Because of the initialization of n fireworks at the beginning of the algorithm, n should be subtracted from F_{max}. Then the total number of generations is divided into n segments and each contains roughly G generations. For every G generations, the current number of fireworks $\hat{n}$ is updated as

$$\hat{n} = \hat{n} - 1. \tag{6}$$

The budget of sparks of the eliminated firework is reallocated to other better fireworks. At the final stage of evolution, only CF survives with all the budget of sparks and thus the aggregation of non-CFs to CF is guaranteed. This elimination mechanism enhances the exploitation ability by giving up unpromising areas gradually and reveals where the true global optimum locates. The procedure of LEFWA is shown in **Algorithm 5**.

Algorithm 5. LEFWA

1: Initialize n fireworks and evaluate their fitness
2: Calculate G using (5)
3: **while** (stopping criterion not met) **do**
4:     **if** current generation is divisible by G and $\hat{n} > 1$ **then**
5:         Eliminate the worst firework
6:         Update $\hat{n}$ using (6)
7:     **end if**
8:     **for** $i = 1$ to $\hat{n}$ **do**
9:         Calculate the number of sparks using (1)
10:        Calculate explosion amplitude using (2)
11:        Generate explosion sparks using **Algorithm 1**
12:        Generate the guiding spark using **Algorithm 2**
13:        Evaluate all the sparks
14:        Select the new firework independently
15:    **end for**
16:    Perform the loser-out tournament using **Algorithm 3**
17: **end while**

3.2 Analysis of LEFWA

The diversity of population decreases gradually due to the last-position elimination mechanism in LEFWA. To solve this problem, LEFWA needs to initialize more fireworks than LoTFWA. This work utilizes the average distance between each candidate and the center of whole population to measure the diversity of population, which is calculated as follows:

$$diversity = \frac{\sum_{i=1}^{n+M}(||x_i - x^c||)}{n + M} \tag{7}$$

where x^c is the center of all candidates and $||x_i - x^c||$ represents the distance between the i-th candidate and x^c. For the fourth function of CEC2013 benchmark [5], Fig. 1 shows the diversity curves of LEFWA as compared to LoTFWA's in two cases, one with the same initial number of fireworks, and the other with a different number. $n_0(\text{LEFWA})$ and $n_0(\text{LoTFWA})$ are the initial number of fireworks in LEFWA and LoTFWA, respectively. We calculate the diversity of population for every 100 evaluations. In each subfigure, X-axis represents the number of calculations and Y-axis represents the diversity of population.

As shown in Fig. 1(a), the diversity of population in LEFWA decreases obviously for every G generations as caused by the last-position elimination mechanism. As a result, the exploration capability of LEFWA is worse than that of LoTFWA. In Fig. 1(b), LEFWA has higher diversity than LoTFWA in the early evolutionary stage because of more initial fireworks. Although the diversity of population in LEFWA decreases along with an evolution process, LEFWA has better capability of exploration at the early evolutionary phase and better exploitation ability at the late evolutionary stage than LoTFWA respectively, which are exactly a feature that evolutionary algorithms should own. In addition, Fig. 1 shows that LoTFWA still maintains a high diversity at the late evolutionary stage, indicating that non-CFs cannot aggregate to CF in the final stage. It is worth mentioning that the reinitialization triggered by the loser-out tournament mechanism makes the diversity of LoTFWA increase at the late stage.

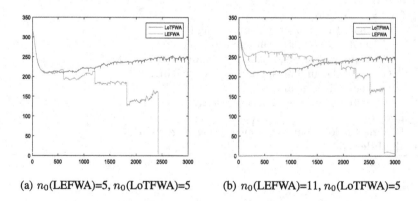

(a) $n_0(\text{LEFWA})$=5, $n_0(\text{LoTFWA})$=5   (b) $n_0(\text{LEFWA})$=11, $n_0(\text{LoTFWA})$=5

Fig. 1. The diversity curve of LEFWA and LoTFWA.

4   Experiments

4.1   Experimental Settings

To show the performance of LEFWA, total 28 functions in CEC2013 benchmark [5] and total 15 functions in CEC2015 benchmark [4] are used, which contain unimodal, multimodal, hybrid and composition functions. For convenience, F1–F28 and F29–F43 represent functions in CEC2013 and CEC2015 benchmark, respectively. For each function, dimension D is set to 30, and the maximum number of fitness evaluations is $10000D$. For a comprehensive comparison, EFWA [8], dynFWA [7], CoFFWA [9], GFWA [2] and LoTFWA [3] are also tested. Their parameter configurations are the same as those in the corresponding references. Each algorithm is run for 51 times independently on each function. At the end of each run, it outputs the error that is defined as $f(\mathbf{X}^*) - f^*$, where $\mathbf{X}^*$ represents the best solution found by it and f^* is the global optimal fitness of a function. Finally, for all algorithms, the means and standard deviations of errors are given.

In LEFWA, all parameter configurations are the same as in LoTFWA. However, as mentioned above, because of the elimination mechanism, the initial number of fireworks in LEFWA n is higher than those in LoTFWA, as listed in Table 1. To be fair, the total number of fitness evaluations in all algorithms is set to the same value, i.e., $10000D$.

Table 1. Parameter configurations

Algorithms	Parameters settings
EFWA	$n = 5, M = 50, \hat{A} = 40$
dynFWA	$n = 5, M = 150, \hat{A} = 40, A_c(1) = 200, \rho^+ = 1.2, \rho^- = 0.9$
CoFFWA	$n = 5, M = 150, \hat{A} = 40, A_c(1) = 200, \rho^+ = 1.2, \rho^- = 0.9$
GFWA	$n = 1, M = 200, \sigma = 0.2, \hat{A} = 40, A_c(1) = 200, \rho^+ = 1.2, \rho^- = 0.9$
LoTFWA	$n = 5, M = 300, \sigma = 0.2, \alpha = 0, A_i(1) = 200, \rho^+ = 1.2, \rho^- = 0.9$
LEFWA	$n = 11, M = 300, \sigma = 0.2, \alpha = 0, A_i(1) = 200, \rho^+ = 1.2, \rho^- = 0.9$

4.2   Experimental Results

The statistical results on CEC2013 and CEC2015 benchmarks are from 51 independent runs, respectively. A Wilcoxon rank sum test is conducted between each algorithm and LEFWA. It tests whether performances of two algorithms are significantly different (with confidence level 95%). The result of such test is shown in Table 2 and presented as a+/b/c−, which means LEFWA is significantly better than/not significantly different from/significantly worse than the corresponding algorithm on a/b/c functions.

Table 2. Wilcoxon test between each algorithm and LEFWA

Benchmark	EFWA	dynFWA	CoFFWA	GFWA	LoTFWA
CEC2013	26+/0/2−	21+/4/3−	22+/4/2−	19+/5/4−	10+/15/3−
CEC2015	12+/3/0−	13+/1/1−	13+/0/2−	12+/1/2−	4+/11/0−
Total	38+/3/2−	34+/5/4−	35+/4/4−	31+/6/6−	14+/26/3−

In CEC2013, LEFWA outperforms all the contenders. The Wilcoxon rank sum test shows that LEFWA significantly outperforms EFWA on 26 functions and dynFWA on 21 functions in a total of 28 functions. Compared to CoFFWA and GFWA, LEFWA significantly outperforms on 22 and 19 functions, respectively. Additionally, LEFWA significantly outperforms LoTFWA on 10 functions and is significantly worse than it on 3 functions. This result indicates that LEFWA has better performance than LoTFWA's. In CEC2015, LEFWA also outperforms all algorithms. The Wilcoxon rank sum test shows that LEFWA significantly outperforms EFWA on 12 functions and dynFWA on 13 functions in total 15 functions. Besides, LEFWA significantly outperforms CoFFWA on 13 functions and GFWA on 12 functions. Additionally, compared with LoTFWA, LEFWA outperforms on 4 functions and is significantly worse on no function.

5   Conclusions and Future Work

This paper reviews LoTFWA that utilizes an independent selection operator and points out its possible slow convergence as caused by non-core fireworks falling into local optima at the late optimization stage. In order to overcome this limitation, this study introduces an elimination mechanism into LoTFWA, resulting LEFWA. The proposed algorithm eliminates the firework with the worst fitness for every G (>1) generations and thus guarantees the aggregation of non-CFs to CF.

Acknowledgement. This work is supported by China NSF under Grants No. 61572359 and 61272271.

References

1. Li, J., Zheng, S., Tan, Y.: Adaptive fireworks algorithm. In: IEEE Congress on Evolutionary Computation (CEC), pp. 3214–3221, July 2014
2. Li, J., Zheng, S., Tan, Y.: The effect of information utilization: introducing a novel guiding spark in the fireworks algorithm. IEEE Trans. Evol. Comput. **21**(1), 153–166 (2017)
3. Li, J., Tan, Y.: Loser-out tournament based fireworks algorithm for multi-modal function optimization. IEEE Trans. Evol. Comput. **22**, 679–691 (2018)

4. Liang, J.J., Qu, B.Y., Suganthan, P.N., Chen, Q.: Problem definitions and evaluation criteria for the CEC 2015 competition on learning-based real-parameter single objective optimization. Technical report. 201411A, Zhengzhou Univ., China and Nanyang Technol. Univ., Singapore, November 2014
5. Liang, J.J., Qu, B.Y., Suganthan, P.N., Hernández-Díaz, A.G.: Problem definitions and evaluation criteria for the CEC 2013 special session on real-parameter optimization. Technical report 201212, Zhengzhou Univ., China and Nanyang Technol. Univ., Singapore, January 2013
6. Tan, Y., Zhu, Y.: Fireworks algorithm for optimization. In: Tan, Y., Shi, Y., Tan, K.C. (eds.) ICSI 2010. LNCS, vol. 6145, pp. 355–364. Springer, Heidelberg (2010). https://doi.org/10.1007/978-3-642-13495-1_44
7. Zheng, S., Janecek, A., Li, J., Tan, Y.: Dynamic search in fireworks algorithm. In: IEEE Congress on Evolutionary Computation (CEC), pp. 3222–3229, July 2014
8. Zheng, S., Janecek, A., Tan, Y.: Enhanced fireworks algorithm. In: IEEE Congress on Evolutionary Computation (CEC), pp. 2069–2077, June 2013
9. Zheng, S., Li, J., Janecek, A., Tan, Y.: A cooperative framework for fireworks algorithm. IEEE/ACM Trans. Comput. Biol. Bioinf. **14**(1), 27–41 (2017)

Planar Thinned Antenna Array Synthesis Using Modified Brain Storm Optimization

Junfeng Chen[1(✉)], Ninjerdene Bulgan[1], Xingsi Xue[2], Xinnan Fan[1], and Xuewu Zhang[1]

[1] College of IOT Engineering, Hohai University, Changzhou 213022, China
chen-1997@163.com, ninjerdene@hhu.edu.cn
[2] College of Information Science and Engineering,
Fujian University of Technology, Fuzhou 350118, China
jack8375@gmail.com

Abstract. Antennas play an important role in the operation of all radio equipment, which is widely used in wireless local area networks, mobile telephony, and satellite communication. The antenna array synthesis seeks steering nulls in the direction of interference and placing the main beam directed to the desired signal. In this paper, the pattern synthesis is modeled as a single-objective combinatorial optimization problem with constraints. The Brain Storm Optimization (BSO) is modified for pattern synthesis of the planar antenna array. Instead of adopting the k-mean clustering, the proposed method follows the Gaussian Mixture Model and also adopted the idea of the discrete Genetic Algorithm (GA) in introducing the binary creating operator into our model. To verify the performances of the proposed method, it is applied to pattern synthesis of the planar antenna array in comparing with the GA. The simulation results show that the proposed BSO algorithm in its modified version has good applicability for the synthesis of thinned planar arrays.

Keywords: Brain Storm Optimization · Thinned planar array · Gaussian mixture model · Binary creating operator

1 Introduction

An antenna array (or array antenna) [1], frequently used in a radar system, is composed of multiple individual antennas which work together to produce a high directive gain or a specified pattern. The thinning is performed by turning off a percentage of elements in an antenna array without causing major degradation in system performance. The advantages that the thinned antenna array [2, 3] has over the completely filled array in terms of cost, weight, power consumption and heat dissipation.

The antenna array thinning can be modeled as a combinatorial optimization problem. It is difficult to design a thinned array optimally due to the exponential increase of n-combinations to tackle as a result of a large number of the array elements. Though, if the array is symmetric, it will halve the number of possibilities for the placement of the elements.

The traditional optimization methods such as conjugate gradient and downhill are not suitable for thinning the large-scale antenna array synthesis as there is an n-infinite number of possible combinations. Swarm intelligence [4, 5] offers a practical way to address the thinning problem. The swarm algorithms make few or no assumptions about the problem and make full use of swarm searching to seeking the optimal combination of the antenna array. Haupt first employed the Genetic Algorithm (GA) to optimize the linear array and planar array with 200 elements [6]. After that, various swarm intelligence tools have been used to the thinned antenna array synthesis, such as GA, Ant Colony Optimization (ACO), Particle Swarm Optimization (PSO), and Differential Evolution (DE).

A planar antenna array is the number of elements connected and arranged in a matrix array and interconnected to produce a directional radiation pattern. Ares-Pena et al. presented a GAs for the pattern synthesis involving linear and planar arrays [7]. Marcano and Duran elaborated on two particular methods for the synthesis of complex radiation pattern for linear and a planar array based on GAs [8]. Villegas developed a parallel GA for the synthesis of arbitrarily shaped beam coverage using planar 2D phased-array antennas [9]. Chen et al. designed a modified real GA for the element position optimization of sparse planar arrays with rectangular boundary [10]. Jain and Mani discussed the basic concepts of antenna array, array thinning and dynamic thinning, and the GA is applied to reduce total number of active elements in the linear and planar arrays [11]. Zhang et al. proposed a GA based on orthogonal design and applied the orthogonal GA to optimize the planar thinned array with a minimum peak side lobe level [12]. Ha et al. introduced the modified compact GA, which had been applied to the optimized synthesis of different-size linear and planar thinned arrays [13]. Cheng et al. proposed a novel hybrid multi-objective optimization algorithm based on the non-dominated sorting genetic algorithm II and validated the good performance of the proposed algorithm on the large planar thinned arrays [14]. Quevedo-Teruel and Rajo-Iglesias used the side lobe level as the desirability parameter and employed the ACO as a useful alternative in the thinned linear and planar arrays design [15]. Li et al. presented an improved PSO for electromagnetic applications, which were concerned with linear as well as planar array [16]. Lanza Diego et al. applied a modified PSO algorithm to planar array synthesis considering complex weights and directive element patterns [17]. Wang et al. introduced a chaotic binary PSO algorithm as a useful alternative for thinning large linear and planar arrays to obtain a low side lobe level [18].

Metaheuristics deliver a set of satisfactory optimal solutions and further room for improvement in search for best ones. One of the latest representatives of Swarm Intelligence Family - Brain Storm Optimization (BSO) algorithm based on human brainstorming has superior properties in evolutionary terms. In this paper, we present the method of optimization of uniformly spaced planar arrays based on a promising metaheuristics - BSO algorithm.

The remainder of this paper is organized as follows. In Sect. 2, the thinning problem of planar arrays is described. In Sect. 3, the BSO is modified based on

278   J. Chen et al.

Gaussian mixture model and the binary creating operator. Simulation experiments and comparisons are provided in Sect. 4. Finally, several conclusive remarks are given in Sect. 5.

2 Problem Formulation for Planar Arrays

A planar array puts both the active and parasitic elements on one plane, making them two dimensional. The antenna beam can be electrically scanned in both azimuth and elevation directions. A schematic diagram of a planar array antenna is given as Fig. 1.

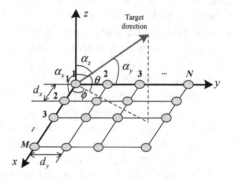

Fig. 1. Geometry of the planar array.

As shown in Fig. 1, the M array elements along the y-direction are uniformly arranged at a pitch of d_y, and the N array elements along the x-direction are uniformly arranged at a spacing of d_x, thereby, forming planar array of a rectangular grid. Assuming that the direction of the target is represented as $(\cos \alpha_x, \cos \alpha_y, \cos \alpha_z)$, the spatial phase difference between the (m, n)-th array element and the $(1, 1)$-th reference array element along the x-axis and the y-axis can be expressed as:

$$\begin{cases} \Delta\phi_x = \frac{2\pi}{\lambda} d_n \cos \alpha_x \\ \Delta\phi_y = \frac{2\pi}{\lambda} d_m \cos \alpha_y \end{cases} \tag{1}$$

where $m \in \{1, 2, \cdots, M\}$, $n \in \{1, 2, \cdots, N\}$. The d_m denotes the distance between the (m, n)-th array element and the $(1, 1)$-th reference array element azimuth, and d_n denotes the (m, n)-th array element and the $(0, 0)$-th reference.

From the geometry illustrated in Fig. 1, the following can be derived.

$$\begin{cases} \cos \alpha_x = \sin \theta \cos \phi \\ \cos \alpha_y = \sin \theta \sin \phi \\ \cos \alpha_z = \cos \theta \end{cases} \tag{2}$$

The phase difference between the (m, n)-th array element and the $(1, 1)$-th reference array element can be expressed as:

$$\Delta\phi_{mn} = \frac{2\pi}{\lambda}(d_n \sin\theta \cos\varphi + d_m \sin\theta \sin\varphi). \tag{3}$$

Let the maximum value of the main beam of the array be (ϕ_0, θ_0). The excitation amplitude and phase of the (m, n)-th element are A_{mn} and α_{mn}, respectively.

$$\alpha_{mn} = \frac{2\pi}{\lambda}(d_n \sin\theta_0 \cos\varphi_0 + d_m \sin\theta_0 \sin\varphi_0). \tag{4}$$

The orientation pattern function of the planar array can be expressed as:

$$
\begin{aligned}
F(\theta, \varphi) &= \sum_{n=1}^{N}\sum_{m=1}^{M} f_{mn}(\phi, \theta) a_{mn} e^{j(\Delta\phi_{mn} - \alpha_{mn})} \\
&= \sum_{n=1}^{N}\sum_{m=1}^{M} f_{mn}(\phi, \theta) a_{mn} e^{j\frac{2\pi}{\lambda}[d_m(\cos\theta\cos\varphi - \cos\theta_0\sin\varphi_0) + d_n(\sin\theta - \sin\theta_0)]}.
\end{aligned}
\tag{5}
$$

In general, the antenna array element is in according with the equiamplitude distribution and omnidirectional, so the amplitude weighting is not required, i.e., $a_{mn} = 1$ and $f_{mn}(\varphi, \theta) = 1$. This implies the pattern function of the planar array can be expressed as:

$$
\begin{aligned}
F(\theta, \varphi) &= \sum_{m=1}^{M} e^{j\frac{2\pi}{\lambda}d_m(\sin\theta\sin\varphi - \sin\theta_0\sin\varphi_0)} \sum_{n=1}^{N} e^{j\frac{2\pi}{\lambda}d_n(\sin\theta\cos\varphi - \sin\theta_0\cos\varphi)} \\
&= |F_1(\theta, \varphi)| \cdot |F_2(\theta, \varphi)|.
\end{aligned}
\tag{6}
$$

where $|F_1(\theta, \varphi)|$ and $|F_2(\theta, \varphi)|$ represent the antenna pattern of the y-direction linear array and the x-direction linear array respectively.

According to the definition of Maximum Side Lobe Level (*MSLL*), the fitness function can be taken as the sum of the maximum sidelobe level of the azimuth pattern and the maximum sidelobe of the pitch pattern:

$$MSLL = \max_{\phi \in S_1}(F(\phi, \theta_0; \phi_0, \theta_0)) + \max_{\phi \in S_2}(F(\phi_0, \theta; \phi_0, \theta_0)). \tag{7}$$

where the S_1 represents the side lobe range of the azimuth pattern at $\theta = \theta_0$ and the S_2 denotes the side lobe region of the pitch-direction pattern at $\phi = \phi_0$.

If the zero-power point of the main lobe of the azimuth pattern is set as $2\varphi_0$, then we have $S_1 = \{\phi | \phi_{\min} \leq \phi \leq \phi_0 - \varphi_0 \cup \phi_0 + \varphi_0 \leq \phi \leq \phi_{\max}\}$.

If the zero-power point of the main lobe of the pitch-direction pattern is $2\psi_0$, then $S_2 = \{\theta | \theta_{\min} \leq \theta \leq \theta_0 - \psi_0 \cup \theta_0 + \psi_0 \leq \theta \leq \theta_{\max}\}$.

Hence, the fitness function is described as $\min_{f}(MSLL)$.

3 The Modified Brain Storm Optimization

3.1 The Basic BSO Algorithm

The BSO algorithm was firstly contributed to Shi in 2011 [19, 20]. It is a global search optimal algorithm, which simulates the proceeding of the human brainstorming and can get the globally best.

The basic BSO generally employs three strategies to produces new candidate solutions and more especially the clustering operator organizes solutions into different groups by using a k-means algorithm. The creating operator is used to produces new candidate solutions by combining existing solutions with a disturbance vector. Selecting the operator determines whether the solutions will be kept into the next generation based on their fitness values. The main procedure of the basic BSO is described as Algorithm 1.

Algorithm 1. Procedure of the basic brain storm optimization algorithm

01. **Initialization**: Randomly generate n potential solutions, and evaluate them;
02. **while** not termination condition **do**
03.   **Clustering**: Cluster n individuals into m clusters by a clustering algorithm;
04.   **Creating**: Randomly select one or two cluster(s) to generate new individual;
05.   **Selection**: The newly generated individual is compared with the existing individual with the same individual index; the better one is kept and recorded as the new individual;
06.   Evaluate the n individuals.
07. **end**

3.2 Clustering with Gaussian Mixture Model

The basic BSO employs the k-means algorithm, which partitions the candidate solutions into k clusters. The k-means algorithm has problems such as non-circular and overlapping situations. It is often not suitable when clusters are not round shaped. Since it uses some distance functions and distance is measured from the clustering center. Another major problem is that data points may be overlapping between the clusters. But they are deterministically assigned to one and only one cluster. To address these problems, we introduce the Gaussian mixture model into the modified BSO version. In this approach, it describes each cluster by its centroid (mean), covariance, and the cluster size.

For $\underline{x} \in \Re^d$, we can define a Gaussian mixture model by making each of the components a Gaussian density with parameters μ_k and $\sum_k$. Each component is a multivariate Gaussian density

$$p_k(\underline{x}|\theta_k) = \frac{1}{(2\pi)^{d/2}|\sum_k|^{1/2}} e^{-\frac{1}{2}(\underline{x}-\underline{\mu}_k)'\sum_k^{-1}(\underline{x}-\underline{\mu}_k)}. \tag{8}$$

with its own parameters $\theta_k = \left\{\underline{\mu}_k, \sum_k\right\}$.

We define the Expectation-Maximization (EM) algorithm for Gaussian mixtures as follows. The algorithm is an iterative algorithm that starts from some initial estimates of Θ (e.g., random), and then proceeds to iteratively update Θ until convergence is detected, where the complete set of parameters is $\Theta = \{\alpha_1, \cdots, \alpha_K, \theta_1, \cdots \theta_K\}$. Each iteration consists of an E-step and an M-step.

E-Step: Denote the current parameter values as Θ. Compute the weight ω_{ik} of data point x_i in cluster k for all data points x_i, $1 \leq i \leq N$ and all mixture components $1 \leq k \leq K$.

M-Step: Now use the weights and the data to calculate new parameter values. Let $N_k = \sum_{i=1}^{N} \omega_{ik}$, i.e., the sum of the membership weights for the k-th component—this is the effective number of data points assigned to component k.

3.3   Clustering with Gaussian Mixture Model

The basic BSO algorithm is initialized utilizing real-number encoding and generates new candidate solutions by using the sigmoid function. The updating formulas are given as follows.

$$x_{\text{offsprings}} = x_{\text{parents}} + \xi \times G(\mu, \sigma). \tag{9}$$

$$x_{\text{parents}} = \begin{cases} x_i^d & \text{one cluster} \\ \omega_1 \times x_i^d + \omega_2 \times x_j^d & \text{two clusters} \end{cases}. \tag{10}$$

where $x_{\text{offsprings}}$ and x_{parents} represent the new generated and the selected solutions from a cluster or two clusters respectively. $G(\mu, \sigma)$ is Gaussian random function with mean μ and standard derivation σ. Superscript d denotes the dimension index. The ω_1 and ω_2 are weight values. The ξ is the coefficient called step-size. It is a logarithmic sigmoid transfer function, which affects the contribution of the Gaussian noise [21, 22].

In the binary BSO, the solution is updated in a continuous version. The difference between binary BSO with continuous version is that the solutions are mapped in terms of probabilities that a bit will change to one. Using this definition, a solution must be restricted within the range [0, 1]. So, a map is introduced to map all real valued-numbers of velocity to the range [0, 1]. The normalization function used here is a sigmoid function as:

$$x'_{ij}(t) = sig(x_{ij}(t)) = \frac{1}{1 + e^{-x_{ij}(t)}}. \tag{11}$$

And the binary candidate solution is obtained using the equation below:

$$x_{ij}(t+1) = \begin{cases} 1 & \text{if } r_{ij} < x'_{ij}(t) \\ 0 & \text{otherwise} \end{cases}. \tag{12}$$

where r_{ij} is a uniform random number in the range [0, 1].

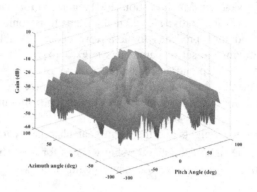

(a) The directional 3D diagram.

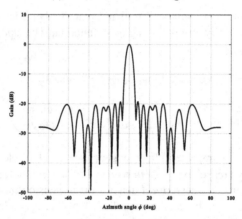

(b) Azimuth pattern.

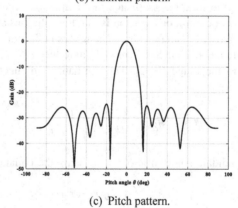

(c) Pitch pattern.

Fig. 2. The directional pattern of the optimized antenna array

4 Experimental Simulation and Result Analysis

The experiments are carried out on a planar array consisting of 20 azimuthal elements and 10 pitched elements. The pitched array is constructed with equal intervals of half wavelength. All array elements are in accord with the equiamplitude and omnidirectional. The wavelength is 1 m, and the array aperture sets as 9.5 m × 4.5 m. The beam pointing angle is $(0°, 0°)$, and the sparse rate is 50%. A sparse array with 100 elements is simulated to minimize the sum of the maximum sidelobe level in the sparse azimuth pattern and the maximum sidelobes in the pitch pattern.

The population size of the modified BSO is 50, and the number of maximum iteration is set to 200 for one execution. The simulation results of the best array are illustrated as Figs. 2 and 3, respectively. Figure 4 shows the best fitness values of two swarm algorithms over iterations.

From Fig. 2, we can see that Fig. 2(a) shows the directional 3D diagram of the thinned antenna array based on the modified BSO algorithm. Figures 2(b) and (c) detail the process of the azimuth pattern and the pitch pattern, respectively. The Fig. 3 shows the element locations of the thinned antenna array using the proposed BSO algorithm.

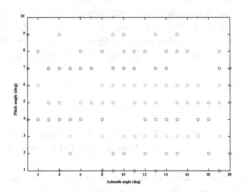

Fig. 3. The element locations of the thinned antenna array

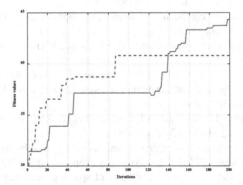

Fig. 4. The fitness evolution curves over iterations.

Figure 4 shows the best fitness curves of the BSO and GA in 200 iterations. Although the GA works well at an earlier stage (before 140 iterations), the modified BSO has the pattern of coming from behind to outperform GA. Therefore, the BSO algorithm has good applicability to the synthesis of the thinned planar arrays.

5 Conclusions

The antenna array thinning problem is a combinatorial optimization problem. This problem has made designing a suitable algorithm for thinning a large-scale antenna array very difficult. This paper presents a new method for optimizing planar antenna array configurations. The modified BSO algorithm is designed on the Gaussian mixture model and the binary creating operator basis. After a successful application of the algorithm to pattern synthesis of the planar antenna array, the simulation results show that the proposed BSO algorithm in its modified version has good applicability for the synthesis of thinned planar arrays over GA.

Acknowledgment. This work is supported by the National Key R&D Program of China (No. 2018YFC0407101), Fundamental Research Funds for the Central Universities (No. 2019B22314), National Natural Science Foundation of China (No. 61403121), Program for New Century Excellent Talents in Fujian Province University (No. GY-Z18155), Program for Outstanding Young Scientific Researcher in Fujian Province University (No. GY-Z160149) and Scientific Research Foundation of Fujian University of Technology (No. GY-Z17162).

References

1. Bevelacqua, P.: Array Antennas (2017). Antenna-theory.com. Accessed 23 Feb 2017
2. Schwartzman, L.: Element behavior in a thinned array. IEEE Trans. Antennas Propag. **15**(4), 571–572 (1967)
3. Schrank, H., Hacker, P.S.: Antenna Designer's Notebook-thinned arrays: some fundamental considerations. IEEE Antennas Propag. Mag. **34**(3), 43–44 (1992)
4. Miller P.: The Smart Swarm: How Understanding Flocks, Schools, and Colonies Can Make Us Better at Communicating, Decision Making, and Getting Things Done. Avery Publishing Group, Inc., Wayne (2010). ISBN 978-1-58333-390-7
5. Chen, J.F., Wu, T.J.: A computational intelligence optimization algorithm: cloud drops algorithm. Integr. Comput. Aided Eng. **21**(2), 177–188 (2014)
6. Haupt, R.L.: Thinned arrays using genetic algorithms. IEEE Trans. Antennas Propag. **42**(7), 993–999 (1994)
7. Ares-Pena, F.J., Rodriguez-Gonzalez, J.A., Villanueva-Lopez, E., Rengarajan, S.R.: Genetic algorithms in the design and optimization of antenna array patterns. IEEE Trans. Antennas Propag. **47**(3), 506–510 (1999)
8. Marcano, D., Durán, F.: Synthesis of antenna arrays using genetic algorithms. IEEE Antennas Propag. Mag. **42**(3), 12–20 (2000)
9. Villegas, F.J.: Parallel genetic-algorithm optimization of shaped beam coverage areas using planar 2-D phased arrays. IEEE Trans. Antennas Propag. **55**(6), 1745–1753 (2007)
10. Chen, K., Yun, X., He, Z., Han, C.: Synthesis of sparse planar arrays using modified real genetic algorithm. IEEE Trans. Antennas Propag. **55**(4), 1067–1073 (2007)

11. Jain, R., Mani, G.S.: Solving antenna array thinning problem using genetic algorithm. Appl. Comput. Intell. Soft Comput. **2012**, 24 (2012)
12. Zhang, L., Jiao, Y.C., Chen, B., Li, H.: Orthogonal genetic algorithm for planar thinned array designs. Int. J. Antennas Propag. **2012**, 7 (2012)
13. Ha, B.V., Mussetta, M., Pirinoli, P., Zich, R.E.: Modified compact genetic algorithm for thinned array synthesis. IEEE Antennas Wirel. Propag. Lett. **15**, 1105–1108 (2016)
14. Cheng, Y.F., Shao, W., Zhang, S.J., Li, Y.P.: An improved multi-objective genetic algorithm for large planar array thinning. IEEE Trans. Magn. **52**(3), 1–4 (2016)
15. Quevedo-Teruel, O., Rajo-Iglesias, E.: Ant colony optimization in thinned array synthesis with minimum sidelobe level. IEEE Antennas Wirel. Propag. Lett. **5**, 349–352 (2006)
16. Li, W.T., Shi, X.W., Hei, Y.Q.: An improved particle swarm optimization algorithm for pattern synthesis of phased arrays. Prog. Electromagn. Res. **82**, 319–332 (2008)
17. Lanza Diego, M., Perez Lopez, J.R., Basterrechea, J.: Synthesis of planar arrays using a modified particle swarm optimization algorithm by introducing a selection operator and elitism. Prog. Electromagn. Res. **93**, 145–160 (2009)
18. Wang, W.B., Feng, Q.Y., Liu, D.: Synthesis of thinned linear and planar antenna arrays using binary PSO algorithm. Prog. Electromagn. Res. **127**, 371–388 (2012)
19. Shi, Y.: Brain storm optimization algorithm. In: Tan, Y., Shi, Y., Chai, Y., Wang, G. (eds.) ICSI 2011. LNCS, vol. 6728, pp. 303–309. Springer, Heidelberg (2011). https://doi.org/10.1007/978-3-642-21515-5_36
20. Shi, Y.: An optimization algorithm based on brainstorming process. In: Emerging Research on Swarm Intelligence and Algorithm Optimization, pp. 1–35. IGI Global (2015)
21. Wang, J., Chen, J., Xue, X., Du, J.: Search strategies investigation in brain storm optimization. Memetic Comput. **10**(4), 397–409 (2018)
22. Chen, J., Cheng, S., Chen, Y., Xie, Y., Shi, Y.: Enhanced brain storm optimization algorithm for wireless sensor networks deployment. In: Tan, Y., Shi, Y., Buarque, F., Gelbukh, A., Das, S., Engelbrecht, A. (eds.) ICSI 2015. LNCS, vol. 9140, pp. 373–381. Springer, Cham (2015). https://doi.org/10.1007/978-3-319-20466-6_40

Refrigerated Showcase Fault Detection by a Correntropy Based Artificial Neural Network Using Fast Brain Storm Optimization

Naoya Otaka[1(✉)], Yoshikazu Fukuyama[1], Yu Kawamura[2],
Kenya Murakami[2], Adamo Santana[2], Tatsuya Iizaka[2],
and Tetsuro Matsui[2]

[1] Graduate School of Advances Mathematical Sciences,
Meiji University, 4-21-1, Nakano, Nakano-ku, Tokyo 164-8525, Japan
naosan1838je@gmail.com, yfukuyam@meiji.ac.jp
[2] Corporate R&D Headquarters, Fuji Electric, Co., Ltd.,
Fuji-machi 1, Hino, Tokyo 191-8502, Japan

Abstract. This paper proposes refrigerated showcase fault detection by a correntropy based Artificial Neural Network (ANN) using Fast Brain Storm Optimization (FBSO). Since there are approximately 50,000 convenience stores in Japan and it is difficult for experts to tune up all of showcase systems with different characteristics. Therefore, an automatic parameter tuning method for various showcase systems such as ANN should be applied. Effectiveness of the proposed method is verified by comparison with conventional least square error (LSE) based ANNs using stochastic gradient descent (SGD) and correntropy based ANNs using Differential Evolutionary Particle Swarm Optimization (DEEPSO) with actual showcase data.

Keywords: Fault detection · Refrigerated showcase ·
Artificial neural network · Correntropy · Fast brain storm optimization

1 Introduction

Refrigerated showcases generally circulate cold air using air fans and maintain temperatures inside the showcases at predetermined temperatures in order to keep temperatures of food and drink in supermarkets and convenience stores. Abnormal conditions that the showcases cannot maintain the predetermined temperatures may occur because of refrigerant leakage and frost formation of refrigerated showcases. Deterioration in food quality may occur when the predetermined temperatures of the showcases cannot be maintained. Accurate fault detection using IoT technologies is crucial for customer service. According to advance in IoT technologies, on-line monitoring of showcase conditions can be realized in order to recognize various abnormal conditions of refrigerated showcases.

Using unsupervised learning techniques including expectation maximization, k-means, and self-organizing maps, a fault detection method of refrigerated showcases has been developed by Santana et al. [1]. Air-conditioners also utilize refrigeration

© Springer Nature Switzerland AG 2019
Y. Tan et al. (Eds.): ICSI 2019, LNCS 11655, pp. 286–296, 2019.
https://doi.org/10.1007/978-3-030-26369-0_27

cycles and an only few methods have been also proposed for air-conditioner fault detection. These methods can be divided into two groups: classic artificial intelligence and integration methods of plural techniques. In classic artificial intelligence techniques, Rossi et al. developed a rule-based fault detection method for vapor compression air-conditioners [2]. York et al. developed a rule-based fault detection system for air handling unit [3]. Han et al. developed a rule-based fault diagnosis expert system for variable air volume (VAV) air handling unit [4]. In integration methods of plural techniques, Li et al. proposed a statistical rule-based fault detection method for package air-conditioners [5]. Han et al. proposed a fault detection method for vapor compression refrigeration systems that integrates support vector machine (SVM) with principal component analysis (PCA) [6].

As of January in 2016, 55,640 convenience stores exist in Japan [7]. Since climatic environments of stores are different in various regions, introduced showcases are different, and a characteristic of each showcase system is different. Therefore, engineers are required to develop different knowledge for fault detection for each showcase using classic artificial intelligence. Namely, it is difficult for engineers to tune up fault detection systems for all showcase systems with different characteristics. Integration methods require engineers to understand the contents of the method and set various parameters by understanding the meaning of the parameters. On the other hand, fault detection models and rules can be generated by machine learning based methods only with learning data automatically.

Artificial neural network (ANN) is one of machine learning techniques and a sort of supervised learning methods. It can generate a fault detection model only with learning data and engineers can utilize it without understanding learning algorithms of ANN such as SGD. Therefore, it can be applied to showcases with different characteristic automatically. However, these conventional ANN based methods have two challenges. The first one is effectiveness of ANN weights learning. Conventionally, SGD has been applied for parameter tuning of ANN [8]. However, using SGD, ANN parameters may be trapped in local minima. Although PSO based ANNs have been utilized for escaping from local minima, it still has a problem of premature convergence [9, 10]. In order to tackle the challenge, the authors have developed DEEPSO based ANN and it has been verified to realize high accuracy for refrigerated showcase fault detection [11]. However, there is still room for improving fault detection accuracy. FBSO is one of the improvement method of Brain storm optimization (BSO) and it has a possibility to overcome the problem [12]. The second one is engineering for handling abnormal data. When abnormal data exist in the learning data, SGD tries to calculate the gradient to the abnormal data and move to the direction which can minimize the difference between the abnormal data and the outputs of the ANN. Therefore, a learned model becomes inappropriate for normal test data. Therefore, when abnormal data exist in learning data for refrigerated showcase fault detection, engineers have to remove the abnormal data for developing an appropriate ANN model. Since it is a heavy workload for the engineer, development of a fault detection method that can reduce the workload for the engineer is one of crucial challenges in this field. Correntropy has been proposed in order to solve this problem [13]. Even if there are abnormal data, correntropy can naturally ignore the data. The authors have developed a correntropy based ANN using DEEPSO for fault detection of refrigerated showcase [11]. The method is verified to realize more accurate fault detection than LSE based ANN using SGD, LSE based ANN using PSO, and LSE based ANN using DEEPSO. Therefore, utilization of correntropy can be effective for handling abnormal data of showcases.

This paper proposes a fault detection method for refrigerated showcase by a correntropy based ANN using FBSO. Effectiveness of the proposed method is verified by comparison with a conventional LSE based ANN using SGD and a correntropy based ANN using DEEPSO with actual showcase data.

2   Refrigerated Showcase Fault Detection

The amount of refrigerant flow and temperatures of various points inside the showcases are measured for management of showcases. Therefore, fault detection of showcases can be realized using the measured sensor data. For example, if measured data of showcases can be gathered and stored in data center through cloud computing, fault detection rules of various stores using ANN can be generated automatically and remote detection can be realized using the learned ANN. For example, when abnormal conditions occur in a showcase of a certain store, an operator confirms the system situation of the showcase using a Web application. Then, the operator dispatches service persons to the store, and the showcase is checked and the service company can respond to the abnormal condition. Such rapid treatment of faults in showcases can be realized according to recent progress of IoT technologies.

A fault detection method has to be developed using normal and abnormal condition data in order to realize on-line fault detection of showcases. This paper assumes offline learning of ANN for fault detection of showcases is executed using stored data in data center and online fault detection is executed using the learned ANN and online data gathered from various stores.

3   Conventional Parameter Tuning Methods of ANN

A multi-layer ANN is a hierarchical neural network composed of input layer, hidden layer, and output layer. The following sigmoid function is usually utilized as an activation function for multi-layer ANN:

$$f(u) = \tilde{f}(u) = \frac{1}{1 + e^{-u}} \tag{1}$$

where u is an input value to the activated function.

Conventionally, a multi-layer ANN is learned by SGD using the following loss function. Weights and biases of a neural network are updated in order to reduce a loss function value. Using SGD, the tuning of ANN weights may be trapped in local minima.

$$E_p = \frac{1}{2} \sum_{j=1}^{J} \left(t_{pj} - o_{pj} \right)^2 \quad (p = 1, \cdots, P) \tag{2}$$

where, E_p is a loss function for pattern p, t_{pj} is p th target data of j th output layer unit, J is the number of output layer units, P is the number of training data.

SGD evaluates LSE using difference between an output value of ANN and a target value. However, a loss function value increases drastically when the difference become large. Therefore, overfitting may occur by LSE based learning in order to reduce the large loss function value.

4 The Proposed Fault Detection Method for Refrigerated Showcase by a Correntropy Based ANN Using FBSO

4.1 Overview of Correntropy [13]

Using LSE, when a difference between an output value of ANN and a target value become large, a loss function value increases drastically. Therefore, whole classification results are influenced by abnormal values. Correntropy is a technique to solve the challenge. A correntropy has been proposed by Liu, Pokharel, and Principe in 2006. The loss function is expressed using the following equation by Correntropy:

$$maxE(o) = \frac{1}{P}\sum_{p=1}^{P} f(o_i - t_i) \tag{3}$$

$$f(o_i - t_i) = \frac{1}{\sqrt{2\pi\sigma^2}} exp\left(-\frac{(o_i - t_i)^2}{2\sigma^2}\right) \tag{4}$$

where σ is a kernel size.

A form of normal distribution is utilized by Correntropy using the difference between an output value of ANN and a target value for evaluation.

Difference between the LSE based method and the correntropy based method can be explained as follows. Loss function values by the LSE using (2) and correntropy based methods using (3) and (4) are shown in Fig. 1(a) and (b). σ in (4) is set to 1 in Fig. 1(b). In Fig. 1 (a), when error is 3, a loss function value is 9 and when error is 4, the value is 16. When errors increase using the LSE based method, loss function values increase drastically. Therefore, since ANN learning by the LSE based method is a kind of minimization problems, learning of weights are largely influenced by the large differences. On the contrary, in Fig. 1(b), when error is 3, a loss function value by correntropy is approximately 0.004 and when error is 4, the value is approximately 0.0001. Therefore, using correntropy, loss function values reduce extremely when errors exceed a certain constant value. Therefore, since ANN learning by correntropy is a kind of maximization problems, learning of ANN weights are not influenced by the large differences. Namely, learning by correntropy based method is performed in order to be suitable for normal data rather than abnormal data.

As shown above, difference of the loss functions largely influences to fault detection results. Learning and test stages by the LSE and the correntropy based methods using different decision boundary functions are shown by Figs. 2 and 3. In the

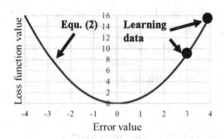 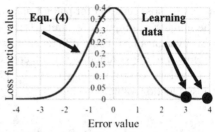

(a) Loss function values by the LSE method using (2) to the differences for two patterns between target values and ANN outputs.

(b) Loss function values by correntropy using (3) and (4) to the differences for two patterns between target values and ANN outputs.

Fig. 1. Loss function values by the LSE method and correntropy for two learning data.

figures, black circle data means normal data and white circle data means fault data. Decision boundary functions in order to classify data are shown by Bold solid curves. Using the LSE based method, the decision boundary function is drastically influenced in order to fit to abnormal data and it is largely bended as shown in Fig. 2(a). Then, at the test stage, using the function, fault detection leads to be incorrect as shown in Fig. 2(b). On the contrary, as shown in Fig. 3(a), the decision boundary function by the correntropy based method is not influenced by abnormal data and appropriate (not overfitted) learning is performed. Then, test data can be correctly classified and improvement of classification accuracy can be expected using the correntropy based method (Fig. 3(b)).

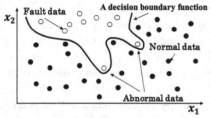 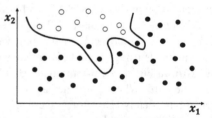

(a) A learning stage using the LSE based method.

(b) A test stage using the LSE based method.

Fig. 2. Learning and test stages using the LSE based method.

The loss function values using correntropy depends on kernel size, σ, in (4). Therefore, σ should be carefully tuned considering various data of the target fault detection problem.

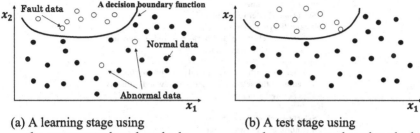

(a) A learning stage using
the correntropy based method.

(b) A test stage using
the correntropy based method.

Fig. 3. Learning and test stages using the correntropy based method.

4.2 Overview of FBSO [12]

BSO is proposed by Shi in 2011 [14] and it is one of evolutionary computation methods. BSO utilizes various procedures, namely, initialization, clustering, generation of new individuals, and selection.

- Initialization: N Individuals are randomly generated.
- Clustering: All individuals are separated into several clusters using k-means method.
- New Individuals Generation: New individuals are generated using the following equations.

$$y_{ij}^k = x_{ij}^k + logsig\left(\frac{0.5 \times k - k\_max}{h}\right) \times rand(0,1) \times N(0,1)_{ij}^k \qquad (5)$$
$$(i = 1, \cdots, N_I, \quad j = 1, \cdots, N_{DV})$$

$$x_{ij}^k = rand(0,1) \times x_{ij1}^k + (1 - rand(0,1)) \times x_{ij2}^k \qquad (6)$$
$$(i = 1, \cdots, N_I, \quad j = 1, \cdots, N_{DV})$$

where y_{ij}^{iter} is a newly generated individual of decision variable j of individual i at iteration k, N_I is the number of individuals, k_max is the maximum number of iteration, h is a coefficient to change slope of log-sigmoid transfer function, N_{DV} is the number of decision variables x_{ij}^k, x_{ij1}^k, and x_{ij2}^k are selected current searching points of decision variable j of individual i at iteration k, $rand(0,1)$ is an uniform random number in the range $(0,1)$, $N(\mu, \sigma)_{ij}^k$ is a Gaussian random real number for decision variable j of individual i at iteration k.

- Selection: The newly generated individual is compared with the current individuals with the same index of individual and record the better one as new individual.

BSO utilizes the k-means method for clustering. It makes the BSO algorithm time-consuming to perform the clustering in every iteration. In order to solve the problem, FBSO utilizes a simple grouping method (SGM) [15] developed for modified BSO instead of k-means method utilized in the original BSO [14]. An algorithm of new individuals' generation is shown in Fig. 4. In the figure, the cluster center is the best evaluated individual instead of the closest individual to the center of the cluster from the distance point of view in k-means method.

```
if rand(0, 1) < P_one
    Select one cluster randomly.
    if rand(0, 1) < P_one_center
        Select the cluster center in the selected cluster, new
        individual is generated using (5)
    else
        Select one individual randomly except the cluster
        center in the selected cluster, and new individual is
        generated using (5)
else
    Select two clusters randomly
    if rand(0, 1) < P_two_center
        Select the cluster centers in the selected cluster, new
        individual is generated using (5) and (6).
    else
        Select two individuals except the centers randomly
        in the selected clusters, and new individual is
        generated using (5) and (6).
```

Fig. 4. An algorithm of new individuals' generation.

The procedures of SGM can be expressed as follows:

- Step. 1 Select M different individuals randomly from the current individuals as cluster centers of M clusters.
- Step. 2 Distances to M cluster centers for all current individuals are calculated, compare the distance values to M cluster centers, and allocate the individual to the closest cluster.

4.3 The Proposed Fault Detection Method for Refrigerated Showcase by a Correntropy Based ANN Using FBSO

The proposed fault detection method for refrigerated showcase by a correntropy based ANN using FBSO is shown in Fig. 5. Learning for the correntropy based ANN using FBSO have three procedures. Firstly, sensor data of the showcases are input into the proposed ANN and outputs are calculated by forward propagation as shown in Fig. 5. Next, loss function value is calculated by correntropy using sum of difference between outputs of ANN and target values using all learning data. Then, weights and biases of ANN are updated based on the FBSO processes to maximize the loss function value by correntropy.

The proposed fault detection algorithm for refrigerated showcases by a correntropy based ANN using FBSO is shown below:

- Step. 1 Initial weights and biases of ANN of all individual are generated within predetermined limits randomly.
- Step. 2 The initial ANN weights and biases of individuals are evaluated by correntropy based loss function values with all learning data of showcase. k is set to 1.
- Step. 3 Weights and biases of individuals are divided into several clusters using the SGM procedure explained in Sect. 4.2.
- Step. 4 Generate new weights and biases of individuals using the new individuals generation procedure explained in Sect. 4.2.

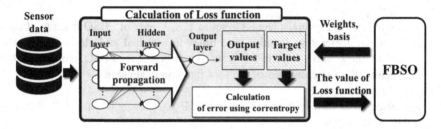

Fig. 5. Learning for the correntropy based ANN using FBSO.

Step. 5 Loss function values of individuals are calculated by correntropy using new weights and biases of ANN with learning data of showcase.

Step. 6 The newly generated weights and biases are compared with the current weights and biases of ANN with the same individual index. The better one is stored as the current weights and biases of the ANN.

Step. 7 When the current iteration number reaches k_max, the procedure can be stopped. Otherwise, $k = k + 1$ and go to Step. 3. Then, repeat the procedures.

5 Simulation

5.1 Simulation Conditions

The proposed correntropy based ANN for refrigerated showcase fault detection using FBSO is applied to actual showcase data for three months. Fault detection results by the proposed correntropy based ANN using FBSO method are compared with fault detection results by the conventional LSE based ANN using SGD and the correntropy based ANN using DEEPSO. Simulation conditions are shown below:

- All showcase data are separated into 30% test data and 70% learning data.
- The number of hidden units is set to 10.
- Sigmoid functions are utilized as activation functions of all layers in the proposed ANN.
- The kernel size of the loss function is set to 1.0 by pre-simulation.
- Abnormal data are included in the learning data at a rate of 5% and 10% randomly (missing rates).
- 90% of normal data are reduced randomly by random under sampling because rates of normal and fault showcase data are imbalanced.
- Since learning results of ANN generally depends on initial weights and biases, the number of trials is set to 30.
- Rates that fault data are classified to be faulty accurately (Fault), rates that normal data are classified to be normal accurately (Normal), and rates of accurate fault detection (Total) are utilized for the evaluations.
- The parameters of FBSO and DEEPSO are shown below:

(a) Common parameters
    The number of individuals(agents) is set to 128, k_max of FBSO is set to 40000.
    DEEPSO evaluates loss function two times for original and clone individuals.
    Therefore, the k_max for DEEPSO is set to half of that for FBSO, namely, 20000
    for keeping the same number of the loss function evaluations.
(b) FBSO parameters
    P_replace is set to 0.1, P_one is set to 0.9, P_one_center is set to 0.7, P_two_-
    center is set to 0.9.
(c) DEEPSO parameters
    The learning parameters τ and τ' are set to 0.4 and 0.001,
    Probability p is set to 0.95, the initial values of B_{ij}^k and C_{ij}^k are set to 0.9 and 0.4.

- The parameters of SGD are shown below:
  Learning rate is set to 0.1, the maximum iteration number of SGD is set to 200000.
  In order to set the same number of the loss function evaluations, the number has to
  be set to 5120000 (128 * 40000). However, the number is set to 300000 because
  SGD is already converged with 300000.
  It is the most important for fault detection of the showcases to minimize influence
  on customers by fault. Therefore, "Fault" evaluations are considered as most
  important.

5.2   Simulation Results

Table 1 shows average values of accuracy of "Total", "Normal", and "Fault" using
various numbers of missing rates for test data by the LSE based SGD, the correntropy
based DEEPSO, and the proposed correntropy based FBSO. In the case of 0%, 5%, and
10% of missing rates, the proposed correntropy based ANN using FBSO can classify
"fault" more accurately than the conventional methods (bold numbers). Namely, even
when abnormal data do not exist in the learning data, the proposed method can classify
"fault" more accurately than the conventional methods. Moreover, when abnormal data
exist in the learning data, there is a possibility that the proposed correntropy based
ANN using FBSO can classify "fault" accurately without engineering.

Table 1. Average values of accuracy using various number of missing rates for test data by the
LSE based SGD, the correntropy based DEEPSO, and the proposed correntropy based FBSO.

Method	Evaluation	Missing rates [%]		
		0	5	10
LSE based SGD	Total [%]	98.603	97.772	97.526
	Normal [%]	99.241	98.587	98.367
	Fault [%]	81.879	79.896	78.996

(*continued*)

Table 1. (*continued*)

Method	Evaluation	Missing rates [%]		
		0	5	10
Correntropy based DEEPSO	Total [%]	99.052	99.012	99.007
	Normal [%]	99.593	99.585	99.583
	Fault [%]	84.832	83.980	83.893
The proposed Correntropy based FBSO	Total [%]	99.124	99.056	99.032
	Normal [%]	99.640	99.614	99.608
	Fault [%]	**85.688**	**84.322**	**83.996**

6 Conclusions

This paper proposes refrigerated showcase fault detection by a correntropy based ANN using FBSO. Effectiveness of the proposed method is verified by comparison with the conventional LSE based ANN using SGD and the correntropy based ANN using DEEPSO with actual showcase data. Using actual showcase data, even if abnormal data exist in learning data, it is verified that the proposed method can classify "fault" more accurately without engineering than the conventional methods.

As future works, for improvement in accuracy of fault detection, various techniques for imbalanced data and applications of various deep learning techniques integrated with evolutionary computation methods will be investigated.

References

1. Santana, A., et al.: Machine learning application for refrigeration showcase fault discrimination. In: Proceedings of Region 10 Conference of IEEE (TENCON) (2016)
2. Rossi, T.M., et al.: A statistical, rule-based fault detection and diagnostic method for vapor compression air conditioners. HVAC&R Res. **3**, 19–37 (1997)
3. Youk, S., et al: Fault detection system using directional classified rule-based in AHU. In: Proceedings of Future Generation Communication and Networking (FGCN) (2007)
4. Han, D., et al.: Automated fault diagnosis method for a variable air volume air handling unit. In: Proceedings of International Conference on Control, Automation and Systems - Society of Instrument and Control Engineers (ICCAS-SICE) (2009)
5. Li, H., et al.: Application of automated fault detection and diagnostics for rooftop air conditioners in California. In: Proceedings of 2004 ACEEE Summer Study on Energy Efficiency in Buildings, pp. 190–201 (2004)
6. Han, H., et al.: PCA-SVM-based Automated Fault Detection and Diagnosis (AFDD) for vapor-compression refrigeration systems. HVAC&R Res. **16**, 295–313 (2010)
7. Number of convenience stores (konbini) in Japan from 2007 to 2016 (in 1,000 s). https://www.statista.com/statistics/810901/japan-convenience-store-numbers/
8. Eberhart, R., et al.: Neural Network PC Tools. Academic Press, Cambridge (1990)
9. Zhang, C., et al.: Particle swarm optimization for evolving artificial neural network. In: Proceedings of IEEE International Conference on Systems, Man, and Cybernetics (SMC 2000) (2000)

10. Kennedy, J., Eberhart, R.: Swarm Intelligence, Morgan Kaufmann (2001)
11. Otaka, N., et al.: Refrigerated showcase fault analysis by artificial neural network using correntropy based differential evolutionary particle swarm optimization. In: Proceedings of System Technology and Smart Facility Workshop of IEE of Japan (2018). (in Japanese)
12. Arai, K., et al.: Dependable parallel multi-population fast brain storm optimization for on-line optimal operational planning of energy plants. In: Proceedings of National Convention of IEE of Japan, pp. 4–229 (2019). (in Japanese)
13. Liu, W., Pokharel, P.P., Principe, J.C.: Correntropy: a localized similarity measure. In: Proceedings of International Joint Conference on Neural networks (IJCNN) (2006)
14. Shi, Y., et al.: Brain storm optimization algorithm: a review. Artif. Intell. Rev. **46**(4), 445–458 (2016)
15. Zhan, Z., Shi, Y., et al.: A modified brain storm optimization. In: Proceedings of the IEEE World Congress on Computational Intelligence (2012)

Swarm Intelligence Algorithms and Improvements

Automatic Diet Generation by Artificial Bee Colony Algorithm

Magda López-López, Axel Zamora, and Roberto A. Vazquez(✉)

Intelligent System Lab, Facultad de Ingeniería, Universidad La Salle,
Benjamin Franklin 45, Col. Condesa, 06140 Mexico City, Mexico
{magda.lopez,jorge.zamora,ravem}@lasallistas.org.mx

Abstract. The overweight in the population has become a problem due to the deficiency on the nutritional contributions, increasing the number of people with diseases. The origin of this problem lies in the way people eat, with a poor nutritional quality and in excessive quantities. To solve this, it is necessary that people consider balance diets with the nutritional expectation and the necessary food to improve people's health and reduce the rates of overweight and obesity. The diet design can be stated as an optimization problem and solved using different algorithms. In this paper, an Artificial Bee Colony (ABC) algorithm has been proposed to automatically design diets considering the physical characteristics of the subjects to find the best diet that satisfies their nutritional requirements using the USDA National Nutrient Database. Particularly, this research is focused on relatively healthy people between 18 and 55 years old to help them to avoid nutritional related diseases. The proposed methodology is compared against particle swarm optimization using the Harris-Benedict equation in order to verify if is capable to achieve the calorie goal.

Keywords: Automatic diet generation · Artificial Bee Colony ·
Basal Metabolic Rate

1 Introduction

Nowadays, the overweight and the obesity in Mexico is generated due to an energy imbalance between the calories consumed and spent. This occurs because of the lack of interest that the people take about their health and their alimentation habits. This makes essential to propose a solution or a plan that can lead the Mexicans through a better and healthier life by generating a change in their alimentation. For this, it is propose to utilize the swarm intelligence to develop automatically balanced diets for the necessities of the individuals. There have been another works that utilized computational algorithms to create balanced diets but with a totally different equations and structure of this project. As implementing a multi-objective optimization algorithm NSGA-II and focusing on diabetic patients [1], or based on the Quantum Genetic Algorithm [2]. There is also a work focused on the generation of tasty calorie restricted diets using

© Springer Nature Switzerland AG 2019
Y. Tan et al. (Eds.): ICSI 2019, LNCS 11655, pp. 299–309, 2019.
https://doi.org/10.1007/978-3-030-26369-0_28

a Differential Evolution algorithm [3] and papers applying the particle swarm optimization algorithm as [4,5].

Although the previous papers provide acceptable results during the diet design, they did not consider relevant information such as price which is a relevant factor for complete the diet for the Mexicans. This represents a challenge for this research to achieve a remarkable difference.

In this paper, it is proposed a methodology to automatically design diets considering physical characteristics of the subjects in order to determine the basal metabolic rate in terms of the Harris-Benedict equation, as a reference to design an accurate diet. The design process is conducted by means of the Artificial Bee Colony (ABC) algorithm using the equivalent portions of food that allow to optimize the quantity of calories with restrictions of macronutrients and price. Additionally, we perform a comparison between the Particle Swarm Optimization algorithm. Moreover, the proposed methodology is focused on people with an age between 18 and 55 (because of the Harris-Benedict equation).

2   Basic Concepts

For understanding the diet automation design is necessary to describe all the concepts related with it. The diet calculations and the ABC algorithm are essential parts of the process. This section described the elements used for design the most suitable diet according with the nutritional expectation.

2.1   Diet Calculation

It is possible to create balanced diets with the nutritional quality required to improve the people's health and reduce the probabilities of being with overweight or obese. The diets vary from each individual according with their physical characteristics and the specific number of calories required; specially with kids, seniors and people with food-related diseases. In this paper is consider individuals between 18 and 55 years old, with purpose of taking people into a healthier life.

The diet problem works as a linear optimization problem as described in [6]. In our paper, the objective is to find a low-cost balanced diet that have the nutrients and caloric requirements for the individuals. The linear problem formula is defined by the objective function (Eq. 1), focused on minimizing the cost of the food for the diet, the constrain (Eq. 2) verify the portions of food in all the nutrients and (Eq. 3) is the definition of the variable's domain p.

$$min \sum_i c_i p_i \tag{1}$$

$$\sum_i m_{ij} p_i \geq b_j, \forall j \in \{0, ...N\} \tag{2}$$

$$p_i \geq 0, \forall i \in \{0, ...F\} \tag{3}$$

where c is the cost of the food, p represents the amount of food, m_{ij} is the amount of nutrients in each food, b denotes the minimal requirement of nutrients, N represents the set of nutrients considered in the problem and F is the set of available foods.

The proposal in this paper includes a different approach of the original solution proposed by Stigler, because it only considered a set of 77 foods. So, we can remark that one of the problems is that it does not have a sufficient selection of food. This makes essential to utilize a different approach for the diet generator. For this, the solution seeks to minimize the calories consumed using Artificial Bee Colony algorithm, based on the requirements of a balanced diet. Since the requirements must comply with the equivalent food portions to cover the caloric needs of a healthy person per day.

The linear problem is defined with several variables that will be described next. A decision variable x_i that means the amount of $Kcal$ by portion of food $i \in [1, 24]$, c_i represents the cost of the portion of equivalent food $i \in [1, 24]$, g_j is percentage of macronutrient $j \in \{1, 2, 3\}$ described in grams, and finally n_{ij} is the number of macronutrients represented in grams [7] $j \in \{1, 2, 3\}$ (fat, protein, carbohydrates) contained in the portion of equivalent food $i \in [1, 24]$. With this information, the linear problem proposed formulations are generated (4)–(7):

$$min| \sum_i x_i - Kcal| \qquad (4)$$

Subject to

$$0 \le x_i \le 5616, \forall i \in [1, 24] \qquad (5)$$

$$\sum_i c_i \le b_i, \forall i \in [1, 42] \qquad (6)$$

$$\sum_i n_{ij} \le g_j, \forall j \in \{1, 2, 3\} \qquad (7)$$

where the grams of protein (Eq. 8) are represented as g_1, the grams of fat (Eq. 9) as g_2, the grams of carbohydrates (Eq. 10) as g_3 and the number of $Kcal$ (Eq. 11) corresponded to (Eq. 11) or (Eq. 12), according to [8].

$$g_1 = \frac{Kcal * 0.30}{4} \qquad (8)$$

$$g_2 = \frac{Kcal * 0.20}{9} \qquad (9)$$

$$g_3 = \frac{Kcal * 0.50}{4} \qquad (10)$$

$$Kcal = 6.4 + (13.7 + w) + 5h - 6.76a \qquad (11)$$

$$Kcal = 655.1 + (9.6 + w) + 1.8h - 4.7a \qquad (12)$$

where the variables a, w and h correspond to the age in years of the subject, weight in kilograms and the height in centimeters respectively. The minimization, generated between the calories of the diet and $Kcal$, states the objective function Eq. 4. The $Kcal$ number established the calories to consume by a healthy person in a day (called Basal Metabolic Rate [9]). The $Kcal$ are calculated by the Harris-Benedict formula, which is based on the age, weight and height of the person and varies depending if is a men (see Eq. 11) or a women (see Eq. 12).

To maintain the amount of carbohydrates, fat and protein under the requirements, the Eq. 5 is used. Equation 6 is use to keep the cost of the diet within budget. The Eq. 7 defines the variable x_i domain.

2.2 Artificial Bee Colony

The Artificial Bee Colony (ABC) algorithm was used to find the best solution to generate an automatic balance diet. ABC algorithm is inspired on the honey bees behavior with the purpose of solving multidimensional problems [10]. The algorithm considers the colony size (CS), the number of food sources (FS) and the limit (L) as control parameters. The limit is the abandoned criteria for a solution. In the ABC model, the bees are the agents that search for rich food sources close to their hive, which means good solutions for the problem. The position of the food source represents the possible solution, and the nectar amount of the source represents the fitness function of the solution.

The first phase is where the scouts bees discover food sources randomly. Equation (13) initialize the solution x_m that can hold n variables, l_i and u_i are the lower and upper bounded values $i \in \{1, ..., n\}$ that the solution can take and r is a random number.

$$x_{mi} = l_i + r(u_i - l_i) \tag{13}$$

In the second phase employed bees search for new food sources v_m using Eq. (14), where x_{mi} is the previous food source $i \in \{1, ..., n\}$, x_{ki} is a food source $i \in \{1, ..., n\}$ randomly selected from the population and ϕ_{mi} is a random number between a range previously defined $[-a, a]$. Then a greedy selection is made between v_m and x_m.

$$v_{mi} = x_{mi} + \phi_{mi}(x_{mi} - x_{ki}) \tag{14}$$

The onlooker bees use probability to choose new food sources. The probability value p_m is obtained by Eq. 15, know as a roulette wheel selection method [11]. Where $fit_m(x_m)$ is the fitness value of the solution x_m.

$$p_m = \frac{fit_m(x_m)}{\sum_{m=1}^{FS} fit_m(x_m)} \tag{15}$$

Scout bees create new solutions when a solution cannot be improved before the abandoned criteria(L). Algorithm 1 is the psudo-code of the ABC algorithm. For more details, see [10].

Algorithm 1 Pseudo-code of ABC

Initialize the first population x_i with Eq. 13.

Evaluate the solution.

while *maximum cycle not met* **do**

> Generate new solutions v_m using Eq. 14 and evaluate them.
>
> Make a greedy selection between v_m and x_m.
>
> Calculate probability p_m for solutions x_m applying Eq. 15.
>
> Select new solutions v_m by onlookers bees from the x_m solutions depending on p_m and evaluate them.
>
> Apply the greedy selection process.
>
> Replace the solutions that were not improved before the abandoned criteria (L) with new ones generated by scout bees.
>
> Memorize the best solution achieved so far

end

---

3   Proposed Methodology

The propose methodology tries to generate automatic diets by applying an Artificial Bee Colony algorithm. In order to do that, this methodology is divided in 4 main steps. The first step is focused on obtaining the nutritional information of the equivalent portions of food. The second step was focused on build a fitness function that allows to measure the quality of the designed diet. The third step was devoted to determine how to code the solution into the particles. Finally, taking into account the solutions generated with ABC, different diets were designed based on a manual nutrition. This section describes these details.

1. Data Source. To solve the problem described, is necessary to obtained the products and their characteristics from a Database, in order to calculate the fitness function. First, the objective function evaluates the data on a .csv (coma separated value) file queried of the data source. This function contains the index of the equivalent portion of food and quantity of energy in Kcal. These parts of the index are contained on the equivalent portion of food, quantity of protein, carbohydrates, fat in grams and the cost in Mexican pesos (MXN). Next, the .csv file is read and saved in a bi-dimensional array until complete a solution index. For every iteration, the solution (24 index array) is evaluated; firstly on the objective function, and then on the fitness function, so, then every index is searched in the bi-dimensional array and pull the information to calculate the fitness. The process continues until it gets the best solution. At this time, the information (food name description, portion and quantity of food to consume) of each index corresponding to a food is searched by a query on the database.

2. Fitness Function. The Caloric Restricted Diet problem has certain constrains in order to find the most feasible solution. There are several techniques to handle constrained problems as unconstrained. The method applied by ABC is a tournament selection operator, where two different solutions are compared by applying the Deb's rules [12] in order to manage the constrains according with

[13]. Equation (16) represents the fitness function, which evaluated the non-viable solutions that are based on the number of violated restrictions. Where f_{max} is the worst feasible solution, $g_j(x)$ is the violated constraint $j \in \{1, ..., m\}$, m is the number of violated constrains and $f(x)$ is as defined in Eq. (4).

$$fit(m_x) = \begin{cases} f(x) & \text{if feasible} \\ f_{max} + \sum_{j=1}^{m} g_j(x) & \text{otherwise} \end{cases} \qquad (16)$$

3. Solution Representation. The solution of the problem will be the best fitness of the food source vector, this will be represented as a 24 integer array. Each item in the array represents the index of a equivalent portion of food in the data source. As it presented in Fig. 1 the array is divided in 7 food groups, Vegetables (V), Fruits(F), Cereals(C), Animal Origin(A), Sugar(S) and Fat(F), considered to design a balance diet.

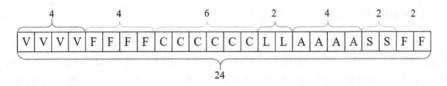

Fig. 1. Structure of the food source represented in a 24 array in terms of different food groups.

4. Diet Design. According with the nutrition manual published by Instituto Mexicano del Seguro Social (IMSS) [14], a balance diet must be composed from 19 to 35 equivalent portions of food, which are divided in 8 food groups that must be eaten through the day, vegtables 4–5, fruits 3–5, cereals 6–11, legumes 1–2, animal origin 2–5, milk 1–3, fat 1–2, sugar 1–2 portion of food. The equivalent portion of food are sorted in the 5 different meals(Breakfast (B), Snack 1 (S1), Lunch (L), Snack 2 (S2) and Dinner (D)), that must be eaten through the day in order to have at least one portion of equivalent food of each group in the main meals(B,L,D), and one or two equivalent portion of food between meals (S1, S2). Table 1 shows the distribution of 24 equivalent portion of foods between the 5 meals of the day. For this paper, 24 items could met the requirements of a caloric restricted diet that is bounded between 1200 Kcal and 2000 Kcal [15]. Milk group is included into the animal origin food group, because of the distribution of the data source used in this work.

4   Experimental Results

In this paper, several experiments were performed to prove the effectiveness of the proposed methodology. The dataset used to perform the experimental tests

Table 1. Distribution of food portions

Food	Vegetables	Fruits	Cereals	Legumes	Animal origin	Fat	Sugar	TOTAL
#Portions	4	4	6	2	4	2	2	24
Breakfast	1	1	2	1	1	1	1	
Snack 1		1						
Lunch	2	1	2		2	1		
Snack 2			1					
Dinner	1	1	1	1	1		1	

was obtained from two sources: the nutritional values was the Standard Reference (SR), from the United States Department of Agriculture Agricultural Research Service USDA National Nutrient Database [16] in the latest update from March 2018; the food cost values were obtained by the monthly average price of food in MXN published by INEGI [17] in the last semester of 2018.

SR database contains more than 7000 food items from several food groups with the nutritional information and food components. The data is presented as a 100 g portion of food and the equivalent nutrients for the portion. Also, the database provided the nutritional information for the amount of a equivalent portion of food, the one used in this work. The data source presents food in several categories included alcoholic beverage, baby food and restaurant food (foods from a specific provider), these ones were not consider into the data set for the experimental tests. The categories used in the experiments were assign to the corresponding food group, Vegetables (V): Vegetables and Vegetable Products with 767 items; Fruits (F): Fruits and Fruit Juices with 345 items; Cereals (C): Breakfast Cereals, Baked Products, Cereals Grains and Pasta with 874 items; Legumes (L): Legumes and Legume Products, Nut and Seed Products with 425 items; Animal Origin and Milk (AO): Sausages and Luncheon Meats, Pork Products, Beef Products,Fish and Shellfish Products, Lamb, Veal and Game Products, Poultry Products, Dairy and Egg Products with 2824 items; Fats (F): Fats and Oils with 214 items; Sugar: Sweets with 325 items.

The control parameter of ABC Algorithm are: Colony Size (CS) set as {5, 10, 12, 16, 20, 22, 24, 28, 30, 36, 38, 40, 44, 45, 50, 60, 70, 80, 90, 100}, the limit for scout bees is calculated by Eq. 17 according to [10].

$$L = (CS * D)/2 \tag{17}$$

where D is the dimension of the problem and is set as D=24. The number of Food Sources is set by Eq. 18 as described in [10]

$$FS = (CS/2) \tag{18}$$

For each parameter configuration, the program was run 30 times aiming to know the best and worst solution, the average of the solution and standard deviation. The caloric goal to reach in these experimental test was 1800 $Kcal$, constrains set as 135 g of protein, 40 g of fat, 225 g of carbohydrates calculated by equations (8–10) and a budged of \$110 MXN, this amount was obtained by the Encuesta Nacional de Ingresos y Gastos de los Hogares (ENIGH) 2016 [18].

The results of the experiments are listed in Table 2, where the first and sixth column represent the control parameters configuration, second and seventh column represent the average solution with standard deviation, third and eight column the best solution, fourth and ninth column the worst solution and the fifth and tenth column the average of $Kcal$ generated by the algorithm. The best solution for each food source configuration is marked in bold and the average evolution of the solution is graphed in Fig. 2.

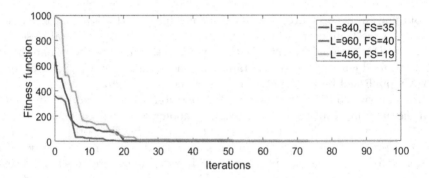

Fig. 2. Average of the solution evolution with the 3 best parameters configurations.

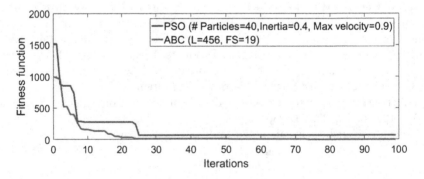

Fig. 3. Comparison of the solution evolution with ABC and PSO.

The constrains values of the best set of parameters are listed in Table 3, where it can be observed that the nutritional restrictions were met without exceeding an error of 10%. The constraint that does not met requirements is the cost, it has an error greater than 15%, this may be due to the variation in prices

Table 2. Experimental results

CS	Average	Best	Worst	Kcal	CS	Average	Best	Worst	Kcal
5	66.53 ± 48.52	0.03	287.87	1823.56	**38**	**0.55 ± 0.43**	**0.00**	**2.96**	**1800.06**
10	149.93 ± 7.62	0.00	608.32	1802.49	40	0.61 ± 0.47	0.01	2.97	1800.11
12	9.84 ± 4.46	0.14	45.87	1801.85	44	0.44 ± 0.29	0.01	3.02	1799.88
16	1.82 ± 1.65	0.01	6.73	1799.97	45	0.28 ± 0.28	0.00	1.20	1800.17
20	23.92 ± 13.93	0.03	87.20	1800.22	50	0.42 ± 0.31	0.00	2.29	1800.00
22	2.92 ± 1.25	0.00	12.23	1800.88	60	0.37 ± 0.24	0.01	1.97	1800.02
24	3.01 ± 1.54	0.032	12.18	1800.75	**70**	**0.35 ± 0.29**	**0.00**	**1.02**	**1800.11**
28	1.52 ± 0.86	0.002	6.45	1800.19	**80**	**0.07 ± 0.09**	**0.00**	**0.32**	**1799.99**
30	10.88 ± 0.75	0.008	5.23	1800.02	90	0.16 ± 0.14	0.00	0.67	1800.01
36	0.34 ± 0.285	0.003	1.00	1800.00	100	0.09 ± 0.11	0.00	0.39	1800.03

in Mexican markets and that the cost obtained by the data source is monthly average. And finally, in the last row of the table are listed the $Kcal$, obtained by the algorithm that has an error of less than 0.1% which means that the ABC algorithm generates good results meeting the nutritional requirements without violating the percentage error of %10 with the exception the cost constraint.

ABC algorithm solution is compared with a solution generated by a Particle Swarm Optimization (PSO) in Fig. 3. The figure shows how faster ABC algorithm is compared with PSO and how the ABC solution almost reach the zero, while PSO does not, and remain in the same value far from zero through several iterations. The table shows the configurations for the control parameters of both algorithms.

Finally, in Table 4 is presented an example of a diet generated by ABC with the configuration on one of the best parameters that reach the caloric goal with

Table 3. Constrains values reached by ABC algorithm.

	Constraint	Reached (L = 840, FS = 35)	Error	Reached (L = 960, FS = 40)	Error	Reached (L = 456, FS = 19)	Error
Protein (g)	≥135	138.36.36	0.0002	138.61	0.0002	136.36	0.0001
Fat (g)	≥40	44.527	0.001	443.648	0.0009	44.543	0.001
Carbs (g)	≥225	233.179	0.0003	229.805	0.0002	229.541	0.0002
Budget (MXN)	≤110	135.97	23.609	142.53	29.572	129.96	18.145
	Kcal desired	Average (L = 840, FS = 35)	Error	Average (L = 960, FS = 40)	Error	Average (L = 456, FS = 19)	Error
Kcal generated	1800	1800.107	5.9E-07	1799.991	4.8E-08	1800.068	3.7E-07

Table 4. Average of the constrains values reached for each parameter configuration

Meal	Kcal	Food	Quantity	Price
Breakfast	28.08	BRUSSELS SPROUTS	0.5 cup	$7.02
	7.7	LIME JUICE	1 fl oz	$1.00
	77.9625	BAGELS	1 oz	$9.30
	140.4	MUFFINS	1 muffin	$8.50
	70.98	TOFU FIRM	0.2 block	$9.50
	273.02	CHICKEN	1 cup, chopped	$16.80
	29.41	APPLE FRUIT BUTTERS	1 tbsp	$1.00
	13.44	MAYONNAISE FAT-FREE	2 tbsp	$0.50
Snack 1	56.24	PEAR	1 half, with liquid	$3.50
Lunch	1.256	RED PEPPERS	1 tbsp	$0.50
	2.0	GREEN PEPPERS	1 ring	$1.00
	167.99	PASTA WITH ADDED SALT	1 cup farfalle	$6.80
	31.92	WHITE BREAD	1 slice crust not eaten	$0.50
	75.65	LAMB	1 oz	$13.50
	177.65	PORK (CHOPS)	3 oz	$7.00
	35.28	ITALIAN SALAD DRESING	1 tbsp	$0.40
	52.44	QUINCES	1 fruit without refuse	$3.60
Snack 2	29.12	GINGERSNAPS COOKIES	1 cookie	$6.50
Dinner	9.288	SESAME CRUNCH	1 piece	$4.81
	72.25	SHRIMP	3 oz	$16.83
	116.7	CEREAL ALPHA-BITS	1 cup	$4.50
	92.13	MANDARIN	1 cup	$4.50
	109.88	YELLOW CORN	1 cup	$5.00
	129.276	DRIED COCONUT MEAT	1 oz	$4.50
Kcal = 1800.062	**Prot = 135.58 g**	**Carbs = 225.193 g**	**Fat = 43.659 g**	**$137.06**

an error of less than 0.1%, in addition to that, the constrains values has an error considered within the parameters of the diet design, with a cost of $137.06 MXN that exceeds the budget by $27.06 MXN.

5 Conclusions

This work described a method to create balanced diets with the nutritional expectation by applying the Artificial Bee Colony (ABC) algorithm. This diets are generated using the physical characteristics of the users and looking to reach the caloric goal in terms of the Harris-Benedict equation. Furthermore, the restrictions of macronutrients and price are considered by the algorithm to achieve the design of an accurate diet.

The results were compared against a similar resource as the Particle Swarm Optimization algorithm (PSO) to identify the best possible solution for the problem. At last, the ABC algorithm had a significant improve in compare with the PSO algorithm. This means, that the error percentage of the ABC was lower and with better results.

Acknowledgment. The authors would like to thank Universidad La Salle México for the support under grant number NEC-10/18.

References

1. Wang, G., Sun, Y.: Applications of MOGA in nutritional diet for diabetic patients. College of Information Science and Technology, Henan University of Technology, Zhengzhou, China (2009)
2. Lv, Y.: Multi-objective nutritional diet optimization based on quantum algorithm. Harbin University of Commerce, Harbin, China (2009)
3. Silva, J.G.R., Carvalho, I.A., Loureiro, M.M.S., da Fonseca Vieira, V., Xavier, C.R.: Developing tasty calorie restricted diets using a differential evolution algorithm. In: Gervasi, O., et al. (eds.) ICCSA 2016. LNCS, vol. 9790, pp. 171–186. Springer, Cham (2016). https://doi.org/10.1007/978-3-319-42092-9_14
4. Lv, Y.: Combined quantum particle swarm optimization algorithm for multi-objective nutritional diet decision making. Harbin University of Commerce, Harbin, China (2009)
5. Rauter, S., Fister, D., Fister, I.: Generating eating plans for athletes using the particle swarm optimization. In: 2016 IEEE 17th International Symposium on Computational Intelligence and Informatics (CINTI) (2016)
6. Stigler, G.J.: The cost of subsistence. J. Farm Econ. **27**, 2 (1945)
7. Food and Agriculture Organization of the United Nations (FAO). Macronutrientes y micronutrientes (2015)
8. María del Carmen Iñarritu Pérez. Elaboración de una dieta
9. Benedict, F.G., Harris, J.A.: A biometric study of human basal metabolism. Proc. Natl. Acad. Sci. U.S.A. **4**(12), 370–3 (1918)
10. Karaboga, D.: An idea based on honey bee swarm for numerical optimization. technical report tr06. Erciyes University, Engineering Faculty, Computer Engineering Department (2005)
11. Goldberg, D.E.: Genetic Algorithms in Search, Optimization And Machine Learning. Addison-Wesley Professional, Boston (1989)
12. Deb, K.: An efficient constraint handling method for genetic algorithms. Comput. Methods Appl. Mech. Eng. **186**, 311–338 (2000)
13. Karaboga, D.: Artificial bee colony algorithm (2010)
14. Instituto Mexicano del Seguro Social (IMMS): Guía de Alimentos para la Población Mexicana. Secretaria de Salud (2010)
15. Marvn Laborde, L., Palicios, B., Pérez Lizaur, A.B.: Sistema Mexicano de Alimentos Equivalentes. Fomento de Nutricin y Salud, A.C. 4th edn. (2014)
16. United States Department of Agriculture Agricultural Research Service (USDA): USDA food composition databases, April 2018
17. Instituto Nacional de Estadística y Geografía (INEGI): Consulta en línea. consulta de precios promedio, July 2018
18. Instituto Nacional de Estadística y Geografía (INEGI): Encuesta nacional de ingresos y gastos de los hogares (enigh), August 2016

A Multi-strategy Artificial Bee Colony Algorithm with Neighborhood Search

Can Sun, Xinyu Zhou$^{(\boxtimes)}$, and Mingwen Wang

School of Computer and Information Engineering,
Jiangxi Normal University, Nanchang 330022, China
xyzhou@jxnu.edu.cn

Abstract. As an effective swarm intelligence based optimization technique, artificial bee colony (ABC) algorithm has become popular in recent years. However, its performance is still not satisfied in solving some complex optimization problems. The main reason is that both of the employed bee phase and onlooker bee phase use the same solution search equation to generate new candidate solutions, and the solution search equation is good at exploration but poor at exploitation. To solve this problem, in this paper, we propose a multi-strategy artificial bee colony algorithm with neighborhood search (MSABC-NS). In MSABC-NS, a multi-strategy mechanism is designed to use two different solution search equations, and a neighborhood search mechanism is introduced to make full use of good solutions. Experiments are conducted on 22 widely used benchmark functions, and three different ABC variants are included in the comparison. The results show that our approach can achieve better performance on most of the benchmark functions.

Keywords: Artificial bee colony · Exploration and exploitation ·
Multi-strategy mechanism · Neighborhood search

1 Introduction

Artificial bee colony (ABC) algorithm is a swarm intelligence based optimization technique, and it has become popular in the community of evolutionary algorithms (EAs) in recent years. Some previous works have pointed out that the performance of ABC is competitive in comparison with other EAs, such as genetic algorithm (GA) [1, 2], particle swarm optimization (PSO) [3, 4], and differential evolution (DE) [5]. The basic ABC is proposed by Karaboga in 2005, which simulates the honeybee's foraging behavior [6, 7]. The basic ABC contains three different kinds of bees, i.e., employed bees, onlooker bees, and scout bees. These three different kinds of bees have different tasks, but they cooperate to maximize the nectar amount, which implies that they cooperate to search the optimal solution of optimization problems.

Although the ABC algorithm has shown good performance, its performance is still not satisfactory in solving some complex optimization problems. Some researchers have indicated that the basic ABC tends to show slow convergence speed. The main reasons possibly include two aspects. On the one hand, the solution search equation in the basic ABC algorithm is good at exploration but poor at exploitation, which leads to an improper balance between the exploration and exploitation capabilities. As we know, a

© Springer Nature Switzerland AG 2019
Y. Tan et al. (Eds.): ICSI 2019, LNCS 11655, pp. 310–319, 2019.
https://doi.org/10.1007/978-3-030-26369-0_29

good balance between the exploration and exploitation capabilities is the key issue for the performance of EAs. On the other hand, different kinds of bees have different tasks, so the responsibilities should also be different. In the basic ABC, however, the same solution search equation is used by both of the employed bees and onlooker bees to generate new candidate solutions, so the performance is limited in this context.

To solve these problems, many different improved ABC variants have been proposed in recent years, and most of them focus on designing new solution search equations. For instances, Zhu et al. [8] proposed a modified ABC variant (GABC) in which the global best solution is integrated into the solution search equation to improve the exploitation capability. Based on the idea of using good solutions, Gao et al. [9] modified the original solution search equation inspired by the DE mutation strategy DE/best/1 in their proposed MABC algorithm. In contrast with the two aforementioned works of using the global best solution, Karaboga et al. [10] designed a neighborhood search mechanism based on the Euclidean distance in their proposed qABC algorithm, which aims to improve the exploitation capability while without losing diversity. Very recently, Cui et al. [11] proposed a modified version of GABC, called MPGABC, in which a multi-strategy of using different solution search equations is designed, and the reported experimental results show the effectiveness and efficiency of MPGABC.

Inspired by the above ABC variants, in this paper, we propose a multi-strategy ABC with neighborhood search (MSABC-NS). As above mentioned, the possible reasons of the deficiencies include two aspects, so we make two corresponding modifications to deal with the deficiencies, respectively. First, we design a multi-strategy mechanism in which two different solution search equations are used through a simple IF-ELSE structure. Second, we introduce a neighborhood search mechanism to make full use of good solutions. It's necessary to point out that our modifications is based on the structure of MPGABC, and the proposed MSABC-NS algorithm can be considered as an improved version of MPGABC to some extent. In the experiments, a suite of widely used 22 benchmark functions is employed to estimate the performance of our approach, and three different ABC variants are included in the comparison. The experimental results show that our approach can achieve better performance on most of the benchmark functions.

The remainder of this paper is organized as follows. We will briefly introduce the basic ABC algorithm in the Sect. 2, while our proposed algorithm will be described in detail in the Sect. 3. The Sect. 4 will show the experiments and the corresponding analysis. The summary of this paper is given in the last section.

2 The Basic ABC Algorithm

The optimization process of the basic ABC algorithm includes four phases, i.e., the initialization phase, the employed bee phase, the onlooker bee phase and the scout bee phase. After initialization phase, ABC turns into a loop of the employed bee phase, the onlooker bee phase and the scout bee phase until the termination condition is met. These three phases have different responsibilities in terms of their roles in the optimization process. In the employed bee phase, the employed bees are responsible for exploration, while the onlooker bees has the responsibility of exploitation in the onlooker bee phase, and the scout bees discards food source which cannot be exploited further. These four phases are described in detail as follows.

(1) The initialization phase

In the initialization phase, the initial food sources are generated randomly according to the Eq. (1). It's worth noting that a food source represents a candidate solution of the optimization problem.

$$x_{i,j} = x_j^{min} + rand(0,1) \cdot \left(x_j^{max} - x_j^{min}\right), \tag{1}$$

where x_i represents the ith food source, x_j^{max} and x_j^{min} represent the boundary of the jth dimension.

(2) The employed bee phase

In the employed bee phase, each employed bee searches a new food source by using the solution search equation listed in the Eq. (2). After all of the employed bees finish their search, they will share the relevant information with the onlooker bees which include the nectar amount and the positions of the food sources.

$$v_{i,j} = x_{i,j} + \emptyset_{i,j} \cdot \left(x_{k,j} - x_{i,j}\right), \tag{2}$$

where x_i represents the current food source or parent candidate solution, v_i indicates the new candidate solution. $\emptyset_{i,j}$ is an uniform random number within the range $[-1,1]$. $j \in \{1,2...,D\}$ is a randomly selected dimension, and D is the dimensionality of the optimization problem. If v_i is better than x_i in terms of the fitness value, then x_i will be replaced with v_i in the next generation. It's worth noting that the fitness value is calculated by using the following Eq. (3), where fit_i and $f(x_i)$ is the fitness value and the objective value of x_i respectively.

$$fit_i = \begin{cases} \frac{1}{1+f(x_i)} \\ 1 + abs(f(x_i)) \end{cases}. \tag{3}$$

(3) The onlooker bee phase

In the onlooker bee phase, onlooker bees will continue to search new food sources, but this is different from the employed bee phase in which each food source has the chance to be searched. Instead, onlooker bees favor searching good food sources based on the received information from the employed bees. The probability of food source whether is selected depends on the fitness value, and the following Eq. (4) is used to calculate the probability.

$$p_i = fit_i / \sum_{j=1}^{NS} fit_j. \tag{4}$$

It can be seen that the bigger the value of fit_i is, the higher probability of being selected for the ith food source. After determining which food source should be selected, the onlooker bees will use the same solution equation listed in the Eq. (2) to generate new candidate solutions.

(4) The scout bee phase

In the scout bee phase, if a food source cannot be exploited for *limit* times, it is considered to be exhausted, and it will be discarded by the scout bee. As an alternative, this discarded food source will be randomly initialized by using the above Eq. (1).

3   The Proposed MSABC-NS Algorithm

3.1   The Multi-strategy Mechanism

In the basic ABC algorithm, both of the employed bee phase and the onlooker bee phase use the same solution search equation to generate new candidate solutions. Due to the strong exploration capability but weak exploitation capability of the solution search equation, the performance of the basic ABC is not satisfactory in solving some complex problems. Therefore, we attempt to design a multi-strategy ABC variant to solve this deficiency, which is beneficial to take the advantages of different strategies.

In fact, there already exist some works about multi-strategy ABC variant. Wang et al. [12] designed a multi-strategy mechanism in which a strategy pool is constructed based on three solution search strategies. When the food source cannot be successfully updated by some solution search strategy, a different new strategy will be randomly selected from the strategy pool to replace the old strategy. However, due to the reason of random selection, the efficiency of the algorithm can be improved further.

Very recently, Cui et al. [11] designed a new multi-strategy mechanism in their proposed MPGABC algorithm in which two different solution search strategies are included. The first strategy is the same with the basic solution search equation, while the second one uses the information of the global best solution to guide search. To control the frequency of these two strategies, a control parameter P is introduced which has significant impact on the performance of MPGABC. However, a fixed value of P is employed, which may hinder the versatility of MPGABC.

Being inspired by the above multi-strategy ABC variants, we attempt to propose a simple but effective multi-strategy mechanism to enhance the performance of ABC. In the algorithm 1, the structure of the proposed multi-strategy mechanism is first given for a clear description. In there, X_{pbest} is a randomly selected food source from a food source set which contains the top N best food sources. The value of N is set to $SN \times q$, SN is the number of food sources and q is a random number in the range $\left[\frac{2}{SN}, 0.1\right]$. $\varphi_{i,j}$ is an uniformly distributed random number in the range $[0, 1.5]$. X_k is a randomly selected food source from the population. $\emptyset_{i,j}$ is an uniformly distributed random number in the range $[-1, 1]$.

Algorithm 1: The proposed multi-strategy mechanism
1. $v_{i,j} = x_{i,j} + \varphi_{i,j} \cdot \left(x_{pbest,j} - x_{i,j}\right)$
2. **if** $fit(v_i) > fit(x_i)$
3. $x_i = v_i$
4. **else**
5. $v_{i,j} = x_{i,j} + \emptyset_{i,j} \cdot \left(x_{i,j} - x_{k,j}\right)$
6. **end**

It can be seen from the algorithm 1, X_{pbest} is a member of the top N food sources which implies it has relatively good fitness value, and it can be considered as an elite solution. What's more, $\varphi_{i,j}$ is set to be larger than 0, this is helpful to push X_i to move toward X_{pbest}, and the convergence rate of the algorithm can be speeded up to some extent. It's worth noting that the value of N is not fixed, which is beneficial to prevent the algorithm from being too greedy [13]. If the food source X_i cannot be improved by the X_{pbest}, the original solution search equation in the basic ABC is used as an alternative. To some extent, this IF-ELSE structure can enhance the exploitation capability while without losing the exploration capability. In addition, the new probability model in the MGPABC algorithm is still kept in our proposed algorithm for the onlooker bees.

3.2 The Neighborhood Search Mechanism

In order to further improve the performance of our approach, the global neighborhood search (GNS) operator proposed by Wang et al. [14] is introduced into our approach. The neighborhood search is to search the vicinity area of candidate solutions for better solutions. In fact, in different EAs, researchers have designed a variety of different types of neighborhood search operations. For example, Wang et al. [14] proposed a global neighborhood search operation to solve the problem of slow convergence speed of PSO algorithm. Although different neighborhood search operations have their own characteristics, they all effectively improve the performance of the corresponding algorithm. In this paper, we directly adopt the GNS operation to further improve the performance of our approach. The GNS operation has a simple structure but good performance, and the Eq. (5) is used in the GNS operation

$$TX_i = r_1 \cdot X_i + r_2 \cdot X_{gbest} + r_3 \cdot (X_a - X_b). \tag{5}$$

In the Eq. (5), TX_i is the candidate solution, X_{gbest} is the global best solution in the population, X_a and X_b are exclusive food sources and they are randomly selected from the population, what's more, they have to be different from X_i. The parameters r_1, r_2 and r_3 are exclusive random numbers within [0, 1], and they have to meet the condition $r_1 + r_2 + r_3 = 1$. A clear demonstration of the GNS operation is presented in Fig. 1. In order to control use frequency of the GNS operation, we set the probability of using the GNS operation to 0.1.

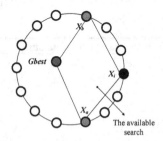

Fig. 1. The global neighborhood search operator.

3.3 Pseudo-code of MSABC-NS

In this paper, we propose an improved ABC variant (MSABC-NS) by combining a simple multi-strategy mechanism with the GNS operator. The pseudo-code of

MSABC-NS is described in the algorithm 2. In there, *FEs* is the number of used fitness function evaluations, and *MaxFEs*, as the stopping criterion, is the maximal number of fitness function evaluations. The control parameter P is set to 0.1, $trial_i$ represents the non-updated times of the i th food source.

Algorithm 2: Pseudo-code of MSABC-NS

1. Randomly generate SN food sources and calculate their fitness values, $FEs = SN$;
2. **while** $FEs \leq MaxFEs$ **do**
3.   /* Employed bee phase */
4.   Rank all the food sources according to their fitness value;
5.   **for** $i = 1$ to SN **do**
6.   Randomly select X_{pbest} and X_k from the population;
7.   Generate a new candidate solution V_i according to the algorithm 1;
8.   Calculate the fitness value of V_i, $FEs = FEs+1$;
9.   **if** $f(V_i) < f(X_i)$ **then**
10.   Replace X_i with V_i;
11.   **end if**
12.   **end for**
13.   /* Onlooker bee phase */
14.   Calculate the probability p_i according to the new probability model;
15.   **for** $i = 1$ to SN **do**
16.   Choose a food source X_j by the roulette wheel selection mechanism;
17.   Randomly select X_{pbest} and X_k from the population;
18.   Generate a new candidate solution V_j by algorithm 1;
19.   Calculate the fitness value of V_j, $FEs = FEs+1$;
20.   **if** $f(V_j) < f(X_j)$ **then**
21.   Replace X_j with V_j;
22.   **end if**
23.   **end for**
24.   /* Scout bee phase */
25.   **if** $\max(trial_i) > limit$ **then**
26.   Replace X_i with a new randomly generated food source according to the equation (1), $trial_i = 0$;
27.   **end if**
28.   /* The global neighborhood search operator */
29.   **for** $i = 1$ to SN **do**
30.   Generate a random number $rand \in [0,1]$;
31.   **if** $rand < P$ **then**
32.   Generate a trial solution TX_i according to the equation (5);
33.   Calculate the fitness value of TX_i, $FEs = FEs + 1$;
34.   **if** $f(TX_i) < f(X_i)$ **then**
35.   Replace X_i with TX_i;
36.   **end if**
37.   **end if**
38.   **end for**
39. **end while**

---

4 Experiments and Analysis

4.1 Benchmark Functions

We use 22 widely used benchmark functions to verify our approach. In these functions, F1–F9 are the unimodal functions, F6 is an uncontinuous step function, F10 is multimodal when its dimension is more than three, and F11–F22 are multimodal functions. The detailed definitions about the functions are listed in the Table 1. For the parameter settings of our approach, SN is set to 50, dimensionality of the functions D is set to 30, $maxFES$ is set to $5000 \cdot D$ and $limit$ is set to $SN \cdot D/2$. Each algorithm is run 25 times per function, the average function values are recorded.

Table 1. The 22 benchmark functions used in the experiments.

Function	Name	Range	Optimum
F1	Sphere	$[-100, 100]^D$	0
F2	Elliptic	$[-100, 100]^D$	0
F3	SumSquare	$[-10, 10]^D$	0
F4	SumPower	$[-1, 1]^D$	0
F5	Schwefel2.22	$[-10, 10]^D$	0
F6	Schwefel2.21	$[-100, 100]^D$	0
F7	Step	$[-100, 100]^D$	0
F8	Exponential	$[-10, 10]^D$	0
F9	Quartic	$[-1.28, 1.28]^D$	0
F10	Rosenbrock	$[-5, 10]^D$	0
F11	Rastrigin	$[-5.12, 5.12]^D$	0
F12	NCRastrigin	$[-5.12, 5.12]^D$	0
F13	Griewank	$[-600, 600]^D$	0
F14	Schwefel2.26	$[-500, 500]^D$	0
F15	Ackley	$[-50, 50]^D$	0
F16	Penalized1	$[-100, 100]^D$	0
F17	Penalized2	$[-100, 100]^D$	0
F18	Alpine	$[-10, 10]^D$	0
F19	Levy	$[-10, 10]^D$	0
F20	Weierstrass	$[-1, 1]^D$	0
F21	Himmelblau	$[-5, 5]^D$	-78.33236
F22	Michalewicz	$[0, \pi]^D$	$-30, -50, -100$

4.2   Verifications of the Proposed Algorithmic Components

Our approach includes two components, i.e., the multi-strategy mechanism and the GNS operator. To verify these two components, two compared algorithms are designed as baselines, i.e., MPGABC-IE and MPGABC-NS. MPGABC-IE represents the MPGABC algorithm only replace its multi-strategy mechanism with our proposed multi-strategy mechanism, while MPGABC-NS only adds the GNS operator. The compared results are shown in the Table 2 and the best results are shown in **boldface**.

As we can see from the Table 2, when compared with MPGABC, MPGABC-IE can get better results on the functions F1, F2, F3, F5, F10, F18 and F20, this implies that the proposed multi-strategy mechanism has shown better performance. Similarly, MSABC-NS has achieved better results on most test functions, and this indicates that the GNS operator indeed improve the performance of the algorithm. After by combing these two components, MSABC-NS has shown the best performance among the included four algorithms.

Table 2. Efficiency of the proposed algorithmic components.

Function	MPGABC	MPGABC-IE	MPGABC-NS	MSABC-NS
F1	6.52E−53	7.80E−57	**6.60E−63**	2.43E−58
F2	8.06E−50	3.88E−54	**1.52E−58**	5.20E−55
F3	4.59E−54	7.82E−58	**5.97E−64**	1.60E−58
F4	3.44E−58	6.40E−45	**2.36E−64**	3.01E−43
F5	9.32E−29	2.12E−32	7.22E−33	**1.96E−33**
F6	1.01E+00	4.55E+00	**2.96E−22**	1.84E−10
F7	**0.00E+00**	**0.00E+00**	**0.00E+00**	**0.00E+00**
F8	4.10E−06	4.13E−06	**0.00E+00**	**0.00E+00**
F9	2.36E−02	2.61E−02	**3.45E−04**	6.06E−04
F10	**1.05E+00**	6.16E−01	2.81E+01	2.60E+01
F11	**0.00E+00**	**0.00E+00**	**0.00E+00**	**0.00E+00**
F12	**0.00E+00**	**0.00E+00**	**0.00E+00**	**0.00E+00**
F13	**0.00E+00**	4.88E−17	**0.00E+00**	**0.00E+00**
F14	**3.82E−04**	**3.82E−04**	**3.82E−04**	**3.82E−04**
F15	3.48E−14	3.50E−14	2.15E−15	**2.01E−15**
F16	**1.57E−32**	**1.57E−32**	**1.57E−32**	**1.57E−32**
F17	**1.35E−32**	**1.35E−32**	2.78E−24	**1.35E−32**
F18	3.86E−08	2.65E−09	9.91E−09	**4.27E−13**
F19	**1.35E−31**	**1.35E−31**	4.39E−03	**1.35E−31**
F20	2.23E−03	1.65E−04	6.56E−04	**1.53E−04**
F21	**−7.83E+01**	**−7.83E+01**	**−7.83E+01**	**−7.83E+01**
F22	**−2.86E+01**	**−2.86E+01**	**−2.86E+01**	**−2.86E+01**

4.3   Compared with Other State-of-the-Art ABCs

In order to further verify the performance of MSABC-NS, we compare it with other three state-of-the-art ABC variants, i.e., GABC, MABC and MPGABC. The brief introductions of these three ABC variants have been given in the Sect. 1. The results are shown in the Table 3 and the best results have been marked in **boldface**. As seen, MSABC-NS also achieved the best performance among the four involved algorithms.

Table 3. Experimental results of MABC, qABC, MPGABC and MSABC-NS.

Function	MABC	qABC	MPGABC	MSABC-NS
F1	4.82E−39	1.34E−15	6.52E−53	**2.43E−58**
F2	4.36E−36	2.70E−20	8.06E−50	**5.20E−55**
F3	3.20E−40	4.65E−22	4.59E−54	**1.60E−58**
F4	2.11E−35	7.13E−51	**3.44E−58**	3.01E−43
F5	5.01E−21	7.78E−23	9.32E−29	**1.96E−33**
F6	9.37E+00	2.89E+00	1.01E+00	**1.84E−10**
F7	**0.00E+00**	**0.00E+00**	**0.00E+00**	**0.00E+00**
F8	6.71E−06	6.78E−06	4.10E−06	**0.00E+00**
F9	2.87E−02	2.91E−02	2.36E−02	**6.06E−04**
F10	3.42E+00	**7.15E−02**	1.05E+00	2.60E+01
F11	**0.00E+00**	**0.00E+00**	**0.00E+00**	**0.00E+00**
F12	**0.00E+00**	**0.00E+00**	**0.00E+00**	**0.00E+00**
F13	1.13E−15	**0.00E+00**	**0.00E+00**	**0.00E+00**
F14	**3.82E−04**	**3.82E−04**	**3.82E−04**	**3.82E−04**
F15	3.06E−14	3.10E−14	3.48E−14	**2.01E−15**
F16	**1.57E−32**	6.85E−13	**1.57E−32**	**1.57E−32**
F17	**1.35E−32**	2.00E−17	**1.35E−32**	**1.35E−32**
F18	**4.44E−17**	1.19E−16	3.86E−08	4.27E−13
F19	**1.35E−31**	2.60E−13	**1.35E−31**	**1.35E−31**
F20	**0.00E+00**	**0.00E+00**	2.23E−03	1.53E−04
F21	**−7.83E+01**	**−7.83E+01**	**−7.83E+01**	**−7.83E+01**
F22	**−2.86E+01**	**−2.86E+01**	**−2.86E+01**	**−2.86E+01**

5   Conclusion

In order to enhance the performance of the basic ABC algorithm, we proposed a multi-strategy ABC with the neighborhood search operator. In the multi-strategy mechanism, two different solution search equations are used through a simple IF-ELSE structure, which aims to take the advantages of different solution search equation. Furthermore, a global neighborhood search operator is introduced into our approach to improve the performance, and this operator is helpful to speed up the convergence rate while without losing diversity. Based on the 22 wildly used benchmark functions, the experimental results have shown the effectiveness of our approach.

Acknowledgments. This work is supported by the National Natural Science Foundation of China (Nos. 61603163 and 61876074) and the Science and Technology Foundation of Jiangxi Province (No. 20151BAB217007).

References

1. Tang, K.S., Man, K.F., Kwong, S., He, Q.: Genetic algorithms and their applications. IEEE Signal Process. Mag. **13**(6), 22–37 (1996)
2. Hunter, A., Chiu, K.S.: Genetic algorithm design of neural network and fuzzy logic controllers. Soft. Comput. **4**(3), 186–192 (2000)
3. Kennedy, J., Eberhart R.: Particle swarm optimization. In: IEEE International Conference on Neural Networks, pp. 1942–1948. IEEE (1995)
4. Kuo, R.J., Wang, M.H., Huang, T.W.: An application of particle swarm optimization algorithm to clustering analysis. Soft. Comput. **15**(3), 533–542 (2011)
5. Price, K., Storn, R., Lampinen, J.: Differential evolution: a practical approach to global optimization. In: ACM Computing Classification. Springer, Berlin (2005)
6. Karaboga, D.: An idea based on honey bee swarm for numerical optimization. Technical report-TR06. Erciyes University (2005)
7. Karaboga, D., Basturk, B.: A powerful and efficient algorithm for numerical function optimization: artificial bee colony (ABC) algorithm. J. Glob. Optim. **39**(3), 459–471 (2007)
8. Zhu, G., Kwong, S.: Gbest-guided artificial bee colony algorithm for numerical function optimization. Appl. Math. Comput. **217**(7), 3166–3173 (2010)
9. Gao, W., Liu, S.: A modified artificial bee colony algorithm. Comput. Oper. Res. **39**(3), 687–697 (2012)
10. Karaboga, D., Gorkemli, B.: A quick artificial bee colony (qABC) algorithm and its performance on optimization problems. Appl. Soft Comput. **23**, 227–238 (2014)
11. Cui, L., et al.: Modified Gbest-guided artificial bee colony algorithm with new probability model. Soft. Comput. **22**, 2217–2243 (2018)
12. Wang, H., Wu, Z., Rahnamayan, S., Sun, H., Liu, Y., Pan, J.: Multi-strategy ensemble artificial bee colony algorithm. Inf. Sci. **279**, 587–603 (2014)
13. Tanabe, R., Fukunaga, A.: Success-history based parameter adaptation for differential evolution. In: IEEE Congress on Evolutionary Computation (2013)
14. Wang, H., Sun, H., Li, C., Rahnamayan, S., Pan, J.S.: Diversity enhanced particle swarm optimization with neighborhood search. Inform. Sci. **223**, 119–135 (2013)

Cuckoo Search Algorithm for Border Reconstruction of Medical Images with Rational Curves

Akemi Gálvez[1,2], Iztok Fister[3], Iztok Fister Jr.[3], Eneko Osaba[4],
Javier Del Ser[4,5], and Andrés Iglesias[1,2(✉)]

[1] University of Cantabria, Avenida de los Castros s/n, 39005 Santander, Spain
iglesias@unican.es
[2] Toho University, 2-2-1 Miyama, 274-8510 Funabashi, Japan
[3] University of Maribor, Smetanova, Maribor, Slovenia
[4] TECNALIA, Derio, Spain
[5] University of the Basque Country (UPV/EHU), Bilbao, Spain
http://personales.unican.es/iglesias

Abstract. Border reconstruction is a key technology in medical image processing, where it is applied to identify and separate different tissues, organs, and tumors in diagnostic procedures. The classical approaches for this problem are based on either linear or polynomial functions to describe the border of the region of interest. However, little effort has been devoted to the more powerful case of rational functions, which extend the polynomial case by including extra degrees of freedom (the weights). As a consequence, rational functions are more difficult to compute. In this paper, we solve the problem by applying a nature-inspired swarm intelligence method called cuckoo search algorithm. The method is applied to two illustrative examples of medical images with satisfactory results.

Keywords: Swarm intelligence · Cuckoo search algorithm ·
Medical imaging · Border reconstruction · Rational curves

1 Introduction

The automatic detection and reconstruction of the borders of objects and areas in images has been a major topic of research in several areas for decades. This problem arises very often in fields such as image processing, pattern recognition, artificial vision, and virtual and augmented reality, to mention just a few. It is also a key technology for medical applications, as it helps to identify and discriminate different tissues and organs for medical visualization in popular non-invasive diagnostic procedures such as computer tomography, magnetic resonance imaging, infrared imaging, dermoscopy, ultrasonography, magnetic resonance spectroscopy, and many others. In fact, medical image processing is one of the most relevant application fields of border detection and reconstruction.

© Springer Nature Switzerland AG 2019
Y. Tan et al. (Eds.): ICSI 2019, LNCS 11655, pp. 320–330, 2019.
https://doi.org/10.1007/978-3-030-26369-0_30

The classical graphical pipeline in automatic medical image processing consists of three stages: (1) image segmentation; (2) feature extraction and feature selection; and (3) classification. Typically, the process starts with a medical image obtained by either of the many clinical procedures based on this technology. While in the past the image was directly used by the medical specialist for visual analysis for diagnostic and therapeutic purposes, the current trend today is to automate the process as much as possible [7,10,11]. However, in many cases the first step of the process is still highly manual: after visual inspection of the image, the medical specialist selects a set of points of the image by clicking with the mouse on the computer screen or a display device. Such points, usually referred to as feature points, correspond to the border between regions of interest (ROIs), usually corresponding to different tissues or organs, or enclosing a possible lesion or tumor. This process is called border detection [2]. After this initial selection of feature points, a computer software applies graphical routines to determine the border of the ROI under analysis, a process called border reconstruction.

The classical procedure in border reconstruction of medical images is to consider a simple polyline connecting consecutive feature points with straight segments. The output of this process is a polygonal enclosing the ROI. Such a polyline gives a rough approximation of the boundary between the ROI and the surrounding background, which is usually enough in many cases, provided that the number of feature points is large enough to describe all the geometry of the border with certain accuracy. However, this procedure can be improved by considering free-form parametric curves, which take advantage of a higher number of degrees of freedom to add extra flexibility to this process. For instance, the polyline does not represent the real process well, as the border of medical images is not generally piecewise linear. In addition, this linear procedure relies on interpolation schemes that enforce the border to pass through *all* feature points. This is often troublesome, as medical data are typically affected by artifacts inherent to manual processes, such as outliers and noise in data. Under such conditions, approximation schemes (that only require the border to pass *near* the feature points) are better suited for this problem [1]. Furthermore, approximation schemes are more advantageous in terms of accuracy, computer memory, and data storage capacity, as the border can be accurately described by a few tens of parameters even for very large collections of feature points. Because of these reasons, in this paper we will consider approximation schemes for this border reconstruction step.

Classical approximation techniques for border reconstruction with free-form parametric curves are primarily based on polynomial schemes, such as the popular Bézier and B-spline curves [6]. Such schemes can be improved by considering some extra real parameters called weights, which allow the user to modify the shape of the curve locally by simply changing the weight of one or several poles of the curve without changing the location of the poles. This is an interesting and valuable feature, as it makes it possible to reduce the degree of the curve significantly without penalizing the approximation accuracy. The resulting parametric curve is no longer a polynomial function but a rational one.

Unfortunately, using rational curves is by far much more difficult than the polynomial case, because some extra variables (the weights) have also to be computed. In addition, the different variables (data parameters, poles, and weights) are strongly related to each other in a highly nonlinear way [3]. As a result, we have to solve a difficult continuous multivariate nonlinear optimization problem that cannot be properly solved in the general case through traditional mathematical optimization techniques.

Our method to solve this problem is based on a nature-inspired metaheuristics called cuckoo search algorithm and introduced by Prof. X.S. Yang in 2009 to solve difficult optimization problems [14]. The algorithm is inspired by the obligate interspecific brood-parasitism of some cuckoo species that lay their eggs in the nests of host birds of other species. Since its inception, the cuckoo search (specially its variant that uses Lévy flights) has been successfully applied in several papers reported recently in the literature to difficult optimization problems from different domains [12,13,15], including data fitting with polynomial curves [5]. However, to the best of our knowledge, the method has never been used so far for border reconstruction of medical images with rational curves.

The structure of this paper is as follows: the fundamentals and main features of the cuckoo search algorithm are discussed in Sect. 2. The problem of data fitting with rational Bézier curves is discussed in Sect. 3. The proposed method to solve the border reconstruction problem is presented in Sect. 4. To illustrate the performance of our method, it is applied in Sect. 5 to perform border reconstruction of two medical images. The paper closes in Sect. 6 with the main conclusions of this contribution and our plans for future work in the field.

2   The Cuckoo Search Algorithm

Cuckoo search (CS) is a nature-inspired population-based metaheuristic algorithm originally proposed by Yang and Deb in 2009 to solve optimization problems [14]. The algorithm is inspired by the brood-parasitism of some cuckoo species that lay their eggs in the nests of host birds of other species with the aim of escaping from the parental investment in raising their offspring. This strategy is also useful to minimize the risk of egg loss to other species, as the cuckoos can distributed their eggs amongst a number of different nests. Of course, sometimes it happens that the host birds discover the alien eggs in their nests. In such cases, the host bird can take different responsive actions varying from throwing such eggs away to simply leaving the nest and build a new one elsewhere.

This interesting and surprising breeding behavioral pattern is the metaphor of the cuckoo search metaheuristic approach for solving optimization problems. In the cuckoo search algorithm, the eggs in the nest are interpreted as a pool of candidate solutions of an optimization problem while the cuckoo egg represents a new coming solution. The ultimate goal of the method is to use these new (and potentially better) solutions associated with the parasitic cuckoo eggs to replace the current solution associated with the eggs in the nest. This replacement, carried out iteratively, will eventually lead to a very good solution of the problem.

In addition to this representation scheme, the CS algorithm is also based on three idealized rules [14, 15]:

Table 1. Cuckoo Search Algorithm via Lévy flights as originally proposed in [14, 15].

Algorithm: Cuckoo Search via Lévy Flights

---

    begin
        Objective function $f(\mathbf{x})$, $\mathbf{x} = (x_1, \ldots, x_D)^T$
        Generate initial population of n host nests $\mathbf{x}_i$ $(i = 1, 2, \ldots, n)$
        while $(t < MaxGeneration)$ or (stop criterion)
            Get a cuckoo (say, i) randomly by Lévy flights
            Evaluate its fitness F_i
            Choose a nest among n (say, j) randomly
            if $(F_i > F_j)$
                Replace j by the new solution
            end
            A fraction (p_a) of worse nests are abandoned and new ones
                are built via Lévy flights
            Keep the best solutions (or nests with quality solutions)
            Rank the solutions and find the current best
        end while
        Postprocess results and visualization
    end

---

1. Each cuckoo lays one egg at a time, and dumps it in a randomly chosen nest;
2. The best nests with high quality of eggs (solutions) will be carried over to the next generations;
3. The number of available host nests is fixed, and a host can discover an alien egg with a probability $p_a \in [0, 1]$. In this case, the host bird can either throw the egg away or abandon the nest and build a new nest in a new location.

For simplicity, the third assumption can be approximated by a fraction p_a of the n nests being replaced by new nests (with new random solutions at new locations). For a maximization problem, the quality or fitness of a solution can simply be proportional to the objective function. However, other (more sophisticated) expressions for the fitness function can also be defined.

Based on these three rules, the basic steps of the CS algorithm can be summarized as shown in the pseudo-code reported in Table 1. Basically, the CS algorithm starts with an initial population of n host nests and it is performed iteratively. In the original proposal, the initial values of the jth component of the ith nest are determined by the expression $x_i^j(0) = rand.(up_i^j - low_i^j) + low_i^j$, where up_i^j and low_i^j represent the upper and lower bounds of that jth component, respectively, and $rand$ represents a standard uniform random number on the open interval $(0, 1)$. Note that this choice ensures that the initial values of the variables are within the search space domain. These boundary conditions are also controlled in each iteration step.

For each iteration g, a cuckoo egg i is selected randomly and new solutions $\mathbf{x}_i(g + 1)$ are generated by using the Lévy flight, a kind of random walk in which the steps are defined in terms of the step-lengths, which have a certain probability distribution, with the directions of the steps being isotropic and random. According to the original creators of the method, the strategy of using Lévy flights is preferred over other simple random walks because it leads to better overall performance of the CS. The general equation for the Lévy flight is given by:

$$\mathbf{x}_i(g + 1) = \mathbf{x}_i(g) + \alpha \oplus levy(\lambda) \tag{1}$$

where g indicates the number of the current generation, and $\alpha > 0$ indicates the step size, which should be related to the scale of the particular problem under study. The symbol $\oplus$ is used in Eq. (1) to indicate the entry-wise multiplication. Note that Eq. (1) is essentially a Markov chain, since next location at generation $g + 1$ only depends on the current location at generation g and a transition probability, modulated by the Lévy distribution as:

$$levy(\lambda) \sim g^{-\lambda}, \qquad (1 < \lambda \leqslant 3) \tag{2}$$

which has an infinite variance with an infinite mean. The generation of random numbers with Lévy flights is comprised of two steps: firstly, a random direction according to a uniform distribution is chosen; then, the generation of steps following the chosen Lévy distribution is carried out. The authors suggested to use the so-called Mantegna's algorithm for symmetric distributions, where "symmetric" means that both positive and negative steps are considered (see [12] for details). Their approach computes the factor:

$$\hat{\phi} = \left(\frac{\Gamma(1 + \hat{\beta}).sin\left(\frac{\pi.\hat{\beta}}{2}\right)}{\Gamma\left(\left(\frac{1+\hat{\beta}}{2}\right).\hat{\beta}.2^{\frac{\beta-1}{2}}\right)} \right)^{\frac{1}{\hat{\beta}}} \tag{3}$$

where Γ denotes the Gamma function and $\hat{\beta} = \frac{3}{2}$ in the original implementation by Yang and Deb [15]. This factor is used in Mantegna's algorithm to compute the step length ς as: $\varsigma = \frac{u}{|v|^{\frac{1}{\hat{\beta}}}}$, where u and v follow the normal distribution of zero mean and deviation σ_u^2 and σ_v^2, respectively, where σ_u obeys the Lévy distribution given by Eq. (3) and $\sigma_v = 1$. Then, the stepsize ζ is computed as:

$$\zeta = 0.01 \varsigma (\mathbf{x} - \mathbf{x}_{best}) \tag{4}$$

where ς is computed as above. Finally, $\mathbf{x}$ is modified as: $\mathbf{x} \leftarrow \mathbf{x} + \zeta.\mathbf{\Psi}$ where $\mathbf{\Psi}$ is a random vector following the normal distribution $N(0, 1)$.

The CS method then evaluates the fitness of the new solution and compares it with the current one. In case the new solution brings better fitness, it replaces the current one. On the other hand, a fraction of the worse nests (according to the fitness) are abandoned and replaced by new solutions so as to increase the exploration of the search space looking for more promising solutions. The rate of replacement is given by the probability p_a, a parameter of the model that has to be tuned for better performance. Moreover, for each iteration step, all current solutions are ranked according to their fitness and the best solution reached so far is stored as the vector $\mathbf{x}_{best}$ (used, for instance, in Eq. (4)). This algorithm is applied in an iterative fashion until a stopping criterion is met.

3 Problem to Be Solved

We assume that the reader is familiar with the free-form parametric curves [8,9]. Mathematically, a *free-form rational Bézier curve* $\boldsymbol{\Phi}(\tau)$ *of degree* η is defined as:

$$\boldsymbol{\Phi}(\tau) = \frac{\displaystyle\sum_{j=0}^{\eta} \omega_j \boldsymbol{\Lambda}_j \phi_j^{\eta}(\tau)}{\displaystyle\sum_{j=0}^{\eta} \omega_j \phi_j^{\eta}(\tau)} \tag{5}$$

where $\boldsymbol{\Lambda}_j$ are vector coefficients called the *poles*, ω_j are their scalar weights, $\phi_j^{\eta}(\tau)$ are the *Bernstein polynomials of index j and degree η*, given by:

$$\phi_j^{\eta}(\tau) = \binom{\eta}{j} \tau^j (1 - \tau)^{\eta-j}$$

and τ is the *curve parameter*, defined on the finite interval $[0, 1]$. By convention, $0! = 1$. Note that in this paper vectors are denoted in bold.

Suppose now that we are given a set of data points $\{\boldsymbol{\Delta}_i\}_{i=1,\dots,\kappa}$ in $\mathbb{R}^{\nu}$ (usually $\nu = 2$ or $\nu = 3$). Our goal is to obtain the rational Bézier curve $\boldsymbol{\Phi}(\tau)$ performing discrete approximation of the data points $\{\boldsymbol{\Delta}_i\}_i$. To do so, we have to compute all parameters (i.e. poles $\boldsymbol{\Lambda}_j$, weights ω_j, and parameters τ_i associated with data points $\boldsymbol{\Delta}_i$, for $i = 1, \dots, \kappa$, $j = 0, \dots, \eta$) of the approximating curve $\boldsymbol{\Phi}(\tau)$ by minimizing the least-squares error, Υ, defined as the sum of squares of the residuals:

$$\Upsilon = \operatorname*{minimize}_{\substack{\{\tau_i\}_i \\ \{\Lambda_j\}_j \\ \{\omega_j\}_j}} \left[\sum_{i=1}^{\kappa} \left(\boldsymbol{\Delta}_i - \frac{\displaystyle\sum_{j=0}^{\eta} \omega_j \boldsymbol{\Lambda}_j \phi_j^{\eta}(\tau_i)}{\displaystyle\sum_{j=0}^{\eta} \omega_j \phi_j^{\eta}(\tau_i)} \right)^2 \right]. \tag{6}$$

Now, taking:

$$\varphi_j^{\eta}(\tau) = \frac{\omega_j \phi_j^{\eta}(\tau)}{\displaystyle\sum_{k=0}^{\eta} \omega_k \phi_k^{\eta}(\tau)} \tag{7}$$

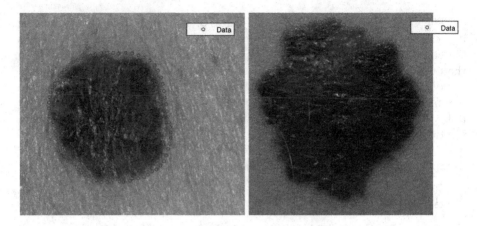

Fig. 1. Original medical images and their corresponding selected border feature points.

Eq. (6) becomes:

$$\Upsilon = \underset{\substack{\{\tau_i\}_i \\ \{\Lambda_j\}_j \\ \{\omega_j\}_j}}{\text{minimize}} \left[\sum_{i=1}^{\kappa} \left(\Delta_i - \sum_{j=0}^{\eta} \Lambda_j \varphi_j^{\eta}(\tau) \right)^2 \right], \qquad (8)$$

which can be rewritten in matrix form as: $\Omega.\Lambda = \Xi$, where: $\Omega = [\Omega_{i,j}] = \left[\left(\sum_{k=1}^{\kappa} \varphi_i^{\eta}(\tau_k)\varphi_j^{\eta}(\tau_k) \right) \right]_{i,j}$, $\Xi = [\Xi_j] = \left[\left(\sum_{k=1}^{\kappa} \Delta_k \varphi_j^{\eta}(\tau_k) \right) \right]_j$, $\Lambda = (\Lambda_0, \ldots, \Lambda_\eta)^T$, for $i, j = 0, \ldots, \eta$, and $(.)^T$ means the transposition of a vector or a matrix. In general, $\kappa >> \eta$ meaning that the system of equations $\Omega.\Lambda = \Xi$ is over-determined. If values are assigned to the τ_i, our problem can be solved as a classical linear least-squares minimization, with the coefficients $\{\Lambda_i\}_{i=0,\ldots,\eta}$ as unknowns. This problem can readily be solved by standard numerical techniques. On the contrary, if the values of τ_i are treated as unknowns, the problem becomes much more difficult. Indeed, since the polynomial blending functions $\phi_j^{\eta}(\tau)$ are nonlinear in τ and so are the rational blending functions $\varphi_j^{\eta}(\tau)$, the least-squares minimization of the errors is a nonlinear continuous optimization problem. Note also that in many practical cases the number of data points can be extremely large, meaning that we have to deal with a large number of unknowns. It is also a multimodal problem, since there might be arguably more than one set of parameter values leading to the optimal solution.

In conclusion, the complex interplay among all sets of unknowns (data parameters, poles, and weights) leads to a very difficult over-determined, multimodal, multivariate, continuous, nonlinear optimization problem. In this work, we are interested to solve this general problem. Instead of making assumption about the values of some free parameters, we include all of them in our computations.

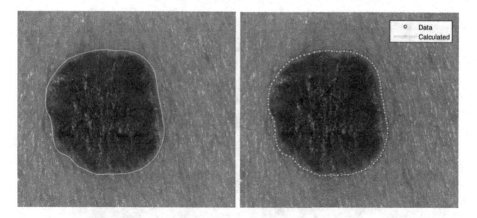

Fig. 2. Graphical results for the first example: image and rational border curve: (left) without and (right) with the feature points.

4   The Cuckoo Search Method

Our approach is based on the application of the cuckoo search method with Lévy flights described in Sect. 2 to our initial input, i.e., the set of feature points $\{\mathbf{\Delta}_i\}_{i=1,\ldots,\kappa}$. We consider an initial parameterization and set of weights, assumed to be random in their respective domains, and apply the cuckoo search on a collection of individuals consisting of the vector $\mathcal{S}^g = \{\mathcal{P}^g, \mathcal{W}^g\}$, where $\mathcal{P}^g = \{\tau_1^g, \ldots, \tau_\kappa^g\}$, $\mathcal{W}^g = \{\omega_0^g, \ldots, \omega_\eta^g\}$, and the superscript g denotes the generation index. The procedure computes the final values of data parameters and weights. Then, inserting them into Eq. (7), we apply least-squares minimization to compute the values of $\{\mathbf{\Lambda}_i\}_{i=0,\ldots,\eta}$ according to Eq. (8).

As it is very well-known, the parameter tuning of metaheuristic methods is largely a problem-dependent issue [4]. Fortunately, the cuckoo search is specially advantageous in this regard. In clear contrast to other metaheuristics that typically depend on several parameters, cuckoo search depends on only two parameters (the population size, n and the probability p_a) so the parameter tuning becomes a much simpler task. In this paper they are set to $n = 100$ and $p_a = 0.25$, as these values have already been used in previous papers with good results [5]. Regarding our stopping criterion, the method was executed for n_{iter} iterations, with n_{iter} set to $50,000$ generations in our examples.

5   Experimental Results

Our method has been applied to two medical images of skin cancer obtained from the digital image archive of the Medical Center, University of Groningen (The Netherlands). They are shown in Fig. 1. The figure shows the original images with a collection of superimposed feature points identified by a trained dermatologist as belonging to the boundary of the skin lesion. Our results for both examples

328 A. Gálvez et al.

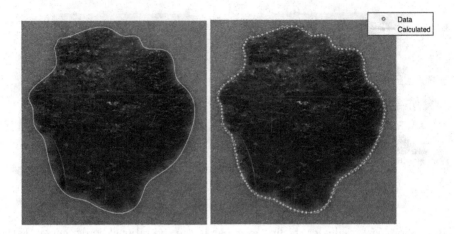

Fig. 3. Graphical results for the second example: image and rational border curve: (left) without and (right) with the feature points.

are shown in Figs. 2 and 3, respectively. The figures show the original medical image and the best reconstructed rational border curve without (left) and with (right) the feature points. From the figures we can see that the method obtains a very good fitting of the data points for both examples. The corresponding convergence diagrams for both examples are shown in Fig. 4.

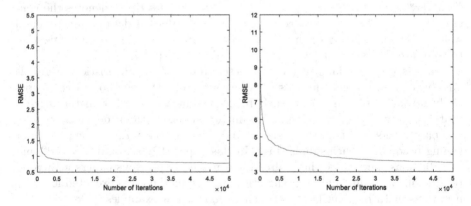

Fig. 4. Convergence diagram for the first (left) and the second example (right).

6 Conclusions and Future Work

In this paper we focus on the problem of border reconstruction for medical images with rational curves. Given a collection of feature points assumed to lie on the boundary of a certain region of interest, the goal is to determine the rational curve that best fits these data points in the least-squares sense. Although this problem has already been addressed in the literature for the polynomial case, it was still unsolved for rational curves, which are more general and flexible but also more challenging, as they include some extra degrees of freedom (the weights) that have also to be computed. The method presented in this paper is based on the cuckoo search algorithm. It has been applied to two examples of medical images with visually satisfactory results. The limiting factor of this method is that it requires many iterations to converge, making it unsuitable for real-time applications. Future work includes the extension of this approach to the case of piecewise rational functions, its generalization to the case of surfaces for volumetric reconstruction, and reducing the number of required iterations.

Acknowledgements. Work supported by projects: PDE-GIR #778035 (EU Horizon 2020 program), #TIN2017-89275-R (Spanish Research Agency, AEI/UE FEDER), P2-0057 & P2-0041 (Slovenian Research Agency) and EMAITEK (Basque Government).

References

1. Abbas, A.A., Guo, X., Tan, W.H., Jalab, H.A.: Combined spline and B-spline for an improved automatic skin lesion segmentation in dermoscopic images using optimal color channel. J. Med. Syst. **38**(80), 1–8 (2014)
2. Celebi, M.E., Iyatomi, H., Schaefer, G., Stoecker, W.V.: Lesion border detection in dermoscopy images. Comput. Med. Imaging Graph. **33**(2), 148–153 (2009)
3. Dierckx, P.: Curve and Surface Fitting with Splines. Oxford University Press, New York (1993)
4. Engelbrecht, A.P.: Fundamentals of Computational Swarm Intelligence. Wiley, Chichester (2005)
5. Gálvez A., Iglesias A.: Cuckoo search with Lévy flights for weighted Bayesian energy functional optimization in global-support curve data fitting. Sci. World J. **11** (2014). Article ID 138760
6. Gálvez A., Iglesias A.: Computational intelligence CSA-based approach for machine-driven calculation of outline curves of cutaneous melanoma. In: Proceedings of Cyberworlds 2018, pp. 270–275. IEEE CS Press (2018)
7. Garnavi, R., Aldeen, M., Celebi, M.E., Varigos, G., Finch, S.: Border detection in dermoscopy images using hybrid thresholding on optimized color channels. Comput. Med. Imaging Graph. **35**(2), 105–115 (2011)
8. Iglesias, A., Gálvez, A.: Memetic electromagnetism algorithm for finite approximation with rational bézier curves. In: Tan, Y., Shi, Y., Buarque, F., Gelbukh, A., Das, S., Engelbrecht, A. (eds.) ICSI 2015. LNCS, vol. 9140, pp. 30–40. Springer, Cham (2015). https://doi.org/10.1007/978-3-319-20466-6_3
9. Iglesias, A., Gálvez, A., Collantes, M.: Global-support rational curve method for data approximation with bat algorithm. In: Chbeir, R., Manolopoulos, Y., Maglogiannis, I., Alhajj, R. (eds.) AIAI 2015. IAICT, vol. 458, pp. 191–205. Springer, Cham (2015). https://doi.org/10.1007/978-3-319-23868-5_14
10. Machado, D.A., Giraldi, G., Novotny, A.A.: Multi-object segmentation approach based on topological derivative and level set method. Integr. Comput. Aided Eng. **18**, 301–311 (2011)

11. Schmid, P.: Segmentation of digitized dermatoscopic images by two-dimensional color clustering. IEEE Trans. Med. Imaging **18**(2), 164–171 (1999)
12. Yang, X.-S.: Nature-Inspired Metaheuristic Algorithms, 2nd edn. Luniver Press, Frome (2010)
13. Yang, X.-S.: Engineering Optimization: An Introduction with Metaheuristic Applications. Wiley, New Jersey (2010)
14. Yang, X.S., Deb, S.: Cuckoo search via Lévy flights. In: Proceedings World Congress on Nature & Biologically Inspired Computing (NaBIC), pp. 210–214. IEEE (2009)
15. Yang, X.S., Deb, S.: Engineering optimization by cuckoo search. Int. J. Math. Model. Numer. Optim. **1**(4), 330–343 (2010)

Quantum Behaved Fruit Fly Optimization Algorithm for Continuous Function Optimization Problems

Xiangyin Zhang[1,2(⊠)] and Shuang Xia[1,2]

[1] Faculty of Information Technology,
Beijing University of Technology, Beijing 100124, China
xy_zhang@bjut.edu.cn
[2] Beijing Key Laboratory of Computational Intelligence and Intelligent System,
Beijing 100124, China

Abstract. In this paper, we study the fruit fly in the fruit fly optimization algorithm (FOA) system moving in a quantum multi-dimensional space and propose a quantum behaved fruit fly optimization algorithm (QFOA) for the continuous function optimization problem. Computational experiments and comparisons are carried out based on a set of benchmark functions. The computational results show the advantage of QFOA to the original FOA.

Keywords: Fruit fly optimization algorithm (FOA) · Quantum ·
Continuous function optimization problem

1 Introduction

Fruit fly optimization algorithm (FOA) is a novel proposed swarm intelligent optimization, which is inspired by the food finding behavior of fruit flies [1]. Recently, FOA attracts researchers' attention and is used to solve more and more optimization problems, for example, the semiconductor final testing scheduling problem [2], UAV path planning [3, 4], general regression neural network optimization [5], parameter tuning for proportional-integral-derivative controllers [6, 7], and so on.

In order to further improve the efficiency and global search ability of the FOA, several improved versions of FOA are proposed by researchers [2–8]. Zhang et al. [3] fuses the phase angle-encoded and mutation adaptation mechanisms into the basic FOA, in which the designed osphresis-based search procedure using the mutation adaptation mechanism enhances the balance of FOA in terms of the exploitation and exploration ability, while the phase angle-based encoded strategy for fruit fly locations helps to achieve the high performance in the convergence process. Pan et al. [8] introduced a new control parameter to adjust the search scope around the fruit fly swarm location adaptively as well as a new solution generating method to enhance the accuracy and convergence rate, and presented the improved fruit fly optimization (IFFO) algorithm.

Y. Tan et al. (Eds.): ICSI 2019, LNCS 11655, pp. 331–340, 2019.
https://doi.org/10.1007/978-3-030-26369-0_31

Sun et al. [9–11] put forward a quantum behaved particle swarm optimization (QPSO) algorithm model from the perspective of Quantum Mechanics view rather than the Newtonian rules assumed in all previous versions of PSO. QPSO was tested on some benchmark functions and experimental results showed that QPSO outperforms PSO. Inspired by their contributions, in this paper, the novel quantum behaved fruit fly optimization algorithm (QFOA) is proposed to solve the continuous function optimization problems. Simulation results on benchmark functions are given to demonstrate the effectiveness and feasibility of the proposed approach.

The rest of this paper is organized as follows. Overview of the basic FOA is described in Sect. 2. Section 3 presents the QFOA in details. Numerical experiment comparisons on the benchmark functions are provided in Sect. 4. Section 5 concludes this paper finally.

2 Fruit Fly Optimization Algorithm

Fruit flies are superior to other species in terms of olfactory and visual senses [1]. When fruit flies look for the food, they use the olfactory organ to sense various odors, and use the visual organ to spot the food.

The FOA is inspired by the behavior of the fruit flies. As the process illustrated in Fig. 1, FOA randomly generates a fruit fly swarm's initial location, and then, the fruit fly is assigned the random direction and distance for following movement. As the food location is unknown, the distance to the origin is estimated. After they arrive at the new positions, the algorithm can find the best position with the results of calculation and judgment. Repeating this process and FOA can finally get the optimal solution. Compared with existing bio-inspired algorithms, FOA is much simpler and straightforward to implement [4], which only takes several lines to code the core part in any programming language.

3 Quantum-Behaved FOA

(1) *Quantum delta potential well model*

According to the quantum theory, objects are described by the wave function $\psi(x, t)$, rather than the position x and velocity v. Any quantum object has the wave-like properties and can exist in many places at once. In the quantum space, the probability of the object appearing on a spot is proportional to the strength module of the wave function on this spot, as follows

$$|\psi(x, t)|^2 \mathrm{d}x\mathrm{d}y\mathrm{d}z = Q\mathrm{d}x\mathrm{d}y\mathrm{d}z \tag{1}$$

where $Q\mathrm{d}x\mathrm{d}y\mathrm{d}z$ is the probability of the object appearing on the spot $x = (x, y, z)$ at time t. Thus, the strength module $|\psi(x, t)|^2$ is the probability density function satisfying the following equation

	STRUCTURE OF FOA
	/* Initialization */
1	Set the generation counter $NC = 0$;
2	Set the number of fruit flies as M_{pop};
3	Randomly initialize the fruit fly swarm's location as $[X_{axis}, Y_{axis}]$;
	/* Iterative search */
4	**while** termination criteria is not satisfied **do**
5	Generation counter $NC = NC + 1$
	/* Search using osphresis */
6	**for** $i = 1 : M_{pop}$ **do**
7	Generate the random direction and distance, and
	$X_i = X_{axis} + random$
	$Y_i = Y_{axis} + random$
9	Compute the distance to the origin:
	$D_i = \sqrt{X_i^2 + Y_i^2}$
10	Calculate the judged value of smell concentration:
	$S_i = 1/D_i$
11	Evaluate the smell concentration judge function (also called fitness function) to get the smell concentrations:
	$Smell_i = f(S_i)$
12	**end for**
	/* Search using vision */
13	Select the fruit fly that has the best smell concentration:
	$index = \arg \max(Smell_i)$
14	**if** $[X_{index}, Y_{index}]$ has the better smell than $[X_{axis}, Y_{axis}]$, **then** The fruit fly uses vision to fly towards the location:
	$X_{axis} = X_{indes}$ and $Y_{axis} = Y_{indes}$
15	**end while**

Fig. 1. Procedure of FOA.

$$\int_{-\infty}^{+\infty} |\psi|^2 dxdydz = \int_{-\infty}^{+\infty} Q dxdydz = 1 \tag{2}$$

In the quantum physics, the motion of objects is described by the Schrödinger's equation as follows

$$i\hbar \frac{\partial}{\partial t} \psi(X,t) = \hat{H}\psi(X,t) \tag{3}$$

where $\hbar$ is a constant called Planck Constant, $\hat{H}$ is the Hamiltonian operator which is given by the following equation

$$\hat{H} = -\frac{\hbar}{2m}\nabla^2 + V(x) \tag{4}$$

where m is the object mass and $V(x)$ denotes the potential field of the object.

(2) *Quantum behaved fruit fly*

Fruit flies search for the food around the location of the fruit fly swarm, and this random search behavior can be replaced by a quantum behavior. We hypothesize the fruit fly swarm move in the quantum space, and each fruit fly searches for the food source in the Delta potential well, of which the location of the fruit fly swarm p_{axis} is the center.

For simplicity, the one-dimensional space is considered here. Thus, if the location of the food source is denoted by x, its potential energy in the one-dimensional Delta potential well is represented as follows

$$V(x) = -\gamma\delta(x - p_{axis}) = -\gamma\delta(y) \tag{5}$$

According to the Schrödinger's equation, the following normalized wave function can be obtained as

$$\psi(y) = \frac{1}{\sqrt{L}}e^{-|y|/L} \tag{6}$$

where L is the characteristic length of Delta potential well. Therefore, the probability density function is as follows

$$Q(y) = |\psi(y)|^2 = \frac{1}{L}e^{-2|y|/L} \tag{7}$$

The above equation is equated to

$$y = \pm\frac{L}{2}\ln\frac{1}{u} \tag{8}$$

where u is the random number uniformly distributed on (0, 1). Hence, we can obtain the food source location that the fruit fly searches for, which is determined as follows

$$x = p_{axis} \pm \frac{L}{2}\ln\frac{1}{u} \tag{9}$$

(3) *Osphresis-based Search using the Quantum Behavior*

In the QFOA algorithm, it assumes that a 1-D Delta potential well exists on each dimension at the swarm center attractor point, and every osphresis-based search behavior of the fruit fly has the quantum properties. The quantum-behaved foraging process of the fruit fly is depicted by the wave function instead of the completely random way.

For the two models of the basic FOA, the quantum-behaved searching mechanism for osphresis-based search are described in details as follows.

In the osphresis-based search process, M_{osp} new locations of the food source are generated in the Delta potential well of which the swarm location (X_{axis}, Y_{axis}) is the center. The quantum-behaved searching mechanism for FOA can be given by

$$\begin{cases} X_i(g+1) = X_{axis} \pm \frac{L_{x,i}}{2} \ln \frac{1}{r_x} \\ Y_i(g+1) = Y_{axis} \pm \frac{L_{y,i}}{2} \ln \frac{1}{r_y} \end{cases} \tag{10}$$

where $i = 1, 2, \ldots, M_{osp}$, r_x and r_y are the random value in the range of [0,1]. $L_{x,i}$ and $L_{y,i}$ are the delta potential well characteristic length of the corresponding dimension, which are determined by the last searching location of the fruit fly based on the olfactory as follows

$$\begin{cases} L_{x,i} = 2b|X_{axis} - X_i(g)| \\ L_{y,i} = 2b|Y_{axis} - Y_i(g)| \end{cases} \tag{11}$$

where g is the current number of iteration and b is contraction-expansion coefficient to control the quantum searching range, which is determined by

$$b = b_1 \, logsig(10 \cdot (0.5 - g/G_{max})) + b_2 \tag{12}$$

where b_1 and b_2 are the two parameters to restrict the value range, namely $b \in [b_2, b_1 + b_2]$.

The implementation procedure of the osphresis-based search using the quantum behavior for fruit flies is as follows (Fig. 2):

	/* *Quantum-behaved search using osphresis* */
1	**for** $i = 1 : M_{osp}$ **do**
2	Calculate the characteristic length
	$L_{x,i} = 2b|X_{axis} - X_i|$,
	$L_{y,i} = 2b|Y_{axis} - Y_i|$;
3	**while** 1 **do**
4	Generate the random direction and distance as follows:
5	**if** *random*>0.5 **then** $X_i = X_{axis} + 0.5\, L_{x,i} \ln(1/r_x)$ **else** $X_i = X_{axis} - 0.5\, L_{x,i} \ln(1/r_x)$;
6	**if** *random*>0.5 **then** $Y_i = Y_{axis} + 0.5\, L_{y,i} \ln(1/r_y)$ **else** $Y_i = Y_{axis} - 0.5\, L_{y,i} \ln(1/r_y)$;
7	Calculate the distance to the origin:
	$D_i = \sqrt{X_i^2 + Y_i^2}$;
8	Calculate the judged value of smell concentration:
	$S_i = 1/D_i$;
9	**if** $S_i \le X_{max}$ and $S_i \ge X_{min}$ **then break;**
10	**end while**
11	Evaluate the smell concentrations: $Smell_i = f(S_i)$;
12	**end for**

Fig. 2. Quantum-behaved search procedure of QFOA.

336 X. Zhang and S. Xia

4 Experimental Comparison

To test the performance of the proposed QFOA, we consider six benchmark problems commonly used in the literature, which are listed in Table 1. For all tested functions, we set the optimum $o = \mathbf{1}^D$ and the dimension $D = 2$ and 10. In this section, we compare the presented QFOA with the basic FOA, IFFO and PSO. The tests are implemented on a computer with Intel(R) Core(TM) i3 3.07 GHz CPU, 4 GB memory, and Window 7. All the algorithms are coded using the Matlab-2009a, and no commercial algorithm tools are used. Due to the randomness nature of swarm intelligence algorithms, the tested algorithms are run 50 times independently for each function and the statistical results are used for the performance evaluation and comparison. The same population size is $M_{osp} = 10D$ and the same maximum number of function evaluation is $fes = 5000D$ for all algorithms.

Table 1. Benchmark functions.

No.	Name	Dim.	Range	x^*	Min
f_1	Shifted Sphere Function	D	[−100,100]	o	0
f_2	Shifted Schwefel's Problem 1.2	D	[−100,100]	o	0
f_3	Shifted Rotated High Conditioned Elliptic Function	D	[−100,100]	o	0
f_4	Shifted Rosenbrock's Function	D	[−10,10]	o	0
f_5	Shifted Rotated Ackley's Function with Global Optimum on Bounds	D	[−32, 32]	o	0
f_6	Shifted Rastrigin's Function	D	[−5.12, 5.12]	o	0
f_7	Shifted Rotated Griewank's Function without Bounds	D	[−600,600]	o	0

Tables 2 and 3 report summary statistics for the optimum values found by the four tested algorithms for benchmark functions with $D = 2$ and $D = 10$ after 50 independent runs, respectively. We compare the best values, the mean values, the max values, and the standard variance of the solutions found. Rank records the performance-rank of seven algorithms for dealing with each benchmark function according to their mean results. The total rank for each algorithm is defined according to their mean rank values over all benchmark problems.

Table 2. Statistical results on benchmark functions with $D = 2$

F	F_{min}		QFOA	FOA	IFFO	PSO
1	0	Min	0	3.39×10^{-7}	8.06×10^{-9}	0
		Mean	0	8.66×10^{-5}	7.04×10^{-6}	0
		Max	0	3.36×10^{-4}	3.30×10^{-5}	0
		Std.	0	8.38×10^{-5}	7.75×10^{-6}	0
		Rank	1	3	2	1
2	0	Min	0	1.13×10^{-6}	1.58×10^{-7}	0
		Mean	6.51×10^{-32}	1.12×10^{-4}	6.86×10^{-5}	0
		Max	1.23×10^{-30}	4.59×10^{-4}	4.93×10^{-4}	0
		Std.	1.82×10^{-31}	9.70×10^{-5}	8.90×10^{-5}	0
		Rank	2	4	3	1
3	0	Min	0	1.26×10^{-3}	2.07×10^{-3}	0
		Mean	0	1.53×10^{-1}	6.56	0
		Max	0	5.61×10^{-1}	9.43×10^{1}	0
		Std.	0	1.42×10^{-1}	1.51×10^{1}	0
		Rank	1	2	3	1
4	0	Min	5.30×10^{-5}	4.65×10^{-5}	3.35×10^{-3}	4.70×10^{-14}
		Mean	1.36×10^{-2}	9.15×10^{-3}	3.05×10^{1}	1.76
		Max	2.89×10^{-2}	4.55×10^{-2}	1.20×10^{2}	2.29×10^{1}
		Std.	7.52×10^{-3}	1.07×10^{-2}	3.31×10^{1}	5.56
		Rank	2	1	4	3
5	0	Min	8.88×10^{-16}	1.44×10^{-3}	7.70×10^{-5}	8.88×10^{-16}
		Mean	2.88×10^{-15}	2.45×10^{-2}	2.68×10^{-3}	8.88×10^{-16}
		Max	1.51×10^{-14}	7.80×10^{-2}	9.03×10^{-3}	8.88×10^{-16}
		Std.	2.70×10^{-15}	1.47×10^{-2}	1.82×10^{-3}	0
		Rank	2	4	3	1
6	0	Min	0	1.56×10^{-6}	3.06×10^{-7}	0
		Mean	0	3.10×10^{-5}	4.38×10^{-3}	2.12×10^{-3}
		Max	0	1.24×10^{-4}	7.68×10^{-3}	7.46×10^{-3}
		Std.	0	2.76×10^{-5}	3.63×10^{-3}	2.77×10^{-3}
		Rank	1	2	4	3
Mean rank			1.5	2.667	3.167	1.667
Total rank			1	3	4	2

The results show that the proposed QFOA performs better than the basic FOA for most functions. The QFOA algorithm gets the smallest variance over the simulations. The convergence curves of the average best function values are displayed in Figs. 3 and 4. QFOA improves the local search ability near the optimal solution and leads to the improved global convergence of FOA.

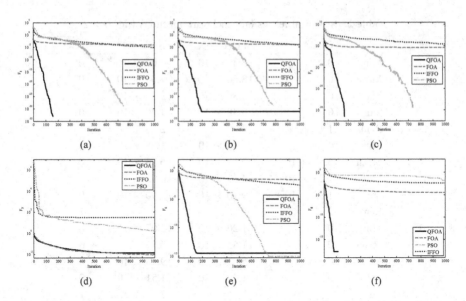

Fig. 3. Comparison of convergence curves on benchmark functions with $D = 2$.

Table 3. Statistical results on benchmark functions with $D = 10$

F	F_{min}		QFOA	FOA	IFFO	PSO
1	0	Min	0	8.03×10^{-2}	6.80×10^{-6}	6.65×10^{-14}
		Mean	4.51×10^{-29}	2.40×10^{-1}	5.90×10^{-5}	8.14×10^{-6}
		Max	2.01×10^{-27}	3.50×10^{-1}	3.10×10^{-4}	3.73×10^{-4}
		Std.	2.84×10^{-28}	5.46×10^{-2}	5.66×10^{-5}	5.27×10^{-5}
		Rank	1	4	3	2
2	0	Min	1.97×10^{-24}	1.53×10^{-1}	1.99×10^{-1}	4.37×10^{-3}
		Mean	5.26×10^{-14}	3.32×10^{-1}	6.96×10^{-1}	2.42×10^{-1}
		Max	2.58×10^{-12}	5.89×10^{-1}	1.44	5.45×10^{-1}
		Std.	3.64×10^{-13}	1.00×10^{-1}	3.66×10^{-1}	1.39×10^{-1}
		Rank	1	3	4	2
3	0	Min	0	3.41×10^{2}	1.41×10^{-1}	5.64×10^{-10}
		Mean	1.09×10^{-12}	9.59×10^{2}	6.08	8.03×10^{-5}
		Max	5.44×10^{-11}	2.12×10^{3}	5.53×10^{1}	1.78×10^{-3}
		Std.	7.70×10^{-12}	3.73×10^{2}	9.68	2.70×10^{-4}
		Rank	1	4	3	2
4	0	Min	2.38	2.03×10^{1}	5.77×10^{-2}	5.25
		Mean	4.26	2.89×10^{1}	2.82×10^{1}	9.36
		Max	8.65	3.98×10^{1}	8.13×10^{-1}	4.96×10^{1}
		Std.	1.56	5.16	2.61×10^{1}	8.92
		Rank	1	4	3	2

(*continued*)

Table 3. (*continued*)

F	F_{min}		QFOA	FOA	IFFO	PSO
5	0	Min	4.44×10^{-15}	9.43×10^{-1}	1.28×10^{-3}	1.28×10^{-6}
		Mean	2.32×10^{-14}	1.45	2.76×10^{-3}	2.39×10^{-4}
		Max	2.42×10^{-13}	1.89	5.08×10^{-3}	2.35×10^{-3}
		Std.	4.34×10^{-14}	2.29×10^{-1}	8.66×10^{-4}	4.66×10^{-4}
		Rank	1	4	3	2
6	0	Min	0	1.06×10^{-2}	9.42×10^{-5}	3.34×10^{-1}
		Mean	4.22×10^{-17}	2.63×10^{-2}	3.71×10^{-2}	4.93×10^{-1}
		Max	6.66×10^{-16}	4.47×10^{-2}	1.16×10^{-1}	6.27×10^{-1}
		Std.	1.10×10^{-16}	7.61×10^{-3}	2.49×10^{-2}	7.22×10^{-2}
		Rank	1	2	3	4
Mean rank			1	3.5	3.167	2.333
Total rank			1	4	3	2

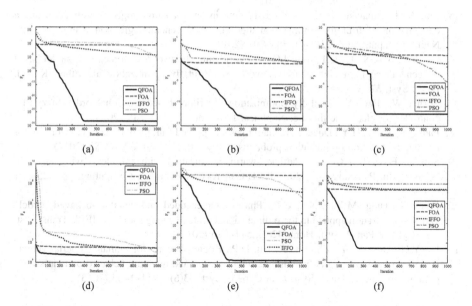

(a)   (b)   (c)

(d)   (e)   (f)

Fig. 4. Comparison of convergence curves on benchmark functions with $D = 10$.

5   Conclusion

FOA is a new evolutionary computation approach. To improve the performance of the FOA, a quantum version of FOA was proposed. QFOA studied the individual fruit fly moving in quantum multi-dimensional space and established a quantum Delta potential well model for the whole fruit fly swarm. Extensive comparative studies were conducted based on various test functions. The experiment results showed much advantage of QFOA to the traditional FOA. Our future work will generalize the QFOA to solve combinatorial and discrete optimization problems.

Acknowledgement. This work is supported by National Natural Science Foundation of China (No. 61703012) and Beijing Natural Science Foundation (No. 4182010).

References

1. Pan, W.T.: A new fruit fly optimization algorithm: taking the financial distress model as an example. Knowl. Based Syst. **26**, 69–74 (2012)
2. Zheng, X.L., Wang, L., Wang, S.Y.: A novel fruit fly optimization algorithm for the semiconductor final testing scheduling problem. Knowl. Based Syst. **57**, 95–103 (2014)
3. Zhang, X.Y., Jia, S.M., Li, X.Z., Jian, M.: Design of the fruit fly optimization algorithm based path planner for UAV in 3D environments. In: Proceedings of 2017 IEEE International Conference on Mechatronics and Automation, pp. 381–386. IEEE, Takamatsu (2017)
4. Zhang, X.Y., Lu, X.Y., Jia, S.M., Li, X.Z.: A novel phase angle-encoded fruit fly optimization algorithm with mutation adaptation mechanism applied to UAV path planning. Appl. Soft Comput. **70**, 371–388 (2018)
5. Lin, S.M.: Analysis of service satisfaction in web auction logistics service using a combination of fruit fly optimization algorithm and general regression neural network. Neural Comput. Appl. **22**(3–4), 783–791 (2013)
6. Li, H.Z., Guo, S., Li, C.J., Sun, J.Q.: A hybrid annual power load forecasting model based on generalized regression neural network with fruit fly optimization algorithm. Knowl. Based Syst. **37**, 378–387 (2013)
7. Sheng, W., Bao, Y.: Fruit fly optimization algorithm based fractional order fuzzy-PID controller for electronic throttle. Nonlinear Dyn. **73**(1–2), 611–619 (2013)
8. Pan, Q.K., Sang, H.Y., Duan, J.H., Gao, L.: An improved fruit fly optimization algorithm for continuous function optimization problems. Knowl. Based Syst. **62**, 69–83 (2014)
9. Sun, J., Feng, B., Xu, W.: Particle swarm optimization with particles having quantum behavior. In: Proceedings of 2004 IEEE Congress on Evolution Computing, pp. 325–331 (2004)
10. Fu, Y.G., Ding, M.Y., Zhou, C.P.: Phase angle-encoded and quantum-behaved particle swarm optimization applied to three-dimensional route planning for UAV. IEEE Trans. Syst. Man Cybern. Part A Syst. Hum. **42**(2), 511–526 (2012)
11. Fu, Y.G., Ding, M.Y., Zhou, C.P., Hu, H.P.: Route planning for unmanned aerial vehicle (UAV) on the sea using hybrid differential evolution and quantum-behaved particle swarm optimization. IEEE Trans. Syst. Man Cybern. Syst. **43**(6), 1451–1465 (2013)

Parameter Estimation of a Nonlinear Hydrologic Model for Channel Flood Routing with the Bat Algorithm

Rebeca Sánchez[1], Patricia Suárez[1], Akemi Gálvez[1,2],
and Andrés Iglesias[1,2]([envelope])

[1] Department of Applied Mathematics and Computational Sciences,
University of Cantabria, Avenida de los Castros s/n, 39005 Santander, Spain
iglesias@unican.es
[2] Department of Information Science, Faculty of Sciences, Narashino Campus,
Toho University, 2-2-1 Miyama, Funabashi 274-8510, Japan
http://personales.unican.es/iglesias

Abstract. Flood routing is a methodology to predict the changes of the flow of water as it moves through a natural river, an artificial channel, or a reservoir. It is widely used in fields such as flood prediction, reservoir design, geographic planning, and many others. One of the most popular and widely used flood routing techniques is the Muskingum model, as it is conceptually simple and only depends on a few parameters that can be estimated from historical inflow/outflow records. However, the estimation of such parameters for the nonlinear case is still a challenging task. In this paper we present a method based on a powerful swarm intelligence technique called bat algorithm to solve the parameter estimation problem of the nonlinear Muskingum model for channel routing. The method is applied to an illustrative example used as a benchmark in the field with very good results. We also show that our method outperforms other state-of-the-art methods in the field such as PSO.

Keywords: Swarm intelligence · Global optimization ·
Bat algorithm · Flood routing · Hydrologic models ·
Parameter estimation

1 Introduction

Flood routing is a very important subject of research in water engineering and other fields. Roughly speaking, flood routing aims at predicting the changes of the rate of flow (discharge) over the time for a given section or point of a river, channel, or reservoir. This problem has many relevant applications in several areas, such as hydrology, flood forecasting, watershed simulations, geographic planning, flood protection, reservoir design, and many others.

Several methods have been described in the literature to address this problem. Among them, the Muskingum method is one of the most popular and frequently

© Springer Nature Switzerland AG 2019
Y. Tan et al. (Eds.): ICSI 2019, LNCS 11655, pp. 341–351, 2019.
https://doi.org/10.1007/978-3-030-26369-0_32

used methods for engineering of rivers and channels owing to its simplicity. This method, originally proposed in 1938 for the Muskingum river in Ohio [10], is indeed very simple to use, as it only depends on two parameters that can be estimated from past inflow and outflow data. The nonlinear Muskingum model is given by the following evolution equations:

$$\frac{dS_t}{dt} = I_t - O_t, \tag{1}$$

$$S_t = K[\chi I_t + (1 - \chi)O_t]^m, \tag{2}$$

where S_t, I_t and O_t denote the values of the storage, inflow and outflow at time t, respectively, K is a storage time constant for the river reach that provides an approximates the flow travel time through the river reach, χ is a weight usually taken values between 0 and 0.3 for stream channels, and m is an exponent introduced to account for the effects of nonlinearity.

In spite of its simplicity, the Muskingum model is still affected by a critical problem: the estimation of its parameters. Finding the correct values for K, χ and m is challenging, because such values cannot be obtained from the historical inflow and outflow hydrographs. This means that a powerful parameter estimation method is absolutely required. As a result, several optimization techniques have already been applied during the last two decades to tackle this issue. Early methods for this problem described in the literature include least-squares method (LSM) [6], Hook-Jeeves pattern search with linear regression, the conjugate gradient and Davidon-Fletcher-Powell method [13], and nonlinear least-squares regression [20]. More recently, two approximate methods based on computing the slopes of the inflow and outflow hydrographs at their intersection point and the computation of such hydrographs at two specific points were described in [1]. Other approach using the Broyden-Fletcher-Goldfard-Shanno (BFGS) method was reported in [5]. The method in [2] is based on the Nelder-mead simplex algorithm. Neither of these methods do guarantee the global optima. Recently, researchers in the field turned their attention towards nature-inspired metaheuristics. They include the use of genetic algorithms [11] and hybrid methods, such as a combination of the modified honey bee colony optimization with generalized reduced gradient methods in [12].

Among the myriad of nature-inspired metaheuristic methods for optimization, those based on swarm intelligence are receiving increasing attention during the last few years because of their ability to cope with problems where little or no information at all is available about the problem [16]. These methods are also very effective for optimization problems where the objective function is not differentiable making gradient-based methods unsuitable, or for problems under difficult conditions (e.g., noisy data, irregular sampling) commonly found in real-world applications. Swarm intelligence methods applied to this problem include harmony search [9], and particle swarm optimization [4], artificial bee colony [14]. A very recent method also considers particle swarm optimization for this problem and investigates the effect of using variable values for the parameters [3].

It is worthwhile to remark that some of the previous methods do not consider the same Muskingum model addressed in this work, but other variations of it. For instance, the method in [3] consider the (simpler) linear Muskingum model, while the method in [1], although also nonlinear, considers a variation of Eq. (2) given by: $S_t = K[\chi I_t^n + (1 - \chi)O_t^n]$. In other words, there are several (qualitatively different) formulations of the Muskingum model so it is important to notice which one is actually under analysis. This observation is crucial to avoid leading our readers to confusion about the real model used in this contribution and its possible relationship with other previous approaches.

In this paper, we address the parameter estimation problem for the nonlinear Muskingum method given by Eqs. (1)–(2). Our approach is based a powerful nature-inspired swarm intelligence technique for global optimization called bat algorithm. The structure of this paper is as follows: the main steps of the procedure for the nonlinear Muskingum model are briefly described in Sect. 2. The bat algorithm is described in detail in Sect. 3 and then applied to our problem in Sect. 4. Our experimental results are briefly discussed in Sect. 5. The paper closes with the main conclusions and some ideas for future work in the field.

2   Procedure for the Nonlinear Muskingum Model

Rearranging Eq. (2), the rate of outflow becomes:

$$O_t = \left(\frac{1}{1-X}\right)\left(\frac{S_t}{K}\right)^{\frac{1}{m}} - \left(\frac{X}{1-X}\right)I_t, \tag{3}$$

Combining Eqs. (1) and (3), we get:

$$\frac{\Delta S_t}{\Delta t} = \left(\frac{1}{1-X}\right)\left(\frac{S_t}{K}\right)^{\frac{1}{m}} - \left(\frac{X}{1-X}\right)I_t, \tag{4}$$

$$S_{t+1} = S_t + \Delta S_t \tag{5}$$

$$O_{t+1} = \left(\frac{1}{1-X}\right)\left(\frac{S_{t+1}}{K}\right)^{\frac{1}{m}} - \left(\frac{X}{1-X}\right)\bar{I}_{t+1}, \tag{6}$$

where $\bar{I}_{t+1} = (I_{t+1} + I_t)/2$. Then, the procedure for the nonlinear Muskingum model given by Eqs. (1)–(2) is based on the following steps:

- **Step 1:** Assume initial values for the three parameters K, χ and m.
- **Step 2:** Calculate the storage S_t using Eq. (2), taking the initial outflow equal to the initial inflow.
- **Step 3:** Calculate the time rate of storage using Eq. (4).
- **Step 4:** Estimate the next accumulated storage using Eq. (5).
- **Step 5:** Calculate the next outflow using Eq. S_t using Eq. (6). I_t will replace $\bar{I}_{t+1}$ when the ratio of storage t and $t + 1$ exceeds 2.
- **Step 6:** Repeat the steps 2–5.

3   The Bat Algorithm

The *bat algorithm* is a nature-inspired swarm intelligence algorithm proposed by Yang in 2010 to solve optimization problems [17–19]. The algorithm is inspired by the echolocation behavior of bats, which is used as a metaphor for a global optimization method and is described by three idealized rules:

1. Bats use echolocation to sense distance and distinguish between food, prey and background barriers.
2. Each virtual bat flies randomly with a velocity $\mathbf{v}_i$ at position (solution) $\mathbf{x}_i$ with a fixed frequency f_{min}, varying wavelength λ and loudness A_0 to search for prey. As it searches and finds its prey, it changes wavelength (or frequency) of their emitted pulses and adjust the rate of pulse emission r, depending on the proximity of the target.
3. It is assumed that the loudness will vary from a (initially large and positive) value A_0 to a minimum constant value A_{min}.

In general, we assume that the frequency f evolves on a bounded interval $[f_{min}, f_{max}]$. For simplicity, we can assume that $f_{min} = 0$, so $f \in [0, f_{max}]$. The rate of pulse can simply be in the range $r \in [0, 1]$, where 0 means no pulses at all, and 1 means the maximum rate of pulse emission. The pseudo-code of the algorithm is shown in Algorithm 1. Basically, it considers an initial population of $\mathcal{P}$ individuals (bats). Each bat, representing a potential solution, has a location $\mathbf{x}_i$ and velocity $\mathbf{v}_i$, initialized with random values within the search space. Then, the pulse frequency, pulse rate, and loudness are computed for each individual bat. The swarm evolves iteratively over generations until the maximum number of generations, $\mathcal{G}_{max}$, is reached. For each generation g and each bat, new frequency, location and velocity are computed as:

$$f_i^g = f_{min}^g + \beta(f_{max}^g - f_{min}^g),\tag{7}$$

$$\mathbf{v}_i^g = \mathbf{v}_i^{g-1} + [\mathbf{x}_i^{g-1} - \mathbf{x}^*]\, f_i^g,\tag{8}$$

$$\mathbf{x}_i^g = \mathbf{x}_i^{g-1} + \mathbf{v}_i^g\tag{9}$$

where $\beta \in [0, 1]$ follows the random uniform distribution, and $\mathbf{x}^*$ represents the current global best location (solution), which is obtained through evaluation of the objective function at all bats and ranking of their fitness values. The superscript $(.)^g$ is used to denote the current generation g.

The best current solution and a local solution around it are probabilistically selected and the search is intensified by a local random walk. For this local search, the solution selected is perturbed locally through a random walk as. $\mathbf{x}_{new} = \mathbf{x}_{old} + \epsilon \mathcal{A}^g$, where ϵ is a uniform random number on the interval $[-1, 1]$ and $\mathcal{A}^g = <\mathcal{A}_i^g>$, is the average loudness of all the bats at generation g.

If the new solution is better than the previous best one, it is probabilistically accepted depending on the value of the loudness. In that case, the algorithm increases the pulse rate and decreases the loudness. This process is repeated for the given number of generations. In general, the loudness decreases once a bat

---

Require: (Initial Parameters)
    Population size: $\mathcal{P}$ Maximum number of generations: $\mathcal{G}_{max}$
    Loudness: $\mathcal{A}$ Pulse rate: r
    Maximum frequency: f_{max} Dimension of the problem: d
    Objective function: $\phi(\mathbf{x})$, with $\mathbf{x} = (x_1, \ldots, x_d)^T$
    Random number: $\theta \in U(0, 1)$
  1: $g \leftarrow 0$
  2: Initialize the bat population $\mathbf{x}_i$ and $\mathbf{v}_i$, $(i = 1, \ldots, n)$
  3: Define pulse frequency f_i at $\mathbf{x}_i$
  4: Initialize pulse rates r_i and loudness $\mathcal{A}_i$
  5: **while** $g < \mathcal{G}_{max}$ **do**
  6:    **for** $i = 1$ **to** $\mathcal{P}$ **do**
  7:       Generate new solutions by adjusting frequency,
  8:       and updating velocities and locations //eqns. (7)-(9)
  9:       **if** $\theta > r_i$ **then**
10:          $\mathbf{s}^{best} \leftarrow \mathbf{s}^g$ //select the best current solution
11:          $\mathrm{ls}^{best} \leftarrow \mathrm{ls}^g$ //generate a local solution around $\mathbf{s}^{best}$
12:       **end if**
13:       Generate a new solution by local random walk
14:       **if** $\theta < \mathcal{A}_i$ *and* $\phi(\mathbf{x_i}) < \phi(\mathbf{x}^*)$ **then**
15:          Accept new solutions
16:          Increase r_i and decrease $\mathcal{A}_i$
17:       **end if**
18:    **end for**
19:    $g \leftarrow g + 1$
20: **end while**
21: Rank the bats and find current best $\mathbf{x}^*$
22: **return** $\mathbf{x}^*$

Algorithm 1: Bat algorithm pseudocode

finds its prey (in our analogy, once a new best solution is found), while the rate of pulse emission decreases. For simplicity, the following values are commonly used: $\mathcal{A}_0 = 1$ and $\mathcal{A}_{min} = 0$, assuming that this latter value means that a bat has found the prey and temporarily stop emitting any sound. The evolution rules for loudness and pulse rate are: $\mathcal{A}_i^{g+1} = \alpha \mathcal{A}_i^g$ and $r_i^{g+1} = r_i^0[1 - exp(-\gamma g)]$, where α and γ are constants. Note that for any $0 < \alpha < 1$ and any $\gamma > 0$ we have: $\mathcal{A}_i^g \to 0$, $r_i^g \to r_i^0$, as $g \to \infty$. In general, each bat should have different values for loudness and pulse emission rate. To this aim, we can take an initial loudness $\mathcal{A}_i^0 \in (0, 2)$ while the initial emission rate r_i^0 can be any value in the interval $[0, 1]$. Loudness and emission rates will be updated only if the new solutions are improved, an indication that the bats are moving towards the optimal solution. As a result, the bat algorithm applies a parameter tuning technique to control the dynamic behavior of a swarm of bats. Similarly, the balance between exploration and exploitation can be controlled by tuning algorithm-dependent parameters.

4   The Method

Bat algorithm has already been applied to data fitting problems [7,8]. Still, to apply bat algorithm described above to our problem, we need to define some important issues. Firstly, we need an adequate representation of the problem. Each bat $\mathcal{B}_j$, representing a potential solution, corresponds to a parametric vector of the free variables of the problem, in the form: $\mathcal{B}_j = (K_j, \chi_j, m_j)$. These parametric vectors are initialized with random values on the intervals $(0, 10)$ for K and m and $(0, 5)$ for χ. We remark however that these constraints apply only for the initial conditions, as we allow the variables to move freely outside such ranges during the execution of the algorithm. Secondly, a fitness function is required for optimization. In our problem, the goal is to predict the outflow given the inflow and then compare the predicted outflow with the observed one. This can be properly done through least-squares minimization. Let O_t and $\bar{O}_t$ be the observed and the predicted outflow at time t, respectively. We consider the least-squares functional LSQ given by the sum of the squares of the residuals:

$$\text{Minimize}(LSQ) = \underset{\{K_j\}, \{\chi_j\}, \{m_j\}}{\text{Minimize}} \left[\sum_{t=1}^{n} (O_t - \bar{O}_t)^2 \right] \qquad (10)$$

where n denotes the number of time instances of the inflow/outflow time series. Finally, we need to address the important issue of parameter tuning. It is well-known that the performance of swarm intelligence techniques depends of a proper parameter tuning, which is also problem-dependent. Due to this reason, our choice has been fully empirical, based on numerous computer simulations for different parameter values. In this paper, we consider a population size of 30 as larger population sizes do increase the CPU times without significantly improving our numerical results. The initial and minimum loudness and parameter α are set to 0.5, 0, and 0.2, respectively. Regarding the stopping criterion, all executions are performed until no further improvement is achieved after 20 consecutive generations.

5   Experimental Results

Our method has been tested on an illustrative example first proposed in 1974 by Wilson [15] and corresponding to a channel routing problem. This example has been widely used as a benchmark for different methods in several previous works. Table 1 reports the values of the observed inflow and outflow (columns 2 and 3) for different time instances, expressed in hours (column 1). All flow results are expressed in cubic meters per second (cms). We also report the numerical results of two previous methods, reported in [11] and [4] and based on genetic algorithms (GA) and PSO respectively, (columns 4 and 5) and the results of our method based on the bat algorithm (column 6). To avoid the spurious effects derived from the randomness of the process, we run 15 independent executions of our method and then consider the average value. This means that the results

Table 1. Observed inflow and outflow hydrographs and computed outflow of two state-of-the-art GA and PSO methods and of our bat algorithm method for the example in the paper (best results are highlighted in bold)

Time (h)	Inflow (cms)	Observed Outflow (cms)	Computed outflow (cms)		
			GA	PSO	Our method
0	22	22	**22.0**	**22.0**	23.0
6	23	21	22.0	22.0	**21.5**
12	35	21	22.4	22.6	**22.2**
18	71	26	26.3	28.1	**26.2**
24	103	34	34.2	32.2	**34.0**
30	111	44	**44.2**	45.0	43.3
36	109	55	56.9	57.0	**55.2**
42	100	66	68.2	67.5	**65.6**
48	86	75	77.1	75.9	**74.4**
54	71	82	83.2	**81.2**	81.0
60	59	85	85.7	**85.6**	84.4
66	47	84	**84.2**	**84.2**	83.5
72	39	80	80.2	79.6	**79.9**
78	32	73	**73.3**	**73.3**	72.5
84	28	64	65.0	65.0	**63.6**
90	24	54	55.8	56.2	**53.8**
96	22	44	46.7	46.5	**45.1**
102	21	36	38.0	37.3	**36.5**
108	20	30	30.9	**29.7**	30.4
114	19	25	25.7	24.3	**25.5**
120	19	22	**22.1**	20.6	22.7
126	18	19	20.4	**19.6**	20.0

Table 2. Parameter values, LSQ error, and improvement rate obtained for the methods in our comparison (best error and and improvement rate highlighted in bold).

Method	SI approach	K	χ	m	LSQ	I.R.
Mohan [11]	Genetic algorithms	0.1033	0.2873	1.8282	38.23	0.00%
Chu and Chang [4]	Particle swarm optimization	0.1824	0.3330	2.1458	36.89	3.50%
Our method	Bat algorithm	3.4580	0.0034	2.3065	**19.59**	**48.78%**

reported in the last column are not those of the best execution (which are even better) but the average of the 15 independent executions. Still, the numerical results obtained with our method are very relevant. A visual comparison between the columns 3 and 5 reveals that our method performs very well, as it is able to capture the real tendency of data for all times instances in the example. This means that our method has a very good predictive capability.

We also compare our results with those of two methods based on GA [11] and PSO [4]. These methods have been primarily chosen for comparison because they are very popular and widely considered state-of-the-art methods in the field and outperform many other methods in the literature for this problem. The best result for each time instance has been highlighted in bold for easier comparison. As the reader can see, our method outperforms these methods for most time instances in this example. This fact becomes evident from Table 2, where we show the optimal parameter values (columns 3–5) along with the LSQ error (column 6) obtained with the three methods (described in columns 1–2), and the improvement rate (column 7) obtained with respect to the worst method (the GA, in this case). Once again, the best results are in bold. Note that our method improves the LSQ error of the GA and PSO methods significantly, with an improvement rate of 48.78% and 46.89% over GA and PSO, respectively.

Our good numerical results are confirmed visually in Fig. 1. The figure depicts the observed inflow and outflow hydrographs as well as the predicted outflow for the PSO and bat algorithm methods used in our comparative work. Note the excellent visual matching between the observed outflow and the outflow predicted by our method. Although the outflow of the PSO method is very close to the

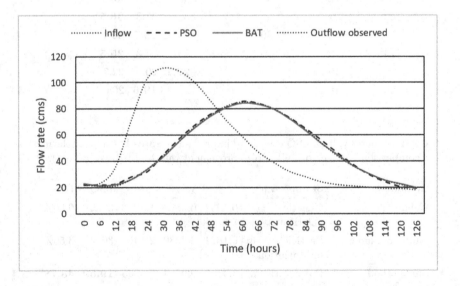

Fig. 1. Observed and predicted inflow and outflow hydrographs for the example computed with the parameter values obtained with PSO and our bat algorithm method.

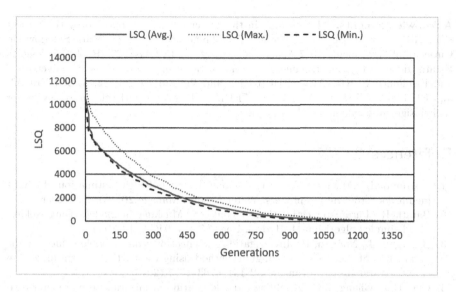

Fig. 2. Convergence diagram of the LSQ error function for the minimum, maximum and average values for 15 different executions.

observed one, ours is even better as it becomes visually indistinguishable from the observed outflow and they overlap each other. This is the best indicator of the good performance of our method for this real-world example.

Finally, Fig. 2 shows the convergence diagram of our method for the maximum, minimum and average values from the 15 independent executions. As shown, the method converges in all cases, and there is no large variation between the different executions, meaning that the method is robust for different executions, a very valuable feature for real-world applications.

6 Conclusions and Future Work

In this paper we present a bat algorithm-based method to solve the parameter estimation problem of the nonlinear Muskingum model, a relevant problem in hydrology, flood forecasting, dam design and other engineering fields. The method is simple to understand and easy to implement. Our computational experiments for a popular real-world channel routing example used as a benchmark in the field show that it performs very well, is robust and outperforms other state-of-the-art approaches in the field. We conclude that it can be safely used for outflow prediction in flood forecasting and in related tasks. Future work in the field includes the extension of this approach to the case of natural rivers and reservoir routing, for which the parameters are expected to behave quite differently. Improving the accuracy of our method even further is also part of our future work in the field.

Acknowledgements. The research in this paper has been supported by the project PDE-GIR of the EU Horizon 2020 research and innovation program, Marie Sklodowska-Curie grant agreement No 778035; the project #TIN2017-89275-R of the Agencia Estatal de Investigación (Spanish Ministry of Science, Innovation and Universities) and EU Funds EFRD (AEI/FEDER-UE); and the project #JU12, of SODERCAN and EU Funds EFRD (SODERCAN /FEDER-UE). We also thank the reviewers for their insightful comments and suggestions.

References

1. Al-Humoud, J.M., Esen, I.I.: Approximate methods for the estimation of Muskingum flood routing parameters. Water Resour. Manage **20**, 979–990 (2006)
2. Barati, R.: Parameter estimation of nonlinear Muskingum models using Nelder-Mead simplex algorithm. J. Hydrol. Eng. **16**(11), 946–954 (2011)
3. Bazargan, J., Norouzi, H.: Investigation the effect of using variable values for the parameters of the linear Muskingum method using the particle swarm algorithm (PSO). Water Resour. Manage. **32**(14), 4763–4777 (2018)
4. Chu, H.J., Chang, L.C.: Applying particle swarm optimization to parameter estimation of the nonlinear Muskingum model. J. Hydrol. Eng. **14**(9), 1024–1027 (2009)
5. Geem, Z.W.: Parameter estimation for the nonlinear Muskingum model using the BFGS technique. J. Irrig. Drain. Eng. **1325**, 474–478 (2006)
6. Gill, M.A.: Flood routing by Muskingum method. J. Hydrol. **363–4**, 353–363 (1978)
7. Iglesias, A., Gálvez, A., Collantes, M.: Multilayer embedded bat algorithm for B-spline curve reconstruction. Int. Comput. Aided Eng. **24**(4), 385–399 (2017)
8. Iglesias, A., Gálvez, A., Collantes, M.: Iterative sequential bat algorithm for free-form rational Bézier surface reconstruction. Int. J. Bio-Inspired Comput. **11**(1), 1–15 (2018)
9. Kim, J.H., Geem, Z.W., Kim, E.S.: Parameter estimation of the nonlinear Muskingum model using harmony search. J. Am. Water Resour. Assoc. **375**, 1131–1138 (2001)
10. McCarthy, G.T.: The unit hydrograph and flood routing. New London. Conf. North Atlantic Division. US Army Corps of Engineers. New London. Conn. USA (1938)
11. Mohan, S.: Parameter estimation of nonlinear Muskingum models using genetic algorithm. J. Hydraul. Eng. **1232**, 137–142 (1997)
12. Niazkar, M., Afzali, S.H.: Application of new hybrid optimization technique for parameter estimation of new improved version of Muskingum model. Water Resour. Manage. **30**(13), 4713–4730 (2016)
13. Tung, Y.K.: River flood routing by nonlinear Muskingum method. J. Hydraul. Eng. **111**(12), 1447–1460 (1985)
14. Vafakhah, M., Dastorani, A., Moghaddam, A.: Optimal parameter estimation for nonlinear Muskingum model based on artificial bee colony algorithm. EcoPersia **3**(1), 847–865 (2015)
15. Wilson, E.M.: Engineering Hydrology. MacMillan, Hampshire (1974)
16. Yang, X.-S.: Nature-Inspired Metaheuristic Algorithms, 2nd edn. Luniver Press, Frome (2010)

17. Yang, X.S.: A new metaheuristic bat-inspired algorithm. In: González, J.R., Pelta, D.A., Cruz, C., Terrazas, G., Krasnogor, N. (eds.) Nature Inspired Cooperative Strategies for Optimization (NICSO 2010), pp. 65–74. Springer, Heidelberg (2010). https://doi.org/10.1007/978-3-642-12538-6_6
18. Yang, X.S.: Bat algorithm for multiobjective optimization. Int. J. Bio-Inspired Comput. **3**(5), 267–274 (2011)
19. Yang, X.S., Gandomi, A.H.: Bat algorithm: a novel approach for global engineering optimization. Eng. Comput. **29**(5), 464–483 (2012)
20. Yoon, J.W., Padmanabhan, G.: Parameter-estimation of linear and nonlinear Muskingum models. J. Water Resour. Plann. Manage. **1195**, 600–610 (1993)

Bacterial Foraging Optimization with Memory and Clone Schemes for Dynamic Environments

Ben Niu[1], Qianying Liu[1], and Jun Wang[2(✉)]

[1] College of Management, Shenzhen University, Shenzhen 518060, China
drniuben@gmail.com, qianying_liu@163.com
[2] School of Computer Science, South China Normal University,
Guangzhou 510631, China
wangjun.scnu@gmail.com

Abstract. Dynamic optimization problems (DOPs) are prevailingly addressed because of their origins from real-world issues. In addition to existing methods that have been developed for evolutionary algorithms to solve DOPs, this paper provides a hybrid memory and clone scheme, called memory-based clone selection, for bacterial foraging optimization algorithms in dynamic environments. Meanwhile, two gene libraries (Random and Non-random) are involved to clone outstanding individuals and dynamically manage the gene hall and memory. This approach not only results in greater diversity and better global search ability, but also enables the algorithm higher adaptability to environmental dynamics and changes. The simulation result generated by a dynamic rotation peak benchmark confirms that proposed memory and clone schemes-based BFO (MCBFO) outperforms standard BFO and PSO in terms of population diversity, convergence rate and searching ability.

Keywords: Bacterial foraging optimization · Dynamic optimization problems · Memory · Immigrants · Clone selection

1 Introduction

As a member of meta-heuristic algorithms, Evolutionary Algorithm (EA) is a type of stochastic search technique enlightened by norms of natural evolution or the behavior of biological groups such as biological evolution, genetics and the social behavior of species. Since EAs can be easily implemented and less restrained on problems to be solved, they have shown broad application prospects in stationary optimization and search problems [1, 2]. However, due to dynamic and uncertain environments, optimization problems are inevitably affected [3].

To better work out dynamic optimization problems (DOPs), aside from quickly and precisely finding the location of global optimum, EAs also should unremittingly track the optima over time, or search a robust solution that works well in a variety of uncertain situations. Since EAs have difficulties in getting rid of an old optimum when converging, DOPs pose a severe challenge to EAs. Nevertheless, enhanced EAs still serves as a good solution for DOPs because these algorithms are normally inspired from the natural and biological evolution subjecting to an ever-changing environment.

© Springer Nature Switzerland AG 2019
Y. Tan et al. (Eds.): ICSI 2019, LNCS 11655, pp. 352–360, 2019.
https://doi.org/10.1007/978-3-030-26369-0_33

In recent decades, an increasing number of scholars have been dedicating to studying EAs for DOPs. Apart from the simplest approach (Restart EAs when a change is detected), there should be other approaches that efficiently utilize computing resources and find similar solutions for DOPs, which include multi-population mechanisms [4], memory schemes [5] and diversity reintroduction [6].

Passino firstly proposed bacterial foraging optimization (BFO) after investigating foraging behaviors of E. coli [7]. BFO has achieved excellent performance in many static benchmark and practical optimization problems [8]. However, there remains an underexplored research area where few scholars have studied BFO in uncertain situations.

This work further explores BFO with explicit memory and clone schemes in order to improve the effectiveness in solving DOPs. Firstly, a dynamic time pattern to update the memory with closet scheme is adopted. Secondly, the clone schemes include random and non-random gene libraries composed of gene fragments of random length to clone elites for generating immigrants to replace the population.

Six different dynamic environments generated by a dynamic rotation peak benchmark are used to verify the effectiveness of MCBFO, BFO, and PSO (Particle Swarm Optimization). Experimental results reveal that MCBFO utilizing both the memory and clone selection outperforms its counterparts.

2 Approaches Developed to EAs for DOPs

Approaches developed to EAs include: memory schemes, multi-population mechanisms and reintroducing diversity. To keep search efficiency while enhance diversity, this paper highlights memory strategies, immigration strategies and immune system cloning strategies.

2.1 Explicit Memory Schemes

The explicit memory scheme of EA in a dynamic environment benefits from the accurate representation of independent storage space. In any new environments, it is capable of explicitly reusing useful information from previous iterations stored in memory. Moreover, memory strategy usually consists of direct memory scheme and associative memory scheme. The direct strategy is to store good individuals in current environment. When detecting changes, it will either reuse the individuals themselves or generate new solutions based on the memory to replace the bad ones, so that the population can adapt to the environment quickly [9]. The associated memory strategy stores good solution and associated environmental information. Such environmental information can be used to similarity metrics for higher efficiency in finding historically optimal solutions that are more relevant to changing environments [10].

2.2 Immigration Strategies

Immigration strategies normally encompass three categories: random immigration, memory immigration, and elite immigration, which facilitate improving search randomness and enhancing group diversity. Such strategies improve randomness and the global search ability of the algorithm and enable individuals' higher probability to escape local optimum and effectively solve the convergence problem of EAs. Furthermore, random immigration is rather simple and consistent with the rules of nature [9]. In each iteration, a probability is used to randomly generate immigrant populations in the search range to replace some individuals in the current population. Memory immigration and elite immigrants integrate the advantages of memory and elites to make the algorithm quickly adapt to the new environment [11]. In addition, memory and elites guide the search direction of immigrant populations, so that the algorithm is able to retain diversity and previous environmental information.

2.3   Cloning Selection

Simões and Costa [12] proposed a GA (Genetic Algorithm) imitating the mechanism of immune system to solve DOPs. During cloning selection, Somatic hypermutation often causes certain variation. To simulate the phenomenon, the algorithm created some gene libraries that comprises many fixed-length gene segments, which are used in a cloning process. These libraries are randomly generated at the beginning of the searching process and remain unchanged. Each individual is subject to a transformation modification with probability p_t. The process of transformation is as follows. Firstly, we choose one gene segment randomly. Then, a transformation location on this gene fragment is randomly selected and recorded. Finally, from the recorded locus, individuals' own genes are replaced with the selected gene segments. By using transformation as a hypermutation operator, EAs can increase population diversity and take advantages of previous useful solution information.

3   Description of Investigated BFO

3.1   Standard BFO

In SBFO, three main bacterial-specific behaviors as chemotaxis, reproduction and elimination and dispersal, are implemented for updating the position of individuals and finding the optimum [7]. The chemotaxis operator moves the bacteria to a better position. The reproduction operator complies with the rule that the fittest bacteria survives while poorly performed bacteria will die. In addition, in the elimination and dispersal operator, the bacteria will be randomly reassigned to a location, thus increasing the randomness of the algorithm.

The SBFO consists of three levels of loops, from the outside to the inside for elimination and dispersal, reproduction, and chemotaxis. Figure 1 shows the flow of the SBFO.

3.2   Memory and Clone Schemes-Based BFO (MCBFO)

Figure 2 presents the pseudo-code of the BFO, which employ memory, cloning selection and immigrants' schemes, referring to MCBFO. MCBFO organically integrates two modules of memory and diversity enhancement. It extracts and preserves favorable

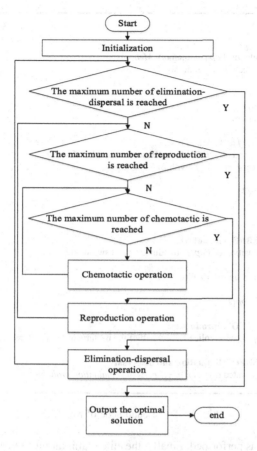

Fig. 1. The flow chart of SBFO

information for the environment, performs dynamic management of memory and gene libraries, and generates immigrant populations based on cloned elites, thereby increasing population diversity and population search range, jumping out of local optimal solutions, and tracking dynamic targets to better solve DOPs.

In the MCBFO algorithm, memory $Mem(T)$ is first randomly generated, and memory is managed according to a dynamic time mode, that is, memory update is performed when an environmental change is detected or $T = T_{Change}$. After each memory updates, the random integer $randi(gap) \in (0, gap)$ will determine when the memory will be updated next time T_{Change}. For the detection of the environment, we adopt simplest method to see whether the average fitness value of the observed population and memory fluctuates greatly.

In this algorithm, two ways are introduced to utilize different memory update methods: if $T = T_{Change}$, then choose the contemporary elite $E(T)$, otherwise choose the previous generation of elite $E(T - 1)$, and find the memory individual $ClMem$ closest to the elite, if it is not as good as the elite, it will be replaced. Subsequently, the SBFO

Initialization
  $T=0$
  $T_{Change}=randi(gap)$
  Initialize population *Pop (0)*, memory *Mem (0)*
  and gene libraries *GL (0)* randomly
End initialization

For (Each elimination)
 For (Each reproduction)
  For (Each chemotaxis)
   evaluate *Pop (T)* and *Mem (T)*
   update *GL(T)* and elite *E(T)*=SelectBestOne*(Pop (T), Mem (T))*
   replace the worst in *Pop (T)* with *E(T-1)*

   *//*update *Pop(T)*

   *//*update *Mem(T)*

   // **perform SBFO' chemotaxis**
   Update the position of *Pop(T)* by tumbling and swimming

   // **immigration based on elite**

   Pop(T+1) = Pop(T)
  End For
  // **perform SBFO' reproduction**
  Evaluate *Pop(T)* and replicate good half of the bacteria in *Pop(T)* to replace the bad half
 End For
 // **perform SBFO' elimination and dispersal**
 randomly generated (*Pop(T)*, p_{ed}) *//* p_{ed} *is the elimination probability*
End For

Fig. 2. The pseudo-code of MCBFO

search procedure was performed. Finally, the elite immigration strategy is executed with the probability P_{Im}. Specifically, a group of $r_{im} * n$ immigrant *Imm(T)* around the elite *E (T)* are cloned and used to replace the worst population in the search population.

For the Cloning selection strategy, unlike [12], this algorithm has three differences. First, [12] has multiple random gene libraries, but this algorithm has only two random and non-random gene libraries, with 30% and 70% gene fragments respectively. Second, the gene library of [12] consists of a series of fixed-length segments, but this article has fragments of random 1–3 lengths. Third, when cloning cells, the original method replaces genes at random location of individuals with randomly selected segments, but we use an aligned transformation strategy [13]. Specifically, two gene libraries are randomly generated initially within the search range. The update method is to randomly update the random library at each iteration. For the non-random library, the tournament selection strategy is adopted. First, two individuals are randomly selected in the population, and then the individual with good fitness is selected. A contiguous gene of the individual is randomly selected as a gene fragment, and the starting position of the fragment is recorded. MCBFO uses an aligned clone transformation strategy. First, it randomly selects a fragment from the gene library. Once the fragment is from a random library, the gene at a random location of the object is replaced; otherwise, the gene at the location recorded before the object is replaced.

4 Experimental Study

4.1 Dynamic Test Environments

We used a dynamic rotation peak benchmark [14] to measure the performance of MCBFO and BFO algorithms in various changing environments. The optimization problem is described as follows:

$$F = \max_{i=1:m}\left(\vec{H_i}(t) \Big/ \left(1 + \overrightarrow{W_i}(t) \cdot \sqrt{\sum\nolimits_{j=1}^{n}\left(x_j - \vec{X}_j^i(t)\right)^2 / n} \right)\right) \tag{1}$$

The $\vec{H}$ and $\vec{W}$ change in six ways: case small step, case large step, case random, case chaotic, case recurrent and case recurrent with noisy.

The parameters of the test problem are set as follows: The number of peaks: $m = 10$; Width range: $w \in [1, 10]$; Width severity is 0.5; Initial width is 5; Dimension: $n = 10$; Search range: $x \in [-5, 5]$; Change frequency: *frequency* = 10000 ∗ n; The number of changes: *numchange* = 5; the rest of the parameters are default.

4.2 The Parameters of the Algorithms

SBFO and MCBFO, the length of chemotaxis step $Csz = 0.2$, the maximum number of swims is set to 4. The probability of elimination: $P_{el} = 0.25$. The max numbers of chemotaxis, reproduction and elimination-dispersal are set as: $Nc = 300$, $Nre = 10$, $Ned = 2$. For PSO, learning rate $C1$, $C2 = 1.49445$ and weight $w = 0.8$. All the experiment runs 10 times, the times of function evaluations are 500000, the size of population $p = 50$.

For MCBFO, the total number of gene fragments: *num_gene* = 30, and random fragments accounted for 0.3, update interval of memory: *gap* = 20, memory, clone and immigration accounts for 0.2, 0.2 and 0.1 percent of the population respectively.

4.3 Experimental Results and Analysis

Figures 3, 4, 5, 6, 7 and 8 show that MCBFO performs better than other rivals in all six dynamic environments. In the top five dynamic environments, the fitness of MCBFO was poor at the beginning of each environmental change, but it can clone a group of immigrants more in line with the current environment according to memories, so that the convergence of the algorithm would quickly exceed the performance of SBFO.

Ultimately, when the environment changes, MCBFO can quickly generate individuals that match the current environment based on the memories, making it outperform traditional BFO and SPSO at the beginning. Above all, this algorithm that clones new individuals based on the gene libraries, is not easy to fall into local optimum and capable of broad global search. In comparison, the performance of SPSO is not satisfying, which may be explained by the fact that linear optimization mechanism is prone to fall into local optimum.

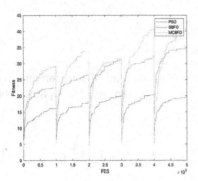

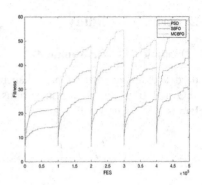

Fig. 3. Convergence curve of small step

Fig. 4. Convergence curve of large step

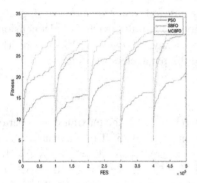

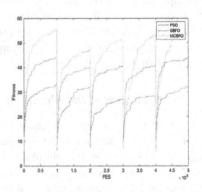

Fig. 5. Convergence curve of random

Fig. 6. Convergence curve of chaotic

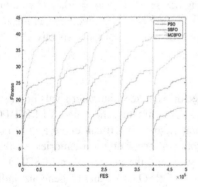

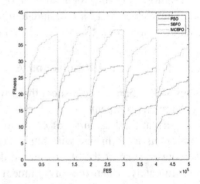

Fig. 7. Convergence curve of recurrent

Fig. 8. Convergence curve of recurrent with noisy

5 Conclusions

This paper provides a bacterial foraging optimization with memory and clone selection to deal with dynamic optimization problems. The function of memories is to store favorable environmental information of the previous generation, which speeds up the convergence rate of algorithm when the environment changes. The cloning strategy that uses two gene libraries to clone elites will drive the population towards the optimal solution while maintain the population diversity.

The effectiveness of the proposed algorithm was verified on a dynamic rotation peak benchmark in the result. As indicated, the proposed MCBFO was an effective technique that outperforms the classical BFO and PSO in tracking dynamic optimal solutions.

Acknowledgements. This work is partially supported by the Natural Science Foundation of Guangdong Province (2016A030310074), Project supported by Innovation and Entrepreneurship Research Center of Guangdong University Student (2018A073825), Research Cultivation Project from Shenzhen Institute of Information Technology (ZY201717) and Innovating and Upgrading Institute Project from Department of Education of Guangdong Province (2017GWTSCX038).

References

1. Hartmann, S.: Project scheduling with multiple modes: a genetic algorithm. Ann. Oper. Res. **102**(1–4), 111–135 (2001)
2. Hartmann, S.: A self-adapting genetic algorithm for project scheduling under resource constraints. Nav. Res. Logistics **49**(5), 433–448 (2002)
3. Branke, J.: Evolutionary Optimization in Dynamic Environments. Kluwer Academic Publishers, Norwell (2001)
4. Branke, J., Kaussler, T., Smidt, C., Schmeck, H.: A multi-population approach to dynamic optimization problems. In: Parmee, I.C. (ed.) Evolutionary Design and Manufacture, pp. 299–307. Springer, London (2000). https://doi.org/10.1007/978-1-4471-0519-0_24
5. Uyar, A.Ş., Harmanci, A.E.: A new population based adaptive domination change mechanism for diploid genetic algorithms in dynamic environments. Soft. Comput. **9**(11), 803–814 (2005)
6. Morrison, R.W., Jong, K.A.D.: Triggered hypermutation revisited. In: Proceedings of the 2000 Congress on Evolutionary Computation, pp. 1025–1032. IEEE, La Jolla (2000)
7. Passino, K.M.: Biomimicry of bacterial foraging for distributed optimization and control. IEEE Control Syst. Mag. **22**(3), 52–67 (2002)
8. Das, S., Biswas, A., Dasgupta, S., Abraham, A.: BFO Algorithm: theoretical foundations, analysis, and applications. In: Abraham, A., Hassanien, A.E., Siarry, P., Engelbrecht, A. (eds.) Foundations of Computational Intelligence Volume 3. Studies in Computational Intelligence, vol. 203. Springer, Heidelberg (2009). https://doi.org/10.1007/978-3-642-01085-9_2
9. Yang, S.: Memory-based immigrants for GA in dynamic environments. In: Proceedings of the 7th Annual Conference on Genetic and Evolutionary Computation, pp. 1115–1122. ACM, New York (2005)

10. Ramsey, C.L., Grefenstette, J.J.: Case-based initialization of genetic algorithms. In: Proceedings of the 5th International Conference on Genetic Algorithms, pp. 84–91. Morgan Kaufmann Publishers Inc, San Francisco (1993)
11. Yang, S.: Genetic algorithms with memory-and elitism-based immigrants in dynamic environments. Evol. Comput. 16(3), 385–416 (2008)
12. Simões, A., Costa, E.: An immune system-based genetic algorithm to deal with dynamic environments: diversity and memory. In: Pearson, D.W., Steele, N.C., Albrecht, R.F. (eds.) Artificial Neural Nets and Genetic Algorithms, pp. 168–174. Springer, Vienna (2003). https://doi.org/10.1007/978-3-7091-0646-4_31
13. Yang, S.: A comparative study of immune system based genetic algorithms in dynamic environments. In: Proceedings of the 8th Annual Conference on Genetic and Evolutionary Computation, pp. 1377–1384. ACM, Seattle (2006)
14. Li, C., Yang, S.: A generalized approach to construct benchmark problems for dynamic optimization. In: Li, X., et al. (eds.) SEAL 2008, LNCS, vol. 5361, pp. 391–400. Springer, Heidelberg (2008). https://doi.org/10.1007/978-3-540-89694-4_40

Genetic Algorithm and Differential Evolution

Evaluation of Genetic Algorithm and Hybrid Genetic Algorithm-Hill Climbing with Elitist for Lecturer University Timetabling Problem

Marina Yusoff[1([⊠])] and Nurhikmah Roslan[2]

[1] Advanced Analytic Engineering Center (AAEC), Faculty of Computer and Mathematical Sciences, Universiti Teknologi MARA, Shah Alam, Selangor, Malaysia
marinay@fskm.uitm.edu.my
[2] Faculty of Computer and Mathematical Sciences, Universiti Teknologi MARA, Shah Alam, Selangor, Malaysia

Abstract. Lecturer university timetabling is an NP-hard real-world problem still needs great attention. The occurrences of the creation of timetable in every university prior to semester starts are compulsory. Its inclusively must cater both hard and soft constraints to satisfy both lecturers and students as the space and time are highly concerned. Genetic Algorithm and Hybrid Genetic Algorithms-Hill Climbing with embedded with elitist mechanism are evaluated with the use of real data sets. The findings have shown Hybrid Genetic Algorithms-Hill Climbing with elitist outperformed Genetic Algorithm with elitist in obtaining an optimal solution. The beauty element offered by Hill Climbing seeking local best individual of the population has given fast convergences with the capability avoiding local optimum. In future, more soft constraints identification of a real problem of lecturer timetabling problem should very much considered as to ensure satisfactions of lecturers and students.

Keywords: Elitist · Genetic Algorithm · Lecturer timetabling problem · Hill-climbing · Optimization

1 Introduction

Timetabling or scheduling is an NP-hard problem that focuses on the allocation of resources over time and space for sets of tasks [1]. Various hard constraints and soft constraints are considered. Many types of timetabling existed from the old times till now as such of nurse shift scheduling [2, 3], airline crew pairing scheduling [4] home health care scheduling [5, 6], job shop scheduling [7, 8] and university timetabling [9–12]. Some of them are still required great attention, especially in the aspect of obtaining an optimum solution. For instance, Lecturer University Timetabling (LTP) with the target of producing a non-clashing timetable still have not reached their most optimum solution as it is very much dependent to the problem details and satisfaction to all soft

© Springer Nature Switzerland AG 2019
Y. Tan et al. (Eds.): ICSI 2019, LNCS 11655, pp. 363–373, 2019.
https://doi.org/10.1007/978-3-030-26369-0_34

constraints. This is evident from the result of Genetic Algorithm (GA) [11, 13], Graph Coloring [14] and Ant Colony Optimization [15]. The criteria to solve is complex as it involves many lecturers, the lecturer's time, many students, courses taken and the availability of the resources such as classrooms, lecture halls and computer labs. For instance, lecturer can request a special classroom for a given course or the maximum learning hour for a student is 4 h [16]. A feasible timetable should be able to fulfil all hard constraints and minimize the number of soft constraints.

Historically, the timetable in a university is done manually whereby the staff in charge will personally allocate the lecturer, student and suitable classroom for that class. This process is very time consuming, complex and still could not reach the goal of a constraint-free timetable after several iterations of the timetabling process. However, only several important constraints are being considered in the manual method. Hence, to overcome this matter, researchers have found a solution which is by using the optimization method to create an automatic timetable generator that is able to produce an optimal or best near- optimal schedule. Hence, it is only right if a viable timetable can be produced to help the lecturers ease their workload and to avoid any clashes in teaching many classes. However, there is still room for improvement in the generation of the result. Thus, a new solution is needed to achieve an optimum lecturer timetable.

This paper addresses the evaluation of hybrid GA-Hill Climbing with elitist to see the performances based on the data sets from Faculty of Computer and Mathematical Sciences, Universiti Teknologi MARA (UiTM), Malaysia. There exists a semi-automatic system to produce a timetable where the academic staff in charge must still key in the data into the system and arrange them one after another. According to the academic staff in charge in the faculty, this process usually takes up to 3 to 4 weeks to finally produce a non-overlapping timetable for the lecturer. The remainder of this article is organized as follows. Section 2 explains the survey for soft constraints identification for LTP. The hybrid GA-Hill Climbing with Elitist (GA-HC-Elitist) is discussed in Sect. 3. Section 4 presents computational results of the comparison between original GA- Elitist and GA-HC-Elitist. Section 5 concludes this paper.

2   Identification of Soft Constraints for Lecturer Timetabling Problem

Prior to identify the constraints of the LTP, a questionnaire was developed based on the adaptation from [17]. A total of 19 questions were asked to the lecturers from the Faculty of Computer and Mathematical Sciences. An analysis was performed from the data gathering. From the 19 questions given, lecturers were asked to rank each question from 1 (most preferred) to 5 (most dislike).

Timestam	Programm	Q1	Q2	Q3	Q4	Q5	Q6	Q7	Q8	Q9	Q10	Q11	Q12	Q13	Q14	Q15	Q16	Q17	Q18	Q19
2018/10/1	Informatic	5	5	3	3	5	3	5	1	4	1	1	1	1	3	3	3	3	4	4
2018/10/1	Informatic	4	4	1	1	4	2	4	3	2	1	1	2	2	4	4	5	5	5	5
2018/10/1	Informatic	5	5	3	4	4	2	3	2	3	2	2	1	1	3	2	2	2	5	5
2018/10/1	Informatic	4	4	3	3	3	1	5	2	3	5	5	1	1	2	2	2	2	4	4
2018/10/1	Informatic	5	5	3	4	4	2	4	1	5	1	1	1	1	4	3	5	3	5	5
2018/10/1	Informatic	5	5	3	5	5	1	5	1	5	2	3	3	1	5	4	4	3	5	2
2018/10/2	Computer	5	5	3	3	3	3	3	1	3	1	2	1	1	5	5	5	5	5	5
Total		33	33	19	23	28	14	29	11	25	13	15	10	8	26	23	26	23	33	30
Average		4.714286	4.714286	2.714286	3.285714	4	2	4.142857	1.571429	3.571429	1.857143	2.142857	1.428571	1.142857	3.714286	3.285714	3.714286	3.285714	4.714286	4.285714
Round off ranking		5	5	3	3	4	2	4	2	4	2	2	1	1	4	3	4	3	5	4

Questions	
1. Teaching 3 lectures event in a day.	11. Lab/tutorial events are scheduled early in the morning (08:00 - 10:00).
2. Teaching 3 lab or tutorial events in a day.	12. Lectures event are scheduled at 10.00 - 12.00.
3. Teaching 2 lectures event in a day.	13. Lab/tutorial events are scheduled at 10.00 - 12.00.
4. Teaching 2 lectures event and 1 lab/tutorial event in a day.	14. Lectures event are scheduled at 12.00 - 14.00.
5. Teaching 2 lab/tutorial events and 1 lecture event in a day.	15. Lab/tutorial events are scheduled at 12.00 - 14.00.
6. Teaching 1 lecture event and 1 lab/tutorial event in a day.	16. Lectures event are scheduled at 14.00 - 16.00.
7. Teaching more than 3 lectures/lab/tutorial event in a day.	17. Lab/tutorial events are scheduled at 14.00 - 16.00.
8. Having any of the two events only in the morning.	18. Lectures event are scheduled at 16.00 - 18.00.
9. Having any of the three events at any point of the day.	19. Lab/tutorial events are scheduled at 16.00 - 18.00.
10. Lectures event are scheduled early in the morning (08:00 - 10:00).	

Fig. 1. Analysis on each question and questions asked

Based on Fig. 1, each question was arranged separately. The total of each mark was summed up and an average score was calculated. The score was then rounded off to determine in which ranking does that question stand between 1 to 5. Each rank was represented by different colors. For instance, question 1 record an average score of 4.714, hence, after rounding off, the result was 5. This indicates that question 1 ranks at point 5 with it being most disliked by almost all lecturers. The color for each question is as shown in Fig. 2.

	MARK	Question Number
1	most preferred	12,13
2	preferred	6,8,10,11
3	neutral	3,4,15,17
4	dislike	5,7,9,14,16,19
5	most dislike	1,2,18

Fig. 2. Colors representing each mark and question number

In Fig. 2, the "Question Number" column represents the question number from 1 to 19 that scores the respective mark. Question number 12 and 13 records rating 1 (most preferred). The question was about having lecture or lab or tutorial events at 10.00 am to 12.00 pm. Most lecturers preferred their class at that time. Secondly, question number 6, 8, 10 and 11 records a mark of 2 which indicated them as preferred. These questions were on having only 2 events in the morning and having any one of the events at 8.00 am to 10.00 pm. Other than that, lecturers do not mind having to teach 2 lecture events a day or teaching 2 lecture events and 1 lab or tutorial event in a day. Some of them also do not mind having classes at 12.00 pm to 2.00 pm and some are even agreed by having lab or tutorial sessions at 2.00 pm to 4.00 pm.

The fourth and fifth questions determine the penalty to be given as they both record criteria lecturers' dislikes most. Question number 5, 7, 9, 14, 16 and 19 were marked at 4 (dislike) hence, they were chosen as the one lecturer dislikes. The question asks for the lecturer's opinion in having 3 events per day, teaching lecture events at 12.00 pm – 2.00 pm or 2.00 pm – 4.00 pm and teaching lab/tutorial events at 4.00 pm – 6.00 pm. Finally, ranking at number 5, question 1, 2 and 18 were chosen as those they dislike most. Those are about teaching 3 lecture events in a day, teaching 3 lab or tutorial events in a day and having to give a lecture at 4.00 pm to 6.00 pm. From this survey, a few soft constraints have been achieved to fulfil the criteria that can satisfy the lecturer's view on their timetable. Two of the soft constraints that must be minimized and considered in this paper are:

- Lecture events are scheduled in the afternoon session (4.00 pm – 6.00 pm)
- Laboratory or tutorial event is scheduled in the afternoon session (4.00 pm – 6.00 pm)

3   Hybrid GA – Hill Climbing with Elitist Solution

3.1   Solution Mapping

This paper addresses the improvement of the solution of LTP in [13]. The chromosome is filled up with a discrete encoding scheme to represent each condition every gene holds. The mapping is illustrated in the Fig. 1.

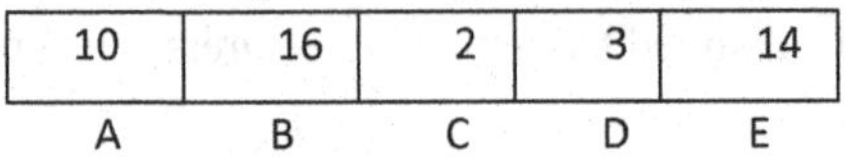

10	16	2	3	14
A	B	C	D	E

Fig. 3. Solution mapping with an example of genes values

Where, Gene A represents Room capacity, gene B represents lecturer teaching hours, gene C represents subjects, gene D represents timeslot and gene E represent courses. The fitness function is based on the penalty scores gained from the soft constraints. The objective is to achieve the minimum sum of all penalties. Higher penalties were given to hard constraints and soft constraint that were most disliked by the lecturers. The 6th and 7th violations were based on findings from Sect. 2, Figs. 3 and 4, Tables 1, 4 and 5.

Table 1. Violation, penalties and type of constraints

No	Violation	Penalties	Constraint
1	Lecturer cannot teach more than 1 course at the same time	50	Hard
2	No room can be occupied by more than one group at the same time	50	Hard
3	No student can attend more than one lecture at the same time	50	Hard
4	The capacity of the classroom should match with the capacity of student group	20	Hard
5	Lecturer cannot teach less than given credit hour	20	Soft
6	Lecture event at 4.00 pm – 6.00 pm	10	Soft
7	Lab/Tutorial event at 4.00 pm – 6.00 pm	10	Soft

Based on the Table 2, the solution generated should not violate any of the violations as it will result in a bad solution. The hard constraints must not be violated while the soft constraint should be minimized as much as possible to achieve a viable schedule. Equation 1 is the fitness function adapted from [17].

$$\text{Minimize } f(x) = \frac{1}{(\text{summation of penalties} + 1)} \tag{1}$$

3.2 Genetic Algorithm - Hill Climbing with Elitist Steps

Basically, the GA-HC-Elitist steps for solving the LTP are as follows:

Step 1: Start the program by initializing the variables such as number of populations, mutation rate, crossover rate, number of elitist, chromosome and number of generations.

Step 2: The initial timetable population will be generated. The chromosome is represented in a string typed variable with a fixed length. Each chromosome represents the possible timetabling solution. The chromosome length depends on the number of classes for the semester. The number of populations will then decide how many chromosomes to be produced. It is important to find the best optimal size of the population and generation because the size will give effect to the computation time and the solution. A big population may result in a longer computation time, but with a more promising result, and a small population will result in a shorter computation time but with lower possibility of a good solution.

Step 3: In this step, the population will be evaluated by measuring the fitness function. The fitness function is defined as in Eq. 1. The sum of penalties is made up from the total hard and soft constraints that have been violated. The constraints are such as those listed in Table 2.

Step 4: At the end of the evaluation, the chromosome that sets the best fitness will be brought forward as parents to be mated for the reproduction process to produce a new off springs. The selection method used is Tournament Selection with Elitist.

Step 5: After the first selection, the solutions will be evaluated to check if it has met the termination criteria. If it has met, then the generation will stop there, and the results will be generated. Otherwise, the next step will be done.

Step 6: The population will undergo crossing over and mutation operators. The crossover method used is the uniform crossover between parent 1 and parent 2 chromosome comparison. Parent 1 will be taken from the selection and parent 2 is the random individual created to allow variance between the two. The crossover will be made based on the result from the probabilities of the solution. The probability of 0.5 has been fixed for the gene swapping and at the end of the crossover phase, off springs will be generated. After that, the mutation phase will take over. In this algorithm, a simple Hill Climbing Optimization is implemented in the mutation phase. Since mutation is used to allow diversity in the solution and to avoid local minima, Hill Climbing fits best at this phase to allow greater power in the local search. The Hill Climbing will generate only fittest individual to be carried out in the next phase. The flow of the Hill Climbing is as follows:

1. Get fittest individual from the current population.
2. Create random individual to perform mutation.
3. Do 1st mutation between the individuals while it fits the mutation probability.
4. Check if the new individual's fitness is greater or lesser than the previous current fitness.
5. If the fitness is lesser than repeat the mutation process by repeating step 2 to 4.
6. If the new individual's fittest is more, then proceed to the next step with the new individual in the population.
7. End.

Step 7: Evaluate the current population and check with the termination criteria. If the criteria have met then move forward to the next step, otherwise repeat from step 3. Each repetition is considered as new generation and the number of generations is updated after each loop.

Step 8: Once the algorithm has reached its end, print the best fit solution as the most optimal solution. Finally, print the timetable solution.

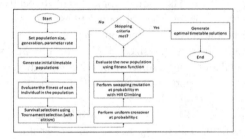

Fig. 4. Flowchart of GA-HC-Elitist

4   Computational Experiments and Findings

4.1   Parameter Setting

The performance of GA-HC-Elitist was tested within such parameter settings as shown in Table 3 and it was compared with GA-Elitist.

Table 2. Parameter setting

Parameter	Value
Number of population	20, 50, 120, 180
Crossover rate	0.7, 0.8, 0.9, 0.95
Mutation rate	0.001, 0.002, 0.005, 0.01
Generation	10, 20, 50, 80

4.2   Comparison Performance Between GA-HC-Elitist and GA-Elitist

The overall analysis on the performance of the two techniques. Each technique has gone through a series of similar parameter tuning and consideration of constraints as shown in Table 2.

Computational Experiment Based on Population Size
This section reports the results from different numbers of population size of 20, 50, 120 and 180 using the LTP datasets from Faculty of Computer and Mathematical Sciences. The constant value of crossover rate = 0.9, mutation rate = 0.001, maximum number of generations of 20, tournament size of 5 are evaluated. As can be seen in Table 3, GA-HC-elitist has obtained better results faster as compared to GA-elitist during the population size of 20. The execution time of GA-HC-elitist is slightly more however it has recorded a penalty of only 40 at a smaller population of 20 compared to GA-elitist that records a penalty of 40 only at the population size 50 with 703 ms. The difference is very small hence this indicates that the implementation of hill climbing only requires a smaller population size to reach a feasible solution. After several consecutive iterations from each population, GA-HC-elitist records a significant decrease in the computation time as the population size grows, whereas, GA-elitist demonstrates inconsistent reading of execution time with the similar method of iterations.

Table 3. Results with different population size

Population size	GA-elitist		GA-HC-elitist	
	Fitness value	Execution time (ms)	Fitness value	Execution time (ms)
20	0.0141	597	0.0244	717
50	0.0244	703	0.0164	687
120	0.0141	667	0.0164	668
180	0.0196	675	0.0123	662

Computational Experiment Based on Crossover Rate
This section reports the results with crossover rates of 0.7, 0.8, 0.9 and 0.95. The constant value of population size = 20, mutation rate = 0.001, maximum number of generations of 20, tournament size of 5. GA-HC-elitist outperformed the GA-elitist in achieving a fitter solution of 0.322580 even though both records the fittest solution at a crossover rate of 0.9. The execution time taken to achieve such fitness was 668 ms which is faster than when reaching the fittest solution at rates 0.7 and 0.9. Although the GA-elitist records a smaller execution time, it still could not beat the fittest solution generated with the assist of the Hill Climbing method.

Table 4. Results with different crossover rate

Crossover rate	GA-elitist		GA-HC-elitist	
	Fitness value	Execution time(ms)	Fitness value	Execution time(ms)
0.7	0.0123	676	0.0164	717
0.8	0.0110	474	0.0244	687
0.9	0.0141	526	0.3226	668
0.95	0.0197	736	0.0164	662

Computational Experiment Based on the Mutation Rate

The mutation rate of 0.005, 0.002, 0.001 and 0.01 has been tested by maximum number of generations of 20, tournament size of 5 are evaluated. With the help of Hill Climbing in mutation, at the rate of 0.001 and 0.1, both have recorded a higher value of fitness in 0.32258. Nevertheless, this occurs since Hill Climbing was working on to get a better solution here. It filters only the fittest solution to be passed on to the next generation. Therefore, it leads to a slightly longer execution time compared to GA-elitist that simply passes on the mutated individual without further filtering.

Table 5. Results with different generation number

Mutation rate	GA-elitist		GA-HC-elitist	
	Fitness value	Execution time(ms)	Fitness value	Execution time(ms)
0.005	0.024	429	0.016	604
0.002	0.014	440	0.014	630
0.001	0.011	499	0.323	579
0.01	0.012	541	0.323	544

Computational Experiment Based on the Number of Generations

A mixture of 10, 20, 50 and 80 generations has been tested alongside other parameter settings. As shown in the Table 6 with the total number of 50 generations set, the fittest solution of 1.0 has been achieved at the 48th generation for GA-HC-elitist as compared to the other technique that managed to get the fittest value at the 67th generation. GA-HC-elitist provides a shorter time was taken to achieve the optimal solution at 2050 ms compared to 9367 ms for GA-elitist. Hence, the GA-HC-elitist has once again proven its efficiency by overcoming the GA-elitist both in smaller population size to achieve fitness and the faster computation time.

Table 6. Results with different number of generations

No of generations	GA-elitist		GA-HC-elitist	
	Fitness value	Execution time (ms)	Fitness value	Execution time (ms)
10	0.0041	440	0.0062	390
20	0.1000	473	0.0164	598
50	0.0444	831	**1.0000**	**2050**
80	**1.0000**	**9367**	1.0000	5467

Computational Results from 15 Experiments

An experiment of 15 consecutive runs was performed by using the optimal parameter settings found from results above. The parameters are population size = 50, crossover rate = 0.9, mutation rate = 0.001, number of generations of 50 and tournament size = 5. It is interesting to note that from the table, it can be clearly seen the GA-HC-elitist has outperformed the GA by achieving 13 times of the best solution, whereas GA-elitist only achieves 8 times of fitness out of 15 experiments. The computation time, however, it differs by quite a number. However, this is because the Hill Climbing has taken a little more time in searching for the best individuals before passing it forward to the next evaluation. Other than that, in an independent wise, the time taken to achieve the optimal result is lesser for GA-HC elitist as compared to GA. The use of the combined local search and global search has enhanced the quality of the solution in getting a faster convergence in GA-HC-elitist. It is true as mentioned in previous studies that GA-HC-elitist can surpass GA in getting a faster optimal solution with a more acceptable computation time (Gopal et al., 2016; Liu et al., 2016). Based on the results from the experiments above, it can be concluded that the GA-HC-elitist outperforms GA-elitist and produces better optimal solutions. GA-HC-elitist method has recorded much better efficiency in finding the solutions for this timetabling optimizer both in the execution time and solution generations. The combination of GA and Hill Climbing Optimization has decreased the number of generations needed to find the fittest solution and it can be done within a shorter time span.

5 Conclusions

This paper proposes GA-HC-elitist to fine tune for a better result for LTP. The evaluation of GA-elitist and GA-elitist were performed with inclusion on identifying the satisfaction factors to create a viable schedule for the lecturers. A survey was done and analyzed to obtain relevant soft constraints that would satisfy the lecturers. The identified soft constraints were added to the list of penalty measures and tested. Several tunings and experiments have been made to the algorithms to ensure that an optimal solution can be gained based on the fixed parameter settings. GA-HC-elitist is outperformed GA-elitist for many occurrences of obtaining an optimal solution. Hill

Climbing Optimization with local search increased the efficiency it through its simple local search in finding the fittest individuals. For future work, it seems a viable for GA-HC-elitist to be tested with large data sets of LTP.

Acknowledgement. Universiti Teknologi MARA a for the grant of 600-IRMI/PERDANA 5/3 BESTARI (096/2018) as well as Faculty of Computer and Mathematical Sciences, Universiti Teknologi MARA, Shah Alam, Malaysia for providing essential support and knowledge for the work.

References

1. Kaleeswaran, A., Ramasamy, V., Vivekanandan, P.: Dynamic scheduling of data using genetic algorithm in cloud computing. Int. J. Adv. Eng. Technol. **5**(2), 327 (2013)
2. Jan, A., Yamamoto, M., Ohuchi, A.: Evolutionary algorithms for nurse scheduling problem. In: Proceedings of the 2000 Congress on Evolutionary Computation. CEC00 (Cat. No. 00TH8512), vol. 1, pp. 196–203. IEEE (2000)
3. Youssef, A., Senbel, S.: A Bi-level heuristic solution for the nurse scheduling problem based on shift-swapping, (978), 72–78 (2018)
4. Deveci, M., Demirel, N.Ç.: Evolutionary algorithms for solving the airline crew pairing problem. Comput. Ind. Eng. **115**, 389–406 (2018)
5. Szander, N., Ros-McDonnell, L., de la Fuente, M.V.: Algorithm for Efficient and Sustainable Home Health Care Delivery Scheduling. In: Mula, J., Barbastefano, R., Díaz-Madroñero, M., Poler, R. (eds.) New Global Perspectives on Industrial Engineering and Management. LNMIE, pp. 315–323. Springer, Cham (2019). https://doi.org/10.1007/978-3-319-93488-4_35
6. Du, G., Zheng, L., Ouyang, X.: Real-time scheduling optimization considering the unexpected events in home health care. J. Comb. Optim. **37**(1), 196–220 (2019)
7. Tan, C.J., et al.: Application of an evolutionary algorithm-based ensemble model to job-shop scheduling. J. Intell. Manuf. **30**(2), 879–890 (2019)
8. Cao, Z., Zhou, L., Hu, B. Lin, C.: An adaptive scheduling algorithm for dynamic jobs for dealing with the flexible job shop scheduling problem. Bus. Inf. Syst. Eng., 1–11 (2019)
9. Hossain, S.I., Akhand, M.A.H., Shuvo, M.I.R., Siddique, N., Adeli, H.: Optimization of University Course Scheduling Problem using Particle Swarm Optimization with Selective Search. Expert Systems with Applications (2019)
10. Leite, N., Melício, F., Rosa, A.C.: A fast simulated annealing algorithm for the examination timetabling problem. Expert Syst. Appl. **122**, 137–151 (2019)
11. Yusoff, M., Othman, A.A.: Genetic algorithm with elitist-tournament for clashes-free slots of lecturer timetabling problem. Indonesian J. Electr. Eng. Comput. Sci. **12**(1), 303–309 (2018)
12. Lindahl, M., Mason, A.J., Stidsen, T., Sørensen, M.: A strategic view of University timetabling. Eur. J. Oper. Res. **266**(1), 35–45 (2018)
13. Ahmad, I.R., Sufahani, S., Ali, M., Razali, S.N.A.M.: A Heuristics Approach for Classroom Scheduling using Genetic Algorithm Technique **9**(3), 10 (2017)
14. Jain, R., Kumar, R.: University Time Table Scheduling Using Graph Coloring (2018)
15. Ashari, I.A., Muslim, M.A., Alamsyah, A.: Comparison performance of genetic algorithm and ant colony optimization in course scheduling optimizing. Sci. J. Inform. **3**(2), 149 (2016)
16. Babaei, H., Karimpour, J., Hadidi, A.: A survey of approaches for university course timetabling problem. Comput. Ind. Eng. **86**, 43–59 (2015)

17. Yang, X.F., Ayob, M., Nazri, M.Z.A.: An investigation of timetable satisfaction factors for a practical university course timetabling problem. In: 2017 6th International Conference on Electrical Engineering and Informatics (ICEEI), pp. 1–5. IEEE (2017)
18. Gopal, G., Kumar, R., Kumar, N., Jawa, I.: Effect of hill climbing in GA after reproduction for solving optimization problems. Int. J. Extensive Res. 3, 79–86 (2015)
19. Liu, Q., Zhou, B., Li, S., Li, A.-P., Zou, P., Jia, Y.: Community detection utilizing a novel multi-swarm fruit fly optimization algorithm with hill-climbing strategy. Arab. J. Sci. Eng. 41(3), 807–828 (2016)

Federated Learning Assisted Interactive EDA with Dual Probabilistic Models for Personalized Search

Yang Chen, Xiaoyan Sun$^{(\boxtimes)}$, and Yao Hu

School of Information and Control Engineering,
China University of Mining and Technology, Xuzhou 221116, China
fedora.cy@gmail.com, xysun78@126.com, 13685131679@163.com

Abstract. Personalized search is essentially a qualitative optimization problem since its target is to find items (as solutions) satisfied by the searcher. Interactive evolutionary computation (IEC) is powerful in solving this problem in view of optimization. The privacy protection when using other users' information in the personalized search, however, has not been concerned when designing IECs. We here present an improved interactive estimation of distribution algorithm (IEDA) with dual probabilistic models by integrating the Federated Learning (FL) proposed for privacy protection. The Federated-SVD is first developed by embedding the singular value decomposition (SVD)-based collaborative filtering into the structure of FL for safely gaining the social preference. The decomposed user and item (solution) features by SVD are uploaded and aggregated in the central service and finally used to construct and update the probabilistic models. The superiority of the enhanced IEDA is demonstrated through ten personalized search cases on movies and TV series.

Keywords: Interactive estimation of distribution algorithm ·
Personalized search · Privacy protection · Federated learning · SVD

1 Introduction

Interactive evolutionary computation (IEC), by involving a person into the evolutionary process to evaluate the individuals, has been concerned for decades due to its superiority in optimizing problems difficult to be exactly depicted with a mathematical model [16], and has been applied to many practical problems, e.g., fashion design, lens optimization, personalized search [12]. Most IECs, however, are developed based on the genetic algorithm strategy since it is simple to be performed. We presented an interactive estimation of distribution algorithm (IEDA) inspired by the personalized search process and applied to laptop search, in which the domain knowledge was extracted to effectively get the initial

---

Supported by the National Natural Science Foundation of China with Grant No. 61876184 and 61473298.

Y. Tan et al. (Eds.): ICSI 2019, LNCS 11655, pp. 374–383, 2019.
https://doi.org/10.1007/978-3-030-26369-0_35

population and then built a probabilistic model using Bayesian model [2]. Further encouraged by our previous work, we turn our view to the deep integration of personalized search and IEDA.

As highly related research fields, personalized search and recommender systems (RSs) share many techniques and insights. In the study of RSs, approaches are grouped into three main streams: content-based, collaborative filtering (CF) and their hybrid techniques. The hybrid ones are more effective, and thus they are more popular in recent years. Many existing improved IECs, e.g., surrogate model assisted ones, can actually be viewed as an enhancement by articulating the content-based filtering technique since the information of the searched solutions in the evolutionary process are fully used to get the possible preference model [2,11]. In [1], Yang et al. proposed the dual probabilistic model assisted interactive estimation of distribution algorithm (DPM-IEDA) for addressing personalized search problems by efficiently incorporating the social preference. The DPM-IEDA adopted the collaborative filtering and the content-collaborative hybrid strategy by constructing a dual-probabilistic model. In such a framework, however, the privacy of the social group is ignored.

Recently, increasing information disclosure cases have raised public's great concerns over their privacy security. As a solution, Google proposed federated learning (FL) in 2017 [10] following the principle of focused collection or data minimization [4]. Local models training and central aggregation, as two main components, consist of the FL process [5,7,10]. The key point is that, with no single piece of privacy data being updated to or stored on the server, only local models' parameters are sent to the center and aggregated to obtain the central model to protect privacy security.

If the FL structure, content-collaborative filtering technique for high efficient recommender can be subtly integrated with IEC, it is possible that we can obtain a powerful intelligent optimization structure for not only effectively explore more satisfied solutions but also without privacy leakage when using the group users information. Motivated by this, we here present a federated learning based interactive EDA, in which the content and collaborative filtering are used to build two probabilistic models from the perspectives of social search preference and the individual one respectively. The framework of integrating federated learning is presented, and a federated collaborative strategy is given in detail.

The main contributions of our work are as follows: (1) FL is integrated with the IEC for keeping the data privacy, which can be a general form and extended with many other learning models for improving IECs' performance. (2) A specific federated collaborative filtering model, i.e. federated singular value decomposition (Federated-SVD), is given for obtaining the social preference on the searched items. (3) Dual probabilistic models for the EDA are provided to enhance the initialization and exploration of the evolution. The remainder of this paper is organized as follows. Section 2 briefly introduces the IEC-assisted personalized search, FL, and CF. And then, Sect. 3 details the proposed algorithm. In Sect. 4, the application of the proposed algorithm together with the experimental results and analyses is addressed. Conclusions are drawn in Sect. 5.

2   Related Concepts

As discussed, personalized search belongs to qualitative optimization problems
that are of no explicit mathematical expression. In the associated studies, user
preference reflected by evaluated items are used and tracked [15]. If the items
to be searched by a person are regarded as discrete solutions, the personalized
search problem can be defined as: $\max f(i)\, i \in D$, where D is the feasible space
of existing items, $f(i)$ is the preferable evaluation on the i-th item but cannot
be explicitly defined and often reflected by the user's interactions. If the item is
encoded into individuals, and the user's preference or evaluations on the item can
be obtained, then IEC is the nature optimization tool. Therefore, the encoding of
item and user preference modeling are the most important issues when applying
IEC to the personalized search. In our previous work [2], we have presented
a method to encode items described with words by use of word2vec. As for
the preference modeling, lots of surrogate assisted IECs have been developed
[2,13,14].

Federated learning was first presented by Google from the viewpoint of keeping the personal data privacy when tracking the possible interests of a user based
on his/her history internet behavior information [5–7,10]. Each user's personal
data are stored only on his/her local mobile devices, and the machine learning
model for extracting his/her preference is built also only on the local device. The
model parameters of all the participated users are then uploaded to the server
and aggregated to get the possible common interest. The aggregated parameters
can then be downloaded to the local devices for further learning and model building. Such process is iterated and the recommended items under this structure
are updated along with the newly stored personal behavior information.

The introduction of Collaborative filtering (CF) is further given here. CF is
greatly popular in Recommender Systems (RSs) [8]. According to the collected
preference from lots of relevant users (social or public preference), CF techniques
make predictions of the interests of a user to items. The existing CF algorithms
can be generally divided into the following two categories: (1) **Memory-based
approaches** are characterized by calculating the similarity between users/items
with the help of rating data, e.g. item-based/user-based top-K recommendations.
(2) **Model-based approaches** predict missing ratings by employing models
that are trained by different data mining or machine learning algorithms, e.g.
latent Dirichlet allocation (LDA), probabilistic latent semantic analysis (pLSA),
and singular value decomposition (SVD).

CF and content-based recommender are very popular and effective in finding
more items interested by the user, but they have not been well articulated with
IEC to get the user's preference model and enhance the explorative performance
of EC.

3 Federated Learning Assisted Interactive EDA with Dual Probabilistic Models

The framework of the proposed algorithm is shown in Fig. 1, and the main contributions of our work are shaded. It is clear that two probabilistic models will be constructed/updated in the IEDA process by designing a federated SVD (CF technique) to extract the public preference and support vector regression (SVR) (content-based strategy) to fetch the current user's interest. The searched items are described with words or documents, therefore, the Doc2Vec learning is used to transfer the words into vectors. This step is time-consuming and can be done offline. With the trained Doc2vec, the public dataset provided by those volunteers or collected before, the user-item matrix can be obtained and the Federated-SVD is applied here to draw the public preference and sent it to construct the first probabilistic model. The population is first generated by sampling the Federated-SVD-based probabilistic model, and the items for the user to evaluate are then sampled with the content-based, i.e. SVR based probabilistic model. Along with the evolution, the current user's interactions and evaluated items will be collected to update the SVR based probabilistic mode to drive the EDA process. Specifically, the key of our work to develop a privacy-preserving CF technique to get the public preference, which will be presented in Sect. 3.1 under the framework of FL; then, the construction of the dual probabilistic models (DPM) and the corresponding entire algorithm (shorted as FL-DPM-IEDA) will be addressed in detail.

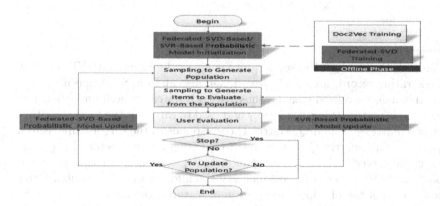

Fig. 1. The framework of federated learning assisted IEDA with dual probabilistic models.

3.1 Federated-SVD

The Federated-SVD presented here is to obtain an estimated interest of user u on the newly appeared or unevaluated i-th item, denoted as $\hat{r}_{ui}$. With such estimations, the probability of selecting the this item can be statistically calculated, and then the public preference induced probabilistic model is easy to be constructed.

Algorithm 1. Federated-SVD.

1: **function** SERVEREXECUTION   ▷ Run on the server
2:     initialize $paras_0$
3:     **for** each round $t = 1, 2, ...$ **do**
4:         $m \leftarrow \max(C \cdot K, 1)$, $S_t \leftarrow$ (random set of m clients)
5:         **for** each client $k \in S_t$ **in parallel do**
6:             $paras_{t+1}^k \leftarrow$ ClientUpdate$(k, paras_t)$
7:         **end for**
8:         $paras_{t+1} \leftarrow \sum_{k=1}^{K} \frac{n_k}{n} paras_{t+1}^k$
9:     **end for**
10: **end function**
11:
12: **function** CLIENTUPDATE$(k, paras_{initial})$ ▷ Run on client k
13:     $paras \leftarrow$ SVD$(paras_{initial})$
14:     return $paras$ to server
15: **end function**

Algorithm 2. Federated-SVD-Based Probabilistic Model Initialization

---

Input: estimated ratings $\hat{r}_i$, threshold $r_{\text{threshold}}$ used to define list L_{search}, estimated probability $\hat{P}_k$
Output: Federated-SVD-based probabilistic model $p = \{..., p_k, ...\}, k \in \{1, ..., k, ..., K\}$
1: **for** $i = 1 \rightarrow n$ **do**
2:     **if** $\hat{r}_i > r_{\text{threshold}}$ **then**
3:         add i to L_{search}
4:     **end if**
5: **end for**
6: sort L_{search} by $\hat{r}$ and evenly arrange the items belonging to L_{search} in categories $L_{\text{search},k}$
7: **for** $k = 1 \rightarrow K$ **do**
8:     **for** $j \in L_{\text{search},k}$ **do**
9:         $p_j = \hat{P}_k * e^{\hat{r}_j} / \sum_1^{|L_{\text{search},k}|} e^{\hat{r}_j}$
10:    **end for**
11:    $len_k \leftarrow |L_{\text{search},k}|$, $a_k \leftarrow 0$, and $b_k \leftarrow 0$
12: **end for**

Compared with SVD, the key improvements of the Federated-SVD are that all users' rating records are locally stored, and also all local SVD algorithms are executed in a decentralized manner; thus, user privacy can be well protected. The rating records matrix R is saved locally and used to carry out the SVD algorithm to get two matrices, P and Q. Matrix P corresponds to the user feature vectors $\{..., p_u, ...\}$, while matrix Q corresponds to the item feature vectors $\{..., q_i, ...\}$. Between the server and users, only parameters $\{..., p_u, ...\}$ and $\{..., q_i, ...\}$ are exchanged. Clearly, these two vectors carry the information of the public data. With the help of the obtained user and item features, the interest of user u to item i, i.e. the rating $\hat{r}_{ui}$ is estimated with the following equation [8]:

$$\hat{r}_{ui} = \mu + b_u + b_i + q_i^T p_u \tag{1}$$

where μ, b_u and b_i are the corresponding average values of R, $R_{u\cdot}$, and $R_{\cdot i}$. They can be calculated with the following equations: $\mu = \frac{\sum_m \sum_n R_{m,n}}{M*N}$, $b_u = \frac{\sum_n R_{u,n}}{N}$, and $b_i = \frac{\sum_m R_{m,i}}{M}$, where M and N are respectively the numbers of users and items. The corresponding pseudo code of Federated-SVD is given in Algorithm 1.

Compared with the traditional SVD and federated learning, our Federated-SVD has two different characterizes. First, the training data composes of two parts, i.e., the public users ratings on their evaluated items and the current users ratings on the same items stored in the local device. The public group has no privacy protection needs but the current user needs privacy protection. Second, the aggregation strategy of the algorithm is different. The user and item feature models after aggregation are denoted as $mode_{\text{UI}}$ and $mode_{\text{I}}$. The terms/parameters of Eq. 1 belong to two groups: the user related $(b_u, \boldsymbol{p}_u)$ and the item related $(b_i, \boldsymbol{q}_i)$. When considering the local matrices, they share the same features of items $(b_i, \boldsymbol{q}_i)$ instead of $(b_u, \boldsymbol{p}_u)$ of users. Undoubtedly, server-side aggregation is reliable for item features. Therefore, for $mode_{\text{UI}}$, local clients set $b_u, \boldsymbol{p}_u, b_i, \boldsymbol{q}_i$ are uploaded and averagely aggregated, while the other mode (I), only $b_i, \boldsymbol{q}_i$ are set with the aggregated parameters. Such an aggregation is beneficial on reducing the communication and computational cost.

3.2 Dual Probabilistic Models

The content-based probabilistic model is constructed with the support vector regression (SVR) that takes evaluated items' content-based features as input and returns the corresponding estimated ratings, i.e. $\hat{r} = \text{SVR}(\boldsymbol{v})$. In the equation, $\boldsymbol{v}$ represents the content-based feature and is in the form of a fixed-length vector. Given the estimated ratings $\hat{r}_l$, the content-based probabilistic model $\boldsymbol{p} = \{..., p_l, ...\}, l \in pop$ is here defined as: $p_l \leftarrow e^{\hat{r}_l} / \sum_1^{|pop|} e^{\hat{r}_l}$, where pop corresponds to the population in IEDA.

Unlike the content-based model that plays the rule of a surrogate to dynamically track the current user's preference, the CF-based one employs the collaborative intelligence reflected by the rating matrix to enhance the power of the presented IEDA, i.e. $\hat{r}_{ui}$. $SVD(\cdot)$ is detailed in Eq. 1, and in it, u and i are the active user and the item to be assessed. With the predicted ratings, the CF-based probabilistic model is then obtained. In the initialization, all the items with the CF-predicted ratings lower than a certain threshold are first filtered out, and the rest are then categorized into K groups, i.e. $\{L_{\text{search},1}, ..., L_{\text{search},k}, ..., L_{\text{search},K}\}$. To category $L_{\text{search},k}$, its CF-based probabilistic model $\boldsymbol{p}_k = \{..., p_j, ...\}, j \in L_{\text{search},k}$ is expressed as: $p_j = \hat{P}'_k * e^{\hat{r}_j} / \sum_1^{|L_{\text{search},k}|} e^{\hat{r}_j}$, where j indexes the items belonging to category $L_{\text{search},k}$, and $\hat{P}'_k$ is the probability of category k.

Federated-SVD-based probabilistic model initialization is detailed in Algorithm 2. As for the implementation of the initialization, details can be found in our previous study [1]. To the items in the evaluation list, the active user conducts interactions, i.e. user evaluation to get their ratings. The evaluation list becomes $s_{e,t}$ used to update two probabilistic models.

4 Experiments and Analysis

4.1 Experimental Settings

Experiments in this Section are divided into: (1) Federated-SVD-assisted recommendations and (2) privacy-preserving FL-DPM-IEDA assisted personalized search. Upon the renowned dataset, MovieLens 20M Dataset [3], the first part given in Sect. 4.2 conducts the experimental comparison between the Federated-SVD and SVD for testifying the effectiveness of the presented privacy-preserving recommender technique. The root-mean-square error (RMSE) is adopted as the metric.

Moreover, the other one in Sect. 4.3 is carried out to demonstrate the superiority of the enhanced FL-DPM-IEDA through the comparisons among it, the basic DPM-IEAD, and interactive genetic algorithm (IGA). Here, two datasets, MovieLens 20M Dataset and Amazon product data [9], are involved. Indicators: (1) **number of found satisfactory items,** to show the searching ability in diversity of the presented IEDA; (2) **average rating,** to illustrate the guidance effectiveness of the group preference model; and (3) **algorithm runtime,** to state the total computational cost and user fatigue. Normally, the number of generations are limited to twenty in IEC since user fatigue is considered [16].

4.2   Federated-SVD-Assisted Recommendations

The experimental setting is given: (1) **The SVD recommender technique executed on local clients,** its corresponding parameters, together with their ranges/values, are as: 100 (Feature Dimension), 5 (Epochs), and {True, False} (Biased). Corresponding to Eq. 1, **Feature Dimension** indicates the dimensions of b_u, b_i, p_u, q_i; if the **Biased** is set as False, the biased terms disappear, and the Equation then becomes $\hat{r}_{ui} = q_i^T p_u$. (2) **The Federated-SVD recommender technique executed on local clients,** its corresponding parameters, together with their ranges/values, are as: 10 (K), {1, 2, 5} (m), 50 (Communication Rounds), and {$mode_I$, $mode_{UI}$} (Initial Mode). K and m indicate the total size number of clients and the size of the participating subset in each communication round. As for the **Initial Mode,** if it is set as $mode_I$, the local SVD only receives b_i, q_i from the server and sets them as the initial value before local training. Otherwise, all parameters including b_u, b_i, p_u, q_i are addressed.

Rather than finely tuning the parameters, the experiments are designed and carried out for offering a basic understanding of the selection of them and their effect on the performance of Federated-SVD. Also, the experiments and corresponding analyses are expected to be a brief guide in practical engineering.

The corresponding results are given in Table 1. This group of experiments is conducted on the proposed Federated-SVD and SVD. The 10_1, 10_2, and 10_5 in the table header correspond to those experiments that are conducted on the FL setting with 10 clients, together with 1, 2, and 5 participating clients in each communication round. Related conclusions are drawn: (1) **Effectiveness of Federated-SVD**: When comparing the 2nd-4th columns and the 5th column, Federated-SVD outperforms SVD. (2) **Initial Mode**: When the first and second rows of the 2nd-4th columns come into focus, Federated-SVD on $mode_I$ achieves better results; moreover, the Federated-SVD on $mode_{UI}$ still performs better than SVD. As previously discussed, features from Eq. 1 belong to two groups: the user related (b_u, p_u) and the item related (b_i, q_i). When considering local matrices, they share the same features of items (b_i, q_i), whereas their user related features vary. The server-side aggregation of user related features causes performance deterioration, which has been experimentally proven. Also, such a mode, i.e. $mode_I$, is beneficial on reducing the communication and computational cost. (3) m: By comparing the 2nd-4th columns, it is not difficult to find the performance corresponding to different values of m slightly fluctuates. So, Federated-SVD is not sensitive to m.

Table 1. Experiment on Federated-SVD.

Initial mode	Federated-SVD @10_1	Federated-SVD @10_2	Federated-SVD @10_5	SVD
$mode_I$	0.764358	0.763886	0.747109	0.915296
$mode_{UI}$	0.846934	0.850753	0.85938	

4.3 Privacy-Preserving FL-DPM-IEDA Assisted Personalized Search

Privacy-preserving personalized search tasks where algorithms are expected to help users locate as many satisfactory items as possible are addressed in this subsection. Two indicators are the average number of found satisfactory items and the bracketed average rating. In order to clearly analyze algorithms, five active users are selected from each dataset, i.e. ten in total. All cases are repeated thirty times for conducting Mann-Whitney U-test. Experimental comparisons among three algorithms on ten cases are conducted, and the results are listed in Table 2. Cells are marked with † when the proposed algorithm outperforms competitors on both metrics and the corresponding results pass the Mann-Whitney U-test with a 0.95 confidence level. The Cell is marked with ‡ when the performance of the proposed algorithm is worse than another competitor(s) on one metric and the corresponding result does not pass the Mann-Whitney U-test with a 0.95 confidence level.

Runtime of compared algorithms is as follows: 0.57s (FL-DPM-IEDA), 0.15s (DPM-IEDA), and 2.83s (IGA). Here are conclusions: (1) When addressing privacy-preserving personalized search tasks, the presented algorithm outperforms all the other compared ones on all cases, except for one case with a slightly worse average rating. (2) When the proposed FL-DPM-IEDA is compared with its original version DPM-IEDA, the proposed one achieves better performance, and its advantages stem from the federated-learning-enhanced CF-based probabilistic model, i.e. Federated-SVD. The corresponding experimental discussions regarding Federated-SVD versus original SVD is given in the previous Sect. 4.2. (3) The basic DPM-IEDA performs better than the IGA; IGA is the worst competitor. (4) The proposed privacy-preserving FL-DPM-IEDA is in the mid-range position and of slightly higher time cost than DPM-IEDA. Since human customers are involved in the process, and they are required to cooperate with algorithms, its performance is acceptable.

382   Y. Chen et al.

Table 2. Experiment on overall performance.

Active user ID	Privacy-Preserving FL-DPM-IEDA	DPM-IEDA	IGA
24661 ∘	**7.30(3.46)**	6.03(3.41) †	6.70(3.35) †
41079 ∘	**6.80(3.59)**	4.97(3.52) †	4.10(3.44) †
33082 ∘	**1.77(2.46)**	1.20(2.34) †	1.00(2.29) †
106939 ∘	**98.07**(4.45)	95.80(**4.48**) ‡	62.80(4.06) †
123352 ∘	**20.73(3.49)**	16.10(3.32) †	12.40(2.98) †
A2EDZH51XHFA9B ◇	**42.73(3.66)**	28.43(3.36) †	33.83(3.31) †
AP3B615GM191G ◇	**138.07(4.39)**	115.73(4.15) †	110.97(4.06) †
A1AISPOIIHTHXX ◇	**117.57(4.36)**	102.27(4.24) †	98.17(4.13) †
A1GHUN5HXMHZ89 ◇	**94.63(4.27)**	86.63(4.20) †	79.53(4.09) †
AER15RIMV8E6D ◇	**103.27(4.26)**	84.73(4.10) †	95.67(4.15) †

∘ Cases are from MovieLens 20M. ◇ Cases are from Movie and TV (5-core), Amazon Dataset.

5 Conclusions

In order to fulfill the urgent need for privacy protection in the personalized search where users' history information is commonly involved, this study proposes the Federated-SVD and then integrates it into the IEDA framework to develop an enhanced FL-DPM-IEDA with two probabilistic models considered. In the extensive experiments, the presented Federated-SVD and FL-DPM-IEDA have experimentally proven their superiorities in the effectiveness and efficiency of helping user locate satisfactory items.

In the future, the privacy-protected personalized search will be studied more deeply for enlarging the application of these techniques. For example, we aim to design a practical IEDA framework that is capable of integrating more different model structures. On the other hand, search diversity will be considered as well.

References

1. Chen, Y., Sun, X., Gong, D., Yao, X.: DPM-IEDA: dual probabilistic model assisted interactive estimation of distribution algorithm for personalized search. IEEE Access **7**, 41006–41016 (2019)
2. Chen, Y., Sun, X., Gong, D., Zhang, Y., Choi, J., Klasky, S.: Personalized search inspired fast interactive estimation of distribution algorithm and its application. IEEE Trans. Evol. Comput. **21**(4), 588–600 (2017)
3. Harper, F.M., Konstan, J.A.: The MovieLens datasets: history and context. ACM Trans. Interact. Intell. Syst. (TIIS) **5**(4), 19 (2016)
4. House, W.: Consumer Data Privacy in a Networked World: A Framework for Protecting Privacy and Promoting Innovation in the Global Digital Economy, pp. 1–62. White House, Washington, DC (2012)

5. Konečný, J., McMahan, B., Ramage, D.: Federated optimization: distributed optimization beyond the datacenter. arXiv Prepr. arXiv:1511.03575 1, 1–5 (2015)
6. Konečnỳ, J., McMahan, H.B., Ramage, D., Richtárik, P.: Federated optimization: distributed machine learning for on-device intelligence. arXiv preprint arXiv:1610.02527 (2016)
7. Konecný, J., McMahan, H.B., Yu, F.X., Richtárik, P., Suresh, A.T., Bacon, D.: Federated learning: strategies for improving communication efficiency. CoRR abs/1610.0(Nips), 1–5 (2016)
8. Koren, Y., Bell, R.: Advances in collaborative filtering. In: Ricci, F., Rokach, L., Shapira, B., Kantor, P. (eds.) Recommender Systems Handbook, pp. 77–118. Springer, Boston (2015). https://doi.org/10.1007/978-0-387-85820-3_5
9. McAuley, J., Targett, C., Shi, Q., Van Den Hengel, A.: Image-based recommendations on styles and substitutes. In: Proceedings of the 38th International ACM SIGIR Conference on Research and Development in Information Retrieval. ACM, pp. 43–52 (2015)
10. McMahan, B., Moore, E., Ramage, D., Hampson, S., Arcas, B.A.: Communication-efficient learning of deep networks from decentralized data. In: Artificial Intelligence and Statistics, pp. 1273–1282 (2017)
11. Sun, X., Gong, D., Jin, Y., Chen, S.: A new surrogate-assisted interactive genetic algorithm with weighted semisupervised learning. IEEE Trans. Cybern. **43**(2), 685–698 (2013)
12. Sun, X., Gong, D., Wei, Z.: Interactive genetic algorithms with large population and semi-supervised learning. Appl. Soft Comput. J. **12**(9), 3004–3013 (2012)
13. Sun, X., Lu, Y., Gong, D., Zhang, K.: Interactive genetic algorithm with CP-nets preference surrogate and application in personalized search. Control Decision **30**(7), 1153–1161 (2015)
14. Sun, X., Zhu, L., Bao, L., Liu, L., Nie, X.: Interactive genetic algorithm with group intelligence articulated possibilistic condition preference model. In: Shi, Y., et al. (eds.) SEAL 2017. LNCS, vol. 10593, pp. 158–169. Springer, Cham (2017). https://doi.org/10.1007/978-3-319-68759-9_14
15. Sun, Y., Liu, W., Qiu, R., Huang, C.: Research development of user interest modeling in China. J. Intell. **32**(5), 145–149 (2013)
16. Takagi, H.: Interactive evolutionary computation: fusion of the capabilities of EC optimization and human evaluation. Proc. IEEE **89**(9), 1275–1296 (2001)

Second Order Differential Evolution
for Constrained Optimization

Xinchao Zhao[1(✉)], Jia Liu[1], Junling Hao[2], Jiaqi Chen[1],
and Xingquan Zuo[3]

[1] School of Science, Beijing University of Posts and Telecommunications,
Beijing 100876, China
xcbupt@126.com
[2] School of Statistics, University of International Business and Economics,
Beijing 10029, China
[3] School of Computers, Beijing University of Posts and Telecommunications,
Beijing 100876, China

Abstract. In this paper, second order differential evolution (SODE) algorithm is considered to solve the constrained optimization problems. After offspring are generated by the second order differential evolution, the ε constrained method is chosen for selection in this paper. In order to show that second order differential vector is better than differential vector in solving constrained optimization problems, differential evolution (DE) with the ε constrained method is used for performance comparison. The experiments on 12 test functions from IEEE CEC 2006 demonstrate that second order differential evolution shows better or at least competitive performance against DE when dealing with constrained optimization problems.

Keywords: Constrained optimization · Evolutionary algorithm ·
Differential evolution · SODE

1 Introduction

Constrained optimization problems (COPs) are mathematical programming problems frequently encountered in the disciplines of science and engineering application. Evolutionary algorithm is usually used to deal with constrained optimization problems due to its excellent performance, but it is essentially an unconstrained optimization evolutionary algorithm, which must be combined with constraint handing technique to solve the constrained optimization problem. Evolutionary algorithm and an appropriate constraint handing technique are combined to form a complete constrained evolutionary optimization algorithm. Among all the evolutionary algorithms, differential evolution (DE) [1] is one of the most important problem solvers.

Differential evolution was introduced by Price and Storn in 1997 [1], and has numerous attractive advantages. First of all, its structure is simple. In addition, it includes few control parameters. More importantly, its search ability, such as, higher search efficiency, higher robustness and lower computational complexity, has been demonstrated in many real-world applications [2, 3].

Y. Tan et al. (Eds.): ICSI 2019, LNCS 11655, pp. 384–394, 2019.
https://doi.org/10.1007/978-3-030-26369-0_36

Due to the above advantages, DE has been frequently applied to solve COPs. Many DE variants optimization have been tailored to tackle COPs [4]. However, few current studies investigate second order differential evolution (SODE) [5] for constrained optimization. To illustrate that second order differential vector is better than differential vector in solving constrained optimization problems, the ε constrained second order differential evolution (εSODE) is proposed in this paper.

The rest of the paper is organized as follows. In Sect. 2 some preliminary knowledge are presented. The proposed εSODE is shown in Sect. 3. The experimental and analytic results are presented in Sect. 4, and the last Section concludes the paper.

2 Preliminary Knowledge

2.1 Constrained Optimization Problems (COPs)

Without loss of generality, a COP can be described as follows:

$$
\begin{aligned}
\text{minimize} \quad & f(\vec{x}), \vec{x} = (x_1, \ldots, x_D) \in S \\
\text{subject to:} \quad & g_j(\vec{x}) \leq 0, j = 1, \ldots, l \\
& h_j(\vec{x}) = 0, j = l+1, \ldots, m \\
& l_i \leq x_i \leq u_i, i = 1, \ldots, D
\end{aligned}
\tag{1}
$$

where $\vec{x} = (x_1, \ldots, x_D)$ is an D dimensional vector, $f(\vec{x})$ is the objective function, $g_j(\vec{x}) \leq 0$ and $h_j(\vec{x}) = 0$ are l inequality constraints and $m - l$ equality constraints, respectively. l_i and u_i are the lower and upper bounds of the i-th decision variable x_i, respectively.

The decision space S is an D-dimensional rectangular space in R^n, in which every point satisfies the upper and lower bound constraints.

The feasible region Ω is defined by the l inequality constraints $g_j(\vec{x})$ and the $(m - l)$ equality constraints $h_j(\vec{x})$. Any point $\vec{x} \in \Omega$ is called a feasible solution; otherwise, $\vec{x}$ is an infeasible solution. The aim of solving COPs is to locate the optimum in the feasible region.

Usually, the degree of constraint violation of individual $\vec{x}$ on the j-th constraint is calculated as follows:

$$
G_j(\vec{x}) = \begin{cases} \max(0, g_j(\vec{x})), & 1 \leq j \leq l \\ \max(0, |h_j(\vec{x})| - \delta), & l+1 \leq j \leq m \end{cases}
\tag{2}
$$

$$
G(\vec{x}) = \sum_{j=1}^{m} G_j(\vec{x})
\tag{3}
$$

where $G_j(\vec{x})$ is the degree of constraint violation on the j-th constraint. δ is a positive tolerance value.

2.2 ε Constrained Method

The ε constrained method was proposed by Takahama and Sakai [6, 7]. The core idea of this method is to divide the individual-based constraint violation degree into different regions by artificially setting the ε value, and in different regions, the feasible solution and the infeasible solution adopt different evaluation methods respectively. The details on how to deal with the constraints, especially in constraint evolutionary optimization, can be found in the references [10, 11].

When comparing two individuals, say $\vec{x}_i^*$ and $\vec{x}_j^*$, $\vec{x}_i^*$ is better than $\vec{x}_j^*$ if and only if the following conditions are satisfied:

$$\begin{cases} f(\vec{x}_i) < f(\vec{x}_j), & if \quad G(\vec{x}_i) \leq \varepsilon \wedge G(\vec{x}_j) \leq \varepsilon \\ f(\vec{x}_i) < f(\vec{x}_j), & if \quad G(\vec{x}_i) = G(\vec{x}_j) \\ G(\vec{x}_i) < G(\vec{x}_j), & otherwise \end{cases} \quad (4)$$

$$\varepsilon(k) = \begin{cases} \varepsilon(0)(1 - \frac{k}{T_c})^{cp}, & 0 < k < T_c \\ 0, & k \geq T_c \end{cases} \quad (5)$$

$$cp = -\frac{\log \varepsilon(0) + \alpha}{\log\left(1 - \frac{k}{T_c}\right)} \quad (6)$$

where ε in Eq. (4) is controlled by Eqs. (5) and (6) and k is the current generation. $\varepsilon(0)$ is the maximum degree of constraint violation of the initial population. T_c is the maximum generation number. According to [8], α is set to 6.

2.3   Classical Differential Evolution

DE consists of four stages, i.e., initialization, mutation, crossover, and selection.

In the initialization stage, *NP* individuals are usually randomly generated from the decision space.

In the mutation operation stage, DE creates a mutant vector $\vec{v}_i$ for each sample $\vec{x}_i$. The two extensively used mutation operators (called DE/rand/1 and DE/best/1) are introduced as follows.

DE/rand/1:

$$\vec{v}_i = \vec{x}_{r_1} + F(\vec{x}_{r_2} - \vec{x}_{r_3}), \quad i = 1, 2, \ldots, NP \quad (7)$$

DE/best/1:

$$\vec{v}_i = \vec{x}_{best} + F(\vec{x}_{r_1} - \vec{x}_{r_2}), \quad i = 1, 2, \ldots, NP \quad (8)$$

where r_1, r_2, r_3 are three random and mutually different integers chosen from [1, NP], and F is a scaling factor and is used to control the amplification of the differential vector.

In the crossover operation stage, the crossover is applied to the parent individual $\vec{x}_i^k$ and its mutant vector $\vec{v}_i^k$. Then a trial vector $\vec{u}_i^k$ is produced.

$$u_{i,j}^k = \begin{cases} v_{i,j}^k, & rand \leq CR \quad or \quad j = j_{rand} \\ x_{i,j}^k, & otherwise \end{cases} \qquad (9)$$

where $rand$ is a uniformly distributed random number between 0 and 1. j_{rand} is a random integer in $[1, NP]$. CR is the crossover probability.

In the selection operation stage, a comparison is conducted between parent individual $\vec{x}_i^k$ and trial vector $\vec{u}_i^k$ to select the better one among them.

$$x_i^{k+1} = \begin{cases} u_i^k, & f(u_i^k) \leq f(x_i^k) \\ x_i^k, & otherwise \end{cases} \qquad (10)$$

2.4   Second Order Differential Evolution

SODE is also composed of four stages, i.e., initialization, mutation, crossover, and selection. Except for the mutation stage, the other stages are the same as those of DE.

In the mutation operation stage, the usually and widely used mutation operations, DE/rand/1, is adopted as analytic model strategies in this paper. In order to efficiently utilize the direction information and the search status of the current population, the second order difference vector mechanism, which is based on the classical mutation strategies, is indicated as in Eqs. (11)–(15).

$$d^k = x_{r1}^k - x_{r2}^k \qquad (11)$$

$$d_1^k = x_{r3}^k - x_{r4}^k \qquad (12)$$

$$d_1^k = x_{best}^k - x_{r4}^k \qquad (13)$$

$$d_2^k = x_{r5}^k - x_{r6}^k \qquad (14)$$

$$d_r^k = d^k + \lambda(d_1^k - d_2^k) \qquad (15)$$

where r1, r2, r3, r4, r5, r6 are different random integers in $[1, NP]$. λ is set as 0.1, which is discussed in reference [5]. x_{best}^k is the best vector in generation k. d_1^k in Eqs. (12) and (13) sets the same variable to different values, which is combined with Eq. (15) to produce different algorithms.

$(d_1^k - d_2^k)$ in Eq. (15) is the second order difference vector. The mutant vector v_i^k is generated as follows:

$$v_i^k = x_{r7}^k + F \cdot d_r^k \qquad (16)$$

where F is a scaling parameter and is set as 0.5. r7 is a random integer in $[1, NP]$.

In this paper, two composing patterns of d_r^k will be used. The first form of d_r^k consists of Eqs. (12) and (14). The second form of d_r^k consists of Eqs. (13) and (14). The first form and the second form based SODE, are denoted as SODErand and SODEbest, respectively.

3 The εConstrained Second Order Differential Evolution

Evolutionary algorithm is a general optimization framework. In order to solve the constraint optimization problems, it must be combined with the appropriate constraint handing technique. Evolutionary algorithm and the constraint handing technique are combined to form a complete constrained evolutionary optimization algorithm. Therefore, while retaining the idea of SODE, this paper adds an ε constrained method to select descendants, which is denoted as εSODErand and εSODEbest, respectively.

3.1 ε SODErand

In this paper, εSODErand uses SODErand mentioned in Sect. 2 to combine with ε constrained method. Its details is given in Algorithm 1.

Algorithm 1: εSODErand

Input: *NP, maxFES, F, CR*

1 k=1; // the generation number
2 Create a random initial population $x_k^i \ \forall i, i=1,...,NP$;
3 *FES=NP*; // FES is the number of fitness evaluations;
4 Get the ε value of the ε constrained method according to Eq.(5);
5 **for** $i=1:NP$
6   Use SODErand to generate a trial vector u_k^i;
7   Apply the ε constrained method to compare x_k^i and u_k^i;
8   Use the better one for the next iteration;
9   *FES=FES*+1;
10 **end for**
11 k=k+1;
12 **Stopping Criterion:** If *FES* ≥ *maxFES*, then stop and output the best solution, else go to Step 4.

3.2 A Subsection Sample

The difference between εSODEbest and εSODErand is the mutation operation stage. The former uses SODEbest mentioned in Sect. 2 to combine with ε constrained method. Its details is given in Algorithm 2.

Algorithm 2: εSODEbest

   Input: *NP, maxFES, F, CR*

1 *k*=1; // the generation number

2 Create a random initial population $x_k^i \; \forall i, i = 1, \dots, NP$;

3 *FES=NP*; // FES is the number of fitness evaluations;

4 Get the ε value of the ε constrained method according to Eq.(5);

5 **for** $i = 1 : NP$

6   Use SODEbest to generate a trial vector u_k^i;

7   Apply the ε constrained method to compare x_k^i and u_k^i;

8   Use the better one for the next iteration;

9   *FES=FES+1*;

10 **end for**

11 *k=k+1*;

12 **Stopping Criterion:** If *FES ≥ maxFES*, then stop and output the best solution, else go to Step 4.

---

4 Experimental Results and Algorithmic Analysis

4.1 CEC2006 Benchmark Functions

In order to check the performance of the proposed algorithms εSODEbest and εSODErand, 12 functions are selected from IEEE CEC2006 [9] as the preliminary test suite, which is described in Table 1.

Table 1. CEC2006 benchmark functions.

Prob.	D	Type of function	LI	NI	LE	NE	Active
g_{01}	20	Nonlinear	9	0	0	0	1
g_{02}	10	Polynomial	0	0	0	1	1
g_{03}	10	Quadratic	3	5	0	0	6
g_{04}	7	Polynomial	0	4	0	0	2
g_{05}	8	Linear	3	3	0	0	6
g_{06}	2	Quadratic	0	0	1	1	1
g_{07}	5	Nonlinear	0	0	3	3	3
g_{08}	10	Nonlinear	0	0	0	0	3
g_{09}	5	Nonlinear	4	34	0	0	4
g_{10}	6	Nonlinear	0	0	4	4	4
g_{11}	15	Nonlinear	0	5	0	0	0
g_{12}	7	Linear	0	1	5	5	6

Where D is the number of decision variables, LI is the number of linear inequality constraints, NI the number of nonlinear inequality constraints, LE is the number of linear equality constraints and NE is the number of nonlinear equality constraints, *active* is the number of active constraints at $\vec{x}$.

4.2 Experimental Settings

In order to show the performance of two proposed algorithms, εDE is chosen to compare with them. In this paper, εDE means to change SODErand in step6 of Algorithm 1 to DE. In addition to the special instructions, the parameters are set as follows.

- Independent running number: RUN = 25.
- Population size: NP = 50.
- Maximum number of function evaluations: maxFES = 240000.

Both parameters, F and CR are initialized to 0.5. Parameter λ is set as 0.1.

It is noteworthy that the feasible rate, i.e., if the algorithm cannot consistently provide feasible solutions in all 25 runs, the running percentage of finding at least one feasible solution is recorded. So, based on the feasible rate, the experimental results are divided into two parts. One part is that the feasible rate of all three algorithms is 100%, and the other part is that there are some algorithms not 100% feasible. The former is called part 1, and the latter part is called part 2.

4.3 Experimental Comparison for Part 1

In the 12 functions, the solutions of 6 functions, include g_{01}, g_{02}, g_{03}, g_{07}, g_{09}, g_{11}, are consistent feasible over all 25 runs. All the final experimental results of the 6 functions over 25 runs, are statistically listed in Table 2, which includes the statistical items of the minimum final result (min), the median final result (median), the average final result (mean) and the standard deviation (std) in multiple runs.

Table 2. Comparison of the results based on CEC2006 functions.

Prob.	Items	εSODErand	εSODEbest	εDE
g_{01}	min	**−8.0361E−01**	−8.0360E−01	−8.0360E−01
	mean	−8.0213E−01	**−8.0315E−01**	−8.0112E−01
	median	**−8.0360E−01**	−8.0359E−01	−8.0359E−01
	std	5.0795E−03	**2.1990E−03**	6.9590E−03
g_{02}	min	**−1.0003E+00**	**−1.0003E+00**	**−1.0003E+00**
	mean	−9.9920E−01	**−9.9972E−01**	−9.9936E−01
	median	−9.9948E−01	**−9.9989E−01**	−9.9960E−01
	std	1.1884E−03	**5.4964E−04**	1.4034E−03
g_{03}	min	**5.1265E+03**	**5.1265E+03**	**5.1265E+03**
	mean	5.1273E+03	**5.1265E+03**	5.1266E+03
	median	**5.1265E+03**	**5.1265E+03**	**5.1265E+03**
	std	3.6150E+00	**5.7052E−02**	5.6944E−01
g_{07}	min	5.3942E−02	**5.1196E−02**	5.3942E−02
	mean	5.4130E−02	**5.3850E−02**	5.3956E−02
	median	**5.3942E−02**	**5.3942E−02**	**5.3942E−02**
	std	9.4131E−04	5.5928E−04	**5.8672E−05**

(continued)

Table 2. *(continued)*

Prob.	Items	εSODErand	εSODEbest	εDE
g_{09}	min	**−1.9052E+00**	**−1.9052E+00**	−1.9052E+00
	mean	**−1.9052E+00**	**−1.9052E+00**	−1.6578E+00
	median	**−1.9052E+00**	**−1.9052E+00**	−1.4307E+00
	std	**4.5325E−16**	9.0649E−16	2.4127E−01
g_{11}	min	3.2972E+01	**3.2910E+01**	3.2985E+01
	mean	3.3166E+01	**3.3123E+01**	3.3216E+01
	median	3.3148E+01	**3.3115E+01**	3.3194E+01
	std	1.2913E−01	**8.6868E−02**	1.4633E−01

Observed from Table 2 two proposed algorithms shows even better results in terms of reliability and accuracy when comparing with εDE. Comparatively speaking, εSODErand performs a little worse than that of εSODEbest. The fact of εSODErand and εSODEbest being better than εDE indicates that SODE has more information utilizing ability for solving constrained optimization problems than DE.

4.4 Boxplot Performance Comparison

To compare the performance of algorithms better, the boxplot analysis is taken for perusal. It can easily show the empirical distribution of all the final data in multiple runs pictorially. In order to better analyze the results, the functions are divided into two parts: Figs. 1 and 2.

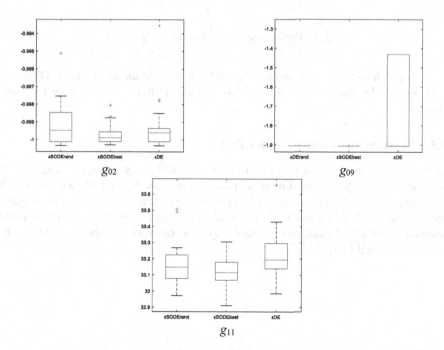

Fig. 1. Performance comparison on g_{02}, g_{09}, g_{11}.

Boxplots are shown in Fig. 1, which shows that both medians and interquartile range of εSODEbest are comparatively lower. The median of εSODErand is lower than that of εDE except for g02 function.

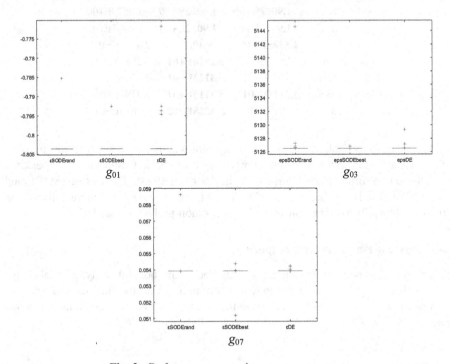

Fig. 2. Performance comparison on g_{01}, g_{03}, g_{07}.

The performance comparison of g01, g03 and g07 are shown in Fig. 2. Observed from Fig. 2, the results of the three algorithms are relatively stable except for some outliers.

4.5 Experimental Comparison for Part 2

In the 12 functions, the solutions of 6 functions, include g_{04}, g_{05}, g_{06}, g_{08}, g_{10}, g_{12}, are inconsistent feasible. To get a more accurate solution, the 6 functions will be run 50 times to get results. The feasible rate, i.e., percentage of runs where at least one feasible solution is found, is recorded if an algorithm fails to consistently provide feasible solutions over all 50 runs. All the final experimental results of the 6 functions are statistically listed in Table 3.

Table 3. Comparison of the results based On CEC2006 functions.

Prob.	Items	SODErand	SODEbest	DE
g_{04}	min	90%	**6.8063E+02**	72%
	mean		**6.8063E+02**	
	median		**6.8063E+02**	
	std		**1.7807E−05**	
g_{05}	min	7.0571E+03	**7.0564E+03**	92%
	mean	7.0682E+03	**7.0646E+03**	
	median	7.0650E+03	**7.0645E+03**	
	std	1.4941E+01	**6.9106E+00**	
g_{06}		8%	8%	0%
g_{08}		4%	0%	0%
g_{10}		4%	4%	0%
g_{12}		96%	98%	90%

Observed from Table 3, two proposed algorithms shows even better results in terms of feasible rate when comparing with εDE. Especially the functions g_{06}, g_{08}, g_{10}, the solutions obtained by εDE are not feasible, but two proposed algorithms significantly improve this phenomenon. This shows that SODE is more suitable for solving constrained optimization problems than DE.

5 Conclusions

A simple modification to SODE is proposed to solve COPs in this paper. The idea is that after producing offspring by the second order differential evolution, the ε constrained method is chosen for selection. εSODErand and εSODEbest on the basis of SODE are proposed. To test the effect of the proposed strategies, they are verified on CEC2006 Benchmark Functions. Experimental results show that second order difference vector has a certain role in dealing with constraint optimization problems. This idea can be hybridized with any DE variants, even for all the swarm intelligence and evolutionary computing methods. So, how to even better utilize the second order difference vector deserves further research.

Acknowledgments. This research is supported by National Natural Science Foundation of China (71772060, 61873040, 61375066). We will express our awfully thanks to the Swarm Intelligence Research Team of BeiYou University.

References

1. Storn, R., Price, K.: Differential evolution: a simple and efficient heuristic for global optimization over continuous spaces. J. Global Optim. **11**(4), 341–359 (1997)
2. Harno, H.G., Petersen, I.R.: Synthesis of linear coherent quantum control systems using a differential evolution algorithm. IEEE Trans. Autom. Control **60**(3), 799–805 (2015)

3. Chiu, W.-Y.: Pareto optimal controller designs in differential games. In: 2014 CACS International Automatic Control Conference (CACS), pp. 179–184. IEEE (2014)
4. Wei, W., Wang, J., Tao, M.: Constrained differential evolution with multiobjective sorting mutation operators for constrained optimization. Appl. Soft Comput. **33**, 207–222 (2015)
5. Zhao, X., Xu, G., Liu, D., Zuo, X.: Second order differential evolution algorithm. CAAI Trans. Intell. Technol. **2**, 96–116 (2017)
6. Takahama, T., Sakai, S.: Constrained optimization by the ε constrained differential evolution with an archive and gradient-based mutation. In: IEEE Congress on Evolutionary Computation, pp. 1–9. IEEE (2010)
7. Takahama, T., Sakai, S.: Efficient constrained optimization by the constrained rank based differential evolution. In: 2012 IEEE Congress on Evolutionary Computation, pp. 1–8. IEEE (2012)
8. Wang, B.C., Li, H.X., Li, J.P., Wang, Y.: Composite differential evolution for constrained evolutionary optimization. IEEE Trans. Syst. Man Cybernet. Syst. **99**, 1–14 (2018)
9. Liang, J., et al.: Problem definitions and evaluation criteria for the CEC 2006 special session on constrained real-parameter optimization. J. Appl. Mech. **41**(8), 8–31 (2006)
10. Li, Z.Y., Huang, T., Chen, S.M., Li, R.F.: Overview of constrained optimization evolutionary algorithms. J. Softw. **28**(6), 1529–1546 (2017)
11. Wang, Y., Cai, Z.X., Zhou, Y.R., Xiao, C.X.: Constrained optimization evolutionary algorithms. J. Softw. **20**(1), 11–29 (2009)

Computability and Stability for Hybrid Algorithms

Nachum Dershowitz[1] and Zvi Retchkiman Königsberg[2]([✉])

[1] School of Computer Science, Tel Aviv University, Ramat Aviv, Israel
nachum.dershowitz@cs.tau.ac.il
[2] Instituto Politécnico Nacional, CIC, Mexico City, Mexico
mzvi@cic.ipn.mx

Abstract. Church's Thesis for discrete algorithms motivates an analogous thesis for dealing with analog algorithms. Specifically, the notions of
analog algorithm and dynamical system are postulated to be equivalent.
Stability for hybrid algorithms is addressed by considering Lyapunov
energy functions for analog algorithms with continuous and discontinuous states.

Keywords: Analog algorithms · Dynamical systems ·
Hybrid systems · Church's Thesis · Stability · Lyapunov functions

1 Introduction

Gurevich [3] has shown that any algorithm that satisfies three intuitive postulates can be step-by-step emulated by an abstract state machine (ASM).
Adding a postulate of effectivity, Dershowitz and Gurevich [2] proceeded to
prove that all notions of effective algorithms for discrete-time models of computation (e.g. Turing machines, Minsky counter machines, Post machines, random
access machines) are covered by their formalization. Bournez, Dershowitz and
Néron [1] then extended that axiomatization to supply a generic notion of analog algorithm and prove completeness results. Their postulates, defining analog
algorithms, are in the same spirit of those given for discrete algorithms. These
notions are reviewed and adapted in the next two sections.

Our study of stability considers Lyapunov energy functions for algorithms
with continuous and discontinuous states. It extends preliminary work for purely
dynamical systems [5] to handle hybrid systems with both discrete and analog
transitions. This is the subject of Sect. 4.

The agents of an artificial swarm system are often hybrid by nature. Stability
is a crucial property for such swarm agents.

2 Computability of Discrete Algorithms

The basic characteristic of a computable function, as formalized in [2,3], is that
there must exist a finite description of an algorithm describing how to compute
the function.

© Springer Nature Switzerland AG 2019
Y. Tan et al. (Eds.): ICSI 2019, LNCS 11655, pp. 395–401, 2019.
https://doi.org/10.1007/978-3-030-26369-0_37

According to this view, a function is computable if: (a) given an input from its domain, it can give the corresponding output by following a procedure (program) that is formed by a finite number of exact unambiguous instructions – possibly relying on unbounded storage space; (b) it returns such output (halts) in a finite number of steps; and (c) if given an input that is not in its domain, it either never halts or it gets "stuck" and fails.

Gurevich [3] proposed a generic model of computation that incorporates these properties in what constitutes a "formal" algorithm, and which is outlined next.

Postulate I (Discrete system). An algorithm is a state-transition system, consisting of a set (or proper class) of states, a subset of which are initial states, and a partial transition function on states that determines the next-state relation. States with no next state are *terminal*.

Postulate II (Abstract state). States are first-order structures with equality, all sharing the same fixed, finite vocabulary, including the scalar (nullary function) true. States and initial states are closed under isomorphism. Transitions preserve the base set (domain), and transitions and isomorphisms commute. The interpretations given by a state x to the function symbols f in the vocabulary of the structure are denoted by $[\![f]\!]_x$, and extended in the usual way to (ground) terms.

Definition 1 (Locations and updates). *If f is a j-ary function symbol in the state vocabulary and $\bar{a}$ is a j-tuple of elements of the base set of a state x, then their combination $f(\bar{a})$ is called a* location. *We denote by $[\![f(\bar{a})]\!]_x$ its interpretation $[\![f]\!]_x(\bar{a})$ in x. When x and y are structures over the same base set and vocabulary, $y \setminus x$ is the set of* updates $\{f(\bar{a}) \mapsto [\![f(\bar{a})]\!]_y : [\![f(\bar{a})]\!]_y \neq [\![f(\bar{a})]\!]_x\}$.

Postulate III (Bounded exploration). There exists some finite set of ground terms over the vocabulary of the states, such that states that agree on the values of these terms also agree on all next-step state changes.

An abstract state machine, or ASM, is a state-transition system in which algebraic states (without predicate symbols) store the values of functions of the current state. Transitions are programmed using a convenient language based on guarded commands for updating individual states. ASMs captures the notion that each step of an algorithm performs a bounded amount of work, whatever domain it operates over, so are central to the succeeding development.

Definition 2 (ASM). *An* abstract state machine (ASM) *is given by a set of algebraic states (without predicate symbols) sharing a vocabulary and closed under isomorphism, a subset of initial states also closed under isomorphism, and a program P, composed of:*

- *assignments $s := u$, for terms s and u over the vocabulary of the states;*
- *conditionals* if q then P *or* if q then P else R, *where q is a conjunction of equalities and inequalities between terms and P and R are programs; and*
- *parallel composition* par $P_1, \ldots P_n$ rap, *for programs $P_1, \ldots, P_n$.*

A program P defines a set of updates $\triangle_P(x)$ for each state x, according to the standard semantics of these programming constructs, each update being of the form $f(\bar{a}) \mapsto b$, for values $\bar{a}, b$ in the base set of x.

Gurevich [3] goes on to prove the following important result.

Theorem 3 (Representation). *For every process satisfying Postulates I–III, there is an abstract state machine (ASM) in the same vocabulary, with the same sets of states and initial states, that emulates it step-by-step, state-for-state.*

To capture the notion of effectiveness, one additional postulate regarding initial states is needed.

Postulate IV (Arithmetical state). Up to isomorphism, all initial states have the natural numbers as their base set, all share the same operations and constants – save input values, and there is exactly one initial state for each possible input. Their operations are all basic arithmetic $(+, -, \times, \div, <)$, or can be programmed by ASMs using only basic arithmetic, or else are completely undefined.

Employing this last postulate, arithmetical ASMs may be defined [2]. With all this information, the Church Thesis is proved.

Theorem 4 (Church's Thesis). *A numeric function is partial recursive if and only if it is computed by a state-transition system satisfying Postulates I–IV. The input is contained in the initial state of a computation and the output in its terminal state.*

Remark 5. We have restricted this presentation to algorithms that work over the natural numbers. However, it is possible to extend it to other possible domains (strings, lists, graphs, etc.) by introducing an encoding notion and the concept of arithmetized algorithm, as done in [2]. No matter what other effective model of computation is chosen, its power of computation will not be increased beyond that given by partial recursive functions. Theorem 3 plays a fundamental role in the proof. See [2] for more details. As a corollary Turing's Thesis is obtained.

3   Effectiveness of Hybrid Algorithms

We are interested next in extrapolating from the above discussion to analog algorithms along the lines suggested by Bournez, Dershowitz, and Néron [1].

Postulate Ia (Dynamical system). A *hybrid* algorithm is a *dynamical system* (T, X, A, φ_t) consisting of a time set T (a monoid with an addition operator + and neutral 0), a metric state space X (with metric d), initial states $A \subseteq X$, and a family of evolution operators $\varphi_t : X \rightharpoonup X$, parameterized by $t \in T$ (but not necessarily defined for all $t \in T$) and satisfying the following two properties: $\varphi_{t+s} = \varphi_t \circ \varphi_s$ and φ_0 is the identity function.

Remark 6. In our definition of dynamical system, it is allowed to have, in general, more than one evolution operator.

Dynamical systems are classified based on the properties of T, X, and φ. The time set T, is it continuous or discrete? Is the state space X finite or infinite? Continuous or discrete? Finite-dimensional or infinite-dimensional? Regarding the evolution map φ_t: is it deterministic or stochastic, autonomous or time-dependent, invertible or not, etc.?

When $T = \mathbb{R} = (-\infty, \infty)$, we speak of a *continuous-time* dynamical system, and when $T = \mathbb{N} = \{0, 1, 2, \cdots\}$ we speak of a *discrete-time* dynamical system. We will consider T equipped with the absolute value as a normed space $(T, |\cdot|)$.

A dynamical system is generally defined by one or more differential or difference equations.

Remark 7. When dealing with continuous dynamical systems determined by ordinary differential equations on $\mathbb{R}^n$, the euclidean metric d is

$$d(x, y) = |x - y| = \sqrt{\sum_{i=1}^{n}(x_i - y_i)^2}, \quad \forall x, y \in \mathbb{R}^n.$$

For discrete dynamical systems determined by difference equations, X equipped with this euclidean metric defines a metric space.

Definition 8 (Computable system). *A dynamical system is said to be* computable *if its family of evolution operators (also called its* trajectories*) are obtained as solutions of its mathematical model.*

Postulate IIa (Abstract state). A hybrid algorithm is an abstract transition system satisfying Postulate II.

Definition 9 (Generator). *An* infinitesimal generator *is a function that maps states to updates, and which respects isomorphisms.*

Definition 10 (Semantics). *A semantics ψ over a class C of sets S is a partial function mapping initial evolutions (non-point evolutions starting at $t = 0$) over some $S \in C$ to an element of S. The infinitesimal generator associated with a semantics ψ maps the state space X, for $x \in X$ such that $\psi([\![f(\bar{a})]\!]_{\varphi_t(x)})$ is defined for all locations $f(\bar{a})$, to the set of updates $\Delta_\psi(x) = \{f(\bar{a}) \mapsto \psi([\![f(\bar{a})]\!]_{\varphi_t(x)}) : f$ in vocabulary of x and $\bar{a}$ in base set of $x\}$.*

Remark 11. When $T = \mathbb{R}$, an example of semantics over the class of sets S containing T is the derivative ψ_{der}, when it exists. When $T = \mathbb{N}$, an example of semantics over the class of all sets would be the function $\psi_{\mathbb{N}}$ mapping f to $\psi_{\mathbb{N}}(f_n) = f_{n+1}, n \in \mathbb{N}$.

Remark 12. From now on, we assume that some semantics ψ is fixed to deal with different types of dynamical system; it could be ψ_{der}, but it could also be another one. However, it is assumed that the class of dynamical systems is restricted to those that guarantee the existence of the respective semantics, and as a result its associated set of updates is well defined. Therefore, not all possible dynamical systems are allowed.

The following corresponds to the Bounded Exploration Postulate, but now for continuous transitions.

Postulate IIIa (Bounded exploration). For any hybrid algorithm, there exists a finite set T of variable free terms over the vocabulary of its states, such that $\Delta_\psi(x) = \Delta_\psi(y)$ for all states x and y that coincide for all terms in T.

Definition 13 (Hybrid algorithm). *A hybrid algorithm is a dynamical system that satisfies Postulates Ia–IIIa.*

In addition to the rules of ASM programs as given in Definition 2, we need dynamic rules.

Definition 14 (Dynamic ASM). *Programs may include statements $Dynamic(f(t_1, \cdots, t_j), t_0)$, where f is a symbol of arity j and $t_0, t_1, \ldots, t_j$ are ground terms. This rule imposes constraints $\psi(f(t_1, \ldots, t_j)) = t_0$ on the updates $\Delta_\psi(x)$.*

The proposed model can adequately describe hybrid systems, made of alternating sequences of continuous evolution and discrete transitions.

Example 15 (Bouncing ball). Let us consider a simple model of a bouncing ball, a classic example of a hybrid dynamical system, whose mathematical model is given by the equations $x'' = -gm$, where g is the gravitational constant and $v = x'$ is the velocity, except that upon impact, each time $x = 0$, the velocity changes according to $v = -kv$, where k is the coefficient of impact. Every time the ball bounces, its speed is reduced by a factor k. Its evolution is described by its associated set of updates of the following program rules

> **if** $x = 0$ **then** $v := -kv$
>
> > **else par** $Dynamic(x, v), Dynamic(v, -gm)$ **rap**

with dynamics ψ_{der}.

Definition 16 (Program). *A ψASM comprises the following: an ASM program, a set S of first-order structures with equality over some finite vocabulary $\mathcal{V}$ closed under isomorphisms with a subset I of S closed under isomorphisms, and a well-defined update set of computations Δ_ψ associated with ψ.*

We are assuming that for each dynamical system, the trajectories can be computed from the description of its dynamical system, as, for example, in the case of nonlinear differential equation, the Lipschitz conditions are satisfied, etc. In other words, not all dynamical systems are contemplated just those that guarantee their existence.

Definition 17 (Unambiguity). *A semantics ψ is unambiguous if for all sets S of first-order structures over some finite vocabulary $\mathcal{V}$ closed under isomorphisms, and for all subsets $S' \in S$ closed under isomorphisms, whenever there exists some φ and a ψASM, then φ is unique.*

Bournez, Dershowitz, and Néron finish their presentation giving their main result (analogous to Theorem 3).

Theorem 18. *Assuming ψ is unambiguous, for every process satisfying Postulates Ia–IIIa, there is an equivalent ψASM.*

Theorem 19 (Church's Thesis for hybrid algorithms). *A dynamical system is computable if and only if a ψASM computes it.*

Proof. If the dynamical system is computable (per Definition 8), there exists an algorithm that computes its trajectories from its mathematical model description and, therefore, the ψASM program will be able to emulate and compute these trajectories by a proper definition of its rules. For the other direction of the implication, given a ψASM that first interprets the fixed dynamical system and then computes its trajectories, we define a numerical procedure that mimics it and therefore computes the dynamical system's trajectories. In fact, its trajectories define an exact mathematical model of themselves.   □

4   Stability of Hybrid Algorithms

We are ready now to consider the stability concept for hybrid algorithms in terms of Lyapunov energy functions. We deal with algorithms whose states are structures with metric space S, d as base set.

Definition 20 (Stability). *Consider a hybrid algorithm. We say that state x with $a \in S$ and time-indexed location $f_{t,t_0}(a)$, where t and t_0 belong to T, is stable if for all $t_0 \in T$ and for all $\varepsilon > 0$ there exists $\delta = \delta(t_0, \varepsilon) > 0$ such that if given $a' \in S$, with $d(a', a) < \delta \Rightarrow d(\llbracket f_{t,t_0}(a') \rrbracket_x, \llbracket f_{t,t_0}(a) \rrbracket_x) < \varepsilon$ for all $t \in T$.*

Chaotic systems are unstable.

Definition 21 (Continuity). *Consider a hybrid algorithm. We say that state x with $a \in S$ and time-indexed location $f_t(a)$ is continuous at $t \in T$ if for all $\varepsilon > 0$ there exists $\delta = \delta(t) > 0$ and state y such that if given $t' \in T$, with $|t - t'| < \delta \Rightarrow d(\llbracket f_t(a) \rrbracket_x, \llbracket f_{t'}(a) \rrbracket_y) < \varepsilon$.*

Definition 22 (Class $\mathcal{K}$). *A continuous function $\alpha : [0, \infty) \to [0, \infty)$ is said to belong to class $\mathcal{K}$ if it is strictly increasing and $\alpha(0) = 0$.*

Postulate E (Bounded energy). The Lyapunov energy function associated with a hybrid algorithm at its starting time point $t_0 \in T$ multiplied by some finite constant $c \geq 1$ bounds the whole Lyapunov energy function, transferred or transformed by the whole algorithm, as the Lyapunov energy function evolves in time.

Theorem 23. *Consider a hybrid algorithm with the possibility of discontinuous states at points* $t_1, t_2, \cdots \in T$. *Assume there exists a Lyapunov function* V : $S \times T \to \mathbb{R}^+$ *and two functions* $\alpha, \beta \in \mathcal{K}$, *such that*

$$\alpha(d(\llbracket f_{t,t_0}(a') \rrbracket_x, \llbracket f_{t,t_0}(a) \rrbracket_x)) \leq V(\llbracket f_{t,t_0}(a') \rrbracket_x, t)$$
$$\leq \beta(d(\llbracket f_{t,t_0}(a') \rrbracket_x, \llbracket f_{t,t_0}(a) \rrbracket_x))$$

for all $a, a' \in S$, $t, t_0 \in T$. *Assume Postulate E and that* $\llbracket f_{t_0,t_0}(a') \rrbracket_x = a'$ *holds, then the hybrid algorithm is stable.*

Proof. We want to show that there exists a $\delta = \delta(t_0, \varepsilon) > 0$ such that given a' with $d(a', a) < \delta \Rightarrow d(\llbracket f_{t,t_0}(a') \rrbracket_x, \llbracket f_{t,t_0}(a) \rrbracket_x) < \varepsilon$ for all $t \in T$. We claim $\delta = \beta^{-1}(\alpha(\varepsilon)/c)$ does the job. Indeed, $d(\llbracket f_{t,t_0}(a') \rrbracket_x, \llbracket f_{t,t_0}(a) \rrbracket_x) \leq \alpha^{-1}(V(\llbracket f_{t,t_0}(a') \rrbracket_x, t)) \leq \alpha^{-1}(cV(\llbracket f_{t_0,t_0}(a') \rrbracket_x, t_0)) = \alpha^{-1}(cV(a', t_0)) \leq \alpha^{-1}(c\beta(d(a', a))) < \varepsilon$, where Postulate E has been used in the second inequality and the equation $\llbracket f_{t_0,t_0}(a') \rrbracket_x = a'$ in the first. $\square$

An example of a stable hybrid algorithm whose Lyapunov function satisfies the conditions imposed by Theorem 23 is the one provided in [4], which consists of a ball in a constant gravitational field bouncing inelastically on a flat vibrating table. It is interesting to see how the Lyapunov function, proposed in the cited paper, monotonically decreases as t increases. In other words, Postulate E holds with $c = 1$.

References

1. Bournez, O., Dershowitz, N., Néron, P.: Axiomatizing analog algorithms. In: Beckmann, A., Bienvenu, L., Jonoska, N. (eds.) CiE 2016. LNCS, vol. 9709, pp. 215–224. Springer, Cham (2016). https://doi.org/10.1007/978-3-319-40189-8_22. http://nachum.org/papers/AxiomatizationAnalog.pdf, https://arxiv.org/pdf/1604.04295v2.pdf
2. Dershowitz, N., Gurevich, Y.: A natural axiomatization of computability and proof of Church's Thesis. Bull. Symbolic Logic **14**, 299–350 (2008). http://nachum.org/papers/Church.pdf
3. Gurevich, Y.: Sequential abstract state machines capture sequential algorithms. ACM Trans. Comput. Logic **1**, 77–111 (2000). http://citeseerx.ist.psu.edu/viewdoc/download?doi=10.1.1.146.3017&rep=rep1&type=pdf
4. Heimsch, T.F., Leine, R.I.: A novel Lyapunov-like method for the non-autonomous bouncing ball system. In: Proceedings of the 7th European Nonlinear Dynamics Conference (ENOC), Rome (2011)
5. Retchkiman, Z., Dershowitz, N.: The Church thesis, its proof, and the notion of stability and stabilization for analog algorithms. Commun. Appl. Anal. **23**, 233–248 (2019)

Swarm Robotics

Stochastic Self-organizing Control
for Swarm Robot Systems

Daisuke Inoue[(✉)], Daisuke Murai, and Hiroaki Yoshida

Toyota Central R&D Labs., Inc., Nagakute, Aichi, Japan
{daisuke-inoue,Daisuke-Murai,h-yoshida}@mosk.tytlabs.co.jp
https://www.tytlabs.com/

Abstract. In swarm robot systems, forming a target shape with autonomously moving robots is an important task. Considering cost and scalability, it is desirable that the observation information required by the robots to form patterns be minimal, whereas the patterns themselves can be as complicated as needed. In this paper, we propose a method of achieving this task under the situation that a scalar value representing a clue to its position is the only information that each robot can observe. We adopted the optimization method proposed by Mesquita et al. [International workshop on hybrid systems: Computation and control, pp. 358 (2008)] as a control method for the swarm robot systems. This method requires neither centralized controllers nor position identification of each robot, and we thus refer to it as "self-organizing control." Compared with existing control methods, the proposed method reduces memory usage and computational complexity. By means of both numerical simulations and experiments with actual robots, we quantitatively confirmed that self-organization was achieved.

Keywords: Swarm robotics · Self-organization · Multi-agent systems

1 Introduction

Swarm robot systems aim at performing complicated tasks with large groups of robots equipped with relatively simple hardware [2,3,13]. Such systems are attracting much attention because of their flexibility, environmental adaptability, and robustness against failure [5,15]. One task proposed for robot swarms is the formation of a target shape while each robot moves autonomously. The task includes several fundamental activities, including *consensus*, in which robots gather in one place, and *coverage*, in which robots are scattered all over a certain field [8,12,17]. In this task, the complexity of the shape that the robots can form depends on the amount of observations made by each robot. For example, when each robot is able to directly obtain its position and orientation using GPS and a gyro sensor, controlling movement towards the target coordinates is easy. However, when a large number of robots is used, it is costly to equip each robot

© Springer Nature Switzerland AG 2019
Y. Tan et al. (Eds.): ICSI 2019, LNCS 11655, pp. 405–416, 2019.
https://doi.org/10.1007/978-3-030-26369-0_38

with sensors, and the lack of sensors makes shape formation very difficult. To circumvent such problems, we studied a method for pattern formation without any individual robot knowing its own position directly; that is, a *self-organizing control* method. Instead of having robots obtain information about their positions, we assumed a situation where each robot can obtain a scalar value representing "the desirability of the current position." One simple example of the scalar value is a light intensity that a robot can observe. In this example, robots gather more densely where the light is strong and more sparsely where the light is weak. Although such a problem setting is similar to a global control problem, in that scalar values are transmitted to the entire group, the situation considered here is more realistic when we consider a massive number of robots, because sending position and orientation directly become less obvious.

In this context, the paper by Mesquita et al. [10] reports a remarkable study. They proposed a method to maximize a certain class of the function $Q : \mathbb{R}^d \to \mathbb{R}$ ($d = 2$ or 3) while letting a large number of virtual agents search in $\mathbb{R}^d$-space according to a certain rule R. As a result of running the agent with this rule, it was shown that the density distribution of the agents converged to the given function Q. Then, the user can know the maximum value of the function, at which the agents exist most densely, after some time elapses. Therefore, in Ref. [10], the rule of each robot's motion was introduced as a means of optimization.

In this study, we applied the method proposed in Ref. [10] to impart self-organizing control to a swarm robots in real space. In other words, by applying the agent paradigm to robots, Q becomes the position clue and R becomes the rule for robot movement, and the density distribution formed by the robots is expected to converge to Q. Because the rule R is probabilistic, we call this method *stochastic self-organizing control*. As compared with conventional methods often used for coverage control in multi-agent systems, such as the ones in Refs. [1, 6, 9], the present stochastic self-organizing control has the following features:

(1) The robots stochastically remain moving, even in a steady state.
(2) The simple algorithms have low computational complexity.
(3) The only necessary information is the value of Q (without self-positions and orientation).

Although (1) is seemingly problematic from the viewpoint of energy consumption, it can provide performance superior to that of deterministic control when there are differences in robot abilities, because the continuous motion keeps robots exchanging their positions within a certain area. Items (2) and (3) mean that the robots can be controlled effectively even when they have small memory and few sensors, respectively; in other words, the proposed method is applicable to a simple, small robot.

The rest of this paper is organized as follows. In Sect. 2, we formulate a shape formation problem and describe the stochastic self-organizing control method. In Sects. 3 and 4, we perform a large-scale simulation and an actual machine experiment. In Sect. 5, we evaluate the performance of the proposed method and discuss future directions for algorithm improvement.

2   Stochastic Self-organizing Control

2.1   Problem Formulation

Consider N mobile robots on $\mathbb{R}^2$-space. Assume that each robot has a unique identifier from 1 to N. The position and velocity of robot i at time $t \in \mathbb{R}_+$ ($\mathbb{R}_+ :=$ $\{a \mid a \in \mathbb{R}, a \geq 0\}$) are denoted by $x_i(t) \in \mathbb{R}^2$ and $v_i(t) \in \mathbb{V}$, respectively, where $\mathbb{V}$ denotes the velocity space of each robot. We make the following assumptions for each robot:

1. $\mathbb{V} = \rho\mathbb{S}$, where $\rho \in \mathbb{R}_+$ is a constant and $\mathbb{S}$ is the unit sphere equipped with a Lebesgue measure $d\mu$. This means that each robot always moves at a constant speed of $\rho > 0$.
2. The robot continuously selects either straight-ahead motion or rotational motion. This method of movement is called *run and tumble*.
3. We define the set $\mathcal{D}$ as $\mathcal{D} := \{f \in L^1(\mathbb{R}^2) \mid f > 0, \int_{\mathbb{R}^2} f(x)dx = 1\}$, and consider $Q \in \mathcal{D}$. Each robot is *not* able to obtain its own position $x_i(t)$ and orientation, but it can measure the value of the function $Q(x_i(t))$.
4. All robots are assumed to move according to the same algorithms. It is also assumed that robots do not communicate with each other, and their density is sufficiently small to avoid collisions. At this time, because the motion of each robot can be regarded as independent, in the following description, the position and speed of the robot are represented by $x(t)$ and $v(t)$, respectively; that is, index i is dropped.

We define $p(x, v, t)$ as the probability density of finding a robot at position x with velocity v at time t. We assume that for each fixed time t, $p(x, v, t) \in L^1(\mathbb{R}^2 \times \rho\mathbb{S})$ holds, when $\mathbb{R}^2 \times \rho\mathbb{S}$ is provided with the product measure $dx \otimes d\mu$. The purpose of the considered control problem is to ensure that

$$\lim_{t \to \infty} \int_{\rho\mathbb{S}} p(x, v, t)d\mu(v) = Q(x). \tag{1}$$

is satisfied by designing rule R. This rule determines the speed $v(t)$ depending on the history of values of the scalar function $\{Q(x(\tau)) \mid \tau \in [s, t], \ s \leq t\}$ observed by each robot.

2.2   Controller Design

Mesquita et al. [10] proposed a method for solving an optimization problem by finding the maximum of a function, say $Q(x)$. This method relies on stochastically selecting the rotational motion of an agent. Here we apply it to achieve our goal in Eq. (1). The probability that a tumble does *not* occur between the time instants t and s is given by

$$\exp\left(-\int_s^t \lambda(x + \tau v, v)d\tau\right).$$ (2)

where $\lambda : \mathbb{R}^2 \times \rho\mathbb{S} \to \mathbb{R}$ is the *tumbling rate*, λ is a design parameter, and $\lambda \in L^\infty(\mathbb{R}^2 \times \rho\mathbb{S})$ holds. At each tumble, the velocity changes to a random value $\bar{v} \in \rho\mathbb{S}$ with probability density T_{v^-}, which may depend on the velocity v^- just before the tumble. This is represented as $\bar{v} \sim T_{v^-}$. T_{v^-} is also a design parameter. In summary, we obtain

$$\dot{x}(t) = v(t),$$
$$\dot{v}(t) = 0,$$
$$v(t) = \begin{cases} \bar{v}, \ \bar{v} \sim T_{v^-} & \text{w. p. } 1 - \exp\left(-\int_s^t \lambda(x + \tau v, v)d\tau\right), \\ v^- & \text{w. p. } \exp\left(-\int_s^t \lambda(x + \tau v, v)d\tau\right). \end{cases}$$ (3)

where the third equation corresponds to rule R.

In Ref. [14], an equivalent expression of Eq. (3), which is a partial differential equation describing the time evolution of the density distribution of the variables, is derived as follows:

$$\frac{\partial p}{\partial t} + v \cdot \nabla_x p(x, v, t) = -\lambda(x, v)p(x, v, t) + \int_{\rho\mathbb{S}} T_{v'}\lambda(x, v')p(x, v', t)d\mu(v').$$ (4)

Equation (4) is interpreted intuitively as follows: on the left-hand side, we find a drift term $v \cdot \nabla_x p(x, v, t)$ corresponding to straight robot movement. On the right-hand side, we find a loss term $-\lambda p(x, v, t)$ that corresponds to robots leaving state (x, v) and a gain term that corresponds to robots transitioning to the next state (x, v).

In [10], λ and T_{v^-} are designed for solving an optimization problem of maximizing $Q(x)$ by means of analyzing Eq. (4). This is expressed as the following theorem:

Theorem 1. ([10]). *Suppose that Q satisfies $Q \in \mathcal{D}$ and $\|\nabla_x \ln Q(x)\| \in L^\infty(\mathbb{R}^2)$. If $T_{v'}$ is designed as a uniform distribution as*

$$T_{v'}(v) = \frac{1}{\mu(\rho\mathbb{S})}.$$ (5)

and λ is designed as

$$\lambda(x, v) = \eta(x) - v \cdot \nabla_x \ln Q(x).$$ (6)

where $\eta(x) = \int_{\rho\mathbb{S}} T_{v'}(v)\lambda(x, v')d\mu(v')$, then, for any $p(x, v, t)$ that satisfies $p(x, v, 0) \in \mathcal{D}$ and Eq. (4),

$$p(x, v, t) \to Q(x), \quad (t \to \infty).$$ (7)

holds in norm.

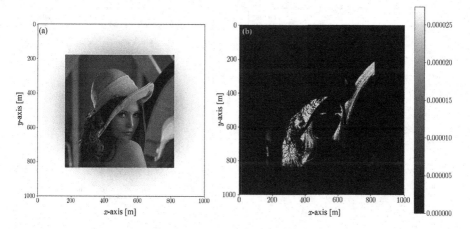

Fig. 1. Scalar value function Q used for numerical calculation. (a): Image of Lena placed in the space $[0,\ 1{,}000]^2\,\mathrm{m}^2$. (b): Image converted to scalar function Q after processing by grayscaling, high contrasting, and normalization.

In Theorem 1, we regard $\eta(\cdot)$ in Eq. (6) as a design parameter and let it be a constant $\bar{\eta} \in \mathbb{R}_+$. This means that the designer chooses the average tumbling rate of each robot in advance. Note that because of this the convergence of the distribution, which is described in Theorem 1, will *not* rigorously hold. The probability of Eq. (2) is then calculated as

$$\exp\left(-\int_s^t \lambda(x(\tau), v(\tau))d\tau\right) = \exp\left(-\int_s^t \bar{\eta} - v \cdot \nabla_x \ln Q(x(\tau))d\tau\right)$$
$$= \exp(-\bar{\eta}(t-s))\frac{Q(x(t))}{Q(x(s))}. \tag{8}$$

In Eq. (8), the size of eta serves as a parameter for controlling the rotation probability as time passes. By using Eq. (8), we can control each robot with the following steps:

1. Set $s \leftarrow t_0$ at the initial time $t = t_0$.
2. Calculate the value $\bar{p} \in [0,1)$ of Eq. (8) at each time t.
3. Generate a uniform random number in the $[0,1]$ section. If it is larger than $\bar{p}$, rotate with an angle sampled from a uniform distribution of $\rho\mathbb{S}$ and reset the value of s ($s \leftarrow t$). If it is smaller than $\bar{p}$, continue traveling straight ahead (no turning).
4. Repeat steps 2 and 3.

As guaranteed by Theorem 1, the distribution $p(x, v, t)$ of the robot is expected to converge to the given function $Q(x)$ using the above steps.

3   Numerical Simulation

We carried out numerical simulation using a large number of robots, namely $40{,}000$. Each robot moves according to the dynamics of Eq. (3), where the speed

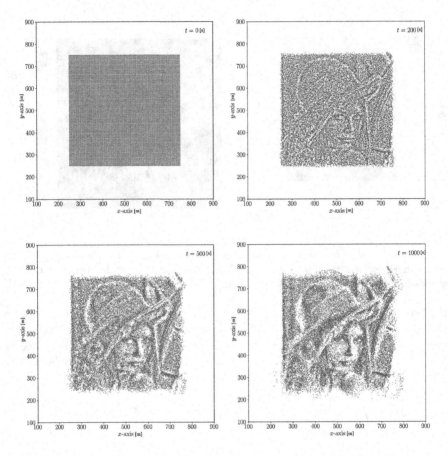

Fig. 2. Trajectory of the movement of 40,000 robots.

of the robot ρ is 0.05 m/s. In the actual computation, Eq. (3) is discretized using Euler approximation at a sampling interval of 1.0 s. The value of $\bar{\eta} = 0.1\,\mathrm{s}^{-1}$ is used as a parameter representing the average rotation rate in Eq. (8). The initial positions of the robot are assumed to be equally spaced in the section $[250,\ 750]^2\,\mathrm{m}^2$. For the scalar value function Q, we used the often used Lena [16] test image, to correspond to the section $[0,\ 1000]^2\,\mathrm{m}^2$, as shown in Fig. 1(a). To convert the original image into a suitable density distribution, we performed the following procedure:

1. Grayscaling: We converted the image to monochrome, and expressed it as scalar value function $\psi : \mathbb{R}^2 \to \mathbb{R}$.

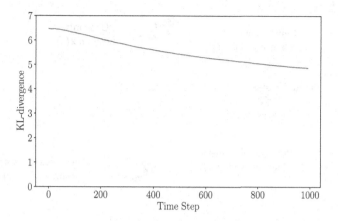

Fig. 3. KL divergence obtained by numerical integration at each time step.

2. High contrasting: To increase the kurtosis of the distribution, we applied the following nonlinear transformation (for details, see Ref. [7]):

$$\phi(q) = \exp(30(\psi(q) - 1)). \tag{9}$$

where $q \in \mathbb{R}$ represents each pixel value of the image.
3. Normalization: The value of each pixel was normalized by the sum of the values of all the pixels, yielding a density distribution.

Figure 1(b) shows a plot of the scalar function Q after performing these operations.

We used the procedure described above to simulate the movement of 40,000 robots, and their resulting trajectories are plotted in Fig. 2. We confirmed that the robots, which were uniformly aligned at the initial time, tended to self-organize into a form of the scalar value function Q representing the image. To evaluate the convergence of the distribution quantitatively, we introduced the following Kullback-Leibler (KL) divergence $d_{\mathrm{KL}}(t; p, Q)$:

$$d_{\mathrm{KL}}(t; p, Q) := \int_{\mathbb{R}^2} \int_{\rho\mathbb{S}} \left(p(x, v, t) \ln \frac{p(x, v, t)}{Q(x)} \right) dx d\mu(v). \tag{10}$$

This is a measure of how the probability distribution p is different from the reference probability distribution Q. Because $d_{\mathrm{KL}}(t; p, Q) \to 0$ $(t \to \infty)$ holds *iff* $p \to Q$ holds, we can regard the smallness of $d_{\mathrm{KL}}(t; p, Q)$ as an evaluation of the proximity of the distributions. Figure 3 shows a time evolution of the value of d_{KL}, obtained by numerically integrating Eq. (10) within the space $[0, 1,000]^2\,\mathrm{m}^2$ discretized into a grid with 10,000 cells. The KL divergence, which was 6.46 at the initial time $t = 0\,\mathrm{s}$, decreased to 4.87 at $t = 10\,\mathrm{s}$, which means that the density distribution $p(x, v, t)$ formed by the robots approached the scalar value function $Q(x)$.

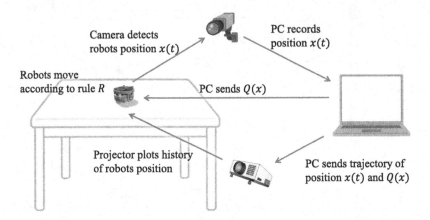

Fig. 4. Experimental setup.

Fig. 5. Robots moving on the stage along with their projected trajectory.

4 Experiment with Robots

In addition to the numerical simulations, we also carried out experiments using actual robots. We employed e-puck 2, a research and educational robot developed by Michael and Francesco [11]. The robot's diameter is as small as 7 cm, and it has a programmable microcontroller. It moves by operating two stepping motors independently, and it carries many sensors, such as infrared proximity sensor, inertial measurement unit, time-of-flight distance sensor, and camera. In addition, these robots can communicate with each other robot or a master PC via Wifi or Bluetooth interface.

Our experimental setup is shown in Fig. 4. Each robot moved on a stage measuring 1×1 m according to the steps described in Sect. 2.2 with the value of Q at its own position. Also, for visualization, a projector displayed the locus of the position of the robots. Figure 5 shows the robots moving on the stage and the

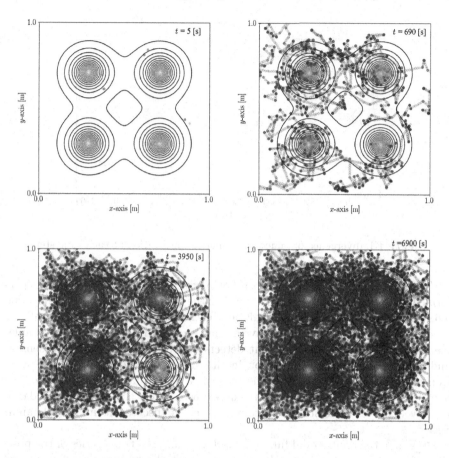

Fig. 6. Trajectory of movement of three e-puck robots.

displayed trajectories. In this experiment, the robots did not sense the function Q; instead, the master PC sent the information to each robot. More specifically, the master PC used the camera above the stage to detect markers applied to the top of each robot and then calculated the value of Q from the marker position. The value of Q was then transmitted to each robot via Bluetooth communication. The reason for employing this procedure to obtain the value of Q, rather than directly sensing it, was to separate the evaluation of the performance of the proposed control method from the evaluation of the sensing performance of the robot. Because the number of Bluetooth simultaneous communication devices was limited, three robots were used in the experiment. In the numerical simulation described in Sect. 3, convergence of the distribution was evaluated by means of a joint distribution of many robots. In this experiment, convergence of the distribution was verified by observing the distribution formed by the trajectory of the position of each robot. This means that we assumed that Ergodicity is established in the system.

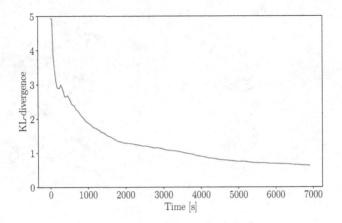

Fig. 7. KL divergence obtained by numerical integration at each time step.

The speed of movement of each robot ρ was $0.02\,\mathrm{m/s}$, and control was performed with the sampling period $0.6\,\mathrm{s}$. For the parameter $\bar{\eta}$, we used the value $0.6\,\mathrm{s}^{-1}$. Unlike the numerical simulation, each robot can collide with walls or other robots because the robots have a finite size. To avoid collisions, we implemented an avoidance function that detects an obstacle using infrared sensors and changes the traveling direction in the direction opposite to the obstacle. Consequently, strictly speaking, the movement algorithm is different from the one described in Sect. 2.2. It was thus expected that the collision avoidance negatively effects the distribution convergence. We discuss this in more detail in Sect. 5.

In Fig. 6, the multimodal function used as Q and the trajectories of the position of robots are visualized. We confirmed that the trajectories of the three robots approached the shape of the given scalar value function Q as time proceeded. Figure 7 shows the plot of the KL divergence (10) at each time step t, which was obtained by dividing the $1 \times 1\,\mathrm{m}$ space of the stage into 14,400 cells and numerically integrating the values on them. The KL divergence, which was 4.92 at the initial time $t = 0\,\mathrm{s}$, decreased to 0.63 at $t = 6,900\,\mathrm{s}$, and it was quantitatively confirmed that the density distribution $p(x, v, t)$ formed by the robots approached the scalar value function $Q(x)$ after sufficient time had elapsed.

5   Discussion and Concluding Remarks

Here, we compare our proposed method with the method proposed by Cortés et al. [6], which is often used for coverage control. Cortés proposed the following method for moving the robots to minimize an evaluation function:

$$\dot{x}_i(t) = -K\left[x_i(t) - g(\mathcal{V}_i(x(t)))\right].$$ (11)

$$g(\mathcal{V}_i(x(t))) := \frac{\int_{\mathcal{V}_i(x(t))} zQ(z)dz}{\int_{\mathcal{V}_i(x(t))} Q(z)dz}.$$ (12)

where $K \in \mathbb{R}_+$ is the gain of the controller and $\mathcal{V}_i(x)$ is called the *Voronoi region*, defined as $\mathcal{V}_i(x) := \{z \in \mathbb{R}^2 | \|z - x_i\| \leq \|z - x_i\| \ \forall j \text{ s.t. } j \neq i\}$. Here, the evaluation function represents the closeness between the distribution formed by the robot swarm and the target shape.

Compared with [6], the computational cost of the proposed method is small. In Ref. [6], integration of the function on the Voronoi region was necessary to obtain the value of g in Eq. (12). In contrast, our method is implemented by only calculating Eq. (8) and a uniform random number at each time step. In addition, in the proposed method, less information is necessary than in the method of Cortés, where the robots need to know their own position and those of neighboring robots to compute their Voronoi regions at each time step. Finally, while Eq. (11) assumes that the robots are able to go straight to the target coordinates, which usually requires them to have their own orientation information, in the proposed method, only the value of $Q(x)$ is used to carry out run and tumble with only the random angle rotation at tumble phases; robots do not need information on their own positions and orientations.

In the proposed method, however, because of its stochastic nature, the probability of collision between robots is expected to be higher than that in the Cortés' method. It is thus necessary for each robot to have a function to avoid collision with other robots, as implemented in Sect. 4. The collision avoidance is regarded as an interaction force acting on the robot. At this time, a new term representing the proximity interaction is added to Eq. (3) as follows:

$$\dot{x}_i(t) = v_i(t),$$
$$\dot{v}_i(t) = f_{ij}(t),$$
$$v_i(t) = \begin{cases} \bar{v}, \ \bar{v} \sim T_{v_i^-} & \text{w. p. } 1 - \exp\left(-\int_s^t \lambda(x_i + \tau v_i, v_i) d\tau\right), \\ v_i^- & \text{w. p. } \exp\left(-\int_s^t \lambda(x_i + \tau v_i, v_i) d\tau\right). \end{cases} \tag{13}$$

where $f_{ij}(t)$ is the interaction term expressing the repulsive force between robot i and robot j. As a result of this term, Eq. (3) is *not* independent for each robot, so that the dimension of the corresponding partial differential equation (4) is N. In the field of statistical mechanics, *mean field approximation*, which averages interactions with surrounding particles and performs approximation, is often applied to decrease the dimension of the system, by means of an appropriate enclosure. However, for proximity interaction, as in our case, the mean field approximation may not be valid, and a different approach is necessary to decrease the dimension. Recently, Bruna et al. [4] proposed an approximation method for systems with proximity interactions, and we are now working on developing a new algorithm incorporating this approximation approach.

Acknowledgement. The authors would like to thank Dr. Yuji Ito for the useful discussions.

References

1. Bandyopadhyay, S., Chung, S.J., Hadaegh, F.Y.: Probabilistic and distributed control of a large-scale swarm of autonomous agents. IEEE Trans. Rob. **33**(5), 1103–1123 (2017)
2. Barca, J.C., Sekercioglu, Y.A.: Swarm robotics reviewed. Robotica **31**(3), 345–359 (2013). https://doi.org/10.1017/S026357471200032X
3. Brambilla, M., Ferrante, E., Birattari, M., Dorigo, M.: Swarm robotics: a review from the swarm engineering perspective. Swarm Intell. **7**(1), 1–41 (2013)
4. Bruna, M., Chapman, S.J., Robinson, M.: Diffusion of particles with short-range interactions. SIAM J. Appl. Math. **77**(6), 2294–2316 (2017)
5. Cao, Y.U., Fukunaga, A.S., Kahng, A.: Cooperative mobile robotics: antecedents and directions. Auton. Robots **4**(1), 7–27 (1997)
6. Cortes, J., Martinez, S., Karatas, T., Bullo, F.: Coverage control for mobile sensing networks. IEEE Trans. Robot. Autom. **20**(2), 243–255 (2004)
7. Izumi, S., Azuma, S., Sugie, T.: Distributed hybrid controllers for multi-agent mass games by a variable number of player agents. Asian J. Control **17**(3), 762–774 (2015). https://doi.org/10.1002/asjc.930
8. Martinez, S., Cortes, J., Bullo, F.: Motion coordination with distributed information. IEEE Control Syst. **27**(4), 75–88 (2007)
9. Meng, Y., Guo, H., Jin, Y.: A morphogenetic approach to flexible and robust shape formation for swarm robotic systems. Robot. Auton. Syst. **61**(1), 25–38 (2013). https://doi.org/10.1016/j.robot.2012.09.009
10. Mesquita, A.R., Hespanha, J.P., Åström, K.: Optimotaxis: a stochastic multi-agent optimization procedure with point measurements. In: Egerstedt, M., Mishra, B. (eds.) HSCC 2008. LNCS, vol. 4981, pp. 358–371. Springer, Heidelberg (2008). https://doi.org/10.1007/978-3-540-78929-1_26
11. Mondada, F., et al.: The E-puck, a robot designed for education in engineering. In: Proceedings of the 9th Conference on Autonomous Robot Systems and Competitions, vol. 1, pp. 59–65. IPCB: Instituto Politécnico de Castelo Branco (2009)
12. Olfati-Saber, R., Fax, J.A., Murray, R.M.: Consensus and cooperation in networked multi-agent systems. Proc. IEEE **95**(1), 215–233 (2007)
13. Şahin, E.: Swarm robotics: from sources of inspiration to domains of application. In: Şahin, E., Spears, W.M. (eds.) SR 2004. LNCS, vol. 3342, pp. 10–20. Springer, Heidelberg (2005). https://doi.org/10.1007/978-3-540-30552-1_2
14. Stroock, D.W.: Some stochastic processes which arise from a model of the motion of a bacterium. Zeitschrift für Wahrscheinlichkeitstheorie und Verwandte Gebiete **28**(4), 305–315 (1974). https://doi.org/10.1007/BF00532948
15. Tan, Y.: Handbook of Research on Design, Control, and Modeling of Swarm Robotics, 1st edn. IGI Global, Hershey (2015)
16. Wakin, M.: Lena (2005). https://www.ece.rice.edu/~wakin/images/
17. Xie, G., Wang, L.: Consensus control for a class of networks of dynamic agents. Int. J. Robust Nonlinear Control: IFAC-Affiliated Journal **17**(10–11), 941–959 (2007)

Framework for Evaluation of Swarm-Based Chemical Reaction Optimization Algorithm

Fabian Schulz[✉] and Carsten Mueller

Baden-Wuerttemberg Cooperative State University,
Lohrtalweg 10, 74821 Mosbach, Germany
informatik@mosbach.dhbw.de, research@ieoca.org

Abstract. Chemical Reaction Algorithm (CRO) is a metaheuristic for optimization inspired by the nature of chemical reactions. A chemical reaction is a natural process of transforming the unstable substances to the stable ones. In this research paper a hybrid chemical reaction optimization algorithm based on local search and global search with an intuitive graphical evaluation framework is presented, which combines the advantages of Chemical Reaction Optimization and Particle Swarm Optimization.

Keywords: Swarm intelligence · Chemical reaction optimization · Framework

1 Foundations

1.1 Chemical Reaction Algorithm

Chemistry is the field of science that studies the chemical properties of matter and its structures [1]. In microscopic view, a chemical reaction starts with unstable molecules with energy. Energy is required for breaking chemical bonds into several molecules. The molecules interact with each other through a sequence of elementary reactions.

The underlying principles of chemical reactions are governed by the first two *laws of Thermodynamics*. The first law (conservation energy) defines that energy cannot be created or destroyed; energy transforms from one form to another and transfer from one entity to another. A chemical reacting system consists of the chemical substances and its surroundings. Each chemical substance possesses potential and kinetic energies, and the energies of the surroundings are symbolically represented by the central energy buffer in CRO [2].

A reaction is endothermic when it requires heat obtained from the surroundings to initialize the reaction process. An exothermic reaction refers to one whose chemical substances give heat to the surroundings. These two reactions are characterized by the initial buffer size (i) positive, reaction is endothermic and (ii) zero, reaction is exothermic. The second law defines that the entropy of the system tends to increase, where entropy is the measure of the degree of disorder.

Potential energy is the energy stored in a molecule with respect to its molecular configuration. Molecules are classified into species based on the fundamental chemical properties. For example, carbon monoxide (CO) and nitrogen dioxide (NO_2) are two different chemical species. The chemical system ($CO + NO_2$) is unstable and the

© Springer Nature Switzerland AG 2019
Y. Tan et al. (Eds.): ICSI 2019, LNCS 11655, pp. 417–428, 2019.
https://doi.org/10.1007/978-3-030-26369-0_39

chemicals finally convert to stable species, CO_2 and NO. The chemical equation which governs this process is described by $CO + NO_2 \rightarrow CO_2 + NO$. This reacting system is realized in multiple stages, described by consecutive sub-reactions: $2NO_2 \rightarrow NO_3 + NO$ and $NO_3 + CO \rightarrow NO_2 + CO_2$.

A chemical reaction results in more stable products with minimum energy and is a step-wise process of searching for the optimal point. At the end of the process, they are converted to those with minimum energy to support their existence.

Molecule is identified by its molecular structure, which characterizes the contained atoms, bond length, angle, and torsion. Energy of the molecules are stored in the form of chemical bonds; bond formation requires energy from outside while bond breakage releases energy to the surroundings. A chemical change of the molecule is triggered by a collision. The two types of collision (i) uni-molecular and (ii) inter-molecular are considered. CRO is a variable population-based metaheuristic [2].

CRO is a multi-agent algorithm and the manipulated agents are molecules. Essential attributes of each molecule include (a) the molecular structure (ω); (b) the potential energy (PE); and (c) the kinetic energy (KE), (d) number of hits, (e) the minimum structure, (f) the minimum PE; and (g) the minimum hit number [3]:

- *Molecular structure* ω captures a solution of the problem. ω is a two-dimensional vector, that represents a point.
- *Potential energy* is the objective function value of the corresponding solution represented by ω. If f denotes the objective function, $PE = f(\omega)$.
- *Kinetic energy KE* is a non-negative number and it quantifies the tolerance of the system accepting a worse solution than the existing one.
- *numbOfHits* counts how many reactions the molecule was involved in
- *minStruct* holds the molecular structure when MinPE was achieved, both together are called information of the best solution in the following
- *minPE* saves the minimum PE the molecule has found
- *minHit* holds the numbOfHits, when MinPE was achieved

Additionally, a *buffer* is required, representing the energy level of the surroundings.

Exothermic reactions transfer energy to the buffer and endothermic can take energy from the buffer.

Following functions are used to find new potential molecular structures:

- NeighbourhoodSearch N1(ω) is finding a potential new molecular structure ω'. N is implemented, as a single step of the Gradient descent of random length between 0 and the constant moveAlongGradeMaxStep.
- NeighbourhoodSearch N2(ω_1, ω_2) generates new molecule structures ω_1' by adding a * ω_2 to ω_1 and ω_2' by adding b * ω_1 to ω_2 with a, b ε [− impactOfOtherMolecule, impactOfOtherMolecule].
- C1(ω) takes a molecular structure ω and generates ω_1 by keeping the first dimension of ω while the second dimension is generated randomly in the search space and ω_2 by keeping the second dimension of ω while the first dimension is generated randomly in the search space.
- C2(ω_1, ω_2) takes two molecular structures ω_1 and ω_2 to create a new molecular structure by adding each dimension of ω_1 and ω_2 in a random proportion.

Also functions for updating the best solution found are defined

- updateMinSolution(M_ω) updates the current best solution of a molecule by the current solution by assigning PE_ω to $minPE_\omega$, ω to $minStruct_\omega$ and numbOf - Hits$_\omega$ to minHit$_\omega$.
- transMinSol(M_ω, $M_{\omega'}$) transfers the information about the minimal solution of $M_{\omega'}$ to M_ω assigning $minPE_{\omega'}$ to $minPE_\omega$, $minStruct_{\omega'}$ to $minStruct_\omega$ and min-Hits$_{\omega'}$ to minHitω.

Chemical Reactions

There are four chemical reactions in CROA. The on-wall ineffective collision and inter-molecular ineffective collision realize the local search and the synthesis and decomposition realize the Exploration of new areas.

On-Wall Ineffective Collision

The on-wall ineffective collision simulates a collision of a molecule with a wall, whereby the molecule is slightly modified. The potential molecular structure ω' is calculated by $N_1(\omega)$ and the numbOfHits$_\omega$ is increased by one.

OnWallIneffectiveCollision
1: **Input:** molecule M_ω
2: $\omega' \leftarrow N_1(\omega)$
3: $PE_{\omega'} \leftarrow f(\omega')$
4: numbOfHits$_\omega \leftarrow$ numbOfHits+1
5: **If** $PE_\omega + KE_\omega \geq PE_{\omega'}$ **then**
6:    Generate a ϵ [KELossrate,1]
7:    $KE_{\omega'} \leftarrow (PE_\omega + KE_\omega - PE_{\omega'})*a$
8:    buffer $\leftarrow$ buffer+$(PE_\omega + KE\omega-$
9:          $PE\omega')*(1-a)$
10:    $\omega \leftarrow \omega'$
11:    $PE_\omega \leftarrow PE_{\omega'}$
12:    $KE_\omega \leftarrow KE_{\omega'}$
13:    **if** $PE_\omega < MinPE_\omega$ **then**
14:       updateMinSolution(M_ω)
17:    **end if**
18: **end if**

It is energetically possible for the molecule to change structures from ω to ω', if

$$PE_\omega + KE_\omega \geq PE_{\omega'} \qquad (1)$$

is accomplished.

In this process, a ratio of the percentage $(1 - a$, $a \epsilon [KELossRate, 1])$ of the surplus of energy

$$buffer \leftarrow buffer + (PE_\omega + KE_\omega - PE_{\omega'}) * (1 - a) \qquad (2)$$

is transferred to the buffer, where *KELossRate* is a constant, describing how much KE is at least kept by the molecule in percentage.

The remaining energy is added as kinetic energy to the molecule.

$$KE_{\omega'} \leftarrow (PE_\omega + KE_\omega - PE_{\omega'}) * a. \qquad (3)$$

ω is replaced with ω' and PE_ω is assigned $PE_{\omega'}$. Finally, it is checked if the molecule has reached a fewer PE_ω than $minPE_\omega$ and if so, *updateMinSolution(ω)* is executed.

Decomposition

The decomposition simulates the splitting of a molecule, whereby one molecule is generated into two new ones. A random large part of the energy can be withdrawn out of the buffer in this process.

Starting with $C_1(\omega)$ two new potential molecular structures are created:

$$\omega_1' \leftarrow \begin{pmatrix} x_\omega \\ y_{generated} \end{pmatrix} \qquad \omega_2' \leftarrow \begin{pmatrix} x_{generated} \\ y_\omega \end{pmatrix} \qquad (4)$$

If

$$PE_\omega + KE_\omega \geq PE_{\omega_1'} + PE_{\omega_2'}. \qquad (5)$$

is fulfilled, the decomposition can occur without external energy.

Two new molecules, $M_{\omega_1'}$ and $M_{\omega_2'}$, are created. The energy surplus

$$(PE_\omega + KE_\omega) - (PE_{\omega_1'} + PE_{\omega_2'}). \qquad (iv)$$

is split up in a random proportion and is distributed to $KE_{\omega_1'}$ and $KE_{\omega_2'}$ in this proportion. If the new molecules haven't reached a lower PE than $minPE_\omega$, the best solution of M_ω is set as their best solution including $minPE_\omega$, $minStruct_\omega$ and $minHit_\omega$. M_ω is destroyed.

If the decomposition cannot occur without external energy, it is examined, whether the reaction can happen with a randomly large part of energy out of the buffer.

If $\delta_1, \delta_2 \in [0, 1]$

```
                Decomposition
1:  Input: molecule Mω
2:  ω1', ω2' ← C1(ω)
3:  PEω1' ← f(ω1') and PEω2' ← f(ω2')
4:  if PEω+KEω ≥ PEω1' + PEω2' then
5:     Edec ← (PEω+KEω) - (PEω1' + PEω2')
6:     goto Step 13
7:  else
8:     Generate δ1, δ2 ∈ [0,1]
9:     Edec ← (PEω+KEω+δ1*δ2*buffer)
10:       -(PEω1'+PEω2')
11:    if Edec ≥ 0 then
12:       buffer←buffer-buffer*(δ1*δ2)
13:       Generate Mω1' and Mω2'.
14:       Generate δ3 ∈ [0,1]
15:       KEω1'←Edec*δ3
16:       KEω2'←Edec*(1-δ3)
17:       if minPEω < PEω1' then
19:          transMinSol(Mω1', Mω)
20:       else
21:          updateMinSolution(ω1')
22:       end if
23:       if minPEω < PEω2' then
24:          transMinSol(Mω2',Mω)
25:       else
26:          updateMinSolution(ω2')
27:       end if
28:       Destroy Mω
29:    else
30:       numbOfHitsω ← numbOfHitsω+1
31:    end if
32: end if
```

$$\delta_1 * \delta_2 * Buffer + PE_\omega + KE_\omega \geq PE_{\omega_1'} + PE_{\omega_2'}.$$

$$(iiv)$$

is fulfilled, the decomposition can occur. Two new molecules are produced through ω_1' and ω_2'. The energy surplus, calculated by

$$\delta_1 * \delta_2 * Buffer + PE_\omega + KE_\omega - PE_{\omega_1'} + PE_{\omega_2'}. \qquad (6)$$

is split up in a random proportion and both molecules in this proportion are assigned as KE. The initial molecule is deleted. The decomposition will not be executed and the $numbOfHits_\omega$ will be increased by one, if there isn't enough energy for it.

Inter-molecular Ineffective Collision

The inter-molecular ineffective collision simulates the collision of two molecules, M_{ω_1} and M_{ω_2}, with low impact. Two new potential molecular structures, ω_1' and ω_2' are found by $N_2(\omega_1, \omega_2)$ resulting into:

$$a, b \in [-impactOfOtherMolecule, impactOfOtherMolecule]$$

$$\omega_1' \leftarrow \begin{pmatrix} x_{\omega_1} + a * x_{\omega_2} \\ y_{\omega_1} + a * y_{\omega_2} \end{pmatrix}. \tag{7}$$

$$\omega_2' \leftarrow \begin{pmatrix} x_{\omega_2} + b * x_{\omega_1} \\ y_{\omega_2} + b * y_{\omega_1} \end{pmatrix}. \tag{8}$$

If

$$PE_{\omega_1} + KE_{\omega_1} + PE_{\omega_2} + KE_{\omega_2} \geq \left(PE_{\omega_1'} + PE_{\omega_2'} \right). \tag{9}$$

is fulfilled, it is energetically possible, and the reaction occurs. The energy surplus

IntermolecularIneffectiveCollision
1: **Input:** molecules $M_{\omega 1}$ and $M_{\omega 2}$
2: ω_1', $\omega_2' \leftarrow N_2(\omega_1, \omega_2)$
3: $PE_{\omega 1'} \leftarrow f(\omega_1')$ and $PE_{\omega 2'} \leftarrow f(\omega_2')$
4: numberOfHit$_{\omega 1} \leftarrow$ numberOfHit$_{\omega 1}$+1
5: numberOfHit$_{\omega 2} \leftarrow$ numberOfHit$_{\omega 2}$+1
6: $E_{inter} \leftarrow (PE_{\omega 1} + PE_{\omega 2} + KE_{\omega 1} + KE_{\omega 2})$
7:       $-(PE_{\omega 1'} + PE_{\omega 2'})$
8: **if** $E_{inter} \geq 0$ **then**
9:    Generate $\delta_1 \in [0,1]$
10:    $KE_{\omega 1'} \leftarrow E_{inter} * \delta_1$
11:    $KE_{\omega 2'} \leftarrow E_{inter} * (1-\delta_1)$
12:    $\omega_1 \leftarrow \omega_1'$
13:    $\omega_2 \leftarrow \omega_2'$
14:    $PE_{\omega 1} \leftarrow PE_{\omega 1'}$ and $PE_{\omega 2} \leftarrow PE_{\omega 2'}$
15:    $KE_{\omega 1} \leftarrow KE_{\omega 1'}$ and $KE_{\omega 2} \leftarrow KE_{\omega 2'}$
16:    **if** $PE_{\omega 1} < MinPE_{\omega 1}$ **then**
21:       updateMinSolution($M_{\omega 1}$)
20:    **end if**
21:    **if** $PE_{\omega 2} < MinPE_{\omega 2}$ **then**
22:       updateMinSolution($M_{\omega 2}$)
25:    **end if**
26: **end if**

$$PE_{\omega_1} + KE_{\omega_1} + PE_{\omega_2} + KE_{\omega_2} - \left(PE_{\omega_1'} + PE_{\omega_2'} \right). \tag{10}$$

is split up in a random proportion and saved as kinetic energy in $KE_{\omega_1'}$ and $KE_{\omega_2'}$. ω_1 and ω_2 are replaced by ω_1' and ω_2'. Has a molecule reached a better solution than held in the information of the best solution, the information of the best solution is replaced with the current solution.

Synthesis

A low KE in a molecule indicates that the local search is completed. The purpose of synthesis is, to transform a new molecule out of two molecules which have a KE below the constant *minimumKE*. ω' is created by $C_2(\omega_1, \omega_2)$.

$$a, b \in [0, 1]$$

$$\omega' \leftarrow \begin{pmatrix} x_{\omega_1} * a + x_{\omega_2} * (1 - a) \\ y_{\omega_1} * b + y_{\omega_2} * (1 - b) \end{pmatrix}. \tag{11}$$

If

$$PE_{\omega_1} + KE_{\omega_1} + PE_{\omega_2} + KE_{\omega_2} \geq PE_{\omega'} \tag{xiv}$$

is fulfilled, the reaction is possible and occurs. A new molecule $M_{\omega'}$ is formed. The $KE_{\omega'}$ is calculated through the energy surplus

Synthesis
1: **Input:** molecules $M_{\omega 1}$ and $M_{\omega 2}$
2: $\omega' \leftarrow C_2(\omega_1, \omega_2)$
3: generate $M_{\omega'}$
4: $PE_{\omega'} \leftarrow f(\omega')$
5: **if** $PE_{\omega 1} + KE_{\omega 1} + PE_{\omega 2} + KE_{\omega 2} \geq PE_{\omega'}$ **then**
6:    $KE_{\omega'} \leftarrow (PE_{\omega 1} + KE_{\omega 1} + PE_{\omega 2} + KE_{\omega 2})$-$PE_{\omega'}$
7:    **if** $minPE_{\omega 1} < minPE_{\omega 2}$ **then**
8:       **if** $minPE_{\omega 1} < PE_{\omega'}$ **then**
9:          transMinSol($M_{\omega'}, M_{\omega 1}$)
10:       **else**
11:          updateMinSolution($M_{\omega'}$)
12:       **end if**
13:    **else**
14:       **if** $minPE_{\omega 2} < PE_{\omega'}$ **then**
15:          transMinSol($M_{\omega'}, M_{\omega 2}$)
16:       **else**
17:          updateMinSolution($M_{\omega'}$)
18:       **end if**
19:    **end if**
20:    Destroy $M_{\omega 1}$ and $M_{\omega 2}$
21: **else**
22:    numbOfHits$_{\omega 1} \leftarrow$ numbOfHits$_{\omega 1}$+1
23:    numbOfHits$_{\omega 2} \leftarrow$ numbOfHits$_{\omega 2}$+1
24:    Destroy $M_{\omega'}$
25: **end if**

$$KE_{\omega'} \leftarrow (PE_{\omega_1} + KE_{\omega_1} + PE_{\omega_2} + KE_{\omega_2}) - PE_{\omega'}. \qquad (12)$$

The information of the best solution of M_{ω_1}, M_{ω_2} and the current solution of $M_{\omega'}$ is stored in $M_{\omega'}$. If the reaction has taken place, M_{ω_1}, M_{ω_2} are destroyed. Has the reaction not taken place the $numbOfHits_{\omega_1}$ and $numbOfHits_{\omega_2}$ are increased by one.

Program Sequence
The program sequence is shown in Fig. 1 and explained in the following. The algorithm is started by a start button and stopped by a stop button described in 5.

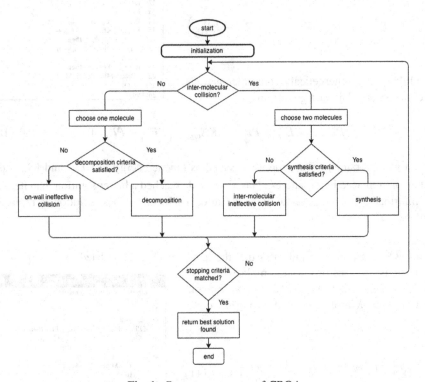

Fig. 1. Program sequence of CROA

Initialization: Random points of the set of solutions of the function are generated in the search space. These points serve as molecular structures ω for the number of molecules that are created. Every molecule has the constant *initialKE* set as KE.

The initial amount of energy in the buffer is assigned the constant *initialBuffer*.

Iterative Reactions: Firstly, it is chosen at random if an inter-molecular or a unimolecular reaction takes place.

Uni-molecular reaction	**Inter-molecular reaction**
A random molecule M_{ω_1} is chosen from the amounts of molecules for the upcoming reaction. If the number of reactions that the molecule has already gone through counted by numbOfHits$_\omega$, exceeds the constant numberOfHitsForDecomposition, the decomposition is carried out. Otherwise, the on-wall ineffective collision is executed.	Two random molecules M_{ω_1} and M_{ω_2} are chosen from the amounts of molecules for the upcoming reaction. If the kinetic energy of both molecules is below the constant minKE, the synthesis is carried out. Otherwise, the inter-molecular ineffective collision occurs.

Stopping Criteria: The algorithm is stopped, if the user presses the stop button.

1.2 Particle Swarm Optimization

Particle Swarm Optimization (PSO) is a nature-inspired metaheuristic method. It was first introduced by Kennedy and Eberhart in 1995 [4]. PSO is inspired by the swarm behavior of birds flocking and utilizes this behavior to guide the particles for search for globally optimal solutions. The population of particles is spread randomly in the search space [5]. The particles are assumed to be flying in the search space.

The velocity and position of each particle is updated iteratively based on personal and social experiences [6]. Each particle possesses a local memory in which the best so far achieved experience is stored. A global memory keeps the best solution found. Sizes of memories are restricted to one. Local memory represents the personal experience of the particle and the global memory represents the social experience of the swarm.

Using randomized correction coefficients are used to maintain the balance between personal and social experience. The philosophy behind the velocity update procedure is to reduce the distance between the particle and the best personal and social known locations. A swarm consists of N particles moving around in a D-dimensional search space. The position of the i-th particle at the t-th iteration is represented by $X_i^{(t)} = (x_{i1}, x_{i2}, ..., x_{iD})$ that are used to evaluate the quality of the particle. During the search process the particle adjusts its position toward the global optimum according to the two factors (i) best position encountered by itself (pbest) denoted as $P_i = (p_{i1}, p_{i2}, ..., p_{iD})$ and the best position encountered by the whole swarm (gbest) denoted as $P_g = (p_{g1}, p_{g2}, ..., p_{gD})$. Its velocity at the t-th iteration is represented by $V_{i(t)} = (v_{i1}, v_{i2}, ..., v_{iD})$. The position at next iteration is calculated according to the following equations:

$$V_i^{(t)} = \lambda(\omega * V_i^{(t-1)} + c_1 * \text{rand}() * (P_i - X_i^{(t-1)} + c_2 * \text{rand}() * (P_g - X_i^{(t-1)})). \quad (13)$$

$$X_i^{(t)} = X_i^{(t-1)} + V_i^{(t)}. \quad (14)$$

where c_1 (cognitive acceleration factor) and c_2 (social acceleration factor) are two positive constants, *rand()* is a random function in the range [0, 1]; ω is inertia factor; and λ is construction factor. The velocities of the particles are within $[V_{min}, V_{max}]^D$. If an element of velocities exceeds the threshold V_{min} or V_{max}, it is set equal to the corresponding threshold.

2 Swarm-Based Chemical Reaction Optimization

The CROA does not converge towards a solution. This is because the molecules do not have a common global knowledge. Through the combination of the CROA and the particle Swarm Optimization, the aim is to reach a common global knowledge and to converge towards the best solutions and thereby examine the local search spaces more effectively. The explorative chemical reactions, synthesis and decomposition, are replaced by the PSO inspired reaction *PSOUpdate*. A hybrid chemical reaction optimization algorithm "Swarm-based Chemical Reaction Optimization" (SCROA) based on local search and global search is developed, which combines the advantages of Chemical Reaction Optimization and Particle Swarm Optimization.

Chemical Reactions
The chemical reactions inter-molecular ineffective collision and on-wall ineffective collision from the CROA are taken on from the SCROA. The decomposition and the synthesis are replaced by the *PSOUpdate*. The explorative property is kept, and a convergence is hereby achieved additionally. The *PSOUpdate* updates the velocity of the molecule and tries to move it towards the direction of the velocity, following the energetic rules defined in CROA. Keeping the same properties of a molecule as in CROA, with the addition of the velocity.

* *Velocity* v_ω captures the current velocity of the molecule
* x_v describes the first dimension and y_v the second dimension of v
* x_ω is equal to the first dimension and y_ω the second dimension of ω
* $minx_\omega$ is equal to the first dimension, $miny_\omega$ second dimension of minStruct$_\omega$
* $minx_{global}$, $miny_{global}$ and $minPE_{global}$ are holding the information about best found solution of all molecules. While $f(minx_{global}, miny_{global}) = minPE_{global}$
* c_1, c_2 and w are the constants of the PSO

PSO-Update
Firstly, the velocity of the molecule is recalculated. This consists of the current velocity weighted with w, the distance to the best result the molecule has achieved weighted with a random factor $r_1 \in [0, 1]$ and c_1, as well as the distance to the best result, which was reached globally weighted with a random factor $r_2 \in [0, 1]$ and c_2.

$$v_\omega \leftarrow \begin{pmatrix} x_{v_\omega} * w + c_1 * r_1 * \left(minx_\omega - x_\omega\right) + c_2 * r_2 * \left(minx_{\text{global}} - x_\omega\right) \\ y_{v_\omega} * w + c_1 * r_1 * \left(miny_\omega - y_\omega\right) + c_2 * r_2 * \left(miny_{\text{global}} - y_\omega\right) \end{pmatrix}. \qquad (15)$$

Afterwards ω' is generated by v_ω and ω. $a \in [0, 1]$

$$\omega' \leftarrow a * \begin{pmatrix} x_{v_\omega} + x_\omega \\ y_{v_\omega} + y_\omega \end{pmatrix}. \qquad (16)$$

If

$$PE_\omega + KE_\omega \geq PE_{\omega'}. \qquad (17)$$

is fulfilled, the molecule can change from ω to ω' without external energy and so the step can be executed. The energy surplus is added as kinetic energy.

$$KE_{\omega'} \leftarrow (PE_\omega + KE_\omega - PE_{\omega'}). \qquad (18)$$

Now ω and KE_ω is updated to ω' and $KE_{\omega'}$.

If it is not possible for the molecule to change from ω to ω' without external energy, a part of the energy from the buffer is tried to be used to make the step possible.

If

```
PSOUpdate
1:  Input: Molecule M_ω
2:  Generate r₁,r₂ ∈ [0..1]
3:  v_ω = (x_{v_ω} * w + c₁ * r₁ * minx_ω + c₂ * r₂ * minx_global
           y_{v_ω} * w + c₁ * r₁ * miny_ω + c₂ * r₂ * miny_global)
4:  Generate a ∈ [0, 1]
5:  ω' ← a * (x_v + x_ω
               y_v + y_ω)
6:  PE_ω' ← f(ω')
7:  if PE_ω + KE_ω ≥ PE_ω' then
8:    KE_ω ← (PE_ω + KE_ω) - PE_ω'
9:    goto step 15
10: else
11:   Generate b₁,b₂ ∈ [0..1]
12:   if PE_ω+KE_ω+Buffer*b1*b2 ≥ PE_ω' then
13:     KE_ω←(PE_ω+KE_ω+Buffer*b1*b2)-PE_ω'
14:     PE_ω ← PE_ω'
15:       numHits_ω ← 0
16:       if PE_ω < minPE_ω then
17:         minx_ω ← x_ω
18:         miny_ω ← y_ω
19:         minPE_ω ← PE_ω
20:         if PE_ω < globalPE then
21:           minx_global ← x_ω
22:           miny_global ← y_ω
23:           minPE_global ← PE_ω
24:         end if
25:       end if
26:   else
27:     numHits_ω ← numHits_ω +1
28:   end if
29: end if
```

$$\delta_1, \delta_2 \in [0, 1]$$

$$\delta_1 * \delta_2 * Buffer + PE_\omega + KE_\omega \geq PE_{\omega'_1}. \qquad (19)$$

is fulfilled, the molecular structure can change. The kinetic energy is now calculated as shown:

$$KE_{\omega'} \leftarrow \delta_1 * \delta_2 * Buffer + PE_\omega + KE_\omega - PE_{\omega'}. \qquad (20)$$

ω and KE_ω is updated to ω' and $KE_{\omega'}$. Has the reaction taken place, it is checked if a better solution is found, than the best ever found solution of the molecule. If a new best is found the information is updated and checked if a new global best solution is achieved and if so, the information about the global best solution is updated.

Program Sequence SCROA

The program sequence of the SCROA is identical of the program sequence of the CROA with two differences:

- Additionally to the initialization described in the CROA, the created molecules are assigned a random velocity v_ω, where each dimension has a value between $-initialMaxLengthVelocityPerDim$ and $initialMaxLengthVelocityPerDim$, where $initialMaxLengthVelocityPerDim$ is a constant.
- The reactions synthesis and decomposition are replaced by the PSOUpdate

3 Parameter

For every combination of algorithm and function a brute force parameter analysis was carried out. Delivering following parameters (Table 1):

Table 1. Results of the parameter analysis

Parameter/Function	Ackley			Rastirgin		
Name	CROA	SCROA	PSO	CROA	SCROA	PSO
c1	–	0	0.242	–	1.425	0.212
c2	–	0.28	0.806	–	1.486	0.644
w	–	0.28	0.688	–	0.845	0.712
keMinLossRate	0.2	0.1429	–	0.72	0.52	–
moleColl	0.36	0.7	–	0.6	0.52	–
minimumKe	16.0	7.0	–	16.0	32.0	–
numberOfHitsForDecomposition	22	40	–	22	16	–
PopSize	24	59	71	24	43	90
minVelocityStep	–	0	–	–	0	–
maxVelocity	–	–	–	–	–	–
MoveAlongGradeMaxStep	0.099	0.066	–	0.186	0.216	–
InitialKE	20.0	50.0	–	33.0	25.0	–
impactOfOtherMolecule	0.970	0.078	–	0.177	0.065	–
initialBuffer	2000	2500	–	1350	1350	–

4 Results

In Fig. 2 the lowest points (minPE) are shown in a boxplot for each function. Those boxplots represent 100.000 executions of each algorithm. The result of the evaluation on the function Ackley and Rastirgin is, that SCROA is significantly superior.

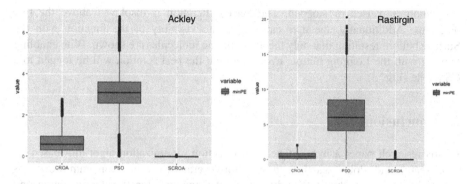

Fig. 2. Results of the functions Ackley and Rastirgin

5 Graphical User Interface

The Graphical User Interface shows the current selected equation plotted in two 360-degree rotatable diagrams. Right above the diagrams, the algorithm can be selected, which should run in the diagram. The molecules are displayed in each diagram by a black dot. The current best-found solution of each algorithm is displayed beneath the diagrams as point (x|y|z). The user chooses one of the following functions with the drop-down menu displayed in the top [7]: Rosenbrock function, Rastirgin function, Ackley function. After selecting a function, the user starts the evaluation. The evaluation can be stopped or paused. Also, the number of Iteration each algorithm executes can be changed with the slider in the Top left between 0 and 100.000, while the

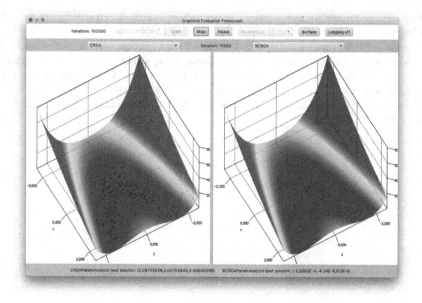

Fig. 3. Graphical user interface

simulation is paused or stopped. The current Iteration is displayed above the two diagrams. Additionally, the user can toggle the visibility of the function with the Surface button, resulting that only the axes and the molecules are shown. With enabling logging with the Logging button, every Iteration the best solution will be logged to a CSV File (Fig. 3).

6 Conclusions

In this research paper a hybrid Chemical Reaction Optimization algorithm based on local search and global search with an intuitive graphical evaluation framework was presented, which combines the advantages of Chemical Reaction Optimization and Particle Swarm Optimization. The Results on the Evaluation have shown that the SCROA has significative performed better than CROA and PSO on different

Benchmark function, which gives reason for further research. An intuitive and interactive Graphical User Interface with 360-degree rotatable diagrams was developed which is used for research and study at Baden-Wuerttemberg Cooperative State University (DHBW) in Mosbach (Germany).

References

1. Montgomery, D.C.: Design and Analysis of Experiments. Wiley, New York (2008)
2. Lam, A., Li, V.: Chemical reaction-inspired metaheuristic for optimization. IEEE Trans. Evol. Comput. **14**(3), 381–399 (2010)
3. Lam, A., Li, V.: Chemical reaction optimization: a tutorial. Memetic Comput. **4**(1), 3–17 (2012)
4. Kennedy, J.: Probability and dynamics in the particle swarm. In: Proceedings of the IEEE Congress on Evolutionary Computation, pp. 340–347 (2004)
5. Kennedy, J., Mendes, R.: Population structure and particle swarm performance. In: Proceedings of the IEEE Congress of Evolutionary Computation, pp. 1671–1676 (2002)
6. Kennedy, J., Eberhart, R. C.: Particle Swarm Optimization. Proceedings of the IEEE International Conference on Neural Networks, 1942–1948 (1995)
7. Pardalos, P.M., Romeijn, H.E.: Handbook of Global Optimization. Kluwer Academic Publishers, Boston (2002)

Mixed Game Pigeon-Inspired Optimization for Unmanned Aircraft System Swarm Formation

Haibin Duan[1]([✉]), Bingda Tong[1], Yin Wang[2], and Chen Wei[1]

[1] School of Automation Science and Electrical Engineering,
Beihang University, Beijing 100083, China
hbduan@buaa.edu.cn
[2] College of Astronautics, Nanjing University of Aeronautics
and Astronautics, Nanjing 211106, China

Abstract. This paper proposes a novel mixed game pigeon-inspired optimization (MGPIO) algorithm for unmanned aircraft system (UAS) swarm formation control. The outer loop controller based on artificial potential field method is designed to transform the UAS swarm formation into abstract movements in the potential field. The inner loop controller based on PIO is designed to solve the optimal UAS position. A novel pigeon-inspired optimization integrated with mixed game theory is proposed to enhance its capacity and convergence speed to solve complex problem while reducing the computational load. This method maintains the capability of the PIO to diversify the pigeons' exploration in the solution space. Moreover, the proposed method improves the quality of the pigeons based on the situation. A series of simulation experiments are conducted compared with basic PIO and Particle Swarm Optimization (PSO) approach. The experimental results verify the feasibility and effectiveness of the proposed method.

Keywords: Pigeon-inspired optimization · Mixed game theory ·
Unmanned aircraft system · Swarm formation

1 Introduction

Unmanned Aircraft System (UAS) has demonstrated repeatedly major potential for diverse applications in military, civilian and public domains [1]. UAS swarm formation control has strong coupling and nonlinearity and no direct mapping relationship between the performance index and the model parameters, the selection of the control input of the close formation model is a key problem. The swarm intelligence optimization algorithm has no special requirements for solving these problems, hence it has obvious advantages in controlling unmanned vehicles, robot path planning and UAS swarm formation.

Pigeon-inspired optimization (PIO) is a novel optimization algorithm, which presented in 2014 [2]. Unlike other swarm-based algorithms such as Particle Swarm Optimization (PSO) and Differential Evolution (DE), PIO uses the special homing ability of pigeons that they combine the sun, the earth's magnetic field and landmarks

Y. Tan et al. (Eds.): ICSI 2019, LNCS 11655, pp. 429–438, 2019.
https://doi.org/10.1007/978-3-030-26369-0_40

to find their destination. However, the basic PIO algorithm is easy to fall into the local optimal solution. Xu et al. proposed a modified method based on PIO to avoid falling into the local optimal value and increase the population diversity by introducing the adjacent-disturbances and integrated-dispatching strategies [3]. Duan and Wang employed PIO approach in the training process of the Echo state network (ESN) to obtain desired parameters [4]. Zhang et al. proposed a novel predator-prey pigeon-inspired optimization (PPPIO) to solve the UAV three-dimension path planning problem in dynamic environment [5]. In this paper, a novel pigeon-inspired optimization integrated with mixed game theory (MGPIO) is proposed to solve the problem for swarm formation of the UAS. PIO is aimed at pigeons' navigation behavior, by simulating its characteristics, to find the global optimal solution.

2 Design of Outer Loop Controller Based on Artificial Potential Field Method

Consider a UAS consisting of n drones in a 3-dimensional Euclidean space, each drone is considered as a particle, then the kinetic model of each drone is described as follows:

$$\dot{P}^i = v^i, m^i \dot{v}^i = u^i - k^i v^i, i = 1, \ldots, n \tag{1}$$

where $\dot{P}^i \in \mathbb{R}^3$ indicates the position vector of drone i, $\dot{v}^i \in \mathbb{R}^3$ indicates the speed vector of drone i, $m^i > 0$ indicates the mass of drone i. $\dot{u}^i \in \mathbb{R}^3$ is the control input value and the $-k^i v^i$ is the speed damping term.

In order to achieve the desired speed of the entire UAS and maintain constant distance between drones, it is necessary to control the speed of UAS to make it consistent and tend to expect speed. At the same time, it is necessary to control the distance between the drones so that the total potential energy is minimized. In summary, the control input u^i of drone i can be described as:

$$u^i = \alpha^i + \beta^i + \gamma^i + k^i v^i \tag{2}$$

where α^i represents the component generated by the artificial potential function in the UAS swarm, it comes from Eq. (3). β^i represents the component which drone i converges with its neighboring drones. γ^i represents the component of drone i speed tending to the desired speed, which depends on the input signal of the leader drone.

The potential function between drone i and its adjacent drone j is:

$$V^{ij}(\|P^{ij}\|) = \ln\|P^{ij}\|^2 + \frac{R_{desire}^2}{\|p^{ij}\|^2} \tag{3}$$

where $P^{ij} = P^i - P^j$ indicates the relative position vector between drone i and drone j. R_{desire} indicates the desired distance between the drone i and drone j [6] in the UAS.

The control input u^i of wingman i includes three dimensions. The first two dimension $u_{1,2}^i$ are the control input in the horizontal direction and the third dimension

u_3^i is in the vertical direction. It is assumed that all drones in the UAS can receive leader's input signal (leader's speed state), the control input $u_{1,2}^i$ can be defined as follows:

$$u_{1,2}^i = -K_p \sum \nabla_{\|P_{1,2}^{ij}\|} V^{ij} - K_v \sum \left(v_{1,2}^i - v_{1,2}^j\right) - m^i \left(v_{1,2}^i - v_{1,2}^1\right) + k^i v_{1,2}^i \qquad (4)$$

where $K_v > 0$ indicates the speed feedback gain factor and $K_p > 0$ indicates the artificial potential field gain factor to control the priority of speed's consistence and the formation.

The control input in the vertical direction u_3^i is defined as follows:

$$u_3^i = -K_h \left(P_3^i - P_3^j\right) - K_v \sum \left(v_3^i - v_3^j\right) - m^i \left(v_3^i - v_3^1\right) + k^i v_3^i \qquad (5)$$

where K_h indicates the altitude feedback gain factor to control the altitude of the formation.

3 Design of Inner Loop Controller Based on Pigeon-Inspired Optimization and Mixed Game Theory

3.1 Pigeon-Inspired Optimization

Pigeons have special navigation capabilities. Pigeons use the sun, the Earth's magnetic field and landmarks to find paths, and use different navigation tools at different stages of the itinerary. When they start flying, the pigeons rely more on navigation tool like compass. In the middle of the itinerary, the navigation tool can be switched to the landmark, this moment the individual pigeons will re-evaluate the route they have experienced and make corrections.

Based on the special behavior of the pigeons during the itinerary, pigeon-inspired optimization uses two different operator models to mimic the different navigation tools in different stages of the pigeon flight.

Map and Compass Operator
The rules in the map and compass operator are defined with the position X_i and the velocity V_i of pigeon i, and the positions and velocities in a D-dimension search space are updated in each iteration. The new position X_i and velocity V_i of pigeon i at the t-th iteration can be calculated as follows:

$$V_i(t) = V_i(t-1)e^{-Rt} + r_1 \left(X_g - X_i(t-1)\right) \qquad (6)$$

$$X_i(t) = X_i(t-1) + V_i(t) \qquad (7)$$

where R is the map and compass factor, r_1 is a random number, and X_g is the current global best position, which can be obtained by comparing the positions among all the pigeons.

As shown in Fig. 1, the best position of the pigeons is developed by using map and compass operator. By comparing the pigeons' positions, the pigeon on the right is the best pigeon. Each pigeon can adjust its flying direction according to (6), which is expressed by the thick arrows. The thin arrows are its former flying direction. The vector sum of these two arrows is its next flying direction.

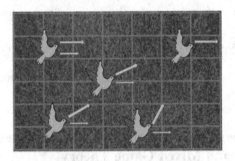

Fig. 1. Map and compass operator model of PIO

Landmark Operator

In the landmark operator, half of pigeons is decreased by N_p in every generation. However, the pigeons are still far from the destination, and they are unfamiliar with the landmarks. Let X_c be the center of some pigeons' position at the t-th iteration, and suppose every pigeon can fly straight to the destination. The position updating rule for pigeon i at t-th iteration can be given by:

$$N_p(t) = \frac{N_p(t-1)}{2} \tag{8}$$

$$X_c(t) = \frac{\sum_{N_p} X_i(t) f(X_i(t))}{\sum_{N_p} f(X_i(t))} \tag{9}$$

$$X_i(t) = X_i(t-1) + r_2(X_c(t) - X_i(t-1)) \tag{10}$$

where r_2 is a random number and f is the quality of the pigeon individual. For maximum problems, $f = f(x)$, for minimum problems, $f = \frac{1}{f(x)+\varepsilon}$, where ε is a constant and $f(x)$ is the cost function.

As shown in Fig. 2, the center of these pigeons is their final destination. Half of the pigeons (pigeons out of the circle) will follow the pigeon, which are close to their destination. The pigeons, which are close to their destination (pigeons in the circle), will fly to their destination very quickly.

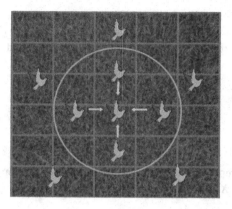

Fig. 2. Landmark operator model in PIO

3.2 Mixed Game Theory

Mixed Strategy Nash Equilibrium

A mixed strategy is a strategy consisting of possible moves and a probability distribution (collection of weights) which corresponds to how frequently each move is to be played. A player would only use a mixed strategy when he is indifferent between several pure strategies, and when keeping the opponent guessing is desirable - that is, when the opponent can benefit from knowing the next move [7].

If each player in an n-player game has a finite number of pure strategies, then there exists at least one equilibrium in (possibly) mixed strategies. If there are no pure strategy equilibria, there must be a unique mixed strategy Nash equilibrium. However, it is possible for pure strategy and mixed strategy Nash equilibria to coexist [8].

Playing the Field

The concept of an 'unbeatable strategy' or an 'evolutionarily stable strategy' is extended to cases in which the payoff to an individual adopting particular strategy depends, not on the strategy adopted by one or a series of individual opponents, but on some average property of the population as a whole, or some section of the population [9, 10].

3.3 Pigeon-Inspired Optimization Integrated with Mixed Game Theory

In the mixed game theory, players can choose different strategies with some kind of probability rather than pure strategies. The basic PIO model is improved by combining mixed game theory (MGPIO) to increase the diversity of the population and improve the feasibility and accuracy of solving the problem of UAS swarm formation.

The velocity and position of pigeon i will be updated as follows:

$$V_i(t) = V_i(t-1)e^{-Rt} + s \cdot r_1 (X_g - X_i(t-1)) + (1-s) \cdot r_2 (X_c - X_i(t-1)) \quad (11)$$

$$X_i(t) = X_i(t-1) + V_i(t) \quad (12)$$

where $s = 1\,or\,0$, which indicates the pigeon's available strategies (following the best pigeon or following the center of the pigeons' position). r_1 and r_2 are random numbers between (0, 1). The probability matrix of the pigeons is defined as:

$$\Pi = \left(\frac{p_1}{p_1 + p_2} \quad \frac{p_2}{p_1 + p_2} \right) \tag{13}$$

$$p_1 = Q_1 \cdot f\left(X_g\right) \tag{14}$$

$$p_2 = Q_2 \cdot f(X_c) \tag{15}$$

where $Q_i, i \in \{1, 2\}$ represent the ratio of strategy i at last iteration, f denotes the fitness value of the position X_g or X_c.

Table 1. Procedure of MGPIO

Step 1	Set parameters and initialize the pigeons' position and velocity
Step 2	Calculate each pigeon's fitness value. Determine the best pigeon's position X_g and center of the pigeons' positions X_c
Step 3	According to Eqs. (13)–(15), fill the probability matrix and decide the strategy in t-th iteration
Step 4	Update positions and velocity. Determine the current optimum solution
Step 5	If $Nc < Nc_{max}$, go to Step 2. Otherwise output the best found solution

Table 1 shows the procedure of the proposed MGPIO.

3.4   Computation Complexity of MGPIO

From the mathematical description of the MGPIO algorithm, the computation complexity of the algorithm can be calculated as follows: Time complexity of the map and compass operator or the landmark operator on one generation is $O\left(DN_p\right)$ because the MGPIO algorithm need to use (11) (12) to update every dimensionality of every pigeon. Since the number of iterations is N_c, we can sum them up and find out the computation complexity of the algorithm which is $O\left(DN_pN_c\right)$.

4   Implementation of UAS Swarm Formation Control

4.1   Process of UAS Swarm Formation

The specific process of UAS swarm formation based on MGPIO is as Table 2.

In summary, the basic idea of the inner and outer loop control method to solve the UAS swarm formation control is: The outer loop controller takes the current cluster

Table 2. Process of UAS swarm formation

Step 1	The current leader drone control input is given and get the status output
Step 2	Use the artificial potential function (3) and get the expected position
Step 3	Use the inner loop controller based on MGPIO and get the control input of the wing-man drones in the UAS and the status output
Step 4	Go to step 1 until the termination condition is reached

state as the controller input, and its output is the expected state at the next moment. At the same, it also provides an optimization target for the inner loop controller. The purpose of improving the MGPIO is to find the optimal control input, so that the difference between actual state and the expected state of the next moment is as small as possible. In the case that the outer loop controller continuously provides the expected state, the inner loop controller continuously solves the corresponding input, and so on, to solve the problems of UAS swarm formation control.

4.2 Comparative Experimental Results

In order to evaluate the performance of our proposed MGPIO algorithm and the effectiveness of UAS swarm formation, a series of experiments compared with basic PIO algorithm and PSO algorithm are conducted in MATLAB R2018a programming environment on a PC with 2.50 GHz CPU.

Assume that there are 6 drones in the swarm, including 1 leader and 5 wingmen. Figures 3, 4 and 5 shows the simulation results when using the MGPIO algorithm.

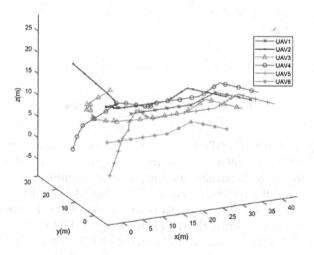

Fig. 3. Simulation result in a 3-D view

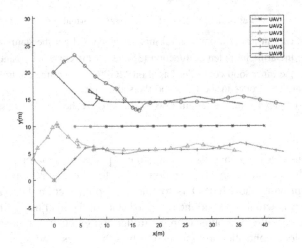

Fig. 4. Simulation result in a top-down view

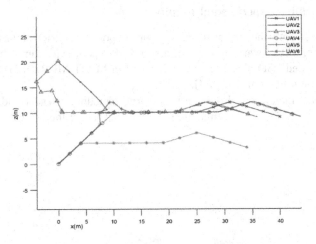

Fig. 5. Simulation result in a side view

From Figs. 3, 4 and 5, MGPIO algorithm could form a stable formation. This is because the MGPIO algorithm have faster convergence speed and it is better at avoiding local minimum. Simulation and comparison experiments verify the feasibility and effectiveness of the proposed method. The comparative evolutionary curves of MGPIO with basic PIO, PSO in artificial potential function (3) is showed in Fig. 6. From evolution curves of three algorithms, it shows MGPIO converged faster than basic PIO and PSO algorithm and the final result of MGPIO is better than the other two algorithms.

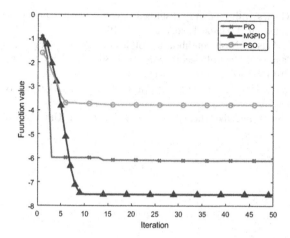

Fig. 6. Comparative evolutionary curves of MGPIO, PIO and PSO

5 Conclusions

The UAS swarm formation is a challenging technical problem. This paper uses the inner and outer loop control to design a UAS swarm formation controller. The outer loop controller selects the artificial potential field function and the mixed game pigeon-inspired optimization algorithm is introduced as a parameter regulator for the inner loop controller. At the same time, the simulation and comparison experiments verify the feasibility and effectiveness of the proposed method, and verify the effectiveness of the MGPIO algorithm by comparing the effects of the UAS swarm form under different inner loop controllers.

References

1. Tzafestas, S., Dalamagkidis, K., Piegl, L., Valavanis, K.: On Integrating Unmanned Aircraft Systems into the National Airspace System. ISCA 2009, vol. 36. Springer, Dordrecht (2009). https://doi.org/10.1007/978-1-4020-8672-4
2. Duan, H., Qiao, P.: Pigeon-inspired optimization: a new swarm intelligence optimizer for air robot path planning. Int. J. Intell. Comput. Cybern. **7**, 24–37 (2014)
3. Xu, X., Deng, Y.: UAV power component-DC brushless motor design with merging adjacent-disturbances and integrated-dispatching pigeon-inspired optimization. IEEE Trans. Magn. **54**, 1–7 (2018)
4. Duan, H., Wang, X.: Echo state networks with orthogonal pigeon-inspired optimization for image restoration. IEEE Trans. Neural Netw. Learn. Syst. **27**, 2413–2425 (2016)
5. Zhang, B., Duan, H.: Three-dimensional path planning for uninhabited combat aerial vehicle based on predator-prey pigeon-inspired optimization in dynamic environment. IEEE/ACM Trans. Comput. Biol. Bioinf. **14**, 97–107 (2017)
6. Duan, H., Qiu, H., Fan, Y.: Unmanned aerial vehicle close formation cooperative control based on predatory escaping pigeon-inspired optimization. Scientia Sinica Technologica **45**, 559–572 (2015)

7. Harsanyi, J.: Games with randomly disturbed payoffs: a new rationale for mixed-strategy equilibrium points. Int. J. Game Theory **2**, 1–23 (1973)
8. Ungureanu, V.: Sets of Nash equilibria in polymatrix mixed-strategy games. Pareto-Nash-Stackelberg Game and Control Theory. SIST, vol. 89, pp. 57–81. Springer, Cham (2018). https://doi.org/10.1007/978-3-319-75151-1_3
9. Sandholm, W.: Evolutionary game theory. In: Computational Complexity, pp. 1000–1029 (2012)
10. Smith, J.: Evolution and the Theory of Games. Cambridge University Press, Cambridge (1982)

Research on UAV Task Assignment Method Based on Parental Genetic Algorithm

Yinping Jia[⊠]

Jiangsu Automation Research Institute, Lianyungang 222006, Jiangsu, China
jiayinping413@163.com

Abstract. Task assignment is one of the important links in UAV combat planning, which has an important influence on the overall combat effectiveness of the system. UAV task assignment is a typical optimization problem. In this paper, an optimization model of the multi-UAV collaborative task assignment problem is firstly established, and then a coding scheme and a sequence number cross method are designed for the multi-UAV multi-task problem, and the two-parent genetic algorithm is used to solve the problem. The results show that the proposed method has the advantages of faster convergence and higher accuracy under the same calculation conditions than the single parent genetic algorithm, and can effectively solve the multi-task assignment problem of multi-UAV.

Keywords: UAV · Task assignment · Genetic algorithm · Coding

1 Introduction

In the face of increasingly complex application environment and diversified operational requirements, single UAV is limited by its own software and hardware conditions, therefore, it has some limitations in use. In order to make up for the limitation of single UAV, cooperative operation of UAV cluster has become a research hotspot in unmanned combat technology. In formation, each UAV has its own characteristics, functions, payloads, combat capabilities and other aspects. Under various constraints, all combat tasks are allocated to UAV formation in a reasonable way to maximize the performance of the system and to give full play to the cooperative work efficiency of UAV formation. This is an important research topic of UAV formation combat system. In order to assign multiple UAVs to perform a group of tasks cooperatively and improve the efficiency of tasks, a reasonable and efficient collaborative control method is indispensable. Therefore, a reasonable collaborative task planning must be carried out for the multi-aircraft system.

UAV mission assignment can be classified into cooperative task assignment and independent task assignment according to the correlation between UAV combat tasks [1], and static task assignment and dynamic task assignment according to the environment of UAV combat tasks [2]. It can also be divided into centralized task allocation, distributed task allocation and hierarchical distributed task allocation according to the way of task allocation [3].

Multi-machine off-line collaborative task planning is a centralized static task planning modeling method. A reasonable mathematical model of task planning must be

Y. Tan et al. (Eds.): ICSI 2019, LNCS 11655, pp. 439–446, 2019.
https://doi.org/10.1007/978-3-030-26369-0_41

established before the optimal algorithm is used for UAV task assignment. The commonly used modeling methods of centralized task planning include multi-trip salesman problem, vehicle routing problem, negotiation model based on market bidding mechanism, network flow model, mixed integer linear programming model and so on. Among them, the multi-traveler-problem model and vehicle routing model are applicable to the multi-UAV coordination of a single type of task.

Different task assignment algorithms can be used for different task planning models, such as evolutionary algorithms, genetic algorithms, tabu search algorithms, and particle swarm optimization algorithms, etc. Genetic algorithm has been widely used in discrete optimization problems. In recent years, the genetic algorithm using serial number coding method is more and more applied to solve the VRP problem and the UAV task assignment problem [4–8], and has achieved some success. Literature [6] regards the UAV task assignment problem as a VRP problem, and then studies the large-scale UAV task assignment method based on parthenogenetic algorithm; In literature [7], a mathematical model is built for the resource scheduling problem in the multi-UAV collaborative system. In the model, each UAV performs an attack task, and the optimization target is the weighted sum of the benefit obtained from destroying the target and the cost of destroying the UAV. Then, the dynamic resource scheduling algorithm based on genetic algorithm is studied. Furthermore, aimed the problem of collaborative mission planning of multi-target group multi-base multi-UAV, a Periodic Fast Search Genetic Algorithm (PFSGA) is proposed in literature [8].

In view of the shortcomings of traditional genetic algorithm in multi-UAV cooperative task assignment, this paper improves the design of coding mode, establishes the corresponding relationship between UAV and task coding segment by adding zero in coding, and in the process of evolution, sequence number crossover and mutation operations are carried out on the task coding and zero at the same time to realize random changes in the task coding and number of each UAV, so that the algorithm has global search capability.

2 UAV Task Assignment Algorithm

The research of task assignment in this paper is aimed at multi-UAV reconnaissance or ground attack tasks in two-dimensional battlefield space. Suppose that an aircraft consisting of M UAVs attacked N different targets on the ground. The UAV set is U and the task set is T, and there is no no-fly zone, terrain obstacles and sudden threats in the battlefield. etc., we define $I \triangleq \{1, 2, \cdots, M\}$ and $J \triangleq \{1, 2, \cdots, N\}$ as subscript sets for UAVs and task targets. In a task assignment, each task is executed only once. Based on the above assumptions, the key to the multi-UAV task assignment using genetic algorithm is to determine the serial number coding method, design the fitness function and genetic operation operator.

2.1   The Chromosome Coding

Genetic algorithm takes the coding of decision variables as the operation object, so the format of chromosome coding has a crucial influence on the performance of the optimization algorithm.

In the traditional multi-UAV task assignment problem, the chromosome encoding method is similar to the "traveling salesman problem", using randomly arranged $1 \sim N$ natural numbers as the chromosome coding, and each chromosome also corresponds to a randomly generated non-negative integer set, which is used to represent the number of tasks assigned to each UAV. In addition, another chromosomal coding method is proposed in the literature [7], which divides chromosomes into M gene segments of the same length, each gene segment corresponding to a task sequence executed by a UAV, and the length is the maximum number of tasks that can be performed by a single UAV. If the number of tasks of the UAV does not reach the maximum number of tasks, 0 is used to complete the vacant position of the gene segment. It can be seen that both coding modes can be applied to multi-UAV multi-target task assignment, but there is a problem that the encoding form is complex, which is not conducive to crossover and mutation operation.

In view of the above problems, this paper has improved the traditional chromosome coding method. The specific coding scheme is as follows:

The code length is $M + N - 1$, which consists of $1 \sim N$ natural numbers and $M - 1$ zeros randomly arranged. Among them, the natural number of $1 \sim N$ represents the task number, and 0 is used to distinguish the coding interval of different drones. Figure 1 is a coding example of a feasible solution for a task assignment problem for a UAV. The figure assumes that the number of UAVs is three and the task targets are ten.

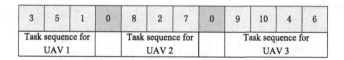

Fig. 1. Example of chromosome length and segmentation

As can be seen from Fig. 1, the chromosome code is divided into three segments by two 0 codes, corresponding to the task sequences of the three UAVs. Each task sequence represents the task number and execution order of a UAV command. For example, the task execution sequence of the UAV 1 is 3-5-1.

This encoding method ensures that each task is executed by a UAV. Based on this coding method, the task number and order of the UAV can be modified by adjusting the order of natural numbers. The number of UAVs that perform the task can be adjusted by adjusting the position of code 0. If code 0 is at the first and the last position of chromosome or two codes 0 are adjacent to each other, it means that there is a UAV that does not participate in task assignment.

When the initial population is created based on this encoding format, the natural numbers $1 \sim N$ are first randomly arranged. Then, among the integers from 0 to N, $m - 1$ numbers are randomly selected as the coding position of 0, and the $m - 1$ zeros are filled into the corresponding position in order.

2.2   Sample Selection

Genetic algorithm is mainly based on Darwin's natural selection process, so the size of the selection intensity plays a key role. The selection process depends on three factors: the sample space, the sample mechanism, and the selection probability. In this paper, the probability-based method is used to select the individuals for operation, and the selected pairs of individuals are cross-operated, and the selected individual individuals are mutated to generate a new population for the next genetic operation. It is worth noting that in the selection process, code 0 can also be selected for crossover and mutation operations to change the number of tasks performed by the UAV. In the process of evolution, it is possible that the optimal solution of a generation is destroyed by the intersection and mutation, which may lead to degradation. This problem is hidden in the commonly used probabilistic selection operation. Therefore, this paper retains the optimal solution of the previous generation as one of the next generation individuals during genetic manipulation.

2.3   Cross and Mutation Operations

Crossover and mutation are the key genetic operations in genetic algorithms. Aiming at the characteristics of chromosome coding in task assignment, a sequence number cross method is proposed in this paper. When a segment of the coding of the parent sample is selected based on probability, the selected coding is sorted from small to large. In order to solve the problem that coding is not unique when coding crossover occurs, the method of sequence number crossover can be used. The coding segments of the two paternal chromosomes are reordered according to each other's sequence number, instead of crossing the coding directly. Figure 2 shows an example of a sequence crossover method.

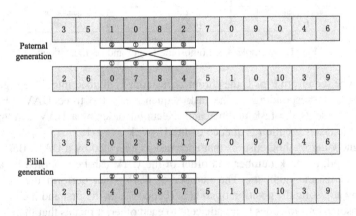

Fig. 2. Sequence number cross operation

For the selected individual, a pair of coded positions are randomly exchanged as a mutation operation to generate a new population for the next genetic operation (Fig. 3).

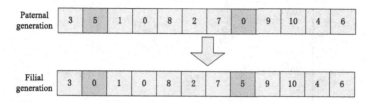

Fig. 3. Variation operation

2.4 Calculation of Individual Fitness Values

The attack cost index is used as the individual adaptive value. The indicators mainly include three aspects: (1) The threat cost of the UAV caused by the execution of the mission; (2) The target value of the UAV attack; (3) Time cost. In this paper, the methods of literature [6] and [7] are used to calculate the individual fitness. The fitness function of each chromosome Y is

$$f(Y) = \sum_{i,j} c_{ij} x_{ij} \tag{1}$$

In this formula, $x_{ij}(i = 1, \cdots, M; j = 1, \cdots, N)$ is a binary decision variable, it can be obtained by decoding the chromosome. It is defined as:

$$x_{ij} = \begin{cases} 1 & UAV\ j\ assigned\ to\ the\ task\ i \\ 0 & other \end{cases} \tag{2}$$

c_{ij} is the threat degree of the i-th UAV, and the calculation formula is as follows:

$$c_{ij} = (1 - P_{kij}) \cdot V \cdot \min_i(TMatrix)/TMatrix(i,j) \tag{3}$$

In formula (3), V is the value index of target i, and is the probability that UAV j is destroyed by enemy target i. TMatrix is the time matrix for UAV j to fly to the target, which makes the total flight distance of each UAV shorter.

3 The Simulation Experiment

In order to test the effectiveness of the parental genetic algorithm on the task assignment of multi-UAV, a simulation example was created and calculated according to the actual combat environment. Take 3 UAVs and 10 mission targets as examples. The location distribution of UAVs and targets is shown in Fig. 4. The number of UAVs is respectively (UAV1, UAV2, UAV3), while the 10 target points that need to be attacked are labeled as 1, 2, ..., 10. Assuming that the threat index for each target is the same (0.8), the probability of destruction of each target to the UAV is shown in Table 1.

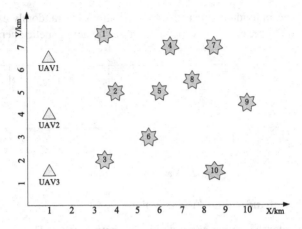

Fig. 4. Example of actual combat environment

Using the parent algorithm to solve the problem, the operating parameters are: genetic algebra 500, population size 60, crossover probability $P_c = 0.5$, mutation probability $P_m = 0.2$. After running for 500 generations, the adaptive value of the optimal individual Y is $f_{opt} = 6.0836$. Figure 5 shows the fitness change curve of a solution with the number of iterations. The optimal solution chromosome coding is shown in Fig. 6.

Table 1. Threat index and destruction probability of the target

	P_{ki1}	P_{ki2}	P_{ki3}	V_i
T_1	0.2	0.3	0.5	0.8
T_2	0.5	0.4	0.1	0.8
T_3	0.2	0.4	0.3	0.8
T_4	0.7	0.6	0.3	0.8
T_5	0.3	0.1	0.6	0.8
T_6	0.7	0.2	0.6	0.8
T_7	0.1	0.4	0.3	0.8
T_8	0.5	0.3	0.2	0.8
T_9	0.4	0.2	0.3	0.8
T_{10}	0.6	0.4	0.1	0.8

It can be seen that the optimal task assignment result is: UAV 1: $1 \to 7$; UAV 2: $5 \to 8 \to 9 \to 6$; UAV 3: $3 \to 2 \to 4 \to 10$.

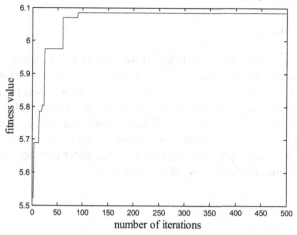

Fig. 5. Fitness evolution curve

Fig. 6. Optimal chromosome coding

In order to verify the effectiveness of the algorithm proposed in this paper, the parental genetic algorithm in this paper and the single parent genetic algorithm in literature [7] were respectively used to solve the above problems, and 100 times of simulation were conducted. The obtained comparison results are shown in Table 2.

Table 2. Comparison of simulation results of two genetic algorithms

	Optimal solution ratio (%)	Average solution algebra of optimal solution
Parental genetic algorithm	91	84.6
Single parent genetic algorithm	64	94.48

By comparison, it can be seen that compared with the single parent genetic algorithm, the parental genetic algorithm converges faster and is less likely to fall into the local optimal solution, which significantly improves the computational ability of the global optimal solution and is more suitable for solving the UAV task assignment problem.

4 Conclusion

In the cooperative control of multi-UAV, reasonable task assignment can effectively improve the combat effectiveness of the formation. In order to solve the problem of UAV multi-task assignment, this paper adopts the parental genetic algorithm and improves the traditional coding method. Through the parental sequence number crossover and mutation operation, the global optimization ability and convergence speed of the algorithm are improved. The simulation results show that compared with the single parent genetic algorithm, the algorithm has faster convergence speed and is less likely to fall into the local optimal solution.

References

1. Ravindran, K.: Task allocation and scheduling of concurrent applications to multiprocessor systems. University of California at Berkeley (2008)
2. Bui, H.N., Han, X., Mandal, S., et al.: Optimization-based decision support algorithms for a team-in-the-loop planning experiment. In: 2009 Proceedings of the IEEE International Conference on Systems, Man and Cybernetics, San Antonio, 11–14 October 2009. IEEE (2009)
3. Chen, X., Qiao, Y.Z., Shenyang Aerospace University: Summary of unmanned aerial vehicle task allocation. J. Shenyang Aerosp. Univ. 33(6), 1–7 (2016)
4. Thangiah, S.R.: Vehicle routing with time windows using genetic algorithms. In: Chambers, L. (ed.) Application Handbook of Genetic Algorithms: new Frontiers, vol. II, pp. 253–277. CRC Press, Boca Raton (1995)
5. Chen, G S., Jose, B., Cruz, J B.: Genetic algorithm for task allocation in UAV cooperative control. In: AIAA Conference on Guidance, Navigation, and Control Austin (2003)
6. Qi, F., De-Yun, Z.: Application of SPGA to large scale task assignment of UCAVs. Fire Control Command Control 31(5), 18–21 (2006)
7. Zhou-Yi, Y.U., Zong-Ji, C., Rui, Z.: On dynamic resource scheduling based on genetic algorithm. Control Decis. 19(11), 1308–1311 (2004)
8. Liu, C., Xie, W., Zhang, P., Guo, Q.: Collaborative mission planning of multi-target group multi-base and multi-UAV. J. Proj. Rocket. Missiles Guid. (2018)

A Comparison Among the Denavit - Hartenberg, the Screw Theory, and the Iterative Methods to Solve Inverse Kinematics for Assistant Robot Arm

Yeyson Becerra[1]([⊠]) , Mario Arbulu[1] , Sebastian Soto[1] ,
and Fernando Martinez[2]

[1] Corporacion Unificada Nacional de Educacion Superior, Bogota, Colombia
{yeyson_becerra,mario_arbulu,sebastian_soto}@cun.edu.co
[2] Universidad Distrital Francisco Jose de Caldas, Bogota, Colombia
fmartinezs@udistrital.edu.co

Abstract. Inverse kinematics solution, for five degree of freedom assistant robot arm, will be described in this work with three different methods. Denavit - Hartenberg approach (D-H), Screw theory and Iterative method will be used. Novel approach of decoupling method will be detailed; after that analytical solution with Paden-Kahan sub problems will be presented, and iterative method will be applied too. Simulations using previous methods will be shown. Finally, results will be compared and discussed.

Keywords: Inverse kinematics · Manipulator motion modelling ·
Decoupling method · Iterative method · Screw method

1 Introduction

Robots are complex mechanisms that integrate multiple technologies to achieve a purpose. The use of robots in manufacturing processes for industrial environments is closely related in production operations, material handling, inspection, execution, assembly, etc.

It is common to use robots to perform repetitive and labor cycles that generally a human can not perform. The manipulators or robotic arms are in the group of multi-functional programmable robots, able to make decisions, respond to orders and communicate with other machines [11,16].

The use of robots in manufacturing processes has led to create several lines of research; where the individual actions of the robot joints are analyzed in detail to execute the desired movement routine. The end-effector position and orientation, and inverse kinematics algorithms can determine the translational or rotational displacement of each and every joint [14].

© Springer Nature Switzerland AG 2019
Y. Tan et al. (Eds.): ICSI 2019, LNCS 11655, pp. 447–457, 2019.
https://doi.org/10.1007/978-3-030-26369-0_42

Inverse kinematics is one of the most important and widely studied problems in robotics. There are multiple mathematical methods to solve the inverse kinematics problem [8,10]. In the present research, kinematic decoupling method, screw-based method and an iterative method are used.

The decoupling method is a closed-form solution that divides the inverse kinematics problem into two problems: position and orientation. This method is appropriated for robots that have an arm and a wrist, where the wrist joint axes are aligned at a point [1]. Defining the position and orientation desired as well as the wrist point, is possible to calculate the 3 first joints that define robot's position (θ_1, θ_2, θ_3). Once the first three joints and end-effector orientation matrix are known [noa], the subsequent joint variables are obtained [13,15].

Screw-based method is used in kinematic study of mechanisms, this theory is mainly used to analyze the position of a kinematic chain. By means of geometric entities, an axis is defined to represent the rotation and translation in a manipulator. This method allows to express angular velocities of the body and linear velocities in a point that coincide with the origin. The instantaneous motion of a rigid body is analyzed in relation to a reference system [20,22,23].

Iterative methods allow to perform calculations from progressive approximations of a seed. Indirect methods give place to a succession of vectors that converge to the solution; the calculation is concluded when the most approximate solution is found after a few iterations [12]. To facilitate the interpretation of movements and positions of the robot, it is necessary to use the Cartesian coordinates x, y, z. The arrangement of the displacement joint is determined to achieve the desired position of the end-effector [17].

In previous reviews of inverse kinematics problem, the following disadvantages were identified: in iterative methods, the computational cost tends to be high, as it takes time to find the correct convergences and to find the most approximate solution [18,22]. In the method based on screws, sub-problems can arise to give solution to the inverse kinematics and the geometric calculations can remarkably hinder the solution, the articular angles are obtained by means of the numerical integration of the joint velocities and errors can appear in the process [21,23]. In kinematic decoupling methods, it is complex to express the kinematics in an arbitrary way and to establish the parameters for the vector equation [13,15]. In the present investigation, all the methods described above are applied and analyzed in a assistant robot arm, at the end, it is determined which is the most efficient method in a real case, with the corresponding mathematical development.

Section 2 of this paper presents the main approach to the problem analyzed. Section 3 solves the problem of inverse kinematics proposed by the closed solution method of kinematic decoupling, screw-based method and open solution with iterative numerical methods. In Sect. 4 the results and discussion of the research are presented, and the methodology used to solve the inverse kinematic problem is described and computational tools are used for the different factors in the robot space with simulations. The conclusions are presented in Sect. 5.

1.1 Contributions

Screw based method has the following contributions:

- Avoiding singularities.
- Paden-Kahan subproblems is an analytical straightforward method for solving manipulator inverse kinematics.

Decoupling method has the following contribution:

- The inverse kinematics problem is divided into two simpler subproblems.

This work compares three different algorithms to solve the inverse kinematics problem in an assistant robot arm. The goal was to identify the more efficient algorithm in terms of reaching a point within the workspace and computation time.

2   Problem Statement

In order to picking objects, the robot should use the better solution for approaching and do the motion. The motion problem for translating an object, from any place to other, implies that the robot should find two hand goals configurations; one for picking the object, and the other one for leaving it.

The picking motion is divided in the following steps: Find the hand robot goal configuration; make the suitable 3D spatial hand trajectories, avoiding external and self collisions, in order to approach close to the goal (path planning); compute the inverse kinematics arm for each point of trajectory (joints trajectories); send to the robot the joints trajectories, in order to reach close hand goal configuration; open the hand, approach to the goal and picking the object; and finally, repeat the same process in order to move the object and to leave it in the second goal configuration. This work is focused in the inverse kinematic solution, and three feasible methods are proposed, which are described in the following sections.

Fig. 1. Assistant robot

3   Proposed Inverse Kinematics Solutions

3.1   Assistant Robot Arm

The manipulation part of assistant robot (Fig. 1) is the NAO humanoid, which is a programmable humanoid developed by the French company Aldebarán Robotics®. Among the features of NAO is that the body of the robot has 25 degrees of freedom and a network of 27 sensors. It also includes elements that allow interacting with the environment including a voice synthesizer, speakers and RGB LEDs. In terms of software, it has a program called choregraphe which works with graphic language. It has a complete development set that works with languages such as C++, Python, JAVA®, .NET and MATLAB® [19].

The research was developed from the arm characteristics of NAO robot, the arm has a total length of 233.7 mm and 5 degrees of freedom (DOF).

3.2   Inverse Kinematics Decoupling Method

The Denavit-Hartenberg (D-H) algorithm was used to solve inverse kinematics for a 5-DOF assistant robot arm. D-H is a systematic method to describe and represent the spatial geometry of kinematic chain elements. This method utilizes a Homogeneous Transformation Matrix (HTM) to describe the relationship between two adjacent rigid elements. HTM relates spatial localization of robot end effector, regarding to coordinates system of robot base [3].

Conventional method to solve inverse kinematic is frequently used to obtain the position of a 3-DOF robot, even though it may be equally used for a 6-DOF robot with a higher complexity. Therefore, it was used decoupling method to solve inverse kinematics for a 5-DOF assistant robot arm. The inverse kinematics problem was divided into two parts; the first one was to obtain the D-H parameters and asses its forward kinematics solution, the second one was to use decoupling method based on D-H parameters and asses its inverse kinematics solution.

To find the forward kinematics solution, it was used the D-H convention [4,9], that is represented as a product of four basic transformations. Where θ_i, d_i, a_i, α_i are the D-H parameters associated with link i and joint i.

As it is indicated in the D-H algorithm [4,9]; the first step was to define coordinates frames in every joint for the 5-DOF humanoid robot arm as shown in (Fig. 2), the second step was to generate the D-H parameters (Table 1), in order to know the forward kinematics solution and start working in the inverse kinematics solution.

The decoupling method split the inverse kinematics problem into two parts; inverse position kinematics and inverse orientation kinematics. To do this, it is necessary to identify the wrist center to separate position from orientation, and setting desired position and desired orientation.

The wrist center for the 5-DOF humanoid robot arm was located in the elbow (joints 3 and 4). The D-H parameters were generated again for 2 joints as shown (Table 2), in order to know the wrist center position, denoted as $\vec{P}_w$, which was a

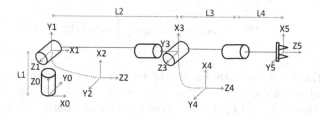

Fig. 2. Coordinate frames

Table 1. D-H parameters for the 5-DOF humanoid robot arm

Joint	θ	d	a	α
1	θ_1	l_1	0	$\pi/2$
2	$\theta_2 + \pi/2$	0	0	$\pi/2$
3	θ_3	l_2	0	$-\pi/2$
4	θ_4	0	0	$\pi/2$
5	θ_5	$l_3 + l_4$	0	0

Table 2. D-H parameters for 2-DOF - kinematic decoupling

Joint	θ	d	a	α
1	θ_1	l_1	0	$\pi/2$
2	θ_2	0	l_2	0

three-vector. The desired position for the end effector was denoted as $\vec{P}_e$, which was a three-vector, see Eq. (2). The l_3 and l_4 were parameters associated to the robot arm (links) and $\vec{z}_5$ was an orientation vector of the HTM.

$$\vec{P}_w = \vec{P}_e - (l_3 + l_4)\vec{z}_5 \tag{1}$$

Inverse kinematics was solved for a robot of 2 DOF, with the D-H parameters shown in Table 2. As a result, the equations listed below that define the first two joints (θ_1 and θ_2) were obtained, see Eqs. (3) and (4).

$$\theta_1 = \arctan \frac{P_{w_y}}{P_{w_x}} \tag{2}$$

$$\theta_2 = \arctan \frac{\frac{P_{w_z}-l_1}{l_2}}{\sqrt{1 - \left(\frac{P_{w_z}-l_1}{l_2}\right)^2}} \tag{3}$$

Once the two first joints were defined for the robot arm, it was necessary to define the next 3 joints. To do this, it was used the orientation matrix, that was represented by R_5^0, see Eq. (5).

$$R_5^0 = [noa] = \begin{bmatrix} n_x & o_x & a_x \\ n_y & o_y & a_y \\ n_z & o_z & a_z \end{bmatrix} = R_2^0 R_5^3 \tag{4}$$

R_5^0 was the desired orientation for the end effector, which had been already defined since the beginning of the inverse kinematics problem. R_2^0 was determined from the values of θ_1 and θ_2, and R_5^3 was the matrix from which joints (θ_3, θ_4 and θ_5) were obtained. The equations are listed below (6), (7), (8)

$$\theta_3 = \arctan \frac{\sin(\theta_1)a_x - \cos(\theta_1)a_y}{-\cos(\theta_1)\sin(\theta_2)a_x - \sin(\theta_1)\sin(\theta_2)a_y + \cos(\theta_2)a_z} \tag{5}$$

$$\theta_4 = \arctan \frac{\sqrt{1 - (\cos(\theta_1)\cos(\theta_2)a_x + \cos(\theta_2)\sin(\theta_1)a_y + \sin(\theta_2)a_z)^2}}{\cos(\theta_1)\cos(\theta_2)a_x + \cos(\theta_2)\sin(\theta_1)a_y + \sin(\theta_2)a_z} \tag{6}$$

$$\theta_5 = \arctan -\left(\frac{\cos(\theta_1)\cos(\theta_2)o_x + \cos(\theta_2)\sin(\theta_1)o_y + \sin(\theta_2)o_z}{\cos(\theta_1)\cos(\theta_2)n_x + \cos(\theta_2)\sin(\theta_1)n_y + \sin(\theta_2)n_z}\right) \tag{7}$$

3.3   Screw-Based Method

Paden and Kahan (P-K) subproblems are used in this subsection, in order to solve the inverse kinematics of 5 DOF humanoid arm (see Fig. 3). At first, forward kinematics is computed by the exponential product of exponential matrices, as following:

$$g_{st}(\theta) = e^{\zeta_1\tilde{\theta}_1} . e^{\zeta_2\tilde{\theta}_2} . e^{\zeta_3\tilde{\theta}_3} . e^{\zeta_4\tilde{\theta}_4} . e^{\zeta_5\tilde{\theta}_5} . g_{st}(0) \tag{8}$$

Where θ is the vector of joint arm rotation angles: θ_1, θ_2, θ_3, θ_4, and θ_5. The ζ_i is the ith joint twist. Furthermore, $g_{st}(\theta)$ and $g_{st}(0)$ are the target, and initial end-effector configuration, respectively.

Next, the P-K subproblems are applied, taking into account the $g_{st}(\theta)$ solution, from the above Eq. (8).

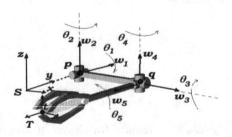

Fig. 3. Humanoid 5 DOF arm screw modeling. Frames S and T, analysis points p,q, and t, i^{th} joint angle θ_i, and axis direction ω_i.

Thus with P-K-2 subproblem, the θ_1, and θ_2 joint angles are obtained as following, by applying screw motions to analysis point q, where the last three joint articulations are crossed:

$$e^{\hat{\zeta_1}\theta_1}.e^{\hat{\zeta_2}\theta_2}.e^{\hat{\zeta_3}\theta_3}.e^{\hat{\zeta_4}\theta_4}.e^{\hat{\zeta_5}\theta_5}.q = q' \qquad (9)$$

As the last three joints are crossed, they do not causes any effect to point q. So, the Eq. 9, turns to: $e^{\hat{\zeta_1}\theta_1}.e^{\hat{\zeta_2}\theta_2}.q = q'$. Being $q' = g_{st}(\theta).g_{st}(0)^{-1}.q$

After that, by applying the last three screws to the point p, where the joints one and two are crossed, the θ_4, and θ_5 joint angles are computed as following:

$$e^{\hat{\zeta_3}\theta_3}.e^{\hat{\zeta_4}\theta_4}.e^{\hat{\zeta_5}\theta_5}.p = p' \qquad (10)$$

Where $p' = e^{-\hat{\zeta_2}\theta_2}.e^{-\hat{\zeta_1}\theta_1}.g_{st}(\theta).g_{st}(0)^{-1}.p$. As, the third axis direction crosses the point p, its rotation θ_3 does not affect to that point. So, the Eq. 10 becomes to $e^{\hat{\zeta_4}\theta_4}.e^{\hat{\zeta_5}\theta_5}.p = p'$, and the P-K-2 subproblem could be applied, to compute the θ_4, and θ_5 joint angles.

And finally, with P-K-1 subproblem, the θ_3 joint angle is obtained, by applying the third screw motion, to the point t, which is the origin of end-effector frame T, as next:

$$e^{\hat{\zeta_3}\theta_3}.t = t' \qquad (11)$$

Being $t' = e^{-\hat{\zeta_2}\theta_2}.e^{-\hat{\zeta_1}\theta_1}.g_{st}(\theta).g_{st}(0)^{-1}.e^{-\hat{\zeta_5}\theta_5}.e^{-\hat{\zeta_4}\theta_4}.t$

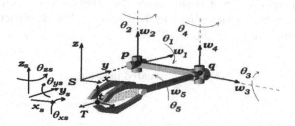

Fig. 4. Humanoid 5 DOF arm screw modeling with floating base S. Frames S and T, analysis points p, q, and t, i^{th} joint angle θ_i, and axis direction ω_i.

The versatility of screws modeling, allows to have a floating base S (see Fig. 4), and introduce it forward in the model, just including the respective screw motions. Where, for a given shoulder position and orientation $(x_s, y_s, z_s, \theta_{xs}, \theta_{ys}, \theta_{zs})$, the forward kinematics is expressed, such as:

$$g_{st}(\theta) = e^{\hat{\zeta_{xs}}x_s}.e^{\hat{\zeta_{ys}}y_s}.e^{\hat{\zeta_{zs}}z_s}.e^{\hat{\zeta_{xs}}\theta_{xs}}.e^{\hat{\zeta_{ys}}\theta_{ys}}.e^{\hat{\zeta_{zs}}\theta_{zs}}....e^{\hat{\zeta_4}\theta_4}.e^{\hat{\zeta_5}\theta_5}.g_{st}(0) \qquad (12)$$

Thus, the inverse kinematics could be solved as before, and only the additional screw motions should be added in the solution. So, the solution including the whole body humanoid, for increasing the robot work space, is easy to extent.

3.4 Iterative Numerical Solution

It was used the Robotics Toolbox for Matlab® to asses the iterative method for a 5-DOF humanoid robot arm. As it is stated in different literature [2,5], these kind of methods offer open solutions to the inverse kinematics problem, due to this, sometimes they lead to no-convergence.

The algorithm used in the Robotics Toolbox is shown in Eq. (13), the solution is computed iteratively using the pseudo-inverse Jacobian of the manipulator; Δ returns the difference between the desired position and the current position, as a 6 element vector of displacements and rotations [6].

$$\dot{\theta} = J^+(\theta)\Delta(F(\theta) - T) \tag{13}$$

The Robotics Toolbox employed the D-H parameters showed in Table 1 to model the robot arm; it was used functions like fkine, ikine, Link and SerialLink to obtain the inverse kinematics solution.

4 Results and Discussion

As it was stated before, iterative methods, sometimes lead to no-convergence; therefore, the iterative algorithm was evaluated for a 5-DOF assistant robot arm, comparing with a kinematic decoupling algorithm, and screw based algorithm, which offer a closed solution for the kinematic chain.

It was used eight different positions for the assistant robot arm, all of them within the work-space, considering length of every link and restrictions of every joint. The positions are described in Table 3.

Table 3. Evaluated positions

$x, y, z, n_x, n_y, n_z, o_x, o_y, o_z, a_x, a_y, a_z$	Kinematic decoupling	Screw based method	Iterative method
(0, −177.40, −25.22, 0, −0.71, 0.71, −1, 0, 0, 0, −0.71, −0.71)	(−pi/2, pi/8, pi, −3pi/8, 0)	(−pi/2, pi/8, pi, −3pi/8, 0)	(−pi/2, pi/8, 0, −3pi/8, 0)
(131.1, 80.4, 146.1, 0.5 −0.71, 0.5, 0.71, 0 −0.71, 0.5, 0.71, 0.5)	(0, pi/4, −pi/2, pi/4, 0)	(0, pi/4, −pi/2, pi/4, 0)	(0, pi/4, pi/2, −pi/4, 0)
(150.97, 147.78, 15.0, −0.5, 0.87, 0, 0, 0, 1, 0.87, 0.5, 0)	(pi/3, 0, pi/2, pi/6, 0)	(pi/3, 0, pi/2, pi/6, 0)	No converge
(114.45, 114.45, −83.47, 0.71, −0.71, 0, −0.61, −0.61, −0.5, 0.35, 0.35, −0.87)	(pi/4, 0, −pi, pi/3, −pi/2)	(pi/4, 0, −pi, pi/3, −pi/2)	Error
(59.68, −100.1, 191.21, −0.07, 0.75, 0.66, −0.99, −0.14, 0.05, 0.13, −0.65, 0.75)	(−pi/6, pi/3, pi/2, pi/6, −pi/4)	(−pi/6, pi/3, pi/2, pi/6, −pi/4)	Error
(189.4, 0, 10.65, 0.5, 0, 0.87, 0, −1, 0, 0.87, 0, −0.5)	(0, pi/6, pi, pi/3, 0)	(0, pi/6, pi, pi/3, 0)	(0, pi/6, 0, −pi/3, 0)
(44.82, −184.07, 15.0, 0.97, −0.26, 0, 0, 0, 1, −0.26, −0.97, 0)	(−pi/4, 0, pi/2, pi/3, 0)	(−pi/4, 0, pi/2, pi/3, 0)	(−pi/4, 0, −pi/2, −pi/3, 0)
(0, 218.70, 15.0, 0, 0, −1, −1, 0, 0, 0, 1, 0)	(pi/2, 0, −pi/2, 0, −pi/2)	(pi/2, 0, −pi/2, 0, −pi/2)	Error

The vectors showed in Table 3 includes position an orientation; the first three elements define position and the rest of them define orientation. Units are in millimeter and angles are in radian.

The decoupling method as well as the screw based method just need the position and orientation of the end-effector and returns the joint positions; while iterative method in Robotics Toolbox needs information from joint positions (forward kinematics solution) to return joint positions. The experiment was as follows:

(a) It was used a forward kinematics algorithm based on D-H parameters to evaluate effectiveness in kinematic decoupling algorithm.
(b) It was defined a random position joint to the forward kinematics algorithm.
(c) The solution from forward kinematics algorithm (position and orientation of end-effector) was introduced to the kinematic decoupling algorithm.
(d) The solution from kinematic decoupling algorithm was compared with the forward kinematics algorithm entrance.
(e) The entrance from forward kinematics algorithm and the solution from kinematic decoupling algorithm were evaluated in the iterative algorithm.
(f) The solutions from overall algorithms (iterative, decoupling, and screws) were compared; identifying differences, errors and no-convergence.

Computational time response was evaluated, in order to find the best solution. For each localization evaluated in Table 3, computational time was measured, with these results, a time average was obtained for each algorithm. The results are show as follows:

- Screw Based Method = 0,45 ms
- Decoupling Method = 0,20 us
- Iterative Method = 0,65 ms

Results describe that Decoupling and Screw based methods find the same solutions; hence, all of them allow approaching the hand to the same points, instead of iterative method not converge at some points. That is, because:

- The analytical methods, (Decoupling and Screw based), make a straightforward solution without any iteration.
- The solution with iterative method for a 5 DOF kinematic chain, with 3D spatial coordinates of the robot end-effector, have six inputs (3 positions coordinates and 3 orientations coordinates), while the kinematics chain have only five degree of freedom, which can only control 3 positions and 2 orientation coordinates at 3D space. So, jacobian matrix is not square, and the pseudo inverse is computed, which causes not convergence at some end-effector configurations.

5   Conclusions

Screws modeling allows a closed straightforward analytical solution, including floating base manipulators. Just using two frames: Base and End-effector ones, and free vectors on SO(3).

Decoupling and Screws based methods allow the same solution with two different approaches:

- Decoupling, with homogeneous transform matrices, that is with frames relationship between each robot joint, and two additional frames: base and end effector.
- Screws, with twist related to each robot joint, that is with free vector direction on each robot joint, and two frames: base and end effector.

The screws method simplified the analytical solution of kinematics chain, and the geometric description of this kind of mechanical systems. The two proposed approaches, one with fixed base, and other with floating base give the same solutions. The floating base approach, allows to move the robot hand motion with wholebody robot displacement.

As it was seen before in results section, the decoupling method is much faster than screw based method and iterative method; nevertheless, the decoupling method does not avoid singularities while screw based method does.

Iterative method is not suitable for this robot arm, because sometimes is not possible the convergence, so there is not solution, for reaching some hand configurations on 3D space.

Acknowledgement. Supported by Corporacion Nacional Unificada de Educacion Superior (CUN), Bogota, Colombia. Project: Assistant robot for home and offices.

References

1. Jin, Y., et al.: Kinematic design of a 6-DOF parallel manipulator with decoupled translation and rotation. IEEE Trans. Robot. **22**(3), 545–551 (2006)
2. Goldenberg, A., Lawrence, L.: A generalized solution to the inverse kinematics of robot manipulators. J. Dyn. Syst. Meas. Control **107**(1), 103–106 (1985)
3. Barrientos, A.: Fundamentos De Robótica, 2nd edn. McGraw-Hill, Madrid (2007)
4. Denavit, J., Hartenberg, R.S.: A kinematic notation for lower-pair mechanisms based on matrices. J. Appl. Mech. **22**, 215–221 (1955)
5. Goldenberg, A., Benhabib, B., Fenton, R.: A complete generalized solution to the inverse kinematics of robots. IEEE J. Robot. Autom. **1**(1), 14–20 (1985). https://doi.org/10.1109/JRA.1985.1086995
6. Corke, P.: Robotics Vision & Control. Springer, Heidelberg (2017). https://doi.org/10.1007/978-3-642-20144-8. ISBN 978-3-319-54413-7
7. Hanaoka, R., Nozaki, T., Murakami, Y.T.: Translation and inclination control for intelligent tension pole based on mode decoupling method. IEEE J. Indus. Appl. **7**(2), 158–165 (2017)
8. Suleiman, W., Ayusawa, K.: On prioritized inverse kinematics tasks: time-space decoupling. In: IEEE 15th International Workshop on Advanced Motion Control, vol. 9, no. 11, pp. 108–113 (2018)
9. Spong, M., Huchinson, S., Vidyasagar, M.: Robot Dynamics and Control. Wiley, India (2008)
10. Khaleel, H.: Inverse kinematics solution for redundant robot manipulator using combination of GA and NN. Al-Khwarizmi Eng. J. **14**(1), 136–144 (2018)

11. Riaño, C., Peña, C.: Application of product development techniques for the development of an anthropomorphic robot. UIS Ingenierias **17**(1), 21–34 (2018)
12. Corke, P.: A simple and systematic approach to assigning Denavit-Hartenberg parameters. IEEE Trans. Robot. **23**(3), 590–594 (2007)
13. Ibarra, J.M., Cisneros, R.: Forward and inverse kinematics for a small-sized humanoid robot. In: International Conference on Electrical, Communications, and Computers, 14 July 2009
14. Zaplana, I.: A novel closed-form solution for the inverse kinematics of redundant manipulators through workspace analysis. Mech. Mach. Theory **121**, 1–27 (2017)
15. Muhammad, A., Andy, H.: Closed-form inverse kinematic joint solution for humanoid robots. In: 2010 IEEE/RSJ International Conference on Intelligent Robots and Systems, 03 December 2010
16. Cardoso, E., Fernandez, A.: Modelos cinemático y dinámico de un robot de cuatro grados de libertad, RIELAC, vol. XXXVIII, no. 3, pp. 56–75 (2017)
17. Santos, V.: Reported anatomical variability naturally leads multimodal distributions of Denavit-Hartenberg parameters for the human thumb. IEEE Trans. Biomed. Eng. **53**(2), 155–163 (2006)
18. Yoshida, E.: Planning 3-D collision-free dynamic robotic planning 3-D collision-free dynamic robotic. IEEE Trans. Robot. **24**(5), 1186–1197 (2008)
19. Hoyos, J., Peña, C.: Towards tool handling by a NAO robot using programming by demostration, Tecno Lógicas, **17**(33), 65–76 (2014)
20. Ribeiro, L., et al.: Screw-based relative Jacobian for manipulators cooperating in a task. In: ABCM Symposium Series in Mechatronics, vol. 3, pp. 276–285
21. Kofinas, N.: Forward and Inverse Kinematics for the NAO Humanoid Robot. Technical University of Crete, Chania (2012)
22. Rocha, C.R., Tonetto, C.P.: A comparison between the denavit-hartenbeg and the screw-based methods used in kinematic modeling of robot manipulators. Robot. Comput. Integr. Manuf. **27**, 723–728 (2011)
23. Arbulu, M., Yokoi, K., Kheddar, A., Balaguer, C.: Dynamic acyclic motion from a planar contact-stance to another. In: 2008 IEEE/RSJ International Conference on Intelligent Robots and Systems, Nice, 2008, pp. 3440–3445 (2008). https://doi.org/10.1109/IROS.2008.4650978

Author Index

Printed in the United States
By Bookmasters